Collaborative and Distributed E-Research:

Innovations in Technologies, Strategies and Applications

Angel A. Juan
IN3 – Open University of Catalonia, Spain

Thanasis Daradoumis
University of the Aegean, Greece, & Open University of Catalonia, Spain

Meritxell Roca
IN3 – Open University of Catalonia, Spain

Scott E. Grasman
Rochester Institute of Technology, USA

Javier Faulin
Public University of Navarre, Spain

Information Science
REFERENCE

Managing Director:	Lindsay Johnston
Senior Editorial Director:	Heather Probst
Book Production Manager:	Sean Woznicki
Development Manager:	Joel Gamon
Development Editor:	Hannah Abelbeck
Acquisitions Editor:	Erika Gallagher
Typesetter:	Russell A. Spangler
Cover Design:	Nick Newcomer, Lisandro Gonzalez

Published in the United States of America by
Information Science Reference (an imprint of IGI Global)
701 E. Chocolate Avenue
Hershey PA 17033
Tel: 717-533-8845
Fax: 717-533-8661
E-mail: cust@igi-global.com
Web site: http://www.igi-global.com

Library of Congress Cataloging-in-Publication Data

Collaborative and distributed e-research: innovations in technologies, strategies, and applications / Angel A. Juan ... [et al.], editors.
    p. cm.
  Includes bibliographical references and index.
  Summary: "This book offers insight into practical and methodological issues related to collaborative e-research and furthers readers understanding of current and future trends in online research and the types of technologies involved"--Provided by publisher.
  ISBN 978-1-4666-0125-3 (hardcover) -- ISBN 978-1-4666-0127-7 (print & perpetual access) 1. Internet research. 2. Group work in research. I. Juan, Angel A., 1972-
  ZA4228.C65 2012
  001.4'202854678--dc23
                    2011039614

British Cataloguing in Publication Data
A Cataloguing in Publication record for this book is available from the British Library.

All work contributed to this book is new, previously-unpublished material. The views expressed in this book are those of the authors, but not necessarily of the publisher.

Editorial Advisory Board

List of Reviewers

Table of Contents

Section 1
Technologies and Strategies

Chapter 1

Lina Markauskaite, University of Sydney, Australia
Mary Anne Kennan, Charles Sturt University, Australia
Jim Richardson, University of Sydney, Australia
Anindito Aditomo, University of Sydney, Australia
Leonie Hellmers, Intersect Australia Ltd., Australia

Chapter 2

Pablo Garaizar, Universidad de Deusto, Spain
Miguel A. Vadillo, Universidad de Deusto, Spain
Diego López-de-Ipiña, Universidad de Deusto, Spain
Helena Matute, Universidad de Deusto, Spain

Chapter 3

Vahid Khatibi, University of Tehran, Iran
Gholam Ali Montazer, Tarbiat Modares University, Iran

Chapter 4

Dukyun Nam, Korea Institute of Science and Technology Information, Republic of Korea
Junehawk Lee, Korea Institute of Science and Technology Information, Republic of Korea
Kum Won Cho, Korea Institute of Science and Technology Information, Republic of Korea

Detailed Table of Contents

Section 1
Technologies and Strategies

Chapter 1

Lina Markauskaite, University of Sydney, Australia

Mary Anne Kennan, Charles Sturt University, Australia

Jim Richardson, University of Sydney, Australia

Anindito Aditomo, University of Sydney, Australia

Leonie Hellmers, Intersect Australia Ltd., Australia

Why and how do researchers collaborate, share knowledge resources, data, and expertise? What kinds of infrastructures and services do they use, and what do they need for the future enhancement of collaborative research practices? The chapter focuses on existing and potential eResearch from a "user" perspective. Drawing on a study of ICT-enhanced research practices and needs conducted at seven Australian universities, it discusses how researchers engage with distributed research and use ICT for collaboration. Findings show significant current engagement of the majority of researchers in collaborative research, their acknowledgement of the potential of eResearch, and researchers' general willingness to engage in collaborative eResearch. While there are some essential differences in the collaboration practices of research students and academics and between practices and challenges in different disciplinary domains, researchers who are more involved in collaborative research also adopt eResearch more extensively, more often use ICT-enhanced collaboration tools, share more of their data, and more often disseminate their findings via digital media.

Chapter 2

Pablo Garaizar, Universidad de Deusto, Spain

Miguel A. Vadillo, Universidad de Deusto, Spain

Diego López-de-Ipiña, Universidad de Deusto, Spain

Helena Matute, Universidad de Deusto, Spain

As a consequence of the joint and rapid evolution of the Internet and the social and behavioral sciences during the last two decades, the Internet is becoming one of the best possible psychological laboratories and is being used by scientists from all over the world in more and more productive and interesting ways each day. This chapter uses examples from psychology, while reviewing the most recent Web paradigms, like the Social Web, Semantic Web, and Cloud Computing, and their implications for e-research in the social and behavioral sciences, and tries to anticipate the possibilities offered to social science researchers by future Internet proposals. The most recent advancements in the architecture of the Web, both from the server and the client-side, are also discussed in relation to behavioral e-research. Given the increasing social nature of the Web, both social scientists and engineers should benefit from knowledge on how the most recent and future Web developments can provide new and creative ways to advance the understanding of the human nature.

Vahid Khatibi, University of Tehran, Iran
Gholam Ali Montazer, Tarbiat Modares University, Iran

Electronic scientific databases (ESDs) such as "ScienceDirect," "GoogleScholar," and "Scopus" became popular in the scientific community, because scientific contents and diverse scientific Web services such as scientific communications and collaborations have taken place electronically in the ESDs. In this way, scientific research has evolved accordingly, yielding electronic research (e-Research) process in which scientists initiate their research, drive it, and reach its determined goals electronically. In this chapter, the authors focus on the ESDs' scientific Web services role in the research process. After representing a classification for the scientific Web services, a comprehensive methodology for the e-Research process is proposed. Also, the effects of scientific Web services on the e-Research process adoption are studied. The findings show that scientific Web services of information storage and sharing, searching, and communications are the most popular and useful Web services in scientific community.

Dukyun Nam, Korea Institute of Science and Technology Information, Republic of Korea
Junehawk Lee, Korea Institute of Science and Technology Information, Republic of Korea
Kum Won Cho, Korea Institute of Science and Technology Information, Republic of Korea

The efficient use of a scientific application service built on a computing environment requires technology that integrates each application service into a workflow so that the workflow is executed in a cooperative environment. There have been a number of attempts to automate research activities as a scientific workflow. However, there are practical problems in the full automation of research activities for a number of simulation programs and researchers. In the cyber environment for Collaborative and Distributed E-Research (CDER), the types of workflows need to be studied and supported separately and with different methodologies. In this chapter, the authors analyze the scientific research and education processes and categorize them into four types: simulation, experiment, collaborative work, and educational activity. They then describe the applications needed for each category. To justify their categorization of the CDER workflow, they examine the workflow of e-AIRS (e-Science Aerospace Integrated Research System), a problem-solving environment for aerospace research.

Paul Longley Arthur, Australian National University, Australia

E-Research is well-established in science and technology fields but is at an earlier stage of development in the humanities. Investments in technology infrastructure worldwide, however, are starting to pay dividends, and a cultural change is occurring, enabling closer collaborations between researchers in a sector that has traditionally emphasized individual research activities. This chapter discusses ways in which the humanities are utilizing digital methods, including: creating and enhancing online collections; building knowledge communities around projects, disciplines, and data; and communicating research results in widely accessible formats. E-Research has brought with it new attitudes, behaviors, and expectations. Topics include the growing opportunities for collaborative and cross-disciplinary approaches, building the information commons, and the need for long-term strategic investment in research infrastructure.

Chapter 6

Christophe Reffay, Ecole Normale Supérieure de Cachan, France & Ecole Normale Supérieure de Lyon, France

Gregory Dyke, Carnegie Mellon University, USA

Marie-Laure Betbeder, Université de Franche-Comté, France

In this chapter, the authors show the importance of data in the research process and the potential benefit for communities to share research data. Although most of their references are taken from the fields of Computer Supported Collaborative Learning and Intelligent Tutoring Systems, they claim that their argument applies to any other field studying complex situations that need to be analyzed by different disciplines, methods, and instruments. The authors point out the evolution of scientific publication, especially its openness and the variety of its emerging forms. This leads them to propose corpora as boundary objects for various communities in the scientific sphere. Data release being itself a complex problem, the authors use the Mulce[1] experience to show how sharable data can be built and made available. Once corpora are considered available, they discuss the potential of their reuse for multiple analyses or derivation. They focus on analytic representations and their combination with initial data or complementary analytic representations by presenting a tool named Tatiana. Finally, the authors propose their vision of data sharing in a world where scientists would use social network applications.

Chapter 7

Paul Smith, National University of Ireland – Galway, Ireland

Sam Redfern, National University of Ireland – Galway, Ireland

In face-to-face work, discussion and negotiation relies strongly on non-verbal feedback, which provides important clues to negotiation states such as agreement/disagreement and understanding/confusion, as well as indicating the emotional states and reactions of those around us. With the continued rise of virtual teams, collaboration increasingly requires tools to manage the reality of distributed e-research and remote work, which is often hampered by a lack of social cohesion and such phenomena as participant multitasking. This chapter discusses important concepts and current issues related to remote research teams and discusses current research in the use of Automatic Facial Expression Recognition Systems (AFERS) in solving some of the inherent problems of the existing online collaboration tools used to support collaborative and distributed research and work. The later half of this chapter describes a proof-of-concept artificial intelligence based software agent (Emotion Tracking Agent, or ETA) developed by the authors for the monitoring of presence and the emotional states of co-workers in virtual research meetings. The agent is intended as an innovative solution to the impaired awareness and attention resulting from continuous task switching or multitasking behaviours of collaborating remote team members. The ETA was developed and integrated into a CVE (Collaborative Virtual Environment), where an initial study was conducted to analyse its benefits and impact on the communicating participants. This chapter describes the results of this study and their implications for the future of distributed e-research and remote work.

Chapter 8

Luis Casillas, University of Guadalajara, Mexico

Thanasis Daradoumis, University of the Aegean, Greece & Open University of Catalonia, Spain

This chapter presents a proposal for modeling / simulating experiments conducted by scientists working in common scientific problems, based on gathering and exploiting knowledge elements produced among them. The authors' approach enables the adaptation of knowledge structures (bounded to scientific problems) and is based on recurrent refining processes that are fed by indicators, which come from collaboration among the scientists involved. This scheme captures a web-based infrastructure, which allows scientists to collaborate on synthesizing experiments online. The proposed model is approached as an ontology that contains scientific concepts and actions. This ontology is linked to the scientific problem and represents both the "common understanding" for such a problem and the way it could be managed by the group. This dynamic ontology will change its structure according to the collaboration acts among scientists. Frequent collaboration over certain elements of the experiment will make them prevail in time. Besides, this process has been defined in a way that provides a global understanding of the scientific treatment that could be applied on any scientific problem. Hence, the ontology represents a virtualization of the scientific experiment. This whole representation is aimed at providing the media for developing e-research among scientists that are working on common problems.

Section 2
Applications and Case Studies

Chapter 9

Jake Rowan Byrne, Trinity College Dublin, Ireland

Brendan Tangney, Trinity College Dublin, Ireland

This chapter discusses a range of topics, including pedagogical concerns, writing practices, existing tools, and human computer interaction approaches, all related to the design of a tool to support PhD candidates with their academic writing. These topics are then used to inform the design of a computer supported collaborative writing tool, CAWriter, which is being developed as part of an ongoing participatory design research project concerned with the creation of a toolkit to support doctoral candidates. This chapter reviews existing tools to support the writing process and explores both the relevant pedagogical and human-computer interaction foundations necessary for the design of such tools. The chapter concludes with a look at a number of initial iterations of the CAWriter tool and the design rationale and approaches used.

Chapter 10

Maria Kordaki, University of the Aegean, Greece

Gabriel Gorghiu, Valahia University Targoviste, Romania

Mihai Bîzoi, Valahia University Targoviste, Romania

Adina Glava, Babes-Bolyai University, Romania

This chapter focuses on the investigation of essential features of a multinational virtual community that can promote effective collaboration and research among its members so as to overcome space, time, and language barriers. Specifically, a multinational Virtual Community Collaborative Space for Sciences Education has been formed in the context of the Socrates Comenius 2.1 European Project: "VccSSe – Virtual Community Collaborating Space for Science Education." In this project, researchers from five European countries (Romania, Spain, Poland, Finland, and Greece) participated in a multinational learning community where blended collaborative learning courses were formed in order to train teachers from these countries in the use of Information and Communication Technologies (ICT) in their real teaching practices. Within this framework, a number of specific software and pedagogical tools were formed to support collaboration and learning for the teachers and the researchers who participated in this virtual community. After the end of these courses, the teachers were asked to design their own virtual experiments and lesson plans and then to implement them in their classrooms. The analysis of the data shows that the researchers-partners of VccSSe effectively used various collaborative methods to produce the previously mentioned software and pedagogical tools. It has been also shown that teachers who participated in the VccSSe project were encouraged—by the use of the collaborative tools provided and the aforementioned collaborative blended course—to develop interesting virtual experiments and use them in their classrooms. Finally, it is worth noting that students who participated in those classes provided favourable feedback related to the implementation of virtual experiments in their everyday learning experiences.

Chapter 11

Javier Faulin, Public University of Navarre, Spain
Angel A. Juan, Open University of Catalonia, Spain
Fernando Lera, Public University of Navarre, Spain
Barry B. Barrios, Northwestern University, USA
Alex Forcada, University of Zaragoza, Spain

This chapter introduces the interrelated concepts of e-Research and e-Mentoring, reviews some recent works related to them, and discusses their importance in a global, Internet-based world. In this chapter, a conceptual framework is proposed to distinguish among the concepts of e-Research, e-Science, and Cyberinfrastructure, which are frequently used synonymously in the existing literature. Then, some issues related to e-Mentoring are discussed, including its characteristics, benefits, challenges, and a review of different Web 2.0 tools that can facilitate and promote e-Mentoring practices in most research organizations. Some personal experiences in e-Mentoring are then related. These experiences involve different universities and international programs, and their study points out several key factors of a successful e-Mentoring collaboration.

Chapter 12

Paolo Diviacco, Istituto Nazionale di Oceanografia e di Geofisica Sperimentale, Italy

A certain number of disciplinary fields are characterized by the intersection of *"soft"* and *"hard"* sciences, resulting in the coexistence of quasi-hermeneutic and nomological approaches. Among the many that correspond to this description, such as medicine or archeology, the author focused on the geo-sciences and in particular on exploration geophysics. Here the inductive/deductive method that characterizes physics meets the abductive approach of geology, creating a very fertile ground for researchers to develop concurrent cognitive models for the same issue. These contrasting visions tend to isolate themselves, thus developing specific knowledge and practices that subsequently make them incompatible. Collaborative research intending to bridge these communities of practices can therefore prove to be problematic, so a form of mediator becomes necessary. Most existing collaborative tools assume that partners share the same perspective on the entities they are working on and therefore these solutions cannot be applied directly to the types of cases this chapter addresses. By exploring geophysics and its peculiarities, one understands its inner dynamics, so that possible solutions can be proposed. These rely on the creation of "boundary objects" capable of bridging different cognitive models. These solutions are based on the integration of diagrams, where concepts and their relations are expressed at an optimal granularity and shared spaces where information can be made available to all partners. These ideas have been implemented in a Web-based Computer-Supported Collaborative Research (CSCR) system that is currently successfully used within many international research projects in this disciplinary field.

Omid Noroozi, Wageningen University, The Netherlands

Harm Biemans, Wageningen University, The Netherlands

Maria C. Busstra, Wageningen University, The Netherlands

Martin Mulder, Wageningen University, The Netherlands

Vitaliy Popov, Wageningen University, The Netherlands

Mohammad Chizari, Tarbiat Modares University, Iran

This chapter presents a case study of Computer Supported Collaborative Learning (CSCL) in the field of human nutrition and health at Wageningen University in The Netherlands. More specifically, this study investigates the effect of the type of collaboration (personal discussion in front of a shared computer vs. online discussion) in CSCL on students' learning outcomes. A pre-test, post-test design was used. Eighty-two students were asked (as an individual pre-test) to design and analyze a study which evaluates a certain dietary assessment method. Subsequently, they were asked to discuss their evaluation studies in randomized pairs. The pairs in one group discussed their task results online and the pairs in the other group discussed their results face-to-face while sharing one computer, in both cases using the CSCL platform Drewlite. As an individual post-test, students had to re-design and re-analyze the same evaluation study. Learning outcomes were measured based on the results of teachers' regular evaluation of students' achievements as well as on the quality of the students' knowledge construction. The results showed that both teachers' marks and the quality of knowledge construction of all students improved significantly from pre-test to post-test. However, the type of collaboration had no significantly different effect. Furthermore, the scores on knowledge construction were consistent with exam results as obtained by teachers' evaluations.

Mayte López-Ferrer, Polytechnic University of Valencia, Spain

This research is within the frame of sociometric studies of science, particularly the application of social networks to co-authorship, and patterns of citations among researchers in Psychiatry and Neurosciences, General Psychology, and Experimental Psychology. This chapter applies Social Network Analysis to information retrieval from a multidisciplinary database; subject headings lists are not considered sufficient or sufficiently flexible to describe relationships between the sciences. The aim is also to identify similarities and differences among these areas according to bibliometric and network indicators. Social Network Analysis used to select scientific articles within a discipline overcomes the rigidity of information retrieval based on a preselected set of topics. Network graphs can be used to show working groups that otherwise would remain hidden. It is useful, also, to overlap networks of co-authorship (explicit relations) and patterns of cited references (implicit relations), which allow comparison between individual author or groups and the whole group. Finally, the author highlights the need to adapt assessment indicators from different scientific areas to allow consideration of the characteristics of diverse disciplines, based not only on the productivity of individual authors, but also their capacity to mediate with other actors and works within the research system.

This chapter describes how Value Networks (VNs) can be applied in multi-stakeholder business and research environments to characterise different approaches to collaboration. In an attempt to highlight some of the issues, the authors compare a couple of communities that adopt different approaches to Knowledge Exchange (KE) and resource discovery. A collaboration framework is used by one of the communities for on-line discussion, chat, and Web conferencing to supplement KE between fairly regular in-person meetings. The other community applies more traditional collaboration tools such as e-mail to supplement face-to-face meetings. One of the research objectives was to establish the extent of multi-dimensional KE, i.e. from academic to business sector, business sector to business sector, and government to business sector. Conditional on successful e-facilitation, a quickening in KE was apparent in the community that used the collaboration framework. This was observed to a lesser or greater extent across all stakeholder groups. E-facilitators are those that engage stakeholders into making on-line submissions. The authors discuss the importance of satisfactory levels of support for collaboration frameworks in community projects. They compare the role of the e-facilitator with a more traditional "business broker" and compare the behaviour of the communities with and without particular collaboration tools. The authors conclude that VNs helped provide a useful characterisation of the roles that the various contributing community elements play and the types of interaction between them.

This chapter presents a comparative analysis of three case studies (all from the field of social and political science) on global e-research collaboration, describing how Information and Communication Technologies (ICTs) are facilitating the overcoming of geographical barriers. Previous research points out that physical e-research collaboration meetings play a relevant role. This chapter explores whether this requirement of physical meetings in e-research collaboration is independent of the scale and complexity of the collaboration established. The findings suggest that high complexity can be achieved using communication tools if the scale of the group is small, while very large groups can collaborate using communication tools if their target is a loose collaboration. However, if the collaboration involves both a large group and a considered complexity of collaboration, establishing a balance between communication tools with the requirement of physical meetings becomes a relevant issue.

Foreword

Over the last half century, research communities across the world have been experiencing a range of noticeable changes in their mundane inquiry practices. Most significant of them have much to do with the emergence of digital research affordances and computer networks. Academic writing has moved from a pen and paper-based mode to digital word processing to collaborative writing platforms. Research dissemination has been supplemented with digital publishing opportunities, which include online journals, websites, blogs, and wikis. Research libraries have been complemented with online databases and powerful search tools. Data gathering has been enhanced by remote digital instruments. Data analysis and discovery processes have been complemented with the possibilities to 'shuffle' around large amounts of digital data and visual representations. In short, at least the part of research activity that constitutes the internal workings of scholarly practice has changed from being material to being digital, from being co-located in physical places to being distributed in virtual spaces—but has research become fundamentally different?

A quick scan through the list of the most prominent scientific discoveries of the 21st century leaves little doubt about the value of digital technologies—neither "Empirical Research on Cause and Effect in the Macro-Economy" nor "The Discovery of the Accelerating Expansion of the Universe through Observations of Distant Supernovae" nor "The Discovery of Quasicrystals"[1] would have been possible without technology-enhanced research instruments, large digital datasets, and computational data analysis and visualization tools. While changes in research practices have perhaps been less universal than some eResearch protagonists expected, the emergence of new disciplines on the borders of traditional scholarship and technological innovation overall leads us to conclude that some changes have been deep in many research fields. New trans-disciplinary research fields—such as bioinformatics, ecoinformatics, cultural informatics, computational linguistics, and learning analytics—increasingly address the most challenging questions of the 21st century.

However, at the core of most radical developments in contemporary research have been not only *the digital* reconstruction in *the material* fabric of scientific practice, but rather noticeable rearrangements in *the social* fabric of knowledge production; this social fabric of knowledge production is reffered to in this book as *collaborative and distributed eResearch.* The move towards more collaborative models of scientific practice can be observed on many levels: from top-down centralized research policies to self-organized forms of networked scholarship. For example, over recent years, the focuses of some governmental research programs have shifted from concentrating research capacities in strong research centers and laboratories to coordinating distributed research capacities by supporting networks, virtual institutes, and other collaboratories.[2] Similar trends can be observed in the seemingly uncoordinated emergence of some distributed virtual research teams that bring together intellectual capacities of researchers with various disciplinary backgrounds and levels of expertise.[3]

Nevertheless, genuine productive collaborative eResearch has been a challenge. For some, this is mainly a technical question: researchers simply need better collaborative research tools, services, and skills. For others, this is a matter of social and epistemological concern, to include disciplinary differences, conflicting mental models, data sharing issues, ethical concerns, and challenges establishing social presence.

One of the most distinct features of this volume is that it approaches the above mentioned issues from a range of perspectives. The chapters, taken together, present a wide-ranging account of collaborative eResearch, addressing technologies, applications, strategies, and practices. Several distinct and complementary threads run throughout the book.

First, the chapters discuss collaborative eResearch in a variety of disciplinary and multidisciplinary contexts, to include social and behavioral sciences, humanities, business, aerospace, geophysics, and education. This broad coverage of disciplinary domains and multidisciplinary fields clearly illustrates that distributed technology-enhanced research is not limited to exact and physical sciences, but rather includes increasingly social domains and the humanities.

Second, the volume presents a variety of aspects concerned with the development of innovative eResearch applications, including eResearch platforms, electronic databases, data sharing tools, and collaborative writing applications. Some chapters discuss new ontology-based system models and other complex system design decisions for distributed collaborative research. They illustrate that the development of new technological affordances is a complex engineering task that requires creativity and conceptual innovation.

Third, a set of chapters report empirical research in which eResearch methodologies have been applied for researching emerging collaborative eResearch practices. These contributions not only show the needs and challenges for understanding the social complexity of digital collaboration, but also illustrate the value of various digital research approaches, such as facial expression recognition, value network analysis, and social network analysis.

The overarching message that emerges from this collection is that many opportunities and challenges for distributed collaborative research unfold as we do eResearch. Scholars who work at this frontier should be involved in continuous innovation by developing new technologies and applications, adjusting their inquiry practices, researching, and fine-tuning what they do as they go. This timely volume offers an important contribution to future development of this technologically, methodologically, and socially complex research domain.

Lina Markauskaite
The University of Sydney, Australia
October 23rd, 2011

ENDNOTES

[1]   These three research achievements have been awarded 2011 Nobel prizes in economics, physics, and chemistry, respectively. Nobel Prize. (2011). *All nobel prizes*. Retrieved 23 Oct 2011 from http://www.nobelprize.org/nobel_prizes/lists/all.

[2]   For examples see recent US and Australian national research funding initiatives: NSF. (2011). Science across virtual institutes (SAVI). *National Science Foundation*. Retrieved 23 October 2011

from http://www.nsf.gov/news/special_reports/savi/index.jsp. NeCTAR. (2011). Virtual Laboratories. *National eResearch Collaboration Tools and Resources NeCTAR*. Retrieved 23 October 2011 from http://nectar.org.au/virtual-laboratory.

[3]   For example, a virtual research group for investigating one massive online open course has emerged just within few months. See: Siemens, G. (2011). *Researching open online courses*. Retrieved 23 October 2011 from http://www.elearnspace.org/blog/2011/07/04/researching-open-online-courses.

Lina Markauskaite is a Senior Lecturer in the Faculty of Education and Social Work and a member of the Centre for Research on Computer-Supported Learning and Cognition at the University of Sydney. Her background is in mathematics, informatics, and communications management. Markauskaite's research investigates students' and trainee teachers' ICT literacy, personal epistemology, and epistemic fluency, eResearch practices, and ICT-enhanced research methods for social sciences, and eResearch in education. She has been the lead researcher of the collaborative study, "Co-Developing eResearch Infrastructure," that investigated technology-enhanced research practices, attitudes, and future requirements at seven New South Wales universities in Australia. Her recent co-edited book, with P. Freebody and J. Irwin (2011), is Methodological Choice and Design: Scholarship, Policy, and Practice in Social and Educational Research from Springer.

Preface

INTRODUCTION

With the ubiquitous nature of technological innovation over the last decades, not only have we seen the growth of new international and distributed research groups, but we are also witnessing the transformation of how scientific research itself is being developed in most traditional face-to-face universities and research centers. These technological innovations have driven the growth of new research opportunities, as researchers from different countries/regions can now interact with colleagues, who have similar research interests, at their convenience and without distance barriers. In effect, in a global world, researchers and research groups do not have to limit themselves to geographic or temporal regions and zones. On the contrary, they now have the opportunity to use Internet-based technologies to collaborate, without physical interaction, with other researchers and groups from different parts of the planet. As a matter of fact, Internet-based technologies and social networks are changing the way in which scientific research is developed worldwide. These technologies include, among others, online environments for collaborative research and work, materials in electronic format, specific subject-related software, groupware, and social network software, and Internet resources and services, e.g. cloud repositories, VoIP and videoconferencing tools, real-time translation services, etc.

Collaborative e-Research refers to the use of Internet-based computing, communication, and information technologies to develop international and distributed scientific research. Hence, it is our understanding that the term e-Research should refer to any kind of collaborative research activity throughout the Internet, in any academic discipline and field (not only Science and Engineering), and including also the design and development of Internet-based environments designed to facilitate this research. Additional issues, related to online collaboration, team management, inter- or multi-disciplinary approaches, research globalization, etc. must also be considered as directly linked to the e-Research domain. Benefits of collaborative e-Research are evident; just to name a few: researchers can interact and share knowledge with other remote researchers with similar interests without having to move from one country to another, international knowledge communities or social science networks can be easily and quickly configured, participation in foreign research projects is promoted, PhD and Master thesis can be co-advised by several senior researchers from different institutions, etc. Therefore, there is little doubt that the Internet is becoming a decisive tool in the international research arena, and, in fact, it is modeling the way scientific research is performed worldwide.

Among the different goals of this book, we can cite the following: (1) identifying and sharing worldwide best practices regarding Collaborative e-Research at an international level; (2) sharing theoretical or applied models and systems used in Collaborative e-Research, including the use of computer-supported collaborative research for international research projects; (3) forecasting emerging technologies and tendencies regarding collaborative e-research and e-research management systems; (4) providing the academic community with a base text that could serve as a reference in research on collaborative e-research; and (5) presenting up-to-date research work on how the Internet is changing international research experiences and practices in a global and Web-based world.

CHAPTER SYNOPSIS

The chapters in this book have been divided into two parts: (1) Technologies and Strategies and (2) Applications and Case Studies. What follows is a chapter-by chapter overview for each of these areas.

Section 1: Technologies and Strategies

In Chapter 1, "*Investigating eResearch: Collaboration Practices and Future Challenges,*" Markauskaite et al. explore open questions in e-Research such as: Why and how do researchers collaborate, share knowledge resources, data, and expertise? What kinds of infrastructures and services do they use, and what do they need for the future enhancement of collaborative research practices? etc. Their findings are based on collaboration practices developed at several universities.

In Chapter 2, "*The Web as a Platform for e-Research in the Social and Behavioral Sciences,*" Garaizar et al. review the most recent Web paradigms (e.g. the Social Web, Semantic Web, and Cloud Computing), as well as their implications for e-Research in the Social and Behavioral Sciences. They also discuss the possibilities offered to social science researchers by the current and future Internet.

In Chapter 3, "*E-Research Methodology,*" Khatibi and Montazer focus on electronic scientific databases and discuss their role in the research process. They also propose a comprehensive methodology for the e-Research process and elaborate on the importance of scientific Web services to the scientific community.

In Chapter 4, "*Collaborative and Distributed e-Research Environment for Supporting Scientific Research and the Education Process,*" Nam et al. analyze the scientific research and education processes in the context of a Cyber-Environment for Collaborative and Distributed e-Research. As a real example, they also examine the workflow of e-AIRS, a problem-solving environment for aerospace research.

In Chapter 5, "*Connecting and Enabling the Humanities: e-Research in the Border Zone,*" Paul Arthur discusses how e-Research is evolving in the humanities. He also analyzes different ways in which researchers in that field are utilizing Internet-based methods.

In Chapter 6, "*Data Sharing in CSCR: Towards In-Depth Long Term Collaboration,*" Reffay et al. examine the importance of data in the research process and the potential benefit for communities to share research data. They propose their vision of data sharing in a world where scientists would use social network applications.

In Chapter 7, "*Artificial Intelligence Supported Non-Verbal Communication for Enriched Collaboration in Distributed E-Research Environments,*" Smith and Redfern discern important concepts and current issues related to remote research teams. They also discuss current research in the use of automatic facial expression recognition systems in the context of collaborative and distributed research and work.

In Chapter 8, "*An Ontological Structure for Gathering and Sharing Knowledge among Scientists through Experiment Modeling,*" Casillas and Daradoumis propose an ontology-based model to support scientific interaction among researchers involved in common problems.

Section 2: Applications and Case Studies

In Chapter 9, "*CAWriter: A Computer Supported Collaborative Tool to Support Doctoral Candidates Academic Writing – A Pedagogical and Human-Computer Interaction Perspective,*" Byrne and Tangney present a collaborative tool to support PhD candidates with their academic writing and analyze a range of related topics, including pedagogical concerns, writing practices, existing tools, and human-computer interaction approaches.

In Chapter 10, "*Collaboration within Multinational Learning Communities: The Case of the Virtual Community Collaborative Space for Sciences Education European Project,*" Kordaki et al. investigate essential features of a multinational virtual community that can promote effective collaboration and research. They describe the Socrates Comenius 2.1 European Project, participated by researchers from five European countries, and some of its main results.

In Chapter 11, "*E-Mentoring: Issues and Experiences in Starting e-Research Collaborations in Graduate Programs,*" Faulin et al. review some recent works related to e-Mentoring and e-Research, discuss the benefits and challenges of e-Mentoring, and depict some personal experiences on the topic.

In Chapter 12, "*Addressing Conflicting Cognitive Models in Collaborative e-Research: A Case Study in Exploration Geophysics,*" Paolo Diviacco describes a Web-based system that is currently used within several international collaborative research initiatives. The system is based on the integration of diagrams, where concepts and their relations are expressed at an optimal granularity, and shared spaces, where information can be made available to all partners.

In Chapter 13, "*Effects of the Drewlite CSCL Platform on Students' Learning Outcomes,*" Noroozi et al. present a case study of Computer Supported Collaborative Learning at Wageningen University in the Netherlands. Moreover, they investigate the effect of the type of collaboration in Computer-Supported Collaborative Learning on students' learning outcomes.

In Chapter 14, "*Social Network Analysis Tools to Understand how Research Groups Interact: A Case Study,*" Mayte Lopez applies Social Network Analysis to information retrieval from a multidisciplinary database and discusses how network graphs can be used to show working groups, overlap networks of co-authorship, and patterns of cited references.

In Chapter 15, "*Collaborative and Distributed Innovation and Research in Business Activity,*" Allan et al. describe how Value Networks can be applied in multi-stakeholder business and research environments to characterize different approaches to collaboration.

Finally, in Chapter 16, "*E-Research Collaboration of International Scope in Social and Political Sciences: Scale and Complexity Linkage with the Requirement of Physical Encounters,*" Mayo Fuster presents a comparative analysis of three case studies on global e-research collaboration. This chapter explores whether the requirement of physical meetings in e-research collaboration is independent of the scale and complexity of the collaboration established.

FINAL WORDS

There are a growing number of available books covering e-learning, computer-supported collaborative work, and, of course, a long history of books covering research issues. However, to the best of our knowledge, this is one of the first international books focused on Internet-based collaborative research, or, simply, collaborative e-research. Accordingly, we expect this book to be a valuable tool for academics and professionals involved in distributed and collaborative research, international research centers, collaborative software developers, as well as instructors implementing courses in computer-supported collaborative work. The text will also be potentially useful for senior year undergraduate or graduate studies in Information Technologies and related fields.

e-Research is an emerging, tech- and social-based, multi-disciplinary, and continuously evolving area of interest for researchers worldwide. With the currently available information, communication, and computing technologies, it is natural to expect that an important part of the next-decade research will be developed by multi-disciplinary and international teams, sharing and analyzing vast amounts of data, performing simulations over distributed computing systems, and using Web-based environments to communicate and collaborate online. If we also consider the rate at which the aforementioned technologies have been evolving during the last decade, and expecting a similar evolution for the following years, we can only say that the best is yet to come.

Angel A. Juan
IN3 - Open University of Catalonia, Spain

Thanasis Daradoumis
University of the Aegean, Greece, & Open University of Catalonia, Spain

Meritxell Roca
IN3 - Open University of Catalonia, Spain

Scott E. Grasman
Rochester Institute of Technology, USA

Javier Faulin
Public University of Navarre, Spain

Acknowledgment

We would like to thank the authors, reviewers, and EAB members for their collaboration and prompt responses to our enquiries, which enabled completion of this book in a timely manner. We gratefully acknowledge the help and encouragement of the editor at IGI Global, Hannah Abelbeck. Also, our thanks go to the staff involved with the production of the book.

Angel A. Juan
IN3 - Open University of Catalonia, Spain

Thanasis Daradoumis
University of the Aegean, Greece, & Open University of Catalonia, Spain

Meritxell Roca
IN3 - Open University of Catalonia, Spain

Scott E. Grasman
Rochester Institute of Technology, USA

Javier Faulin
Public University of Navarre, Spain

September 15, 2011

Section 1
Technologies and Strategies

Chapter 1
Investigating eResearch:
Collaboration Practices and Future Challenges

Lina Markauskaite
University of Sydney, Australia

Mary Anne Kennan
Charles Sturt University, Australia

Jim Richardson
University of Sydney, Australia

Anindito Aditomo
University of Sydney, Australia

Leonie Hellmers
Intersect Australia Ltd., Australia

ABSTRACT

Why and how do researchers collaborate, share knowledge resources, data, and expertise? What kinds of infrastructures and services do they use, and what do they need for the future enhancement of collaborative research practices? The chapter focuses on existing and potential eResearch from a "user" perspective. Drawing on a study of ICT-enhanced research practices and needs conducted at seven Australian universities, it discusses how researchers engage with distributed research and use ICT for collaboration. Findings show significant current engagement of the majority of researchers in collaborative research, their acknowledgement of the potential of eResearch, and researchers' general willingness to engage in collaborative eResearch. While there are some essential differences in the collaboration practices of research students and academics and between practices and challenges in different disciplinary domains, researchers who are more involved in collaborative research also adopt eResearch more extensively, more often use ICT-enhanced collaboration tools, share more of their data, and more often disseminate their findings via digital media.

DOI: 10.4018/978-1-4666-0125-3.ch001

BACKGROUND AND AIMS

National and international research agendas almost universally acknowledge that successful solutions of global issues and future social, cultural, and scientific innovation fundamentally rely on distributed scholarly practices and research collaborations, such as the sharing and integration of data, resources and knowledge, remote collaborative access to scientific instruments, and pooled human expertise (Atkins, et al., 2003; Hey, Tansley, & Tolle, 2009). Many countries, including Australia, have made significant strategic investments in developing general and discipline-specific data repositories, virtual laboratories and other shared technology-enhanced research infrastructures often known under several broad umbrella terms, such as 'eResearch,' 'Cyberinfrastructure,' 'eInfrastructure,' 'eScience,' 'eHumanities,' 'eSocial Sciences,' and 'The Grid' (ACLS, 2006; Atkins, et al., 2003; DEST, 2006; http://www.e-irg.eu/images, 2009; NCRIS Committee, 2008). Some pioneering collaborative research projects have demonstrated successful uptake of new research infrastructures and significant benefits of collaborative research practices (e.g., see Hey, et al., 2009). However, experiences from some other technology-enhanced collaborative projects have suggested that researchers involved in such collaborative research also face a range of challenges, and such research collaborations have not been as successful as it was initially expected (Borgman, 2007; Haythornthwaite, et al., 2006; Lawrence, 2006; Meyer, 2009). Further, the uptake of collaborative research practices and new infrastructures beyond pilot projects tend to be slower and less transformative than initially planned (Foster & Gibbons, 2005). Among key questions for further development of eResearch are the widening adoption of technology-enhanced research practices and the sustainability of 'proof-to-concept' developed eResearch tools and services (Halfpenny, et al., 2009).

eResearch infrastructure developers face significant challenges and tensions in meeting current researcher demands and simultaneously creating infrastructure for the desired future (Ribes & Finholt, 2009). On the one hand, effective technological infrastructures for data sharing, communication, remote data analysis, and other distributed research tasks are important enablers of collaborative discovery and innovation. On the other hand, many barriers for collaborative research tend to be not technological, but rather social, cultural and organizational, such as lack of researchers' willingness and engagement, difficulties managing information, ethical concerns, and legal issues (David, 2006; Haythornthwaite, et al., 2006; Jirotka, et al., 2005; Lawrence, 2006). Further, researchers' scientific challenges, their ways of doing collaborative research and their needs for eResearch infrastructures and support vary considerably within and across disciplines and research fields (Bos, et al., 2007; Fry, 2006; Laterza, Carmichael, & Procter, 2007). In order to create infrastructures and services that meet researchers' expectations and epistemic practices now and in the future, eResearch implementers and funders need initially to understand existing research questions, current challenges and practices, and future research visions.

Why and how do researchers collaborate, share knowledge, resources, and expertise? What encourages researchers and what prevents them from engaging in collaborative eResearch practices? What kind of infrastructures, services and support do they need? How do they envision collaborative eResearch in the future of their field?

In order to answer these questions, this chapter discusses findings about distributed research practices and collaboration from a broad survey-based study on Information and Communication Technology (ICT)-enhanced research practices which was conducted at seven Australian universities. The chapter has three main objectives: (a) to present a snapshot of current traditional and ICT-enhanced collaboration practices in various disciplines in the Australian eResearch context; (b) to discuss researchers' needs for eResearch services and support and their vision about the role of collaborative eResearch for future progress of their research field; (c) to explore some existing coherences and differences between 'top-down' collaborative research visions expressed in 'grand' eResearch strategies and projects on the one hand, and 'bottom-up' researcher experiences and views of effective collaborative practices on the other.

This exploration is both distinct and limited in several specific ways. First, it is based on empirical data collected in the Australian eResearch context, which has been little explored in mainstream sociological eResearch literature. Second, it provides an account of eResearch potential and challenges from an ordinary 'ICT user-researcher' perspective. This perspective is quite distinct from the accounts of eResearch developers and early adopters, which are more often reported in similar literature (e.g., Barjak, et al., 2009), yet this user perspective is fundamental for developing productive ways forward (Ribes & Finholt, 2009).

This chapter is structured as follows. The following two sections introduce the Australian eResearch context and review ICT-enhanced collaboration practices and challenges reported in the literature. The next section describes the approach and procedure of the empirical study. The following results section provides a snapshot of researchers' answers about their collaboration and distributed practices, and explores some differences between the practices of academics and research students, researchers from different disciplinary domains, and those already involved in various kinds of research collaboration. The final section discusses key findings and major implications. Among key insights are some noticeable discrepancies among current researchers' ICT-enhanced collaboration practices, their short-term needs for eResearch services and support, and their thinking about eResearch potential in their research domain. Further, the section highlights a noticeable discrepancy, in researchers' thinking

about eResearch roles and challenges between two distinct modes of distributed research: (a) 'team-based' collaboration that extends possibilities, but comfortably fits with familiar research routines; and (b) 'grand' distributed collaboration that requires new coordination practices and additional efforts.

AUSTRALIAN ERESEARCH CONTEXT

The use of ICT in research is not a new phenomenon—in fact the development of academic networks and ICT infrastructures for research and education has been part of international and national strategies in many countries, including Australia, for several decades (De Roure, et al., 2003; Korporaal, 2009). eResearch as an independent initiative in Australia emerged in the background of similar international developments, in the mid 2000s (Paterson, et al., 2007). This development was marked by the launch of an eResearch Coordinating Committee that released an Australian eResearch Strategy and Implementation Framework, which outlined an eResearch vision and its key elements (DEST, 2006). As this document states:

"The vision for eResearch in Australia is that Australian researchers will enhance their contribution to world-class research endeavours and outcomes, through the use of advanced and innovative information and communications technologies. The vision encourages researchers to participate in the technological revolution that offers the power to undertake research on a scope previously unattainable—to work collaboratively and globally and improve their research as a result." (p. vii).

This strategy resulted in a number of programs outlined in the National Collaborative Research Infrastructure Strategy's Roadmap (NCRIS Committee, 2008) and targeted investments intended to enhance collaboration, assist researchers in managing large datasets, and provide high speed computing and innovative analysis tools. These national infrastructures and services are delivered in partnerships with state-based eResearch initiatives, such as Intersect in NSW and VeRSI in Victoria. Funded initiatives include two broad sets of programs. One group of programs covers a variety of aspects related to the development of generic eResearch infrastructure and services, such as development of research data commons, shared access methods, large data collections, high performance computing and extended bandwidth (NCRIS, 2011). The second set of programs is more focused on the development of discipline-specific services and tools, including eResearch resources for medical research, humanities, social sciences and arts. Examples of such disciplinary projects are Collaborative Visualisation Tools for Creative eResearch (Aus-e-Stage); Integration and Annotation Services for Australian Literature Communities (Aus-e-Lit); Data Management for Microscopy, Imaging, Neutron and X-Ray Facilities (DataMINX); Data Integration and Access Services for Biodiversity (DIAS-B); National Criminal Justice Research Data Network (NCJRDN); and Marine and Climate Data Discovery and Access Project (MACDDAP) (ARCS, 2011). More recently announced eResearch Collaboration Tools and Resources and Research Data Storage Infrastructure programs, part of a new national Super Science Initiative, also aim to support both multi-purpose and more problem- and discipline-specific eResearch tools and virtual laboratories.

Concurrent with, and related to, these developments were programs addressing the accessibility, visibility and dissemination of research data and outputs. The national government recognized that accessibility to research presents significant challenges for researchers and the public and that some areas—such as data and information access, management and preservation—need

significant attention and investment. It addressed this need by providing funding for a number of schemes such as institutional repositories with an early focus on accessibility and dissemination of research publications (Kennan & Kingsley, 2009), and more recently by concentrating on data curation, sharing, and accessibility through the development of data commons (Clarke, Harrison, & Searle, 2009; Paterson, et al., 2007).

Overall, Australian eResearch and research information infrastructure initiatives recognize that enabling infrastructures include more than just technology, but also researchers' expertise, leadership, and governance, ICT management and support. Nevertheless, much funding and attention has been directed towards development of new 'hard' infrastructures, tools and services rather than 'soft' programs for user capacity building and engagement with eResearch. 'Social side' and 'social shaping' of eResearch in Australia, has received less attention than in other countries, such as the UK, The Netherlands, and other North American and European counties (Barjak, et al., 2009; Ribes & Finholt, 2009; Ribes & Lee, 2010; Woolgar, 2004; Wouters & Beaulieu, 2007).

LITERATURE REVIEW: ICT-ENHANCED COLLABORATION PRACTICES AND CHALLENGES

Any understanding of ICT-enhanced collaboration practices and challenges must begin from the understanding of collaboration among researchers more generally. This section focuses on three major aspects of research collaboration: (a) the research process; (b) data sharing and re-use; and (c) research dissemination. It initially reviews some major insights from the sociological literature into practices, motives and impediments for collaborative research and then extends this discussion to include the literature on ICT-enhanced research infrastructures.

Research collaboration is complex and manifests in many ways, such as co-investigation on research projects, sharing and integration of data and information, remote collaborative access to scientific instruments, pooled human expertise and shared authorship (Borgman, 2007; Katz & Martin, 1997). Participants in collaborative research can be active or passive in one or more phases of research (Katz & Martin, 1997). Collaboration can occur simultaneously or in an indirect or serial manner (Borgman, 2007).

Previously much research has been conducted by lone researchers, or co-located teams (Katz & Martin, 1997) where most team members had similar disciplinary background, but this has changed over recent decades. Needs for more collaborative forms of research arise from factors such as the increased complexity and scope of research problems requiring multi-, inter-, and trans-disciplinary approaches linking specialised expertise, needs in some scientific projects for expensive instruments and computational power, and pressure from some funders (Katz & Martin, 1997). Despite these encouragements and prevailing opinion that high productivity correlates with collaboration, it is recognised that collaboration is difficult and that collaboration over distance even more so (Barjak, et al., 2009; Borgman, 2007; Olson, Zimmerman & Bos 2008).

Disciplines vary in their practices in a number of ways, from the objects of their investigations and the methods they use, to the dissemination methods and types of publications they favour and the ways they collaborate (Meadows, 1998). Generally, researchers in physical sciences collaborate more than those in the social sciences and humanities (Becher & Trowler, 2001). Further, within disciplines experimentalists tend to collaborate more than theoreticians (Katz & Martin, 1997).

Facilitating collaboration, particularly distributed collaboration, is one of the primary goals of eResearch. The scale, scope and focus of eResearch collaborations can vary from large "virtual organisations" together tackling broad global problems, such as those using the "collaboratory" model (Olson, Zimmerman, & Bos, 2008), to small scale collaborations with a narrower focus, such as teams working on specific issues and analyzing shared data sets together (Borgman, 2007; Hey & Trefethen, 2008).

Adopting ICT-enhanced collaboration practices is not an easy process, and typically demands attention and development over time (Bos, et al., 2007; Jirotka, et al., 2006; Laterza, et al., 2007; Lawrence, 2006). For example, reviewing the process of collaborative eResearch adoption by a group of scientists and engineers, Olson and colleagues (2008) note that much of the early focus was on using the Internet to exchange large amounts of data, provide access to high-end computing resources and share instrumentation. Over time this collaboration grew to include more human interaction and a broad range of joint activities.

Sharing data is core to eResearch collaboration. Data can be re-used to reproduce and validate original findings, to advance the original research or open another line of enquiry sometimes using vast amounts of data collected over time and from various sources. The literature speaks of a "deluge" of scientific and research data (Hey, et al., 2009; Hey & Trefethen, 2003; Wilson, et al., 2007) and the importance of capturing and managing it for use beyond its original community, purpose, and time. Data value increases as it is interconnected, networked, shared, used, and re-used (Borgman, 2007). Vast amounts of complex and varied data are being generated and collected, and too often this data is lost or discarded as researchers move, projects complete and storage technologies evolve (Henty, et al., 2008; Markauskaite, et al., 2009). For better collaborative exploration and exploitation of data as it exponentially grows, the data must be better understood and managed (Karasti, Baker, & Halkola, 2006).

Data is heterogeneous and some datasets can be extremely large. Different disciplines have different types of data ranging from large gigabyte-scale files in crystallography through databases and spreadsheets to small text files of interviews in humanities research (Borgman, 2007; Carlson & Anderson, 2007; Henty, et al., 2008). To re-use data, researchers need to understand its provenance, content, the conditions it was collected under, access restrictions and many other details (Edwards, et al., 2009; Hey & Trefethen, 2008; Miles, et al., 2007; Wu, Heok, & Tamsir, 2007). This heterogeneity can present technical and social challenges, and analysis is required of the data characteristics, its production, and the communication *mores* of the community the data serves before data management can occur (Cragin, et al., 2010). Data sharing "…is a complex social process involving trust, incentives, disincentives, risks, and intellectual property" (Borgman, 2007, p. 360). As evidence shows, researchers rarely have the desire, skills or resources to prepare their data for deposit or public sharing in repositories (Cragin, et al., 2010; Henty, et al., 2008).

Data, especially in the social sciences and humanities are often "complex, fuzzy, discursive, inconsistent" (Barjak, et al., 2009, p. 586). There are data licensing, privacy and confidentiality concerns which in turn may cause high costs for preparing data for sharing and re-use (Bishop, 2005; Edwards, et al., 2009; Parry & Mauthner, 2005; Tan, et al., 2009). At the same time, little scientific credit is gained by sharing data sets. Ownership rights in data generated in a collaborative project might be difficult to assign, yet the data themselves may have substantial financial value. Finally, new applications are typically context specific, and their transfer to new contexts brings substantial challenges. Some of these issues can be solved with the development of applications that are secure and that implement data access and rights management protocols, but these are not yet available for all types of data.

At the same time as developments in eResearch infrastructure are beginning to provide the ability to access, search, and share data in digital reposi-

tories, new developments are taking place in ways of disseminating final research outputs and publications. Research builds on what has gone before, and to do so, researchers must have access to it; research is incomplete until it is communicated, used, disseminated and further developed within a community (Borgman, 2007). The results of research can be documented and shared in a variety of forms from letters and memos, to journal articles and books. At present in most disciplines the primary form of scholarly communication is still via articles usually published in journals and book chapters or disseminated at conferences (Kling & Callahan, 2003). These forms maintain their importance in dissemination as they demonstrate desirable characteristics for scholars seeking to disseminate their work: the research is accessible by others in the present and the future; there is publicity so that other interested scholars can be made aware of it (journal subscriptions, indexing, abstracting); it is demonstrated as trustworthy having gone through some sort of peer review or other certification; and it registers and acknowledges who carried out the work (Borgman, 2007; Kling & McKim, 1999; Prosser, 2005).

Changing technologies from the 1970s—computers, the Internet, and search engines—have shifted the dominant form of dissemination from printed journals to electronic journals (Kling & McKim, 1999). The online provision of scholarly publications comes in many formats, such as individual electronic journals, publisher collections of journals, aggregator collections of articles (often subject-based and provided by commercial organisations as an adjunct to their existing indexing and abstracting services). While access channels and media have changed, the basic structure and relations of production of scholarly communication or dissemination have not changed much. Journals and other research outputs are mainly available to those who pay for subscriptions or whose institutions do so (Houghton & Oppenheim, 2010; King & Tenopir, 2011). An open access movement which promotes free online access to research outputs and data has developed, providing an alternative access to some scholarly outputs through the infrastructure of institutional and disciplinary repositories and connected networks of those repositories, indexed and searchable over the internet (Lynch & Lippincott, 2005).

A great deal of work has gone into the development of repositories (Payette, et al., 1999; Smith, et al., 2003; Van de Sompel, et al., 2004). There is some evidence that increased access through open access repositories may potentially increase the use of the work, its visibility, and therefore its impact and citations of research (Brody, Harnad, & Carr, 2006; Swan, 2010). However, many repositories are less than comprehensive. Studies that examine open access typically find that communication of findings, recognition of work, promotion and tenure are major motives for researchers to publish, and they do not always see these aims being furthered in open repositories. Among their reported concerns are lack of interest, knowledge or time, issues with copyright, and concern about plagiarism (Kennan, 2007; Rowlands & Nicholas, 2006; Swan & Brown, 2005).

The Internet has fostered other developments such as e-lists, blogs, wikis, RSS Feeds, chat technologies, and other Web 2.0 tools, which enable more democratic collaboration and dissemination. These tools and 'grey literature' associated with informal scholarly communication and collaboration do not undergo traditional peer review or other institutionalized certification. However, as their use matures, new forms of more informal, dynamic peer review may emerge (Hey & Trefethen, 2008).

To bring together our discussions on data and dissemination, it is evident that the Internet and eResearch infrastructure can do more than just disseminate or make available the full text of research papers and data. In principle, they can integrate data with the literature to create a world that allows researchers and readers to see the whole knowledge production cycle (Fink, et al., 2008; Hey, Tansley, & Tolle, 2009; DeRoure

& Frey, 2007; Seringhaus & Gerstein, 2007). For example, readers of publications can not only see and use the original data, but also redo the analysis or combine the data with other data for other purposes. As Lynch (2009) says, such scholarly communications can be a "vehicle for *building up communities* and for a form of large-scale *collaboration* across space and time" (p. 178).

Infrastructure, service and support requirements will differ depending on the discipline and the nature of the research. Borgman (2007) observes that whereas almost all research data are created by, and for, scientific purposes, a significant portion of data used in social research consists of data created by other parties for other purposes, for example, government, business, and mass media. Furthermore, the social sciences and humanities use highly heterogeneous datasets. This creates complex semantics and interoperability challenges and makes "one size fits all" approaches to infrastructure development and support unsuitable for research in these domains (Barjak, et al., 2009).

Studies investigating eResearch uptake provide some initial insights into several aspects that might support broader researcher engagement with eResearch. For example, Dutton and Meyer (2009) report that while respondents believe that many new scientific questions will require eResearch tools to answer them, many researchers are still uncertain, or have no opinion, about what these questions are. They also notice that recent graduates are more likely to be interested in, and knowledgeable about, eResearch. This, and other research (Pearce, 2010), also found that disciplinary differences were not a barrier in the uptake of eResearch tools, and that a wide variety of tools were already in use. Some researchers who collaborate using eResearch infrastructure, do so largely because colleagues or potential collaborators encourage them to. Other catalysts include seed funding, interesting research that requires eResearch infrastructure (Barjak, et al., 2007), the connection between eResearch projects and their potential user communities, and support infrastructure such as developers to hand and training resources. Differing research communities have differing needs, so analysis of the practices, communication and collaboration relations, and social organization of different research fields is required to find out how these needs can be supported (Barjak, et al., 2009). Successful collaboration projects in eResearch development were found to have strategies in place ensuring that domain and computer scientists work together in co-development of technologies and services (Barjak, et al., 2009).

Researchers report that barriers to the adoption of eResearch collaboration practices include lack of information on usefulness and applicability to research problems, perceptions about insufficient practicality and applicability, and perceptions about infrastructures being developed by technologists in isolation from the researchers who will use them. Benefits of eResearch are most likely to reach new communities of scholars via highly regarded researchers in their own field, and eResearch initiatives are encouraged to engage these highly regarded researchers to assist in promotion (Barjak, et al., 2007). Other barriers include lack of funding, costs, lack of qualified staff and the need for more information and training (Barjak, et al., 2007; Dutton & Meyer, 2009).

However, little is known about how researchers' engagement with different research collaborations relates to specific ICT use for collaboration practices; how researchers view the role of collaborative eResearch in the future of their field; and what kinds of support might assist them to attain their eResearch visions.

With this background, we now turn to results from our study.

APPROACH AND PROCEDURE

The study called "Co-Developing eResearch Infrastructure: Technology-Enhanced Research Practices, Attitudes, and Requirements" was conducted using a Web-survey. It covered three main eResearch areas: (a) data management, retention, and sharing; (b) technology-enhanced research methods, tools, and services; (c) research collaboration and dissemination. Participants were asked to respond to 40 questions, most of which required them to choose from a range of options and allowed a short comment, while eight questions asked participants to provide open narrative answers. About 10 questions focused on distributed and collaborative research practices, such as data sharing, research communication and dissemination (Appendix 1). The main results from the analysis of participants' answers to these questions are presented in this chapter.

The survey was administered in two phases at seven Australian Universities in the state of New South Wales: (a) four universities completed the study in May-June 2009; and (b) three others did so in October-November 2009. Email invitations were distributed to all academic staff, research students and research support staff via universities' internal mailing lists. The survey was targeted at all researchers and research students, including those who do not use ICT for research yet, therefore the invitation explicitly stated that "We are interested in your research practices and opinions, whatever your discipline, and whatever the extent of ICT use in your research."

After the survey was closed, the multiple-choice questions were analysed using relevant statistical techniques with SPSS. On the basis of participants' answers, five grouping variables were created: (a) disciplinary clusters; (b) career stage; (c) degree of collaboration; (d) scale of collaboration; and (e) nature of collaboration (Table 1). These variables were used to explore some major differences between answers of: researchers from different disciplinary areas; research students and academic staff; and researchers involved in different kinds of collaboration in various degrees. Only differences that were significant at level $p < .05$ are discussed in this paper.

Table 1. Grouping variables and categories used in the analysis of survey data

Grouping variables	Categories
Disciplinary clusters	1. *Social fields* – humanities, arts and social sciences 2. *Biomedical fields* – biological, health and medical sciences 3. *Physical fields* – physical sciences, chemical sciences, IT, engineering and mathematics 4. *Multidisciplinary* – a combination of all three or any two of the above categories
Career stage	1. *Research students* – full time and part time postgraduate research students 2. *Academic staff* – full time, part time and honorary academics at all stages of career: early career, middle career and experienced researchers
Degree of collaboration	*1. Nearly all research is individual* *2. About half research is collaborative* *3. Nearly all research is collaborative* Note: This category is based on participants' answers to the question without further regrouping.
Scale of collaboration	1. *International* – participants involved in research collaborations on international scale, such as partnerships with universities from other countries 2. *National* – participants involved only in research collaborations that occur within the country, including other national universities and non-university partners 3. *Local* – participants involved only in research collaborations that occur within their institution, including their research group, other research groups within their faculty and other faculties within their university 4. *Individual* – participants not involved in collaborative research
Nature of collaboration	1. *Beyond university* – researchers engaged in some collaborations with non-university partners, such as non-university research agencies and non-academic partners 2. *University* – researchers engaged in collaborations with university partners only, including local partnerships and other national and international universities

Answers to the open-ended questions were explored for patterns independently using both manual coding and automatic text visualisation. First, written answers were categorised using human coding and explored for most-common categories using statistical techniques. Second, written texts were pre-processed and visualised creating "word clouds" with *Wordle* Web-based software (Feinberg, 2009). Most frequent words and phrases used by participants in their answers were further explored and triangulated with the results of human coding. To obtain more contextualised visual representation of answers, texts were initially pre-processed by detecting 10-15 most frequently used adjectives and linking these adjectives to the following nouns, forming phrases. For example, words "Digital" (adj.) and "Repository" (noun) were linked into the phrase "DigitalRepository."

It is important to note some limitations. First, the sample of this study was not representative of the whole university research population in Austra-lia or NSW and findings cannot be generalised to this population. For example, the ratio of academic staff and research students was about 3.5 in the sample, while the ratio of academics and research students in all Australian universities is about 1.4 (i.e., 49,942 academics and 34,821 research students, full-time equivalent as of 2008) (Universities Australia, 2010). However, the survey sample was large (864 respondents) compared with similar studies that have been completed in this domain (e.g., Barjak et al. [2007] – 560 responses, Dutton and Meyer [2009] – 526 responses), and it had participants from various disciplines, with different levels of research experience and involved in various kinds of research collaboration (see next section). Therefore, the results for these subgroups were examined separately, and presented findings primarily aim to provide insight into the differences between these subgroups.

Second, three different grouping variables were used to investigate how different aspects of research collaboration were related to researchers' use of ICT-enhanced collaboration technologies, data collection, sharing, and dissemination practices. While these variables reflected distinct aspects of collaboration, as it could be expected, they were interrelated (Spearman's rho was between 0.17 and 0.25, with the largest association between the scale and degree of collaboration). As these variables reflected distinct aspects of collaboration they were all included in analysis and analysed separately. Possible implications from those associations were, when possible, made explicit in the results section and should be taken into account in the interpretation of findings.

RESULTS

Participants' Background

In total, 864 participants took the survey and 703 (81%) of them completed it to the end. Varying disciplines were well represented in the sample. The largest percentage of participants (22%) indicated Medical and Health Sciences as one of their major disciplines. Between 10% and 12% of participants indicated one or several of the following four disciplines: (a) social science, humanities, arts; (b) biomedical sciences; (c) information computing and communication sciences; and (d) education. Overall, three major disciplinary clusters were almost equally represented in the sample. Similar numbers (29%) of participants were from social fields and biomedical fields, and slightly fewer participants (25%) were from physical fields. As researchers were allowed to indicate all relevant disciplinary areas in which they specialise, about 18% of them listed disciplines that belonged to different disciplinary clusters indicating that they were involved in multidisciplinary research. A number of participants in the latter category listed computer sciences as one of their disciplinary areas, but overall this category included diverse combinations, such as medical sciences and mathematics.

About 70% of participants were academic staff; 20% were postgraduate research students; 8% were other university staff (mainly general staff, librarians, research assistants, and ICT and research support), and the remaining 2% were visiting and honorary academics. Different levels of research experience were quite evenly represented among the academic staff: 27% of participants were early career researchers; 22% were middle career researchers and 21% were senior researchers[1].

About 42% of participants answered that they had heard of the term eResearch before the survey, while other 58% had not heard this term before, indicating that the respondents represented different levels of awareness about eResearch. Overall, only one-third (33%) of research students were aware about eResearch; this was followed by a larger proportion of academic staff (42%) and other university staff (58%)[2]. Such relatively high awareness among other university staff reflected that some of participants from this category were involved in provision of information services, ICT support and other services related to eResearch.

Research Collaboration Practices: Extent, Loci, and Scale

Respondents were asked to indicate how much of their research was collaborative. Almost half (46%) the participants indicated that nearly all their research was collaborative, about one-third (32%) indicated that about half of their research was collaborative, while the remaining 21% responded that nearly all their research was individual (Figure 1). Researchers from social fields were involved in collaborative research least often, with more than one-third (35%) of them stating that nearly all their research was individual and less than one-third (32%) of them indicating that nearly all their research was collaborative.

There were striking differences between research students and academic staff. While more than two thirds (68%) of research students indi-

Figure 1. Involvement of academics and research students in collaborative research in different disciplines

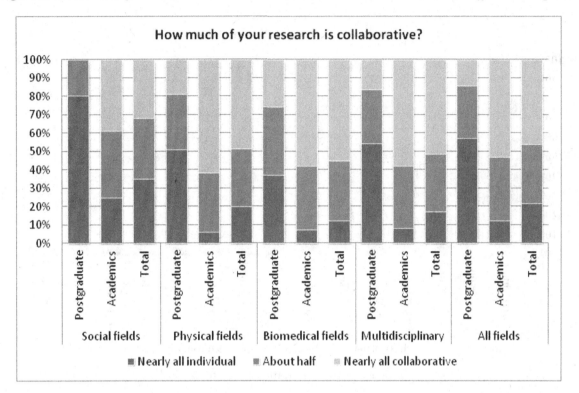

cated that almost all their research was individual, only 12% of academics gave this answer. While significantly larger proportions of students from biomedical, physical and multidisciplinary fields were involved in collaborative research than students from social fields, nevertheless differences between academics and research students were significant in all disciplinary fields.

Participants who were more involved in collaborative research were also more likely to indicate that they had heard about eResearch. These answers ranged from 34% of researchers, nearly all of whose research was individual, to 46% of those almost all of whose research was collaborative.

Participants were asked to indicate places in which their research collaborations typically occurred. The majority of researchers collaborated within their research groups (70%), with other universities within Australia (52%), and internationally (51%). Fewer researchers collaborated outside their research group but within the same faculty or other faculties within the same university, 37% and 30% respectively. Overall, a majority of researchers were involved in more than one kind of partnership, and only 7% stated that they did not collaborate at all. Significantly fewer research students than academics were involved in all kinds of collaboration and about one third (31%) of students indicated that they were not involved in any collaboration. Nevertheless, more than half (54%) of students indicated that they collaborated in their research group and about one quarter (24%) said that they collaborated with universities outside Australia. Only a small minority of students (9%-16%) were involved in all other types of local and national collaboration.

According to the largest scale of collaboration, the loci of partnership were grouped into four embedded categories: (a) individual (i.e., no collaboration); (b) local; (c) national; and (d) international (see Table 1).

Figure 2. Scale of research collaboration of academics and research students in different disciplines

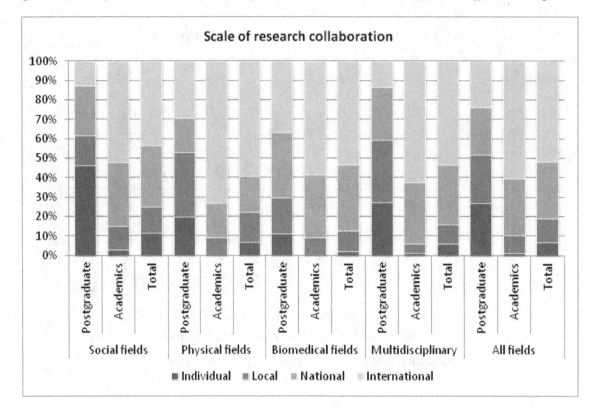

Only 7% of participants were not involved in any collaboration, 12% collaborated only locally, 30% on the national scale and 51% collaborated internationally (Figure 2). In physical fields the majority (59%) of researchers collaborated on the international scale and about three times fewer (19%) researchers collaborated only nationally. In the other two clusters, and in multidisciplinary fields, fewer (43%-53%) researchers were involved in international collaborations, whereas about one third (32%-35%) collaborated on the national scale. There were also significant differences in the loci of collaboration between academic staff and research students. Most noticeably, a significant proportion of students collaborated only locally (25%), while just 9% of academics collaborated only on this scale.[3]

Research partnerships also ranged across university and non-university sectors. A slightly larger percentage (51%) of researchers collaborated only within the university sector, and a

slightly smaller percentage (49%) collaborated within and beyond the university sector. In the latter group, one third (33%) of collaborations involved non-academic partners and just above one-fifth (22%) of collaborations involved non-university research agencies[4]. A majority of researchers from multidisciplinary fields and about half of researchers from biomedical fields collaborated beyond academia, 63% and 51% respectively. However, only 44% of researchers from social and physical fields were involved in such partnerships. Fewer than 1% of researchers who collaborated beyond the university sector did not collaborate within it.

Communication Technologies in Collaborative Research

Respondents were asked to indicate what kinds of technologies they used for communication and project management in their collaborations and how often they used them. Face to face meetings remained an important form of communication that was used often by 60% of participants and occasionally by the other 38%. The most common media for research collaboration used often or occasionally by more than 93% of respondents were emails and telephone. Between 29% and 57% of researchers also at least occasionally used various ICT-based tools for synchronous communication such as audio and videoconferencing, but fewer than 15% of researchers used these tools often. Collaboration media for asynchronous communication (other than email) were used less often and by fewer researchers. For example, fewer than one third of participants used Web 2.0 tools (33%), collaborative document writing (26%) and social networking (18%) even occasionally, and only between 12% and 14% used any of these tools often. Further, about 95% of respondents did not use virtual research environments and about 88% did not use special project or task management tools.

Various communication tools were used differently in various disciplinary clusters. In particular, researchers from biomedical fields more often than researchers from physical fields used some traditional media communication tools, such as the telephone. For example, more than 63% of researchers in biomedical fields used the telephone often and only 2% did not use it; meanwhile only 37% of researchers in physical sciences used telephone often and nearly 18% of researchers did not use the telephone at all. In contrast, a significantly larger proportion of researchers from physical disciplines than those in the biomedical disciplines often used ICT-based communication and sharing tools, such as Web 2.0 (20% and 2%, respectively), file sharing (24% and 9%), collaborative writing (11% and 2%), and videoconferencing (24% and 2%). This was despite the fact that researchers in physical fields were generally less intensively involved in collaborative research than researchers in biomedical fields. It was interesting to note that most intensive

users of social networking tools were researchers from social disciplines, where 27% of participants used this media at least occasionally. This was in sharp contrast to biomedical fields, where only 9% of researchers used this medium.

Generally, academic staff tended to use communication technologies more intensively than research students, and these differences were statistically significant for telephone, email, audio conferencing, videoconferencing and file sharing. This finding partly reflected lesser need for communication media among research students, who were generally less involved in collaborations, since researchers who were involved in collaborative research to a lesser degree tended also to use a similar range of communication tools less often. Nevertheless, students used some of collaboration tools less often than academics independently of the degree of their involvement in research collaborations. For example, two thirds (66%) of academics about half of whose research was **collaborative** at least occasionally used audio conferencing, whereas just above one third (35%) of research students about half of whose research was collaborative did so.

Further, it was interesting to note that 75% of researchers who were involved only in local collaborations communicated face-to-face often, while just above half (56%-58%) of researchers who collaborated nationally or internationally communicated often in this way. In contrast, the latter two groups significantly more frequently used a range of technologies, including the telephone (particularly those who were involved in national collaborations), email, audio and videoconferencing, Web 2.0 tools, file sharing and social networking (Figure 3).

Dissemination of Research Findings

Respondents were asked to indicate what kinds of dissemination methods and technologies they used and how often they used them for disseminating their findings. Conventional publishing (e.g.,

Figure 3. Communication tools used often or occasionally by researchers who were involved in individual research only and collaborative research on local, national, and international scales

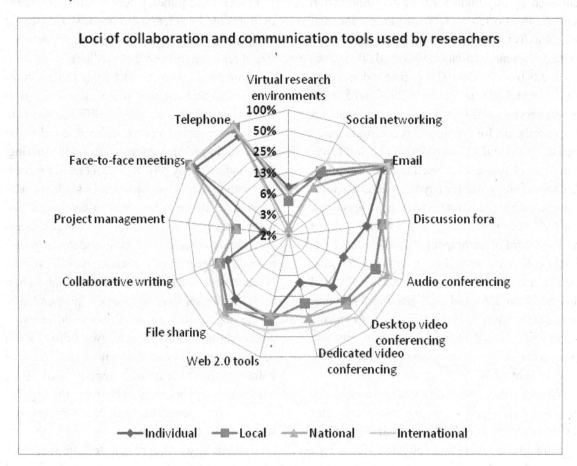

journals, books, proceedings) was the main form of research dissemination used often or occasionally by almost all (97%) researchers. About two-thirds (67%) of participants also at least occasionally published in online proceedings, 60% published in e-journals and 46% published in open access e-journals. Between 38% and 45% of participants used institutional, project or personal websites, blogs or wikis and institutional repositories to disseminate their research findings. However, less than one-fifth (15%-19%) of researchers used digital disciplinary repositories for disseminating their research or published in open access, commercial or scientific societies' e-books. Overall, researchers on average indicated more than four dissemination channels out of twelve that they

used at least occasionally (M = 4.5, SD =2.55, n =738, $Median$ = 4; $Mode$ = 5). However, more than half (56%) of researchers often used one or two main dissemination strategies (M = 1.9, SD = 1.78, n = 738, $Mode$ = 1, $Median$ = 2).

Similar proportions of researchers from all disciplinary fields disseminated their findings via open e-journals. Nevertheless, there were some significant differences between the disciplines in many other forms of dissemination. Most noticeably, researchers from biomedical fields more often published in traditional journals than researchers from other fields, whereas researchers from physical fields more often used various digital forms of dissemination. For example, 5% and 44% of researchers from biomedical and physical fields respectively indicated that they disseminated their research findings via digital disciplinary repositories. It was interesting to note that a relatively large proportion of researchers from social fields also used various digital forms to disseminate their findings, but the majority of them did this occasionally rather than often.

Research students tended more often than academics to disseminate their findings via e-books, while academics more often than research students used conventional publishing, e-journals and project wikis. Overall, academics on average used often or occasionally a slightly broader range of dissemination strategies: academics $M = 4.7$, $SD = 2.50$, $n = 551$; students $M = 4.1$, $SD = 2.72$, $n = 135$; respectively, $t = 2.218$, $p < .05$.

Some forms of research dissemination were also associated with the degree and scale of research collaboration. Some of these differences were distinct for academics and research students. Most notably, academics who were more involved in collaborative research also significantly more often disseminated their results via departmental and project websites, but they and less-collaborating researchers used equally often all other forms of dissemination, including conventional publishing, individual websites, wikis and repositories. In contrast, research students used all digital forms similarly often, independently of the degree of their research collaboration. However, research students who were more involved in collaborative research disseminated their findings significantly more often via conventional publishing. Specifically, more than four-fifths (82%) of students whose almost all research was collaborative used often conventional publishing, while just above half (54%) of students whose only half of research was collaborative did this and only 38% of those almost all of whose research was individual published often in conventional scholarly sources. This result indicated that research students involved in collaborative research perhaps have more opportunities to be co-authors of joint peer reviewed research papers.

Overall, some digital forms of research dissemination—such as digital repositories, departmental, project and personal websites—were apparently more often used by those who collaborated on a broader scale and particularly by those who were involved in international partnerships (Figure 4). For example, 54% of researchers who collaborated on international scale disseminated their findings via departmental websites, while only 37% of researchers who only collaborated nationally and 33% of those who were involved only in local collaborations did this.

Enhancing Digital Collaboration and Dissemination

Respondents were asked to suggest three main areas of research collaboration and dissemination that would most benefit from ICT support. The range and frequency of common words and phrases used in participants' answers are represented in Figure 5. Among many other needs, the largest number of researchers indicated the following three areas: (a) needs related to web-based technologies, such as project websites, wikis and blogs for enhancing general online presence (36%); (b) a range of needs related to data and information handling and sharing, such as data archiving in online data repositories (33%); and (c) synchronous communication, such as videoconferencing (28%). Researchers also often indicated a range of needs related to e-publishing, and a need for tools for shared work in online spaces, such as project management software, virtual research environments, and collaborative document writing.

Data Collection and Sharing Practices

Respondents were asked to indicate how often and in which ways they obtained their data. A very large majority at least occasionally collected or created data themselves (94%) or as part of a team (89%); and a large majority (71%) indicated that

Figure 4. Dissemination strategies used often or occasionally by researchers who were involved in individual research only and collaborative research on local, national, and international scales

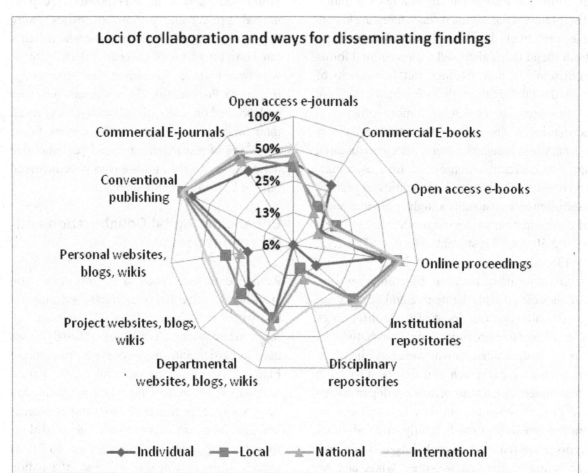

they often collected data themselves. A significant majority of participants also obtained data directly from other researchers (71%), data archives and repositories (59%), and third party organisations (58%), but most researchers did this occasionally, 52%, 34% and 42% respectively. Similarly, about one quarter (26%) of participants occasionally obtained data from commercial online sources, but only 6% did this often. Overall, researchers on average indicated just less than four sources out of seven that they used at least occasionally ($M = 3.9$, $SD = 1.43$, $n = 704$, *Median* = 4, *Mode* = 3). However, two-thirds of researchers (66%) often obtained their data in one or two major ways ($M = 1.9$, $SD = 1.17$, $n = 704$, *Mode* = 2, *Median* = 2).

Overall, the results indicated that the majority of researchers often collected data themselves or as a part of research teams and, while they obtained data from a variety of sources, 61% of researchers used secondary data sources only occasionally. Nevertheless, a large minority (39%) of researchers indicated at least one secondary source that they used often.

There were significant disciplinary differences in how researchers obtained their data (Figure 6). Just less than three-quarters (72%) of researchers from biomedical fields often collected their data as a part of project team, whereas just over half (55%) the researchers from physical fields and less than half (47%) from social fields did this. In contrast,

Figure 5. One hundred words and phrases most often used by participants to describe the areas of research collaboration and dissemination that would benefit from ICT support: size of text reflects frequency of use.[5]

a large minority (44%-48%) of researchers in the latter two fields at least occasionally re-used data collected by others, while only 27% of researchers from biomedical fields did this. It is interesting to note that researchers from the social and physical fields obtained existing data in rather distinct ways as well. Specifically, about-one third (33%) of researchers from physical fields often obtained their datasets directly from other researchers, while only 10% of researchers from social fields often obtained their data directly from other researchers. In contrast a relatively large proportion of researchers from social fields at least occasionally used data from third party research organizations (70%) and commercial online sources (46%), while fewer researchers from physical fields ever obtained their data in these two ways, 54% and 20% respectively.

The degree of involvement in collaborative research was associated with specific data collection methods in particular ways. Specifically, researchers whose larger proportion of research was collaborative, more often collected data as a part of their research teams and more often obtained data directly from other researchers. For example, a little more than half (52%) of those for whom almost all of their research was individual occasionally or often obtained data directly from other researchers, while more than three-quarters (78%) of researchers almost all of whose research was collaborative did this. In contrast, researchers for whom nearly all of their research was individual, significantly more often obtained data from archives and repositories and commercial online sources (Figure 7).

As fewer research students than academics were involved in research collaborations, fewer research students than academics collected data as a part of research teams (68% and 94%, respectively) or received data directly from other researchers (62% and 74%, respectively). While a similar and relatively large proportion (59%) of academics and research students obtained data via third party organizations, in contrast, significantly more students than academics often obtained data in this way, 26% and 16%, respectively. Many of these differences between research students and academics remained significant even when the degree of their collaboration was taken into account. For example, 62% of academics for

Figure 6. Ways used often to obtain data by researchers from different disciplinary fields

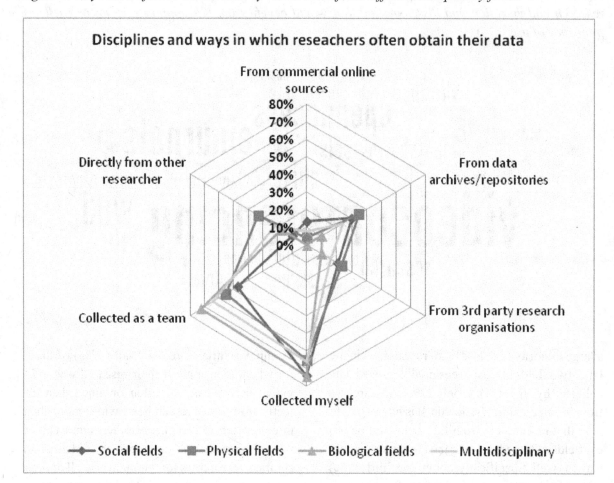

whom about half of their research was collaborative often collected their data as a part of a team and 13% often obtained data from third party organizations, whereas only 46% of research students for whom about half of their research was collaborative often collected their data as a part of team and 29% often obtained from third party organizations.

Respondents were asked if they would allow researchers from outside their team or project to access their research data. Half of participants (50%) did not allow access to any of their data, while 41% allowed access to some of their data and only 9% provided access to all their data. The largest majority (62%) of researchers who did not allow access to the data were those from social

fields. This was followed by a slightly smaller majority (55%) of researchers from biomedical fields who also did not share their data. In contrast, significantly more researchers from physical fields shared at least some of their data, and only slightly more than one-third of them (36%) did not allow access to any of their data. Researchers who were more involved in collaborative research typically also allowed access to more of their data to other researchers beyond their project team. For example, only 29% researchers nearly all of whose research was individual shared at least some of their data, while nearly double that (59%) of researchers nearly all of whose research was collaborative did so.

This latter finding was mirrored in the differences in data sharing patterns between research

Figure 7. Degree of involvement in collaborative research and ways used often or occasionally to obtain data

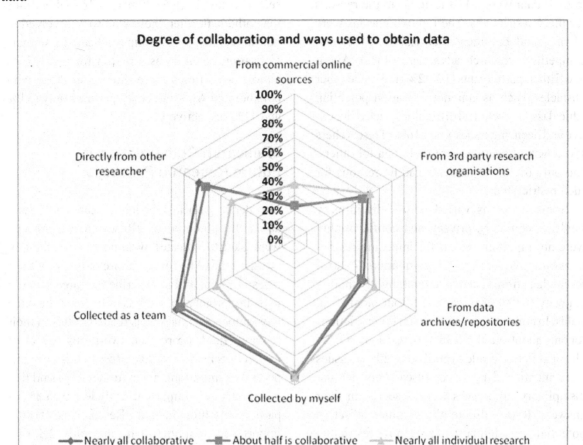

students and academics: while only about one-third (34%) of research students provided access to at least some of their data, more than half (54%) of academics did so. This difference reflected lesser student involvement in research collaborations and was insignificant once the degree of collaboration was taken into account. For example, quite similar proportions of research students and academics for whom almost all research was individual did not provide access to any of their data, 73% and 69% respectively.

Of those researchers who allowed access to their data, about three-quarters (74%) provided privately negotiated access. Slightly more than one-third (35%) of participants also published data online; 29% submitted data when they pub-

lished in e-journals; 22% deposited their data to repositories; and only 14% provided access via a third party. Researchers in biomedical fields exhibit quite different data sharing practices than the other two fields. For example, only 10% of researchers from biomedical fields published data online, whereas 88% provided privately negotiated access. In contrast, 44% and 69% of researchers in social fields, and 49% and 67% of researchers in physical fields respectively published online and privately negotiated access to their data. Nevertheless, there were no significant differences between the data sharing practices of academics and research students, and these data sharing strategies were not related to the involvement in collaborative research.

Participants who applied restrictions on access to their data were asked to indicate the reasons for these restrictions. The top two reasons were privacy and confidentiality issues (58%) and competitive research advantage (43%). About one fifth of participants (19-22%) indicated other obstacles, such as commercialisation potential, ethical issues, technical difficulties, lack of incentive and licensing issues. Only 16% of researchers saw a lack of usefulness of their data for others, and only 6% of respondents had no reasons for such restrictions.

Some concerns varied across disciplinary fields. Specifically, privacy and confidentiality were an important reason for imposing restrictions on access for almost three-quarters (73%) of researchers from social fields and slightly smaller majority (64%) of researchers from biomedical fields. In contrast this was a reason for restrictions for only about one-third (36%) of researchers from physical fields. While overall other ethical issues were mentioned by fewer researchers, similar disciplinary differences were observed in their answers. Rather differently, commercialisation potential was an important reason for restricting access to their data for about one quarter (23%-25%) of researchers from the biomedical and physical fields, and only for 9% of researchers from social fields. More than one quarter (28%) of researchers from physical fields also noted technical difficulties, but this was an important concern for significantly fewer researchers in biomedical and social fields, 17% and 14% respectively. It is interesting to note that there were no differences between the obstacles indicated by academic staff and research students, except for lack of incentive. The latter reason was mentioned by 21% of academic staff and only 10% of students.

There was no association between the degree of involvement in collaborative research and reasons for restrictions, but the scale and nature of collaboration were associated with some obstacles. For example, competitive research advantage, licensing and technical difficulties were important concerns for significantly larger proportion of researchers involved in international collaborations than others. Further, those who were involved in non-university partnerships indicated commercialisation potential as a reason for restrictions almost three times more often than those who collaborated with university partners only (31% and 11% respectively).

eResearch Collaboration in Future Research Practices

In order to gain insight into researchers' views about the potential of eResearch, participants were asked to indicate how important they thought eResearch will be for the future progress of their research field, and to describe the three specific most important applications of ICT and the three most important challenges related to this in their research field. More than two-thirds (69%) of researchers answered that eResearch is very important or important, and a further 21% said that it is moderately important. Only less than 8% of participants thought that eResearch is of little importance or unimportant, and only 2% said that eResearch is not relevant to their research. There were no significant differences between the answers of researchers from various disciplinary fields, at various stages of career or involved in various kinds of collaborative research to different extents. This indicated that researchers from all domains and with different experiences saw quite significant potential for eResearch.

Researchers indicated a broad range of future applications of ICT important for their research fields. 'Analysis,' 'access,' 'storage,' 'data' and 'collaboration' were the most frequent words used to describe these applications and emerging opportunities in participants answers (Figure 8). Interpretative analysis and categorisation of these responses showed that the largest number (46%) of researchers who answered this question mentioned new analytical opportunities related to data-driven and computation-intensive methods, such as data mining, modelling, visualisation, as well as other ICT-based analytical tools. About one third (31%) of participants listed various applications and opportunities related to data, such as management, archiving, access and sharing. About one quarter (26%) of researchers indicated applications directly related to research collaboration, such as opportunities to work on projects with overseas partners, jointly analyse data and write papers.

In the answers about the most important challenges for the application of ICT in their research field now and in the near future, participants frequently mentioned 'support,' 'access,' 'storage,' 'data,' and lack of resources, including time and funding (Figure 9). More than one quarter (29%) of researchers indicated the lack of specialised and general ICT expertise needed to harness eResearch opportunities. Slightly fewer researchers (27%) indicated concerns related to data storage, management and sharing, and similar number of researchers (27%) expressed concerns about ICT policies and administration. Only 8% of researchers indicated concerns related specifically to collaboration, such as competition or difficulties of working in a team, indicating that researchers

overall did not have significant concerns that would prevent them from engaging in collaborative eResearch practices.

DISCUSSION

This chapter has analysed some findings about research collaboration from a larger study on eResearch practices and needs for support (Markauskaite, Aditomo & Hellmers, 2009, 2011), and specifically has focused on the analysis of ICT-enhanced collaboration practices and challenges reported by researchers from seven universities in the Australian state of New South Wales (NSW). The sample, as noted previously, was not representative of the university research population in Australia or in NSW, and the findings cannot be generalized to these populations. Nevertheless, the survey sample was large, and it well represented researchers from various disciplinary fields, at various career stages and involved in various kinds of collaboration. The findings, therefore, are primarily instructive for understanding disciplinary differences, and how researchers' experience

Figure 8. One hundred words and phrases most often used by participants to describe the most important future applications of ICT in their research field[6]

Figure 9. One hundred words and phrases most often used by researchers to describe the most important challenges for the application of ICT in their research fields now and in the near future[7]

and involvement in various kinds of collaboration relate to their eResearch practices.

Less than half the researchers had previously heard about eResearch, indicating that general awareness about eResearch was rather limited, but as was found in some earlier studies conducted primarily in the European countries (Barjak, et al., 2007; Dutton & Meyer, 2009), many researchers were positive about ICT use in research and collaboration, and acknowledged significance and potential of ICT-enhanced research practices for research progress in their fields. Many researchers were involved in some kinds of collaboration, with only 7% of participants not involved in any collaboration at all. Nevertheless, there were significant differences between research students and academics and disciplinary fields and, overall, not all researchers collaborated equally intensively. In general, results indicated that those who collaborated more intensively also tended to use ICT-enhanced collaboration tools and dissemination strategies more often, and shared more of their data than those who collaborated less.

There were essential gaps between the widespread adoption of some general purpose ICT-enhanced communication and collaboration tools, such as email, and the much less common use of specialised research collaboration tools, such as virtual research environments and project management software. Further, significant number of researchers indicated their willingness to adopt some synchronous communication tools, data and information sharing technologies, such as videoconferencing, wikis, blogs and file sharing. These tools generally do not require researchers to codify their knowledge or significantly (re) structure their data, and therefore perhaps could be more easily integrated with existing research practices, in comparison with other technologies for distributed research that require compliance with standards and the restructuring of data, such as integrated data repositories.

A significant proportion of researchers see virtual communication and collaboration among the three most important aspects of eResearch for research progress in their field. While many researchers indicated that they need support in this eResearch area at this stage, very few researchers mentioned that collaborative eResearch might be an important challenge in future. This positive vision nevertheless was primarily related to team-based collaboration, and did not encapsulate data management and sharing that were also perceived as important challenges.

Results of the study indicate that researchers from different disciplinary fields collaborated to different extents and were involved in different types of collaboration, confirming again that ways of doing research and patterns of collaboration vary across different research fields and disciplinary communities (Becher & Trowler, 2001; Katz & Martin, 1997; Meadows, 1998). Further, this study indicates that researchers from different fields also tend to use different media for collaborating and disseminating. The biomedical fields appeared to be intensive users of the telephone, most likely reflecting that these fields have more established collaboration traditions, while social sciences were more intensive users of social networking reflecting that these fields are more receptive to new digital scholarship practices and open forms of dissemination (Greenhow, Robelia, & Hughes, 2009). Rather differently, physical scientists were intensive users of many teamwork tools such as Web 2.0 approaches, collaborative writing and videoconferencing, reflecting that some forms of team-based collaboration, such as those captured through measures of co-authorship (Borgman, 2007), are more pervasive in this research cluster.

A number of researchers mentioned data as one of most important future eResearch application areas. Interestingly, some of them referred to storage, archiving and management, rather than sharing, integration or re-use of these data resources. A number of researchers also indicated that they see data and data management as important challenges, and that they need support in this area.

Only half of researchers provided access at least to some of their data. The largest group of researchers who did not enable access to their data were those from the social fields. As reported in the literature (Barjak, et al., 2009; Borgman, 2007), data de-identification and "cleansing" for ethical reasons require substantial work and some-times may be impossible, particularly in social sciences. Overall, the two major reasons for not sharing data were privacy and confidentiality, and competitive research advantage, with the former being a barrier for significantly larger proportions of researchers in social fields, and the latter for significantly larger proportions in biomedical and physical fields.

Traditional publishing was still the main way for disseminating findings demonstrating that changes in the form of scholarly dissemination over the last decade have not been very large (Borgman, 2007; Kling & McKim, 1999). Never-theless, a number of researchers indicated several common areas of ICT-enhanced dissemination in which they need support. Researchers particularly saw as beneficial "in-house" dissemination approaches, such as institutional or project websites, wikis and blogs, and integrated disciplinary and institutional repositories. However, very few researchers mentioned ICT-enhanced dissemination among the most important aspects for future progress of their research field, and it was rarely mentioned as a future challenge. This finding reflects the ready availability of Web 2.0 tools and the existence of institutional repositories in Australian universities (Kennan & Kingsley, 2009). What is perhaps required more here is the time to investigate and learn to use existing infrastructure, and technical assistance with initial setup and maintenance.

Overall, while researchers still focused on more traditional one-to-many dissemination in their answers about current needs, this focus shifted towards collaborative knowledge creation practices in their answers about future eResearch potential. Least advanced, most promising and most challenging aspects of collaborative eRe-search were data-related collaborative research practices. While researchers often mentioned technical needs and challenges, many of their concerns were related to their own expertise and needs for technical support—what David (2006) called "soft infrastructure."

Overall, there was a noticeable difference between researchers' views about two kinds of collaboration, that we term "team-based" collaboration and "grand" collaboration. Team-based collaboration primarily includes distributed joint work on specific research projects that could be supported by videoconferencing, document sharing, collaborative authoring tools and other group work software. Such distributed yet more focused collaboration sits comfortably with familiar collaborative research routines, and was generally seen by researchers as an enabler of more productive current or near future research practices.

Large-scale "grand" collaboration encompasses shared data repositories, secure virtual organizations and other large-scale infrastructures. Such large-scale collaboration is more open and unpredictable. It typically requires new coordination efforts (e.g., adjusting research routines, standardizing data resources) and, overall, has less immediate and tangible benefits. This mode of eResearch collaboration was also acknowledged by researchers as a big future opportunity, which comes with many challenges. While development of infrastructures for such large-scale collaboration is often supported by large national investments, researchers saw it as a big challenge that requires their time, expertise, support, and other efforts.

An alarming finding of this study was low involvement of research students in collaborative research. Almost two thirds of research students reported that nearly all their research was individual and about one third indicated not being involved in any collaborative research. This finding suggested several important implications. First, about half of research students collaborated in their research groups, yet this also indicated that many research students did not view their research degree supervision as collaboration. Meanwhile, as noticed in the literature, the supervisor's role is a combination of teaching, learning and collaboration, and, in some domains, publications based on the student's higher degree research are often co-authored by the student and supervisors

(Kyvik & Smeby, 1994; Maxwell & Smyth, 2011). Second, the results indicated that students made less use of ICT collaboration tools. This finding was not surprising taking into account that students were less involved in collaborations, and supports results from the "researchers of tomorrow" study conducted recently in the UK, which indicated that while "X generation" doctoral students might be proficient ICT users, they are risk averse and only like to use new technologies when they see a clear benefit (Carpenter, et al., 2010). Nevertheless, even those students who were involved in collaborations tended to use some communication technologies less often than academics. Thirdly, students who are not involved in collaborations were significantly less often involved in established scholarly dissemination practices. This finding indicates that research students involved in collaborative research have more opportunities to gain experience of publishing in peer reviewed journals.

Taken as a whole, these findings indicated that research higher degree students gain little experience of working collaboratively in distributed (disciplinary and multidisciplinary) research teams and little experience of using communication technologies in their research work. While, overall, they express favourable attitudes about technologies and collaboration, the individualistic nature of postgraduate research provides few opportunities to engage in research collaboration.

CONCLUSION AND FUTURE WORK

Drawing on a study of ICT-enhanced research practices and needs conducted at seven Australian universities, this chapter has discussed how researchers engage with distributed research and use ICT for collaboration. Results show significant current engagement of the majority of researchers in collaborative research, their acknowledgement of the potential of eResearch, and researchers' general willingness to engage in collaborative eResearch.

Findings also indicate some important relationships between researchers' general collaboration practices and their use of ICT for this purpose. While there are some significant differences in the collaboration practices of research students and academics and between practices and challenges in different disciplinary domains, researchers who are more involved in collaborative research also more often use ICT-enhanced collaboration tools; share more of their data; and more often disseminate their findings via digital media.

Results indicate two important discrepancies and tensions between researchers' current practices of ICT use in their research and their thinking about future eResearch opportunities and challenges. First, there are some essential differences between researchers' current practices, their short-term needs for eResearch services and support, and their forward thinking regarding the potential for eResearch in their research domain. eResearch collaboration is reported by respondents as one of the most important eResearch opportunities for enhancing their scholarly practices. While many researchers acknowledge that they currently need support in this area, few of them consider it might be a future challenge. Secondly, there is a noticeable discrepancy between two modes of collaboration: (a) 'team-based' collaboration that primarily includes distributed joint work on specific projects; and (b) 'grand' collaboration that is open, has fewer tangible and immediate outcomes, and requires new coordination efforts. While the former mode of eResearch is generally seen by researchers as an enabler of more productive current or near future practices, the latter mode of eResearch collaboration is a future opportunity and a grand challenge that requires effort and support.

This study has provided some important insights into various aspects of research collaboration, to include researchers' general collaboration practices, their use of communication technologies for collaborative research, ICT-enhanced dissemination of research findings, and data collection and sharing practices. As our results indicate, researchers have different needs for eResearch and experience different challenges in each of these areas of ICT use for research collaboration. More focused follow-up studies should be conducted to investigate further most important specific issues, such as research publishing and dissemination strategies and motives, data sharing issues and incentives, and researchers' needs for discipline-specific collaboration environments, services, and support. In-depth studies are also needed to investigate research students' ICT-use practices and reasons for their low engagement in collaborative research.

ACKNOWLEDGMENT

The work reported in this paper was initiated and part-funded by University of Sydney ICT (Tools and Frameworks for Research Collaboration project) and Intersect Australia Ltd. The authors would like to thank the DVCs/PVCs for Research of all participating universities for their cooperation, and all participants of this survey for their time and willingness to contribute. Main ethics clearance was granted by the University of Sydney Human Research Ethics Committee.

REFERENCES

ACLS. (2006). *Our cultural commonwealth: The final report of the American council of learned societies commission on cyberinfrastructure for the humanities and social sciences*. Washington, DC: American Council of Learned Societies Commission on Cyberinfrastructure for the Humanities and Social Sciences.

ARCS. (2011). NeAT projects. *Australian Research Collaboration Service*. Retrieved February 24, 2011, from http://www.arcs.org.au/index.php/services/ research-community-projects/ 266-research-community-custom-projects-redone.

Atkins, D. E., Droegemeier, K. K., Feldman, S. I., Garcia-Molina, H., Klein, M. L., & Messer-schmitt, D. G. (2003). *Revolutionizing science and engineering through cyberinfrastructure. Report of the National Science Foundation Blue-Ribbon Advisory Panel on Cyberinfrastructure*. Arlington, VA: National Science Foundation.

Barjak, F., Lane, J., Kertcher, Z., Poschen, M., Proct-er, R., & Robinson, S. (2009). Case studies of e-infra-structure adoption. *Social Science Computer Review*, *27*(4), 583–600. doi:10.1177/0894439309332310

Barjak, F., Wiegand, G., Lane, J., Kertcher, Z., Poschen, M., Procter, R., et al. (2007). *Accelerating transition to virtual research organization in social science (AVROSS): First results from a survey of e-infrastructure adopters*. Paper presented at the Third International Conference on e-Social Science. Ann Arbor, MI. Retrieved February 24, 2011, from http://ess.si.umich.edu/ papers/ paper141.pdf.

Becher, T., & Trowler, P. R. (2001). *Academic tribes and territories*. Philadelphia, PA: Society for Research into Higher Education & Open University Press.

Bishop, L. (2005). Protecting respondents and enabling data sharing: Reply to Parry and Mauthner. *Sociology*, *39*(2), 333–336. doi:10.1177/0038038505050542

Borgman, C. L. (2007). *Scholarship in the digital age: Information, infrastructure, and the internet*. Cambridge, MA: The MIT Press.

Bos, N., Zimmerman, A., Olson, J., Yew, J., Yerkie, J., & Dahl, E. (2007). From shared databases to com-munities of practice: A taxonomy of collaboratories. *Journal of Computer-Mediated Communication*, *12*(2). doi:10.1111/j.1083-6101.2007.00343.x

Brody, T., Harnad, S., & Carr, L. (2006). Earlier web usage statistics as predictors of later cita-tion impact. *Journal of the American Society for Information Science and Technology*, *57*(8), 1060–1072. doi:10.1002/asi.20373

Carlson, S., & Anderson, B. (2007). What are data? The many kinds of data and their implications for data re-use. *Journal of Computer-Mediated Communication*, *12*(2). doi:10.1111/j.1083-6101.2007.00342.x

Carpenter, J., Wetheridge, N., Smith, N., Good-man, M., & Struijvé, O. (2010). *Researchers of tomorrow*. London, UK: British Library/JISC.

Clarke, S., Harrison, A., & Searle, S. (2009). *Schol-arly information repository services at Monash University*. Paper presented at the International Association of Technical University Libraries (IA-TUL) 30th Annual Conference. Leuven, Belgium.

Cragin, M. H., Palmer, C. L., Carlson, J. R., & Witt, M. (2010). Data sharing, small science, and institutional repositories. *Philosophical Trans-actions of the Royal Society A: Mathematical, Physical and Engineering Sciences, 368*(1926), 4023-4038.

David, P. A. (2006). Towards a cyberinfrastructure for enhanced scientific collaboration: Providing its 'soft' foundations may be the hardest part. In Kahin, B., & Foray, D. (Eds.), *Advancing Knowl-edge and the Knowledge Economy* (pp. 431–454). Cambridge, MA: MIT Press.

De Roure, D., Baker, M. A., Jennings, N. R., & Shadbolt, N. R. (2003). The evolution of the grid. In Berman, F., Fox, G., & Hey, A. J. G. (Eds.), *Grid Computing: Making the Global Infrastructure a Reality* (pp. 65–100). West Sussex, UK: Wiley.

De Roure, D., & Frey, J. (2007). *Three perspec-tives on collaborative knowledge acquisition in e-science*. Paper presented at the Workshop on Semantic Web for Collaborative Knowledge Acquisition (SWeCKa). Hyderabad, India.

DEST. (2006). *An Australian e-research strategy and implementation framework: Final report of the e-research coordinating committee*. Sydney, Australia: Australian Government.

Dutton, W., & Meyer, E. (2009). Experience with new tools and infrastructures of research: An exploratory study of distance from, and attitudes toward, e-research. *Prometheus, 27*(3), 223–238. doi:10.1080/08109020903127802

e-IRG. (2009). *E-IRG white paper 2009.* Retrieved February 24, 2011, from http:// www.e-irg.eu/ images/ stories/ publ/ white-papers/ e-irg_white_ paper_ 2009_ final.pdf.

Edwards, P., Farrington, J. H., Mellish, C., Philip, L. J., Chorley, A. H., & Hielkema, F. (2009). E-social science and evidence-based policy assessment: Challenges and solutions. *Social Science Computer Review, 27*(4), 553–568. doi:10.1177/0894439309332305

Feinberg, J. (2009). *Wordle.* Retrieved February 22, 2011, from http://www.wordle.net.

Fink, J. L., Kushch, S., Williams, P. R., & Bourne, P. E. (2008). Biolit: Integrating biological literature with databases. *Nucleic acids research, 36*(2), W385-W389. Retrieved February 24, 2011, from http:// nar.oxfordjournals.org/ content/ 36/ suppl_2/ W385.full.

Foster, N. F., & Gibbons, S. (2005). Understanding faculty to improve content recruitment for institutional repositories. *D-Lib Magazine, 11*(1). Retrieved February 24, 2011, from http:// www. dlib.org/ dlib/ january05/ foster/ 01foster.html.

Fry, J. (2006). Coordination and control across scientific fields: Implications for a differentiated e-science. In Hine, C. (Ed.), *New Infrastructures for Knowledge Production: Understanding e-Science* (pp. 167–188). Hershey, PA: IGI Global. doi:10.4018/978-1-59140-717-1.ch008

Greenhow, C., Robelia, B., & Hughes, J. E. (2009). Learning, teaching, and scholarship in a digital age: Web 2.0 and classroom research: What path should we take now? *Educational Researcher, 38*(4), 246–259. doi:10.3102/0013189X09336671

Halfpenny, P., Procter, R., Lin, Y.-W., & Voss, A. (2009). Developing the UK-based e-social science research program. In Jankowski, N. (Ed.), *E-research: Transformation in Scholarly Practice* (pp. 73–90). New York, NY: Routledge.

Haythornthwaite, C., Lunsford, K. J., Bowker, G. C., & Bruce, B. C. (2006). Challenges for research and practice in distributed, interdisciplinary collaboration. In Hine, C. (Ed.), *New Infrastructures for Knowledge Production: Understanding e-Science* (pp. 143–166). Hershey, PA: IGI Global. doi:10.4018/978-1-59140-717-1.ch007

Henty, M., Weaver, B., Bradbury, S. J., & Porter, S. (2008). *Investigating data management practices in Australian universities.* Canberra, Australia: Australian Partnership for Sustainable Repositories (APSR).

Hey, A. J. G., Tansley, S., & Tolle, K. M. (2009). *The fourth paradigm: Data-intensive scientific discovery.* Palo Alto, CA: Microsoft Research.

Hey, T., & Trefethen, A. (2003). The data deluge: An e-science perspective. In *Grid Computing: Making the Global Infrastructure a Reality* (pp. 809–824). New York, NY: Wiley.

Hey, T., & Trefethen, A. (2008). E-science, cyberinfrastructure, and scholarly communication. In Olson, G. M., Zimmerman, A., & Bos, N. (Eds.), *Scientific Collaboration on the Internet* (pp. 15–31). Cambridge, MA: MIT Press.

Houghton, J., & Oppenheim, C. (2010). The economic implications of alternative publishing models. *Prometheus, 28*(1), 41–54. doi:10.1080/08109021003676359

Jirotka, M., Procter, R., Hartswood, M., Slack, R., Simpson, A., & Catelijne, C. (2005). Collaboration and trust in healthcare innovation: The eDiaMoND case study. *Computer Supported Cooperative Work, 14*(4), 369–398. doi:10.1007/ s10606-005-9001-0

Jirotka, M., Procter, R., Rodden, T., & Bowker, G. (2006). Special issue: Collaboration in e-research. *Computer Supported Cooperative Work, 15*(4), 251–255. doi:10.1007/s10606-006-9028-x

Karasti, H., Baker, K. S., & Halkola, E. (2006). Enriching the notion of data curation in e-science: Data managing and information infrastructuring in the long term ecological research (LTER) network. *Computer Supported Cooperative Work: The Journal of Collaborative Computing, 15*(4), 321–358. doi:10.1007/s10606-006-9023-2

Katz, J. S., & Martin, B. R. (1997). What is research collaboration? *Research Policy, 26*(1), 1–18. doi:10.1016/S0048-7333(96)00917-1

Kennan, M. A. (2007). Academic authors, scholarly publishing, and open access in Australia. *Learned Publishing, 20*(2), 138–146. doi:10.1087/174148507X185117

Kennan, M. A., & Kingsley, D. A. (2009). The state of the nation: A snapshot of Australian institutional repositories. *First Monday, 14*(2). Retrieved February 24, 2011, from http:// firstmonday.org/ htbin/ cgiwrap/ bin/ ojs/ index.php/ fm/ article/ view/ 2282/ 2092.

King, D. W., & Tenopir, C. (2011). Some economic aspects of the scholarly journal system. *Annual Review of Information Science & Technology, 45*, 295–366.

Kling, R., & Callahan, E. (2003). Electronic journals, the internet, and scholarly communication. *Annual Review of Information Science & Technology, 37*(1), 127–177. doi:10.1002/aris.1440370105

Kling, R., & McKim, G. (1999). Scholarly communication and the continuum of electronic publishing. *Journal of the American Society for Information Science American Society for Information Science, 50*(10), 890–906. doi:10.1002/(SICI)1097-4571(1999)50:10<890::AID-ASI6>3.0.CO;2-8

Korporaal, G. (2009). *AARNet 20 years of the internet in Australia: 1989-2009*. Sydney, Australia: AARNet.

Kyvik, S., & Smeby, J.-C. (1994). Teaching and research: The relationship between the supervision of graduate students and faculty research performance. *Higher Education, 28*(2), 227–239. doi:10.1007/BF01383730

Laterza, V., Carmichael, P., & Procter, R. (2007). The doubtful guest? A virtual research environment for education. *Technology, Pedagogy and Education, 16*(3), 249–267. doi:10.1080/14759390701614363

Lawrence, K. (2006). Walking the tightrope: The balancing acts of a large e-research project. *Computer Supported Cooperative Work, 15*(4), 385–411. doi:10.1007/s10606-006-9025-0

Lynch, C. (2009). Jim Gray's fourth paradigm and the construction of the scientific record. In Hey, A. J. G., Tansley, S., & Tolle, K. M. (Eds.), *The Fourth Paradigm: Data-Intensive Scientific Discovery*. Palo Alto, CA: Microsoft Research.

Lynch, C. A., & Lippincott, J. K. (2005). Institutional repository deployment in the united states as of early 2005. *D-Lib Magazine, 11*(9), 1082–9873. doi:10.1045/september2005-lynch

Markauskaite, L., Aditomo, A., & Hellmers, L. (2009). *Co-developing eresearch infrastructure: Technology-enhanced research practices, attitudes and requirements*. Retrieved February 24, 2011, from http:// www.intersect.org.au/ docs/ eResearch%20 survey%20 full%20 reportv1.0_ noelene.pdf.

Markauskaite, L., Aditomo, A., & Hellmers, L. (2011). *Co-developing eresearch infrastructure: Technology-enhanced research practices, attitudes and requirements. Full technical report: Round 2*. Sydney, Australia: Intersect & the University of Sydney.

Markauskaite, L., Hellmers, L., Kennan, M. A., & Richardson, J. (2009). *eResearch practices, barriers and needs for support: Preliminary study findings from four NSW universities*. Paper presented at the 3rd eResearch Australasia Conference. Retrieved February 24, 2011, from http:// www.eresearch. edu.au/ docs/ 2009/ era09_ submission_ 55.pdf.

Maxwell, T. W., & Smyth, R. (2011). Higher degree research supervision: From practice toward theory. *Higher Education Research & Development, 30*(2), 219–231. doi:10.1080/07294360.2010.509762

Meadows, A. J. (1998). *Communicating research.* San Diego, CA: Academic Press.

Meyer, E. T. (2009). Moving from small science to big science: Social and organizational impediments to large scale data sharing. In Jankowski, N. (Ed.), *E-Research: Transformation in Scholarly Practice* (pp. 147–159). New York, NY: Routledge.

Miles, S., Groth, P., Branco, M., & Moreau, L. (2007). The requirements of using provenance in e-science experiments. *Journal of Grid Computing, 5*(1), 1–25. doi:10.1007/s10723-006-9055-3

NCRIS. (2011). *eResearch infrastructure.* Sydney, Australia: National Collaborative Research Infrastructure Strategy. Retrieved February 24, 2011, from https:// www.pfc.org.au/ bin/ view/ Main/ WebHome.

NCRIS Committee. (2008). *Review of the national collaborative research infrastructure strategy's roadmap.* Sydney, Australia: DEEWR.

Olson, G. M., Zimmerman, A., & Bos, N. (2008). *Scientific collaboration on the internet.* Cambridge, MA: The MIT Press.

Parry, O., & Mauthner, N. (2005). Back to basics: Who re-uses qualitative data and why? *Sociology, 39*(2), 337–342. doi:10.1177/0038038505050543

Paterson, M., Lindsay, D., Monotti, A., & Chin, A. (2007). DART: A new missile in Australia's e-research strategy. *Online Information Review, 31*(2), 116–134. doi:10.1108/14684520710747185

Payette, S., Blanchi, C., Lagoze, C., & Overly, E. (1999). Interoperability for digital objects and repositories. *D-Lib Magazine, 5*(5), 1082–9873. doi:10.1045/may99-payette

Pearce, N. (2010). A study of technology adoption by researchers. *Information Communication and Society, 13*(8), 1191–1206. doi:10.1080/13691181003663601

Prosser, D. C. (2005). Fulfilling the promise of scholarly communication – A comparison between old and new access models. In *Die Innovative Bibliothek: Elmar Mittler zum 65* (pp. 95–106). Berlin, Germany: Geburtstag.

Ribes, D., & Finholt, T. A. (2009). The long now of infrastructure: Articulating tensions in development. *Journal of the Association for Information Systems, 10*(5), 375–398.

Ribes, D., & Lee, C. (2010). Sociotechnical studies of cyberinfrastructure and e-research: Current themes and future trajectories. *Computer Supported Cooperative Work, 19*(3), 231–244. doi:10.1007/s10606-010-9120-0

Rowlands, I., & Nicholas, D. (2006). The changing scholarly communication landscape: An international survey of senior researchers. *Learned Publishing, 19*(1), 31–55. doi:10.1087/095315106775122493

Seringhaus, M., & Gerstein, M. (2007). Publishing perishing? Towards tomorrow's information architecture. *BMC Bioinformatics, 8*(1). Retrieved February 24, 2011, from http:// www.biomedcentral.com/ content/ pdf/ 1471-2105-8-17.pdf.

Smith, M. K., Barton, M., Bass, M., Branschofsky, M., McClellan, G., Stuve, D., et al. (2003). Dspace: An open source dynamic digital repository. *D-Lib Magazine, 9*(1). Retrieved February 24, 2011, from http:// www.dlib.org/ dlib/ january03/ smith/ 01smith.html.

Swan, A. (2010). *The open access citation advantage: Studies and results to date.* Southampton, UK: University of Southampton.

Swan, A., & Brown, S. (2005). *Open access self-archiving: An author study.* Truro, UK: Key Perspectives Limited.

Tan, K. L. L., Lambert, P. S., Turner, K. J., Blum, J., Gayle, V., & Jones, S. B. (2009). Enabling quantitative data analysis through e-infrastructure. *Social Science Computer Review*, *27*(4), 539–552. doi:10.1177/0894439309332647

Universities Australia. (2010). *Australian universities data snapshot 2010*. Retrieved February 24, 2011, from http:// www.universitiesaustralia.edu. au/ resources/ 389.

Van de Sompel, H., Payette, S., Erickson, J., Lagoze, C., & Warner, S. (2004). Rethinking scholarly communication. *D-Lib Magazine*, *10*(9), 1082–9873. doi:10.1045/september2004-vandesompel

Wilson, A., Rimpilainen, S., Skinner, D., Cassidy, C., Christie, D., & Coutts, N. (2007). Using a virtual research environment to support new models of collaborative and participative research in Scottish education. *Technology, Pedagogy and Education*, *16*(3), 289–304. doi:10.1080/14759390701614413

Woolgar, S. (2004). *Social shaping perspectives on e-science and e-social science: The case for research support*. Oxford, UK: University of Oxford.

Wouters, P., & Beaulieu, A. (2007). Critical accountability: Dilemmas for interventionist studies of e-science. *Journal of Computer-Mediated Communication*, *12*(2). doi:10.1111/j.1083-6101.2007.00339.x

Wu, P. H. J., Heok, A. K. H., & Tamsir, I. P. (2007). Annotating web archives - Structure, provenance, and context through archival cataloguing. *New Review of Hypermedia and Multimedia*, *13*(1), 55–75. doi:10.1080/13614560701423620

KEY TERMS AND DEFINITIONS

eResearch: A set of research activities that use advanced information and communication technologies, including computer networks, large shared databases, remote research instruments, and computational power.

Research Students: Postgraduate university students that pursue higher research degrees, such as doctor of philosophy or professional doctorate.

Academic Staff: Teaching and research, and research only university academics at all stages of career.

Disciplinary Clusters: Three broad groups of academic disciplines and fields of study: social fields (humanities, arts and social sciences); biomedical fields (biological, health and medical sciences); physical fields (physical sciences, chemical sciences, IT, engineering and mathematics).

ENDNOTES

[1] Terms "respondents," "researchers," and "participants" all refer to the survey sample and are used interchangeably in this chapter. The term "academics" refers to academic and honorary staff only, while the term "research students" refers to postgraduate research students.

[2] In the rest of this chapter we include other university staff that work in specific disciplinary fields in making comparisons between disciplines, but exclude them from comparisons between academic staff and research students.

[3] The rest of the chapter analyses differences separately between researchers involved in collaboration to different extents and between researchers at different career stages. However, in interpreting findings, we take into account lesser involvement of research students in research collaboration.

[4] Some researchers were involved in both types of non-university collaboration.

[5] Word clouds produced using *Wordle* Web-based software (Feinberg, 2009).

[6] See endnote 5.

[7] See endnote 5.

[8] This number indicates question number in the original survey instrument.

APPENDIX: QUESTIONS FROM THE SURVEY

Research Project: "Co-Developing eResearch Infrastructure: Technology-Enhanced Research Practices, Attitudes, and Future Requirements"

3. Please identify your major disciplinary area(s)[8].

Check all that apply.

21 - Science (General)
22 - Social Sciences, Humanities and Arts (General)
23 - Mathematical Sciences
24 - Physical Sciences
25 - Chemical Sciences
26 - Earth Sciences
27 - Biological Sciences
28 - Information, Computing and Communication Sciences
29 - Engineering and Technology
30 - Agricultural, Veterinary and Environmental Sciences
31 - Architecture, Urban Environment and Building
32 - Medical and Health Sciences
33 - Education
34 - Economics
35 - Commerce, Management, Tourism and Services
36 - Policy and Political Science
37 - Studies in Human Society
38 - Behavioural and Cognitive Sciences
39 - Law, Justice and Law Enforcement
40 - Journalism, Librarianship and Curatorial Studies
41 - The Arts
42 - Language and Culture
43 - History and Archaeology
44 - Philosophy and Religion
98 – Other

5. Please indicate your current primary role.

Postgraduate research student
Academic/research staff: Early career
Academic/research staff: Middle career
Academic/research staff: Senior/long experience
Emeritus, honorary, visiting or adjunct appointment
Other. If other, please specify

6. Prior to this survey, had you heard of the term "eResearch"?

Yes
No

10. How much of your research is collaborative?

Nearly all collaborative
About half
Nearly all individual

11. Indicate where your research collaborations occur.

Check all that apply.

Within my research group
Outside my research group within my faculty
With other faculties within my university
With other universities within Australia
With universities or institutions in other countries
With non-university research agencies (e.g. CSIRO)
Beyond academia, with industry partners
None (i.e. I am not involved in collaborative research)
Other. If other, please specify

12. When you collaborate, how often do you use the following technologies for communication and project management?

1 - Don't use; 2 - Use occasionally; 3- Use often

Face to face meetings
Telephone calls
Email
Discussion fora (e.g. e-lists)
Audio conferencing, audio meetings
Video conferencing via desktop or laptop software
(e.g. Skype)
Video conferencing in a dedicated room or facility
(e.g. Access Grid)
Web 2.0 content management tools (e.g. wiki, blog)
File and document sharing tools (e.g. file repositories)
Collaborative document writing tools
(e.g. Google Docs)
Special project and task management tools (e.g. trac, dotProject)
Virtual research environments (VRE)
Social networking software (e.g. Facebook)
Other. If other, please describe

13. Which of the following methods and technologies do you use to disseminate research findings?

1- Don't use; 2- Use occasionally; 3- Use often

Conventional publishing (e.g. journals, books, proceedings)
eJournals published by commercial publishers or scholarly societies
Open access eJournals
eBooks published by commercial publishers or scholarly societies
Open access eBooks
Online conference proceedings
Digital institutional repository or archive

Digital disciplinary repository or archive
(e.g. arXiv, SSRN)
Departmental/institutional website, blog or wiki
Project website, blog or wiki
Personal website, blog or wiki
Other. If other, please describe

14. List up to 3 main areas of research collaboration and dissemination that would most benefit from ICT support.

16. How often do you use data obtained in the following ways?

1- Don't use; 2- Use occasionally; 3- Use often

Collected or created by yourself
Collected or created as part of a team
Acquired directly from another researcher or team
Acquired from academic data archives or repositories
Acquired from third party research organisations
(e.g. the Australian Bureau of Statistics, OECD)
Acquired from commercial online sources (e.g. Lexis-Nexis, Financial Times, Euromonitor)
Other. If other, please describe

20. Do you allow researchers from outside your team/project to access your research data?

No, none of the data
Yes, some of the data
Yes, most of the data

21. If yes, in which of the following ways do you typically provide access to your data?

Check all that apply.

Publish data online (e.g. on a public project website)

Deposit data to open data repositories
Submit data for publishing when I publish papers
    in eJournals
Allow access my data via privately negotiated access
Access to my data is provided by a third party
    (e.g. the experimental facility, institution,
    funding body)
Other. If other, please describe

22. If there are restrictions on accessing your data, what are the reasons for these restrictions?

Check all that apply.

Competitive research advantage
Commercialisation potential
Privacy and confidentiality issues
Other ethical issues
Licensing issues
Technical difficulty of making data available
Lack of incentive to make data available
Lack of usefulness of my data to others
Other reasons. If other, please describe
None

29. Have you heard about or used services provided by the following Australian bodies?

1- Never heard of them; 2- Heard of them;
3- Used their services

AAF - Australian Access Federation

ANDS - Australian National Data Service
ARCS - Australian Research Collaboration Service
Intersect - an eResearch Consortium of
    NSW Universities
NCI - National Computational Infrastructure
NCRIS - National Collaborative Research
    Infrastructure Strategy

30. List up to 3 specific ICT technical or human support areas that would enhance your research capacities.

31. How important, do you think, is eResearch for the future progress of your research field?

Very important
Important
Moderately important
Of little importance
Unimportant
Not applicable (ICT is essentially irrelevant)

32. Write up to 3 phrases that describe the most important future applications of ICT in your research field.

33. Write up to 3 phrases that describe the most important challenges for the application of ICT in your research field now and in the near future.

Chapter 2
The Web as a Platform for E–Research in the Social and Behavioral Sciences

Pablo Garaizar
Universidad de Deusto, Spain

Miguel A. Vadillo
Universidad de Deusto, Spain

Diego López-de-Ipiña
Universidad de Deusto, Spain

Helena Matute
Universidad de Deusto, Spain

ABSTRACT

As a consequence of the joint and rapid evolution of the Internet and the social and behavioral sciences during the last two decades, the Internet is becoming one of the best possible psychological laboratories and is being used by scientists from all over the world in more and more productive and interesting ways each day. This chapter uses examples from psychology, while reviewing the most recent Web paradigms, like the Social Web, Semantic Web, and Cloud Computing, and their implications for e-research in the social and behavioral sciences, and tries to anticipate the possibilities offered to social science researchers by future Internet proposals. The most recent advancements in the architecture of the Web, both from the server and the client-side, are also discussed in relation to behavioral e-research. Given the increasing social nature of the Web, both social scientists and engineers should benefit from knowledge on how the most recent and future Web developments can provide new and creative ways to advance the understanding of the human nature.

DOI: 10.4018/978-1-4666-0125-3.ch002

WEB-BASED RESEARCH IN PSYCHOLOGY: TWO DECADES OF JOINT EVOLUTION

Cognitive psychology has traditionally kept a special relationship with computer science. In fact, the "cognitive revolution" usually refers to the joint developments that took place in the mid 1950's and 1960's in computer science and psychology, together with those of other cognitive sciences (linguistics, philosophy, anthropology, and neuroscience). Initially, psychologists were interested in computers mainly because they provided a novel and interesting model on how the brain might work (Gardner, 1985). Behaviorists had complained that cognitive concepts were difficult to apprehend in mechanistic and reductionist terms and that they should, therefore, always be avoided in scientific psychology. However, computer science showed for the first time that simple, mechanic devices were also able to process information and perform many cognitive tasks that had sometimes been assumed to remain beyond the realm of science. Soon, psychologists proposed that the human brain was just a peculiar type of computer and that the mind was a kind of software running on this "hardware." Moreover, cognitive scientists started to describe cognitive processes in a program-like manner and even tried to simulate these processes in standard computers (Newell & Simon, 1972).

For a long time, this was the main role played by computers in cognitive psychology. However, during the 1980's, when computers became cheaper and the recently developed high-level programming languages made their use more accessible, psychologists started to use computers with a new purpose in mind. Instead of just using them as an abstract model of how the mind works, psychologists began to use computers as an additional tool in their experiments. Computers simplified the presentation of stimuli to participants and the registration of many types of responses to those stimuli. In fact, any researcher with rudimentary programming skills could easily conduct classical laboratory experiments with only the help of a desktop computer. The old laboratory in which a different apparatus had to be used for each different experiment was soon substituted by laboratories in which computers were used to run all types of experiments, including tasks as different as: a) spatial navigation through different types of mazes, b) memory tasks with different lists of words, or with images or sounds, c) reading comprehension studies using different types of stories and distracting stimulation, d) reaction-time studies, e) subliminal perception involving words or images or sounds presented so rapidly that they could not be consciously processed, f) Pavlovian and operant conditioning including visual or auditory stimuli as well as different types of responses (from keyboard to mouse to vocalizations), g) divided attention, h) social dilemmas, or any other interesting research question a psychologist could think of. Thus, by the time the World Wide Web was created, in the early 1990's, most experimental psychologists were already used to having computers in their labs and using them extensively in their experiments. It was only a matter of time before some researchers made the first steps towards taking advantage of the new opportunities offered by the Internet as a multipurpose and world-wide psychology laboratory. There is no doubt that this world-wide laboratory is also of great value to other social and behavioural sciences interested in human behaviour, beliefs, attitudes, and social relations. These include education, economics, marketing, anthropology, sociology, and politics, but this list is certainly not complete. Indeed, any scientific discipline interested in how people reason, learn, relate to each other, process information, and respond to it, should benefit from using the Web as a platform for e-research. Although focusing on examples from our own field of expertise, experimental psychology, the present chapter should become a useful guide for other social sciences as well.

From its very beginning at the Conseil Européen pour la Recherche Nucléaire (CERN) in the early 1990's, the World Wide Web has been closely linked to the academic world. During the past two decades, we have witnessed its technological evolution and how social science researchers have been taking advantage from its capability to engage participants around the whole world to perform larger, more insightful, and valid experiments. The advantages of conducting psychological research over the Internet soon became clear. Probably the most remarkable one is that the Internet made it relatively easy to access extraordinarily large samples, something that is usually beyond the possibilities of the traditional psychological laboratory. In fact, this is still the main reason many researchers decide to conduct experiments over the Internet (e.g., Nosek, 2005). This feature of Internet-based experiments becomes especially relevant when researchers are interested in determining whether a nonsignificant statistical result reflects a genuine absence of effects or a simple lack of statistical power (Bar-Anan, De Houwer, & Nosek, 2010; Ratliff & Nosek, 2010). Moreover, this methodology does not only allow the recruitment of many participants but also can be used to target very peculiar populations which would otherwise remain inaccessible (Mangan & Reips, 2007; Vernberg, Snyder, & Schuh, 2005).

However, in spite of these and other advantages, Internet-based research methods also pose important methodological problems. In general, researchers have little control over the conditions in which online participants conduct the experimental task. They cannot even make sure of whether the participants have been paying attention to the task or of whether they have correctly understood the instructions. Moreover, the participant can enter the Web site of the experiment several times and submit data repeatedly. Although there are some technical measures that can be used to avoid or reduce the negative impact of these and related meth-

odological problems (Birnbaum, 2004; Reips, 2002), many of these solutions pose their own problems as well. It is not surprising that the pioneers of Internet-based research usually had to face a high level of scepticism in the evaluation of their studies.

In this situation, the first step that had to be made before Internet-based methods could be trusted was to carefully assess the impact of conducting a study over the Internet, in relation to the traditional laboratory. Therefore, many researchers started to replicate well-known effects over the Internet or to conduct studies simultaneously in the laboratory and over the Internet, so that the results of both methodologies could be contrasted. This work was done both to assess the validity of online questionnaires and surveys (Buchanan & Smith, 1999; Schmidt, 1997a), on the one hand, and the validity of experimental procedures, on the other (Birnbaum, 1999; Birnbaum & Wakcher, 2002; Dandurand, Shultz, & Onishi, 2008; Matute, Vadillo, & Bárcena, 2007; Matute, Vegas & Pineño, 2002; Steyvers, Tenenbaum, Wagenmakers, & Blum, 2003; Vadillo, Bárcena, & Matute, 2006; Vadillo & Matute, 2009, 2011). It was particularly important to show that effects could be replicated over the Internet even when delicate dependent measures, such as reaction times, were used (McGraw, Tew, & Williams, 2000). In general, the main result of this research was that, with very minor exceptions, online methods could be trusted and that the drawbacks of this methodology were clearly compensated by its many advantages.

A second step towards the generalization of e-research in psychology was the development of experimental software that could be easily used by researcher to develop their own experimental applications. Although most cognitive psychologists were used to having to learn some programming languages in order to design their experiments, during the '90's and even today, few of them have the necessary skills to adapt these experiments to the Internet environment.

Therefore, many researchers started to develop simple design tools that could be used to generate survey forms (Birnbaum, 2000; Schmidt, 1997b) or more complicated experimental tasks (Reips & Neuhaus, 2002) without much technical knowledge of Internet-based programming.

After two decades of joint evolution, the Internet has become a highly valuable research tool for many experimental psychologists. They do not only regularly use the Internet to conduct experiments and large correlational studies. They are also using it to gather other types of information such as, for instance, psycholinguistic data about the frequency of words in several languages (Lahl, Göritz, Pietrowsky, & Rosenberg, 2009), or the susceptibility of people to cognitive illusions and biases such as the illusion of control (Matute, Vadillo, Vegas, & Blanco, 2007). Moreover, the increasing access of the general population to the Internet is also providing psychologists with new research topics that need to be explored (e.g., Internet abuse, cyberbullying) and with novel ways of delivering psychological interventions to the population (e.g., Botella et al., 2008a, 2008b, 2009). As we will show below, the recent developments in the Web 2.0 and the future Semantic Web bring new and yet unexplored possibilities for e-research in social sciences.

THE NEW WEB PARADIGMS AND THEIR IMPLICATIONS FOR E-RESEARCH IN THE SOCIAL SCIENCES

The Future of the Web is yet unclear, but some approaches like Social Web, Semantic Web, and Cloud Computing have been used widely and can still be substantially improved. In this section we will describe the new scenarios enabled by them in terms of e-research in the social and behavioral sciences, and we will also glimpse at the possibilities offered to social scientists by future Internet proposals.

The Social Web

Despite of the fact that even from its first stages of development at the early 1990's the World Wide Web (WWW) had a flexible and collaborative design that allowed users to create new links and content, it was not until the beginning of the 21st century that this possibility became true by virtue of the technological and methodological evolution popularly known as the Web 2.0 (Di-Nucci, 1999; O'Reilly, 2005) or the Social Web (Hoschka, 1998).

For the last two decades, Web users have moved forward from simply carrying out hypertextual data transfers to the socialization of many aspects of their lives. The Web has evolved towards the "Read/Write Web," achieving one of the goals initially proposed by its designers (Berners-Lee & Cailliau, 1990). Describing this new stage of the Web as the "Social Web" seems more appropriate, since the adoption of the new technologies and methodologies involved has not been as abrupt or revolutionary as the term "Web 2.0" might suggest, but through a progressive process of socialization. There may be differences between both terms when explaining the origin of the change, but there is no such discrepancy when considering its effects. O'Reilly (2005) defines Web 2.0 applications as services that get better the more people that use them. Over the last 15 years, the Web has grown from an information-centered network (i.e., "information superhighways") into a people-centered social media in which user-generated content is crucial. This trend is likely to continue further, considering that Future Internet aims at favoring user-empowerment (i.e., two users making the same search with the same keywords being at different locations and having different web profiles will obtain different search results).

Two are the foundations of this Social Web: users and data. Users generate content with different levels of implication (from merely being part of a social media site to publishing and editing multimedia content, rating or tagging it, or providing recommendations and reviews), attract more users, and reshape platforms and Web services in terms of content (e.g., fixing errors) and purpose (e.g. creating new ways of using them, not defined by their designers). Data is the fuel that drives social media, regardless of whether it is generated by users or by other online services. Instead of conforming vast repositories of unrelated information, the Social Web's data is available in several standard formats, ready to be remixed, completed or updated by third-party services. As stated by Engeström (2009), people do not just connect to each other using social media. They connect through "shared objects," and good online services (e.g. Youtube, Flickr, Delicious) allow people to create social objects that add value to the rest of the users, and subsequently to the whole social media.

Both these aspects of the Social Web can enhance e-research in social and behavioral sciences in two different ways. On the one hand, the Social Web allows using methodological approaches that would be unfeasible otherwise, providing cheap and effective ways to engage people in participating in experiments, or taking advantage from the sharing features of social media to distribute and process experimental data. On the other hand, the success of the Social Web has significant consequences from a psychological point of view, in terms of new or implicit behaviors in social media. Thus, the Social Web can be a good means for improving research methodology and, at the same time, an object of e-research in psychology.

Improving Research Methodology through the Social Web

Many authors agree that the popularization of computational technology provides a new way to do science. Wolfram (2002) remarks the power of using computers when facing complex problems, even through simple programs, delegating the tedious calculations to machines. According to Shneiderman (2008), new kinds of science are

needed to study the integrated interdisciplinary problems at the heart of socio-technical systems. This Science 2.0 combines the methods of traditional science (i.e., hypothesis testing, predictive models, and the need for validity, replicability, and generalizability) with the opportunities offered by the Social Web to collect and process real-time empirical data. E-research in the social sciences is also involved in this evolution. In addition to academic social networks (e.g., Academia. edu, Mendeley, ResearchID, SciLink), general purpose social networks (e.g., Facebook, Twitter, MySpace) can be used to spread scientific findings or even to discuss them. The idea of achieving insightful conclusions through open debates in social media is still very controversial for many reasons (e.g., irrelevant or non-accurate contributions, reputation, non-disclosure agreements). Nevertheless, there is no such debate about using the social media as a way to recruit participants for experiments. Many social science experiments can take advantage from the wide range of ways to push information provided by the Social Web. It is easy to publish information regarding the experiment or to recruit potential participants using tags, categories, recommendations, groups, or fan-pages, without annoying other people with unsolicited notifications that could be considered as spam. Due to all the hints provided by user-generated content, the Social Web is able to hit very specific targets and avoid general and ineffective ways of promotion (Anderson, 2006). Thus, e-researchers in social sciences can reach very specific participants in studies that would be extremely difficult or even unfeasible without the social features of the Web.

Apart from the increase in the number and prevalence of participants in social sciences experiments, the Social Web provides several techniques to analyze and exploit user-generated content. Virtually all social media services allow interacting with their data through Application Programming Interfaces (APIs). APIs allow consuming a Web service without using a browser to browse through service's Website (e.g., using a mobile phone application) contents. Features derived from APIs are often underestimated by non-programmers. Using a real-life comparison, APIs can be shown as "delivery services" of a restaurant. If a family does not want to prepare dinner, they can either go to a restaurant or call to a delivery service. There are also mixed alternatives, like going to a restaurant and order a take-away meal, or even pay for a catering service at home. Coming back to Web services, the meal is the content that users need, and the delivery service is the API. There are some restaurants without delivery service that force customers to go to their place for a meal, as API-less Web applications do; and there are some other restaurants which provide both alternatives (local or delivery), and customers can decide whether it is worth going to the restaurant or it is better to have dinner at home.

Moreover, by using APIs, third-party developers can aggregate social services to create new ones, called "mash-ups" (e.g., an application that mixes cartographic information provided by Google Maps with beautiful pictures of nearby places gathered from Flickr, with no need to have an explicit agreement between the providers of those APIs [Google and Yahoo!]). Another interesting feature of social media APIs is that they allow to access, collect, and analyze huge amounts of useful information. Older methodologies, like traditional offline experimentation or even online experimentation with no use of social media, can handle tens, hundreds, or thousands of participants. But using the APIs provided by social media, millions of interactions can be handled in real time. Eventually, the range provided by the API is able to cover the whole target population of the study, but it can sometimes be more limited in wide-range studies due to technical and economic reasons. Nevertheless, going from thousands to millions of interactions is a significant leap in e-research. For instance, Twitter's public APIs allow to access to the 1% of all real-time 'tweets'—messages sent via Twitter—to third-party applications. The

third-party applications using Twitter APIs can apply to be whitelisted, which allows upgrading their quota and access to the 10% of all Twitter content. This means a huge number of 2 to 20 million tweets per day for regular and whitelisted applications, respectively.

Providing ways to build a third-party applications' ecosystem is at the core of all successful social media platforms. The case of Facebook is particularly remarkable because it enables the creation of successful business models within the social network (e.g., Zynga, the social videogame company behind FarmVille, got over $1 million in revenue a day during 2010 thanks to Facebook), boosts the use of the Facebook fan-pages by companies, and provides several interfaces to publish outside-generated content in Facebook, or vice versa, Facebook content in third-party platforms. If Facebook's benefits from interconnectivity are considerable, Twitter's are outstanding. Although it is still unclear whether Twitter can be considered a social network like Facebook or not (Kwak, Lee, Park, & Moon, 2010), Twitter describes itself as an "information network" where users find, curate, and deliver content, rather than socialize. Twitter users focus less on their social graph and more on information broadcasting. Paradoxically, Twitter's limitations are its biggest strengths: Its home page is extremely simple compared with other social media, text-based content and 140-character limitations encourage focusing on crucial information and the subscription-based social graph allows asymmetric relationships between users. Contrary to Facebook's symmetric relationships, where "friendship" is always bi-directional, a Twitter user can follow another user (i.e., subscribe to other user's tweets), while not being followed by her. The simplicity of Twitter's Web interface contrasts with the large set of rich clients that extend the capabilities of the platform through an intensive API usage. Metaphorically, we can see Twitter as a government that builds highways (i.e., Twitter servers and network bandwidth), sets the regulations to use them (i.e., APIs descriptions), and provides standard and simple vehicles (i.e., Twitter Web page). Users can choose to drive these standard vehicles or get others more adapted to their needs (e.g., motorbikes, trucks, etc.; or their equivalents in mobile Twitter clients, blogging Twitter publishing buttons, etc.), as long as they fulfil the regulations. This is a standard feature of most social media platforms, but it is more evident in Twitter because of the extreme simplicity of its Web interface and the myriad of third-party clients. As Cheng and Evans (2009) found, in 2009 TweetDeck was the most popular non-Twitter.com publishing tool with a 19.7% market share, and more than half of Twitter users (55%) used something other than Twitter.com. In 2010, as stated by Twitter's CEO (Williams, 2010), just 25 percent of the content is generated from Twitter.com. That is, 75 percent of traffic comes from outside Twitter.com through the ecosystem provided by public APIs.

Twitter is a good example of the success that public APIs can reach, but the rest of social media (e.g., Facebook, Youtube, Flickr) are also seizing the opportunity to offer content outside their platforms and enabling mixing their contents: Facebook users can share Youtube videos in their fan-pages or walls, blog editors can embed slideshows from Flickr and add social media links at the end of each post to share it across the Social Web, LinkedIn (a business-oriented social network) users can include Slideshare presentations in their resumes. Using APIs is not exclusive for social media, though. Wherever a dynamic map is needed, Google is providing it through Google Maps API.

Social sciences e-researchers must take into account the fact that most of the Social Web's data is being heavily used and reused. Accounting reused information should be done carefully. On the one hand, researchers should avoid populating their local databases with multiple copies of the same information. On the other hand, information reusage may imply relevance, and should be analyzed on its own. Suh, Hong, Pirolli, and Chi (2010) studied the variables that predict Twit-

ter content reusage ("retweetability," the ability of being retweeted—forwarded—when posting content). Agichtein, Castillo, Donato, Gionis, and Mishne (2008) question the simple metrics used when analyzing social media, and introduce a general classification framework for combining the evidence coming from different sources of information, that can be tuned automatically for a given social media type and quality definition.

The Social Web's public APIs are not the panacea to all problems related to content. Sometimes they are inadequate, insufficient or too complex to use. In those cases, e-researchers should look for third-party APIs with extra functionality or a wider range of provided information formats. GNIP.com is probably the best example of a third-party API provider, as it supplies its own APIs for more than 30 different social media (e.g., Facebook, Twitter, Youtube, Flicrk, Worpdress). For instance, GNIP.com provides several Twitter-related APIs with interesting extra features ("GNIP Premium Twitter feeds"), like access to the 50 percent of all Twitter content, delivered in real time (GNIP Twitter Half-hose), a stream of all Twitter statuses containing URLs, delivered in real time too (GNIP Twitter Link Stream), or statuses that mention any given user (GNIP Twitter User Mention Stream). The main drawback of this kind of services is its price, not suitable for low-budget research initiatives. Even so, there are academic institutions that offer third-party social media APIs for free, but under some restrictions (e.g., limited date ranges, sample sizes, storage quotas) due to the costs involved in maintaining the service (Gaffney, Pearce, Darham, & Nanis, 2010).

Finally, when no API is provided to access relevant information from service providers, e-researchers still have some alternatives. The first one is to take advantage from "Web feeds" (also known as "Web syndication"), if they are available. Web applications use web feeds to publish updated content in a standard way (i.e., using XML-based formats like RSS or Atom). Newspapers are probably the best example to illustrate the Web feed concept. In a newspaper's Web site, information is arranged by relevance and topicality. If someone wants to be informed, she should periodically access that Web site and look for new content. As this can be very difficult for some news, newspapers offer a publicly available time-ordered news list as a Web feed. Gathering the new content of a Web site is extremely easy when Web feeds are available. The main difference between API-based queries and Web feeds is that using the former allows advanced queries, whereas the later is limited to the last updates. Coming back to the previous comparison between APIs and pizza deliveries, a Web feed would be like a delivery where customers cannot order the pizza they want, but the last pizza that came out from the oven. The second alternative when no API is provided is a technique called "Web scraping." Using Web scraping techniques, a researcher can convert human-readable data provided by a web site and defined in HyperText Markup Language (HTML) into raw data defined in an XML dialect or other data formats, and subsequently store and process it by means of a content analyzer. There are many problems related to Web scraping: (a) The HTML code of some Web sites is not easy to parse to extract valuable data, (b) Small changes in Web site's HTML code have large impact in the gathering process, and (c) Extracting data from Web sites and using it in third-party services can sometimes violate Terms of Use and content license of the service provider.

In conclusion, there are many interesting features of the Social Web that can be very useful for e-research. Firstly, the Social Web is an excellent platform to promote ongoing experiments and to disclose findings, encouraging discussions about them and reaching a large-scale pool of people interested in participating in experiments. Secondly, the Social Web's stress on data reuse allows researchers to collect and process huge amounts of original information, using social media public APIs, third-party APIs, or even more complex techniques like Web feeds or web scraping.

The Social Web as the Object of E-Research in Psychology

Over the last decade, the Social Web has gone through various stages (i.e., blogs, wikis, social networks, location-based social networks). The social component of the Web is a key factor to understand why so many technologies are now considered obsolete, and why the findings of research studies conducted a few years ago no longer apply to the current situation. Linden and Fenn (2003) created a graphic representation of the maturity, adoption and social application of specific technologies to characterize the over-enthusiasm or "hype" and subsequent disappointment that typically happens with the introduction of new technologies. As shown in Figure 1, a typical "hype cycle" consists of five phases:

1. "Technology Trigger": The new technology is presented to the public with a proof of concept, trying to achieve media coverage.
2. "Peak of Inflated Expectations": Everyone wants to use the new technology. Media organisations show it as the solution to every problem. There may be some successful applications of a technology, but there are typically more failures.
3. "Trough of Disillusionment": Over-enthusiasm vanishes and technology fails to be successful in all proposed scenarios. Media usually abandons the topic and the technology.
4. "Slope of Enlightenment": The technology is improved and adapted to those specific situations where it was successful (less than expected during the "Peak of Inflated Expectations," but more than discarded during the "Trough of Disillusionment").
5. "Plateau of Productivity": The benefits of using the technology are widely demonstrated and accepted. The technology becomes increasingly stable and evolves in second and third generations.

Figure 1. Gartner's hype cycle phases (adapted from Linden & Fenn, 2003)

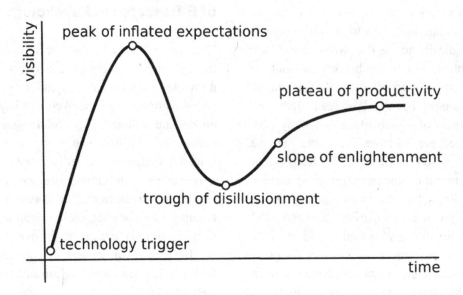

Blogging, like all technologies related to the Social Web, passed through the different phases of adoption, very similar to this "hype cycle." The number of blogs was consistently doubled every 6 months from 2003 until 2006 (see Figure 2), but needed 320 days to double in 2007 (Sifry, 2007). In 2008, there were 600,000 blog posts per day, less than in 2007 (Winn, 2009). Did blogging reach the "Peak of Inflated Expectations" at the end of 2006? It is very likely that the success of Facebook and Twitter influenced in this decrease of blogging usage, but this can also be related to the fact that blogs were presented as the solution to all Web needs during the period from 2003 and 2007 (e.g., comercial promotion, e-learning, research, multimedia portfolios). The over-enthusiasm was answered with the creation of companies focused in blog analysis (e.g., Technorati, BlogPulse, Google Blog Search), but some of them changed their target when blogging became less popular. Nowadays, blogs are close to the "Slope of Enlightenment," as they are being used for the specific purpose they were created for. This crazy growth of expectations around the Social Web was described by Engeström (2009) as

"butterfly flights," as they fly higher and higher, and suddenly descend to the floor. The same happens with social media adoption when they lose the users' interest (e.g., Six Degrees, Friendster, MySpace). Thus, exponential growth rates (Fisch, 2006) should be considered cautiously in the Social Web, because they can be a sign of being at the "Peak of Inflated Expectations."

E-research in psychology has dealt with blogging by studying the causes and consequences of being a blogger. Even though there are diverse motivations for blogging (Nardi, Schiano, Gumbrecht, & Swartz, 2004), some authors suggest that it can be predicted from the big five personality traits (Digman, 1990): People who score high in openness to new experience and high in neuroticism too are more likely to be bloggers (Guadagno, Okdie, & Eno, 2007). Similarly, Hsu and Lin (2008) proposed a model based in the Theory of Reasoned Action (TRA) where ease of use, enjoyment, and knowledge sharing (i.e., altruism and reputation) explain 78 percent of the variance of being a blogger; and social factors (e.g. community identification) and attitude toward blogging explain 83 percent of the variance

Figure 2. Weblogs cumulative (March 2003 - April 2006). Weblogs reached the "Peak of Inflated Expectations" at the end of 2006 (© 2007, Technorati.com. Used with permission).

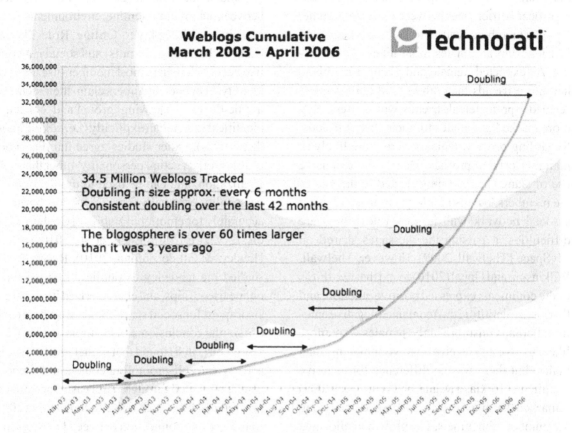

of continuing to blog. In relation to the consequences of being a blogger, Baker and Moore (2008) found that intending bloggers were more psychologically distressed and more likely to use venting and self-blame to cope with their stress than non-bloggers. Intending bloggers also scored lower on measures of social provisions and were less satisfied with their number of online and offline friends when compared to non-bloggers. Consistent with the similarities between blogging and writing a diary, many of the benefits related to writing a diary (Smyth, 1998) have been found to also be present in blogging.

Despite the fact that wikis did not attract the attention of many e-researchers in psychology, Amichai–Hamburger, Lamdan, Madiel, and Hayat (2008) studied personality characteristics of Wikipedia members (i.e., "wikipedians"), and found that Wikipedia members locate their real me on the Internet more frequently than non-Wikipedia members. They also found significant differences in agreeableness, openness, and conscientiousness, which were lower for the Wikipedia members, and an interaction between Wikipedia membership and gender: Introverted women were more likely to be Wikipedia members as compared with extroverted women.

There is no doubt that online social networks have been hot topics for e-research in psychology. MySpace was the first online social network to reach an audience of more than 100 million people (Adest, 2006), creating huge expectations for this new way to socialize. Thelwall (2008) studied the motivation of MySpace members, finding significant differences between male and female. Female members tended to be more interested in friendship and males more interested in dating. As expected, female and younger members had more friends than others, and both genders seemed to prefer female friends, with this tendency more marked in females for their closest friends. Regarding privacy, females were more likely to maintain private profiles. Due to the extensive use of slang (i.e., not only related to the age of the members, but also for being online and using a social network with its own rules) there are difficulties in parsing the messages shared on MySpace (Thelwall, 2009). However, Thelwall, Wilkinson, and Uppal (2010) found that two thirds of the comments expressed positive emotion, and that just a minority (20%) contained negative emotion. Perhaps unsurprisingly, females were more likely to give and receive positive comments than males, but there was no difference for negative comments. Torkjazi, Rejaie, and Willinger (2009) remarked the "hype cycle" of MySpace analyzing the number of members. The growth of allocated user IDs in MySpace was exponential until 2007 (i.e., "Peak of Inflated Expectations") followed by a sudden and significant slow-down in 2008 (i.e., "Trough of Disillusionment") motivated by an increase in the popularity of Facebook. Hargittai (2007) verified the struggle for new members between Facebook and MySpace and found significant differences according to their socio-economic situation. Students whose parents had lower levels of schooling were more likely to be MySpace members, whereas students whose parents had higher levels of education were more likely to be Facebook members.

Facebook offers a reasonable trade-off between standardization and customization for members' profiles. Both characteristics are interesting from a researcher perspective: Having standard features makes profiles easily comparable, and customizations can be correlated with many other variables (e.g., personality traits, mental disorders). Zhao, Grasmuck, and Martin (2008) found differences between anonymous online environments (e.g., Massively Multiplayer Online Role-Playing Games, chat rooms, forums) and social networks like Facebook, where most members use their real identity. Facebook members claim their identities implicitly (i.e., showing group and consumer identities) rather than explicitly (i.e. talking about themselves). Other studies agree that Facebook profiles reflect actual personality rather than self-idealization, and can be used to predict owner's personality, especially for extraversion, but not so accurately for emotional stability (Gosling, Gaddis, & Vazire, 2007; Back, et al., 2010; Correa, Hinsley, & Gil de Zúñiga, 2010). Rosen (2007) studied the tendency to publicly trumpet one's online friendships, and characterized it as a narcissistic quest for social status. Several authors came to a similar conclusion. For example, Buffardi and Campbell (2008) found that higher levels of social activity and self-promoting content in Facebook can be predicted through narcissistic personality self-reports. Ellison, Steinfield, and Lampe (2007) found a strong connection between Facebook use and perceived social capital. Social networks help to maintain relationships as people move from one offline community to another (e.g., when students graduate from high school or college). Such connections could have strong payoffs in terms of jobs, internships, and other opportunities, even in online environments. Lerman and Galstyan (2008) found evidence of it analyzing the impact of the "social graph" in social news Websites (e.g., Digg, Reddit, StumbleUpon): Users tend to like stories submitted by friends and stories their friends read and liked.

Another important issue related to Facebook is privacy. There is a tendency for social media users to value privacy, security, and trust, but there are still inconsistent concerns about them. For instance, Acquisti and Gross (2006) found that social networks users are mildly concerned about who can access their personal information and how it can be used, but not concerned about the information itself, mostly because they are the publishers of the content shared on the social network, and because they believe to have some control on its access. Moreover, there are many social motivators against privacy when using social networks, like having fun or allowing the social network to be a useful tool by sharing enough information. Fogel and Nehmad (2009) concluded that general privacy and identity information disclosure concerns are more salient to female than male (e.g., greater percentages of male than female display their phone numbers and home addresses on social media). Social media around "social objects" (Engeström, 2009) offers a wider range of alternatives to deal with privacy. Lange (2007) analyzed social relationships among youth on Youtube, identifying various degrees of "publicness" in video sharing. Considering the anonymity and the access restriction as factors, four combinations could happen (i.e., public account with unrestricted content, anonymous account with unrestricted content, public account with restricted content, and anonymous account with restricted content). Lange remarked the use of two strategies to leverage anonymity while sharing content: (a) "publicly private," in which video maker's identities were revealed, but content was relatively private because it was not widely accessed, and (b) "privately public," where content was widely accessible, but detailed information about video maker's identities was limited. However, anonymity and privacy are not the same thing, and social media users should realize that both are important.

As mentioned before, Twitter is not really a social network, but an information network. Perhaps the most interesting issue regarding Twitter is related to the fact that users reshaped the network, creating new ways of using it: (a) When users needed a short way to answer a message, they added an "@" to the username to mean it; (b) "RT" or "retweet" was unofficially created to express that the content is not original, but forwarded from other user; and (c) as there was

no tagging system on Twitter, users started to prepend a "#" to words to be considered as tags by other users. Months later Twitter administrators realized that these new codes were "de facto" standards among the users and implemented them as official features. Taking into account its fast evolution in less than 5 years, studies published in the last years should be considered within its context, as their conclusions are not likely to apply to current Twitter activity. For instance, Java and Song (2007) concluded that the most common use of Twitter was talk about daily routine. This could be true in 2007, but nowadays people use Twitter with other purposes. Moreover, other particular characteristics of Twitter, like its text-based only content, asymmetric relationships (e.g., @aplusk, Ashton Kutcher user on Twitter follows less than a thousand users, but is followed by more than 6 million users), or similar functionality for mobile users, make Twitter a great platform for e-research in social sciences. Cha, Haddadi, Benevenuto, and Gummadi (2010) analyzed influence in Twitter and found that popular users who have a large number of followers are not necessarily influential in terms of spawning retweets or mentions (e.g., a tweet from Ashton Kutcher is not more likely to be forwarded or mentioned just because the extraordinary number of followers). Furthermore, a concerted effort (e.g., limiting tweets to a single topic) seems to be the best way to gain influence in Twitter. Conversely Suh, Hong, Pirolli, and Chi (2010) found that the number of followers and "following" (i.e., followees), as well as the age of the account, seem to affect influence in Twitter in terms of "retweetability," while, interestingly, the number of past tweets does not predict retweetability of a user's tweet. It is also interesting the fact that URLs and hashtags have strong relationships with retweetability, confirming the shift of typical Twitter activity from daily routine to information sharing. Perhaps some of the controversial issues can be explained examining the topology of the social graphs. Mislove, Marcon, Gummadi, Druschel, and Bhattacharjee (2007) stated that online social networks have structures that differ from other networks, in particular the Web. Social networks have a much higher fraction of symmetric links and also exhibit much higher levels of local clustering.

Location Based Social Networks (LBSN) go further in the real-time social media mobility (e.g., FourSquare, Gowall, Whirl). As LBSN users tend to be Twitter members, all of them are tightly connected with it, providing multiple ways to automatically publish their content on Twitter. This can be also problematic. Humphreys, Krishnamurthy, and Gill (2010) found that about a quarter of tweets included information regarding when people are engaging in activities and where they are. Educating users about the ways in which personal information can be used for alternative purposes (i.e., related to user's privacy, security or even safety) is an important step in media literacy.

Given the aforementioned privacy and security issues in social networking, several radical approaches for social media are being tested. For example, Diaspora is a distributed social network that provides a decentralized alternative to services like Facebook. The project is currently under development by Grippi, Salzberg, Sofaer, and Zhitomirskiy (2010), and works by letting users set up their own server of the social network, or by using a server of a trusted organization. Diaspora servers interact to share status updates and other social data. Being open source software, it can be audited by security experts and checked for backdoors or other privacy leaks. With a decentralized schema, the members of an institution concerned about privacy, security, and trust (e.g., the Department of Defence of the United States of America) can use the Diaspora server set up by their own IT department, and still socialize with the rest of the social network with no risk. Path.com offers another new concept: The personal network. Each path member creates her own personal network limited to her 50 closest friends (Morin, 2011). This limit is based on the "Dunbar's number," a theoretical cognitive limit to the number of

people with whom one can maintain stable social relationships (Dunbar, 1992). Although, Dunbar's research suggested 150 as the maximum number of social relationships, the network expands in factors of roughly 3 (i.e., ~5 closest friends, ~20 people with regular contact, ~50 people considered within the personal network, and ~150 stable social relationships). It is still too soon to assess such revolutionary approaches, but all of them suggest that there is much work to do in the Social Web in terms of privacy, security, and trust.

The Semantic Web

When Berners-Lee, designer of the World Wide Web, described the Semantic Web with Hendler and Lassilla (Berners-Lee, Hendler, & Lassila, 2001), the evolution of the Web appeared to be targeted towards a machine-readable World Wide Web (i.e., using metadata to describe meaningfully the content of the Web), and not through the socialization of the technologies involved (i.e., the Social Web). Initially, Berners-Lee underestimated the Web 2.0 phenomenon (Lanningham, 2006), considering that most of the alleged new features were already present in his original World Wide Web design (i.e., the "Read/Write Web"). He dreamed about a new Web where machines would be able to understand and work with the data transferred on interactions between people or other machines (i.e., textual or multimedia content, web links, user interactions), and prevent people from tedious and repetitive procedures that could be accomplished through machines talking to other machines (Berners-Lee & Fischetti, 1999). If so much data is already published on the Web, why do we still need to compare or aggregate it manually? For instance, a Semantic Web approach of "buying the cheapest flight from one place to another" would provide the automatic mechanisms to gather all the information from diverse sources, understand and integrate it into a semantic reasoner, and get the best offer among all processed ones.

Although the Semantic Web is a much bigger step compared with the Social Web, its current development status is promising but limited. The main reason is technological. Adapting a Web designed for humans (i.e., full of ambiguous and incomplete information, multimedia content without textual transcription, or broken links) to a machine-readable one is not a trivial task. The Social Web is the Web of people. Social media users generate, consume and share content. The Semantic Web is the Web of data. Semantic data provide enough meta-data to allow for automatic processing. Old hyper-text formats are too limited for this purpose, so new formats are needed. Semantic web formats should be able to describe data, define data properties, relationships among data, data classes or models, and logic rules to process data without human help. The World Wide Web Consortium (W3C) launched the Semantic Web Activity, where a big number of Working Groups are developing and adapting the Semantic Web standards (e.g., RDF Working Group to define Resource Description Framework, RDF format, SPARQL Working Group to define SPARQL Protocol and RDF Query Language, SPARQL format, and so forth).

Designing the standard formats to build the Semantic Web is very important, but more actions have to be taken towards achieving a machine-readable World Wide Web. The next step should be to start describing Web data using semantic formats, creating ontologies that explain and describe relationships between concepts (Chandrasekaran, Josephson, & Benjamins, 1999). Under the field of the Semantic Web, an ontology is a formal representation of knowledge about a specific domain. Within an ontology, concept properties and relationships between them are explicitly described using a restricted vocabulary that allows automatic reasoning about them. Thus, defining and using ontologies are key factors for the Semantic Web's success, but it is not an easy task and experts are needed to supervise and correct the ontology defining process. Besides, in most of the cases experts cannot formally describe their domain of expertise and the formalization process may lead to a loss of accuracy.

Ontologies are valuable tools used to process large amounts of data. They are often confused with taxonomies—hierarchical, experts-made—or even folksonomies (Vander Wal, 2004)—non-hierarchical, amateurs-made. Both taxonomies and ontologies need experts to be precisely defined, but while taxonomies are focused on classifying, ontologies provide enough semantic metadata to enable automatic reasoning about the data. Perhaps, recurring to a widely-used example is the easiest way to understand ontologies better. There are different versions of the beer ontology, but regardless the semantic format used to describe it, all of them are very similar. Figure 3 shows a beer ontology (http://www.purl.org/net/ontology/beer.owl) that describes almost everything related to beer: Types of beer, ingredients, regions where beer is produced, awards and associations related to beer brewery, beer festivals, and so on. Expert knowledge about beer brewery is needed to create the beer ontology, because it has to be able to accurately describe every concept related to beer. Combining the beer ontology with a semantic reasoner and other Web services, a Semantic Web service would be able to fulfil complex queries like "show me the closest bars serving a pale ale beer with caramel, ordered by distance and beer price."

Considering that data is the raw material of scientific research, the Semantic Web (i.e., the Web of data) is tightly related to e-research. Indeed, Engelbrecht and Dror (2009) suggest that cognitive psychology can contribute to the development of ontologies for semantic technologies and the Semantic Web in two different ways: (a) The efficiency with which activities that involve domain experts (e.g. knowledge elicitation and ontology authoring) are carried out and the utility of the resulting ontologies can be improved by considering human information processing and its limitations, and (b) the human cognitive system, in general, and human knowledge representation,

Figure 3. Partial view of a beer ontology (http://www.purl.org/net/ontology/ beer.owl)

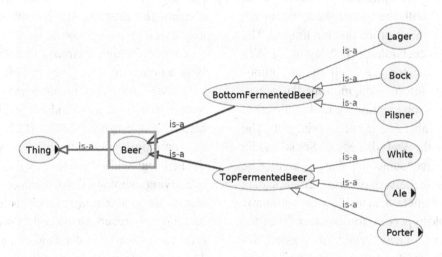

in particular, can act as a model for the structure of ontologies.

While it is essential to take into account the cognitive abilities of experts to create ontologies, it is also important to consider the opportunities that the Semantic Web could provide. Bairoch (2009) pictured the current situation: "It is quite depressive to think that we are spending millions in grants for people to perform experiments, produce new knowledge, hide this knowledge in an often badly written text and then spend some more millions trying to second guess what the authors really did and found." If all scientific knowledge published in thousands of peer-reviewed journals were stored using semantic formats, automatic reasoning could be used to infer vast amounts of new implicit knowledge, refuting established models, completing preliminary studies, or foreseeing new fields of research. W3C's Scientific Publishing Task Force was created with this goal. Actually, Aleman-Meza et al. (2006) went further in reanalyzing published data when they proposed a Semantic Web application that detects Conflict of Interest (COI) relationships among potential reviewers and authors of scientific papers.

W3C decided to encourage the use of Semantic Web technologies for Health Care and Life Sciences (with focus on biological science and translational medicine), for many reasons: (a) these domains have to process huge amounts of complex (and not simplifiable) data, (b) there is a high level of interaction in managed data (e.g., interactions between molecules through well-known processes generate new molecules with different effects), (c) data sources are very heterogeneous and diverse, (d) the benefits are crucial for humanity. However, there are still some bad practices related to "in silico" (i.e., computer-based) experiments. Good and Wilkinson (2006) criticized researchers that prefer to develop their own and lesser-quality technological solutions in order to increase the number of publications and citations, which is precisely the opposite of the main goal of the Semantic Web. Having more and better applications using Life Science Identifier systems (LSID), Resource Description Framework (RDF), Web Ontology Language (OWL), and Semantic Web Services should discourage the use of non-standard technologies.

What would be the psychological equivalent of large genomic databases? There is no direct equivalent, but as explained before, the Social Web generates millions of single interactions among social media users that could be semantically analyzed to extract opinions, emotions and feelings and to infer new knowledge from them. Opinion Mining (computer science) or Sentiment Analysis (computational linguistics) are two promising fields of research specialized on content analysis (Pang & Lee, 2008). Some Web-focused companies are currently developing semantic parsers for social media content (e.g., Semiocast provides semantic APIs for Facebook and Twitter content), and many researchers are applying data mining techniques to information shared in social media. In two similar studies, Mislove and colleagues (Mislove, et al., 2010; Mislove, et al., 2010) created cartograms (i.e., maps where geometry or space is distorted in order to convey the information of a variable) based on the evolution of political topics on Twitter through time. Sakaki, Okazaki, and Matsuo (2010) proposed an algorithm to detect earthquakes in real time by social sensors (i.e., social media activity). In a similar way, Asur and Huberman (2010) found significant correlations between box-office revenues of movies and social media activity prior to their public release. Finally, many other authors (Specia & Motta, 2007; Van Damme, Hepp, & Siorpaes, 2007) have worked on the integration of the Social Web and the Semantic Web, trying to take advantage of the best features of both approaches.

Despite being so promising, the Semantic Web will not be widely available within the next few years, due to the technological and human resources involved. However, "Linked Data" (Berners-Lee, 2006) is an attempt to progress towards a more realistic application of Semantic Web, where a cut-down data model empowered by the rich expressivity of new semantic standards (especially a combination of RDF and OWL, termed as RDFS++) is used to define vocabularies and instance data which are interlinked. Thus, a global knowledge graph (see Figure 4) is being enabled under the auspices of Linking Open Data initiative (Bizer, Heath & Berners-Lee, 2009), linking and bringing together concepts and re-

lationships about different knowledge domains. An interdisciplinary and global science could arise from Open Data (Uhlir & Schroeder, 2007).

In the meantime, less ambitious approaches, like microformats or "lowercase semantic web"—also known as "decaffeinated Semantic-Web" or "lower-s semantic web"—(Khare, 2006), can provide semantic features to the Web through simple semantic annotations (e.g., a non-semantic Web service can offer semantic features using microformats to express the language of each Web page with a simple "lang" property: <html lang="es">). These annotations are often invisible to users but enable valuable third-party web applications and e-research initiatives. For example, each message or "tweet" transferred via Twitter contains not only the 140 characters sent by the user to the social network, but also tens of metadata fields regarding dates, location, user preferences, scope of the message and so forth (indeed, the text of the message only represents the 5-10% of the whole tweet, depending on the personal settings of the sender). Reips and Garaizar (2011) used geo-location related metadata of millions of Twitter messages to create iScience Maps (http://maps.iscience.deusto.es), a service that allows researchers to assess via Twitter the effect of specific events in different places as they are happening and to make comparisons between cities, regions, or countries and their evolution in the course of an event.

Web-based research should be aware of this kind of solutions and apply them, when available.

New Paradigm Addressed by Future Internet

The current Internet, with billions of users worldwide is a great success in terms of connecting people and communities, but it was designed in the 1970s for purposes quite different from today's heterogeneous needs and expectations. The current Internet has grown beyond its original expectations and beyond its original design

Figure 4. Linking open data cloud diagram (© 2011, Richard Cyganiak and Anja Jentzsch: http://lod-cloud.net/. Used with permission)

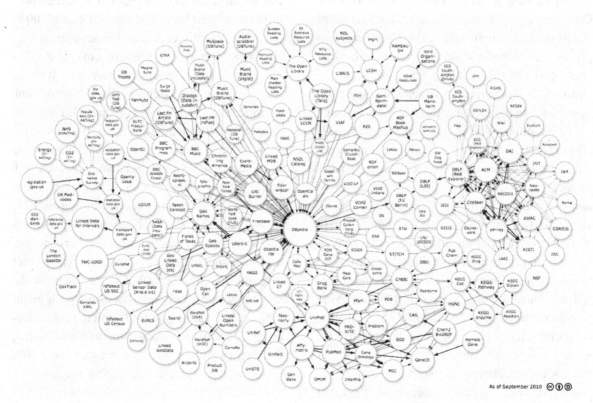

objectives. Many partial solutions have been progressively developed and deployed to allow the Internet to cope with the increasing demands in terms of user connectivity and capacity. There is a growing consensus among the scientific and technical community that the methodology of continuously "patching" the Internet technology will not be able to sustain its continuous growth, and to cope with it at an acceptable cost and speed. The current Internet architecture is progressively reaching a saturation point in meeting increasing user's expectations and behaviors, as well as progressively showing inability to efficiently respond to new technological challenges (i.e., in terms of security, scalability, mobility, availability, and manageability, but also of socio-economical challenges).

Future Internet is a new term which summarizes the efforts made by international asso-

ciations (e.g., GENI, AKARI, Future Internet) to progress towards a better Internet, either through (a) small, incremental evolutionary steps, or (b) complete redesigns (clean slate) and architecture principles. It should offer all users a secure, efficient, trusted, and reliable environment, that allows open, dynamic, and decentralized access to the network and adapt its performance to the users' needs and context.

Figure 5 illustrates how the 4 pillars of Future Internet rely on the Future Internet networking infrastructure foundation: (a) Internet by and for people, (b) Internet of contents and knowledge, (c) Internet of services, and (d) Internet of things (Gershenfeld, Krikorian, & Cohen, 2004; Papadimitriou, 2009). All the elements of the Future Internet (foundation and pillars) need each other and are mutually dependent. New services and applications are a prerequisite for investments in

Figure 5. Future Internet foundation and pillars (adapted from Gershenfeld, Krikorian, & Cohen, 2004)

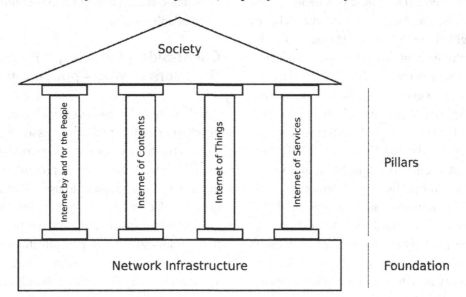

new infrastructure, since Infrastructure without necessary capabilities cannot support new services and applications (i.e., technology pull). New infrastructure technologies open new opportunities for new services and applications (i.e., technology push). Therefore, cooperation between all stakeholders is required for a successful Future Internet.

Considering how all of these new approaches redefine the relationship between users and technology, their implications for e-research in Social Sciences are clear: Not only because of the methodological changes that will come, but also because of the wide range of new scenarios and their psychological and social implications.

THE WEB AS A PLATFORM

The most recent advances in the architecture of the Web allow using it as an excellent platform to deploy social science experiments over the Internet. In this section we will discuss the specific implications for e-research in social sciences of those improvements, both on the server and the client-side.

Server-Side Technology: WOA, REST, Cloud Computing

The Web as a platform defines its services using Web Oriented Architecture (WOA), a design and modelling methodology that extends Service Oriented Architecture (SOA) to web applications. WOA represents information as resources that will be handled by user-agents (browsers) and Web servers through a simple Representational State Transfer (REST) mechanism. In other words, simple interfaces using XML and Hyper-Text Transfer Protocol (HTTP). Regarding the infrastructure, Cloud Computing provides a platform to develop and deploy Web applications offered as services that can be consumed without knowledge about its use and the implementation of its resources.

This set of technologies and design methodologies fosters the vision of the Web as a platform to develop and deploy all kind of applications, including social science e-research ones, empowering them with distributed, scalable (i.e., capable of not degrading the service upon increasing demand), and underlying technology agnostic services.

Although Web 2.0 has more commonly been known as the Social Web, some researchers have also highlighted another important facet of it: It transforms the Web into an application platform. This is explained by the fact that there are numerous services or functions published on the web as proven by the site programmableweb.com, where thousands of services, mainly offering easy to consume Representational State Transfer (REST) interfaces—a well-know approach to export functionality through the HTTP protocol—and smart combinations and aggregations of them in the form of Web mash-ups are published. Learning this publicly available (most often free) web-accessible functionality is very easy at first, developers only need to understand the methods, parameters and results returned by its Application Programming Interfaces (APIs). Therefore, they have given place to remarkable innovation in mash-up creation from the active Web developer community.

Furthermore, the emergence of a new computing paradigm, namely Cloud Computing, where data and services lie in highly scalable data centers which can be ubiquitously accessed from any Internet-connected device, is addressing two key aspects for reliably pushing (migrating) application functionality to the Internet: scalability and ease of deployment. Cloud Computing can be defined as a pool of abstracted, highly scalable, and managed (supervised and controlled) compute infrastructure capable of hosting (running) end-customer applications and billed by consumption. Interestingly, Cloud Computing makes available a service hosting infrastructure for Web application server-side deployment through easily consumed REST interfaces. Remarkably, Cloud Computing is designed to make more computing and storage resources available in a dynamic manner as the demand for the consumption of a given Web application grows in time. Big companies such as Google, Microsoft, and Amazon offer compelling Cloud Computing solutions on top

of which e-research applications could be easily and scalably hosted.

Client-Side Technology: From Browsers to Web Application Players

Thanks to the last decade's technological and social developments, the Web is progressively becoming something that cannot only be browsed, but also used for specific purposes. At present, it is becoming less and less frequent to use a Website just to have a look at news or to "jump" from one site to another, with no particular purpose in mind. Instead, many traditional desktop applications are being replaced by equivalent programs offered as Web services (e.g., Gmail instead of the traditional email client, Youtube instead of the multimedia player, Google Docs instead of the classical word processors) that can be accessed by Web user-agents (i.e., web-browsers), now more similar to "application players" than to simple Internet browsers.

As we have already discussed, part of this evolution from static websites to current Web applications can be seen as the result of the natural development of the technologies that support the Web (i.e., Cloud Computing, WOA). However, the evolution of web user-agents has played an important role too, providing an execution environment increasingly similar to that of the traditional desktop applications. Many of these improvements have been made possible by the Hypertext Application Technology Working Group (WHATWG), an initiative of the developers of the main web user-agents (i.e., Apple, Mozilla, and Opera) aimed at extending and updating the hypertext definition language used to design Web sites (i.e., HTML) so that it can support the main functionalities of most applications, such as local storage, exchanging messages between documents, drag-and-drop features, browsing history management, or 2D immediate sketching, among others. The efforts made by the WHATWG, with the support of the W3C, gave rise to the specification of HTML5, which includes many of these improvements (Hickson, 2011).

Let's analyze in detail the most important implications of HTML5 for e-research in social sciences. First, the "canvas" object for 2D sketching, the drag-and-drop events or the timed multimedia playing allows social science researchers to design experiments that, until this very moment, could only be conducted with desktop applications. Given that the Web is increasingly being accessed from mobile devices, one can achieve several goals by being able to drag-and-drop elements directly with the fingers or by synchronizing the interaction with multimedia elements: (a) the development of more attractive experiments, (b) the possibility of interacting with the experiment almost anywhere and in any circumstances, thanks to the use of Web standards, and, most importantly, (c) the study of psychological processes that can hardly be explored with the limited interactivity of traditional PCs. HTML5 also offers interesting possibilities for Internet-based surveys, as it provides a new API for web forms that allows to edit documents, send data from one form to another, or even manage browsing history. Both types of studies, either interactive or form-based, can benefit from the local-storage functions offered by HTML5, so that experiments do not depend on the users' connectivity, which can facilitate longitudinal studies and also naturalistic experiments conducted outside the laboratory. An additional contribution of these standards to the new Semantic Web is their support for microdata management, brief semantic labels that can help to make inferences about the type of experiment being conducted, its published results or the relationship between that experiment and similar ones conducted by the same research team or related people.

In spite of these new possibilities, both WHATWG and W3C continue working on new specifications that allow Web user-agents to better compete with desktop applications. For instance, Web workers have been designed to accomplish background tasks (e.g., complex calculations). Similarly, Web storage, Web sockets, and server-sent events can be used for a better integration of Web applications. The Geolocation API allows to place on a given map any web interaction in an automatic manner. Finally, other data formats can be imported to HTML by means of SVG (vectorial graphs) or MathML (mathematical equations). The implications of all these tools for e-research are promising, not only because of the specific contributions made by each of them, but also because of the more general transition from an hypertext- and form-based Web to a different Web in which almost everything in a desktop is possible and the Web user-agents provide all the necessary functions to simplify this task.

CONCLUSION

Throughout this chapter, the different approaches of the Web as a platform for the development of social science experiments have been fully considered, from simple standalone web experiments to Cloud Computing based services accessed by Web application players. Researchers cannot only run their traditional experiments on the Internet to get larger and more representative data, as has become usual during the last decade, but they can also benefit from the new Web technologies and the increasingly social character of the Web.

The Social Web can be used as a research platform to collect data that can be used to contrast psychological or sociological theories on how people interact, reason and feel in different settings. Likewise, the recent developments in Cloud Computing and in the design of Web-user agents will allow conducting more interactive and realistic experiments on the Internet. Moreover, the way people interact and behave on the Internet may not be a mere reproduction of the offline social behaviour. The peculiarities of this medium and the impact it might have on behaviour, as well as the personal factors that influence their use, are becoming important issues in current social science research. Psychological research can also make an important contribution by endowing people with the cognitive skills necessary to grasp knowledge in this vast universe of information, while protecting their privacy.

Although our discussion has focused mainly on our own area of expertise, experimental psychology, other social sciences, such as marketing, sociology, politics, economics, education, or anthropology, should benefit to a similar extent from these new technologies. During the next years, the combined efforts of these disciplines and computer scientists will surely provide new and intriguing insights on human behaviour.

ACKNOWLEDGMENT

Support for this research was provided by Grants IT363-10 and IT458-10 from the Education, Universities, and Research Department of the Basque Government.

REFERENCES

Agichtein, E., Castillo, C., Donato, D., Gionis, A., & Mishne, G. (2008). *Finding high-quality content in social media*. Paper presented at the ACM Web Search and Data Mining Conference. Palo Alto, CA.

Aleman-Meza, B., Nagarajan, M., Ramakrishnan, C., Ding, L., Kolari, P., Sheth, A. P., et al. (2006). Semantic analytics on social networks: Experiences in addressing the problem of conflict of interest detection. In *Proceedings of the 15th International Conference on World Wide Web,* (pp. 407-416). New York, NY: ACM Press.

Anderson, C. (2006). *The long tail: How endless choice is creating unlimited demand.* London, UK: Random House Business Books.

Asur, S., & Huberman, B. A. (2010). *Predicting the future with social media*. Retrieved from http:// www.hpl.hp.com/ research/ scl/ papers/ socialmedia/ socialmedia.pdf.

Back, M. D., Stopfer, J. M., Vazire, S., Gaddis, S., Schmukle, S. C., Egloff, B., & Gosling, S. D. (2010). Facebook profiles reflect actual personality, not self-idealization. *Psychological Science, 21,* 372–374. doi:10.1177/0956797609360756

Bairoch, A. (2009). *The future of annotation/ biocuration*. Paper presented at the 3rd Biocuration Conference. Berlin, Germany.

Baker, J. R., & Moore, S. M. (2008). Distress, coping, and blogging: Comparing new MySpace users by their intention to blog. *Cyberpsychology & Behavior, 11,* 81–85. doi:10.1089/ cpb.2007.9930

Bar-Anan, Y., De Houwer, J., & Nosek, B. A. (2010). Evaluative conditioning and conscious knowledge of contingencies: A correlational investigation with large samples. *Quarterly Journal of Experimental Psychology, 63,* 2313–2335. doi:10.1080/17470211003802442

Berners-Lee, T. (2006). Linked data. *International Journal on Semantic Web and Information Systems, 4*(1), W3C.

Berners-Lee, T., & Cailliau, R. (1990). *WorldWideWeb: Proposal for a hypertexts project*. Retrieved from http:// www.w3.org/ Proposal.html.

Berners-Lee, T., & Fischetti, M. (1999). *Weaving the Web*. San Francisco, CA: Harper.

Berners-Lee, T., Hendler, J., & Lassila, O. (2001). The semantic Web. *Scientific American, 284,* 35–43. doi:10.1038/scientificamerican0501-34

Birnbaum, M. H. (1999). Testing critical properties of decision making on the Internet. *Psychological Science, 10,* 399–407. doi:10.1111/1467-9280.00176

Birnbaum, M. H. (2000). SurveyWiz and FactorWiz: JavaScript web pages that make HTML forms for researchers on the Internet. *Behavior Research Methods, Instruments, & Computers, 32,* 339–346. doi:10.3758/BF03207804

Birnbaum, M. H. (2004). Human research and data collection via the Internet. *Annual Review of Psychology*, *55*, 803–832. doi:10.1146/annurev.psych.55.090902.141601

Birnbaum, M. H., & Wakcher, S. V. (2002). Web-based experiments controlled by JavaScript: An example from probability learning. *Behavior Research Methods, Instruments, & Computers*, *34*, 189–199. doi:10.3758/BF03195442

Bizer, C., Heath, T., & Berners-Lee, T. (2009). Linked data - The story so far. *Journal on Semantic Web and Information Systems*, *5*(3), 1–22. doi:10.4018/jswis.2009081901

Botella, C., Gallego, M. J., Garcia-Palacios, A., Baños, R. M., Quero, S., & Alcañiz, M. (2009). The acceptability of an Internet-based self-help treatment for fear of public speaking. *British Journal of Guidance & Counselling*, *37*(3), 297–311. doi:10.1080/03069880902957023

Botella, C., Gallego, M. J., García-Palacios, A., Baños, R. M., Quero, S., & Guillen, V. (2008a). An Internet-based self-help program for the treatment of fear of public speaking: A case study. *Journal of Technology in Human Services*, *26*(2-4), 182–202. doi:10.1080/15228830802094775

Botella, C., Quero, S., Baños, R. M., García-Palacios, A., Bretón-López, J., Alcañiz, M., & Fabregat, S. (2008b). Telepsychology and self-help: The treatment of phobias using the Internet. *Cyberpsychology & Behavior*, *11*(6), 659–664. doi:10.1089/cpb.2008.0012

Buchanan, T., & Smith, J. L. (1999). Using the Internet for psychological research: Personality testing on the World Wide Web. *The British Journal of Psychology*, *90*, 125–144. doi:10.1348/000712699161189

Buffardi, L. E., & Campbell, W. K. (2008). Narcissism and social networking web sites. *Personality and Social Psychology Bulletin*, *34*, 1303–1314. doi:10.1177/0146167208320061

Cha, M., Haddadi, H., Benevenuto, F., & Gummadi, K. P. (2010). *Measuring user influence in Twitter: The million follower fallacy.* Paper presented at the 4th International AAAI Conference on Weblogs and Social Media. Washington, DC.

Chandrasekaran, B., Josephson, J. R., & Benjamins, V. R. (1999). What are ontologies, and why do we need them? *IEEE Intelligent Systems*, *14*, 20–26. doi:10.1109/5254.747902

Dandurand, F., Shultz, T. R., & Onishi, K. H. (2008). Comparing online and lab methods in a problem-solving experiment. *Behavior Research Methods*, *40*, 428–434. doi:10.3758/BRM.40.2.428

DiNucci, D. (1999). Fragmented future. *Print*, *53*(4), 32.

Ellison, N. B., Steinfield, C., & Lampe, C. (2007). The benefits of Facebook "friends": Social capital and college students' use of online social network sites. *Journal of Computer-Mediated Communication*, *12*, 1143–1168. doi:10.1111/j.1083-6101.2007.00367.x

Engelbrecht, P. C., & Dror, E. I. (2009). How psychology and cognition can inform the creation of ontologies in semantic technologies. In Y. Kiyoki, T. Tokuda, H. Jaakkola, X. Chen, & N. Yoshida (Eds.), *Proceeding of the 2009 Conference on Information Modeling and Knowledge Bases XX*, (pp. 340-347). Amsterdam, The Netherlands: IOS Press.

Engeström, J. (2009). *Building sites around social objects.* Paper presented at the Web 2.0 Expo. San Francisco, CA.

Fisch, K. (2006). *Did you know?* Retrieved from http://thefischbowl.blogspot.com/2006/08/did-you-know.html.

Fogel, J., & Nehmad, E. (2009). Internet social network communities: Risk taking, trust, and privacy concerns. *Computers in Human Behavior*, *25*, 153–160. doi:10.1016/j.chb.2008.08.006

Gaffney, D., Pearce, I., Darham, M., & Nanis, M. (2010). *Presenting 140Kit: An open, extensible research platform for Twitter*. Retrieved from http:// www.webecologyproject.org/ 2010/ 07/ presenting-140kit/.

Gardner, H. (1985). *The mind's new science: A history of cognitive revolution*. New York, NY: Basic Books.

Gershenfeld, N., Krikorian, R., & Cohen, D. (2004). The Internet of things. *Scientific American, 291*, 76–81. doi:10.1038/scientificamerican1004-76

Good, B. M., & Wilkinson, M. D. (2006). The life sciences semantic web is full of creeps! *Briefings in Bioinformatics, 7*, 275–286. doi:10.1093/bib/bbl025

Gosling, S. D., Gaddis, S., & Vazire, S. (2007). *Personality impressions based on Facebook profiles*. Paper presented at the International Conference on Weblogs and Social Media. Boulder, CO.

Hargittai, E. (2007). Whose space? Differences among users and non-users of social network sites. *Journal of Computer-Mediated Communication, 13*, 276–297. doi:10.1111/j.1083-6101.2007.00396.x

Hickson, I. (2011). *HTML5: A vocabulary and associated APIs for HTML and XHTML*. W3C Editor's Draft 16 February 2011. Retrieved from http:// dev.w3.org/ html5/ spec/ Overview.html.

Hoschka, P. (1998). CSCW research at GMD-FIT: From basic groupware to the Social Web. *ACM SIGGROUP Bulletin, 19*, 5–9.

Hsu, C. L., & Lin, J. C. (2008). Acceptance of blog usage: The roles of technology acceptance, social influence, and knowledge sharing motivation. *Information & Management, 45*, 65–74. doi:10.1016/j.im.2007.11.001

Humphreys, L. M., Krishnamurthy, B., & Gill, P. (2010). *How much is too much? Privacy issues on Twitter*. Paper presented at the Conference of the International Communication Association. Singapore.

Java, A., & Song, X. (2007). Why we Twitter: Understanding microblogging usage and communities. In *Proceedings of the Joint 9th WEB-KDD and 1st SNA-KDD Workshop,* (pp. 56-65). Baltimore, MD: WEBKDD Press.

Khare, R. (2006). Microformats: The next (small) thing on the semantic Web? *IEEE Internet Computing, 10*, 68–75. doi:10.1109/MIC.2006.13

Kwak, H., Lee, C., Park, H., & Moon, S. (2010). What is twitter, a social network or a news media? In *Proceedings of the 19th International conference on World Wide Web,* (pp. 591–600). ACM.

Lahl, O., Göritz, A. S., Pietrowsky, R., & Rosenberg, J. (2009). Using the world-wide-web to obtain large-scale word norms: 190,212 ratings on a set of 2,654 German nouns. *Behavior Research Methods, 41*, 13–19. doi:10.3758/BRM.41.1.13

Lange, P. G. (2007). Publicly private and privately public: Social networking on YouTube. *Journal of Computer-Mediated Communication, 13*, 361–380. doi:10.1111/j.1083-6101.2007.00400.x

Lanningham, S. (2006). *DeveloperWorks interviews: Tim Berners-Lee*. Retrieved from http:// www.ibm.com/ developerworks/ podcast/ dwi/ cm-int082206txt.html.

Lerman, K. (2006). *Social networks and social information filtering on Digg*. Retrieved from http:// arxiv.org/ PS_cache/ cs/ pdf/ 0612/ 0612046v1.pdf.

Lerman, K., & Galstyan, A. (2008). *Analysis of social voting patterns on Digg*. Paper presented at WOSN 2008. Seattle, WA.

Linden, A., & Fenn, J. (2003). *Understanding Gartner's hype cycles*. Strategic Analysis Report R-20-1971. New York, NY: Gartner Research.

Mangan, M. A., & Reips, U.-D. (2007). Sleep, sex, and the Web: Surveying the difficult-to-reach clinical population suffering from sexsomnia. *Behavior Research Methods*, *39*, 233–236. doi:10.3758/BF03193152

Matute, H., Vadillo, M. A., & Bárcena, R. (2007). Web-based experiment control software for research and teaching on human learning. *Behavior Research Methods*, *39*, 689–693. doi:10.3758/BF03193041

Matute, H., Vadillo, M. A., Vegas, S., & Blanco, F. (2007). Illusion of control in internet users and college students. *Cyberpsychology & Behavior*, *10*(2), 176–181. doi:10.1089/cpb.2006.9971

Matute, H., Vegas, S., & Pineño, O. (2002). *Utilización de un videojuego para estudiar cómo interfiere lo nuevo que aprendemos sobre lo que ya sabíamos*. Paper presented at 1er Congreso Online del Observatorio para la CiberSociedad. Retrieved from http:// www.cibersociedad.net/congreso/ comms/ g10matute-el-al2.htm.

McGraw, K. O., Tew, M. D., & Williams, J. E. (2000). The integrity of web-delivered experiments: Can you trust the data? *Psychological Science*, *11*, 502–506. doi:10.1111/1467-9280.00296

Mislove, A., Lehmann, S., Ahn, Y., Lazer, D., Lin, Y., Onnela, J., & Rosenquist, J. N. (2010). *Mapping the conversation: Political topics and geography on Twitter*. Retrieved from http://election.ccs.neu.edu/.

Mislove, A., Lehmann, S., Ahn, Y., Onnela, J., & Rosenquist, J. N. (2010). *Pulse of the nation: U.S. mood throughout the day inferred from Twitter*. Retrieved from http:// www.ccs.neu.edu/ home/ amislove/ twittermood/.

Mislove, A., Marcon, M., Gummadi, K. P., Druschel, P., & Bhattacharjee, B. (2007). *Measurement and analysis of online social networks*. Paper presented at IMC 2007. San Diego, CA.

Newell, A., & Simon, H. (1972). *Human problem solving*. Englewood Cliffs, NJ: Prentice Hall.

Nosek, B. A. (2005). Moderators of the relationship between implicit and explicit evaluation. *Journal of Experimental Psychology*, *134*, 565–584.

O'Reilly, T. (2005). What is Web 2.0: Design patterns and business models for the next generation of software. *International Journal of Digital Economics*, *65*, 17–37.

Pang, B., & Lee, L. (2008). Opinion mining and sentiment analysis. *Foundations and Trends in Information Retrieval*, *2*, 1–135. doi:10.1561/1500000011

Papadimitriou, D. (2009, August 1st). Future Internet: The cross-ETP vision document. *European Technology Platform*.

Ratliff, K. A., & Nosek, B. A. (2010). Creating distinct implicit and explicit attitudes with an illusory correlation paradigm. *Journal of Experimental Social Psychology*, *46*, 721–728. doi:10.1016/j.jesp.2010.04.011

Reips, U. D. (2002). Standards for Internet-based experimenting. *Experimental Psychology*, *49*, 243–256. doi:10.1026//1618-3169.49.4.243

Reips, U.-D., & Garaizar, P. (2011). Mining Twitter: Microblogging as a source for psychological wisdom of the crowds. *Behavior Research Methods*, *43*, 635–642. doi:10.3758/s13428-011-0116-6

Reips, U. D., & Neuhaus, C. (2002). WEXTOR: A Web-based tool for generating and visualizing experimental designs and procedures. *Behavior Research Methods, Instruments, & Computers*, *34*, 234–240. doi:10.3758/BF03195449

Rosen, C. (2007). Virtual friendship and the new narcissism. *New Atlantis (Washington, D.C.)*, *17*, 15–31.

Sakaki, T., Okazaki, M., & Matsuo, Y. (2010). Earthquake shakes Twitter users: Real-time event detection by social sensors. In *Proceedings of the 18th International World Wide Web Conference*. New York, NY: ACM.

Schmidt, W. C. (1997a). World-wide web survey research: Benefits, potential problems, and solutions. *Behavior Research Methods, Instruments, & Computers*, *29*, 274–279. doi:10.3758/BF03204826

Schmidt, W. C. (1997b). World-wide web survey research made easy with www survey assistant. *Behavior Research Methods, Instruments, & Computers*, *29*, 303–304. doi:10.3758/BF03204832

Shneiderman, B. (2008). Science 2.0. *Science*, *319*, 1349–1350. doi:10.1126/science.1153539

Specia, L., & Motta, E. (2007). Integrating folksonomies with the semantic web. In *Proceedings of the European Semantic Web Conference (ESWC 2007)*. Innsbruck, Austria: Springer.

Steyvers, M., Tenenbaum, J. B., Wagenmakers, E.-J., & Blum, B. (2003). Inferring causal networks from observations and interventions. *Cognitive Science*, *27*, 453–489. doi:10.1207/s15516709cog2703_6

Suh, B., Hong, L., Pirolli, P., & Chi, E. H. (2010). *Want to be retweeted? Large scale analytics on factors impacting retweet in Twitter network*. Paper presented at the Second IEEE International Conference on Social Computing (SocialCom 2010). Minneapolis, MN.

Thelwall, M. (2008). Social networks, gender and friending: An analysis of MySpace member profiles. *Journal of the American Society for Information Science and Technology*, *59*, 1321–1330. doi:10.1002/asi.20835

Thelwall, M. (2009). MySpace comments. *Online Information Review*, *33*, 58–76. doi:10.1108/14684520910944391

Thelwall, M., Wilkinson, D., & Uppal, S. (2010). Data mining emotion in social network communication: Gender differences in MySpace. *Journal of the American Society for Information Science and Technology*, *61*, 190–199.

Torkjazi, M., Rejaie, R., & Willinger, W. (2009). *Hot today, gone tomorrow: On the migration of MySpace users*. Paper presented at the WOSN 2009. Barcelona, Spain.

Uhlir, P. F., & Schroeder, P. (2007). Open data for global science. *Data Science Journal*, *6*, 36–53. doi:10.2481/dsj.6.OD36

Vadillo, M. A., Bárcena, R., & Matute, H. (2006). The internet as a research tool in the study of associative learning: An example from overshadowing. *Behavioural Processes*, *73*, 36–40. doi:10.1016/j.beproc.2006.01.014

Vadillo, M. A., & Matute, H. (2009). Learning in virtual environments: Some discrepancies between laboratory- and Internet-based research on associative learning. *Computers in Human Behavior*, *25*, 402–406. doi:10.1016/j.chb.2008.08.009

Vadillo, M. A., & Matute, H. (2011). Further evidence on the validity of web-based research on associative learning: Augmentation in a predictive learning task. *Computers in Human Behavior*, *27*, 750–754. doi:10.1016/j.chb.2010.10.020

Van Damme, C., Hepp, M., & Siorpaes, K. (2007). *Folksontology: An integrated approach for turning folksonomies into ontologies*. Paper presented at the 4th European Semantic Web Conference. Innsbruck, Austria.

Vander Wal, T. (2004). *Folksonomy*. Retrieved from http:// vanderwal.net/ folksonomy.html.

Vernberg, D., Snyder, C. R., & Schuh, M. (2005). Preliminary validation of a hope scale for a rare health condition using web-based methodology. *Cognition and Emotion, 19*, 601–610. doi:10.1080/02699930441000256

Williams, E. (2010). *Keynote*. Paper presented at Chirp, the official Twitter Developer Conference. San Francisco, CA.

Wolfram, S. (2002). *A new kind of science*. Champaign, IL: Wolfram Media.

ADDITIONAL READING

Almeida, A., Orduña, P., Castillejo, E., Lopez-de-Ipiña, D., & Sacristan, M. (2011). Imhotep: An approach to user and device conscious mobile applications. *Personal and Ubiquitous Computing, 15*, 419–429. doi:10.1007/s00779-010-0359-8

Anderson, C. A., & Bushman, B. J. (2001). Effects of violent video games on aggressive behavior, aggressive cognition, aggressive affect, physiological arousal, and prosocial behaviour: A meta-analytic review of the scientific literature. *Psychological Science, 12*, 353–359. doi:10.1111/1467-9280.00366

Back, M. D., Stopfer, J. M., Vazire, S., Gaddis, S., Schmukle, S. C., Egloff, B., & Gosling, S. D. (2010). Facebook profiles reflect actual personality, not self-idealization. *Psychological Science, 21*, 372–374. doi:10.1177/0956797609360756

Balicer, R. D. (2007). Modeling infectious diseases dissemination through online role-playing games. *Epidemiology (Cambridge, Mass.), 18*, 260–261. doi:10.1097/01.ede.0000254692.80550.60

Bargh, J. A., & McKenna, K. Y. A. (2004). The Internet and social life. *Annual Review of Psychology, 55*, 573–590. doi:10.1146/annurev.psych.55.090902.141922

Birnbaum, M. H. (Ed.). (2000). *Psychological experiments on the Internet*. San Diego, CA: Academic Press.

Birnbaum, M. H. (2004). Human research and data collection via the Internet. *Annual Review of Psychology, 55*, 803–832. doi:10.1146/annurev.psych.55.090902.141601

boyd, D. M., & Ellison, N. B. (2008). Social network sites: Definition, history, and scholarship. *Journal of Computer-Mediated Communication, 13*, 210-230.

Garcia-Zubia, J., Orduña, P., Lopez-de-Ipiña, D., & Alves, G. R. (2009). Addressing software impact in the design of remote laboratories. *IEEE Transactions on Industrial Electronics, 56*, 4757–4767. doi:10.1109/TIE.2009.2026368

Giles, J. (2011). Social-bots infiltrate Twitter and trick human users. *New Scientist, 209*(2804), 28. doi:10.1016/S0262-4079(11)60614-3

Gómez-Goiri, A., Emaldi-Manrique, M., & López-de-Ipiña, D. (2011). A semantic resource-oriented middleware for pervasive environments. *CEPIS UPGRADE, 12*, 6–16.

Gómez-Goiri, A., & López-de-Ipiña, D. (2011). On the complementarity of triple spaces and the web of things. In *Proceedings of the 2nd International Workshop on the Web of Things (WoT 2011)*, (pp. 12:1-12:6). ACM.

Killingsworth, M. A., & Gilbert, D. T. (2010). A wandering mind is an unhappy mind. *Science, 330*, 932. doi:10.1126/science.1192439

Kraut, R., Kiesler, S., Boneva, B., Cummings, J., Helgeson, V., & Crawford, A. (2002). Internet paradox revisited. *The Journal of Social Issues, 58*, 49–74. doi:10.1111/1540-4560.00248

Kraut, R., Patterson, M., Lundmark, V., Kiesler, S., Mukopadhyay, T., & Sherlis, W. (1998). Internet paradox: A social technology that reduces social involvement and psychological well-being? *The American Psychologist, 53*, 1017–1031. doi:10.1037/0003-066X.53.9.1017

López-de-Ipiña, D., Díaz-de-Sarralde, I., & García-Zubia, J. (2010). An ambient assisted living platform integrating RFID data-on-tag care annotations and Twitter. *Journal of Universal Computer Science, 16*, 1521–1538.

Matute, H., & Vadillo, M. A. (2007). Assessing e-learning in web labs. In Gomes, L., & García-Zubía, J. (Eds.), *Advances on Remote Laboratories and e-Learning Experiences* (pp. 97–107). Bilbao, Spain: University of Deusto.

Matute, H., Vadillo, M. A., & Bárcena, R. (2007). Web-based experiment control software for research and teaching on human learning. *Behavior Research Methods, 39*, 689–693. doi:10.3758/BF03193041

Matute, H., Vadillo, M. A., & Garaizar, P. (2011). Web based experiment control software for research on human learning. In Seel, N. M. (Ed.), *Encyclopedia of the Sciences of Learning*. Berlin, Germany: Springer Verlag. doi:10.3758/BF03193041

Matute, H., Vadillo, M. A., Vegas, S., & Blanco, F. (2007). Illusion of control in Internet users and college students. *Cyberpsychology & Behavior, 10*, 176–181. doi:10.1089/cpb.2006.9971

Orduña, P., & García-Zubia, J. Irurzun, J., & López-de-Ipiña, D. (2011). Accessing remote laboratories from mobile devices. In C. Li (Ed.), *Open Source Mobile Learning: Mobile Linux Applications*. Hershey, PA: IGI Global.

Vadillo, M. A., Bárcena, R., & Matute, H. (2006). The internet as a research tool in the study of associative learning: An example from overshadowing. *Behavioural Processes, 73*, 36–40. doi:10.1016/j.beproc.2006.01.014

Vadillo, M. A., & Matute, H. (2009). Learning in virtual environments: Some discrepancies between laboratory- and Internet-based research on associative learning. *Computers in Human Behavior, 25*, 402–406. doi:10.1016/j.chb.2008.08.009

Vadillo, M. A., & Matute, H. (2011). Further evidence on the validity of web-based research on associative learning: Augmentation in a predictive learning task. *Computers in Human Behavior, 27*, 750–754. doi:10.1016/j.chb.2010.10.020

Valkenburg, P. M., & Peter, J. (2009). Social consequences of the Internet for adolescents: A decade of research. *Current Directions in Psychological Science, 18*, 1–5. doi:10.1111/j.1467-8721.2009.01595.x

Vazire, S., & Gosling, S. D. (2004). e-Perceptions: Personality impressions based on personal websites. *Journal of Personality and Social Psychology, 87*, 123–132. doi:10.1037/0022-3514.87.1.123

KEY TERMS AND DEFINITIONS

API: Application Programming Interface, a layer or interface between different software programs aimed to facilitate their uncoupled interaction.

Cloud Computing: Provides a platform to develop and deploy web applications offered as services that can be consumed without knowledge about its use and the implementation of its resources.

Future Internet: The efforts made by international associations to progress towards a better Internet that should offer all users a secure, efficient, trusted, and reliable environment to enable open, dynamic, and decentralized access to the network and adapt its performance to the users' needs and context.

HTML5: The Fifth revision of the HTML standard, a language for structuring and presenting content for the World Wide Web.

Linked Data: An attempt to progress towards a more realistic application of Semantic Web, where a cut-down data model empowered by the rich expressivity of new semantic standards (especially a combination of RDF and OWL, termed as RDFS++) is used to define vocabularies and instance data which are interlinked.

SaaS: Software as a Service, a software delivery model in which software and its associated data are provided as services hosted in Cloud Computing based servers.

Semantic Web: A machine-readable World Wide Web using metadata to describe meaningfully the content of the web.

Social Web: A new approach of the Web, also known as Web 2.0, that emphasizes user-generated content and user interactions in web applications.

Chapter 3
E–Research Methodology

Vahid Khatibi
University of Tehran, Iran

Gholam Ali Montazer
Tarbiat Modares University, Iran

ABSTRACT

Electronic scientific databases (ESDs) such as "ScienceDirect," "GoogleScholar," and "Scopus" became popular in the scientific community, because scientific contents and diverse scientific Web services such as scientific communications and collaborations have taken place electronically in the ESDs. In this way, scientific research has evolved accordingly, yielding electronic research (e-Research) process in which scientists initiate their research, drive it, and reach its determined goals electronically. In this chapter, the authors focus on the ESDs' scientific Web services role in the research process. After representing a classification for the scientific Web services, a comprehensive methodology for the e-Research process is proposed. Also, the effects of scientific Web services on the e-Research process adoption are studied. The findings show that scientific Web services of information storage and sharing, searching, and communications are the most popular and useful Web services in scientific community.

INTRODUCTION

As studied in epistemology, humans appeal to various methods to acquire knowledge. These are classified into four modes: authoritarian, mystical (or intuitionistic), rationalistic, and scientific (Mouley, 1970). In authoritarian mode, we refer our propositions to authorized persons to validate their correctness, whereas in the rationalistic mode, we rely mainly on sagacity to reason our propositions. Also, the mystical mode focuses on intuitive perceptions. The last mode, the scientific method, is considered as the most popular way to acquire knowledge, allowing us to formulate, examine, test, and verify our hypotheses in various disciplines (Krige & Pestre, 1997). Whatever the aims of their works, scientists use the same underlying steps to organize their research (Trefil, 2001): (1) they make detailed observations about objects or processes, either as they occur in nature

DOI: 10.4018/978-1-4666-0125-3.ch003

or as they take place during experiments; (2) they collect and analyze the information observed; and (3) they formulate a hypothesis that explains the behavior of the phenomena observed.

Recent applications of information and communication technologies (ICTs) have a strong social impact on society and daily life. One of the aspects of society that has been transforming is the way of learning and teaching (Parikh & Verma, 2002). In recent years, we have seen exponential growth in electronic learning (e-Learning) such as Internet-based learning through Web services. E-learning is defined as an innovative approach for facilitating well designed, media-equipped, interactive and learner-friendly education for anybody, anywhere, and at any time by applying various digital sources along with other educational methods, provided through open, flexible, and well-distributed educational systems (Comercher, 2006). Thus e-Learning can take place at people's work or at home and at the time they are available (Kabassi & Virvou, 2004). Other benefits of using e-Learning are: an opportunity for overcoming the limitations of traditional learning, such as distance, time, and budget; equal opportunities for getting education no matter where you live, how old you are, what your health and social status is; better quality and variety of lecture materials; new consortia of educational institutions, where many specialists work in collaboration and use shared resources; and students get the freedom to receive knowledge, skills, and experience from other universities (Georgieva, Todorov, & Smrikarov, 2003).

One of the main resources in e-Learning is electronic scientific databases (ESDs), which represent the various scientific Web services to scientists and researchers. Scientific research has flourished with the use of ESDs, so as scientists now initiate their research, drive it, and reach its determined goals electronically. This evolution is the breakthrough from the regular research process towards the electronic research (e-Research) process. E-Research can be useful for both novice and experienced (Anderson & Kanuka, 2003). In this chapter, we first study the scientific Web services of the ESDs thoroughly, and then, a comprehensive methodology for the e-Research process is proposed. Also, the effects of scientific Web services on the e-Research process adoption are studied. For this purpose, an appropriate questionnaire is prepared and delivered to graduate students in engineering and management disciplines of Tarbiat Modares and Amirkabir universities, located in Tehran, Iran, to assess scientific Web services' usages in their scientific researches.. The obtained data of the scientific Web services' usages are analyzed, and their results are reported.

This chapter is organized as follows: After discussing e-Science and e-Research, we represent the findings of an electronic scientific databases study. In following, a comprehensive methodology for the e-Research process is proposed. At last, the scientific Web services' effects on the e-Research process adoption are analyzed.

E-SCIENCE AND E-RESEARCH

The relatively new field of electronic science (e-Science) provides a real opportunity to transform regular science by enabling students, teachers, and research scientists to engage in authentic scientific enquiry, collaboration, and learning (Schroeder, 2008; Underwood, Smith, Luckin, & Fitzpatrick, 2008). The UK National e-Science Centre asserts that e-Science will change the dynamic of the way science is undertaken, describing the rapidly evolving field as being about global collaboration in science and developing the next generation's infrastructure that will enable it (NeSC, 2007). E-Science is about both new ways of doing science and the technologies that enable them. Researchers in education have seen the potential for e-Science to also support new ways of learning and have explored these in several projects. For a review of e-Science in education see Woodgate and

Fraser (2005), who offer the following definition for e-Science: "The use of ICT in education, to enable local and remote communication and collaboration on scientific topics and with scientific data." This definition rightly places the emphasis on the learning activities to be supported while deliberately avoiding mention of specific "new technologies" to enable these. This contrasts with the wider definition of e-Science which, while still focusing on the activity to be supported, clearly points to the need for new infrastructure to enable this; an infrastructure that enables flexible, secure, coordinated resource sharing among dynamic collections of individuals, institutions, and resources (NeSC, 2007).

Many recent science education and technology projects clearly fall within the definition of e-Science in education provided above and are essentially about resource sharing. Educational e-Science projects typically have one or more of the following characteristics:

- Access to remote resources, such as sensors (Underwood, et al., 2008)
- Electronics laboratories (Burbidge & Grout, 2006) and telescopes (e.g., Faulkes Telescope[1])
- Collaboration with science projects by contributing computing resources (e.g., climateprediction.net[2], ProteinFolding@home[3])
- Collaboration with science projects by providing human resources to gather data (e.g., Walking with Woodlice[4])
- The use of tools to support communication between remote participants around scientific enquiry activities, e.g., between learners in different schools (Pea, et al., 1997; Smith, Luckin, Fitzpatrick, Avramides, & Underwood, 2005), between learners in school and out on field trips (Kravcik, Kaibel, Specht, & Terrenghi, 2004) and between learners, teachers and remote science experts (Underwood, et al., 2008).

It is often claimed that such collaborations can lead to improved learner attitudes towards science and the understanding of real science and scientists (Beare, 2007; Scherz & Oren, 2006).

A novel field of e-Science has been developed, called e-Research, based on information and communication technologies' application in the research process (Anderson & Kanuka, 2003; Meyer & Schroeder, 2009). The term "e-Research" encapsulates research activities that use a spectrum of advanced ICT capabilities and embraces, according to (Sargent, 2006), new research methodologies emerging from increased access to:

- broadband communications networks, research instruments and facilities, sensor networks, data repositories with their associated data standards and management tools, and high performance computing resources;
- software and infrastructure services that enable a trust and sharing relationship to be established between researchers and the wide variety of data repositories, computers, systems, and networks on which they depend; and
- application and discipline-specific tools such as graphics intensive visualization, simulation software, and interactive tools that provide a human interface, allowing researchers to interact with each other and with their instruments, computational facilities, and data resources.

E-Research capabilities serve to advance and augment rather than replace traditional research methodologies. According to Sargent (2006), there is a growing dependence on the following e-Research capabilities to:

- discover knowledge, whether held in digital or physical forms;

- access data as well as the software services that are being made available to manipulate or analyze this data;
- synthesize, curate, and disseminate new knowledge efficiently; and
- facilitate interactivity and research collaboration, allowing researchers to work seamlessly from desk-to-desk within and between organizations.

The main factors that enable researchers to increase their use of ICT are:

- their awareness of the full potential of ICT to enhance their research;
- the availability of an interconnected fabric of underlying shared service resources that facilitate access to diverse datasets, collaboration, and interoperability, regardless of the discipline of the researcher or computer platform being used;
- the ease of access to, and expert support of, ICT resources; and
- the skills and abilities of the researchers themselves to make full use of the ICT services and facilities at their disposal.

The amount and range of benefits from the use of e-Research methodologies will vary between researchers and disciplines, according to their needs, awareness, and skills, and the availability of the necessary support, expertise, and physical resources.

ESDs have great effects on the e-Research process. Scientists can initiate their research, drive it, and reach its determined goals by using the ESDs' scientific Web services. Both novice and experienced researchers can use the e-Research process to enhance their research programs. It encompasses how information technology, such as Internet, changes, evolves, improves, and yet often complicates the research process. e-Research aims to update the regular research process and to give researchers the greatest benefit of information and communication technologies. E-Research encompasses the normal research process augmented by the benefits of Internet tools in gathering both qualitative and quantitative data and then analyzing and disseminating the results (Anderson & Kanuka, 2003).

ELECTRONIC SCIENTIFIC DATABASES AND THEIR WEB SERVICES

Electronic scientific databases, similar to digital libraries, are advanced academic repositories that offer scientific information through appropriate contents and services (Buckland, 2008; Chowdhury & Chowdhury, 2003; Moreira, Goncalves, Laender, & Fox, 2009). In this way, two approaches are observed; one on the access and retrieval of digital content, and the other on the collection, organization, and service aspects of digital resources or artifacts that cannot be represented or distributed in printed formats (Xie, 2006). As a key pillar of the e-Research process, electronic scientific databases play a critical role in the achievement of this developed research process. Today, Internet and its most famous service, the Web service, have great potentiality for establishing ESDs, and in this way are the most popular platforms for implementing ESDs. To examine the various ESDs on the Internet and their scientific Web services, we studied 42 ESDs as follows: CiteSeer, Directory of Open Access Journals (DOAJ), Institute of Engineering and Technology/ Information Service for Physics, Electronics, and Computing (IET/INSPEC), Library and Information Sciences Abstracts (LISA), National Administration of Space and Aeronautics/Astrophysics Data System (NASA/ ADS), Open Access Journals Gateway (Open J-Gate), Stanford Public Information Retrieval System (SPIRS), The Collection of Computer Science Bibliographies, Thompson-Reuters Services (formerly Institute for Scientific Information [ISI]) including Web of Knowledge (WOK), Web of Science (WOS), Essential Science Indicators (ESI) and Journal Citation Reports (JCR), Scopus, Association of Computing Machinery (ACM) digital library, arXiv, AtyponLink, Blackwell Synergy, Cambridge Scientific Abstracts (CSA), E-Prints in Library and Information Science (E-LIS), Excerpta Medica Database (EMBASE), HighWire, Institute of Electrical and Electronic Engineers (IEEE) Digital Library, IngentaConnect, JSTOR (Journal Storage), National Bureau of Economical Research (NBER), Ovid, ProQuest, PubMed, Research Papers in Economics (RePEc), ScienceDirect, Sens Public, Social Sciences Research Network (SSRN), Wiley InterScience, Emerald, SpringerLink, GoogleScholar, HubMed, King Medical Library Engine (KMLE) Medical Dictionary, Libra, LivRe, Scirus, CiteULike, RefWorks, 2Collab, and EndNote Web. In the next step, the ESDs' scientific Web services are studied, and then classified into 10 categories which are as follows:

- scientific communications:
  ○ e-mail
  ○ news groups and forums
  ○ Weblogs
  ○ virtual social networks
- scientific information storage and sharing; scientific e-Publishing:
  ○ scientific e-Journals and e-Zines
  ○ e-Theses and e-Dissertations
  ○ e-Encyclopedias, e-Dictionaries, and e-Maps
- scientific searching:
  ○ scientific search engines
- scientific multimedia and Webcasting:
  ○ texts, pictures, audios, videos, graphics, animations, and interactive programs
  ○ e-Conferences and Webinars
- scientific collaborations:
  ○ e-Workspaces in scientific projects

  ○ scientific discussions in chat rooms
  ○ scientific funding opportunities
  ○ scientists and researchers introduction
  ○ scientific call for papers (CFPs)
- collective intelligence:
  ○ online encyclopedias with user-generated content
- scientific indexing:
  ○ indexing the papers of various journals
  ○ indexing the journals in various disciplines
- scientific citation analysis:
  ○ assessment of the papers citation
  ○ determination of the most cited researchers and universities
- online scientific reference libraries:
  ○ management of the scientific references on the Web
- scientific Web applications:
  ○ grid computing
  ○ decision support and expert systems on the Web

Scientific communications are very similar to regular communications, but performed via electronic channels, e.g. email, Weblogs and virtual social networks. Essentially, some of the electronic services are substituting for the regular physical ones. For instance, the regular communication mechanisms such as physical letter postage have been influenced by information technology; the new ways of electronic communication have gained popularity, and even in some cases substituted their more traditional counterparts. Scientific information storage and sharing is the electronic publication of scientific information, called scientific e-Publishing. Scientific searching is enhanced by special search engines, such as "Scirus"[5], which are designed to index, search, and represent only scientific information. Scientific multimedia and Webcasting services are using audio, video, animation, and other multimedia features to participate in scientific events, such as teleconferences and Webinars. Scientific collaboration is the use of ICT to form a new scientific workspace between scientists and researchers to conduct their research processes. Collective intelligence is a relatively new field in which information is generated by the users, e.g. Wikis like "Wikipedia"[6], allowing users to extend their knowledge by using this intelligence, and also contributing to the improvement of others' intelligence. Scientific indexing services index the papers in various journals or the journals in various disciplines. Scientific citation analysis services assess citations to the papers, and in this way, can determine the most cited researchers and universities. Online scientific reference libraries provide a new way for researchers to manage their scientific references on the Web. Scientific Web applications are special software programs on the Web that facilitate the scientific affairs of researchers in various disciplines by providing customized services.

Among the mentioned categories, five categories (scientific information storage and sharing [e-Publishing], scientific indexing, scientific citation analysis, scientific searching, and online reference libraries) are primal, and are observed frequently in ESDs. According to these categories, the 42 studied ESDs are classified as follows:

- **Scientific indexing**: CiteSeer, Directory of Open Access Journals (DOAJ), Institute of Engineering and Technology/Information Service for Physics, Electronics, and Computing (IET/INSPEC), Library and Information Sciences Abstracts (LISA), National Administration of Space and Aeronautics/Astrophysics Data System (NASA/ADS), Open Access Journals Gateway (Open J-Gate), Stanford Public Information Retrieval System (SPIRS), and the Collection of Computer Science Bibliographies.

- **Scientific citation analysis:** Thompson-Reuters Services (formerly Institute for Scientific Information [ISI]) including Web of Knowledge (WOK), Web of Science (WOS), Essential Science Indicators (ESI) Journal Citation Reports (JCR), and Scopus.

- **Scientific information storage and sharing (e-Publishing):** Association of Computing Machinery (ACM) Digital Library, arXiv, AtyponLink, Blackwell Synergy, Cambridge Scientific Abstracts (CSA), E-prints in Library and Information Science (E-LIS), Excerpta Medica Database (EMBASE), HighWire, Institute of Electrical and Electronic Engineers (IEEE) Digital Library, Emerald, SpringerLink, IngentaConnect, JSTOR (Journal Storage), National Bureau of Economical Research (NBER), Ovid, ProQuest, PubMed, Research Papers in Economics (RePEc), ScienceDirect, Sens Public, Social Sciences Research Network (SSRN), and Wiley InterScience.

- **Scientific search engines:** GoogleScholar, HubMed, King Medical Library Engine (KMLE) Medical Dictionary, Libra, LivRe, and Scirus.

- **Online scientific reference libraries:** CiteULike, RefWorks, 2Collab, and EndNote Web.

Most of the studied ESDs are in the scientific information storage and sharing category, whereas the fewest number of ESDs are in the online scientific reference libraries category. Figure 1 shows the quantitative status of the studied ESDs based on their scientific Web services. Induction of this result to all ESDs on the Web indicates that most of the scientific Web services belong to scientific e-Publishing, and then to scientific indexing, searching, citation analysis, and online reference libraries categories, sequentially. It should be noted that some of the ESDs, such as citation analysis databases, are very rare, but their tasks are very special in contrast to others.

Figure 1. Quantitative status of the studied ESDs based on their scientific Web services

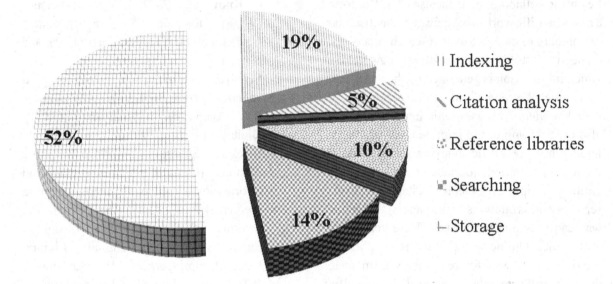

‖	Indexing
＼	Citation analysis
⁘	Reference libraries
◢	Searching
⊢	Storage

E-RESEARCH METHODOLOGY

In this section, we propose a comprehensive methodology for the e-Research process. Various electronic technologies, such as handheld computers, satellite imagery, Computer Aided Design (CAD), virtual realities, etc., have had a strong impact on the developments of scientific affairs (Monahan, McArdle, & Bertolotto, 2008). But, since the Internet has flourished and yielded a new era in communications and learning, we have focused on the use of the Internet and its Web services in science and research in the proposed methodology.

Problem Proposal

Similar to regular research methodology, the first step in the e-Research process methodology is the proposal of the problem, because the research is usually initiated for a subjective or objective problem, and then research questions are determined to discover the problem solution, whether problems are proposed by private companies or government institutions (external organizations),

or the researcher him- or her-self proposes the problem. Research of the first type could be titled "request-based research" and the second, "offer-based research," respectively.

Recognition of Problem Subject

After the proposal of the problem, its subject should be recognized. At this step, researchers undertake a comprehensive literature review to study the latest developments on the research problem. Also, it should be determined that the same research has not been done, and the research target should be narrowed and made precise. The best practice in this regard is the literature review of scientific resources which can be done easily and thoroughly using e-Research methods.

Literature Study

In this step, the researchers should study the literature related to their subject carefully, so as to extract peer-reviewed scientific documents through searching the various resources. Representation of a large share of scientific resources in digital formats can be found in general e-Databases, discipline-specific e-Databases, citations and patents searching, abstract journals, open access journals, scientific search engines, and general e-Resources such as e-Books, e-Maps, e-Theses, etc.

One of the main services used in the e-Research process is scientific searching, which provides scientists with the information in conference proceedings, journal papers, theses documents, and even patent specifications, so as scientists can find the most suitable and appropriate contents related to their research subject. In addition to general purpose search engines such as "Google"[7] and "Yahoo"[8], some scientific search engines like "Scirus" and "GoogleScholar"[9] are proposed specifically in this regard. Also, the searching service is included in almost all ESDs, such as "ScienceDirect"[10], "SpringerLink"[11], "Scopus"[12], and "ProQuest"[13].

Electronic encyclopedias can be used as complementary general references in almost all scientific disciplines, allowing scientists to reach the huge pools of information provided by famous encyclopedias such as "Britannica"[14] and "Encarta"[15] to augment their research contents. These websites usually require subscription fees to show the full versions of their articles to interested scientists. Also, electronic versions of dictionaries are provided online. Scientists can access famous dictionaries such as "Oxford"[16] and "Webster"[17] to know the meanings of the words and phrases electronically. Also, special websites such as "AcronymFinder"[18] help scientists know the abbreviations and acronyms in different disciplines.

Scientists need to narrow down the research problem to make it a suitable one. In this regard, they determine the keywords of their research, so they can recognize the related concepts and works of their field of study, and therefore can compare that research results with theirs. For this purpose, the thesaurus search of ESDs such as "Scopus" and "ProQuest" is a useful Web service that assists scientists in finding the related keywords of their

research topic. Another method is to browse the indices of ESDs such as "NASA/ADS"[19] which classify the research topics in a hierarchical mode. In this way, scientists can find the appropriate topics and keywords in each branch of a scientific discipline.

Finding the hottest research subjects is another useful Web service in ESDs, which can be done via a citation review and analysis service, so scientists can recognize the most cited scientific works. This service, represented in special ESDs, such as "Thompson-Reuters' Web of Science," "Scopus," and "CrossRef"[20], is developed via digital technologies because without using these technologies, it is very difficult, and in some cases impossible, to gather all the citations to the scientific peer-reviewed contents.

Prevention of Plagiarism

Plagiarism avoidance is a main ethical principle in research. Copying what somebody else has written or taking somebody else's idea and trying to pass it off as original is illegal and prohibited. It is recommended that the researcher investigates that the same research has not been completed and published. Some websites such as "PlagiarismDetect"[21] can assist to scientists in resolving this issue, and after being assured that no research with the same subject has been published, they can follow their research process.

Finding Key Researchers

Finding the key researchers in specific scientific domains is another Web service embedded in some ESDs such as "Scopus" and "Cambridge Scientific Abstracts" (CSA)[22]. In this way, scientists can identify the most active researchers in their domain of study, allowing scientists to study their publications and also communicate with them electronically to resolve their problems or even collaborate with them to conduct joint research projects.

Proposing a Solution

After a comprehensive review of the research subject in various scientific resources, the researcher recognizes all the problem aspects and also the previous suggested solutions. In the next step of the e-Research methodology, a solution for the problem should be proposed, which is considered the most important stage in the research methodology, so as scientists suggest a new theory or method for solving the problem whereas novel e-Science methods can be used in regard to the e-Research methodology.

Suggesting a Solution

In regular research methodology, scientists suggest a new theory or solution for the research problem through deep thinking. For this purpose, various research approaches including rationalistic/naturalistic, retrospective/prospective, conclusion-oriented/decision-oriented can be followed, and also different research methods can be exploited which have two classifications according to the research target and data gathering. Based on the research target, research methods are divided into basic, applied, and Research and Development (R&D) types, and based on data gathering, they are divided to descriptive (non-experimental) and experimental classes. The descriptive research method class itself is divided into various methods including survey, correlation, action research, case study, and ex-post facto research.

Using Novel e-Science Methods

As noted earlier, because of vast developments in information technology, it is used in solving problems, but despite its capabilities, automation of solving problems is not yet provided, and we cannot rely only on the technology to solve a scientific problem at the moment. Nevertheless, information technology may facilitate this stage via several methods including grid computing, scientific social networks, consultations with scientists, providing standards, software codes, scientific datasets, etc. Also, it is anticipated that artificial intelligence (AI) may automate problem solving by providing thinking machines in the future, and, in this way, we can rely on intelligent technologies to propose the best solutions for our research problems. Also, many scientists need access to the appropriate datasets to examine their proposed methods. Some ESDs such as the machine learning repository of the University of California, Irvine (UCI)[23] assist scientists in this stage too, by providing various datasets via sponsors or donators for free or with usage fees.

Obtaining Financial Aid (Grants and Funds)

If the research problems are proposed by private companies or government institutions (request-based research), they will be sponsored by these organizations, but in offer-based research, the scientists usually need sponsors to support their research to provide technical equipment, laboratory tools, and human resources. In this regard, appropriate Web services are implemented in some ESDs such as "ProQuest's Community of Science" (COS)[24] that provide scientists with financial opportunities, available grants, and even fellowship opportunities. In this way, scientists can find and exploit the best opportunities to support their research. Participating in scientific research groups is another regular way to acquire scientific and financial support. Cyberspace also provides another novel medium to join researchers in a specific domain via electronic communications, allowing scientists to define, drive, and finish their research with the collaboration of each other electronically. Some ESDs such as ACM's Special Interest Groups (SIGs)[25] and IEEE's Sections[26] provide such opportunities for scientists to participate in research and scientific affairs.

Suggested Solution Testing

After proposing the solution, it should be tested to validate its correctness and usefulness. The testing stage of the research methodology is considered the most crucial pillar of the research method because the main intention of the research method is the testing stage, which applies assessment mechanisms on the proposed theories and hypotheses. In regular research methodology, several test mechanisms exist for solution assessment, including the reliability and validity assessment. It should be noted that the essence of the solutions' assessment and validation yields two deductive and inductive approaches which itself implies two types of deductive and inductive sciences.

Acceptance, Rejection, or Modification of the Suggested Solution

After testing the proposed solution, the acquired results imply acceptance, rejection, or modification of the solution. If the solution is accepted, the researcher goes to the next step of the methodology, but if rejected, the researcher revises it, and if possible, the researcher corrects and modifies it and then tests the revised solution again. Otherwise the suggested solution is rejected and the researcher goes to the next step of the methodology.

Reporting Research Findings

After proposing the research solution and its examination, scientists should report the research findings. Research report preparation includes comprehensive review and report of related literature, previous works' results and their analysis, citation of the used references, representation of the contents from general topic to details, well-organized structure, precise report of research components including research plans, measurement instruments, research methods, experiments and results analysis, attention to research ethical principles, and legible writing.

Online Referencing

As shown above, citation of the used references is one of the main aspects of scientific reports. For this purpose, scientists can use online reference libraries to manage their scientific references on the Web. Gathering the citation information of the research references according to the journal or conference styles is one of the time-consuming tasks in the research process. Some ESDs such as "RefWorks"[27] and "CiteULike"[28] can assist in this regard, so as after extracting the citation information of the selected references electronically, they adapt them according to the journal style or reference library software formats such as "EndNote"[29] and "BibTex"[30]. Also, we can use the journals or conferences paper templates, e.g. the EndNote journal or conference templates, to represent our solution in the scientific communities.

Finding Publications and Conferences (Calls for Papers)

Since information technology developments including the Internet make information distribution instant all over the world, the journals' and conferences' calls for papers have been facilitated through Web, allowing scientists to collaborate and present the findings of their research in the scientific communities through the appropriate and respective conferences, congresses, symposiums, colloquiums, and workshops of their research interests, and also learn the new advancements taking place in their domain of study. Some websites such as "WikiCFP"[31], "ConferenceAlerts"[32], and "AllConferences"[33] provide dedicated services in this regard. Also, the Call For Papers (CFPs) of the peer-reviewed journals and their special issues are included in some of the ESDs.

The novelty and validity of the research should be investigated, and that is handled through the peer-review process. Authors usually submit their research papers to conferences and journals to be reviewed for publication. In this stage, ESDs can assist the scientists in several ways. Almost all the conferences and journals have dedicated websites through which they receive manuscripts and then dispatch them to reviewers. After finalizing the review process, they send the reviewers' comments and final decisions to the authors. The whole process takes place electronically. As a famous instance of this Web service, "Elsevier" Editorial Service (EES)[34] can be mentioned. It was developed for almost all the journals from the publisher, "Elsevier"[35]; it handles the above mentioned process electronically. The other ways to represent the research results include magazines, workshops, patent registration, etc.

The electronic presentation of the research results is a novel approach in scientific information publication. After acceptance of the papers, they are usually published on the journal's website prior to their print version, which is called "articles in press" or "pre-print" versions, as represented in some ESDs such as "ScienceDirect." Teleconferences, Webinars, and virtual workshops are also novel presentation methods, allowing authors to participate or present their papers electronically via appropriate tools such as webcams and fast network connections.

Scientists can register the systems, products, algorithms, and even ideas as patents to protect their intellectual property, so as they will be recognized as the legal owners of them. Some offices are responsible for the reviewing and registering the patents, among which are the United States Patent and Trademark Office (USPTO)[36], European Patent Office (EPO)[37], and Japan Patent Office (JPO)[38]. Also, scientists can search the patent specifications in the aforementioned websites in addition to "Scopus" patents[39] and "Google" patents[40].

Usage Analysis of the Research Results

As a subordinate in research methodology, scientists can access the usage analysis of their research findings reports. The patent usages or paper citations are represented in some ESDs such as "Scopus" and "Google." They can be used to recognize the hottest research topics and applications, and also are considered the main criteria in the assessment of scientists and universities.

Documentation of the Research Process

At the last step of the e-Research process, the experiences during all the research stages should be documented, which can be done electronically too. Then, the challenges, weaknesses, shortcomings, and strengths, besides the open research areas in the studied domain, should be proposed and documented. The proposed methodology for the e-Research process is shown in Figure 2, Figure 3 and Figure 4.

ANALYSIS OF SCIENTIFIC WEB SERVICES' EFFECTS IN THE E-RESEARCH PROCESS ADOPTION

To invest effectively in scientific Web services, we need to know the importance and applicability of these services in the scientific community (Lopez-Fernandez & Rodriguez-Illera, 2009; Xie, 2008). In this way, we can determine the investment priorities, allowing the most popular services to obtain more funds. After that, the adoption and development of the e-Research process in the scientific community will be facilitated.

To evaluate the importance, applicability and effects of scientific Web services in the adoption of the e-Research process, we prepared a questionnaire to measure the effect various scientific Web services have had in the scientific community, and in this way, their ranking is also determined. In this questionnaire, we asked the audience to represent their opinions about scientific Web services' importance, applicability, and effect degrees in their research processes through the 1-10 scoring system. For this purpose, we selected 176 graduate students in the engineering and manage-

Figure 2. E-research process methodology

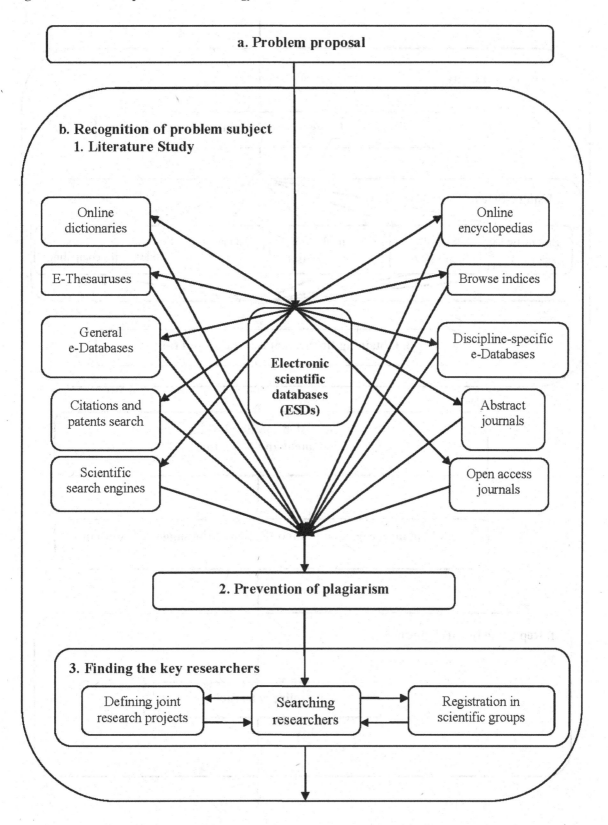

Figure 3. E-research process methodology continued

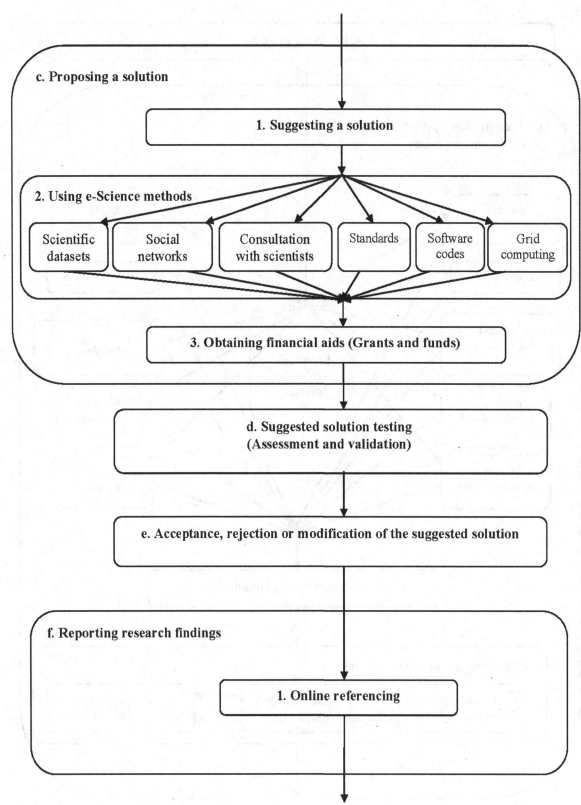

Figure 4. E-research process methodology continued

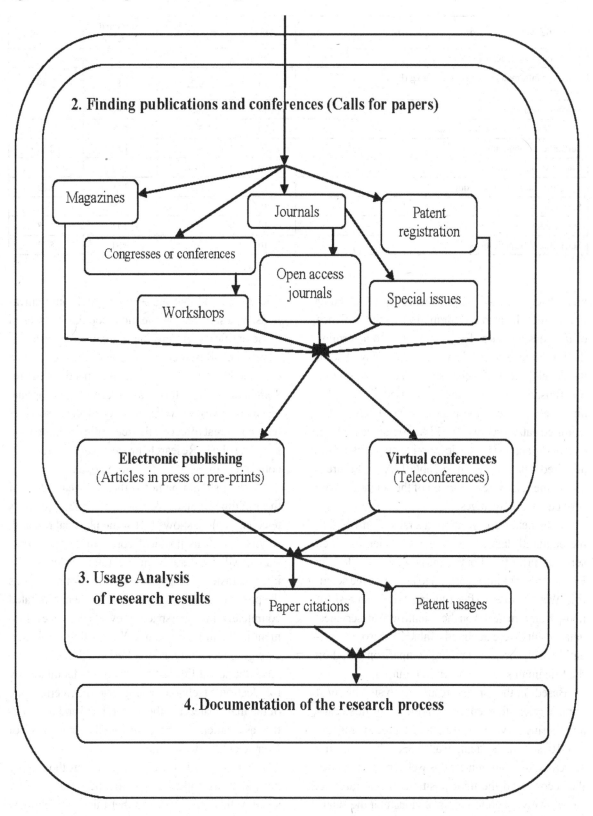

Table 1. The scientific Web services' descriptive statistics

Scientific Web service score	Min.	Max.	Average	Standard deviation	Variance
Scientific communications	5	10	6.89	1.75	3.08
Scientific information storage and sharing (E-publishing)	7	10	9.32	1.87	3.49
Scientific searching	5	10	8.58	1.46	2.12
Scientific multimedia and Webcasting	3	10	6.41	1.89	3.6
Scientific collaborations	4	10	7.54	1.61	2.58
Collective intelligence	3	10	6.5	1.78	3.2
Scientific information indexing	4	10	6.27	2.19	4.82
Scientific citation analysis	5	10	6.04	2.29	5.1
Online scientific reference libraries	3	10	6.08	2.18	4.78
Scientific Web applications	3	10	5.62	2.31	5.32

ment disciplines of Tarbiat Modares and Amirkabir universities, located in Tehran, Iran, as the audience of the questionnaire. They were asked to determine the importance scientific Web services have had in the development of their research. After organizing the finished questionnaires, we used Cronbach's alpha test to check the internal consistency of the acquired data. A score of 0.827 was obtained for their reliability analysis. The descriptive statistics of the acquired data are shown in Table 1. Also, Figure 5 shows the relative comparison of the scientific Web services' score averages.

In the next step, we applied a ranking method to the acquired data to determine the scientific Web services' priorities. For this purpose, we selected the Friedman's ranking algorithm to prioritize the scientific Web services. After running Friedman test (of non-parametric tests) on the scientific Web services' data, results were acquired (Table 2). Also, the scientific Web services' ranking comparison based on the Friedman's test is shown in Figure 6.

Based on the ranking results analysis, the most popular scientific Web service is the scientific storage and sharing service, whose effect degree average, in a 1-10 scoring system, was 9.32. The scientific searching and communications Web services obtained the second and the third positions in the ranking, respectively. Therefore, it is obvious that the scien-

tific storage and sharing, searching and communications Web services are the most popular services in the scientific community, have great effects on adoption of the e-Research process, and hence should be expanded to come up with the new needs of the researchers, and for this reason, are the appropriate places to invest. The desirability of these services has had a great affect on the scientific community in adopting the e-Research process easily, the more convenient the service, the more popular it was.

Also, it should be noted that the weak score of the multimedia and Webcasting services, such as teleconferences, shows that some physical research services, such as physical conferences and workshops, will be durable in the future, because the idiosyncrasies of these physical sessions, such as the presence sense and eye contact, are not imitated completely in cyberspace. Nevertheless, development in the multimedia and Webcasting service by emerging technologies may resolve this issue, too. Also, the scientific citation analysis is facilitated by the electronic technologies, such as the Internet; one of the main criteria in the researchers' and universities' assessment has become the citation analysis of their scientific documents.

Some of the scientific Web services are thoroughly new, such as collective intelligence. But the low score of this service shows that this relatively new

Figure 5. Scientific Web services' score averages comparison

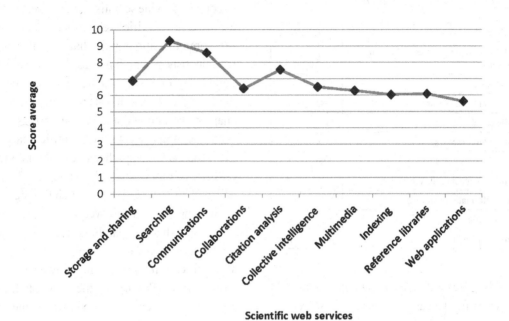

Figure 6. Scientific Web services ranking comparison based on the Friedman's test

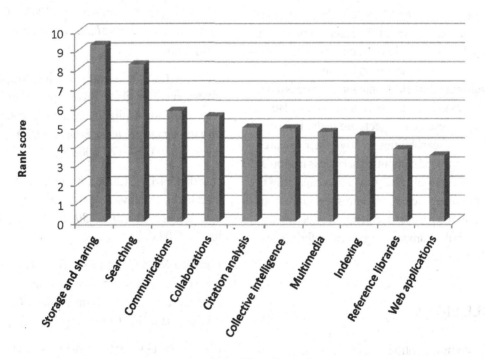

Table 2. The scientific Web services ranking scores based on the Friedman's algorithm

Scientific Web service	Score	Rank
Scientific information storage and sharing (E-publishing)	9.27	1
Scientific searching	8.23	2
Scientific communications	5.82	3
Scientific collaborations	5.5	4
Scientific citation analysis	4.91	5
Collective intelligence	4.86	6
Scientific multimedia and Webcasting	4.68	7
Scientific information indexing	4.5	8
Online scientific reference libraries	3.77	9
Scientific Web applications	3.45	10

field needs more extensive partnership of scientists to be a scientific standard reference for researchers. Improvement in the information quality analysis, verification, and assurance methods is the primal way to do this. Also, the scientific Web applications have not shown their real capabilities in the development of the research process yet; so one of the open research areas in the e-Research process is the proposition of the appropriate Web applications to assist in the resolution of the research problems of various disciplines. The most crucial point in the e-Research process is the research problem solution step, which is not fully electronic and still needs more enhancements to integrate its various aspects. But at present, some research projects are using information technology capabilities to drive their research process, e.g. the grid computing service is a popular method to integrate all the computation capacities to perform massive calculations in a short amount of time, used in the particle acceleration experiments' calculations in the European Organization for Nuclear Research (CERN).

CONCLUSION

Scientific communication via the Internet and its famous Web service, especially through electronic scientific databases such as "ScienceDirect" and "Scopus," provide scientists with scientific contents and diverse scientific Web services including scientific communications and collaborations. Therefore, the scientists' research process has evolved accordingly based on ESDs and their Web services, called the electronic research (e-Research) process. In this chapter, the authors studied the various scientific Web services and electronic scientific databases, and then proposed a comprehensive methodology for the e-Research process, which focused on the Internet and its Web services. The research findings analysis showed that the scientific Web services of information storage and sharing, searching, and communications are the most popular and applicable services in the scientific community, and therefore have had a great affect on the adoption of the e-Research process. Also, the research findings showed some physical research services, such as physical conferences and workshops, will be durable in the future.

REFERENCES

Anderson, T., & Kanuka, H. (2003). *E-research: Methods, strategies and issues*. Boston, MA: Pearson Education.

Beare, R. (2007). Investigation into the potential of investigative projects involving powerful robotic telescopes to inspire interest in science. *International Journal of Science Education, 29*(3), 279–306. doi:10.1080/09500690600620938

Buckland, M. K. (2008). Reference library service in the digital environment. *Library & Information Science Research, 30*, 81–85. doi:10.1016/j.lisr.2008.03.002

Burbidge, M., & Grout, I. (2006). *Evolution of a remote access facility for a PLL measurement course*. Paper presented at the 2nd IEEE International Conference on e-Science and Grid Computing. New York, NY.

Chowdhury, G. G., & Chowdhury, S. (2003). *Introduction to digital libraries*. London, UK: Facet Publication.

Comercher, M. (2006). *E-learning concepts and techniques*. Bloomsburg, PA: Bloomsburg University.

Georgieva, G., Todorov, G., & Smrikarov, A. (2003). *A model of a virtual university: Some problems during its development*. Paper presented at the 4th ACM International Conference on Computer Systems and Technologies: E-Learning. New York, NY.

Kabassi, K., & Virvou, M. (2004). Personalised adult e-training on computer use based on multiple attribute decision making. *Interacting with Computers*, *16*, 115–132. doi:10.1016/j.intcom.2003.11.006

Kravcik, M., Kaibel, A., Specht, M., & Terrenghi, L. (2004). Mobile collector for field trips. *Journal of Educational Technology & Society*, *7*(2), 25–33.

Krige, J., & Pestre, D. (1997). *Science in the twentieth century*. Newark, NJ: Harwood Academic.

Lopez-Fernandez, O., & Rodriguez-Illera, J. L. (2009). Investigating university students' adaptation to a digital learner course portfolio. *Computers & Education*, *52*, 608–616. doi:10.1016/j.compedu.2008.11.003

Meyer, E. T., & Schroeder, R. (2009). Untangling the web of e-research: Towards a sociology of online knowledge. *Journal of Informetrics*, *3*(3), 246–260. doi:10.1016/j.joi.2009.03.006

Monahan, T., McArdle, G., & Bertolotto, M. (2008). Virtual reality for collaborative e-learning. *Computers & Education*, *50*, 1339–1353. doi:10.1016/j.compedu.2006.12.008

Moreira, B. L., Goncalves, M. A., Laender, A. H. F., & Fox, E. A. (2009). Automatic evaluation of digital libraries with 5SQual. *Journal of Informetrics*, *3*, 102–123. doi:10.1016/j.joi.2008.12.003

Mouley, G. L. (1970). *The science of educational research*. London, UK: Van Nastrand Reinhold.

NeSC. (2007). *Definition of e-science*. Retrieved 10 January, 2010, from http://www.nesc.ac.uk/nesc/define.html.

Parikh, M., & Verma, S. (2002). Utilizing internet technologies to support learning: An empirical analysis. *International Journal of Information Management*, *22*, 27–46. doi:10.1016/S0268-4012(01)00038-X

Pea, R., Gomez, L., Edelson, D., Fishman, B., Gordin, D., & O'Neil, D. (1997). Science education as a driver of cyberspace technology development. In Cohen, K. C. (Ed.), *Internet Links for Science Education: Student–Scientist Partnerships* (pp. 189–220). New York, NY: Plenum. doi:10.1007/978-1-4615-5909-2_12

Sargent, M. (2006). *An Australian e-research strategy and implementation framework*. Canberra, Australia: E-Research Coordinating Committee.

Scherz, Z., & Oren, M. (2006). How to change students' images of science and technology. *Science Education*, *90*, 965–985. doi:10.1002/sce.20159

Schroeder, R. (2008). E-sciences as research technologies: Reconfiguring disciplines, globalizing knowledge. *Social Sciences Information. Information Sur les Sciences Sociales*, *47*(2), 131–157. doi:10.1177/0539018408089075

Smith, H., Luckin, R., Fitzpatrick, G., Avramides, K., & Underwood, J. (2005). *Technology at work to mediate collaborative scientific enquiry in the field*. Paper presented at the 12th International Conference on Artificial Intelligence in Education (AIED 2005). New York, NY.

Trefil, J. (2001). *The encyclopedia of science and technology*. London, UK: Routledge.

Underwood, J., Smith, H., Luckin, R., & Fitzpatrick, G. (2008). E-science in the classroom – Towards viability. *Computers & Education*, *50*, 535–546. doi:10.1016/j.compedu.2007.07.003

Woodgate, D., & Fraser, D. S. (2005). E-science and education 2005: A review. *Joint Information Systems Committee (JISC)*. Retrieved 10 January, 2010, from http://www.jisc.ac.uk/uploaded_documents/ACF2B4.pdf.

Xie, H. I. (2006). Evaluation of digital libraries: Criteria and problems from users' perspectives. *Library & Information Science Research, 28*, 433–452. doi:10.1016/j.lisr.2006.06.002

Xie, H. I. (2008). Users' evaluation of digital libraries (DLs): Their uses, their criteria, and their assessment. *Information Processing & Management, 44*, 1346–1373. doi:10.1016/j.ipm.2007.10.003

KEY TERMS AND DEFINITIONS

Electronic Science (E-Science): Use of ICT in science development to enable local and remote communication and collaboration on scientific topics and with scientific data.

Electronic Scientific Databases (ESDs): Similar to digital libraries, they are advanced academic repositories that offer scientific information through appropriate contents and services.

Scientific Web Services: The Web services specially proposed for scientific affairs and research which are classified into 10 categories in this chapter including scientific communications, information storage and sharing, searching, collaborations, etc.

Collective Intelligence: a relatively new field in which information is generated by the users, e.g. Wikis like "Wikipedia," so as users can extend their knowledge by using this intelligence, and also contribute to improve the others' intelligence.

E-Research Process: Dependent on the electronic developments in science and research such as ESDs and their scientific Web services, the scientists' research process is evolved accordingly, so as the electronic research (e-Research) process emerged in which scientists initiate their research, drive it, and reach its determined goals electronically.

E-Research Methodology: a comprehensive methodology for using information technologies in the regular research development, proposed in this chapter, mainly focused on the usage of Internet and its Web services in science and research.

Prevention of Plagiarism: Plagiarism avoidance is considered as a main ethical principle in research, so as copying what somebody else has written or taking somebody's else's idea and trying to pass it off as original is illegal and prohibited.

Scientific Citation Analysis Service: This service assesses citations to the papers, and in this way, can determine the most cited researchers and universities.

Online Referencing: A scientific service in some ESDs such as "RefWorks" and "CiteU-Like" which extracts the citation information of the selected references electronically, and adapts them according to the journal style or reference library software formats such as "EndNote" and "BibTex." In this way, online scientific reference libraries provide a new way for researchers to manage their scientific references on the Web.

ENDNOTES

[1] Faulkus Telescope Project. (2011). *Webpage.* Retrieved from http://faulkus-telescope.com/.

[2] Climate Prediction Project. (2011). *Webpage.* Retrieved from http://www.climateprediction.net/.

[3] Stanford. (2011). *Folding@home distributed computing project.* Retrieved from http://folding.stanford.edu/.

[4] Natural History Museum. (2011). *Walking with woodlice project.* Retrieved from http://www.nhm.ac.uk/woodlice/.

[5] Scirus. (2011). *Scientific search engine.* Retrieved from http://www.scirus.com/.

[6] Wikipedia. (2011). *User-generated content encyclopedia.* Retrieved from http://www.wikipedia.org/.

[7] Google. (2011). *General search engine.* Retrieved from http://www.google.com/.

[8] Yahoo. (2011). *General search engine.* Retrieved from http://www.yahoo.com/.

9   Google Scholar. (2011). *Scientific search engine*. Retrieved from http://scholar.google.com/.

10 Sciencedirect. (2011). *Elsevier's online scientific repository*. Retrieved from http://www.sciencedirect.com/.

11 Springerlink. (2011). *Springer's online scientific repository*. Retrieved from http://www.springerlink.com/.

12 Scopus. (2011). *Elsevier's scientific citation database*. Retrieved from http://www.scopus.com/.

13 UMI. (2011). *Proquest online scientific database*. Retrieved from http://www.umi.com/pqdauto.

14 Encyclopedia Britannica. (2011). *Online version*. Retrieved from http://www.britannica.com/.

15 Encyclopedia Encarta. (2011). *Online version*. Retrieved from http://encarta.msn.com/.

16 Oxford Dictionary. (2011). *Online version*. Retrieved from http://www.oxfordlanguage-dictionaries.com/.

17 Webster Dictionary. (2011). *Online version*. Retrieved from http://www.merriam-webster.com/.

18 Acronymfinder. (2011). *Acronyms and abbreviations database*. Retrieved from http://www.acronymfinder.com/.

19 NASA. (2011). *Astrophysics data system*. Retrieved from http://www.suo-nasaads.com/.

20 CrossRef. (2011). *Online citation database*. Retrieved from http://www.crossref.org/.

21 PlagiarismDetect. (2011). *Plagiarism detection database*. Retrieved from http://www.plagiarismdetect.com/.

22 CSA. (2011). *Subset of Proquest database*. Retrieved from http://www.csa.com/.

23 UCI. (2011). *Machine learning repository of UCI university*. Retrieved from http://archive.ics.uci.edu/ml/.

24 COS. (2011). *ProQuest's community of science database*. Retrieved from http://www.cos.com/.

25 ACM. (2011). *Association of computing machinery's special interest groups*. Retrieved from http://www.acm.org/.

26 IEEE. (2011). *Institute of electrical and electronic engineers' sections*. Retrieved from http://www.ieee.org/.

27 Refworks. (2011). *Online reference library website*. Retrieved from http://www.refworks.com/.

28 Citeulike. (2011). *Online manipulation of scientific references library*. Retrieved from http://www.citeulike.org/.

29 EndNote. (2011). *Reference library management software*. Retrieved from http://www.endnote.com/.

30 BibTex. (2011). *Reference library software*. Retrieved from http://www.bibtex.org/.

31 Wikicfp. (2011). *Wiki call for papers*. Retrieved from http://www.wikicfp.com/.

32 ConferenceAlerts. (2011). *Alerts of conferences website*. Retrieved from http://www.conferencealerts.com/.

33 AllConferences. (2011). *Conference lists in difference scientific disciplines*. Retrieved from http://www.allconferences.com/.

34 EES. (2011). *Online editorial service*. Retrieved from http://ees.elsevier.com/.

35 Elsevier. (2011). *Webpage*. Retrieved from http://www.elsevier.com/.

36 US Patent Office. (2011). *Webpage*. Retrieved from http://www.uspto.gov/.

37 European Patent Office. (2011). *Webpage*. Retrieved from http://www.epo.org/.

38 Japan Patent Office. (2011). *Webpage*. Retrieved from http://www.jpo.go.jp/.

39 Scopus. (2011). *Patents*. Retrieved from http://www.scopus.com/.

40 Google Patents. (2011). *Webpage*. Retrieved from http://www.google.com/patents/.

Chapter 4

Collaborative and Distributed e-Research Environment for Supporting Scientific Research and the Education Process

Dukyun Nam
Korea Institute of Science and Technology Information, Republic of Korea

Junehawk Lee[1]
Korea Institute of Science and Technology Information, Republic of Korea

Kum Won Cho
Korea Institute of Science and Technology Information, Republic of Korea

ABSTRACT

The efficient use of a scientific application service built on a computing environment requires technology that integrates each application service into a workflow so that the workflow is executed in a cooperative environment. There have been a number of attempts to automate research activities as a scientific workflow. However, there are practical problems in the full automation of research activities for a number of simulation programs and researchers. In the cyber environment for Collaborative and Distributed E-Research (CDER), the types of workflows need to be studied and supported separately and with different methodologies. In this chapter, the authors analyze the scientific research and education processes and categorize them into four types: simulation, experiment, collaborative work, and educational activity. They then describe the applications needed for each category. To justify their categorization of the CDER workflow, they examine the workflow of e-AIRS (e-Science Aerospace Integrated Research System), a problem-solving environment for aerospace research.

DOI: 10.4018/978-1-4666-0125-3.ch004

INTRODUCTION

In terms of computational science, the Collaborative and Distributed E-Research (CDER) environment is similar to the science gateway in e-Science defined as "large scale science that will increasingly be carried out through distributed global collaborations enabled by the Internet." Science Gateway (Wilkins-Diehr, 2007) provides not only an access interface for computing resources, information, and instruments, but also an intelligent environment, i.e., a cyber environment (Myers & McGrath, 2007), wherein users can retrieve useful information and use research tools. Through this interface, users are able to conduct computer simulations to verify and understand existing or proposed theories. The efficient use of a scientific application service built on a computing environment requires technology that integrates each application service into a workflow so that the workflow is executed in a cooperative environment. The business community has tried to automate business processing steps, and the computer industry supplied tools to help with this. In e-Science, research activities have been automated as a scientific workflow (Barga & Gannon, 2007; Leymann & Roller, 2000). However, the full automation of research activities with a number of stand-alone software programs has practical problems. For the cyber environment for Collaborative and Distributed E-Research (CDER), we need to study the types of workflows and support each type separately with different methodologies.

In this chapter, we analyze the research flows for CDER and describe the essential functionality of the workflow system, even when the system does not fully automate the entire research process. To do this, the workflow expected in CDER is categorized into four types. The first type describes the workflow for simulations on remote computing resources that involve supercomputers or grid resources. The second type is for experiments involving large-scale equipment. The third type describes the workflow for collaborative work. Finally, the fourth type describes workflow for educational activity. The CDER can assist students in understanding natural phenomena in class in areas such as computational fluid dynamics, bioinformatics, and computational chemistry. The educational activities (Kim et al., 2006) have different characteristics to research activities. For example, in an educational activity, students might run a sample simulation simultaneously for a limited time to acquire knowledge, including using a science gateway.

To justify our categorization of the CDER workflow, we examine the workflow of e-AIRS (e-Science Aerospace Integrated Research System) (Kim, et al., 2006), a problem-solving environment for aerospace research. We explain the characteristics of the CDER workflow, which benefits business and scientific workflows, based on the analysis of the e-AIRS system. Here, we also describe the necessary applications and functionalities for the workflow.

RELATED WORK

Directed Acyclic Graph Manager (DAGMan) (Frey, 2002) allows users to submit a number of jobs with workflows using Condor, and provide the interface for various types of workflows. The goal of DAGMan is the automation of managing complex workflows, including the job submission process. The weakness of DAGMan is the lack of supporting control flow, such as conditional branch and iteration, because Directed Acyclic Graph (DAG) is limited in how it represents the dependency of each step. Pegasus (Deelman, et al., 2003), using the DAGMan execution engine, constructs executable workflows based on the information of workflow instances and usable resources. It makes it possible for users to design a workflow at the application level, regardless of the status of computing resources and the execution environment.

Triana (Taylor, et al., 2003) is a workflow environment that provides an intuitive graphical user interface, allows users to build their own services, and also provides several services for control or logic, such as loops and if clauses. In order to access grid infrastructures, Triana uses the Grid Application Toolkit (GAT) (Seidel, et al., 2002). GAT defines generic APIs for accessing Grid services. Because GAT focuses on executing collective services, it is not adequate to design the entire experimental process, which includes experiment planning, offline experiments, and collaborative works with GAT.

Taverna (Oinn, et al., 2004) is a workflow system currently used in bioinformatics. It helps compose data-centric workflows that require data stored in distributed databases. These workflows can be used as templates for an *in silico* experiment. Taverna focuses on supporting data integration, fault tolerance, and user-friendly interfaces. To the best of our knowledge, it does not support an environment for collaborative work among e-Science researchers.

Kepler (Ludäscher, et al., 2006) is based on the Ptolemy II system (Brooks, et al., 2005), a platform for heterogeneous and concurrent modeling and design. Kepler's strength is that it provides plenty of services for solving ecological, geological, and biological problems, and also supports various databases and grid systems. In addition, Kepler supports various workflow control strategies. However, Kepler lacks sufficient support for collaborative research, because its basis, Ptolemy II, was not intended to support collaborative workflows.

P-GRAGE Portal (Kacsuk & Sipos, 2005) is a Web-based environment for the development, execution, and monitoring of workflows on various grid platforms. In the portal layer, it plays the role of a bridge between grid platforms, and makes it possible to design workflows via a Graphical User Interface (GUI) with executable components, such as sequential jobs, Message Passing Interface (MPI) jobs, or Parallel Virtual Machine (PVM) jobs.

CATEGORIZATION OF COLLABORATIVE AND DISTRIBUTED E-RESEARCH ACTIVITIES

Considerable effort has been expended in developing a comprehensive method for automating repetitive and complicated workflows in the business and science field.

However, scientific and the business workflow systems have several differences in their requirements (Barga & Gannon, 2007). Typically, scientists create scientific workflows, and frequently change the workflow as their research progresses. Thus, scientific workflow systems tend to require a more user-friendly interface and a more reliable system for creating, executing, and modifying workflows. In addition, because scientific workflows usually involve different types of simulation tasks and data, the proposed scientific workflow systems (Taylor, et al., 2003; Oinn, et al., 2004) support simulations on grids or large-scale computing resources, and also managing a large dataset to help large-scale research processes. Business workflows are constructed using professional software, and are less dynamic. Scientific workflows tend to be executed in a trial-and-error fashion, whereas business workflows are more routine in nature. In addition, unlike scientific workflows, business workflows consist of tasks that require interaction with users.

To support CDER activities, we can define the workflow system for e-Research as a combination of the different features of business and scientific workflows, as depicted in Figure 1. To define the essential functions for enabling collaborative and distributed e-Research workflows, it is important that we characterize the typical workflow types frequently used in e-Research. Therefore, we categorized e-Research workflows into four types: simulation, experiment, collaborative work, and educational activity.

Figure 1. Characteristics of e-research workflows

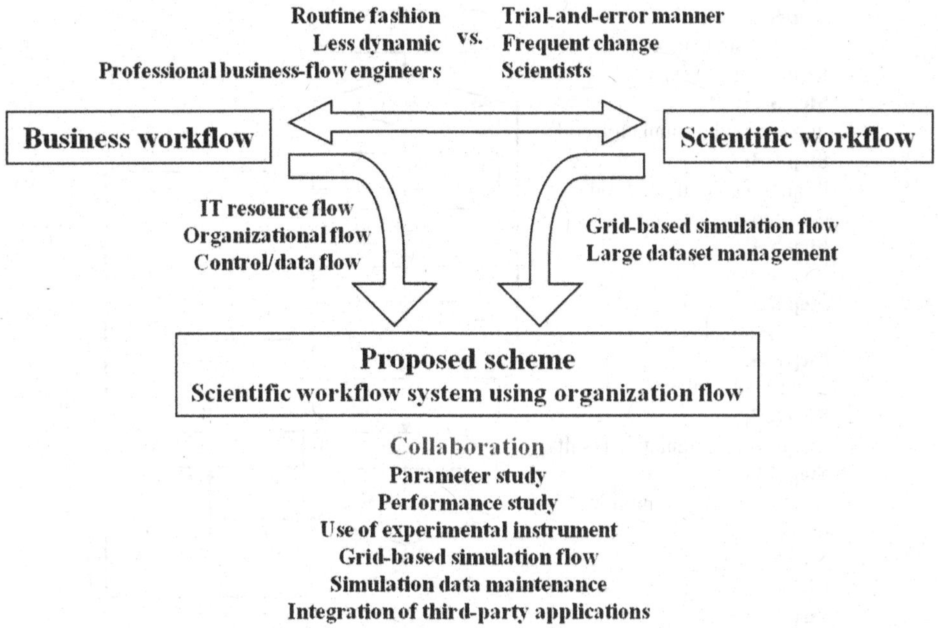

Simulation

Figure 2 shows the workflow for computer-aided simulation, which can be executed on large-scale, remote computing facilities, such as supercomputers, grid resources, or clusters. For simulations, we need to adopt the features of a scientific workflow, such as using grid resources and managing a large dataset.

To run a simulation, researcher needs the code for analysis, or the compiled binary code. If the source code or binary code is already installed on computing resources (as is the case with researchers who already have the simulation program), the simulation can be done with less effort (Step S-5). Otherwise, researchers need to implement a simulator themselves (Step S-2). This new simulator is not deployed on the computing resources. In many cases, when running a job on large-scale, remote computing facilities, administrator approval is required before installing and running user-implemented applications. In this case, researchers need to request that system administrators deploy their simulation program to the computing resources (Step S-3). After deployment, all data required for running the simulation should be transferred to the computing resources (Step S-4). When the input data is prepared, the simulation program can be run (Step S-5). The results can be obtained after the job completes (Step S-6). Researchers then examine the results and further analyze the simulation results (Step S-7). According to the simulation results, researchers may want to run more simulations with different settings (Step S-8). In this case, they prepare a new simulation, with altered settings, and run it (Step S-9a). In other situations, researchers may want to changes the simulation code itself. In such a case, the process returns to the implementation step (Step S-2). The results generated from these repetitive simulations should be stored together, and should be tagged with their simulation environments, such as parameter settings, simulation codes, and dates, in order to allow results to be compared.

Figure 2. Computer-aided simulation workflow

Step S-1:
Does the simulation code
for the scheme exist?
Step S-2:
Implement the simulation code
Step S-3:
Request deploying the code
on computing resources
Step S-4:
Prepare input data
Step S-5:
Run the simulation code
Step S-6:
Download results
Step S-7:
Examine the simulation results
Step S-8:
Need further simulations with
different data sets
Step S-9a:
Change the parameter
Step S-9b:
Modify the simulation code?

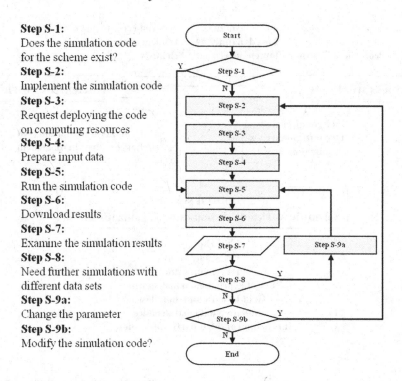

Experiment

Experimental work and collaborative work are associated with business workflows. Typically, each experimental activity needs to be approved, because it may deal with large-scale or expensive equipment. Thus, the first task is to write a proposal for the experiment and request approval. This procedure is described in Figure 3. When a researcher makes a proposal for an experiment (Step E-1), a supervisor or operator of the equipment must accept or decline the proposal (Step E-2). If permission is granted, the researcher can perform the experiment by sending the data required for the experiment (Step E-3). If permission is denied, the process ends. When the experiment is completed, the operator of the experimental equipment uploads the result data to the system, and the researcher may download the results for further analysis (Steps E-4, E-5).

Collaboration

Assigning a work item to a suitable individual is a common task in the field of business process management (Leymann & Roller, 2000). An example is a company groupware system. As in the business field, an e-Research process may require more than one researcher, as some tasks might require special abilities or knowledge. In this case, the tasks need to be distributed to suitable researchers, as in the field of business process management, in order to complete the research process. The first step in assigning a task to another individual is to send a request, including the information required to perform the task (Step C-1). This assignment can be sent to more than one individual (e.g. for polling opinions). In such cases, the set of replies can be aggregated as one result. When a task assigned to an individual is completed, the researcher can download the results (Step C-2) and analyze them further (Step C-3) (see Figure 4).

Figure 3. Experiment workflow

Step E-1:
Write the experiment proposal

Step E-2:
Confirmed?

Step E-3:
Send data for experiment

Step E-4:
Download results

Step E-5:
Examine the experiment results

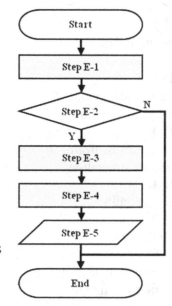

Figure 4. Collaborative research activity workflow

Step C-1:
Request the collaborative work from the researcher in charge

Step C-2:
Download results

Step C-3:
Examine the results

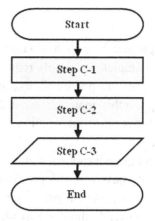

Education

One of the purposes of e-Research is to provide more effective higher education. As scientific and engineering research becomes more complex and involves many disciplines, there is a greater need to provide educational programs to help students better understand the systematic behavior of scientific phenomena and overall research procedures. In such cases, the e-Research environment can be used as a means to train students to understand the big picture of research procedures. The distinctive characteristic of educational activity is that the same workflows are executed repetitively, with the same parameters and input data, by the many students who participate in a class. Because the purpose of utilizing an e-Research environment is to teach students how to set up a simulation and understand the entire research process, the actual execution of a simulation is not as important.

Figure 5. Education workflow

Step D-1:
Prepare input data and
set parameters
Step D-2:
Is there a result generated
with the same condition
Step D-3:
Return the results from
the previous simulation
Step D-4:
Download results
Step D-5:
Run simulation
Step D-6:
Store the result to the repository
along with the simulation
conditions
Step D-7:
Examine the results

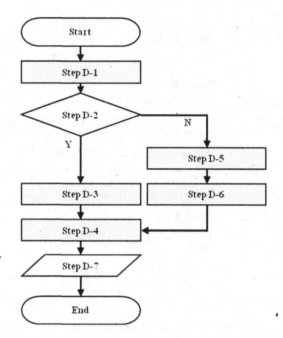

Therefore, the duplicated execution of a task can be assumed to be complete by simply returning the same results from the previously executed simulation. To support this approach, the system should store the provenance information of an educational activity.

Figure 5 depicts the educational e-Research workflow. The flow starts with the preparation of input data and the simulation parameters by the students (Step D-1). If there are available simulation results, generated with the same parameters and input data, the result is retrieved from storage (Step D-3). If there are no existing simulation results with the specified conditions, the simulation is performed as discussed in the simulation activity description (Step D-5). After the simulation is completed, the simulation results are saved to the repository, along with the simulation conditions (Step D-6). Finally, the simulation results can be downloaded and analyzed by the student (Step D-4, D-7).

CASE STUDY: E-AIRS

In this section, we discuss our categorization types by analyzing a case study of the e-Science Aerospace Integrated Research System (e-AIRS) (Kim, et al., 2006), a problem-solving environment used by aerospace researchers. The e-AIRS system supports numerical wind tunnel analyses (Ludewig, et al., 2004) by Computational Fluid Dynamics (CFD) simulation. A wind tunnel is experimental equipment developed to assist studying the effects of air moving over or around solid objects. CFD simulation is a complex method of computer modeling that, if applied well, can recreate the real-world behavior of liquids and gases in a virtual environment.

Figure 6 describes the analyzed scenario. Here, researchers generate the models for the experiment and examine the variations in the fluid and its related characteristics while changing several parameters. Essentially, a wind tunnel experiment is conducted multiple times to examine the fluid dynamic phe-

Figure 6. e-AIRS workflow

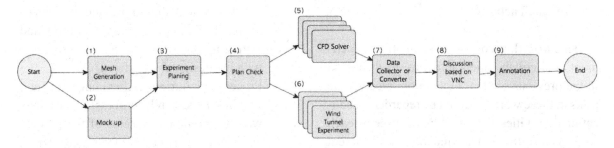

nomena while changing the target fluid dynamic parameters. However, owing to the high cost of wind tunnel experiments, they are only conducted for a small number of cases, and CFD simulations are used to examine the remaining conditions. The steps followed in the scenario are as follows:

- Mesh generation – Mesh data of the selected model is required to perform a CFD simulation. In this step, a researcher who is in charge of mesh modeling creates the mesh data based on the CAD data of the model, and stores the created mesh data in a specific storage location.
- Mock up modeling – For a wind tunnel experiment, a mock-up of the target model is necessary, and is produced by a mock-up modeling expert.
- Experiment planning – After the mesh and the mock-up are produced, a detailed experiment plan is created. The plan includes the objectives of the experiment and the specific values of the variables for each experimental case. In addition, a decision is made for each experimental case on whether it will be analyzed in a wind tunnel experiment or via a CFD simulation.
- Examination of the experiment plan – Because wind tunnel experiments are very costly and complex, and because CFD simulations require relatively significant computing resources, the experiment plan must

be confirmed by supervisors, according to a set of rules.
- Simulation by CFD solver – Experiments based on a CFD simulation are performed using a large amount of grid resources. Each simulation is scheduled and executed by a parameter sweep algorithm that changes the variables for each simulation, as specified in the experiment plan.
- Wind tunnel experiment – Each experiment case, including the specified variables, are handed over to the wind tunnel operator in this step. The operator then performs the experiment as requested, and stores the resulting experiment data in a specified location.
- Collecting and integrating the result – In this step, the results generated in the CFD simulations and wind tunnel experiments are collected and integrated into one examinable data file. The integration of the results facilitates the analysis and sharing of the data.
- Sharing results and discussion – The researchers in charge of analyzing the data share and discuss the data that was collected and integrated in the previous step. During the discussion, the researchers make decisions regarding the next plan.
- Storing the results in a database, with annotation – After analyzing the target model, the resulting data and a summary of the discussion are stored in a database so that

they are accessible in the course of related research activity.

This workflow consists of simulation, experiment, and collaboration activities, as discussed in the previous section. In addition, most of the tasks in these workflows can be regarded as educational activities if this workflow is used to teach students how to set up a wind tunnel experiment with computational fluid dynamics simulations.

REQUIRED FUNCTIONALITY

Based on the categorization of e-Research activities and the example workflow of aerodynamics research, it is possible to enumerate a comprehensive functionality list required to conduct e-Research processes.

The following list summarizes the essential functionality of a workflow system for a CDER process, according to the e-AIRS environment case study:

- Collaborative research – Most research processes are accomplished in a collaborative manner, rather than by a single researcher. Thus, the problem-solving environment necessitates a system that can support communication among researchers and the sharing of results.
- Service management – Each research process is composed of a number of tasks. In the e-AIRS case study, this included a mesh generation task, simulation with a CFD solver, and wind tunnel experiments. Therefore, service management is a critical function in the workflow of a research system. A workflow system should provide necessary functionality for deploying and managing a service.
- Workflow modeling – An interface for supporting the modeling of a workflow is a basic requirement for an e-Research work-

flow system. A workflow system for the e-AIRS system should provide functionality for designing a research workflow and setting up one or more research processes with the designed workflow.
- Process monitoring – After composing and running a research process, researchers want to monitor the status of the process and interactively control the process based on its status. Therefore, an e-Research workflow system should provide both a process monitoring and process control function.
- Security – While executing an experiment in an e-Research environment, researchers need to use various resources, such as computing resources, experimental instruments, and data storage. These resources may have different security mechanisms. Therefore, supporting various security mechanisms is an important requirement for an e-Research workflow system.
- Distributed data management – In e-AIRS system, researchers need to access distributed data, for instance, a researcher's laptop, computing resources, and large data storage devices. Therefore, an environment for accessing heterogeneous data storage is necessary.
- Access to distributed computing resources – As described in previous section, the e-AIRS system submits computing jobs to grid resources to solve CFD problems. Consequently, an e-Research system should provide a means to submit a job to specific computing resources.
- Provenance management – An e-Research system needs to manage the provenance of a simulation and its results, including the validation of research results. The system should record and store execution information for each instance of an e-Research workflow, and the results from each simulation. This includes the simulation

environment, such as input parameter information and input file information. With well-implemented provenance management functionality, an educational activity can easily be constructed by using the provenance information for each simulation program.

This essential functionality can be implemented by integrating various existing, legacy software applications. In Table 1, we summarize the application types according to each of the subtasks in typical e-Research activities in order to define the required functionality more precisely. For example, in the simulation workflow, for step S-1, it is necessary to access the repository of the simulation codes or applications. If researchers store codes in a repository whenever they develop them, the repository can become more valuable as the number of codes grows. One example is the National Grid Service (NGS) applications repository. In Step S-2, the system can use a simple editor or Integrated Development Environment (IDE), such as Eclipse. If a new simulation code needs to be run on remote computing resources, the code must be deployed on specific resources. Therefore, in Step S-3, it is necessary to request that the system administrator deploy this code via the application deployment request interface. Steps S-4 to S-6 are common remote computing resource use cases of the stage-in, run, and stage-out procedures. In Step S-7, graph generation tools, such as Gnuplot, are used to examine the results. Steps S-8 and S-9 require an interface for changing the parameters, enabling researchers to conduct a parameter study. Recently the authors proposed a scheme for the parameter sweep (Kim, et al., 2007).

In the experiment workflow, for Step E-1, a page is required to request the experiment, along with the appropriate information. In Step E-2, it should be possible to confirm whether the experiment has been accepted. Steps E-3 and E-4 use a data transfer tool, such as a GUI-based FTP

Table 1. Application types for workflow support

Workflow	Step ID	Application type
Simulation	S-1	Simulation code (Application) repository
	S-2	Code editing environment
	S-3	Application deployment request page
	S-4	Data transfer supporting tool
	S-5	Job submission service
	S-6	Data transfer supporting tool
	S-7	Graph tool and performance study
	S-8	Parameter study
	S-9a	Problem solving environment
	S-9b	-
Experiment	E-1	Experiment proposal page
	E-2	Settlement page
	E-3	Data transfer supporting tool
	E-4	Data transfer supporting tool
	E-5	Graph tool and performance study
Collaborative work	C-1	Work item request page
	C-2	Data transfer supporting tool
	C-3	Data browser
Education	D-1	Data transfer supporting tool
	D-2	Provenance information repository
	D-3	-
	D-4	Data transfer supporting tool
	D-5	Job submission service
	D-6	Provenance information repository
	D-7	Graph tool and performance study

application. Lastly, in Step E-5, as in Step S-7, the results are examined.

Collaborative work is typical in a business workflow. A work item can be assigned to a capable person via the work item request page in Step C-1. After finishing the requested work, results are downloaded via the data transfer tool in Step C-2, and examined in Step C-3.

Educational workflows are not that different from the other types of workflows. According to our categorization in the previous section, the biggest difference between an educational work-

Figure 7. Proposed architecture of e-research workflow system

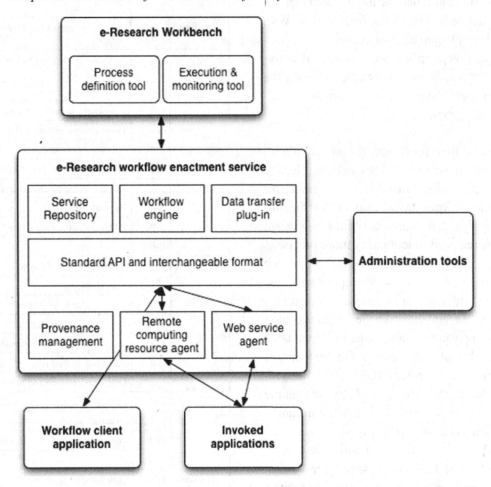

flow and other workflows is that an educational workflow requires provenance information of simulations in order to compare simulation environments, such as input parameters and input files. Therefore, to search for simulations with the same conditions (Step D-2), education workflows should access a provenance management system. In addition, when a simulation is completed, all information regarding the simulation should be stored in the provenance management system, as described in Step D-6.

Architecture

As shown in Figure 7, the CDER workflow system can be designed based on the workflow

reference model (Hollingsworth, 1994) of the Workflow Management Coalition (WfMC). The proposed architecture consists of three basic components. The first one is known as the e-Research workbench. The workbench is a user interface enabling researchers to model, run, and monitor the workflow, and communicate with other researchers. The second component is the e-Research workflow enactment service, which executes and maintains the modeled workflow. It includes the service repository for managing all services that can be executed within the system, a workflow engine for assigning and scheduling each task to appropriate resources, and the data transfer plug-in for communication with various storage resources. In addition, e-Research workflow enactment service provides two modules to deal with invoked applications: the remote computing resource agent and the web service agent. The provenance management component controls all metadata related to the execution of each task in the e-Research workflow system. The third component is the set of administration tools for the e-Science workflow enactment service, which manages all administrative activities.

CONCLUSION

In this chapter, we analyzed the characteristics of the CDER workflow and described the necessary applications and functionality for the workflow. To do this, we categorized the expected workflow in the CDER environment into four types: simulation, experiments, collaborative work, and educational activity. This categorization, along with the proposed workflow system architecture and its functionality, can be used as a reference for designing the CDER workflow.

Scientific application services on a computing environment are varied. Therefore, the existing approach is to develop domain-specific science gateways. This is because the user requirements, including the interface expected by users, is slightly different, even if the core technology supporting the CDER workflow is common and can be shared. Thus, we can define a core set of reusable components for building new applications, called the Application Framework. The application service uses the framework for setting up and submitting High Performance Computing (HPC) jobs, and monitors the job progress through job monitoring components provided in the framework. In the near future, we plan to develop a science gateway supporting the CDER workflow for the computational fluid dynamics field with supercomputers and clusters. Through the science gateway, users will be able to conduct

computer simulations to verify and understand both existing and new theories.

REFERENCES

Barga, R., & Gannon, D. (2007). Scientific versus business workflows. In *Workflows for E-Science: Scientific Workflows for Grids* (pp. 9–16). Berlin, Germany: Springer.

Brooks, C., Lee, E. A., Liu, X., Neuendorffer, S., Zhao, Y., & Zheng, H. (Eds.). (2005). *Heterogeneous concurrent modeling and design in java*. Berkeley, CA: University of California.

Deelman, E., Blythe, J., Gil, Y., Kesselman, C., Mehta, G., & Vahi, K. (2003). Mapping abstract complex workflows onto grid environments. *Journal of Grid Computing*, *1*(1), 25–39. doi:10.1023/A:1024000426962

Frey, F. (2002). *Condor dagman: Handling inter-job dependencies*. Retrieved from http:// cs.wisc.edu/ condor/ dagman/.

Hollingsworth, D. (1994). The workflow reference model. *Workflow Management Coalition*. Retrieved from http://www.wfmc.org.

Kacsuk, P., & Sipos, G. (2005). Multi-grid, multi-user workflows in the P-GRADE portal. *Journal of Grid Computing*, *3*(3-4), 221–238. doi:10.1007/s10723-005-9012-6

Kim, B., Nam, D., Suh, Y., Lee, J., Cho, K., & Hwang, S. (2007). Application parameter description scheme for multiple job generation in problem solving environment. In *Proceedings of the International Conference on e-Sceince and Grid Computing*, (pp. 509-515). IEEE Press.

Kim, Y., Kim, E., Kim, J. Y., Cho, J., Kim, C., & Cho, K. W. (2006). e-AIRS: An e-science collaboration portal for aerospace applications. In *Proceedings of the High Performance Computing and Communications Conference*, (vol 4208), (pp. 813-822). IEEE Press.

Leymann, F., & Roller, D. (2000). *Production workflow: Concepts and techniques*. Upper Saddle River, NJ: Prentice Hall.

Ludäscher, B., Altintas, I., Berkley, C., Higgins, D., Jaeger, E., & Jones, M. (2006). Scientific workflow management and the Kepler system. *Concurrency and Computation, 18*(10), 1039–1065. doi:10.1002/cpe.994

Ludewig, T., Hauser, J., Gollnick, T., & Paap, H. (2004). *JUSTGrid – A pure Java HPCC grid architecture for multi-physics solvers using complex geometries*. Paper presented at the 42nd AIAA Aerospace Sciences Meeting and Exhibit. Washington, DC.

Myers, J., & McGrath, R. (2007). *Cyberenvironments: Adaptive middleware for scientific cyberinfrastructure*. Paper presented at the 6th International Workshop on Adaptive and Reñective Middleware. New York, NY.

Oinn, T., Addis, M., Ferris, J., Marvin, D., Senger, M., & Greenwood, M. (2004). Taverna: A tool for the composition and enactment of bioinformatics workflows. *Bioinformatics (Oxford, England), 20*(17), 3045–3054. doi:10.1093/bioinformatics/bth361

Seidel, E., Allen, G., Merzky, A., & Nabrzyski, J. (2002). GridLab: A grid application toolkit and testbed. *Future Generation Computer Systems, 18*(8), 1143–1153. doi:10.1016/S0167-739X(02)00091-2

Taylor, I., Shields, M., & Wang, I. (2003). Triana applications within grid computing and peer to peer environments. *Journal of Grid Computing, 1*(2), 199–217. doi:10.1023/B:GRID.0000024074.63139.ce

Wilkins-Diehr, N. (2007). Special issue: Science gateways – Common community interfaces to Grid resources. *Concurrency and Computation, 19*(6), 743–749. doi:10.1002/cpe.1098

ENDNOTES

[1]   Corresponding author

[2]   This work was supported in part by the EDucation-research Integration through Simulation On the Net (EDISON) Project funded by the Ministry of Education, Science and Technology, the Republic of Korea.

Chapter 5
Connecting and Enabling the Humanities:
e-Research in the Border Zone

Paul Longley Arthur
Australian National University, Australia

ABSTRACT

E-Research is well-established in science and technology fields but is at an earlier stage of development in the humanities. Investments in technology infrastructure worldwide, however, are starting to pay dividends, and a cultural change is occurring, enabling closer collaborations between researchers in a sector that has traditionally emphasized individual research activities. This chapter discusses ways in which the humanities are utilizing digital methods, including: creating and enhancing online collections; building knowledge communities around projects, disciplines, and data; and communicating research results in widely accessible formats. E-Research has brought with it new attitudes, behaviors, and expectations. Topics include the growing opportunities for collaborative and cross-disciplinary approaches, building the information commons, and the need for long-term strategic investment in research infrastructure.

INTRODUCTION

In today's era of ubiquitous computing and global online connectivity, e-research is enriching research across a growing range of academic disciplines. Its reach is extending beyond the science and technology fields where it originated, and is now "penetrating the social sciences and humanities, [though] sometimes with differences in accent and label" (Jankowski, 2009). This chapter discusses some of the ways in which humanities researchers are embracing new digital resources, formats and modes of collaborating in order to further the traditional goals of humani-

DOI: 10.4018/978-1-4666-0125-3.ch005

ties research, "to better understand ourselves, our history, and our cultural heritage" (Cole, 2007).

Humanities researchers constitute a very large and diverse community whose intellectual contribution is vitally important to social, cultural, and economic wellbeing. Their research encompasses "the study of society, identity, economy, business, governance, history, culture and creativity," a vast field that "links universities, government agencies, collecting institutions and creative industries with policy development and with communities" (Strategic Roadmap, 2011, p. 45). The field typically includes disciplines such as archaeology, arts, classical studies, cultural and communication studies, English, history, languages, linguistics, literature, philosophy and religion. The use of digital tools, services and methodologies is impacting on how records of human culture and history are created, stored, interpreted and accessed, and humanities research practices are changing, but it is a gradual process. E-Research in the humanities includes activities such as: creating and enhancing online collections; building knowledge communities around projects, disciplines and data; and communicating research results in widely accessible formats.

Topics covered in this chapter include the growing opportunities for collaborative and interdisciplinary approaches, building the information commons for public benefit, and the growing need for strategic investment in research infrastructure to support the humanities. Humanities e-research initiatives in Australia are highlighted as a specific example that is aligned with and reinforces recent international policy directions.

BACKGROUND

Extending e-Research to the Humanities

Computers have been used in humanities research for more than 50 years, and yet the benefits of digital methods, especially those that have evolved over the past two decades, have only recently begun to be widely understood in the academic community. This is in spite of the fact that in some circles, there was a very early awareness of the value of computing in the humanities[1]. The following statement, from the American Council of Learned Societies (ACLS) in 1966, remains relevant today: "*Of course* computers should be used by scholars in the humanities, just as microscopes should be used by scientists... [t]he facts and patterns that they—and often they alone—can reveal should be viewed not as the definitive answers to the questions that humanists have been asking, but rather as the occasion for a whole range of new and more penetrating and more exciting questions" (Blitzer, 1966). Forty years on, in 2006, the ACLS report, *Our Cultural Commonwealth*, was a call to action for the humanities sector. It argued that a better coordinated approach to managing and building the online information commons was an urgent priority and a responsibility to be taken seriously. The report notes that "with many new works [of scholarship] accessible and understood only through digital media," purpose-designed solutions must be developed for the humanities sector; the "creation, curation, and preservation of information" requires advanced systems, but these cannot simply be borrowed from the sciences (Our Cultural Commonwealth, 2006, p. i). Applying the term 'cyberinfrastructure' to the humanities (a term given currency through a 2003 report of the National Science Foundation), the report recommended major investment in infrastructure funding on a national and international scale so that digital scholarship in this sector could become "cumulative, collaborative, and synergistic" (Our Cultural Commonwealth, 2006, p. i). Similar concerns were noted in the European context (ESFRI, 2008b, p. 16).

To date, digital technologies have more naturally supported existing methodologies and patterns of work in the sciences than they have in the humanities. However, we are now at a critical moment in the history of digital penetration into the realms of non-science research. For many humanities researchers, the digital revolution has remained external to them. It was something occurring in another space—on the science side of the university, in the fast-changing IT innovation sector, somewhere out there in the nebulous realm of the internet, or in new kinds of animation and special effects in films. Towards the end of the twentieth century as emails increasingly consumed their working days and electronic transfer of information became more common, humanities researchers were still not in a position to see or predict the wealth of new possibilities that would open up for them very rapidly. In contrast to the history of computerization of scientific research, the digital dimension typically entered their lives not from within the academic sphere, as had occurred in the sciences, and not in an organized way through the purchase of specialized equipment and software, but from the public realm, haphazardly and by chance. With the emergence of search engines and then the sudden upsurge of social media in the past decade, many humanities researchers began to discover and take advantage of the new opportunities. Others could see no benefit in doing so. Libraries and museums played a leading role. They were the first to establish large-scale databases, digitization programs and policies, and other digital resources for humanities research. In universities, however, the uptake tended to be spasmodic and individual. It is this early history of isolated and unplanned engagement that can explain the relatively dispersed and disconnected nature of digital resources in the humanities. It can also explain the absence, until very recently, of a coherent vision for the future and therefore the time-lag in investment.

Terminology and Definitions

In the humanities there is much confusion around the term 'e-Research' due to the fact that 'e-Research' and 'e-Science' have come to be used almost interchangeably, giving the impression that this kind of research is more relevant to the sciences than it is to the humanities. There is also a "notable discrepancy in terminology used in different countries, leading to a lack of clarity" (ESFRI, 2008a), with e-research being the term favored in Europe and in Australasia and e-science traditionally used in Britain (Jirotka, et al., 2006, p. 251). In the USA 'cyberinfrastructure' has been the commonly adopted term. The most widely applicable definitions of e-research take a broad view, clearly accommodating research practices beyond the sciences. The UK based Joint Information Systems Committee (JISC), for example, provides the following definition:

e-Research refers to the development of, and the support for, information and computing technologies to facilitate all phases of research processes. The term e-Research originates from the term e-Science but expands its remit to all research domains, not just the sciences. It is concerned with technologies that support all the processes involved in research including (but not limited to) creating and sustaining research collaborations and discovering, analysing, processing, publishing, storing and sharing research data and information. Typical technologies in this domain include: Virtual Research Environments, Grid computing, visualisation services, and text and data mining services. (JISC e-Research, 2012)

The Monash University e-Research Centre in Australia explains it in the following terms, again without privileging specific disciplines:

e-Research is the use of IT, communications and Information Management (IM) technologies to do better research and to do research collaboration better. E-Research enables researchers to draw on perspectives and resources from a range of participants, in order to develop new insights and new solutions to complex problems. It involves the use of technology to draw people together, where technology is the facilitator to researcher collaboration.... From a multi-national blog that provides a new academic forum on art theory, to multi-disciplinary research drawing together databases on climate change from England, the USA and Australia, e-research is changing the face of research around the world. (Monash e-Research, 2012)

In the humanities sector there have in fact been very few projects that can accord with the definition of e-research as 'data-intensive, large-scale information sharing and collaboration,' which is how it is most commonly understood in the sciences. A 2007 report, prepared as part of the UK Arts and Humanities Research Council Workshops on E-Science, made this point, noting that "humanities scholars will undoubtedly develop research requiring the enhanced processing power offered by grid technologies, [but] at present few humanities projects present problems whose resolution would benefit from such technologies" (Shepherd, 2007, p. 7).

Confusion over terminology complicates international comparisons between projects and limits productive dialogue. Worldwide, the range of digital work in the humanities is broad, and there are already terms and expressions that overlap confusingly under the umbrella term of 'e-Research,' and closely related to this, the 'digital humanities.' They include fields and sub-fields (such as cultural informatics, virtual heritage, archaeological computing, and historical GIS), activities and processes (such as text encoding, 3D rendering, visualization, animation, and modeling), formats and proto-genres (such as online encyclopedias, cultural atlases, database narratives, multimedia documentaries, and virtual museums), as well as numerous other approaches and methods. These new terms and emerging subfields are indicative of the transformations in traditional research practices in the humanities that are occurring.

E-Research, as it is understood in this chapter, is not a 'field'; rather, it is a layer of technology-driven links—between people, between stores of data, and across physical spaces—that underpins and facilitates collaboration. A fundamental principle of e-research in all its forms is that it offers an enhanced capacity for connectedness—connectedness of information in and between databases, connectedness between the sciences and humanities, between experts and the public, and between communities across the world. With this have come new patterns of working, new attitudes, new behavior, and new expectations.

CREATING NETWORKED KNOWLEDGE ENVIRONMENTS

Barely imaginable a few decades ago, the idea of global networks of knowledge has now become a part of the commonplace reality of our world. Academics generally had the privilege of early access to digital networking tools and for many humanities academics this has meant experiencing the full sweep of the digital revolution at close hand through the transformation of the basic daily tools of their trade—from pen and paper to laptop computer, from book to iPad, from real to virtual and from the shelves of the library to vast databases. Such changes have not only enabled but *imposed* new ways of working in the humanities. However, in the early years, the changes entered the humanities research environment slowly and unsystematically, with individuals taking advantage of the new technologies in opportunistic and arbitrary ways, rather than via institutionally coordinated planning frameworks. In the humanities, researchers were not so much enticed as swept towards a networking culture by the first wave of the digital revolution.

Key Issues

Digital technology is now playing a major role in research and teaching across the humanities and recent technical breakthroughs have led to developments that have revolutionized some areas of activity. For example, fundamental changes in approach to preservation and archiving have been brought about by the growth of digital repositories, and the newly flexible formats and protocols for database design and information architecture are leading to new and open formats and standards. Developments such as these have had an impact on most disciplines in the humanities and they have changed the dominant research culture, over a relatively short period, to one that now openly welcomes the application of digital technologies in social and cultural research. New communities of researchers and practitioners have emerged, made up not only of humanities subject experts, but also computer scientists, communication professionals and policy-makers, a mix that was uncommon even a decade ago. As a result, novel research topics are being formulated, and a new language, used by a new generation of scholars, is evolving.

However, in the humanities the outputs that are most highly valued institutionally continue to be in conventional, mostly non-electronic, forms (sole-authored books, monographs and journal articles). Some of these are practically "invisible in terms of online traces, particularly when compared to the highly-cited online-only physics article" (Meyer & Schroeder, 2009, p. 246). Digital publication formats that make use of the hyper-media environment to present information and interpretation in new ways are not yet fully recognized as serious academic outputs and remain in a phase of very early development. In the humanities there is a critical need "to bridge the divide between the building of multimedia digital repositories, and the publishing of research outcomes that exploit the interactive potential of digital media" (Jakubowicz, 2007).

While the growing alliance between humanities research and information technologies is a bridge that now spans and links sectors and research practices, the humanities have their own pressing issues at this time of transformation. They include:

- Managing and benefiting from the multiple ways in which research communities can be created and leveraged in networked information environments;
- Devising ways to better measure and, in the process, place a higher value on digital research and production;
- Supporting large-scale approaches underpinned by shared technology solutions, including the application of quantitative approaches in fields that have emphasized qualitative methodologies;
- Developing visualization and modeling techniques for wide application across the disciplines of the humanities;
- Fostering common protocols, languages and standards to enhance the interoperability of data collections;
- Training staff and students to the levels of digital literacy required for communicating, presenting and preserving knowledge in online environments;
- Exploring new modes of digital publishing and archiving to guard against data obsolescence; and
- Attracting higher levels of funding to provide the infrastructure required to underpin and support e-research in the humanities.

Fostering Collaboration

Because collaboration within and across teams is a fundamental characteristic of scientific research, the collaborative practices of e-research were quickly embraced by the scientific community. For scientists e-research is an extension of their traditional culture: it expands possibilities and enhances long-established patterns of working. Scientists can rapidly transfer or compare unprecedented amounts of information and use high-definition, real-time imaging and other equally data-intensive applications. As a powerful set of tools and services that allows researchers to delve more deeply and deliver results more quickly and accurately than ever before, e-research has given the sciences worldwide a huge injection of new energy and is speeding up the pace of discovery and innovation. The humanities, by contrast, have not been well-positioned to derive corresponding benefits from the high-speed transfer, sharing and collaborative analysis of large amounts of data. Diane Goldenberg-Hart explained the challenges in these terms, in her 2004 report *Libraries and Changing Research Practices* on the ARL/CNI Forum on e-Research and Cyberinfrastructure:

Unlike the sciences, the humanities face a more difficult challenge ... because knowledge communities are more difficult to foster, data tends to emerge from human experience rather than scientific enquiry, there is less dependency on information technology, and a bigger challenge in promoting a payoff from the use of information technology and digital information. (Goldenberg-Hart, 2004)

The core of the problem is that humanities researchers have not been accustomed to working collaboratively. The strongest tradition in this sector has been that of the solitary researcher, reading, working with words and ideas, testing them in debate perhaps, and writing them down. Research on changing attitudes of researchers has shown that some are "marked by ambivalence," resisting change and believing "the internet may not replace the need for some more traditional forms of scholarly communication" (Genoni, et al., 2006, p. i). Others may see the benefits for the larger community, but not for themselves: "while individuals may accept the overall value of such a foundation, they do not necessarily see a direct benefit…" (Goldenberg-Hart, 2004).

However, the Web 2.0 environment that underpins social media services in their many forms is a readily available platform that is now so easily and commonly used that it has greatly facilitated collaborative modes of user access to and participation in the creation of knowledge in the humanities. Rudimentary as they may seem at first when compared with the highly specialized data-sharing services developed for scientific research, publicly available Web 2.0 services are proving to be a key tool for e-research in the humanities. Twitter, for example, is commonly cited as the single most useful communication tool for the digital humanities community, bringing like-minded humanities scholars together *en masse*. Other popular social media services are being incorporated into nationally significant online data services such as the National Library of Australia's long-running PictureAustralia project[2] in which the functionality includes Flickr-based photo sharing. Users contribute their own photographs and have the chance to add to the collection. This kind of involvement of non-specialists in creating and contributing to online digital resources is an important point of distinction between the humanities and the sciences. There are many potential benefits for researchers in being able to engage with "more idiosyncratic, unpredictable, and democratic genres of expression" (Bollier, 2003). However, incorporating social media does also present hazards. It can result in "a rolling mess of participation," as one commentator has put it (Kelly, 2008). Scientists are not faced with this problem, at least not to the same extent.

Social media services are being used effectively to link humanities experts with the public and allowing humanities researchers to form their own large online communities. However, the promise of secure, private, virtual spaces for focused online collaboration and data sharing is yet to be realized. In the immediate future it is likely that more projects will experiment with widely supported wiki software to facilitate secure information sharing, peer review and other aspects of project-driven collaboration. The wiki software Confluence, for example, was used very successfully by the Australian Research Council-funded Network for Early European Research (NEER), based at the University of Western Australia[3].

The Principle of Public Benefit

The depositing of research data and publications in digital repositories is now being mandated by many institutions and this will bring about a change in attitudes over time. Humanities researchers are increasingly contributing to a digital information commons. Whereas the commons once took the form of a physical meeting place (Yelling, 1977; Turner, 1984), today's information commons are virtual spaces that give users access to a vast variety of electronically published resources. The information commons can be defined in various ways, including as "intangible assets including public knowledge and creative production not legally privatized through copyright or made available for free public access through other legal arrangements" (Bollier, 2002). Taken in the broadest sense, the internet itself represents one vast information commons which crosses national, public, private and institutional boundaries. For humanities and social sciences research, the information commons has been primarily facilitated by libraries and by major national and state collecting institutions, all of which share an interest in the dissemination of cultural information for the benefit of society (Kranich, 2004; Lee, 2003). Programs such as the Open Archives Initiative and Data Documentation Initiative, which grew out of the open access and institutional repository movements, are working to ensure better consistency, interoperability and access between systems, institutions and sectors.

Central to the concept of the commons is the goal that information should be freely available for the public benefit while respecting the historical circumstances, ownership and motivations for presenting and sharing information. Core principles are free expression, fair use and equitable access to digital resources. Because there is a growing range of formats and interfaces for user access to digital content, the idea of the commons is moving further away from the traditional concept of a shared meeting space towards the e-research model of a distributed information community.

Ongoing issues to be addressed include: technical considerations, specifically the establishment of access standards such as single sign-on principles, as well as mechanisms for interoperability of information systems; policy implications, especially for intellectual property, copyright and privacy, allowing for levels of scholarly and general public utilization; and data management, particularly in relation to aligning the policies and practices of universities, collecting institutions and government agencies with those of individual researchers.

Case Study: Australian Humanities e-Research

The Australian case described here outlines the progress that has been made in one national context over a period of a decade to the point where the government is readying itself for potential large-scale investment in humanities e-research infrastructure. Australia is set apart from many other countries, including the USA and some European nations, in that its research community relies almost entirely on government funding, and the government takes a centralized approach that suits the country's very large land size and relatively small population. However, the history of the adoption of e-research in the humanities in Australia over the past decade mirrors experiences in other parts of the world, and current developments in Australia are broadly representative of a range of key trends internationally.

In Australia, humanities e-research activities have been expanding significantly over the past decade since the e-Humanities Gateway launched its major online database of Australian digital projects in 2002[4]. In June 2007, the inaugural eResearch Australasia conference, held at the University of Queensland, featured presentations from humanities researchers alongside scientists and information technology experts. These included an interim report from the Australian Academy of the Humanities on a major Australian Research Council-funded survey, undertaken in 2006, gauging attitudes to and areas of adoption of new technologies in the humanities[5]. In November 2007 the Academy centered its annual symposium on the theme of 'Humanities Futures: New Methods and Technologies for Humanities Research' to address directly the impact of technological innovation across the disciplines of the humanities[6]. The eResearch Australasia conferences have been held annually since 2007 and feature humanities research as a key component. State-based e-research agencies such as the Victorian eResearch Strategic Initiative (VeRSI)[7] and, in the state of New South Wales, Intersect[8], now routinely work in conjunction with national programs such as the Australian National Data Service (ANDS) to support humanities-related projects in the higher education and cultural sectors. One example is the recent Museum Metadata Exchange project[9]. With the recent formation of the Australasian Association for Digital Humanities in April 2011, there is now a body that can potentially provide advocacy and leadership to draw the humanities e-research community together, identify priorities and influence the scale and direction of investment in infrastructure.

As in the UK context, Australian humanities e-research projects often involve the "curation of very large stores of digital images, or exploitation of archives of large video and audio files," and this presents issues related to scale and manageability (Shepherd, 2007, p. 7). Some of Australia's most highly regarded university-led e-research projects in this sector include Austlit: The Australian Literature Resource[10], PARADESIC (Pacific and Regional Archive for Digital Sources in Endangered Cultures)[11], and the projects of the Archaeological Computing Laboratory at the University of Sydney that are built on the Heurist reference database for e-research[12]. A common theme that links these diverse projects is the goal of capturing, preserving, building upon and articulating the richness of Australian culture and history for current and future generations.

So far, in Australia, the investment in research infrastructure for the humanities has been channeled through small and mid-size initiatives rather than through a large coordinated program. The recently released *2011 Strategic Roadmap for Australian Research Infrastructure Discussion Paper*, however, underlines the importance of large-scale and interconnected social and cultural research in the Australian knowledge economy. It proposes an "online knowledge network," envisaged as a "distributed national e-research facility to underpin transformational Australian research that will advance our understanding of cultures and communities" (Strategic Roadmap, 2011, p. 45)[13]. This national plan provides for e-research solutions to unite researchers in diverse disciplines and aims to bring together nationally significant data collections as a 'hub and spoke' network through an interface directly accessible via desktop computers. It aims to "revolutionise research in this fundamentally important field," providing services and tools "to create, capture, store, share, manage, manipulate and analyse diverse data collections and resources, and it would link individuals with virtual research communities" (Strategic Roadmap, 2011, p. 45). The authors explain the rationale behind the proposed e-research facility by highlighting the fragmented nature of Australia's leading digital projects in the humanities, many of which were conceived in isolation, and remain closed and non-interoperable:

Australia has a wide range of data collections and digital resources that play a crucial role in our understanding of cultures and communities. Internationally respected projects such as the Australian Dictionary of Biography, AustLit and Pacific and Regional Archive for Digital Sources in Endangered Cultures (PARADISEC) are examples. However, these collections and resources are dispersed amongst multiple locations, institutions and agencies, and they mostly take the form of stand-alone, subject-specific repositories with very different information architectures. Re-

searchers working collaboratively using digital tools and services to address pressing issues of national and global significance require access to complex data sets that are interoperable. In order to identify, manage and improve these nationally important collections, and make them accessible and usable, it is necessary to develop standards, services and environments through a nationwide approach and on a vastly expanded scale. (Strategic Roadmap, 2011, p. 48)

Providing hardware and software in itself is not sufficient. Promoting education and training for 21st century social and cultural research underpinned by ICT is crucial in building the necessary core competencies, domain specific skills and best practices. (Strategic Roadmap, 2011, p. 48)

Pilot projects would be developed in order to demonstrate the benefits of the national-level, integrated and data-centric approach proposed. The Australian discussion paper refers to the various iterations of the European research infrastructure strategy roadmap over the past five years as a potential model to follow. The 2008 report of the Social Sciences and Humanities Roadmap Working Group to the European Strategy Forum on Research Infrastructures (ESFRI, 2008b) noted that five of the six research infrastructure proposals referred to in the 2006 ESFRI Roadmap (ESFRI, 2006) were successful in gaining European Commission funding for 'Preparatory Phase' projects. These have proven to be sound, targeted investments that demonstrate to other research communities in the humanities and social sciences the potential rewards of large-scale infrastructure projects. The projects are: the Council of European Social Science Data Archives (CESSDA)[14]; Common Language Resources and Technology Initiative (CLARIN)[15]; Digital Research Infrastructure for the Arts and Humanities (DARIAH)[16]; European Social Survey (ESS)[17]; and the Survey of Health, Ageing and Retirement in Europe (SHARE)[18]. DARIAH and CLARIN

are of particular relevance to researchers in the humanities, arts and social sciences. DARIAH spans an existing network of data centres and services to form an infrastructure for the arts and humanities to give access to resources on the cultural heritage of Europe. CLARIN aims to bring an accessible archive of language resources and technology within reach of researchers in all disciplines but especially those working in the humanities and social sciences.

The next stage of the Australian roadmapping process will be to develop further the vision of an interconnected online knowledge network by tailoring existing e-research solutions to the specific needs of the humanities community. The sector is made up of "broad and diverse fields with multiple entry points for researchers," and this has implications for the design of large-scale infrastructure, as noted in the European context (ESFRI, 2008b, p. 21). The European experience has shown that any development of e-research infrastructure must be undertaken within an overarching framework of key principles and long-term goals such as: "increasing the availability of quality comparative data"; "enhancing data modelling"; developing "data integration and language tools"; enabling "access to research resources and materials through integrated systems and processes"; and including "the digitization, enhancement and repurposing of key analogue data resources" (ESFRI, 2008b, p. 9). Underlying all of these is the need for large-scale, coordinated digitization programs.

FUTURE RESEARCH DIRECTIONS

During the past few years the levels of commitment to and investment in establishing interconnected knowledge networks that facilitate collaboration in practical and sustainable ways, both within individual countries and across international boundaries, have increased greatly. Many major infrastructure projects have been established and others are being initiated or proposed. New networks and organizations that promote and facilitate e-research policy and practice are being formed. We have yet to fully grasp the huge potential of these developments for e-research communities, especially for the humanities.

The Humanities in Transition

The April 2011 Research Information Network (RIN) Report, *Reinventing Research? Information Practices in the Humanities*, was published in a series that seeks to "understand how researchers within a range of disciplines find and use information, and in particular how that has changed with the introduction of new technologies" (RIN, 2011, p. 6). The range of humanities disciplines referred to in this report is suitably broad, and accordingly there is a wide variety of approaches and methodologies surveyed. The report finds that text and images tend to be a core focus in this sector, but, as the report notes, researchers "use and also create a wide range of information resources, in print, manuscript and digital forms" (RIN, 2011, p. 6). The authors conclude that, while humanities scholars are often perceived to be working largely on their own and only collaborating informally in highly-dispersed networks, the situation has begun to change. Referring to a series of six case studies, the report suggests that existing investments in technology infrastructure for the humanities worldwide, while relatively modest, are beginning to pay dividends and that cultural change is taking place.

Growing collaboration between institutions is demonstrated by formal affiliations such as centerNet, a worldwide network of more than 200 digital humanities centers. Individual researchers in the humanities are also engaging with or forming large communities, and are increasingly establishing links with those working in science and technology disciplines. One of the largest such communities is HASTAC (Humanities, Arts, Science and Technology Advanced Collabora-

tory), made up of a vast network of "humanists, artists, social scientists, scientists and engineers committed to new forms of collaboration across communities and disciplines fostered by creative uses of technology[19]." These trends towards internationalization and formation of large networks are likely to continue until a critical mass of engaged researchers has been achieved.

International Trends in e-Research Infrastructure Investment

Recent reports on e-research in the humanities internationally have identified the need for major infrastructure investments to underpin a changing culture of research that values and responds to the opportunities offered by new technologies. European nations have led the way in responding to this need by supporting large-scale collaborative initiatives formulated to have maximum research benefit as well as public benefit. The investment in e-research infrastructure in Europe over the past five years shows trends towards:

1. *Cross-disciplinary integration of infrastructure and research practices*, with the aim of developing a "broader infrastructural system, which could incorporate and support additional RIs [Research Infrastructures] and research networks within the SSH [Social Sciences and Humanities]" (ESFRI, 2008b, p. 6). This has included finding common ground between the humanities and the sciences and identifying opportunities for building digital resources and tools that are either shared or adapted for re-use between these sectors[20].

2. *Moving from centralised solutions to a model of interoperable systems working in large-scale distributed arrangements.* Whereas past approaches have emphasized "centralisation and the establishment of large-scale European-wide institutions," the newer approach is to focus on "standardiza-

tion, the power of emerging information and communication technologies, harmonization of data access restrictions and strengthening of and collaboration among already established groups and organisations engaged in the development of the European Research Area" (ESFRI, 2008b, p. 13).

3. *Recognising the importance of non-technological factors*, including the need for training, awareness building, encouraging change in research practices and the ongoing refinement of policies. For the humanities, the challenge goes far beyond "fibre-optic cables, storage area networks or basic communication protocols." Issues related to user access, as well as legal and financial conditions and arrangements, have been found to "have a greater impact on the availability of data to the research community than do technological solutions" (ESFRI, 2008b, pp. 13-14).

Project Bamboo[21] is an example of a global project for the humanities that demonstrates the trend in point (2) above towards research becoming "increasingly distributed across larger-scale and multi-institutional collaborations" (Meyer & Schroeder, 2009, p. 246). Described as "a multi-institutional, interdisciplinary effort that brings together humanities scholars, librarians, and information technologists," it is tackling the question, "How can we advance arts and humanities research through the development of shared technology services?" A 2010 Andrew W. Mellon Foundation grant of USD$1.3 million to an international consortium of ten partner universities launched Phase 1 of the Bamboo Technology Project (to run 2010-2012)[22]. This follows a planning and consultation stage in 2008-10 that involved over 600 individual experts from 115 institutions. Phase 1 will offer scalable environments for digital scholarship through the development of tools for content management, collaboration and connection with collections and web services. The project

will also develop the underlying infrastructure that partner institutions can use to "sustain and connect research applications and collections" with the aim of better integrating and supporting data and tools. This will include customizing and adapting for the humanities a tool originally created for the sciences, HUBzero[23]. A planned Phase 2 will set out to "define how e-research environments can evolve to support increasingly complex and large-scale forms of corpora scholarship across the disciplines"—a goal that would enable all that was learnt from this project to be fed back into other areas, including, ultimately, even the sciences.

CONCLUSION

Digital tools and techniques have been transforming the sciences for half a century. They have been used in humanities research, but to a lesser extent, and there has been a different pattern of development. While the utilization of e-research practices is at an earlier stage in the humanities, the greatly increased rate of activity and the rapidly growing number of large-scale new initiatives provide an indication of their current impact and their transformational potential for the future. Meanwhile, the quantitative evidence base relating to humanities practices and investment is underdeveloped. This is in part due to the fact that e-research is defined and understood very differently between countries and across institutions. Even comparing relative investment is difficult; science funding, for example, is often appropriated for technology-driven humanities projects when separate and direct sources of funding are not available.

Collaboration between the sciences and the humanities and all the disciplines within them will be greatly enhanced as e-research enters the humanities mainstream. E-Research has the capacity not only to change the way humanities research is carried out, but also to fundamentally alter the assumptions, processes, and ultimately the very questions that researchers address. The digital revolution has delivered, to an extraordinary extent, the promise of the democratization of knowledge. Citizens have access to specialist and non-specialist information as never before. But this freedom brings with it a new world of responsibilities and dangers, including for data security and longevity. And despite the abundance of cultural information online, with billions of pages accessible at the click of the mouse, the vision of a "true network of cultural heritage information" to support advanced collaborative research in this sector is far from being realized (ESFRI, 2008b, p. 16).

There is no doubt that the integration of e-research into humanities work practices requires greater national and international investment. Progress continues to be hampered by a critical lack of access to online content. This can be explained in terms of a general shortfall in investment in infrastructure and digitization programs as well as a range of other factors such as: fragmentation of existing high-value resources; restrictions of format; major gaps in data collections; and a lack of database interoperability and accessibility. But perhaps the greatest barrier to extending e-research to the humanities continues to be a resistance to change from the sector itself. Its conventional work practices are very well-established and there has historically been a reluctance to adopt new approaches that rely on fast-changing technology. For all the demonstrated advantages of e-research in other sectors, technology-enabled approaches in the humanities continue to occupy a border zone between old and new ways of working.

REFERENCES

ACLS. (2006). *Our cultural commonwealth: The report of the American council of learned societies commission on cyberinfrastructure for the humanities and social sciences*. Retrieved April 3, 2011 from http:// www.acls.org/ cyberinfrastructure/ ourculturalcommonwealth.pdf.

Blitzer, C. (1966). This wonderful machine: Some thoughts on the computer and the humanities. *ACLS Newsletter, 17*(4).

Bollier, D. (2002). Reclaiming the commons. *Boston Review*. Retrieved March 10, 2011 from http:// bostonreview.net/ BR27.3/ bollier.html.

Bollier, D. (2003). Artists, technology and the ownership of creative content. *Cultural Commons Portal*. Retrieved March 10, 2011 from http://www. culturalcommons.org/ comment-print.cfm?ID=10.

Cole, B. (2007). *Opening address by chairman of the national endowment for the humanities*. Paper presented at the Using New Technologies to Explore Cultural Heritage Conference. Retrieved April 13, 2011 from http:// www.neh. gov/ DigitalHumanities/ Conference_07Oct/ DH_Conference.html.

ESFRI. (2006). *European roadmap for research infrastructures report*. Retrieved April 3, 2011 from http:// ec.europa.eu/ research/ infrastructures/ pdf/ esfri/ esfri_roadmap/ roadmap_2006/ esfri_roadmap_ 2006_en.pdf.

ESFRI. (2008a). *European roadmap for research infrastructures, update*. Retrieved April 3, 2011 from http:// ec.europa.eu/ research/ infrastructures/ pdf/ esfri/ esfri_roadmap/ roadmap_2008/ esfri_roadmap_ update_2008.pdf.

ESFRI. (2008b). *European roadmap for research infrastructures, social sciences and humanities roadmap working group report*. Retrieved April 12, 2011 from http:// ec.europa.eu/ research/ infrastructures/ pdf/ esfri/ esfri_roadmap/ road-map_2008/ ssh_report_ 2008_en.pdf.

Genoni, P., Merrick, H., & Willson, M. (2006). Scholarly communities, e-research literacy and the academic librarian. *The Electronic Library, 24*(6), 734–746. doi:10.1108/02640470610714189

Goldenberg-Hart, D. (2004). *Libraries and changing research practices*. Retrieved April 15, 2011 from http:// www.arl.org/ forum04/ #proceedings.

Henninger, D. (2010). Commentary – World. *Wall Street Journal*. Retrieved from http://www.wsj.com.

Jakubowicz, A. (2007). Bridging the mire between e-research and e-publishing for multimedia digital scholarship in the humanities and social sciences: An Australian case study. *Webology, 4*(1). Retrieved April 16, 2011 from http:// www.webology.org/ 2007/ v4n1/a38.html.

Jankowski, N. (Ed.). (2009). *E-research: Transformation in scholarly practice*. New York, NY: Routledge.

Jirotka, M., Procter, R., Rodden, T., & Bowker, G. (2006). Editorial: Special issue, collaboration in e-research. *Computer Supported Cooperative Work, 15*(4), 251–255. doi:10.1007/s10606-006-9028-x

Kelly, K. (2008). World wide brain. *Age*. Retrieved March 10, 2011 from http:// businessnetwork. theage. com.au/ articles/ 2005/ 11/ 18/ 3491.html.

Kranich, N. (2004). *The information commons: A public policy report*. Retrieved March 10, 2011 from http:// www.fepproject.org/ policyreports/ infocommons.II.html.

Lee, D. (2003). Constructing the commons: Practical projects to build the information commons. *Knowledge Quest, 31*(4), 13–15.

Meyer, E., & Schroeder, R. (2009). Untangling the web of e-research: Towards a sociology of online knowledge. *Journal of Informetrics, 3*(3), 246–260. doi:10.1016/j.joi.2009.03.006

Research Information Network. (2011). *Reinventing research? Information practices in the humanities report*. Retrieved April 15, 2011 from http:// www.rin.ac.uk/ our-work/ using-and-accessing-information-resources/ information-use-case-studies-humanities.

Shepherd, D. (2007). *The access grid in collaborative arts and humanities research, final report of the arts and humanities research council (AHRC) workshops: E-science*. Retrieved April 16, 2011 from http:// www.ahessc.ac.uk/ files/ active/ 0/ AG-report.pdf.

Strategic Roadmap. (2011). *2011 strategic roadmap for Australian research infrastructure discussion paper*. Canberra, Australia: Australian Government. Retrieved April 7, 2011 from http:// www.innovation.gov.au/ science/ researchinfrastructure/ Pages/ default.aspx.

Turner, M. (1984). *Enclosures in Britain 1750-1830*. London, UK: Macmillan.

Yelling, J. A. (1977). *Common field and enclosure in England 1450-1850*. Hamden, CT: Archon Books.

ADDITIONAL READING

Anderson, T., & Kanuka, H. (2003). e-*Research: Methods strategies and issues*. Boston, MA: Pearson Education.

Barrett, A. (2005). The information-seeking habits of graduate student researchers in the humanities. *Journal of Academic Librarianship, 31*(4), 324–331. doi:10.1016/j.acalib.2005.04.005

Borgman, C. L. (2007). *Scholarship in the digital age: Information, infrastructure, and the internet*. Cambridge, MA: MIT Press.

British Academy. (2005). *E-resources for research in the humanities and social sciences: A British academy policy review*. London, UK: British Academy.

Buchanan, G., Cunningham, S. J., Blandford, A., Rimmer, J., & Warwick, C. (2005). Information seeking by humanities scholars. In *Proceedings of the 9th European Conference on Research and Advanced Technology for Digital Libraries,* (pp. 218-229). Berlin, Germany: Springer.

Burton, O. V. (Ed.). (2002). *Computing in the social sciences and humanities*. Urbana, IL: University of Illinois Press.

Castells, M. (1996). *The rise of the network society*. Oxford, UK: Blackwell.

Cole, C., & Craig, H. (Eds.). (2003). *Computing arts 2001: Digital resources for research in the humanities*. Sydney, Australia: University of Sydney.

ESFRI. (2009). *European roadmap for research infrastructures, implementation report*. Retrieved April 3, 2011 from http:// www.europarl.europa. eu/ meetdocs/ 2009_2014/ documents/ itre/ dv/ esfri_implementation_ report_2009_/ esfri_implementation_ report_2009_en.pdf.

Europa. (2007). *Trends in European research infrastructures: Analysis of data from the 2006/07 survey*. Retrieved April 3, 2011 from http:// ec.europa.eu/ research/ infrastructures/ pdf/ survey-report-july-2007_ en.pdf.

Europa. (2009a). *Emerging trends in socio-economic sciences and humanities in Europe: The METRIS report*. Retrieved April 3, 2011 from http:// ec.europa.eu/ research/ social-sciences/ pdf/ metris-report_ en.pdf.

Europa. (2009b). *FP7 socio-economic sciences and humanities, indicative strategic research roadmap 2011-2013*. Retrieved April 3, 2011 from http:// ec.europa.eu/ research/ social-sciences/ pdf/ roadmap-2011-2013-final_ en.pdf.

Europa. (2010). *Synergies between FP7 and structural funds for research infrastructures, report*. Retrieved April 3, 2011 from http:// ec.europa. eu/ research/ infrastructures/ pdf/ synergies-fp-sfmappingesfriprojects. pdf.

Genoni, P., Willson, M., & Merrick, H. (2009). E-research and scholarly community in the humanities. In Jankowski, N. W. (Ed.), *E-Research Transformation in Scholarly Practice* (pp. 91–108). London, UK: Routledge.

Hess, C., & Ostrom, E. (2003). Ideas, artifacts, and facilities: Information as a common-pool resource. *Law and Contemporary Problems, 66*(1), 114–118.

Houghton, J. W., Steele, C., & Henty, M. (2003). *Changing research practices in the digital information and communication environment*. Canberra, Australia: Department of Education, Science and Training.

Inman, J. A., Reed, C., & Sands, P. (Eds.). (2004). *Electronic collaboration in the humanities: Issues and options*. Mahwah, NJ: Lawrence Erlbaum.

JISC e-Research. (2012). *Website*. Retrieved 18 January 2012, from http://www.jisc.ac.uk/whatwedo/themes/eresearch.aspx.

Kirkham, R., Pybus, J., Bowman, A. K., Crowther, C., Fraser, M., & Jirotka, M. (2006). *Building a virtual research environment for the humanities: Report of the user requirements survey*. Oxford, UK: Oxford University/JISC. Retrieved April 3, 2011 from http:// bvreh.humanities.ox.ac.uk/ files/ User_requirementsBVREH. doc.

Mattelart, A. (2000). *Networking the world, 1794-2000*. Minneapolis, MN: University of Minnesota Press.

Monash e-Research. (2012). *Website*. Retrieved 18 January 2012, from http://www.monash.edu. au/eresearch/about/services.html.

O'Gorman, M. (2006). *E-crit: Digital media, critical theory and the humanities*. Toronto, Canada: University of Toronto Press.

OECD. (2008). *Global science forum, report on roadmapping of large research infrastructures*. Retrieved April 3, 2011 from http:// www.oecd. org/ dataoecd/ 49/ 36/ 41929340.pdf.

Rizzuto, C. (2010). *Inspiring excellence research infrastructures and the Europe 2020 strategy.* Retrieved April 3, 2011 from http:// ec.europa. eu/ research/ infrastructures/ pdf/ esfri/ home/ esfri_inspiring_ excellence.pdf.

Turner, G. (2008). *Towards an Australian humanities digital archive: Scoping paper.* Canberra, Australia: Australian Academy of the Humanities.

KEY TERMS AND DEFINITIONS

Cultural Informatics: Cultural information management in online environments.

Digital Humanities: The application of computing methods to humanities scholarship.

e-Humanities: A variant on 'digital humanities' (see above).

Humanities Computing: A term sometimes used interchangeably with 'digital humanities' (see above). While this term is longer established it is now less commonly used.

Hyper-Media: Interactive media in networked information environments.

Virtual Heritage: Information technology for the recording and display of cultural heritage. Virtual heritage is the more common term in Australasia, with 'cultural heritage and technology' favored in Europe.

ENDNOTES

[1] The term 'humanities' is used in this chapter to refer to the range of disciplines generally covered by the terms 'arts,' 'social sciences,' and 'humanities.'

[2] Picture Australia. (2011). *Website.* Retrieved April 15, 2011, from http://www.pictureaustralia.org.

[3] Confluence. (2011). *Website.* Retrieved April 15, 2011, from http://www.atlassian.com/ sofware/confluence/default.jsp.

[4] e-Humanities Gateway. (2011). *Website.* Retrieved from http://www.rihss.usyd.edu. au/research/projects/ehumanities_gateway. shtml. The e-Humanities Network and Gateway, supported by the Australian Research Council, the University of Sydney, the University of Newcastle, and the Australian Academy of the Humanities, offered great promise but has become inactive.

[5] Academy Survey. (2011). *Website.* Retrieved April 15, 2011, from http://www.humanities. org.au/Policy/HumTech/default.htm.

[6] Academy Symposium. (2011). *Website.* Retrieved April 15, 2011, from http://symposium.humanities.org. au.

[7] VeRSI. (2011). *Website.* Retrieved April 16, 2011, from https://www.versi.edu.au/.

[8] Intersect. (2011). *Website.* Retrieved April 16, 2011, from http://www.intersect.org.au/.

[9] Powerhousemuseum. (2011). *Website.* Retrieved April 16, 2011, from http://www. powerhousemuseum.com/museumexchange/index.php/archives/ 145.

[10] Austlit. (2011). *Website.* Retrieved April 16, 2011, from http://www.austlit.edu.au/.

[11] PARADISEC. (2011). *Website.* Retrieved April 16, 2011, from http://www.paradisec. org.au/.

[12] Archaeological Computing Laboratory. (2011). *Website.* Retrieved April 16, 2011, from http://www.acl.arts.usyd.edu.au.

[13] The author of this article was a member of the Expert Working Group that advised the Australian Government on matters relating to research infrastructure in the humanities in early 2011, which led to the publication of the Discussion Paper referred to here.

[14] CESSDA. (2011). *Website.* Retrieved April 16, 2011, from http://www.cessda.org/.

[15] CLARIN. (2011). *Website.* Retrieved April 16, 2011, from http://www.clarin.eu/external/.

[16]   DARIAH. (2011). *Website.* Retrieved April 16, 2011, from http://www.dariah.eu/.

[17]   European Social Survey. (2011). *Website.* Retrieved April 16, 2011, from http://www.europeansocialsurvey.org/.

[18]   Share Project. (2011). *Website.* Retrieved April 16, 2011, from http://www.share-project.org/.

[19]   HASTAC. (2011). *Website.* Retrieved April 15, 2011, from http://www.hastac.org.

[20]   An example of a formal international structure for networked cross-disciplinary research is the Australian Research Council's recently launched 'Centre of Excellence for the History of the Emotions.' Writing in the *Australian* newspaper Luke Slattery describes it as "a collaboration between 11 universities – five Australian and six European….[It] is funded to the tune of $24.25million across 7 years and puts Australian researchers into a global orbit with colleagues working over a range of disciplines." Luke Slattery, 'Centre to uncover the essence of Humanity.' Slattery, Luke. (2011, June 1). Centre to uncover the essence of humanity. *The Australian*, p. 29.

[21]   Project Bamboo. (2011). *Website.* Retrieved July 14, 2011, from http://www.projectbamboo.org/about/.

[22]   Phase 1 partner institutions are: Australian National University, Indiana University, Northwestern University, Tufts University, University of California, Berkeley, University of Chicago, University of Illinois, Urbana-Champaign, University of Maryland, University of Oxford, and University of Wisconsin, Madison.

[23]   HUBzero, a platform to create dynamic websites for scientific research, was developed by Purdue University. HUBzero. (2011). *Website.* Retrieved from http://hubzero.org.

Chapter 6
Data Sharing in CSCR:
Towards In–Depth Long Term Collaboration

Christophe Reffay
Ecole Normale Supérieure de Cachan, France & Ecole Normale Supérieure de Lyon, France

Gregory Dyke
Carnegie Mellon University, USA

Marie-Laure Betbeder
Université de Franche-Comté, France

ABSTRACT

In this chapter, the authors show the importance of data in the research process and the potential benefit for communities to share research data. Although most of their references are taken from the fields of Computer Supported Collaborative Learning and Intelligent Tutoring Systems, they claim that their argument applies to any other field studying complex situations that need to be analyzed by different disciplines, methods, and instruments. The authors point out the evolution of scientific publication, especially its openness and the variety of its emerging forms. This leads them to propose corpora as boundary objects for various communities in the scientific sphere. Data release being itself a complex problem, the authors use the Mulce[1] experience to show how sharable data can be built and made available. Once corpora are considered available, they discuss the potential of their reuse for multiple analyses or derivation. They focus on analytic representations and their combination with initial data or complementary analytic representations by presenting a tool named Tatiana. Finally, the authors propose their vision of data sharing in a world where scientists would use social network applications.

DOI: 10.4018/978-1-4666-0125-3.ch006

INTRODUCTION

In the research process, data is crucial and often hard to collect. Researchers spend a lot of time designing studies and collecting, transforming, analyzing, or interpreting data. Once analyzed and communicated in some publication by a local research team, data is often lost and can't be re-used by anybody. This means that other researchers have no access to original data to deepen their understanding by replicating an analysis or comparing their own results on the same data with a slightly different analysis method.

In this chapter, we would like to draw the state of the art in data sharing among research communities and, in particular, to report the results of the Mulce project[1]. This project's main results are the design and creation of a data structure and a corresponding platform to share learning and teaching corpora. These results give the community a way to access, share, analyze and visualize learning and teaching corpora.

This work has been motivated by the lack of impact of research results in the real world of online learning. In the CSCL (Computer Supported Collaborative Learning) research for example, a very wide range of indicators on collaboration have been designed and prototyped in a particular context but almost none of them are reused in other situations or contexts. We argue in this chapter that our research community should be able to widen the validity of its results by sharing data, tools and analyses performed with these tools.

In their work on the coding and counting analysis methodology, Rourke, Anderson, Garrisson, and Archer (2001) have pointed out the weakness of our research domain. Replicability, reliability and objectivity need to be improved in our work. The main idea of research collaboration is well expressed by (Chan, et al., 2006) in the following terms:

"There is urgent need of putting together complementary strengths and contexts and combining our insights as rapidly as possible to make a greater impact and further elevate our research quality at the same time. Research generally has had a small voice in national educational outcomes; we can speak louder if we speak together." (Chan et al., 2006)

Considering e-Research as an efficient way to meet and collaborate, this chapter suggests that e-collaboration could provide emerging communities with tools and virtual places to actually share their data, analyses and results in order to improve their theories, knowledge and tools. Although the focus of our work is on CSCL, we argue that this proposal is not limited to this domain or even to its contributing disciplines, and that the core ideas and benefits of our proposal can be extrapolated to other fields of research.

In the remainder of the chapter, we first examine current trends in scientific publication and the central role played by data in the scientific process. We then highlight the particular problem posed by data collection and replication in learning-related research and examine the state of the art for data sharing within this context. The Mulce proposal for constructing and sharing learning and teaching corpora is presented in detail, followed by the Tatiana framework for creating and re-using analytic representations. We conclude by drawing up our vision of data sharing within the learning sciences field and describe how other fields can draw upon our experience to construct data and analysis sharing models of their own.

Evolution in Scientific Publication

Who is producing knowledge? Nowadays, this process is no longer limited to academic researchers and prestigious journals. Civil society including local, national and international organizations is bringing its truth in various areas like economy, education, environment science, etc. Forms of publication are also evolving from classical journal articles to virtual exhibitions, datasets, software tools, etc., or any combination of these elements allowing participants to find new spaces to further explain, demonstrate, or exemplify their theories with renewed modes of creativity.

For many reasons, open access is becoming the rule. Because of the unacceptable delay of release of articles in scientific journals, in comparison to the fast obsolescence of their results, physicists prefer the Open Archives Initiative. Gentil-Beccot, Mele, and Brooks (2009) shows that 97% of the publications used by the community of nuclear research scientists, were freely available as pre-prints. It also indicates that publications that are available as preprints are cited 5 times more than others, and that the citation peak occurs before the release of the journal publication. In the footprints of physicians, considering that knowledge, published in scientific journal, should be accessible for anybody in the world (including developing countries), many scientific communities have oriented part of their articles toward open access journals. The Directory of Open Access Journals (http://www.doaj.org/), created in 2002, counted (at the end of year 2002) 31 journals coming from 7 countries. In August 2011, the DOAJ counts 6920 indexed open journals coming from 112 countries. More recently, many publishers (either private or public) joined in the Open Access Scholarly Publishing Association (http://www.oaspa.org/), created in 2009 and organized their first conference in Lund (Sweden) in September 2009. In their discussions, we should mention the questions of economic models, transparency (scientific quality, reviewing process, metadata of their publications), impact factor, prestige, software tools (e.g. Open Journal Software) (PKP, 2010; Edgar & Willinsky, 2010), citations and references links persistence (e.g.: Digital Object Identifier) (Bilder, 2009) and the variety of publication types (exhibition spaces, datasets, books, articles, etc.). An ambitious project entitled "Sponsoring Consortium for Open Access Publishing in Particle Physics" (http://www.scoap3.org) presented by Mele (2009) is building a new economic model

where publication costs would be endorsed by each country, according to the number of articles they submit. Considering the rate of scientific production in some domains (e.g. medicine), it is simply impossible for a single researcher or even for a well organized team, to keep up to date. Consequently, using semantic web techniques, a new format, namely "nano-publication" is suggested by Velterop (2009). Such a nano-publication would represent only the substrate of the published results in the form of RDF statements indexed in an open access database so that all researchers may be able to catch any new statement they are directly concerned with.

These few examples illustrate the speed, magnitude and depth at which the scientific publication process is evolving. We think that time has come for us to surf this wave in order to help our research community to share not only the articles and results, but also data and even analysis processes (methods or tools) that produce these results. The next two sections recall the central role of data in the scientific process and the importance for sciences that consider complex situations to share their data collections.

Data: At the Very Core of the Research Process

Most (if not all) areas of research involve a cycle with the following steps: define a research question, collect data, transform data in various ways, and produce statements which are the answer to the research question (Fisher & Sanderson, 1996). The epistemological framework within which research is conducted will define the kinds of question, data, analysis methodology and type of answer which are acceptable. For example, hypothetico-deductive research will typically require setting up a research question with competing hypotheses, collecting data in various conditions, performing statistical analysis and producing statements about robustness of results across conditions, or of causality/correlation between conditions and results. Certain fields of research (typically study of human behavior in authentic situations) have broad epistemological agreement that certain kinds of data can be collected with no research question in mind or that data collected with regard to a given research question is generic enough to be used to answer different questions (e.g. the Augmented Multi-Party Interaction [AMI] meeting Corpus [Carletta, 2007], telephone conversations [Godfrey, et al., 1992], etc.). Given that one of the major costs of research is data collection, it makes economical sense to exploit and share data as much as possible.

Furthermore, within collaborations at various levels (grad students and faculty supervisors, in the context of a laboratory or of a project, etc.), not only should data be shared, but sharing the various analytic representations created during data analysis can also be beneficial: better reliability can be achieved in subjective analysis if identical independent analyses are performed (De Wever, Schellens, Valcke, & Van Keer, 2006), researchers can collaborate to extend the applicability of an analytical method to a new domain of application (e.g. Lund, Prudhomme, & Cassier, 2007), researchers can spread the workload (Goodman, et al., 2006), or can combine the insights of several analysts (e.g. Prudhomme, Pourroy, & Lund, 2007). Last, in situations where different epistemologies are united around shared data, the lack of commensurability between methodologies and between acceptable types of results can result in data being the only focal point from which productive discussion and mutual understanding is possible.

King (2007), involved in the *Dataverse* project (http://www.dataverse.org), found many benefits for the scientific community to make the data available. We can summarize some of them here:

- **Recognition** for the author: any other researcher that would reuse his/her data would of course cite the corresponding publication, increasing its value and then,

the value of the collection it belongs to, i.e.: book, journal or conference proceeding. Articles in journals with replication policies that make data available are cited three times as frequently as otherwise equivalent articles without accessible data (Gleditsch, Metelits, & Strand 2003).

- **Transparency**: making the data verifiable, authorized and persistent should give more credit to results of a publication.
- **Replication**: in many complex situations, it is unfeasible to replicate the study in exactly the same conditions. In such situations, replication of analysis can be performed on the original data if they are shared.

Data Sharing to Face Complexity in Education Science

In education science and education technology, situations involving (several) human beings are far too complex to be replicable. For example, let us suppose that a publication shows a result R_1 in a situation S_1. If another team attempts to reproduce in S_2, the same situation as S_1 (same pedagogical scenario, same instructor, same school, same level, same age, etc.) for the next cohort of learners, it is not certain at all that result R_1 will be confirmed in situation S_2. There are a number of factors already pointed out in the literature, that may be the source of this: the higher experience of the instructor; the simple fact that learners are different; the world changes between S_1 and S_2 (news, crisis, art, technology, etc.) or even a slightly different timetable for learners that brings the observed sessions at an earlier or later time... Especially when we deal with collaboration or interaction analysis, we know that learners build their interaction on their own experience. In the constructivist theory, this is even considered as a basic hypothesis for learning in general. This experience being in constant evolution for everybody, a same learner cannot be in the same conditions for two sequential situations S_1 and S_2. Experience being unique for anybody, two different learners cannot be considered in the same conditions in a given situation. It is even more complex to replicate a given situation (S_1) for a group of learners because you have to take into account not only the (sum of) experience variation between these two groups of learners, but also the history of interaction between pairs of participants (learners and instructor).

Until now, the most frequent case in our scientific field is that we can read a publication that shows results on a given situation, but we have no access to the data collection from which these results have been derived. In most of the cases, we only have a general description of the situation, the data collection and the derivation processes. This state of facts prevents the scientific community from deeper discussion; better comparisons and understanding that could be obtained by the following new derivation processes in case of data sharing:

- Replication of the (same) analysis on the same data using the same analysis process either to understand in detail the analysis process or to verify it;
- Replication of the analysis on the same data but using a different analysis process for comparison of analysis processes;
- Derivation of a secondary analysis on the same data, for example trying to find other results on a different facet of the same data;
- Derivation of a complementary analysis on the same data that builds new results by using the previous outputs;
- Analysis of correlation between results (of different facets) of the same data collection.

When studying collaboration or interaction in learning groups, one way to face the complexity of such situations is to get various analyses with different points of view, in order to evaluate the

conditions under which various results co-occur in the different derivations of a given dataset.

Beyond all these new possible derivations, the community would also gain in maturity by exchanging analysis process experiences, teaching and learning more consensual processes and having an available test bed for anybody who wants to perform such analysis processes. In addition, for the technological part of our research, these available data collections may also be useful to test or calibrate new instruments or indicators. Finally, for the most studied collection data, the corresponding situation gains in accuracy on different facets and becomes interesting (for tests) for its well known characteristics. For the most popular datasets, this can lead to well referenced datasets.

Instead of having hundreds of unclassified learning situations, where the data of each are available only to the researchers that built them, we argue that our communities would gain maturity and deepen their understanding by sharing some of the representative situations. Such data could be used as a test-bed for the variety of indicators or methods to analyze various facets of the collaboration.

The Potential of Links between Data, Analysis, and Results

For scientific fairness, data should be available for all discussants. Exposing data and analyses (and not only results) has great potential: deeper understanding and argumentation, articulation of various analyses on the same data. This can lead to in depth discussion of results or relation between complementary results brought by different disciplines. From a methodological point of view, as is the case for any multi-disciplinary project, again, this can also induce a wider spread of methods and tools among involved disciplines.

Considering the structural links between a dataset, its various derivative analysis processes and results, this can lead to a hierarchical representation (i.e. a tree) where the root would be the initial shared dataset and the nodes the derivative analyses, publication and results. As already mentioned by (King, 2007), the fact that a given publication is associated with a data collection makes its analysis process replicable. As well known properties of in- and out-degrees in Social Network Analysis, we can hypothesize that: the longer the list of results and publication that derive from a single dataset (high out-degree for the dataset), the higher the citation index for dataset and derivative publications will be.

DATA SHARING: AN OVERVIEW OF RELATED WORKS

For the Intelligent Tutoring System (ITS) field, the PSLC DataShop presented in (Koedinger, et al., 2008) provides a data repository including datasets and a set of associated visualization and analysis tools. These data can be uploaded as well-formed XML documents that conform to the Tutor_message schema. The goal is to improve the Intelligent Tutoring Systems (ITS) the data are logged from. The datasets are fine-grained, principally automatically generated by ITS and focus on action/feedback interaction between learners and (virtual) tutor tools.

In the CSCL community, a very interesting framework: DELFOS (Osuna, et al., 2001) provides similar proposals as the Mulce project. It defines an XML based data structure (Martinez, et al., 2003) for collaborative actions in order to promote interoperability (between analysis tools), readability (either for human analysts or automated tools) and adaptability to different analytic perspectives. Some of these authors joined the European research project on Interaction Analysis (JEIRP–IA) and reported in (Martinez, et al., 2005) a template describing Interaction Analysis tools and a common format. This common format should be automatically obtained from Learning Support Environments (by an XSL transformation)

and either directly processed by new versions of Interaction Analysis tools, or automatically transformed in their original data source format to be processed by previous versions of theses tools. The resulting common format focuses more on technical interoperability than on learning context or human readability. The context is given for fine grain interaction.

In the Mulce structure, the learning situation and the research context are described as wholes, possibly in different formats (IMS-LD, LDL, Mot-Plus, simple text document, etc.) If they conform to IMS-LD, their identified included objects can be referred to by the list of acts that is recorded in the instantiation part. The nature of sharing perspectives is very different: in the JEIRP, the goal is to share a schema structure, whereas the Mulce platform's main objective is to share the data collections.

For this last issue, impressive work has been done in the Dataverse Network project described in (King, 2007). We agree with the members of this project that datasets have to be made available, or at least identified and recorded in a fixed state in order to make sure that data used for a given publication are the same as those identified and (hopefully) made available for other researchers.

In the Mulce project, we provide a technical framework to describe an authentic situation, described by a formal or informal learning design or detailed guidelines, with a representative number of actual participants, according to a research protocol. We also: define a "Learning and teaching Corpus," provide a technical XML format for such a corpus to be sharable and we are currently developing a technical platform for researchers to save, browse, search, extract and analyze online interactions in their context. The main idea of the Mulce project is to provide contextualized interaction data connected to published results.

Considering today's available technology, Markauskaite and Reimann drew an ideal research world in (Markauskaite & Reimann, 2008) where grid computing, middleware services, tools managing remote resources, open access to publications and data repositories, open and interactive forms of peer review process, constitute great potential for e-research. We globally share the same vision for the future of research. Even if we consider that the path to reach this ideal vision is rather long, the main contribution of this chapter can be considered as a modest but concrete step in this direction by presenting an example of data structure for a teaching and learning corpus (Letec) as well as a framework for analytic representation and manipulation (Tatiana).

Availability of data should enable deeper scientific discussion on previously published results. Other researchers may be able to verify or replicate the methods proposed. It becomes possible to compare methods on the same data and then discuss the result or the efficiency of the methods. This way, different analyses can be done on the same set of interaction data. Data may also be connected or compared to other available data. As another example of benefits (for the data provider) of data sharing, let us conclude with these illustrating words:

"Everybody makes mistakes. And if you don't expose your raw data, nobody will find your mistakes." -Jean-Claude Bradley (Wald, 2010)

MAKING DATA SHARABLE

Even if the willingness to share is a necessary element, unfortunately, it is far from being enough to make a collected raw dataset sharable with other researchers. According to our experience (Reffay, et al., 2008; Reffay & Betbeder, 2009), we consider that a given dataset is sharable, if it verifies at least the following properties:

- The context (of the situation) is explicit;
- The structure (of the dataset) is explicit and data are saved in files in open formats;

- The data are free of sensitive and personal information. Rights of publication and use are stated;
- The dataset is referenced by a unique identifier.

These properties are described in more detail in the following subsections.

Make the Context Explicit

Let us refer to an *internal* researcher when dealing with a researcher who belongs to the team that built the situation (or study) or collected or structured the dataset. Conversely, we will refer to an *external* researcher when s/he did not take part of any of those processes. Then, the context elicitation of the situation (or study) is the process that collects all (implicit) information in the internal researcher's head or notes and organizes it in a document (or structure) so that external researchers can find all useful elements when interpreting the data themselves (interaction, learner's production, etc.). Even if this concept of context elicitation is easy to understand, it may be very difficult to achieve in the concrete acts and choices. In fact, the perimeter of *useful information* is different from one analysis to another, from one theory to another and even from one researcher to another. Moreover, some information that could be useful for a specific analysis (e.g. sociological/cultural/linguistic), may be undesirable for ethical reasons (e.g.: ethnic or geographical or cultural/linguistics origins). Now, even if some constraints are irreconcilable in very specific cases, we argue (1) that a lot of other analysis can be done without this undesirable information and (2) that special contracts between respectable research teams are often possible and may lead to an arrangement that may be of benefit to both.

As a positive side effect, even without making the data available for other teams, the simple fact of making the context explicit for any other research also serves the internal research team itself and confers longevity (or even immortality) to the dataset. Newcomers (newly recruited researchers) in the team will be able to re-use this dataset and discuss it with their colleagues despite the fact they are *external* researchers for this dataset. This can help in building a common ground/culture in a research team.

Make the Structure Explicit

We showed in the previous section that explicit context makes data readable (interpretable) for humans. In this section, we argue that explicit structure renders them human and machine readable (usable, computable). The main advantage of a well organized dataset is that any information (contained in the dataset) is easy to find for a human and possible to retrieve for an automated process. The very important corollary is that, if you can't find fixed information, it means this information does not exist in the dataset. In other words: every piece of information may have a single position in the dataset or may be duplicated in (or linked to) any other possible (logical) places.

Being related to computation tools used by the target scientific community, the data may be prepared for these tools in the corresponding formats. Otherwise, the structure should (at least) enable an automated translation to transform the selected format in the target tool's format. Note that it is not the responsibility of the dataset holder to produce the automated translation process. But if such a process already exists, it may be interesting (for the rest of the community) that the selected format (in which data have been actually stored) work as a direct input of this process. The various automated transformation processes may flourish afterwards and be built by some external researchers, interested in transforming the data into a specific (new) format. For the dataset, the ease of use may increase its value. In the CSCL Community, the XML based data structure proposed in (Martinez, et al., 2003) is a common format that enables centralized interoperability.

In order to enable such automated transformations, it is very important (for independence and longevity) to save original data in open formats (txt, rtf, csv, xml, bmp, mpeg, etc.) or very widely used formats (pdf, xls, sql, jpeg, avi, or mov).

Data being often heterogeneous and split into several files, it may be convenient to consider several levels of structure: a global level making clear where metadata, data, information, complementary resources, are and how they are related to one another, and a local or specific level, where we can find individual pieces of data (typically a text, a data table, an XML structure, …) whose organization must be explicit so that readers can take advantage of each of their information pieces. In the Mulce project we adopted the IMS-CP standard integration content package. Such a package is basically composed of a manifest (XML file) structured according to the corresponding schema (XSD) and a "content" folder containing any type and number of heterogeneous files. The last part of the manifest (list of referenced resources) describes and locates each of these files. The first part is generally dedicated to metadata; an arbitrary number of internal parts may be used to describe more specific data or information. We found XML particularly interesting for different reason: (1) it's increasingly widely adopted by different research communities, (2) it is simultaneously formal and malleable and (3) local tag names and parameters make the structure explicit in the innermost parts of wide and long lists repeating headers in each element description. This means that parts of an XML structure can be cut and paste maintaining their comprehensibility. Moreover, identifiers and references in XML structures may avoid repetition of key information or heavy blocks. These are good means to ensure coherence in the data structure.

Consider Ethical Perspectives

It is of particular importance to take into account rights and ethical aspects of data when dealing with long term conservation and widespread dissemination. Data may be free of sensitive (religion, ethnic, health specificities, etc.) and personal information (name, addresses, etc.). Either the dataset depositor received the appropriate permission from participants for all videos, photos and documents where they can be identified, or all documents have been anonymized (photos or videos blurred, names replaced by pseudonyms in text documents). Anonymization may be difficult and time consuming to achieve for some datasets. This may discourage some researchers from sharing their data. We argue that more support may be given to researchers to help them in this task. Efficient anonymization process and tools for each type of data may be developed to support researchers. Now, in case of interaction data in learning session, when participants are aware that they are taking part in a research experiment, sensitive data may not appear. Moreover, ethical committees may take into account the context of the experiment (data genesis) that should influence the risk (for participants) to release these data. Sometimes, ethical committees request destruction of data after a fixed period of time and put some restrictions on data diffusion.

Currently, research foundations such as NSF (that modified its policy in January 2011), are requesting for researchers who want to be funded to provide an explicit plan for data management and a justification in the case they don't share their data. Another initiative: the Panton Principles (www.pantonprinciples. org) were publicly launched in February of 2010. Four months later, about 100 individuals and organizations had endorsed the Principles. According to Pollock:

"It's commonplace that we advance by building on the work of colleagues and predecessors standing on the shoulders of giants. In a digital age, to build on the work of others we need something very concrete: access to the data of others and the freedom to use and reuse it. That's what the Panton Principles are about."

STRUCTURE OF THE CORPUS: THE MULCE PROPOSAL

The Mulce Project

We know how hard it is to build authentic learning situations. When we launched the Mulce project (Mulce, 2010), we thought it would be useful to add some more work on a data collection to structure and document it so that it could be reused later by other researchers or even be ourselves. As we had no ready-made structures to pack a Learning and Teaching Corpus (LETEC), we decided to define one, tentatively reusing standard bricks. One of the basic principles was to pack together a general description of the corpus with an arbitrary number of heterogeneous files. This brought us to use the IMS-CP (2011) specification to build our general package structure presented in the next section. We reused IMS-LD (2011) for context description (Learning Design and Research Protocol) and IMS-MD (2011) for general metadata of the corpus. However, we built a new XML schema for the core component (namely Instantiation) that can contain the data (production and interaction) of the learning situation.

Description of the Package Structure

In this section, we first present the main phases involved in this methodological process. Then, we give the derived definition of a "learning and teaching corpus" and explore the structure of its main components.

Building and Recording Interaction in an Online Course

A general organization for an online study is illustrated in Figure 1.

In a first stage, the educational scenario is described at an abstract level, by defining the educational prerequisites and objectives, the abstract roles (learner, tutor, etc.), the learning ac-

Figure 1. Building a research study for an online course: chronology

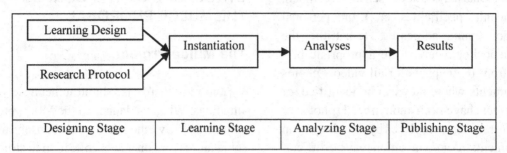

tivities and the support activities with their respective environments (abstract tools, e.g. chat, forum, etc.) When the course has to be observed for a research study, the researchers define on the one hand the research questions and objectives and on the other hand the list of observable events to be logged. This documentation makes explicit the research protocol or context of the study: i.e. what will be evaluated, are there pre- or post- tests, or participant interviews or questionnaires? In the second stage, the learning situation actually takes place. The abstract roles (designed in both parts of the first stage) are endorsed by real participants, and abstract environments have been implemented in particular platforms including identified tools and virtual (instantiated) spaces. This is the instantiation phase where embodied learners and tutors actually run the activities and identified processes or researchers collect their observable actions (interactions and productions). Specific activities designed in the research protocol may also take place during this period: e.g. pre- or post- tests, interviews, etc. At the end of the learning stage, i.e. when learners and tutors are gone, the collected data can be structured and analyzed by researchers. These analyses hopefully lead to research publications that summarize the context and the methodology and emphasize the results. The data collection is generally not disseminated.

Both documentations of the design phase describe the context of the experimentation. The instantiation phase produces the core data collection that is analyzed in the third stage. In order to make this data collection sharable with external researchers, we show how the various phases presented above become the main components of the corpus defined hereafter.

Learning and Teaching Corpus (Letec): Definition

We define a Learning and Teaching Corpus as a structured entity containing all the elements resulting from an on-line learning situation, whose context is described by an educational scenario and a research protocol. The core data collection includes all the interaction data, the course participants' production, and the tracks, resulting from the participants' actions in the learning environment and stored according to the research protocol. In order to be sharable, and to respect participant privacy, these data should be anonymized and a license for their use be provided in the corpus. A derived analysis can be linked to the set of data actually considered, used or computed for this analysis. An analysis consisting in a data annotation/transcription/transformation, properly connected to its original data, can be merged into the corpus itself, in order for other researchers to compare their own results with a concurrent analysis or to build their complementary analysis upon these previous shared results.

The definition of a Learning and Teaching Corpus as a whole entity comes from the need of explicit links, between interaction data, context and analyses. This explicit context is crucial for an external researcher to interpret the data and to perform their own analyses.

The general idea of this definition intends to grasp the context of the data stemming from the course to allow a researcher to look for, understand and connect this information even though he was not present during the learning (data collection) stage.

Corpus Composition and Structure

The main components of a Letec: Learning and Teaching Corpus (see Figure 2) are:

- The Instantiation component, the heart of the corpus, which includes all the interaction data, productions of the on-line course participants, completed by some system logs as well as information characterizing participants' profiles.
- The Context concerns the educational scenario and the optional research protocol.

- The License component specifies both corpus publisher's (editor) and users' rights and the ethical elements toward the participants of the course. A part of the license component is private, held only by the person in charge of the corpus. Only this private part may contain some personal information regarding the participants of the course.
- The Analysis component contains global or partial analyses of the corpus as well as possible transcriptions.

The Mulce structure aims at organizing the components of the corpus in a way that enables linking subparts of components together. For example a researcher, while reading a chat session (in the instantiation component), must be able to read the objectives of the activity in which this chat session took place (the activity is described in the pedagogical context, i.e. Learning Design component).

Figure 2. Teaching and learning corpus: the main components in a content package

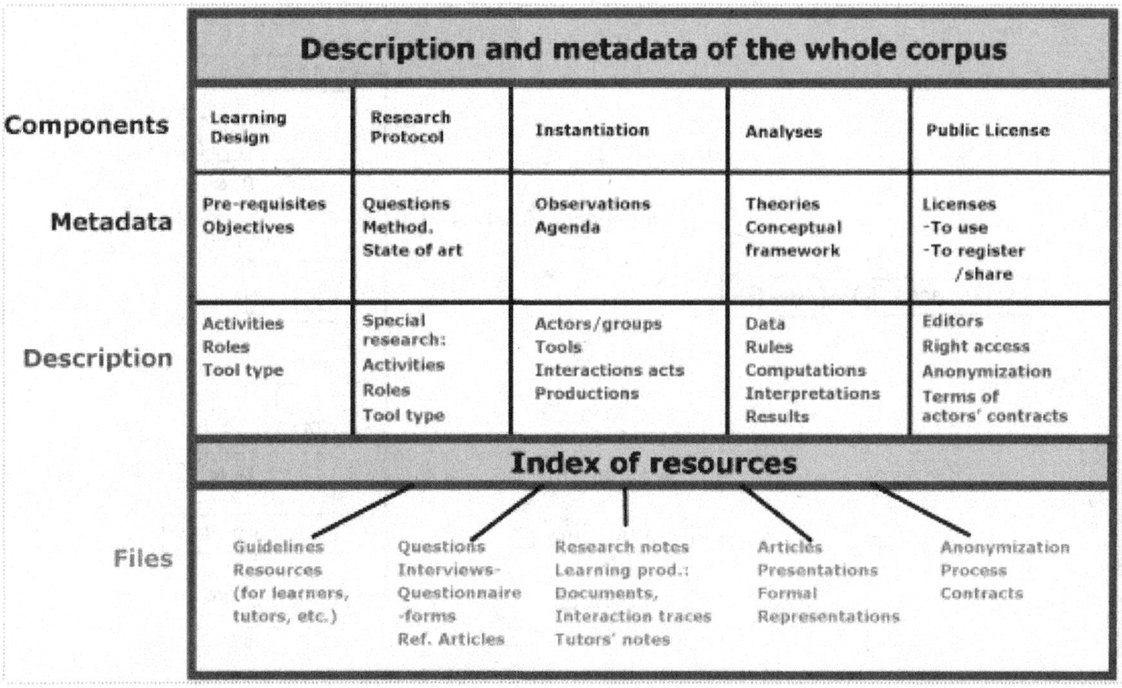

Description and metadata of the whole corpus					
Components	Learning Design	Research Protocol	Instantiation	Analyses	Public License
Metadata	Pre-requisites Objectives	Questions Method. State of art	Observations Agenda	Theories Conceptual framework	Licenses -To use -To register /share
Description	Activities Roles Tool type	Special research: Activities Roles Tool type	Actors/groups Tools Interactions acts Productions	Data Rules Computations Interpretations Results	Editors Right access Anonymization Terms of actors' contracts
Index of resources					
Files	Guidelines Resources (for learners, tutors, etc.)	Questions Interviews- Questionnaire -forms Ref. Articles	Research notes Learning prod.: Documents, Interaction traces Tutors' notes	Articles Presentations Formal Representations	Anonymization Process Contracts

A standard exchange format is also required to download the whole corpus.

Considering these constraints, we chose the IMS-CP formalism (2011) as the global container. This XML formalism fits these constraints by expressing metadata, different levels of description, and an index pointing to the set of heterogeneous resources. In this container, each component is described as an "organization" element of the IMS-CP structure. Each of these can be structured either as basic IMS-CP organization or a more specific one. For example, Learning Design and Research protocol components can use IMS-LD structure as their organization model. If they are only described by a simple text, this text can be defined as an "item" element of the basic IMS-CP organization. For the Analyses component, we generally use a standard IMS-CP organization model. However, the Instantiation component is more specific and has to capture and organize the collected tracks of the situation, played out by the participants. It is the central component where all interaction data and logs may be recorded. In the Mulce project, we decided to define a special XML scheme for this organization: the Structured Interaction Data model (mce_sid, 2011). The next section gives the most important concepts of this model.

Description of the Core Component: Instantiation

The hierarchical structure of the learning stage is captured in the *workspaces* element that contains a sequence of *workspace* elements (see Figure 3). The *workspaces* element may also define: a list of *places* that organizes the space (i.e. each *place* element defines a reference and description of a virtual or physical place like chat room or classroom), a list of *sessions* that splits the time into meaningful periods (i.e. each *session* element defines a reference and description for a dedicated

Figure 3. Extract of the XML schema: the workspaces element

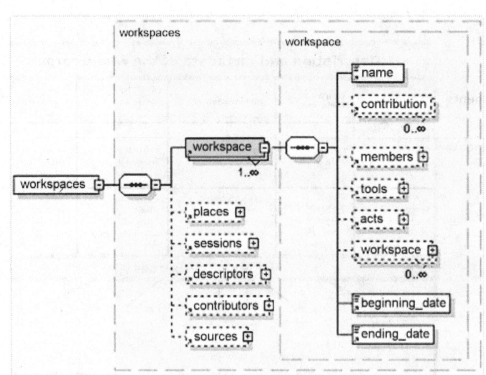

period of time like a chat session or any other [mainly] synchronous activity), a list of *descriptors* or tags that may be used by researchers in their analysis (by associating interaction acts to a set of these descriptors) in order to categorize or count units for each category, the complete list of *contributors* (researchers, developers, compilers, recorders, inputers, etc.) for the corpus and the list of *sources* (i.e. a *source* element is generally a reference to an audio or video record).

A *workspace* is generally linked to a learning activity (of the pedagogical scenario). It encompasses all the events observed during this activity, in the tool spaces provided for this activity, for a given (instantiated) group of participants. As shown in Figure 3, a *workspace* description includes its *members* (references to the participants registered in the learning activity), starting and ending dates, the provided *tools* and the tracks of interaction (*acts*) that occurred in these tools. In order to fit the hierarchical structure of learning and support activities, a *workspace* can recursively contain one or more *workspace* elements.

The lists of *places*, *sessions*, *descriptors*, *contributors* and *sources* defined in the *workspaces* element can be referenced by *workspace*, *contribution*, or *act* elements. For example, *descriptors* may list identified categories so that each act of the acts element list could refer to one or more of these categories. This principle enables browsing of the interaction data in many different ways, independent of the concrete storage organization in the XML document.

Our specification describes communication tools and their features with a great level of precision. The corpus builder can specialize/particularize the schema (i.e., restrict it) to fit the specific tools and features proposed to the learners in a specific learning environment. In the meantime, if a tool cannot be described with the specification, one can augment the schema by adding new elements, in order to take into account the tool's specificities. Restriction and extension are the mechanisms we offer to corpus builders,

to adapt our specification to their specific tools or analysis needs.

Moreover, recursive *workspace* descriptions enable the corpus compiler to choose the grain at which he needs to describe the environment. Thus, a workspace can be used to describe a complete curriculum, a semester, a module, a single activity or a work session (a concept generally related to synchronous learning activities). The workspace concept represents the space and time location where we can find interaction with identified tools. This concept has the same modularity as the EML learning units (Koper, 2001; Mce_sid, 2011).

Devices and tools within which interaction occurs can be as different as a forum, a blog, a chat or collaborative production tools (e.g., a conceptual map editor, a collaborative word processor, a collaborative drawing tool).

Interaction tracks are stored according to the *act*'s structure presented in Figure 4. All actions, wherever they come from, are described by an *act* element. An *act* necessarily refers to its *author* identifier (defined in the members list—Figure 3), and a *beginning_date*. Depending on the nature of the act (*act_type*), an optional ending_date can be specified. The *act_type* element is a selector. The actual content (or value) of the act depending on its type, is stored in the appropriate structure.

For example, a *chat act* (see Figure 5) can have the type in/out (participant entering/leaving), it may contain a *message*, can be addressed to all the workspace members or to a specific one (e.g. if it is a private message). A *chat act* can contain an attached document (*file*) which in turn is described by a *name*, a *type* and a *date*.

Optional element *comment* (Figure 4) contains a sequence typed text of any type and can be used to store researchers' annotations. The last optional element of the *act*'s structure (*any*) leads to any extension not provided in our schema.

This XML Schema defines the storage structure for many act types, e.g.: forum message, chat act,

Figure 4. Extract from the XML schema: the act concept

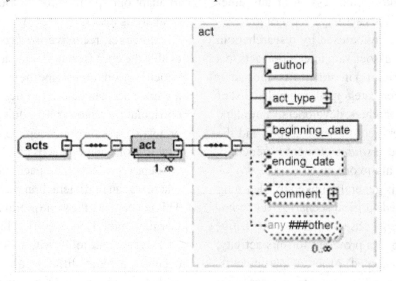

transcribed voice act, blogs and more. This chapter only gives some of the main ideas of this schema, but the complete schema for structured information data is available online (Mce_sid, 2011).

The definition, composition and structure of a Learning & Teaching Corpus have been presented in the sections above. The next one explains how these data structures can be available throughout Open Archives and specific platforms.

MAKING YOUR DATA AVAILABLE

At this point, we can consider that data structure is explicit and context has been documented. When data are correctly aggregated in a formalized package, we have to specify some metadata according to the search need users may have. In our case of learning and teaching corpora (in Language learning field) we decided to use the following metadatasets:

- IMS-MD (2011): general metadata for a content package, including Dublin Core specifications (Powell, Nilsson, Naeve, Johnston & Baker, 2008);
- LOM (2002): Learning Object Meta-data;

- OLAC (2007) meta-data: Open Language Archive Community: collections of data in various languages or concerning languages.

Because metadata characterize data, they can serve several objectives: an object description summary, detailed characterization of the object in various classifications, specific description for referencing, etc. Even if a given corpus is not intended to be widely spread on the network, it could be important (for authorship and precedence reasons) to define its metadata and make them widely available.

In the Mulce project, the 34 objects named corpora (currently registered) can be entirely downloaded by any registered user (Mulce Platform, 2011). Each of these objects encapsulates its own metadata. An exhaustive list of all (general) metadata of all registered objects is stored and maintained in the static repository (i.e. a simple XML file available at a specified URL [Mulce-SR, 2011]). This XML file is harvested daily by the OLAC server that makes them widely visible and responds to any OAI request concerning the Mulce collection. This way, we can be sure that our objects are widely visible and searchable on the web. Moreover, each of the corpora has a unique

Figure 5. Extract from the XML schema: the chat act concept

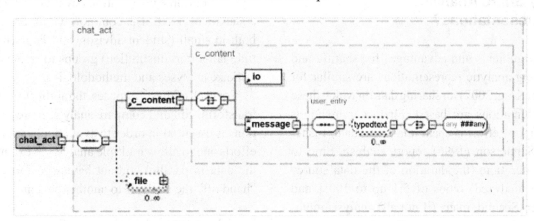

identifier that can be cited by any researcher who may reuse its content for: scientific discussion, comparative or complementary analysis.

LINKING DATA AND ANALYSES

Once the infrastructure for sharing data has been considered and has been put in place, the natural question of what can be done with these data arises. Already, in the Mulce structure of a corpus, we consider that transcriptions might form part of the primarily shared data and assign a component for analyses on that corpus. In various fields of research (e.g. Conversational Analysis vs. Content Analysis), different standards are expected of transcription and different "authority" is given to the transcription. In conversational analysis (Sacks, Schegloff, & Jefferson, 1974), Jeffersonian notation is used for a transcription which includes pauses, vowel lengths, overlaps between speakers and voice intonation. Such a transcription is kept as objective as possible but is nevertheless not generally considered an acceptable substitute for the original audio or video. On the other hand, for Content Analysis (De Wever, Schellens, Valcke, & Van Keer, 2006), a transcription can be more subjective, including the editorialisation of sentences (which do not naturally exist in spoken language), and the omission of false starts. The

subjectivity of the transcription is embraced and subsequent analyses usually trust the transcription as a proxy for the video.

Such practices hint at the idea that secondary artifacts and representations, constructed from the primary data during the analytic process, have different roles in different scientific communities. They are also judged "valid" by a variety of standards. For example in Content Analysis, utterances are typically coded according to a coding scheme laid out by the researcher. A second researcher codes a subset of the data, using the same scheme. The Kappa statistic (Cohen, 1968) is then used to assess the extent to which agreement amongst the researchers is better than chance.

In both the examples of transcription and coding, the researcher constructs an object which is later to be used as a substitute for, or in combination with, the original data. In this section, we examine such analytic artifacts in the field of CSCL. We first examine some of the roles they could play if they were shared in the same way that we suggest data be shared throughout this chapter. We then present a case study describing our experience in sharing data as the focus of a series of workshops in multivocal CSCL analysis. Last we describe the Tatiana framework, which lays out the requirements and a proposed solution for describing and sharing a subset of these "secondary" analytic artifacts.

Why Share Analytic Representations?

The arguments and advantages for sharing and re-using analytic representations are similar for those (King, 2007) for sharing data on which these representations are based. First, a tremendous amount of effort is spent analyzing data. Fisher and Sanderson (1996) report analysis time to sequence time (the duration of the data source being analyzed) ratios of 5:1 up to 100:1 and higher. Second, many (if not all) analysis methods (e.g. Content Analysis) insert steps between the primary data and the final result. How is a reviewer to evaluate an analysis if only the primary data and not the coded data are made available to them? Third, new analyses can be performed more quickly and find results that are more profound by taking a previous analysis as a starting point, rather than as a competing analysis. Such a hermeneutic view is common in fields which analyze corpora that will no longer be extended (e.g. the Bible for theological research, Corpus Iuris Civilis for legal research, etc.).

Furthermore, there are many advantages to analyzing within a team. As exemplified by Content Analysis, several analytic methodologies use inter-rater reliability to validate a new analytic artifact. In this method, two researchers independently perform the same subjective analytic manipulation and compare their resulting artifacts for which a certain amount of agreement must be met. Well modeled analytic representations can easily allow such agreement to be computed automatically. Goodman et al. (2006) describe an analytic tool which they use to distribute the workload among several analysts. Making it easy to piece together the resulting analytic fragments removes the reluctance a coordinator might otherwise feel. Prudhomme, Pourroy, and Lund (2007) describe an analysis in which the multiple perspectives of argumentation and collaborative design iteratively come together to show how multiple criteria are leveraged to evaluate solutions, much in the same way that multiple justifications are used to defend a statement. Last, it is common within projects both in small (student-advisor) and large (multiple laboratory/institution) groups to refine and criticize analyses and methodologies.

For each of these purposes, the ability to share, transform, edit and compare analytic representations is essential in order to avoid duplication of efforts and to allow multiple analysts to examine the data in parallel without having to formally "hand off" the analysis to another person.

Building Inter-Disciplinarity: An Experience

In the field of CSCL, there is a common agreement in the positive value of collaborative learning. However, there is some disagreement as to exactly what constitutes collaborative learning and why it should be educationally effective (Suthers, 2006). The diversity of epistemological beliefs and research methodologies has led several researchers to question how such a plurality could become a source of productive scientific discourse rather than disagreement or balkanization. A series of 5 workshops were conducted, from 2008 to 2011, to address this issue. Some preliminary results of this effort were reported in Suthers et al. (2011). Initial workshops focused on examining five analytic dimensions: epistemological assumptions, purpose of analysis, units of interaction that are taken as the basis of analysis, representations of data and analytic interpretations, and analytic manipulations taken on these representations. Discussions about these dimensions proved productive but did not indicate how or whether different approaches could be reconciled. Sharing of datasets and multiple analyses on these datasets was then investigated, but it was frequently hard to determine to what differences in interpretation were due without being able to return to the primary data. In the final two workshops, to as great an extent as possible, analytic representations were shared and used to combine multiple viewpoints.

In one case study based on these workshops, Dyke et al. (2011) describe three analyses, which originally appeared to be so different as not to be able to inform each other. It was shown how a single visualization combining the viewpoint of two analysts directly on the primary data could illustrate the differences in belief the analysts had about collaborative learning.

Creating Reusable Analytic Representations: Tatiana

In this last case study, the Tatiana analysis tool (Dyke, Lund, & Girardot, 2009; Dyke, Lund, & Girardot, 2010) was used both to perform the initial analyses and to combine these analyses into a single representation. Tatiana is based on a framework which answers several requirements for analytic representation creation and sharing: the necessity of being able to use analytic representations both in combination with each other and with the primary data; the ability to create and share analytic representations based on a previously shared corpus; and the ability to combine and re-use existing analytic representations.

Tatiana (Trace Analysis Tool for Interaction ANAlysts) is an environment (and an underlying conceptual framework) designed for manipulating various kinds of analytic representations, in particular those that present a view on event-based data. We call these representations replayables, because they can be replayed in a similar fashion to a video. They are one of the major kinds of representations that researchers construct to analyze computer-mediated interaction.

Tatiana is built on a number of core concepts and components. Tatiana replayables can be created either automatically (through import) or by hand. Once created, all replayables in Tatiana benefit from Tatiana's four core functionalities: transformation, enrichment, visualization and synchronization.

Transformations

Replayables can be transformed (again, automatically or manually) and exported. As replayables are made up of events (with each event having a set of facets or properties), a transformation results in the creation of a replayable containing new events or a new sequence of existing events. Automated import, transformation and export works through the application of what we call filters. These are objects that combine scripts into a workflow. Scripts are small programs written in XQuery to perform a specific operation, such as transforming a file in the corpus into data Tatiana can understand, excluding certain kinds of events from a replayable, finding certain kinds of events in a replayable, combining multiple replayables, etc. A filter might combine a new script for data import from the interaction log data produced by a new kind of tool with an existing script that only shows the actions of a particular subset of students. Manual transformations include the ability to delete, reorder, re-group and split events.

Enrichment

All replayables within Tatiana can be enriched by analysis generated by the researcher. Such enrichment is the equivalent of adding new columns in a table or, in other words of adding new facets to previously existing events. There are currently three kinds of enrichments supported by Tatiana: free-form annotation, categorization, and graphs. Categorization is simply a way of annotating the verbal transcripts from a restricted list of words and can be used for coding, labeling and adding keywords. The list of categories available can be edited at any time thus allowing for an evolving analysis scheme. Graphs allow researchers to explicitly mark relationships between events. As enrichments annotate the data in a standoff notation, they can be shared separately from the original corpus and can also be opened in concert on the same representations, much in the same way as multiple map overlays can be placed on top of a single map to add in multiple geographical features.

Visualization

All replayables within Tatiana can be visualized in different viewers, which do not modify the underlying abstract nature of the replayable but merely style it appropriately for examination by a human. There currently exist two kinds of viewers: a table view, with one row per event and columns for each of the event's properties and a graphical timeline. The graphical timeline is a first attempt at assisting the automated creation of visualizations. It presents each event as a graphical object whose graphical properties (color, shape, size, position, etc.) can be set according to the properties of the event (user, tool, timestamp, analysis category, etc.). Tatiana is extensible, allowing new kinds of views to be created, affording new

ways of visualizing data. The ability to create and configure multiple visualizations, in concert with transformation and enrichment contributes to the ability to re-use and combine previously existing analytic artifacts.

Synchronization

Finally, all visualizations of replayables in Tatiana can be synchronized with each other (cf. Figure 6) and also with data viewed in external replayers such as media players. Synchronized replay means that when a timestamp is selected in the "remote control," the video players (and other external replayers) are instantly navigated to that timestamp, and the events matching that timestamp in the currently visualized replayables are highlighted. Furthermore, selecting an event in a visualized replayable will again navigate all the other views to that moment in time. For example, during analysis of a video and its transcription in

Figure 6. Various replayables visualized in Tatiana: traces of a shared text editor (top left), transcription (middle left), writing units (top center), visualization of reformulation (bottom left), synchronized with external tools, DREW replayer (top right), video player (middle right), remote control (bottom right)

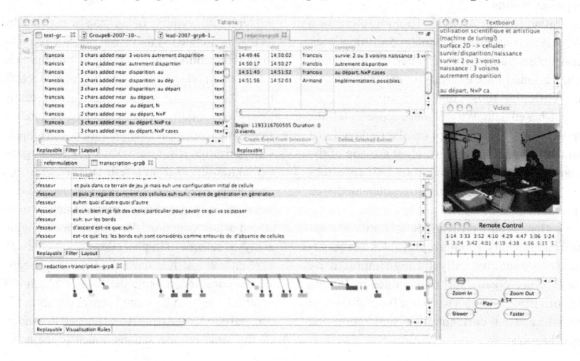

Tatiana, if a researcher clicks on a time stamped utterance in the table view, this action causes the replayer to bring the video to this point. Information on the dynamics of the interaction in thus provided, which is oftentimes difficult to discern in static log traces. Zooming in on particular episodes becomes possible. In general, such linking between replayables is very useful for limiting the amount of information displayed in a single visualization, with the knowledge that further information is available in other visualizations on demand. Synchronization is the main answer to the necessity of being able to use multiple analytic artifacts in concert.

Beyond Tatiana

The framework presented above is limited to analytic representations which preserve the notions of time and ordered events. It excludes notions such as aggregations (e.g. number of utterances by each speaker), experimental conditions, social networks, etc. It does, however provide a model for how reusable analytic representations can be created. This model, and Tatiana (or any other tool) could be extended to encompass new kinds of representations while considering how they could be integrated with the existing notion of replayables.

Already, some of the corpora available on the Mulce platform include analyses in the Tatiana format. However, while the analytic representations are reusable in concert with each other, they do not currently interoperate with other parts of the corpus (learning context, research context, etc.). Nevertheless, because of the commitment to open standards throughout, once it is more clearly understood what purpose such interoperability might serve, it should be relatively straightforward to implement new tools to facilitate combined use.

While Tatiana may superficially appear to be an analysis tool and its associated data format, we believe that the underlying concept of a replayable and its associated operations provide not only the means for static interoperability, where one analysis tool uses another tool's data as input, but also a means for dynamic interoperability, where multiple tools showing multiple analytic representations are open together in real time and coordinate to enable a better understanding of the underlying data.

It is not only interesting to reuse a shared corpus to add a new analysis of its data; in (Reffay, et al., 2011) we show how a new tool may offer new possibilities to analyze interaction data in terms of social cohesion. But we also show that the research questions (being new for a given tool) may lead to interesting adaptation of these tools that should make them able to support new analyses or extend data that they can use as entry.

CONCLUSION

In this chapter, we recalled the importance of data in the research process and showed the implication of sharing this data. Thus, the road for data (and analysis) sharing is long and our work only represents an initial step, which we hope can serve as an example to researchers in other fields who feel the need for data sharing within their community. In the Mulce project findings recalled in this chapter, we have detailed that: explicit context (both of the learning situation and the research situation), explicit structure (both of the data and subsequent analyses), and a regard for ethical issues are prerequisites for successful data sharing. As an explicit example, we presented in details the general structure of a Mulce corpus as a package that can be referenced and downloaded.

We have also described the Tatiana tool, designed for manipulating various kinds of analytic representations. This tool enables both to perform the initial analysis and to combine these analyses into a single representation by producing synchronized replayable and analytic representations. More generally, with the Tatiana framework, we argue for a thorough understanding of the analytic representations common in a field, of the operations for moving from one representation to another (starting at the original data), and of the means for understanding how multiple analytic representations can inform each other. The current state of the framework only integrates a limited number of kinds of analytic representations (those in which time is a dimension) and is as yet not fully able to work with statistics, aggregations, experimental conditions, etc.

Within our field, at least, there nevertheless remain many obstacles to encouraging researchers to share their data. In particular, it is not immediately obvious that publication of a dataset will pay off in terms of recognition, especially on the part of institutions. Furthermore, journals may be reluctant to impose data sharing, both with regard to submitters who might see it as to high a barrier and to reviewers who already perform a time-consuming task which is not of direct benefit to them. Finally, we are conscious that structuring the data can be a heavy workload as different data types need to be formatted according to the schema. Similarly, adopting new analysis tools for creating interoperable analytic representations requires learning to use them and that they adequately replace existing tools. Although we have only few comparative analyses on the same dataset, we think that this work is an encouraging step towards sharing research data.

As with any system where the benefits are indirect and long-term, while the profitability of a functioning solution in the long term is plain to see, the means of bootstrapping the system are less obvious. As data are increasingly shared, we will be better able to find new ways to manage, describe and combine analytic viewpoints on it.

OUR VISION: THE ROLE OF DATA SHARING IN CSCR

From the contents of this chapter, our vision for the role of data sharing is clear, and may at first glance appear simplistic. Because it promotes recognition, transparency, and replication, we see it as a means by which our field (indeed, many fields) can move forward, with stronger results, built on a multi-faceted understanding. The particular cost of data collection and difficulty of replication in technology enhanced learning, not to mention the variety of epistemologies for subsequent analyses renders the question of data and analysis sharing all the more important and timely for us.

Considering this arising need and emerging service of data sharing, the most efficient way to share is still to be determined. On the one hand, institutions are putting pressure on researchers to release their results, publications and data, especially for publicly funded research. The type of repository targeted by these institutions is rather formal and the benefits for the researchers are not clear. On the other hand, social network applications, both for personal or professional purposes, are evolving quickly and tend to encompass a variety of services. In these social network applications, every type of relationship may lead to a specific sociograms for the research community that can help newcomers to socialize or leaders to better build or manage projects. These relationships may be as diverse as: "attended a given scientific event," "share common research topics/tag," "co-authored a publication," "co-worked in the same project/team/laboratory," etc. These applications being centered either on individuals or on specific objects shared by individuals (interests, conferences, journals, projects, team, laboratories, etc.), we see at least two reasons for these communities to adopt data sharing: the first would to consider a shared corpus as a scientific publication and the second to use it as an attracter (intermediary object) between researchers who worked on it either as contributor or as analysts. In the SNA theory, we can hope that two scientists sharing the same corpus as contributors are strongly related to each other and the link between a contributor and an analyst may show a concrete involvement of the analyst to engage scientific discussion and collaboration on related or complementary topics (based on the same data as boundary object). Our idea is that such a link is extremely useful to build bridges between communities (complementary analysis) and may lead to in-depth long-term collaboration.

Following this vision that considers shared data as attracters in a widely connected social network, we can expect that widely reused data, providing a variety of analyses and results, would become more and more attractive and play constructive roles for the communities as a boundary object disseminating methods, tools, epistemologies and results. We think this is a way towards better adoption of our research tools and results and finally contributing a more significant impact to society. However, we are not expecting that thousands of researchers will rapidly join as earlier contributors. Because of the cost of data (and methods and tools) adoption, and those of analysis contribution, we are rather expecting that these costs may work as efficient filters preventing noise of superficial communication in the scientific relationships. It should result in a small heavily concerned and engaged community that may easily consider co-publication and project building. In a sense, it would promote a new way of networking where ties between researchers are stronger, communities' doors are more widely opened and visible, so that any contributor is welcome but where the entry ticket (the first contribution for a newcomer) is rather expensive in terms of work. The strength of this approach stems from the openness of data and transparency of analysis processes that should attract newcomers and lead them to better understanding situations, methods and results. Researchers are not the only ones who would be able to reuse these data and analysis processes; this would also be of interest to programmers that would like to test their tools for robustness by attempting to treat the data of the corpus, or implementing alternative processes among those already used in the derived analyses. Their contribution may be either a new tool proposal for the research community, or an application tool that may have real impact to society.

REFERENCES

Bilder, G. W. (2009). Video presentation of Cross-Ref by its boss: Geoff W. Bilder. In *Proceedings of the 1st Conference on Open Access Scholarly Publishing*. Lund, Sweden. Retrieved from http://river-valley.tv/ tag/ geoff-bilder/.

Carletta, J. (2007). Unleashing the killer corpus: Experiences in creating the multi-everything AMI meeting corpus. *Language Resources and Evaluation Journal, 41*(2), 181–190. doi:10.1007/s10579-007-9040-x

Chan, T., Roschelle, J., Hsi, S., Kinshuk, , Sharples, M., Brown, T., & Hoppe, U. (2006). One-to-one technology-enhanced learning: An opportunity for global research collaboration. *Research and Practice in Technology Enhanced Learning, 1*(1), 3–29. doi:10.1142/S1793206806000032

Cohen, J. (1968). Weighed kappa: Nominal scale agreement with provision for scaled disagreement or partial credit. *Psychological Bulletin, 70*(4), 213–220. doi:10.1037/h0026256

De Wever, B., Schellens, T., Valcke, M., & Van Keer, H. (2006). Content analysis schemes to analyse transcripts of online asynchronous discussion groups: A review. *Computers & Education, 46*(1), 6–28. doi:10.1016/j.compedu.2005.04.005

Dyke, G., Lund, K., & Girardot, J.-J. (2009). Tatiana: An environment to support the CSCL analysis process. In *Proceedings of the International Conference on Computer Supported Collaborative Learning,* (pp. 58-67). Rhodes, Greece: ACM.

Dyke, G., Lund, K., & Girardot, J.-J. (2010). Tatiana: Un environnement d'aide à l'analyse de traces d'interactions humaines. *Technique et Science Informatiques, 29*(10), 1179–1205. doi:10.3166/tsi.29.1179-1205

Dyke, G., Lund, K., Jeong, H., Medina, R., Suthers, D. D., van Aalst, J., et al. (2011). Technological affordances for productive multivocality in analysis. In *Proceedings of the International Computer Supported Collaborative Learning,* (pp. 454-461). Hong Kong, China: ACM.

Edgar, B. D., & Willinsky, J. (2010). A survey of the scholarly journals using open journal systems. *Journal Scholarly and Research Communication.* Retrieved June 27, 2011, from http:// pkp.sfu.ca/ files/ OJS Journal Survey.pdf.

Fisher, C., & Sanderson, P. (1996). Exploratory sequential data analysis: Exploring continuous observational data. *Interaction, 3*(2), 25–34. doi:10.1145/227181.227185

Gentil-Beccot, A., Mele, S., & Brooks, T. (2009). Citing and Reading behaviours in high-energy physics: How a community stopped worrying about journals and learned to love repositories. *Scientometrics, 84*(2), 345–355. doi:10.1007/s11192-009-0111-1

Gleditsch, N. P., Metelits, C., & Strand, H. (2003). Posting your data: Will you be scooped or will you be famous? *International Studies Perspectives, 4*(1), 89–97.

Godfrey, J., Holliman, E., & McDaniel, J. (1992). SWITCHBOARD: Telephone speech corpus for research and development. In *Proceedings of ICASSP, 1992,* 517–520.

Goodman, B. A., Drury, J., Gaimari, R. D., Kurland, L., & Zarrella, J. (2006). *Applying user models to improve team decision making.* Retrieved April 10, 2008 from http:// mitre.org/ work/ tech_papers/ tech_papers_07/ 06_1351/.

IMS-CP. (2011). Instructional management system content package, version 1.2. *Public Draft 2 Specification.* Retrieved from http:// www.imsglobal.org/ content/ packaging/.

IMS-LD. (2011). Instructional management system learning design, version 1. *Specification.* Retrieved from http:// www.imsglobal.org/ learningdesign/.

IMS-MD. (2011). *Instructional management system meta-data. version 1.3, final specification.* Retrieved from http:// www.imsglobal.org/ metadata/.

King, G. (2007). An introduction to the dataverse network as an infrastructure for data sharing. *Sociological Methods & Research, 36*(2), 173–199. doi:10.1177/0049124107306660

Koedinger, K. R., Cunningham, K., Skogsholm, A., & Leber, B. (2008). An open repository and analysis tools for fine-grained, longitudinal learner data. In *Proceedings of the First International Conference on Educational Data Mining,* (pp. 157-166). ACM.

Koper, R. (2001). Modelling units of study from a pedagogical perspective: The pedagogical metamodel behind EML. *Technical Report OUNL June.* Retrieved from http:// dspace. ou.nl/ bitstream/ 1820/ 36/ 1/ Pedagogical%20 metamodel%20 behind%20 EMLv2.pdf.

LOM. (2002). Learning technology standards committee of the IEEE. *Draft Standard for Learning Object Metadata.* Retrieved from http:// ltsc. ieee.org/ wg12/ files/ LOM_1484_ 12_1_v1_ Final_Draft.pdf.

Lund, K., Prudhomme, G., & Cassier, J.-L. (2007). Using analysis of computer-mediated synchronous interactions to understand co-designers' activities and reasoning. In *Proceedings of the International Conference on Engineering Design.* Paris, France: IEEE Press.

Markauskaite, L., & Reimann, P. (2008). Enhancing and scaling-up design-based research: The potential of e-research. In *Proceedings of International Conference for the Learning Sciences,* (pp. 27-34). Utrecht, The Netherlands: ACM.

Martinez, A., De la Fuente, P., & Dimitriadis, Y. (2003). Towards an XML-based representation of collaborative action. In *Proceedings of International Conference on Computer Supported Collaborative Learning Conference,* (pp. 14-18). Bergen, Norway: ACM.

Martinez, A., Harrer, A., & Barros, B. (2005). Library of interaction analysis tools. *Deliverable D.31.2 of the JEIRP IA*. New York, NY: KaleidoScope. Mce_sid. (2011). *Full schema for the structured information data (instantiation component) of a Mulce corpus*. Retrieved from http:// lrl-diffusion.univ-bpclermont.fr/ mulce/ metadata/ mce-schemas/ mce_sid.xsd.

Mele, S. (2009). *SCOAP3: Sponsoring consortium for open access publishing in particle physics*. Paper presented at the First Conference on Open Access Scholarly Publishing. Lund, Sweden. Retrieved from http:// river-valley.tv/ media/ conferences/ oaspa2009/ 0301-Salvatore_Mele/.

Mulce. (2010). *French national research project 2006-2010*. Retrieved from http:// mulce.org.

Mulce Platform. (2011). *Multimodal learning and teaching corpora exchange*. Retrieved from http:// mulce.univ-bpclermont.fr:8080/ PlateFormeMulce/.

Mulce-SR. (2011). *Static repository for the Mulce collection*. Retrieved from http://lrl-diffusion. univ-bpclermont.fr/ mulce/ metadata/ repository/ mulce-sr.xml.

OLAC. (2007). Open language archives community. *University of Pennsylvania*. Retrieved from http:// www.language-archives.org/.

Osuna, C., Dimitriadis, Y., & Martínez, A. (2001). Using a theoretical framework for the evaluation of ksequentiability, reusability and complexity of development in CSCL applications. In *Proceedings of the European Computer Supported Collaborative Learning Conference*. Maastricht, The Netherlands: ACM.

PKP. (2010). *Public knowledge project*. Retrieved from http:// pkp.sfu.ca/ about.

Powell, A., Nilsson, M., Naeve, A., Johnston, P., & Baker, T. (2008). DCMI abstract model. *Dublin Core Metadata Initiative*. Retrieved from http:// dublincore.org/ documents/ abstract-model/.

Prudhomme, G., Pourroy, F., & Lund, K. (2007). An empirical study of engineering knowledge dynamics in a design situation. *Journal of Desert Research, 3*, 333–358. doi:10.1504/JDR.2007.016388

Reffay, C., & Betbeder, M.-L. (2009). Sharing corpora and tools to improve interaction analysis. In *Proceedings of the 4th European Conference on Technology Enhanced Learning*, (pp. 196-210). Springer.

Reffay, C., Chanier, T., Noras, M., & Betbeder, M.-L. (2008). Contribution à la structuration de corpus d'apprentissage pour un meilleur partage en recherche. *Sciences et Technologies de l'Information et de la Communication pour l'Éducation et la Formation, 15*, 185–219.

Reffay, C., Teplovs, C., & Blondel, F.-M. (2011). Productive re-use of CSCL data and analytic tools to provide a new perspective on group cohesion. In *Proceedings of International Conference on Computer Supported Collaborative Learning*. Hong Kong, China: ACM.

Rourke, L., Anderson, T., Garrisson, D. R., & Archer, W. (2001). Methodological issues in the content analysis of computer conference transcripts. *International Journal of Artificial Intelligence in Education, 12*, 8–22.

Sacks, H., Schegloff, E. A., & Jefferson, G. (1974). A simplest systematics for the organisation of turn-taking for conversation. *Language, 50*, 696–735. doi:10.2307/412243

Suthers, D. D. (2006). Technology affordances for intersubjective meaning-making: A research agenda for CSCL. *International Journal of Computer-Supported Collaborative Learning, 1*(3), 315–337. doi:10.1007/s11412-006-9660-y

Suthers, D. D., Lund, K., Rosé, C., Dyke, G., Law, N., & Teplovs, C. (2011). Towards productive multivocality in the analysis of collaborative learning. In *Proceedings of CSCL 2011*, (pp. 1015-1022). Hong Kong, China: ACM.

Velterop, J. (2009). *Nano publications*. Paper presented at the first Conference on Open Access Scholarly Publishing. Lund, Sweden. Retrieved from http://river-valley.tv/ media/ conferences/ oaspa2009/ 0201-Jan_ Velterop/.

Wald, C. (2010). *Scientists embrace openness*. Retrieved from http:// sciencecareers.sciencemag. org/ career_magazine/ previous_issues/ articles/ 2010_04_09/ caredit. a1000036.

KEY TERMS AND DEFINITIONS

Analytic Representation: Intermediary representation resulting from a transformation or analysis process.

Data Sharing: making a data set (issued from a research project) available, understandable and re-usable for researchers not involved in the project that collect the data.

Learning and Teaching Corpus: a Learning & Teaching Corpus is a structured entity containing all the elements resulting from an on-line learning situation.

LETEC: Learning and Teaching Corpus.

Mulce Structure: Conceptual organization of a Learning and Teaching Corpus including learning design, research protocol, structured interaction data, analytic representation and license. The corresponding XML schema is available here: http:// lrl-diffusion.univ-bpclermont.fr/mulce/metadata/ mce-schemas/mce_sid.xsd

Replayable: Core concept of the Tatiana software: analytic representations issued from event-based data.

Replication: Run either the same analysis method or comparable one on the same dataset for training or verification.

Tatiana: Trace Analysis Tool for Interaction ANAlysts. (http://code.google.com/p/tatiana/).

ENDNOTE

[1]   Mulce is a French 3-year project (funded by the French National Research Agency), led by T. Chanier. More information can be found here: http://mulce.org.

Chapter 7
Artificial Intelligence Supported Non–Verbal Communication for Enriched Collaboration in Distributed E–Research Environments

Paul Smith
National University of Ireland – Galway, Ireland

Sam Redfern
National University of Ireland – Galway, Ireland

ABSTRACT

In face-to-face work, discussion and negotiation relies strongly on non-verbal feedback, which provides important clues to negotiation states such as agreement/disagreement and understanding/confusion, as well as indicating the emotional states and reactions of those around us. With the continued rise of virtual teams, collaboration increasingly requires tools to manage the reality of distributed e-research and remote work, which is often hampered by a lack of social cohesion and such phenomena as participant multi-tasking. This chapter discusses important concepts and current issues related to remote research teams and discusses current research in the use of Automatic Facial Expression Recognition Systems (AFERS) in solving some of the inherent problems of the existing online collaboration tools used to support col-laborative and distributed research and work. The later half of this chapter describes a proof-of-concept artificial intelligence based software agent (Emotion Tracking Agent, or ETA) developed by the authors for the monitoring of presence and the emotional states of co-workers in virtual research meetings. The agent is intended as an innovative solution to the impaired awareness and attention resulting from con-tinuous task switching or multitasking behaviours of collaborating remote team members. The ETA was developed and integrated into a CVE (Collaborative Virtual Environment), where an initial study was conducted to analyse its benefits and impact on the communicating participants. This chapter describes the results of this study and their implications for the future of distributed e-research and remote work.

DOI: 10.4018/978-1-4666-0125-3.ch007

INTRODUCTION

In modern work/research environments, the activities of teleconferencing and other forms of virtual meetings have become increasingly important due to the growing number of businesses and research institutions using distributed workers based in many different countries and locations around the world (Lojeski, Reilly, & Dominick, 2007). Many companies such as Intel (70%), IBM (40%), and Sun Micro Systems (nearly 50%) already have high percentages of virtual and distributed workers and researchers (Lojeski, Reilly, & Dominick, 2007). Some of these workers are based at home or abroad or travel frequently and for these individuals, virtual conferencing is the most convenient and economical means of communication with colleagues and clients.

One of the inherent problems in remote meetings as described in the literature relates to multitasking in both traditional (Benbunan-Fich & Truman, 2009) and virtual work and research environments (Appelbaum, Marchionni, & Fernandez, 2008). Successfully managing worker multitasking and providing solutions to specific multitasking disadvantages is of key importance to future work practices (Black & Hearne, 2008).

Much consideration has been given to the effect of multitasking on a user's attention and performance in a virtual meeting. The problem lies in the fact that during virtual meetings (and to a lesser extent face-to-face meetings), participants often juggle more than one task, whether it be checking emails, browsing the internet or performing other work or non-work activities (Lojeski, Reilly, & Dominick, 2007). Our contention is that this is not a 'bad' thing that should be constrained but rather we seek to provide an innovative mechanism to assist users in these situations.

In this chapter we discuss the use of real-time Automatic Facial Expression Recognition Systems (AFERS) in solving some of the common and inherent problems associated with current online collaboration tools used in the support of collaborative and distributed e-research. These problems include poorly supported non-verbal communication and an increased propensity of collaborators to engage in distracting multitasking or task switching behaviours. A prototype Emotion Tracking software Agent (ETA) of our own design is presented and discussed later in this chapter, along with a description of its integration and testing within an online research CVE (Collaborative Virtual Environment). This discussion is then used as a mechanism for further exploration of the issues obstructing the continued advancement of collaborative e-research and remote work tools and the potential benefits of an AFERS in reducing these issues. The developed ETA is aimed for use in remote work and online collaboration tools such as teleconferencing, video conferencing and a variety of groupware such as collaborative virtual environments (CVEs) and other forms of VEs. The main purpose of the agent is as a tool to help support online interactions by providing a real-time form of automatic non-verbal communication interface along with, by use of a number of methods, increasing online collaborators' attention and emotional awareness in virtual meetings.

REMOTE WORK/RESEARCH AND MULTITASKING

In the last decade the popularity of remote work amongst employees in many diverse employment sectors has increased significantly. This is largely due to the increase in availability of specialised information technology software and hardware allowing virtual meetings between increasingly larger groups of people to become possible, removing the restrictions which once curbed the organisation of work activities. Modern companies are outsourcing work contracts throughout the world and are no longer limited by the boundaries of on-site employees. The same can be said for research institutions and the concept of "virtual teams" is becoming a global phenomenon allowing researchers to carry out complex and ambitious projects regardless of their distance from their base of operations or their collaborators.

Remote work has become necessary for a number of reasons in our modern economy, but its original intention first surfaced as a result of employer's attempts to accommodate female employees whose responsibilities to their families would otherwise have prevented their abilities to commit to fulltime employment (Christensen, 1988; Kraut, 1989; Huws, Korte, & Robinson, 1990). Over time the concept of remote work or telecommuting grew in popularity and effectiveness and became an important employment strategy used by companies in satisfying highly skilled workers and managerial professionals to retain their employment and ensure their continued interest in their professional roles.

Disability also remains a reason for telecommuting as many professionals with impaired mobility or other health conditions are unable to commute regularly between their homes and work base and therefore remote work is a viable option in retaining their current employment positions. For these professionals, telecommuting has become a necessity and the continued development of effective remote work and collaboration tools is imperative in the removal of any limitations which may hinder the successful and efficient completion of their work related duties.

Other individuals may choose to telecommute for reasons of flexibility in working hours or simply because their employment requires their frequent use of telecommunication technologies and it is not necessary for their daily travel to a central work office in the successful completion of their professional duties. Remote workers may also be forced to travel frequently on business trips requiring their constant usage of teleconferencing technologies to successfully coordinate collaborative work with their colleagues while they are on the road. In the last ten to fifteen years it has become more common that companies and

research institutions have begun to actively encourage remote working among their employees due to the cost accompanying the maintenance of a physical workspace (Nolan & Galal, 1998; Westfall, 1998).

Remote research is also a growing area which has become more prominent in recent years, supporting both distributed workers and cross-institutional research projects. E-Research is sometimes supported by Virtual Research Environments (VREs), a type of Collaborative Virtual Environment which is closely related to Virtual Education Environments. Although they have been available for a significant amount of time, VREs and remote collaborative research have only recently been considered as a separate field from Computer Supported Cooperative Work/ Learning (CSCW or CSCL). This emerging field has come to be known as Computer Supported Cooperative Research (CSCR).

Due to the fact that this is a relatively new field of study, there is very little current literature available regarding the issues that may arise in the design of systems for supporting collaborative research groups remotely interacting with each other over significant distances (Hinze-Hoare, 2007).

VIRTUAL TEAMS

Organisations have begun to adopt the strategy of utilising what is now referred to as "virtual teams" which are multinational groups of employees who are entirely composed of remote researchers/workers distributed over large distances. Such teams have the added advantage of, when organised correctly in terms of research hours and roles, providing the organisation with an effective twenty four hour work day within which to schedule project activities.

Choice of Technology

Recent advancements in communication and collaboration tools and technology has been the single most influential factor in the growth of remote work/research and virtual teams as a viable strategy in our modern economic climate. Such tools are often available for free which increases the incentive to integrate their use into our everyday professional lives.

The simplest and most common of these tools are email clients and instant messengers such as Gmail, Hotmail, Skype, and Windows Live Messenger which are widely used in both a personal and professional capacity. More specialised tools aimed for use by the professional population include groupware applications for remote document management, virtual conferencing systems such as teleconferencing and videoconferencing packages and systems such as meeting managers and virtual whiteboards for support of group decision making in virtual meeting environments. All of these tools are suited for different remote or collaborative tasks, and studies have shown that utilising the appropriate tool for a particular activity or situation increases the effectiveness of remote participant communication within virtual teams and all forms of remote collaboration (Ancona & Caldwell, 1990; Leonard, et al., 1998).

Advantages of Remote Research/ Work and Virtual Teams

The most obvious benefits of remote work and research are those of financial and time related savings due to the lack of need to daily commute between accommodation and work base (this applies mostly to home based telecommuters) (Stanek & Mokhtarian, 1998; Nilles, 2000). In situations where employment must cease due to the fact that an employee/researcher, for whatever reason, is forced to move a large distance away from his/her work place, remote working is a viable option to ensure retention of current employment.

It has been shown that remote commuters have significantly increased abilities to dynamically schedule their work processes and time over the restricted nine to five work hours of their non-

remote staff colleagues (Bélanger, 1999; Malone, 1997). This amount of flexibility allowed by remote participation in organising one's professional time means both family and personal lives of employees/researchers can be easier managed which results in increased staff satisfaction. Literature in this area of research also indicates that job satisfaction is significantly higher among remote commuters in comparison to onsite regular staff (DuBrin & Barnard, 1993).

Remote collaboration also provides the opportunity for large teams of professionals based in globally distributed locations to collaborate on projects in circumstances where it would have not been possible or viable to collaborate in physically face-to-face meetings. This is particularly important for collaborative research projects, where the norm is increasingly to bring together the complementary skills of two or more geographically separated research laboratories.

Problems Associated with Virtual Teamwork

Many problems have been highlighted in the literature relating to the shortcomings of remote work and virtual teamwork. These range from communication problems among collaborators due to poor choice of tools or technology, to cultural and organisational difficulties caused by geographical and ethnic barriers. Lack of face-to-face interaction is another major disadvantage of remote collaboration due to the many aspects of communication and interaction which are not sufficiently supported by modern remote interaction tools. Interpersonal relationships between colleagues are also difficult to form from such distances and many telecommuters and virtual collaborating professionals note isolation as a major disadvantage. It is widely believed that in order to maximise the success of virtual collaboration strategies, organisations should reduce as much as possible the sense of isolation experienced by their remote staff members (Handy & Mokhtarian, 1995; Belanger & Collins, 1998; Johnson, 1998).

Problems which have adverse effects on productivity and efficiency during traditional face-to-face professional gatherings can also have a serious impact on virtual meetings between geographically dispersed team members. Research in the last decade (Hogan, Kelly, & Craik, 2006; Spink, Ozmutlu, & Ozmutlu, 2002; Vega, 2009) into multitasking behaviours among our modern media rich society has uncovered unwanted effects caused by such activities as continuous attention switching, which was once believed to be an efficient use of a person's time and a useful strategy for effective organisation of multiple work tasks. Studies of the human brain (Ishizaka, Marshall, & Conte, 2001; Rubinstein, Meyer, & Evans, 2001) have now produced evidence of undesirable effects such as forms of memory loss and wasted and inefficient use of time related to the constant switching between projects or tasks in a work related context. In virtual teamwork all these factors still apply but the issue of lack of attention while on conference calls or other forms of remote meetings due to multitasking behaviour, is an even larger problem in such situations than in a non-virtual work framework.

Human Multitasking

In the following sections we summarise the viewpoint of and research conducted upon multitasking behaviours in the cognitive and information sciences in order to expose the negative effect of multitasking on human ability, in order to clarify the need for solutions to its behavioural disadvantages.

Human multitasking is the phenomenon of an individual appearing to handle multiple tasks at one time. In reality the individual is in fact splitting his or her attention between these tasks since the human brain is incapable of actually processing more than a single task at any given time. Due to this splitting of attention between

tasks, he/she ultimately pays more attention to one at the expense of another. It is believed that this phenomenon results in wasted time due to the regular occurrence of human context switching and the increase of error in these tasks due to lack of adequate attention.

Research has been conducted since the early 1990s, on the nature and limitations of the human brain in dealing with multitasking. Many of the studies conducted have concluded that in general, a person shows heavy interference even if two relatively simple practical tasks are performed simultaneously (Gladstones, Regan, & Lee, 1989; Pashler, 1994). Many researchers believe from their experiences that the planning of action in the human brain forms a bottleneck which effectively limits the brain's capabilities of dealing with more than a single task at any one time (Hallowell, 2007). Due to this, the human brain is unable to completely focus during multitasking leading to longer task completion times and more frequent occurrences of error.

Psychiatrist Edward Hallowell has described extreme human multitasking as akin to attention deficit/hyperactivity disorder. It has been linked to a new condition known as "Attention Deficit Trait" which is claimed to be widespread in the business world (Rosen, 2008). A number of studies using functional Magnetic Resonance Imaging (fMRI) have been carried out in order to determine the activity which occurs in the physiology of the human brain during the engagement of "task-switching" (i.e. multitasking behaviour). Psychologist René Marois found evidence using this technique, of a "response selection bottleneck" that is caused in the brain during instances where it is forced to deal with multiple stimuli simultaneously. He states that this bottleneck results in wasted or lost time as the brain determines which of the tasks to carry out (Dux, et al., 2006). Another Psychologist, David Meyer, has a different theory which asserts that what actually happens inside the human brain is a process called "adaptive executive control" instead of a bottleneck and this process "schedules task processes appropriately to obey instructions about their relative priorities and serial order" (Meyer, et al., 1995). Even though this is a more optimistic view of multitasking, his research has also discovered that multitasking itself contributes to the brain's release of a number of stress hormones and adrenaline which can result in long term health problems and loss of short-term memory if left uncontrolled.

Psychologist Russell Poldrack has determined that multitasking negatively affects people's learning capabilities. Poldrack's work revealed through the scanning of the brains of a number of individuals, that during active multitasking, different areas of a person's brain are used for learning and information collection than if they were not distracted from a singular task (Foerde, Poldrack, & Knowlton, 2007). These areas of the brain are less efficient in information retrieval and have reduced flexibility in relation to learning.

Multitasking research in the cognitive sciences has frequently been mentioned in the press with multiple studies being published relating to the negative effects of mobile phone use on the driving performance of people in cars and other automotive vehicles (Strayer & Johnston, 2001). These studies resulted in laws being passed in many countries to reduce this kind of multitasking behaviour. Despite multitasking behaviour's importance in cognitive science, it is only recently that the research field of information science has begun to devote time to its understanding. Recently multitasking has begun to emerge as a fundamental process that underpins information behaviour resulting in its growth in theoretical and practical significance among information scientists.

Many interactive technologies do not provide support for the management of the multitasking behaviours of their users (Wickens, 1992) and interest is growing especially among employers and organisational behaviourists who are concerned about multitasking in work environments, partly due to the explosion of popularity and availability of modern information devices (Holstein, 2006). In

cognitive psychology there is extensive research literature on multitasking, concurrent information processing and task switching (Burgess, 2000; Pashler, 2000). The negative impact on productivity caused by multitasking over diverse tasks types (Rubinstein, Meyer, & Evans, 2001) is further supported by the theory that the ability of humans to perform multiple simultaneous mental processes is limited by the capacity of a central mechanism. This is known as the single channel theory (Schweickert & Boggs, 1984).

Differences have also been identified between prioritised and unprioritised multitasking and dual tasking situations (Ishizaka, Marshall, & Conte, 2001) through studies and analysis of multitasking in situations such as driving (Waller, 1997).

Human Task Switching

The phenomenon of 'task switching' has been accepted as an essential component of multitasking and a detailed review in relation to cognitive science is available in (Monsell, 2003). Due to the belief that task switching and multitasking are one and the same, research into multitasking in cognitive science focuses primarily on the costs to the individual of switching tasks in comparison to task repetition or non-task switching. Much experimental research has been carried out into these negative impacts and the executive control processes and the cognitive architecture involved in these rapid task switching occurrences have been described and studied in detail (Allport, Styles, & Hsieh, 1994; Rubinstein, Meyer & Evans, 2001).

The effect of such behaviour on memory is also an area which has received much attention. In (Logan, 2004) a description is given of the role of working memory in executive control during task switching. (Miyake & Shah, 1999; Baddeley, Chincotta, & Adlam, 2001) contains a summary of all current theories of working memory. The main drawback with this form of memory is its limitations in capacity (Anderson, Reder, & Lebiere, 1996) and it has been shown that during task switching, information is lost from working memory due to interference or decay (Waugh & Norman, 1965). A description of how long-term memory and working memory combine together in the process of multitasking or task switching is given in (Anderson, Reder, & Lebiere, 1996; Baddeley & Logie, 1999).

In cognitive science the study of communication observes multitasking from a multi-channel or multi-media viewpoint. In a multitasking situation a user may make use of a channel or medium at the same time as engaging with other media. This phenomenon is known as 'media multitasking' and attracts much interest due to the prevalence of multitasking among today's media proficient young people.

Media multitasking is the simultaneous use of several diverse media, such as television, the Internet, computer games, text messages, telephones, and e-mail. The amount of new media trends appearing such as Facebook, Twitter, Hi5 and the multitude of games and other tasks these websites offer to users causes many people to constantly switch between one media to another. Media multitasking is a widespread and increasing occurrence today in our heavily online oriented information lead society.

Multitasking in Remote Work/ Research Situations

An important current topic in the literature relates to the advantages and disadvantages of multitasking in both traditional and virtual work environments (Appelbaum, Marchionni, & Fernandez, 2008). Successfully managing worker multitasking and providing solutions to specific multitasking disadvantages is of key importance to future work practices.

Receiving much attention in this area is the effect of multitasking on a user's attention and performance in a virtual meeting (Lojeski, Reilly, & Dominick, 2007). In modern work environments, teleconferencing and other forms

of virtual meetings have become increasingly important due to the number of companies and institutions employing distributed personnel based in many different countries and locations around the world. The problem lies in the fact that during virtual meetings and even in face-to-face meetings, remote worker participants often juggle multiple tasks, from checking emails or browsing the internet to performing other work or non-work activities. This is certainly due in part to the lack of social pressure to attend fully to a meeting when colleagues are unaware of your behaviour. However, we believe that being forced to fully attend to all aspects of a meeting may be an inefficient use of one's time when some agenda items may be of lesser personal relevance: it is often better to support multitasking and mitigate against its negative effects than to stop it from happening at all.

In the area of collaborative e-research, multitasking and attention distraction can also present difficulties as most of the issues relating to remote work are equally applicable to remote research. The fields of CSCR, CSCW and CSCL are largely related in many conceptual themes, but the difference between them is determined by the differentiation between work, learning and research practices. It has become apparent from recent studies that learning is a specialised form of work and research is a specific form of learning (Hinze-Hoare, 2007). While research is essentially a learning activity, it differs in the fact that it is a highly structured and refined process. As stated by Barnett, "research is the creation of new knowledge" (Barnett, 2004)

The main differences in CSCW, CSCL and CSCR which differentiate them for use with our ETA are the users themselves. It can be said that people whose work fits into the domain of CSCW are a more dispersed demographic in terms of occupation, intelligence and motivation, while most people would view researchers to be more internally motivated and like-minded. It can be assumed that the majority of researchers, since they are often not 'forced' to participate in a project, are therefore more motivated than the typical CSCW worker. However, a person's attention span is limited whether they are a basic worker or high level researcher (Dukette & Cornish, 2009). A person's motivation does not always dictate their interest in specific tasks, especially the more monotonous housekeeping meetings which may occur in day to day research. An individual's attention cannot be guaranteed to be entirely focused on every research task/topic which may arise in a remote meeting or group interaction. Some researchers are more interested in specific topics or aspects of a project than others and may not pay sufficient attention to other aspects of a group discussion due to their own focus on matters more related to their own research. In this regard researchers are not immune to attention distraction or multitasking behaviours, especially during remote research discussions where the lack of face-to-face contact can leave increased opportunity to conduct side tasks if topics are not of pressing interest to these individuals. We contend that, although differences exist, and multitasking may be a lesser problem in eResearch than in typical CSCW, the underlying problem remains true.

A survey conducted in 2004 (Gilbert, 2004) of 385 respondents reports that 90% of all conference call participants engage in multitasking during conference calls. Some of the activities named by these respondents were unrelated work (70%), email or instant messaging (50%), eating (35%), muting for side conversations (35%), surfing the web (25%) and even driving (12%). Considering the amount of information, both non-verbal and verbal, which these conference call participants may have missed it is not surprising that multitasking in industry is something which many company leaders and management are becoming more and more concerned about. This not only translates into inefficient communication, but ultimately reduces the medium's effectiveness, causing a possible obstacle to further growth of teleconferencing technology and its continued adoption

in industry. The future of remote collaboration whether in a work or research context, therefore depends on the development of solutions to its inherent problems and limitations such as the negative impact of such multitasking scenarios.

Attention and awareness are important elements in communication and collaborative work, in order to fully understand and follow the reactions and sentiments of co-workers. Unfortunately when people multitask during a conference call they miss certain information points due to lack of attention, and in addition to this, they miss important non-verbal information transmitted by participants which can provide valuable insight into their reactions to proposed information and specific topics brought up during the meeting (Vlaar, Van Fenema, & Tiwari, 2008).

Multitasking in Information Behaviour

Information behaviour refers to all human conduct related to sources and channels of information, including both active and passive information seeking, and information use (Wilson, 2000). This behaviour also includes face-to-face communication between people, as well as passive reception of information from such media as TV advertisements, where recipients have no real intention to act on the received information.

Models of multitasking and task switching during information behaviour have been described which include cognitive, cognitive style, and individual differing variables (Spink & Park, 2005). One study (Spink, et al., 2007) investigated the multitasking information behaviours of the users of one of Brentwood and Wilkinsburg Public Libraries in Pittsburgh through the use of questionnaires. The study revealed that of the 96 library users who were involved in the investigation, 63.5 percent engaged in multitasking information behaviours and a mean of 2.5 topic changes and 2.8 topics per library visit was also observed. An important result from this study was the fact that a large amount of people who seek information in libraries search for multiple topics and engage in multitasking behaviours.

In (Spink & Cole, 2007, 2006a, 2006b) it is argued that when information is added to a multitasking situation the process becomes increasingly complex and the user's behaviour may involve a mixture of cognitive and physical actions on two or more tasks simultaneously or in sequence and may include switching between different information tasks. Unlike other scientific areas, information behaviour research tends to view multitasking behaviours as an essential element of the information-behaviour process that need to be carefully studied, allowed for, and facilitated in the design of information systems.

Tackling Multitasking Behaviour

In the research field of human factors, the science of understanding the properties of human capability, multitasking is an important topic in the creation of cognitive models which allow human operators to control and act properly in multidimensional environments successfully. In this research field, the notion of multitasking corresponds to "the ability to integrate, interleave and perform multiple tasks and/or component subtasks of a larger complex task" (Salvucci, Kushleyeva, & Lee, 2004). Examples of such architecture/ modeling of multitasking have been created for application to tasks such as driving, piloting and air traffic control (Aasman, 1995; Jones, et al., 1999; Lee & Anderson, 2001). In summary, research in this field has primarily focused on the development of supervisory and control interfaces using these cognitive models and architecture in order to ensure that individuals undertaking important tasks, where multitasking is both dangerous and unacceptable, are kept in a focused and alert state (Cole, Spink, & Waller, 2008). Other fields such as online collaboration are currently lacking in developed technology to tackle multitasking or task switching behaviours.

In the research field of Human Computer Interaction (HCI), which encompasses the study of personal interactions with the means of computer technology and thus is heavily related to online and remote interactions, multitasking is described as a process of human/user interruption. According to (McFarlane, 1997), interruptions are "unanticipated requests for switching between different tasks during multitasking." In Tsukada, Okada, and Matsushita (1994) a practical discussion is given of the process and concepts behind work carried out by individuals or groups in Computer Supported Cooperative Work/Research (CSCW/R) enabled office environments in which an individual may be responsible for progressing numerous projects simultaneously. HCI views the problem of multitasking as when people are interrupted from a task which they are performing alongside another subtask, they must return to the task which needs attention and interrupted them, causing themselves to often forget where they are in the subtask, which can lead to wasted time and energy. This is termed 'prospective memory failure' which is the inability to remember the task that you must perform (Ellis & Kvavilashvili, 2000). According to O'Connail and Frohlich (1995) task interruptions at work has been attributed as one of the most common reasons for prospective memory failure. Unfortunately with the current state of research and work it is not always possible to only concentrate on a single project, hence forcing employees to multitask in order to keep on top of numerous projects which they may be required to be working on. This brings forward the dilemma whereby workers and researchers are unable to avoid multitasking behaviours.

Through the years, HCI research has focused its efforts on the negative effects of multitasking, task switching and interruptions on the performance of tasks, and on the consequences of interruptions on time efficiency and human safety. HCI research has found that multitasking affects performance speed as well as causing people to perform differently on interrupted tasks (Gillie & Broadbent,

1989; Kreifeldt & McCarthy, 1981; Cabon, Co-blentz, & Mollard, 1990). See McFarlane (2002) for a full review of interruption and multitasking literature in HCI.

It is clear from the research described up to this point that multitasking is widespread in both the business and research world. It is also evident that such behaviour needs to be controlled since the advantages of multitasking are evident in theory, but the negative effects it may cause outweigh the prospective positives in many cases. The prospects of efficiently juggling multiple tasks have clear advantages in the modern work and research environment. Hence we conclude that it is necessary to remove the negative while retaining the positive aspects of this phenomenon. Most research to date has focused on preventive measures against multitasking but we believe that a more effective solution may lie in supporting collaborative interactions by instead reducing the negatives associated with this form of behaviour: the reality is that researchers and information workers today need to attend to many meetings that are of peripheral importance to them, or that a meeting may move between topics of greater and lesser importance to them. Forcing participants to abandon other tasks while attending these meetings is not a good solution.

In the next section we will discuss current research conducted on automatic facial expression recognition and how it can be used to support communicative and collaborative online interactions.

AUTOMATED FACIAL EXPRESSION RECOGNITION SYSTEMS (AFERS)

Research into automated facial expression recognition in online interactions has primarily focused on supporting communication modes among users of virtual environments. The communication requirements of collaborative virtual interaction environments and other online interaction spaces are complex and the required responsiveness,

reliability and scale of information transfer can vary significantly between applications, contexts and scenarios (Snowdon, et al., 2004). It is important that the communication modes employed in real world human-to-human communication are implemented in virtual interaction environments if the goal of efficient and effective interaction during collaborative situations is to be reached. These modes include verbal, visual and non-verbal communication of all known forms.

Verbal communication has received much development success in current online interaction applications in the last decade with the advent of voice over IP communication. Visual modes such as one-to-one video calls and conferencing have also received much attention and with the recent increases in bandwidth and internet connection speeds, applications for video calling are popular among businesses and research institutions. The support for non-verbal modes of communication in online interactions is yet to be refined and facilitated sufficiently. One-to-one non-verbal communication is dealt with quite adequately by simple video conferencing products, but when larger numbers of users attempt to communicate or collaborate in a virtual meeting the software begins to show its limitations in non-verbal communication support.

Some work has been done in developing alternative methods of providing support for non-verbal communication in online interactions. The most common methods used entail the provision of gestures, facial expressions and body language displayed on an avatar which represents the user's virtual self within the virtual environment (Verhulsdonck, 2007). These gestures are generally triggered by mouse or keyboard input on the side of the user. Currently there are no commercially available or marketed solutions and very little published research which aim to sufficiently provide such gestures or non-verbal feedback from real-time tracking of a user's facial expressions or body language which are usable in large scale online interactions such as virtual meetings.

Much of the work conducted into the synthesis and recognition of emotions through non-verbal signals has been conducted for application to the field of Human Computer Interaction (HCI) with the goal of creating natural human-machine interfaces (Cowie, et al., 2001; Fragopanagos & Taylor, 2005). Another application domain for automated analysis of facial expressions which has received interest is its use in behavioural science and medicine (Khosrowabadi, et al., 2010). Recent uses of AFERS include deception detection (Ryan, et al., 2009) and automatic feedback during teaching (Whitehill, Bartlett, & Movellan, 2008), but most research of late has tended to revolve around developing more efficient techniques for accurate, fast and robust facial expression recognition.

Automatic facial expression recognition focuses on the problems related to the representation and classification of the static or dynamic characteristics of the deformations of facial components and their special relations which form the basis of facial expressions (Chibelushi & Bourel, 2002). Systems designed for automatic recognition of facial expressions are commonly structured as a sequence of processing blocks built around a conventional pattern recognition model. These blocks include image acquisition (using cameras or other imaging devices), preprocessing (processing the image and removing skewing or distortion caused by camera or head angle before being sent to the next phase for feature extraction), feature extraction (identifying points on the user's face representing known facial features such as nose or eyes), classification (classifying patterns formed by features using a classifier such as a neural network) and post-processing (performing any extra processing before beginning work on next image) (Chibelushi & Bourel, 2002).

The preprocessing stage is one of the most important due to the extent of distortions caused by head rotation, distance from camera and varying head and facial feature proportions. The methods used to solve these problems commonly involve some form of standardisation or normalisation

of the input image before the data is sent to the recognition system itself. Typically, this involves geometric correction in order to ensure adherence to a standard image which exhibits an ideal facial pattern. These standardisation techniques ensure that all affine transformations such as skewing, rotation or scaling do not affect the data being tested.

The feature extraction stage is where individual facial features such as eyes, nose and mouth are located and extracted from the image. The feature extraction stage is very important in Facial Expression Recognition (FER) since the extracted feature's positions and orientation are what forms the facial expression. The final classification stage consists of comparisons between the extracted facial image and a database of known facial expressions for classification and production of recognition output. This classification stage is generally achieved by the use of a neural network trained on a large set of facial expressions as its training data.

Evaluating the Accuracy of AFER Systems

The objective comparison of the recognition accuracy of multiple AFER system can be problematic. This is partially due to the fact that some systems can be developed to recognise different expressions using Facial Action Coding System Action Units (FACS AUs) while others may be created to recognise prototypic emotions. Another aspect which makes comparison difficult is the fact that the databases on which different AFER systems are tested can have a dissimilar number of images used; be taken in different lighting conditions; image resolution and quality can vary and the subjects used to construct the databases can vary in ethnicity, age, and gender. While the majority of such databases are constructed from images of subjects directly facing the camera under artificial laboratory conditions, some also exist which are compiled using more natural data sets in which the subjects head position and posture vary. Due to the varying conditions of datasets used in the literature, it is only possible to make very basic comparisons between the accuracy of differing AFER systems.

In most literature, the accuracy of an AFER system is generally described in term of the percentage of correctly identified emotions from a number of images (e.g. 85% accuracy would mean 85 out of 100 images were classified correctly and 15 were misclassified). This is the most common method of measuring accuracy with systems which, similar to our own ETA, are designed to recognise prototypic emotions. For systems developed to recognise emotions using FACS AUs, the above method of measuring accuracy is not adequate. A more sophisticated measure of recognition accuracy is used in FACS based systems, whereby the area under the Receiver Operator Characteristics curve (also known as the A' statistic which is a graphical plot of the sensitivity or true positive rate versus false positive rate of a binary classifier system), generated from the recognition results, takes into account both the true positive and false positive rates of the classifier. Most literature on AFER systems represents accuracy results only in percentage correctly classified form.

Facial Expression Databases

The human face is capable of displaying an extremely large number and variety of facial expressions. Due to this expansive range of possible facial expressions, it is difficult to collect a sufficient database that samples this space in a meaningful way (Jain & Li, 2005). There are significantly fewer databases existing for AFER than those for identity or facial recognition (see Table 1). As mentioned earlier, there are two methods employed for the description of facial expressions. There are two main classes of AFER databases which are categorised from the choice of description method employed (FACS AUs [Kanade, Cohn, & Tian, 2000] or prototypic emotional expressions [Lyons, et al., 1998]).

Table 1. Commonly used expression recognition databases (Jain & Li, 2005)

Database	No. of Subjects	No. of Expressions	Image Resolution	Video/ Image
JAFFE	10	7	256 × 256	Image
U. Maryland	40	6	560 × 240	Video
Cohn-Kanade	100	23	640 × 480	Video

The major facial expression recognition databases used in the literature are shown in Table 1. This table lists the number of subjects used for facial expressions in each database, the number of individual expressions portrayed by each subject and the image or video resolution of the facial expression data. Since our work uses specialised hardware to facilitate emotion recognition we were unable to use any of these databases in testing of our own system and instead conducted our own analysis from the facial expressions trained on our neural network and compared them to the accuracy of human subjects viewing the same facial expressions recorded as video (this is described later in this chapter).

SOFTWARE AGENT SOLUTION

Recent research and development conducted by our team has produced a prototype software agent whose primary use is the tracking of emotional states of remote collaboration participants in a virtual work/research environment. This Emotion Tracking Agent (ETA) is intended to inform participants of important changes in emotional states of fellow collaborators and in doing so increase their attention to and awareness of the meaning of important information presented by co-workers. The main aim of this solution is to reduce the lack of attention and awareness caused by multitasking and continuous task switching behaviours. The agent primarily acts as a user's "attention assistant," alerting them when they need to pay attention. It is integrated into our Collaborative Virtual Environment research platform 'VRCGroups,' illustrating its use in one of its intended contexts.

The ETA is designed to track and identify all 6 of Paul Ekman's primary emotions (i.e. anger, disgust, sadness, happiness, surprise, and fear) (Ekman, 1980) while prompting users of the emotional states of fellow meeting participants. Non-universal emotions such as agreement and confusion are dealt with on a person to person basis, allowing a user to record their facial cues for training the neural network inside the application. Non-universal emotions are more relevant than universal emotions in a collaborative research context, since they convey the bulk of emotions that occur in non-aggressive communication and negotiation. However, they are less useful for assessing accuracy and comparing the ETA with human performance.

ETA Information Modes

Since the aim of our software agent is to increase users' emotional awareness and attention in a remote meeting, the users are prompted with information relating to other participant's emotional states in three separate communication modes. These modes are vocal (a recorded message prompts the user of fellow collaborator's emotional states), textual (a chat message is sent to the user informing them of the emotion change of a fellow environment user)

and visual (an emoticon icon appears over the head of the user whose emotional state has changed allowing easy identification of the user's avatar). The user also has the ability to specify which co-workers they are interested in receiving information about, to ensure that they are not bombarded with unwanted information.

The textual message is sent to the virtual environment's chat window (see Figure 1) in a highlighted text format to draw more attention to the event and specifies the name of the participant about whom the information involves. The vocal message is played directly through the user's speakers simultaneously with the textual message and the visual message takes the form of an emoticon representing the user's mood floating above the head of their avatar (see Figure 2). Each emoticon used in the visual mode is a separate colour and reflects the colour of the text alert in the chat window to allow a user who is familiar with the use of the system to easily distinguish between emotions if they are aware of which colour stands for each emotion.

Options Window

The integrated ETA agent also provides an options menu which is used to allow users to record their own variations of non-universal emotions and save these recorded data as training groups for the ETA's neural network to learn to recognise for

Figure 1. The chat window displaying emotion alert message to user

later use. The window also contains a graphical display showing a 3D avatar head which reflects the user's facial movements by moving the corresponding facial muscles on a 3D model (see Figure 3).

ETA Architecture

For this research it was necessary to be able to capture and analyse facial movements. However since the main focus of the research was being able to classify the emotion represented by these facial movements and not in the capture or feature tracking aspect, then as much as possible it was desirable to use pre-existing hardware and software to capture the facial movements flaw-

lessly. In order to simplify the image acquisition and preprocessing stages, a specialist optical motion capture, an Optitrack FLEX: C120 was used (developed by the company NaturalPoint (2010) (see Figure 4). This camera is an integrated image capture and processing unit which uses a B&W CMOS imager to capture 120 frames of video per second and an onboard image processer which transfers marker data over standard USB to a computer for display and post processing. The camera preprocesses the image to remove most light, preventing anything from being retained unless it is very bright. The camera contains a ring of 12 infrared LEDs which are used to illuminate the tracking markers which are made of a highly reflective material (see Figure 5). The Software

Figure 2. Users' avatars with emoticons displayed above their heads (avatar on left displays surprise and on the right displays happiness)

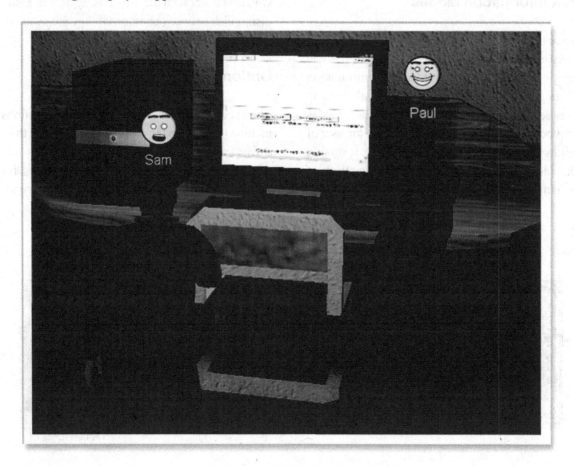

Figure 3. The ETA options window with its various controls and avatar head model which reflects the user's facial expressions

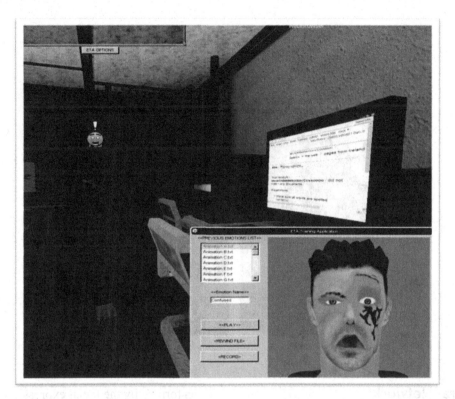

Development Kit (SDK) provided with the camera allows developers to track these markers and write their own tracking applications.

Tracking Device Setup

During tracking the FLEX: C120 camera was mounted on a tripod 14cm from a mounting platform of 8.5cm height (see Figure 5). The camera was positioned so that the lens and LEDs were fully visible above the top of the laptop screen as illustrated in Figure 6.

The camera was positioned approximately 50 centimetres from the user's head during trials and the user attempted to keep his head as steady as possible since the current preprocessing standardisation methods do not allow for large out of plane head movement.

Tracking Marker Setup

Eight self adhesive luminous tracking markers are physically placed on the user's face in positions which have been calculated to be areas of high significance to the expression of facial displays of emotion (Zhang, 1999). Another 3 markers are also placed in positions which have been shown to be of very little significance to facial expression and subject to minimal movement (Zhang, 1999). These 3 extra markers are used as stabilisation points and are mainly employed in preprocessing and standardisation of the other 8 marker's coordinates before input to the ETA neural network (used for classification of emotion). Figure 7 illustrates the marker positions on a user's face highlighting the 3 standardisation markers.

Figure 4. Front and side views of the chosen tracking solution, the Optitrack FLEX: C120 developed by Naturalpoint (NaturalPoint, 2010)

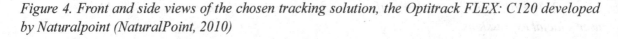
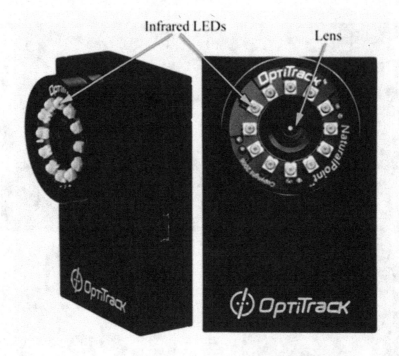

ETA Neural Network

The main classification of emotion is performed using a feed-forward multilayer perceptron neural network, which uses a back-propagation learning algorithm with 'early stopping' to prevent over-fitting or over training of the network (Stergiou & Signanos, 1996). For our prototype the neural network was trained on 40 snapshots of each primary emotion (from the 6 mentioned earlier) taken from our FLEX: C120 tracking device. The output of the network took the form of 6 output values ranging from 0 to 1, each separate value representing the probability of its corresponding emotion being the emotion identified from the image.

The raw input data sent to the neural network took the form of the 11 facial marker's 2D co-ordinates (see Figure 7). This raw data is then preprocessed to remove scaling, rotation and other distortions which may prevent the underlying pat-terns formed by the facial expression from being represented correctly for classification by the ETA neural network. Once preprocessing is completed, the data is then converted to an appropriate input scheme used to accentuate the underlying facial expression patterns in the dataset. Four main candidate input schema were considered for this final stage of the standardisation process. These schemes used varying methods to describe the underlying patterns in the datasets, ranging from representing the data by various geometric distances between markers to specific angle computations between chosen markers. The resulting schemae were compared by cluster analysis to determine which method served to most effectively highlight the similarities between datasets representing equivalent emotions. The final input representation scheme settled upon for use in the ETA neural network took the form of 15 specific angles between various markers (see Figure 8).

Figure 5. FLEX: C120 camera setup displaying tripod and mounting platform

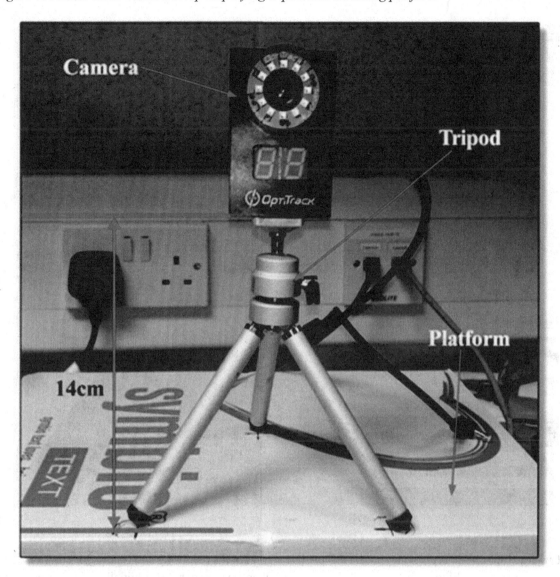

The initial code for the neural network was taken from (Chopra, 2009) and is open source written in C++ which has been extended and edited for our purposes. The completed neural network consists of three separate layers: the input layer, a single hidden layer where most of the classification is performed and a final output layer in which a single emotion is identified as the dominant among Ekman's universal prototypic emotions (see Figure 9). As illustrated in Figure 9 there are 15 nodes in the input layer representing the angles computed using the input representation scheme, 15 nodes in the hidden layer and 6 nodes in the output layer (one for each of the emotions the network has been trained to recognise).

The network's hidden layer is where most of the process of producing the output value for each of the six nodes in the output layer is performed. Once these have been computed an output interpretation model is used to make the final emotion classification from the values of each of the out-

Figure 6. FLEX: C120 camera positioned above screen of Lenovo W500 Thinkpad notebook

put nodes. Each node represents one of the primaries proposed by Ekman.

The finished neural network was trained using 40 instances of each emotion (270 in all) and 10 instances were recorded separately for each emotion and used as validation sets for early stopping and prevention of over-fitting. The neural network was also programmed to ensure at least 10000 training iterations were achieved before the early stopping algorithm was allowed to halt the learning process. This was used to reduce the chance of the network training terminating prematurely.

For the recording and training of emotion other than those the network is initially trained to recognise (such as non-universal emotions like uncertainty or confusion), an interface is provided to re-train the network using the newly recorded emotion data. For efficient training the network should also be given a number of instances of the emotion for testing and validation purposes (the ETA uses 10 sets of coordinates as validation sets for the prototypic emotions) which will allow the early stopping training function to prevent over-training of the network.

The next section will describe the evaluation tests performed in order to assess the performance of the ETA neural network and a description is given of

Figure 7. Positions of tracking markers placed on a user's face. The 3 highlighted markers are those used in preprocessing to calculate and remove affine transformations distorting the input data.

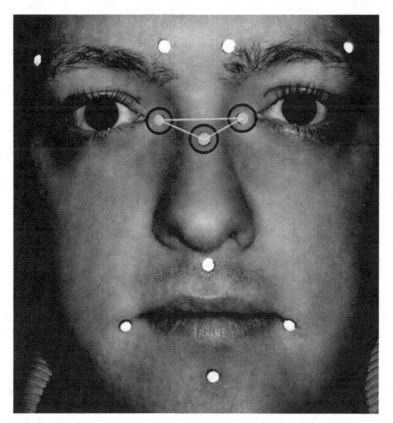

an implementation study which was performed to gauge the effect of the ETA on a number of users in a communication context.

ETA ASSESSMENT AND PERFORMANCE EVALUATION

The neural network which forms the heart of the emotion recognition system for our ETA was evaluated in a number of experimental tests designed to gauge its ability to recognise each of the 6 primary emotions. The network's abilities were also compared to the emotion recognition capacity of a group of human participants tested on videos of the same facial expressions, in order to ascertain that it operated with at least the abilities of a human observer. This also ensured its

performance was adequate for its real-time usage requirement, as a substitute for a user's eyes in keeping track of the non-verbal communication of other users outside his/her field of view. The final testing of this software agent required both its integration within a virtual meeting environment that supports multi-modal remote collaboration, and an implementation study performed in order to evaluate its contribution to reducing the negative effects of multitasking among users in remote meetings.

Our first test involved the recording of a user's facial movements using the FLEX: C120 camera and a digital video camera simultaneously. The experiment was conducted as a benchmark for evaluation of the recognition ability of the ETA's neural network in comparison with human subjects. The videos recorded using the digital camera

Figure 8. Illustration of 15 angles used in current analysis for the angle input representation scheme. Angles are labeled in order from a to o.

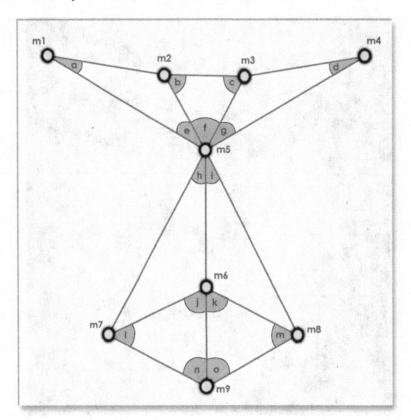

were shown to a group of 15 subjects who were instructed to identify which of the 6 primary emotions each video portrayed. The data recorded by the motion tracking camera (i.e., the coordinates of facial markers) were presented to the ETA's neural network in the same order as the videos were given to the experiment participants.

Experimental Results

The results of the experiment assessing the ability of 15 human subjects to identify emotions from video produced an average of 78.15% recognition rate (i.e. an average of 78.15% of the videos shown to the participants, were identified correctly). Falling between the high average emotion recognition accuracy of 89% published in (Susskind, et al., 2007) and the relatively low recognition accuracy

of 69% published in **(Zucker, et al., 2008),** our results appear to be consistent with previous studies.

The results achieved by our ETA's neural network on the same dataset yielded a 95.93% recognition rate, indicating that the neural network used in this research exceeds the accuracy of human observers when detecting primary emotion from facial movements. In order to assess the ETA further it was necessary to perform a study in which the agent was integrated into a virtual meeting environment. This study is described in the next section.

Implementation Study

A study was conducted with two main objectives: to illustrate the use of the ETA agent in its intended role and to evaluate the completed prototype agent. The study involved evaluating the benefits of the

Figure 9. The basic structure of the ETA neural network

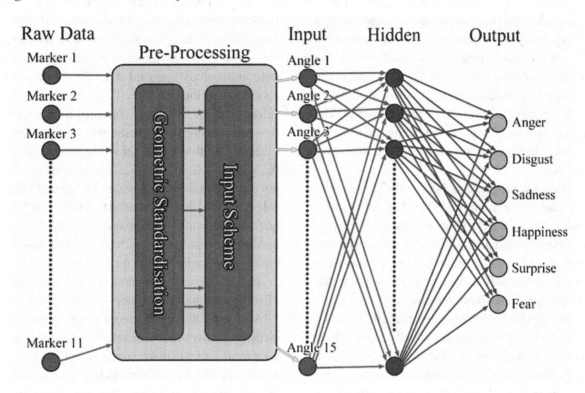

ETA in relation to a multitasking user's understanding of information presented to him/her during the study and his/her perceived effectiveness of the agent in increasing emotional awareness and attention in the test environment. The Collaborative Virtual Environment (CVE) used in this study was *VRCGroups (Virtual Reality Collaboration Groups)*, a virtual research and teaching environment created during an earlier project by members of our research team. VRCGroups is a fully functional LAN based collaborative virtual environment which provides text and voice chat facilities along with application and work sharing tools for user collaboration. Within the VRC-Groups meeting environment, users are able to log into a virtual university or office workspace and interact and work together on shared work files or take part in virtual meetings.

The implementation study involved analysing the experiences of a number of individuals in the VRCGroups environment, both with and without

the use of the ETA, with the goal of measuring their emotional awareness under a heavy multitasking situation and to evaluate the impact of the agent on their communication abilities. The study consisted of two stages, both of which involved a number of participants engaging in a simulated remote meeting where they were required to juggle multiple tasks in parallel while also paying attention to another user's presentation. The first stage required participants to complete their tasks without the help of the ETA and the second saw the ETA functionality included.

The main task given to the subjects involved listening to a presenter talk about a topic and to provide feedback in the form of emotions perceived and meaning of the presented message. A mixed quantitative and qualitative questionnaire was used to determine a participant's emotional awareness in both stages and to determine the participant's perception of the meaning of presented messages during the study. Another survey was used at the end of the second stage to allow participants to give feedback on the perceived benefits or disadvantages instigated by the introduction of ETA functionality. In order to induce multitasking, a side-task in the form of a short IQ-style test was also given to the participants, to complete in parallel with the main emotion identification and perception survey. The results of this side-task were not important but the effect it had on the participants of the study was imperative.

Any learning effects between both stages of the study were minimised since both stages took place a month apart and none of the subjects were given any feedback about the results of either stage. In both stages of the study, the participants were observed but only to the extent of ensuring that all aspects of the study ran smoothly. No further interaction between study subjects and the observer was conducted to ensure any added negative effect or extra variables introduced would be minimised. Any effect caused by the subjects being aware that they were under observation should not have a significant impact on the study outcome since both stages equally shared this experience. It is of course possible that being observed may have reduced the subject's propensity to become distracted or multitask but such effects would have meant that any positive observations from the study would merely be increased in a less controlled environment such as in a real remote collaboration situation.

Implementation Study Results

Participants of the study observed that, with the inclusion of the ETA, they were capable of concentrating on the side task more due to the abundance of emotional information provided which made the understanding of the meaning of the presented information much easier. Subjects also stated that the juggling of two tasks is much easier if one of the tasks is aided by the ETA and it is clear when the increased accuracy of the subject's descriptions in stage 2 is considered, that the overall interaction seems to have benefited significantly.

Another remark made by subjects in interview indicated that concentration was never really a large problem in either stage but they did note that it was definitely easier to focus and concentrate in the study's second stage. Some subjects revealed that their strategy for dealing with the side-task in the first stage consisted of choosing the easiest of the given questions to perform first, in order to allow more time to concentrate on the main presentation task. This was apparently not a problem during the second stage and most subjects stated that they tended to go from the first question sequentially to the last due to the lack of need to concentrate as much on the main task to the degree required in the initial stage.

In relation to emotional awareness, a number of subjects remarked in interviews that once the ETA informed them of the emotion being portrayed on the presenter's face during the interaction, they were more aware of that emotion in the presenter's vocal tone and the emotions in his voice seemed clearer and more pronounced. It was also noted that the ETA made it easier for them to recognise and distinguish problem emotions such as the negative emotions of *anger*, *disgust* and *fear* which were identified by subjects as being harder to differentiate or detect from the presenter's vocal tone alone in stage 1 of this study. Positive emotions such as *happiness* and *surprise* were noted as easier to recognise from vocal tone than their negative counterparts.

The effect of the information offered by the ETA was evident from the descriptions given by the subjects in the second stage of this study (where the ETA supported the interactions) from their use of the names of emotions prompted by the ETA in their described meanings recorded in this stage.

The use of more concise and detailed language during the second stage of this study by the majority of subjects indicated an increase in understanding of the underlying message portrayed by the presenter. The usage of words such as "might be," "seems," "maybe," or "it appears to be" were prevalent in stage 1 giving the impression of a lack of certainty and sureness in the subject's descriptions. During the second stage it was clear from the predominance of terms such as "definitely" or "does not" or "is not" or "is," that there was a clear increase in the subject's confidence and certainty in their answers. This improvement in the certainty levels of the study participants suggested a positive reaction to the inclusion of the ETA which complemented the previously observed increases in the subject's understanding and emotional awareness.

Implementation Study Implications

During the implementation study many conclusions and observations have been made in relation to the effect of the integrated software agent solution on users communicating in a virtual environment and their resulting abilities to deal with multiple tasks.

This completed research represents a framework on which future developed applications for the support of remote work can be built upon using the scientifically verified approach and high level design decisions used. The agent solution has been demonstrated to allow online collaborators to more easily perform multiple tasks when one or more of these tasks involve a communicative interaction supported by the ETA. The results of this work has illustrated that the application of such an emotion tracking agent to remote work tools can have the capability to increase collaborating user's understanding of vocal communication and increase their attention and ability to concentrate on the ETA supported interactions.

The methods used in this project to attempt to alleviate the problems caused by remote worker multitasking are not only useful in this task, but also represent a non-verbal communication interface which enriches the communication process within these virtual work and research environments.

Through this implementation study we can conclude that there is a clear benefit to the emotional awareness of users when the agent is supporting

an online interaction, and that users experienced increases in their abilities to focus and concentrate on the interaction and other side interactions as a result of this. The most notable limitations of our system uncovered by the study related to difficulties relating to such vocal subtleties as sarcasm, where facial expressions may not always reflect a person's true emotions, leading to increased confusion in certain situations. This limitation serves to further highlight the importance of non-universal emotions and states in a collaborative interaction: our future work includes a study involving non-universal emotions.

CONCLUSION

The agent solution developed during the completion of this research, has been demonstrated to allow workers to more easily perform multiple tasks when one or more of these tasks involve a communicative interaction supported by the ETA. The results of this work have illustrated that the application of such an emotion tracking agent to remote collaboration tools has the capability to increase collaborating user's understanding of vocal communication and increase their attention and ability to concentrate on the ETA supported interactions while engaged in side-tasks. Such increased communicative abilities between collaborating users will help bridge the gap between real world and virtual world interactions and if such an agent is developed further to a commercially available product built on commonly available hardware (removing the need for physically applied markers), then it would represent an important step forward in remote work/research supporting technology.

The research related to the tracking and recognition of non-verbal displays of emotion carried out during this research project has demonstrated the importance of facial expression in the portrayal of emotion and meaning in an online communicative interaction between two or more collaborating persons. It was evident from observations made during the implementation study that without the accompaniment of facial expressions during a communicative interaction, the listening parties may exhibit difficulties in extracting the full meaning of vocally communicated messages. Clear improvements to user's understanding and confidence in the correctness of extracted meaning were observed upon the introduction of the ETA prototype into the communicative process. During the implementation study it was also observed that the non-verbal feedback provided by the ETA adds to a user's ability to more clearly understand messages from other participants where the person's facial expressions are not directly in view of the user.

Although there are a number of facial expression recognition applications which have been developed previously by researchers, the application of real-time emotion recognition from facial expression has not before been applied to the reduction of multitasking drawbacks and the enhancement of users' attention and awareness in a remote work context.

FUTURE RESEARCH DIRECTIONS

Due to the fact that a wide range of fields have been drawn upon and applied to this research, a wide variety of important research problems have been uncovered. A number of these apply primarily to remote collaboration itself, while others are of more general interest to emotion recognition, non-verbal communication interfaces and cognitive science and psychology applications. Since this chapter's focus is on remote research we will however only discuss this area.

The limitations uncovered by assessment of the chosen research methodologies have highlighted a number of further research studies which will be of benefit to the additional assessment of the developed ETA in relation to remote worker/ researcher multitasking. Through analysis of the results, the implementation study appears to have fallen short, in certain respects, of fully simulating remote worker multitasking. In order to better analyse the agent's benefits to multitasking remote interaction participants, we are currently undertaking a more detailed case study in which the ETA is employed in a real collaborative research situation over an extended time period.

In addition to this more detailed case study, the methods used in increasing the attention and emotional awareness of multitasking remote meeting participants may be further improved by selectively using the 3 modes of presenting the emotions recognised by the ETA (vocal, textual and visual) in order to be less intrusive to the user and to maximise the visibility of the message without interfering with ongoing interactions. Possible directions could include using vocal mode only in the situation where a user is unable to clearly see other modes, such as when users are not currently paying attention to their computer monitors, perhaps while attending to other unrelated tasks or away from keyboard. Using the textual or chat message mode would be more beneficial to users who frequently made use of such chat facilities in the environment. Visual mode may be useful as a default if neither text nor vocal are appropriate choices.

Another more obvious direction to take in furthering this research is the replacement of the optical motion capture device with a webcam using robust image processing techniques to provide feature extraction and input for the ETA neural network. This would not only be more practical and less intrusive but also more economical if such an emotion recognition agent is to be eventually developed into a commercial product. Use of the ETA without specialised equipment beyond those required for remote work would minimise the boundaries which may arise from the extra expense and expertise needed to operate specialist technology. Much work has been done in developing efficient image processing algorithms for facial expression recognition in recent years and further research into the application of these algorithms for the ETA would undeniably benefit the future of our work.

It is also evident that future implementations of the ETA should apply greater focus on the support for tracking and recognition of non-universal emotions and states such as confusion, agreement and (dis)interest. The primary emotions used in the proof of concept prototype agent are not particularly useful in real-life collaborative interactions, and thus research in order to extend the emotion recognition architecture to better deal with such states and emotions would be of great benefit.

Another aspect of facial movement which was not addressed during the discussed project is the dynamic characteristics of facial deformations during the display of facial expression. Our research to date has involved analysis of only the static characteristics of facial expression and has not taken into account such concepts and transitions between emotions or emotion intensity. Such concepts may be better dealt with if the ETA was capable of analysing sequences of images as opposed to a single static snapshot of an individual's facial expression. Future research into the extension of the emotion recognition architecture to include such dynamic characteristics may also be of benefit to the overall agent.

REFERENCES

Aasman, J. (1995). *Modeling driver behaviour in Soar*. Leidschendam, The Netherlands: KPN Research.

Allport, A., Styles, E., & Hsieh, S. (1994). Shifting intentional set: Exploring the dynamic control of tasks. In Umita, C., & Moscovitch, M. (Eds.), *Attention and performance XV: Conscious and Nonconscious Information Processing* (pp. 421–452). Cambridge, MA: MIT Press.

Ancona, D., & Caldwell, D. (1990). Information technology and work groups: The case of new product teams. In Galegher, J., Kraut, R., & Egido, C. (Eds.), *Intellectual Teamwork: Social and Technological Foundations of Cooperative Work* (pp. 173–190). Hillsdale, NJ: Erlbaum.

Anderson, J. R., Reder, L. M., & Lebiere, C. (1996). Working memory: Activation limitations on retrieval. *Cognitive Psychology, 30*(3), 221–256. doi:10.1006/cogp.1996.0007

Appelbaum, S. H., Marchionni, A., & Fernandez, A. (2008). The multitasking paradox: Perceptions, problems and strategies. *Management Decision, 46*(9), 1313–1325. doi:10.1108/00251740810911966

Baddeley, A., Chincotta, D., & Adlam, A. (2001). Working memory and the control of action: Evidence from task switching. *Journal of Experimental Psychology, 130*(4), 641–657. doi:10.1037/0096-3445.130.4.641

Baddeley, A., & Logie, R. H. (1999). Working memory: The multiple-component model. In Miyake, A., & Shah, P. (Eds.), *Models of Working Memory: 110 Annual Review of Information Science and TechnFology Mechanisms of Active Maintenance and Executive Control* (pp. 28–61). Cambridge, UK: Cambridge University Press.

Barnett, C. (2004). Pro-poor dissemination: Increasing the impact of research. *Development in Practice, 14*(3), 432–439.

Bélanger, F. (1999). Workers' propensity to telecommute: An empirical study. *Information & Management, 35*(3), 139–153. doi:10.1016/S0378-7206(98)00091-3

Belanger, F., & Collins, R. (1998). Distributed work arrangements: A research framework. *The Information Society, 14*, 137–152. doi:10.1080/019722498128935

Benbunan-Fich, R., & Truman, G. E. (2009). Multitasking with laptops during meetings. *Communications of the ACM, 52*(2), 139–141. doi:10.1145/1461928.1461963

Black, J., & Hearne, S. (2008). *Effective leadership of international virtual project teams*. Denver, CO: PMI Global Congress.

Burgess, P. W. (2000). Realworld multitasking from a cognitive neuroscience perspective. In Monsell, S., & Driver, J. (Eds.), *Control of Cognitive Processes: Attention and Performance XVIII* (pp. 465–472). Cambridge, MA: MIT Press.

Cabon, P., Coblentz, A., & Mollard, R. (1990). Interruption of a monotonous activity with complex tasks: Effects of individual differences. In *Proceedings of the Human Factors Society 34th Annual Meeting*, (pp. 912-916). HFS Press.

Chibelushi, C. C., & Bourel, F. (2002). *Facial expression recognition: A brief tutorial overview*. Retrieved from http:// homepages.inf.ed.ac.uk/ rbf/ CVonline/ LOCAL_COPIES/ CHIBELUSHI1/ CCC_FB_ FacExprRecCVonline. pdf.

Chopra, P. (2009). *Neural network base code*. Retrieved on 3 January, 2010 from http://paraschopra.com/.

Christensen, K. (1988). *The new era of home-based work*. Boulder, CO: Westview Press.

Cole, C., Spink, A., & Waller, M. (2008). Multitasking behaviour. In Cronin, B. (Ed.), *Annual Review of Information Science and Technology* (pp. 93–118). Medford, NJ: Information Today.

Cowie, R., Douglas-Cowie, E., Tsapatsoulis, N., Votsis, G., Kollias, S., Fellenz, W., & Taylor, J. G. (2001). Emotion recognition in human-computer interaction. *IEEE Signal Processing Magazine, 18*(1), 32–80. doi:10.1109/79.911197

DuBrin, A., & Barnard, J. (1993). What telecommuters like and dislike about their jobs. *Business Forum, 18*(3), 13.

Dukette, D., & Cornish, D. (2009). *The essential 20: Twenty components of an excellent health care team*. Pittsburgh, PA: RoseDog Books.

Dux, P. E., Ivanoff, J., Asplund, C. L., & Marois, R. (2006). Isolation of a central bottleneck of information processing with time-resolved fMRI. *Neuron, 52*(6), 1109–1120. doi:10.1016/j.neuron.2006.11.009

Ekman, P. (1980). *The face of man: Expressions of universal emotions in a New Guinea village*. New York, NY: Garland STPM Press.

Ellis, J., & Kvavilashvili, L. (2000). Prospective memory in 2000: Past, present and future directions. *Applied Cognitive Psychology, 14*(7), 1–9. doi:10.1002/acp.767

Foerde, K., Poldrack, R. A., & Knowlton, B. J. (2007). Secondary task effects on classification learning. *Memory & Cognition, 35*, 864–874. doi:10.3758/BF03193461

Fragopanagos, N., & Taylor, J. G. (2005). Emotion recognition in human-computer interaction. *Neural Networks: Emotion and Brain, 18*(4), 389–405.

Gilbert, A. (2004). Can't focus on the teleconference? Join the club. *C-Net*. Retrieved on January 3, 2010 from http:// news.cnet.com/ Cant-focus-on-the-teleconference-Join-the-club/ 2100-1022_3-5494304.html.

Gillie, T., & Broadbent, D. (1989). What makes interruptions disruptive? A study of length, similarity, and complexity. *Psychological Research, 50*, 243–250. doi:10.1007/BF00309260

Gladstones, W. H., Regan, M. A., & Lee, R. B. (1989). Division of attention: The single-channel hypothesis revisited. *Quarterly Journal of Experimental Psychology: Human Experimental Psychology 41*(A), 1-17.

Hallowell, R. (2007). *Crazy busy: Overstretched, overbooked, and about to snap! Strategies for handling your fast-paced life*. New York, NY: Ballantine Books.

Handy, S., & Mokhtarian, P. (1995). Planning for telecommuting: Measurement and policy issues. *Journal of the American Planning Association. American Planning Association, 61*(1), 99–111. doi:10.1080/01944369508975623

Hinze-Hoare, V. (2007). CSCR: Computer supported collaborative research. *University of Southampton*. Retrieved on October 14, 2008 from http:// arxiv.org/ abs/ 0711.2760.

Hogan, M. J., Kelly, C., & Craik, F. (2006). The effects of attention switching on encoding and retrieval of words in younger and older adults. *Experimental Aging Research, 32*(2), 153–183. doi:10.1080/03610730600553935

Holstein, W. J. (2006, June 7). The workplace. *International Herald Tribune*, p. 22.

Huws, U., Korte, W., & Robinson, S. (1990). *Telework: Towards the elusive office*. Chichester, UK: John Wiley and Sons.

Ishizaka, K., Marshall, S. P., & Conte, J. M. (2001). Individual differences in attentional strategies in multitasking situations. *Human Performance, 14*(4), 339–358. doi:10.1207/S15327043HUP1404_4

Jain, A. K., & Li, S. Z. (2005). *Handbook of face recognition*. Secaucus, NJ: Springer-Verlag New York.

Johnson, S. (1998). Teleworking service management – Issues for an integrated framework. In *Teleworking: International Perspectives* (pp. 185–206). New York, NY: Routledge.

Jones, R. M., Laird, J. E., Nielsen, P. E., Coulter, K., Kenny, P., & Koss, F. (1999). Automated intelligent pilots for combat flight simulation. *Artificial Intelligence Magazine, 20*, 27–42.

Kanade, T., Cohn, J., & Tian, Y. (2000). Comprehensive database for facial expression analysis. In *Proceedings of the Fourth IEEE International Conference on Automatic Face and Gesture Recognition (FG 2000)*, (pp. 484-490). Grenoble, France: IEEE Press.

Khosrowabadi, R., Heijnen, M., Wahab, A., & Chai Quek, H. (2010). *The dynamic emotion recognition system based on functional connectivity of brain regions*. Paper presented at the 2010 IEEE Intelligent Vehicles Symposium. San Diego, CA.

Kraut, R. (1989). Telecommuting: The trade-offs of home work. *The Journal of Communication, 39*(3), 19–47. doi:10.1111/j.1460-2466.1989.tb01038.x

Kreifeldt, J. G., & McCarthy, M. E. (1981). Interruption as a test of the user computer interface. In *Proceedings of the 17th Annual Conference on Manual Control*, (pp. 655-667). ACM.

Lee, F. J., & Anderson, J. (2001). Does learning of a complex task have to be complex? A study in learning decomposition. *Cognitive Psychology, 42*, 267–316. doi:10.1006/cogp.2000.0747

Leonard, D., Brands, P., Edmondson, A., & Fenwick, J. (1998). Virtual teams: Using communications technology to manage geographically dispersed development groups. In Bradley, S., & Nolan, R. (Eds.), *Sense and Respond: Capturing Value in the Network Era* (pp. 285–298). Boston, MA: Harvard Business School Press. doi:10.1142/9789814295505_0014

Logan, G. D. (2004). Working memory, task switching, and executive control in the task span procedure. *Journal of Experimental Psychology. General, 133*(2), 218–236. doi:10.1037/0096-3445.133.2.218

Lojeski, K. S., Reilly, R., & Dominick, P. (2007). Multitasking and innovation in virtual teams. In *Proceedings of the Hawaii International Conference on System Sciences*, (p. 44b). IEEE.

Lyons, M., Akamatsu, S., Kamachi, M., & Gyoba, J. (1998). Coding facial expressions with gabor wavelets. In *Proceedings of the Third International Conference on Face & Gesture Recognition (FG 1998)*, (p. 200). ACM.

Malone, T. (1997). Is 'empowerment' just a fad? Control, decision-making, and information technology. *Sloan Management Review, 38*(2), 23–35.

McFarlane, D. C. (1997). *Interruption of people in human-computer interaction: A general unifying definition of human interruption and taxonomy*. Washington, DC: Naval Research Laboratory. Retrieved on January 5, 2009 from http:// www.interruptions.net/literature/McFarlane-NRL-97.pdf.

McFarlane, D. C. (2002). Comparison of four primary methods for coordinating the interruption of people in human-computer interaction. *Human-Computer Interaction, 17*(1), 63–139. doi:10.1207/S15327051HCI1701_2

Meyer, D. E., Kieras, D. E., Lauber, E., Schumacher, E. H., Glass, J., & Zurbriggen, E. (1995). Adaptive executive control: Flexible multiple-task performance without pervasive immutable response-selection bottlenecks. *Acta Psychologica. Discrete and Continuous Information Processing, 90*(1/3), 163–190.

Miyake, A., & Shah, P. (Eds.). (1999). *Models of working memory: Mechanisms of active maintenance and executive control*. Cambridge, UK: Cambridge University Press.

Monsell, S. (2003). Task switching. *Trends in Cognitive Neuroscience, 7*(3), 134–140. doi:10.1016/S1364-6613(03)00028-7

NaturalPoint. (2010). *Optical motion capture specialists*. Retrieved on January 4, 2010 from http://www.naturalpoint.com.

Nilles, J. S. (2000). *Integrating telework, flextime, and officing for workforce 2020*. Indianapolis, IN: Hudson Institute.

Nolan, R., & Galal, H. (1998). Virtual offices: Redefining organizational boundaries. In Bradley, S., & Nolan, R. (Eds.), *Sense and Respond-Capturing Value in the Network Era* (pp. 299–320). Boston, MA: Harvard Business School Press.

O'Connail, B., & Frohlich, D. (1995). Time space in the workplace: Dealing with interruptions. In *Proceedings of the Conference on Human Factors in Computing Systems,* (pp. 262-263). ACM.

Pashler, H. (1994). Dual-task interference in simple tasks: Data and theory. *Psychological Bulletin, 116*(2), 220–244. doi:10.1037/0033-2909.116.2.220

Pashler, H. (2000). Task switching and multitask performance (tutorial). In Monsell, S., & Driver, J. (Eds.), *Control of Cognitive Processes: Attention and Performance* (pp. 277–309). Cambridge, MA: MIT Press.

Rosen, C. (2008). The myth of multitasking. *The New Atlantis, 20*, 105-110. Retrieved on February 4, 2010 from http:// www.thenewatlantis.com/ publications/ the-myth-of-multitasking.

Rubinstein, J. S., Meyer, D. E., & Evans, J. E. (2001). Executive control of cognitive processes in task switching. *Journal of Experimental Psychology. Human Perception and Performance, 27*(4), 763–797. doi:10.1037/0096-1523.27.4.763

Ryan, A., Cohn, J. F., Lucey, S., Saragih, J., Lucey, P., de la Torre, F., & Rossi, A. (2009). Automated facial expression recognition system. In *Proceedings of the IEEE International Carnahan Conference on Security Technology*. IEEE Press.

Salvucci, D. D., Kushleyeva, Y., & Lee, F. J. (2004). Toward an ACT-R general executive for human multitasking. In *Proceedings of the Sixth International Conference on Cognitive Modeling,* (pp. 267-272). ACM.

Schweickert, R., & Boggs, G. J. (1984). Models of central capacity and on currency. *Journal of Mathematical Psychology, 28*(3), 223–281. doi:10.1016/0022-2496(84)90001-4

Snowdon, D., Churchill, E., Frécon, E., & Roberts, D. (2004). Communication infrastructures for inhabited information spaces. *Inhabited Information Spaces, Computer Supported Cooperative Work. Computer Science, 29*, 233–267.

Spink, A., Alvarado-Albertorio, F., Naragan, B., Brumfield, J., & Park, M. (2007). Multitasking information behavior: An exploratory study. *Journal of Librarianship and Information Science, 39*(3), 177–186. doi:10.1177/0961000607080420

Spink, A., & Cole, C. (2006a). New directions in human information behaviour. In *Annual Review of Information Science and Technology* (p. 116). Berlin, Germany: Springer.

Spink, A., & Cole, C. (2006b). Human information behaviour: Integrating diverse approaches and information use. *Journal of the American Society for Information Science and Technology, 57*(1), 25–35. doi:10.1002/asi.20249

Spink, A., & Cole, C. (2007). Multitasking framework for interactive information retrieval. In *New Directions in Cognitive Information Retrieval* (pp. 99–112). Berlin, Germany: Springer.

Spink, A., Ozmutlu, H. C., & Ozmutlu, S. (2002). Multitasking information seeking and searching processes. *Journal of the American Society for Information Science and Technology, 53*(8), 639–652. doi:10.1002/asi.10124

Spink, A., & Park, M. (2005). Information and non-information task interplay. *The Journal of Documentation, 61*(4), 548–554. doi:10.1108/00220410510607516

Stanek, D., & Mokhtarian, P. (1998). Developing models of preference for home-based and center-based telecommuting: Findings and forecasts. *Technological Forecasting and Social Change, 57*, 53–74. doi:10.1016/S0040-1625(97)00070-X

Stergiou, C., & Signanos, D. (1996). *Neural networks*. Retrieved on June 28, 2010 from http:// www.doc.ic.ac.uk/ ~nd/ surprise_96/ journal/ vol4/ cs11/ report.html#The Back-Propagation Algorithm.

Strayer, D. L., & Johnston, W. A. (2001). Driven to distraction: Dual-task studies of simulated driving and conversing on a cellular telephone. *Psychological Science, 12*(6), 462–466. doi:10.1111/1467-9280.00386

Susskind, J. M., Littlewort, G., Bartlett, M. S., Movellan, J., & Anderson, A. K. (2007). Human and computer recognition of facial expressions of emotion. *Neuropsychologia, 45*, 152–162. doi:10.1016/j.neuropsychologia.2006.05.001

Tsukada, K., Okada, K. I., & Matsushita, Y. (1994). The multi-project support system based on multiplicity of task. In Proceedings *of the 18th Annual International Computer Software and Applications Conference*, (pp. 358-363). ACM.

Vega, V. (2009). Seminar on the impacts of media multitasking on children's learning & development. *Stanford University*. Retrieved on February 4, 2010 from http:// multitasking.stanford.edu/ Multitasking Background Paper.pdf.

Verhulsdonck, G. (2007). Issues of designing gestures into online interactions: Implications for communicating in virtual environments. In *Proceedings of the 25th Annual ACM International Conference on Design of Communication (SIGDOC 2007)*, (pp. 26-33). ACM.

Vlaar, P. W. L., Van Fenema, P. C., & Tiwari, V. (2008). Cocreating understanding and value in distributed work: How members of onsite and offshore vendor teams give, make, demand, and break sense. *MIS Quaterly*, *32*(2), 227–255.

Waller, M. J. (1997). Keeping the pins in the air: How work groups juggle multiple tasks. In *Advances in Interdisciplinary Studies of Work Teams* (*Vol. 4*, pp. 217–247). Stamford, CT: JAI Press.

Waugh, N. C., & Norman, D. A. (1965). Primary memory. *Psychological Review*, *72*, 89–104. doi:10.1037/h0021797

Westfall, R. (1998). The microeconomics of remote work. In Igbaria, M., & Tan, M. (Eds.), *The Virtual Workplace* (pp. 256–287). Hershey, PA: IGI Global.

Whitehill, J., Bartlett, M., & Movellan, J. (2008). *Automatic facial expression recognition for intelligent tutoring systems*. Paper presented at the CVPR Workshop on Human Communicative Behavior Analysis. New York, NY.

Wickens, C. D. (1992). *Engineering psychology and human performance*. New York, NY: HarperCollins.

Wilson, T. D. (2000). Human information behaviour. *Informing Science*, *3*(2), 49–56.

Zhang, Z. (1999). Feature-based facial expression recognition: Sensitivity analysis and experiments with a multilayer perceptron. *International Journal of Pattern Recognition and Artificial Intelligence*, *13*(6), 893–911. doi:10.1142/S0218001499000495

Zucker, U., Radig, B., & Wimmer, M. (2008). *Facial expression recognition – A comparison between humans and algorithms*. Retrieved on January 7, 2010 from http:// www9-old.in.tum.de/ people/ wimmerm/ lehre/ sep_zucker/ sep_zucker. pdf.

Chapter 8
An Ontological Structure for Gathering and Sharing Knowledge among Scientists through Experiment Modeling

Luis Casillas
University of Guadalajara, Mexico

Thanasis Daradoumis
University of the Aegean, Greece & Open University of Catalonia, Spain

ABSTRACT

This chapter presents a proposal for modeling / simulating experiments conducted by scientists working in common scientific problems, based on gathering and exploiting knowledge elements produced among them. The authors' approach enables the adaptation of knowledge structures (bounded to scientific problems) and is based on recurrent refining processes that are fed by indicators, which come from collaboration among the scientists involved. This scheme captures a web-based infrastructure, which allows scientists to collaborate on synthesizing experiments online. The proposed model is approached as an ontology that contains scientific concepts and actions. This ontology is linked to the scientific problem and represents both the "common understanding" for such a problem and the way it could be managed by the group. This dynamic ontology will change its structure according to the collaboration acts among scientists. Frequent collaboration over certain elements of the experiment will make them prevail in time. Besides, this process has been defined in a way that provides a global understanding of the scientific treatment that could be applied on any scientific problem. Hence, the ontology represents a virtualization of the scientific experiment. This whole representation is aimed at providing the media for developing e-research among scientists that are working on common problems.

DOI: 10.4018/978-1-4666-0125-3.ch008

INTRODUCTION

Most of the activities developed by humans are based on sets of concepts and the relationships among such knowledge elements. The human's understanding of the environment is defined by the concepts and ideas acquired before. These elements are organized as nets of perceptions in which the relationships are modeled by links of proximity. The nets of concepts provide meaning by clustering related ideas. These meaningful structures could be understood as ontologies.

Our proposal aims at defining an innovative approach for the simulation of experiments through a formal process of gathering and sharing the knowledge from activities related to research, which results in defining an ontological structure. This ontology has dynamic capabilities in order to allow the addition of new slots for knowledge categories, concepts and relationships. The elements of the ontology can be shared among the researchers on common projects, with the purpose of establishing a *common understanding* of a scientific challenge and the topics to be observed and managed along the experimentation experience.

Scientists collaborating on the same scientific problem could modify the already defined structure, and such changes are allowed for all the collaborators. Researchers do not need to vote expressly for concepts (topics) or relationships, since the prolonged use of such elements will imply their confirmation, and the forgotten elements will eventually disappear.

Different tools could be used to build an artificial ontology with standardized format. The resulting construction could be shared among the scientists involved in the same research. We are proposing an abstract tool that may be fed by this model, where the concepts as well as their relationships are immediately shown.

This proposal is, by some means, framed by the regular understanding for e-science suggested by Atkins et al. (2003) and Jankowski (2007). We are trying to fulfill the remaining tasks in the simulation of experiments. In most of the cases, e-science is committed to offer information resources and is frequently focused on social sciences. The spirit of the e-science proposals is the capture of the web-based infrastructure. Thus, our proposal might be rather settled in the way of e-science experimentation, as explained by Walton and Barker (2004). The advance in information and communications technologies has enabled an innovative understanding for the web and its new capabilities allow an enhanced simulation of natural and/or technical phenomena.

KNOWLEDGE GRIDS AS ONTOLOGIES

It is a fact that knowledge has become an asset for most of the organizations, which are conscious about the resources of awareness and the ways to manage them. Knowledge, by itself, is hard to define and its handling is rather difficult. In such context, any knowledge managing technique acquires some attention from people related to the creation, storing and handling of knowledge. One of the most frequent mechanisms used to manage knowledge is grids (Li & Liu, 2007; Goble, et al., 2005; Zettsu, et al., 2008).

Every concept has its own charge of knowledge, which is a piece of information or even a piece of primitive knowledge. In order to represent a higher level of meaning, concepts can be assembled as nets. Along the process of assembling the nets of knowledge, the semantics bound to the nets becomes complex. Thus the action of assembling is important for meaning, although meaning does not depend on the assembling by itself, it depends on the concepts involved and the kind of relationships established among these concepts. Not every connection of concepts will imply meaningful structures. The connections should be rationally founded in the common understanding of reality.

The human brain is always trying to relate the stimuli, arriving from the environment, to the elements already stored by the previous experiences. The brain's goal is to produce meaning to the current experience. The network of concepts, made during this linking process in the brain, is able to produce meaning. Artificial grids of knowledge could produce the very same support for dealing with synthetic concepts.

According to the Stanford Encyclopedia of Philosophy[1], *"ontology is the study of what there is."* The classical approach of ontology is bound with the mere existence of things. More recently, the concept of ontology has been associated to the capacity of machines to *synthetically* represent entities from the real world. Hence, concepts from reality could eventually be represented throughout ontological representations in machines.

Grids of knowledge can be understood as ontology. A synthetic ontology, from this perspective, can hold a family of concepts related to the understanding about some field of knowledge. These concepts are bound among themselves to form a grid.

RELATED WORK

The e-science seeks to provide order and support for the recent transformations in the science endeavors. In the current context of advanced technologies for information and communications, there is an infrastructure that undergirds modern societies. Science is undoubtedly seizing such infrastructure (Jankowski, 2007).

The report from Atkins et al. (2003) is highly focused in the exploitation of the available cyber-infrastructure. According to them, there is a revolution in science due to advances in information and communication technologies. This revolution is based in the innovative capabilities to successfully **emulate reality in the digital dimension**. Specifically, these authors argue *"...the classic two approaches to scientific research, theoretical / analytical and experimental / observational, have been extended to in silico simulation and modeling to explore new possibilities and to achieve new precision... "* (p. 4); with important achievements in Forestry, Ocean Science, Environmental Science, and Engineering, Space Weather, Computer Science and Engineering, Information Science and Digital Libraries, Biology / Bioinformatics, Medicine, Physics, Astronomy, Engineering, Materials Science and Engineering, and Social and Behavioral Sciences.

For Jankowski (2007) e-science is strongly supported by key aspects of the information and communication technologies, which are: *"1. International collaboration among researchers; 2. Increasing use of high-speed interconnected computers, applying Grid architecture; 3. Visualization of data; 4. Development of Internet-based tools and procedures; 5. Construction of virtual organizational structures for conducting research; 6. Electronic distribution and publication of findings."*

Besides, Jankowski (2007) has identified specific fields in the e-science activity: *"1. Managing collaboration and communication among researchers separated by distance; 2. Developing and using Internet-based tools for data collection, analysis, and visualization of findings; 3. Archiving and providing access to data; 4. Publishing and disseminating results."*

In this context, there is a clear need of mechanisms to successfully represent diverse phenomena in the digital dimension. Since 1960's, computers had been used formally in the scientific field. The tasks that used to be assigned to computers were mainly connected to calculations in iterative, recurrent and concurrent contexts. More recently, the advances in computers' graphics allowed improved simulations. Nowadays, computers are not the actor using "brute force" anymore. Of course, they will do the calculations needed; however, the main goals have changed. The goal for computers in this context is to support the collaboration among scientists, in the already mentioned fields for e-science.

According to Anandarajan and Anandarajan (2010), scientists have worked for the last decades under a quite regular fashion: isolated groups of researchers developing solutions (*ideas, projects, and inventions*), based on common understanding for a problem and its solution. For these editors, the advent of the Web technologies paraphernalia has established a new comprehension for collaboration among researchers: social networks and collaboration tools have enabled the knowledge sharing. In this context, they argue: "*...currently, tens of thousands of researchers are using research networks, ushering in a new paradigm for research. In this paradigm, collaboration is made much easier, and sharing of research knowledge is instant. Synergies from routine collaboration will yield huge advances in research productivity and innovation...*" (p. v).

One of the mechanisms that could support such forms of collaboration is the knowledge representation through formal structures. If it is admitted that there is knowledge underlying in the scientific problems, knowledge representation achieves forcefulness. The act of "sharing knowledge" would narrow under a standardized scheme, making available an improved capability to model advanced concepts of the analyzed problem.

During the last decade the ontology-based approach has become a goal in diverse fields related with knowledge handling. Human interaction through artificial channels requires meta-structures for representing and handling the knowledge involved. Unfortunately the practice of the ontology's design and its managing imply the resolution of complex challenges. Ontology mapping has a range of options to be modeled (Kalfoglou & Schorlemmer, 2003).

Newman et al. (2009) have proposed a complete framework for: "*1. Facilitate management and sharing of Research Objects (ROs); 2. Support a social model; 3. Provide an open extensible environment; 4. Provide a platform to action research.*"

Their project (*myExperiment*), is a model that has been influenced by these four capabilities in order to provide the support to the scientists' interaction. *myExperiment* is based on a Resource Description Framework (RDF), this description is aimed at sharing definitions of experiments. These specifications include different components, such as contributions and experiments involved. This approach is an important reference regarding the backbone for the knowledge required in *e-Research*. Unfortunately the Newman's proposal does not include clear ideas regarding the interaction processes among scientists and it focuses on the complexity bound to the ontology mapping.

There is another group interested in sharing high level knowledge among scientists. The project FEARLUS-G of Pignotti et al. (2004), which allows large scale experiments distributed among participants throughout a semantic grid. Pignotti's group has understood that scientific research always involves collaboration between individual scientists. They are clear about the Internet's capability to share and distribute data, but they noticed that such channel does not offer a natural way to manage and coordinate computational resources. There is a set of models under the FEARLUS project. They are oriented to provide semantics to atomic elements bound to the experiment. The aim is to provide an infrastructure for simulating the collaboration that would happen among scientists cooperating under the same ceiling. This infrastructure could handle experiments involving participants from remote locations. The main constraints from FEARLUS project is that is focused in specific domains related to land use research, although their discoveries are useful in general approaching for social/scientific interaction.

The project STIN (Walker & Creanor, 2009) is an effort to go beyond the eLearning experience to explore the relationships between people and technology. The most interesting aspect from this project is the fact that its authors recognize networks as a way / tool to capture the complexity of relationships among people through technology artifacts. The STIN's framework is capable to handle different levels of resolution. Another interesting aspect from their proposal is the elements used to build the network, which is composed by objects and properties involved in the learning process instead of people as the center of the network. Unfortunately STIN project does not reach the following step in the semantics stair, the ontology approach.

David (2004) makes an astonishing utterance regarding the capability of scientists to perform e-research in the scopes provided by modern ICT's. This author recognizes the significant advance in information and communication technologies, as well as the internet computing and grid technologies. Nevertheless, the author also argues that *"engineering breakthroughs alone will not be enough to achieve the outcomes envisaged for these undertakings. Success in realizing the potential of e-Science—and other global collaborative activities supported by the 'cyber-infrastructure'—if it is to be achieved, will more likely be the resultant of a nexus of interrelated social, legal and technical transformations"* (p. 3). Hence, a technical effort, as the presented in this chapter, will provide a framework or, at least, a tool for gathering, handling and sharing the knowledge related to certain scientific activities. Our proposal tries to enhance the effects of data and information related to scientific research. According to David (2004), *"scientific research collaboration is more and more coming to be seen as critically dependent upon effective access to, and sharing of digital research data. Equally critical are the information tools that facilitate data being structured for efficient storage, search, retrieval, display and higher level analysis, and the codified and archived information resources that may readily be located and reused in new combinations to generate further additions to the corpus of reliable scientific knowledge"* (p. 5-6); our proposal could be framed in such understanding for e-science.

MODEL DEFINITION

The idea is to allow the collaboration among scientists through a common framework. This structure is composed by a set of concepts and the relationships among them. Under the assumption that: *it is possible to deal with a specific problematic through the treatment for a set of variables, ranging along a group of values*, the problem's decomposition will be oriented to gathering the main variables of the problem. The collaborative stages that have been considered for this experiment simulation model are:

- Discovering variables (direct and indirect). Variables are filtered to achieve an optimal list.
- Defining ranges for variables. Ranges are filtered to achieve an optimal definition of values.
- Building a Cartesian product to merge the variables through their ranges.
- Applying constrains to filter the set of *tuplets* resulting from the Cartesian product.
- Binding specific resulting *tuplets* to specific states in the contextual reality of the studied problem. Hence, defining a list of problem states based on *tuplets* of values.
- Defining or establishing possible actions over a studied problematic situation.
- Applying constrains to filter up to an optimal list of actions.
- Merging the discovered states of the problem with the resulting actions that are allowed in the context of the problem.

Discovering Variables Bound to the Problem / Solution

We understand every concept bound to the problem / solution as a specific assembly of variables. In order to compose this ensemble of variables, scientists should coordinate to discover and define the most significant aspects of the scientific problem. The set of variables could be classified as direct and indirect variables. Direct variables have an immediate influence in the outcome of the studied problem; meanwhile the indirect ones have an effect on the situation through the affection over direct variables or even other indirect variables. Understanding that every variable will imply specific dealing efforts, the list of variables must be filtered in order to achieve an optimal list. This list should have only the most representative indicator for the problem, but it should not miss any influent aspect of the problem / solution. Coordination among collaborating scientists is required in order manage this optimal list of variables.

Defining Ranges for Variables

Once the whole set of variables has been defined and refined, scientists should work over the definition for the ranges to every variable. This definition of ranges includes the data type specification for every variable. Some variables could have a declarative or qualitative specification for their range, e.g. a temperature could be expressed as "very cold," "cold," "warm," "hot," and "very hot." The use of these declarative elements will allow a handling with higher semantics for the aspects related to the problem.

Discovering and defining the variables and their ranges is a *non computable task*. These processes are clearly related to mental performance in humans, which remain away from current computers capabilities. It clearly demands some assistance from humans. Nevertheless, some automatic elements can be integrated in order to assist the scientists while they are collaborating in defining these main aspects, concepts and relationships of the problem. Distributed applications can support the sharing of knowledge among the researchers involved. Hence, a tool for cooperative work could be adapted to allow the variables' definitions and their ranges.

Merging Variables to Define the States of the Problem

The ranges of variables, resulting from the previous stage, are merged through a Cartesian product. This task is clearly assignable to machines. The wide list of ensembles of variables must be analyzed by the group of collaborating researchers. At this point, the task is oriented to discriminate those ensembles that do not have compatibility with problem understanding. This is an important activity. If redundant or incompatible ensembles are kept, the problem could become not amenable or even illogical for the approach. Two ideas are central in order to achieve this goal: on the one hand, the scientists involved are able to vote for the ensembles they consider as crucial. On the other hand, a set of constraints must be defined. If every ensemble resulting from the Cartesian product is understood as a configuration of the analyzed scope, we believe that these configurations are the states of the scientific problem. Thus, the constraints are defined as a set of states which represent the unreal or unpractical configurations of the problem.

Eventually, the list of states of the problem will be strictly defined by the cooperative work of the scientists involved in the treatment of the studied problem. At the same time, these states are the elements for constructing the ontology.

Defining the Applicable Actions for Problem / Solution

A set of scientific activities must be defined by the group of researchers. In this case, scientists must propose sets of activities. These activities are analyzed by the whole group. Once again, they will vote and confront them with the constraints (at this point, the constraints to perform certain action). Activities could be defined in different phases. At first, every activity is defined only by the name. Later on, the conceptualization of the activities should be specialized through the definition of inner steps. This exercise will allow the detection of redundant or missing activities. Inner steps could be established as a narrative inside a script.

It is possible to use a CSCW tool to undertake this task. In the first phase, a forum would be useful for providing the actions' listings. In the following phase, which concerns the activities' bodies, common spaces could be created to allow placing in the proposals; these spaces could be assessable by the collaborators.

Building the Network of States and Actions

The refined set of activities is merged with the states through a graph. The resulting network combines the different states of the problem, as nodes, and the actions which are responsible of the state changes, as edges. This network is the kernel for the ontology's construction. A sketch of this graph is shown in Figure 1. This figure shows a segment from a diagram for states' transition. It is built with the possible states and actions, in the scientific scope, bound to the problem. This diagram models the common awareness among scientists collaborating in the same problem.

The network of states and actions could be understood as a synthetic representation of the experiment. The main advantage of having this representation is the possibility to share and replicate the experiment among scientists throughout the cyber-infrastructure. It is also possible for scientists to operate the experiment and simulate the performance, without the necessity of being *in situ*. Hence, scientists can collaborate in the same experiment even if they are in different geographical places. A distributed approach is allowed. The number of variables and the fine tuning in the actions elected for the problem implies an improved granularity available for the scientific management.

This network is the ontology linked to the specific scientific problem. Its elements are bound

Figure 1. A segment from a diagram for states' transition

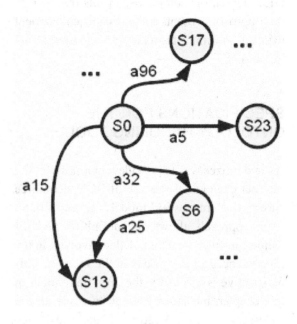

to the variables through the states (nodes) and the scientific actions through the edges.

Use of the Ontology

This ontology could be understood as the plastic representation of the hypotheses that are supporting the research effort. This is an important achievement for this model. This plastic representation could be always matched with the actual results during the experiment's development, as well as the capacity to correct the hypotheses or the tasks to perform. Hence, the ontology becomes a map to guide the research efforts made by the different participants, which constitutes a common reference built democratically by the participants.

Regarding the control of the interaction among the scientists, the model will be measured from the perspective of affiliation networks proposed by Faccioni and Panzarasa (2006). This approach is aimed at discovering the amount of knowledge transferred among the social actors collaborating in common spaces. These quantitative elements will provide additional semantics on the interaction acts shown by participants in the common research effort. Given the complexity of this framework, this approach presents a significant achievement to grasp "meaning" from the collaboration among humans.

SPECIFICATIONS FOR THE ONTOLOGY-HANDLING TOOL

A standardized way to provide semantics over the Internet channels is the use of RDF "Resource Description Framework" model (Tauberer, 2006). Such approach allows the definition and /or naming for pieces of knowledge involved in the transferences among nodes in the Internet. This perspective is useful for the proposed model in this chapter, but is not enough to cover all the necessary aspects to represent the knowledge involved, which has different semantic-levels.

According to the arguments in the previous sections, scientists must agree over the variables and scientific actions that are bound to the problem or experiment to be handled by the group. As it would be understood, the nature of these elements will differ among the experiments or problem regarded. Besides, the scientists and even scientific groups will have different understanding for the very same problem. Thus, the understanding and therefore the RDF for a scientific problem are strongly bound to such problem and the approach established by the people involved. This situation will imply the production of an RDF that can be used only in the analyzed problem. Although this treatment is valid and useful for dealing with a specific problem, it is not useful for dealing with any scientific problem. An additional structure for definitions must be considered. This additional arrangement contains definitions for global elements that are useful for any scientific treatment.

The higher level definitions in the upper RDF are aimed at gathering the main concepts and actions from any scientific challenge. As mentioned in the previous section, such elements are the direct and indirect variables as well as the scientific actions that can be performed over the variables. This meta-structure is the backbone for supporting a common handling for scientific problems. The lower level is bound to specific aspects of the problem, although is compatible to the higher understanding provided by the upper RDF. This lower RDF has definitions for concrete variables, states, actions and events from the scientific problem.

Meta-definitions can be defined as a framework for guiding the scientific efforts. The standard RDF provides mechanisms to crumble the knowledge into small pieces (Tauberer, 2006). The primitive elements of knowledge are organized as triplets and some rules are included to provide meaning. According to Tauberer (2006), an RDF document is built on the following bases: *"1. A fact is expressed as a Subject-Predicate-Object triple, also known as a statement. It's like a little English sentence. 2. Subjects, predicates, and objects are given as names for entities, also called resources (dating back to RDF's application to metadata for web resources) or nodes (from graph terminology). Entities represent something, a person, website, or something more abstract like states and relations. 3. Names are Uniform Resource Identifiers (URIs), which are global in scope, always referring to the same entity in any RDF document in which they appear. 4. Objects can also be given as text values, called literal values, which may or may not be typed using XML Schema datatypes."*

Hence, the graphical understanding for an ontology can be modeled as metadata that explains the treatment for a scientific problem. Figure 2 sketches the ontology both for the upper level of the scientific treatment for a problem and the breakdown of the associated complexity.

The RDF that can be built from the upper ontology for scientific problems, shown in Figure 2, is roughly approached through the tabular notation that is shown in Table 1. This approach is applied during the treatment of scientific problems and the effort to reach a solution. As such,

Figure 2. Graphical representation for the general ontology approach

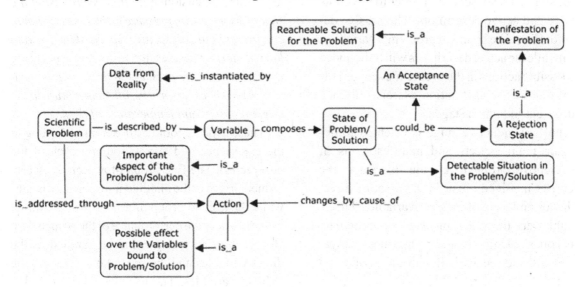

it can be understood as the ontology that supports an automated breakdown of the complexity in scientific problems.

Now, we have enough elements to build the RDF of the upper ontology meant for scientific problems. In order to achieve this knowledge representation, the first stage is to use a notation that mimics the tabular representation shown in Table 1. This representation style is called "Notation 3" or simply N3 (Tauberer, 2006). An advantage of this specification is that the notion of the underlying graph prevails and it is possible to grasp the elements organization from the reading. The next step is to build the RDF/XML standard representation, which is more compatible to the computer's approach but it is more obscure regarding the graph view.

Once the upper RDF has been defined, the following task is to build the lower RDF. This new effort is oriented to discover the specific aspects of the problem, based on the approach proposed through the higher ontology (represented in the upper RDF). During this task, it is precise to gather all the knowledge elements bound to the problem. These elements are gathered under the higher ontology's basis. Hence, the scientific

Table 1. Tabular representation for the general ontology approach

Start Node	Edge Label	End Node
Scientific Problem	is_described_by	Variable
Scientific Problem	is_addressed_through	Action
Variable	is_a	Important Aspect of the Problem / Solution
Variable	is_instantiatied_by	Data from Reality
Variable	composes	State of Problem / Solution
Action	is_a	Possible effect over the Variables bound to Problem / Solution
State of Problem / Solution	is_a	Detectable Situation in the Problem / Solution
State of Problem / Solution	could_be	An Acceptance State
State of Problem / Solution	could_be	A Rejection State
State of Problem / Solution	changes_by_cause_of	Action
An Acceptance State	is_a	Reachable Solution for the Problem
A Rejection State	is_a	Manifestation of the Problem

problem must be observed in order to unveil its passive and active descriptors. The passive descriptors could be bound to problem's variables; meanwhile the active descriptors will be bound to the possible actions in the problem's scope. This effort requires an abstraction exercise, divided in different inductive stages.

The first inductive stage is oriented to detect the main aspects and manifestations of the scientific problem. During this stage, the scientists involved must define a set of direct variables and a set of indirect variables. Direct variables are those that produce an immediate effect on problem's situation when they change; meanwhile indirect variables produce collateral effects in the problem. All scientists involved in the problem could provide sets of variables. A Problem / Solution administrator could collect those proposals and build unified lists of variables. At this point all the proposed variables are added and only those similar variables are combined into one common-identification. The discrimination of variables will be done automatically when a variable is left behind because some other variables are more effective to model the treatment of the problem.

These lists of variables, once defined, are treated through the assignment of ranges for every variable. The ranges are established, as it was mentioned before, through discrete elements. The use of discrete elements settles any exuberance of the problem. The variables are combined using a Cartesian product, which generates a set of *tuplets* that model the understanding of the problem, for the scientists involved, within the different dimensions that have been regarded as valid for the problem /solution. Every *tuplet* represents a possible state of the problem.

This inner approach to the scientific problem can be shown throughout an example: *the design of an intelligent suspension of a car*, which will have the goal of providing automatic-response to changes in the road and driving conditions. This is shown in Figure 3. Some interesting aspects

in the car suspension are: *oil pressure inside the shock absorbers, oil pressure in the steering pump, compression in coil springs, speed of the car and lateral inertia;* besides, the following aspects are interesting too: *air pressure in tires, oil temperature in the shock absorbers, oil temperature in the steering pump and temperature of tires.*

These aspects could be different according to the experience and abstraction approach of the observer(s). The first group of aspects is clearly influencing over the intelligent suspension; meanwhile the second group of aspects has not direct influence over the performance of the suspension. Hence, the first group could be handled as the direct variables and the second one refers to the indirect variables. The following stage consists in defining discrete ranges for the variables. Table 2 shows the discrete ranges for those variables that have been considered a direct. These variables, as well as the acronyms that shorten the variables' names, play an influencing role in an intelligent suspension. Once again, the discrete ranges could be different according to the approach of every person.

In addition, Table 3 shows the discrete ranges for those variables considered as indirect influence for the problem. It is understood that indirect

Figure 3. Graphical model for the hydraulic steering system analyzed

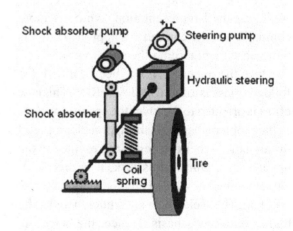

Table 2. Discrete ranges for the variables considered as direct

Oil pressure inside the shock absorbers (OPISA)	High
	Medium
	Low
Oil pressure in the steering pump (OPISP)	High
	Medium
	Low
Compression in coil springs (CICS)	Very shaky
	Frequent and heavy
	Frequent but brief
	Regular but intense
	Regular and brief
	Sporadic but intense
	Sporadic and brief
	Soft
Speed of the car (SOC)	First quintile
	Second quintile
	Third quintile
	Fourth quintile
	Fifth quintile
Lateral inertia (LI)	Left high
	Left medium
	Left low
	Equilibrium
	Right low
	Right medium
	Righ high

Table 3. Discrete ranges for the variables considered as indirect influence in an intelligent suspension, as well as the acronyms that shorten the variables' names

Air pressure in tires (APIT)	High
	Medium
	Low
Oil temperature in the shock absorbers (OTISA)	Very hot
	Hot
	Temperate
	Cold
	Very Cold
Oil temperature in the steering pump (OTISP)	Very hot
	Hot
	Temperate
	Cold
	Very Cold
Temperature of tires (TIT)	Very hot
	Hot
	Temperate
	Cold
	Very Cold

variables will influence the scientific problem through the changes they produce over the direct variables.

It is the time now for the variables to get mixed. In order to finish this task, the ranges of the variables are combined using the Cartesian product. Due to the simplification achieved for representing the problem's milestones, the effort to combine the ranges of the variables can be performed by an automatic algorithm.

A program could automatically produce the set of *tuplets* from merging the variables. Every *tuplet* is one of the possible states for the scientific problem according to the abstraction approach that supports the group of variables elected. Box 1 contains a subset of 945000 states found to the problem.

The following stage consists in defining the set of possible actions over the variables detected. Sometimes it is not possible to modify a variable's manifestation, such as modifying the time of continuing to passing, stopping it or returning it. Nevertheless, a set of actions must be made for all the variables that can be changed. All those variables that cannot be changed must be treated as implicit changes, bound to time or other unhandled events.

Box 1. A subset of the states bound to the scientific problem of the intelligent suspension

```
State: 0
Directs[opisa(High), opisp(High), cics(Very shaky), soc(First Quintile),
li(Left High)]
Indirects[apit(High), otisa(Very Hot), otisp(Very Hot), tit(Very Hot)]

State: 1
Directs[opisa(High), opisp(High), cics(Very shaky), soc(First Quintile),
li(Left High)]
Indirects[apit(High), otisa(Very Hot), otisp(Very Hot), tit(Hot)]
…

State: 427341
Directs[opisa(Medium), opisp(Medium), cics(Very shaky), soc(Third Quintile),
li(Right Medium)]
Indirects[apit(Medium), otisa(Cold), otisp(Cold), tit(Hot)]

State: 427342
Directs[opisa(Medium), opisp(Medium), cics(Very shaky), soc(Third Quintile),
li(Right Medium)]
Indirects[apit(Medium), otisa(Cold), otisp(Cold), tit(Temperate)]

State: 427343
Directs[opisa(Medium), opisp(Medium), cics(Very shaky), soc(Third Quintile),
li(Right Medium)]
Indirects[apit(Medium), otisa(Cold), otisp(Cold), tit(Cold)]
…

State: 944997
Directs[opisa(Low), opisp(Low), cics(Soft), soc(Fifth Quintile), li(Right
High)]
Indirects[apit(Low), otisa(Very Cold), otisp(Very Cold), tit(Temperate)]

State: 944998
Directs[opisa(Low), opisp(Low), cics(Soft), soc(Fifth Quintile), li(Right
High)]
Indirects[apit(Low), otisa(Very Cold), otisp(Very Cold), tit(Cold)]

State: 944999
Directs[opisa(Low), opisp(Low), cics(Soft), soc(Fifth Quintile), li(Right
High)]
Indirects[apit(Low), otisa(Very Cold), otisp(Very Cold), tit(Very Cold)]
```

It now possible to build a network in which the nodes are the states generated by merging the variables' ranges and the edges of the network are the actions and the implicit changes detected. This structure can be made through automatic media. Every state is faced to every action and implicit change detected, and every edge is modeled by considering the current state and the following one (as a leap of state). The resulting graph can be understood as a state transition diagram, which mimics the experiment according to certain approach. Hence the experiment can be modeled as a set of triplets, in which every triplet contains the code in Box 2.

These edges are not arbitrarily established; they are settled on the basis of the discrete ranges defined for the variables. If a certain state has the oil pressure in the steering pump as medium and the action of pumping more oil is performed, the oil pressure in the steering pump will increase and might reach the state of *high*. Therefore, the algorithm that creates the edges has to follow up a set of rules in which the behavior of variables is described under the effect of actions and implicit changes.

The first approach of the graph will be somehow *overcrowded* with transitions, as a natural effect of the computer's action which mixes blindly all of the states with all of the change factors. The rules will control the uncontrolled growing, but some redundant growing will happen in some branches of the definition. This collateral congestion could be handled by the natural interaction among scientists. All those underused transitions will receive less voting and eventually will be disregarded of the synthetic experiment.

Hence, the lower RDF must be constructed under the same perspective used to build the upper one, but now considering the concrete variables of the scientific problem and their discrete ranges,

the possible actions and the implicit changes are detected. A distributed tool, based on web, could handle these RDF definitions in order to manage their contents and enable the collaboration through the supervision of the use of each element. All those overused elements will imply a rhetorical invitation to maintain such element in the approach and all those underused elements will be a tacit invitation for removing them from the approach. Besides, a *system manager* or *collaboration supervisor* could always receive queries from scientists for adding or removing elements according to the own expertise or the own practical experiment definition.

DISCUSSION

The model presented in this work is a new proposal for modeling the knowledge undergirding scientific problems. Such a representation of knowledge can be used for supporting a series of tasks. The tasks considered during the construction of this proposal are the experiment modeling / simulation and the sharing of knowledge among scientists. Due to the nature of the representation proposed, RDF/XML, these tasks can be undertaken automatically by systems designed for such purpose. There are a series of feasible advantages from the perspective of this model:

- Scientists collaborating have the chance to narrow the exuberance that is bound to certain scientific problems, by synthesizing its treatment as a list of tasks. Though the act of following lists could kill creativity, our proposal provides some looseness regarding *collaboration mechanisms* and *human intervention* to **fix** or **complete** the approach taken for the problem/solution.

Box 2.

```
<tuplet_current_state, tuplet_following_state, action_or_event>
```

- The synthetic representation of experiments can travel along the Internet channels, enhancing the chances to capture the cyber-infrastructure. This representation can be easily replicated and shared among collaborators, while it provides ways for gathering feedback from specialists in the group, independently where they are.

- The RDF/XML representation for the experiment allows standardized transference and exploitation for the model. Different tools can grasp the meaning stored in the structure. The resulted ontology can feed adapted tools for virtual reality. Artificial agents could mimic the actors of the problem by performing as indicated in the diagram of the states and transitions, as explained by Walton and Barker (2004).

- Automatic testing tools could be implemented to run the tests over different aspects of the problem. Or, even, to verify automatically the presence of constraints disregarded by collaborating scientists. These tools can be fed with the proposed ontology.

CONCLUSION

Our proposal is aimed at creating a model that can support the scientific interaction among researchers involved in common problems. This very first step, described in this chapter, aims at creating procedures to approach effectively the scientific problem to be managed by the group. Such knowledge is used to build an artificial representation of the experiment. We believe that most of scientific problems could be approached by this perspective and, therefore, could be handled by the proposed model. Our method has the capacity to capture the main aspects linked to scientific problems: variables (direct and indirect), ranges for variables, states of the problem/solution, actions over the variables, implicit changes and state transitions. These elements, presented in synthetic fashion in machines, enable the idea that scientific problems can successfully be emulated in synthetic scopes, capturing the cyber-infrastructure. This is an important achievement, since a synthetic representation demands specific knowledge from the concrete object / situation represented; this knowledge, once isolated and represented in machines, promotes the enforcement of the indicators linked to complexity's control. By enabling this knowledge in machines, the synthetic representation can be easily transferred through regular channels that actually are used to transfer data and information in the Internet, as suggested by David (2004). The pending tasks in this project are the design of the interaction/collaboration model among participants and the implementation of the model in specific platforms. Nevertheless, the model is already defined; the whole design and implementation could also imply the development of a framework that supports the interaction among scientists cooperating in common problems.

ACKNOWLEDGMENT

This work has been partially supported by the FP7 European project ALICE, under grant FP7-ICT-2009-5-257639

REFERENCES

Anandarajan, M., & Anandarajan, A. (2010). *E-research collaboration: Theory, techniques and challenges*. Berlin, Germany: Springer-Verlag.

Atkins, D., Droegemeier, K., Feldman, S., Garcia-Molina, H., Klein, M. L., & Messina, P. (2003). Revolutionizing science and engineering through cyberinfrastructure: Report of the national science foundation blue-ribbon advisory panel on cyberinfrastructure. *National Science Foundation.* Retrieved June 16th 2011, from www.nsf.gov/ cise/ sci/ reports/ atkins.pdf.

David, P. A. (2004). Towards a cyberinfrastructure for enhanced scientific collaboration: Providing its 'soft' foundations may be the hardest part. *Oxford Internet Institute, Research Report No. 4, August 2004*. Retrieved June 30th 2011, from http://www.oii.ox.ac.uk/ resources/ publications/ RR4.pdf.

Faccioni, M., & Panzarasa, P. (2006). Knowledge transfer within affiliation networks. In *Proceedings of the IEEE International Engineering Management Conference*, (pp. 226-230). IEEE Press.

Goble, C., Stevens, R., & Bechhofer, S. (2005). The semantic web and knowledge grids. *Drug Discovery Today, 2*(3), 225–233. doi:10.1016/j.ddtec.2005.08.005

Jankowski, N. (2007). Exploring e-science: An introduction. *Journal of Computer-Mediated Communication, 12*(2). Retrieved June 15th 2011, from http://jcmc.indiana.edu/ vol12/ issue2/ jankowski.html.

Kalfoglou, Y., & Schorlemmer, M. (2003). Ontology mapping: The state of the art. *The Knowledge Engineering Review, 18*(1), 1–31. doi:10.1017/S0269888903000651

Li, H., & Liu, L. (2007). A decentralized resource discovery based on keywords combinations and node clusters in knowledge grid. In *Proceedings of the Intelligent Computing 3rd International Conference on Advanced Intelligent Computing Theories and Applications,* (pp. 738-747). Qingdao, China: Springer.

Newman, D., Bechhofer, S., & De Roure, D. (2009). *myExperiment: An ontology for eResearch*. Paper presented at the Workshop on Semantic Web Applications in Scientific Discourse in Conjunction with the International Semantic Web Conference. Washington, DC.

Pignotti, E., Edwards, P., Preece, A., Gotts, N., & Polhill, G. (2004). FEARLUS-G: A semantic grid service for land-use modelling. In *Proceedings of the ECAI-04 Workshop on Semantic Intelligent Middleware for the Web & the Grid,* (vol 111). IEEE Press.

Tauberer, J. (2006). What is RDF? *O'Reilly XML from Inside Out*. Retrieved February 4th, 2011 from http://www.xml.com/ pub/ a/ 2001/ 01/ 24/rdf.html.

Walker, S., & Creanor, L. (2009). The STIN in the tale: A socio-technical interaction perspective on networked learning. *International Forum of Educational Technology & Society, 12*(4), 305–316.

Walton, C., & Barker, A. (2004). An agent-based e-science experiment builder. In *Proceedings of the 1st International Workshop on Semantic Intelligent Middleware for the Web and the Grid,* (pp. 247-264). Valencia, Spain.

Zettsu, K., Nakanishi, T., Iwazume, M., Kidawara, Y., & Kiyoki, Y. (2008). Knowledge cluster systems for knowledge sharing, analysis and delivery among remote sites. In *Proceeding of the 2008 Conference on Information Modelling and Knowledge Bases XIX,* (pp. 282-289). Amsterdam, The Netherlands: IOS Press.

KEY TERMS AND DEFINITIONS

Cyberinfrastructure: The set of cybernetic implements which constitute the support to different services and functionality.

E-Science: The set of resources offered to support science practice throughout Internet channel.

Experiment Modeling: Achieving a synthetic representation of an experiment.

Knowledge Grid: A set of concepts linked through different abstract or concrete bounds.

Knowledge Transfer: The transference of concepts: ideas, awareness, etc. regarding a matter.

Online Collaboration: People collaborating throughout Internet channels: mainly the Web.

Ontology Mapping: Gathering pieces from reality and insert them into the slots bound to main concepts.

ENDNOTES

[1]   Stanford. (2011). *Website*. Retrieved from http://plato.stanford.edu/.

Section 2
Applications and Case Studies

Chapter 9
CAWriter:
A Computer Supported Collaborative Tool to Support Doctoral Candidates Academic Writing – A Pedagogical and Human–Computer Interaction Perspective

Jake Rowan Byrne
Trinity College Dublin, Ireland

Brendan Tangney
Trinity College Dublin, Ireland

ABSTRACT

This chapter discusses a range of topics, including pedagogical concerns, writing practices, existing tools, and human computer interaction approaches, all related to the design of a tool to support PhD candidates with their academic writing. These topics are then used to inform the design of a computer supported collaborative writing tool, CAWriter, which is being developed as part of an ongoing participatory design research project concerned with the creation of a toolkit to support doctoral candidates. This chapter reviews existing tools to support the writing process and explores both the relevant pedagogical and human-computer interaction foundations necessary for the design of such tools. The chapter concludes with a look at a number of initial iterations of the CAWriter tool and the design rationale and approaches used.

INTRODUCTION

This chapter provides an overview for those interested in designing systems to support PhD candidates with academic writing. It highlights a broad range of areas in the literature from peda-

gogical concerns, existing systems and Human Computer Interaction methods and approaches needed to develop prototype designs. The chapter then explores the design of a Web-based Computer Supported Collaborative Learning/Work (CSCL/W) tool to support doctoral candidates with their academic writing. It looks at best practices, strategies and existing approaches to support the

DOI: 10.4018/978-1-4666-0125-3.ch009

PhD candidate with their academic writing. It is the aim of this chapter to provide the reader with a good foundation from which they can develop their own designs.

Pedagogical theories and practices on doctoral training generally emphasis the social and collaborative nature of learning (Boud & Lee, 2008; Hopwood & McAlpine, 2007; Leshem, 2007; McCotter, 2001). Community of Practice (Johnson, 2001; Lave & Wenger, 1991; Miao, Fleschutz, & Zentel, 1999; Wenger, 1998; Wenger & Snyder, 2000), Cognitive Apprenticeship (Lave & Wenger, 1991), and Peer Learning (Boud & Lee, 2005) provide the theoretical frameworks to describe the social environment and practice in which doctoral candidates can be supported in the transition from novice researchers to legitimate members of the academic community.

The pedagogical literature specifically addressing computer science doctoral training, the context in which this research is taking place, is limited but a noticeable exception is an ACM taskforce paper on research methods in computing (Holz, et al., 2006) which extends Bloom's taxonomy of higher order thinking skills (Bloom, Krathwohl, & Masia, 1956) for the domain of computer science doctoral training education. The extended framework covers "core skills," such as synthesis, evaluation and analysis, which are largely applicable to all scientific disciplines and a set of "specific skills." These specific skills include selecting papers, analysing the literature, writing research proposals and evaluating results.

Although Holz et al and others regard writing as a central activity in research, doctoral candidates often receive little support in this area beyond the one-to-one meetings with their supervisor (Paré, Starke-Meyerring, & McAlpine, 2009). Aitchison and Lee (2006) argue that writing skills are best acquired through engagement with a community of practice and through apprenticeship. They also suggest that writing is a *"knowledge-creating"* rather than merely knowledge-recording activity. This view is supported by Sharples (1999), who

argues writing is a creative design process. These works do not deal specifically with the processes involved in academic writing, therefore this chapter describes, in detail, a largely paper based, approach to dissertation writing, the "Single System" (Single & Reis, 2009), is described in detail. The "Single System" provides a comprehensive peer supported model for dissertation writing which resonates with both the arguments for collaboration, mentioned above, and the features found in a number of innovative writing tools.

After an initial discussion on research and writing skills, and underlying pedagogical foundations for their acquisition, the chapter discusses tools which help with the writing process. Writer's Assistant (Sharples, Goodlet, & Pemberton, 1989) and iWeaver (Shibata & Hori, 2002, 2008) are described as examples of innovative tools to support non-linear approaches to writing. Concept mapping tools are also examined. Given the arguments in the literature that both collaboration and community of practice are central to doctoral training, key concepts from the field of Computer Supported Collaborative Work (CSCW) and Computer Supported Collaborative Learning (CSCL) are introduced and their implications for the design of writing tools are explored.

Against the background of the ideas introduced, the chapter describes how a Participatory Design (PD) and Participatory Action Research (PAR) approach is being followed in the iterative development of the CAWriter writing tool, which is in turn part of a larger virtual research environment project to support computer science doctoral candidates in mastering and utilising a range of research skills.

PEDAGOGICAL PRACTICES IN DOCTORAL TRAINING

Understanding the best practices and strategies within any domain is an essential element when designing a tool. This section reviews the pedagogical theories which are relevant to doctoral training. It includes Communities of Practice (CoP) (Johnson, 2001; Lave & Wenger, 1991; Miao, et al., 1999; Wenger, 1998; Wenger & Snyder, 2000), Cognitive Apprenticeship (Lave & Wenger, 1991), and Peer Learning (Boud & Lee, 2005).

"A community of practice is an intrinsic condition for the existence of knowledge, not least because it provides the interpretative support necessary for making sense of its heritage. Thus, participation in the cultural practice in which any knowledge exists is an epistemological principle of learning. The social structure of this practice, its power relationships, and its conditions for legitimacy define possibilities for learning (i.e. for legitimate peripheral participation)." (Lave & Wenger, 1991)

As described by Lave and Wegner's the concept of a Community of Practice (CoP) acts as an interpretive framework within which doctoral learning occurs in a sociocultural-historical context (Cumming, 2008). Three principles summarise the characteristics of a community of practice: a shared domain of interest, engagement in mutual learning and knowledge sharing, and a shared repertoire of resources (Leshem 2007). In both the works of Leshem & Cumming (2008) they suggest that the application of the CoP concept to doctoral programmes can support candidates in their learning of research practices. This may be achieved by fostering and developing communities that encourage the sharing of experience, knowledge and practice and in fostering legitimate participation both with their peers and supervisors.

Cognitive Apprenticeship builds on the traditional craft apprenticeship model where the learner acquires, develops and uses skills obtained from the practices of experts, through observation and collaboration in an authentic social context (Brown, Collins, & Duguid, 1989). In this view, and that of situated learning, the locus of learning expands beyond the more traditional interpretation

of learning taking place within the individuals' mind, to that of more socially distributed processes, in what Lave and Wegner call *"legitimate peripheral participation"* in a *"community of practice."* Here the focus is on situated activities rather than simply the transference of factual knowledge. Participation not only influences the learner, but also the social practice in which the learner and experts are engaged.

In keeping with the views taken by (Boud & Lee, 2005; Hopwood & McAlpine, 2007), it is appropriate to view the doctoral process as a good example of a cognitive apprenticeship model in operation, where the student learns from expert supervisors, research staff and peers, gradually moving towards "full participation" within the community.

Boud and Lee (2008) challenge the dominant focus on supervision and *"provisionism"* and suggest that a more appropriate pedagogic discourse should draw on the familiar notion of *"peer"* from the world of research. They support the notion that research occurs as part of a CoP and view the research environment as a pedagogical paradigm in and of itself. They argue that the doctoral process has had little in the way of pedagogic practices applied to it and that it is approached almost wholly from a supervision perspective rather than that of teaching.

In this context the term *"peer"* has two meanings, first in the sense of learning from and with fellow students, co-workers and collaborators. Secondly in the sense of becoming a research peer moving from the vertical relationship of supervisor-student towards a more horizontal relationship of researcher to researcher.

RESEARCH AND WRITING SKILLS

Despite the range of pedagogical theories discussed above, there is little that deals explicitly with the research skills needed by the novice researcher in their transition to legitimate members of the academic community. The following section addresses this shortfall, with a discussion of both research and writing skills applicable to doctoral candidates.

Holz et al. Framework of Research Skills for Computer Science

Holz et al. describe the research skills computer science researchers need to master (Holz, et al., 2006). The framework extends Bloom's taxonomy (Bloom, et al., 1956) of higher order thinking skills to encompass the *"core skills"* needed in computer science and scientific disciplines in general. They categorise core research skills as ranging across a number of areas including: Organisational, Expressive, Cognitive and Meta-Cognitive. Of particular interest are those skills listed under cognitive skills, as these are rarely supported in existing virtual research environments (Carusi & Reimer, 2010).The cognitive skills are:

Synthesis:

"Establishing a whole new creation by combination of ideas from different sources, in a way that formats and molds will be created, and will stand at the basis of the new creation." (Bloom, et al., 1956)

Analysis:

"A thorough study to comprehend the structure of the learned content, its formal and logic way of organization, in order to detect the elements, outlooks, and methods this content is based upon." (Bloom, et al., 1956)

Evaluation:

"Judging the values in the ideas through use of standards of estimations, that will determine the accuracy level, purposefulness and practicality of the details." (Bloom, et al., 1956)

Melioration:

"The skill of selecting the appropriate amalgam of information and applying it to a solution of problems in situations, which arise at different times and places, thereby meliorating the amalgam." (Holz, et al., 2006).

Computation:

"At a loss for a better word, we termed the ability to cognitively manipulate active abstract objects computation." (Holz, et al., 2006).

It is evident that these skills are invaluable to computer science research students, and with the exception of "computation," may be generalisable across any scientific discipline. Holz et al. also list a set of specific research skills associated with research. Specific research skills emphasis early writing related activities such as reviewing and analysing the literature, writing research proposals, through to the final presentation of a written thesis.

Writing in Doctoral Education

Lee and Aitchison (2009) highlight that academic research writing is a crucially important, yet inadequately supported process in doctoral education as opposed to undergraduate studies.

"when it comes to doctoral-level candidature, however, there has been almost deafening silence. Instead, asParé et al. [2009] note, apart from one-to-one work with supervisors, doctoral students in many disciplines are left to learn the normalising ways of writing and speaking in their research communities by observation and trial and error. And, as they demonstrate, supervisors are often poorly equipped to address the need." (Lee & Aitchison, 2009)

Lee and Aitchison (2009) emphasise the benefits of engagement with a community of writing practice, such as writing groups, for both the acquisition of writing skills and an in-depth understanding of how knowledge is created. The suggestion that writing is a *"knowledge-creating"* rather than merely knowledge-recording activity is further supported by Sharples where he suggests that writing may be viewed as a creative design process (Sharples, 1999). This is traced back to the knowledge transforming model of writing found in the Bereiter and Scardamalia work in *"The Psychology of Written Composition"* (Scardamalia & Bereiter, 1987).

In Sharples work there is regular reference to visualisation representations, during the planning stages right through to the construction of arguments as one develops one's prose. These visualisations come in a range of different forms including; note networks, mind maps and flow charts. This suggests that graphical and semiological representations are important throughout the writing process.

Although insightful the aforementioned ideas do not provide a comprehensive guide to dissertation and academic writing. The next section looks at an approach that provides an explicit step-by-step guide to dissertation writing that fits in well with concepts previously discussed and offers an excellent basis for a scaffold upon which to design a tool.

Single's System for Dissertation Writing

Single & Reis (2009) set out a comprehensive guide, the "Single System," which covers a number of different phases involved in the production of a doctoral dissertation. This system supports the CoP, CA, and Lee and Aitchison's references to reading and writing groups as it involves a significant amount of collaboration, in the form of group work and seminars.

The process starts with what Single refers to as "interactive reading" which provides the student with the opportunity to familiarise themselves with the "expectations, structures, formats, and styles" found within the writing in their academic field(s) of study. This higher level study of writing allows them to cover future reading in a faster and more efficient manner. During the interactive reading phase, rough notes are sketched on the document highlighting various aspects e.g. the main point, results, theoretical approaches or methodologies etc.

"Interactive note taking" follows on from interactive reading. Here one collects the rough notes into more coherent notes on the paper, book or the text one is reading, and adds any other relevant information, such as quotes. If well written these notes can negate the need to refer back to the original paper later on.

"Citable notes" are created from a synthesis of the interactive notes. These should be small notes that contain references and the "active ingredient" of the literature. The citable notes should help categorise and theme the literature so as to relate to one's own thesis topic. The idea being that a lot of time can be saved when it comes to writing prose, as one may refer to the citable note when outlining and then refer to the relevant interactive note if necessary. Again this reduces the need to refer back to the original papers.

The authors of this chapter argue that moving through the stages as presented so far in the "Single System" helps support the core cognitive skills of synthesis, analysis, evaluation and melioration. Creating coherent "interactive notes" necessitates analytical skills. Moving from interactive notes to citable notes requires the student to engage in synthesis, evaluation and melioration as they bring the ideas from a number of sources together into an original form.

Once the student has a good grounding in the literature, it is time to make an attempt at a research focus statement. Single describes a focus statement as a clear and concise guiding paragraph of between one and four sentences that communicates the essence of the dissertation. It is meant to focus the student's research direction and stop them veering off and wasting time in unnecessary areas. It must be concise, yet compelling to the student as they will be spending a number of years on the topic.

Single recommends group work for writing the focus statement, where groups of two ask a series of questions to explore the research domains they are interested in. Although the focus statement is a guiding tool for the student, there is no reason that it cannot change over time, as formulating it is an iterative process. The only thing that remains the same is that it is still concise and compelling.

After the focus statement has been formulated, a one-page outline is created. This outline regularly follows one of three common dissertation formats: thematic, data analytical, or journal article. The first step is to brainstorm about where their work sits in the big picture, here a range of questions explore the implications and relevancy of their research beyond the scope that they would normally consider. The brainstorming should also tackle issues such as sources of data, methodologies, possible findings and theoretical concepts. Next, three main themes are to be highlighted from the students citable notes and understanding of the topic, again these are preliminary and may change, but act as guidance in the process. These themes take their place as headings within the overall dissertation format as discussed above.

The long outline develops from the one-page outline. The headings from the one-page outline are expanded to include their own focus statements and sub-headings. Citable notes are then inserted into the appropriate sections, thus bringing references with them. This ultimately creates the basic structure of the dissertation on which to work.

A regular writing routine is recommended; meaning writing time should be set aside and adhered to. This provides time not only to write new content put also to revise previous writing. Single also suggests setting up a writing network to help work on ideas and motivate each other to write. Achieving a regular writing routine should also satisfy the need to attain the meta-cognitive skill of self-regulation, as set out by Holz et al.

Revision can take two forms, at the structural level or at the paragraph level (Single & Reis, 2009; Sharples, 1999). The structural level is organisational in nature, whereas the paragraph level dictates the flow and style of the work.

Single suggests a number of methods for paragraph level revision. One method to highlight is the idea of "smoothing," where each paragraph discusses one concept only. This may be achieved through numerous iterations, finally achieving one concept per paragraph. Single also suggests looking at the work of Strunk (2006), *The Elements of Style,* as a reference when looking at sentences and paragraphs at a micro-editing level.

The "Single System" provides an excellent scaffold upon which to design a comprehensive tool to support dissertation writing. A number of innovative writing tools have been developed with functionality that coincidently reflect a number of the tasks found in the "Single System," the following section will explore two of these in brief.

WRITING RELATED TECHNOLOGIES

The idea that we can use machine and tools to support our cognitive faculties has been suggested in many other works including some previously mentioned cognitive models such as cognitive apprenticeship, situated learning, and others (Resnick, 1987; Lave & Wenger, 1991; Skagestad, 1993; Wenger & Snyder, 2000) and probably most famously in a research context with Vannevar Bush's vision of the Memex (Bush, 1945). This section explores a number of existing technologies that are of relevance to research and writing activities, before discussing how these technologies may inspire designs to support the writing process.

Writing Tools: Writer's Assistant and iWeaver

The Writer's Assistant was developed primarily to focus on both the linear and non-linear activities involved in the writing process, rather than the simple linear functionality found in standard word-processor (Sharples, et al., 1989). Sharples et al. provide an overview of writing tasks and how they may be represented (Table 1). One of the main innovative outputs of the Writer's Assistant is the idea of multiple views of the emerging document. The notes view allows the writer to express ideas as notes and place them into an associative network. The linear view allows the writer to view the text from beginning to end and perform standard text editing activities. Finally the structured view allows the writer to create and alter the structure of the linear text.

Table 1. The representation space for writing (Sharples, et al., 1989) (© 1989, Intellect Ltd. Used with permission)

Organization of Item	Type of Item	
	Uninstantiated	**Instantiated**
Unorganized	1 Techniques: Brainstorming Representations: Idea Labels	2 Techniques: Note-taking (verbatim) Collecting Quotes Representations: Notes
Non-Linear Organization	3 Techniques: Following a thread Writing a dialectic Representations: Network of idea-labels	4 Techniques: Organizing notes Filing Representations: Network of notes
Linear Organization	5 Techniques: Linear planning Outlining Representations: List of idea labels Table of contents	6 Techniques: Drafting text Revising text Copying text Representations: Linear text

iWeaver (Shibata & Hori, 2002, 2008) is a more recent work that builds on Writers Assistant, and it also provides multiple representations of document. The representations differ from the Writer's Assistant in that it uses what they call a "ContextMap" view instead of a "Notes Network." They argue that the ContextMap view is easier to transform into linear text and requires fewer graphical objects to describe relations, using proximity and location rather than the arrows and lines of Writers Assistant's Notes Network. The OutlineTree and DocumentView are similar to the structured and linear views in the Writer's Assistant.

The Oultine view, although innovative at the time Writier's Assistant was developed, is now common in a number of modern word processors. However, there is little in modern word-processors that have adopted anything similar to the ContextMap or Notes Network paradigms. Modern concept and mind mapping programs would be the closest tools to resemble both of these views.

Concept Mapping

The work on both Writer's Assistant and on writing as creative design suggest that an essential part of the writing process is planning, brainstorming and the networking of notes and ideas (Sharples, 1999; Sharples, et al., 1989).

Concept maps have been advocated as beneficial in managing and developing a learners knowledge structures (Novak, 1998). Collaborative concept mapping is also discussed as being a practical way of capturing and negotiating collective knowledge in a group or team, making it potentially helpful for doctoral candidates when discussing their work with peers and supervisors.

Trochim (1989) suggests that concept mapping may be useful both in the planning and evaluation of group projects. This is supported in a doctoral setting by Leshem's (2007) work on developing conceptual frameworks for the early planning of doctorial research, utilising both concept maps and group work. This potentially opens up the possibility of sharing a common interface across a range of different tasks throughout the research project from planning, writing and evaluation.

A number of existing concept-mapping tools exist such as C-map (http://cmap.ihmc.us/), Vue (http://vue.tufts.edu/) and KPE (http://www.kp-lab.org/tools/knowledge-practices-environment). KPE is of particular interest as it provides a range of web-based collaborative tools for knowledge work and has a sociocultural pedagogy at its foundation (Kosonen, Ilomäki, & Lakkala, 2008). Such collaborative technologies have become commonplace today.

Computer Supported Collaborative Learning/Work

As the pedagogical theories related to doctoral training generally calls for a social view to the learning process, collaboration is an essential element of any design, whether it is for the support of supervisor-student relationship, peer writing/ reading groups or collaboration on an academic paper or thesis. Fitting with the theme that doctoral training is a collaborative and social practice, the "Single System" involves workshop and seminars, and purports the benefits of reading and writing groups. This implies that any technology developed to support the process would benefit from collaborative technologies that support these social practices.

Awareness of other users' location and perspectives is a recurring theme in work on shared workspaces in both Computer Supported Collaborative Learning and Computer Supported Collaborative Work (CSCL/W) (Buder & Bodemer, 2008; Cox & Greenberg, 2000; D. Suthers, 2001; Suthers, 2006).

Cox and Greenberg's (2000) work on supporting interpretation using groupware provides an insight how users can collaborate critically on various pieces of information, an issue relevant to any design looking at supporting groups during the writing process. In Cox and Greenberg's work there are elements not too different to the map and network nodes found in the Writers Assistant and iWeaver, yet it in this case the aim is collaboration. The additions suggested here include support for sketching, shared/similar workspace, free form annotation, creation and movement of data in the space. They also use multiple views to navigate the space and information, this again has similarities with concept mapping tools.

Buder and Bodemer's (2008) work about supporting controversial discussion explores augmenting the interface to display group awareness indicators. These indicators show at a glimpse the other users agreement and perception of controversial ideas. These prompts may be combined with work on supporting argumentation (Ravenscroft & McAlister, 2008) in order to create relevant prompts to further the conversation, argumentation being an essential skill in any scientific discipline, thus a skill all doctoral candidates should acquire.

Although the ideas in the previous sections provide good basis from which we can construct a tool, but they do not provide a comprehensive guide as to how we may go about the design of such a tool to support writing. The next section looks at Human Computer Interaction approaches that can be used to design of such tools.

HUMAN-COMPUTER INTERACTION APPROACHES

Contemporary Human-Computer Interaction (HCI) theories support the idea that we use machines and tools in support of our cognitive faculties. Two theories that purport this idea, Distributed Cognition and Activity Theory, have been extensively used in designing HCI interfaces (Holland, et al., 2000; Wright, et al., 2000; Fjeld, et al., 2002; Halverson, 2002; Collis & Margaryan, 2004; Blandford & Furniss, 2006; Jaworski & Goodchild, 2006; Rogers, 2006; Matthews, et al., 2007; Engeström, 2008) and help bridge the gap between theory and practice. They also complement the pedagogical theories used to describe doctoral training, suggesting the convergence of ideas in both educational research and HCI fields.

The following section briefly explores the more popular HCI theories and frameworks used to elucidate the cognitive elements involved that need to be considered when designing any interface. We explore Distributed Cognition, Activity Theory and Cognitive Dimensions as three central theories to consider when planning a design. We suggest that Cognitive Dimension provide the clearest set of guiding principles to the broadest audience as they offer non-specialist and specialist a method for evaluating a design. A brief discussion on alternative evaluation methods found in HCI practice (Dix, Finlay, & Abowd, 2004; Lazar, Feng, & Hochheiser, 2009; Muller, Matheson, Page, & Gallup, 1998) provides the reader with basic techniques that they may deployed when designing interfaces in general. Following on from the higher level concepts in HCI and evaluation methods, user centred design approaches such as future technology workshops (Vavoula & Sharples, 2007), participatory design (Muller, 2003) and meta-design (Fischer, 2003; Fischer, Rohde, & Wulf, 2007; Giaccardi, 2005; Giaccardi & Fischer, 2008) are explored.

Distributed Cognition

Distributed cognition is a framework that looks at cognition as system that is distributed socially, temporally and externalised (Holland, et al., 2000), which contrasts with the more traditional ideas where cognition would classically be viewed as solely occurring in the learner's head. This can be useful to get an overview of a particular learning situation, the people involved, their roles, and what artefacts are used to support it.

Distributed cognition is good as a general framework to conceptualise a cognitive system, but does not emphasis a step-by-step guide to the process (Halverson, 2002) making it difficult to

analyse and distinguish the multifaceted nature of the doctoral program.

Activity Theory

Activity theory builds largely on the work of Vygotsky, as discussed above, where cognition is mediated via external stimulus such as tools, language and social interactions. Engeström (2000) developed this further by adding details such as community, rules of activity and the division of labour. This provides a very rich and detailed framework under which to explore activity.

Activity theory allows for a more granular view of activities, whether they are sub-activities or larger motivational activities. Although it provides a richer framework to explore activities it can be harder to learn initially due to its complex conceptual structure (Halverson, 2002).

There are also suggestions that Activity Theory may be good for highlighting tensions in varied activities (Hopwood & McAlpine, 2007) that may be involved within a complex social process such as the professional development of a PhD candidate i.e. activities related to the PhD thesis and professional development such as teaching, attending conferences, workshops, etc.

Cognitive Dimensions

Cognitive dimensions provide the designer with a framework to both help in the development and evaluation of an *"information-based artefact"* (Green, 1989; Green & Blackwell, 1998). They focus more on broad, easy to understand dimensions with which a non-specialist can either design to support or evaluate an existing system against. There is a trade-off between ease of use and the level of depth of analysis, meaning that it may not be suitable for highly detailed analysis but should make an excellent choice for non-specialists and those collaborating with participants unfamiliar with HCI techniques.

Although Green developed 13 dimensions in the original framework, another work that focuses on Cognitive Dimension of idea sketches is of more relevance (Wood, 1993). Wood's Cognitive Dimensions were developed based on both Green's dimensions and on observation and interviews conducted with PhD students as they collaborated together while preparing papers for publication. Despite this work's age, it is still highly relevant to the is issue of designing tools to support academic writing as it provides a comparison to conventional media, such as pen and papers, and makes explicit reference to "mind maps" and "spider diagrams," both of which are relevant to the design of concept mapping spaces and how they ultimately relate to the production of a written document. Wood's provides a set of 8 main Cognitive Dimensions with a number of sub dimensions (Table 2).

These dimensions may be used to inform early prototypes and tackle usability issue early on in the process. They may also be used later in the process in order to evaluate an existing design and inform improvements or alterations to the design. The next section explores other methods that are commonly used to evaluate and improve existing prototypes.

Evaluation

There are a number of reasons one would want to use evaluation methods in a HCI project. Assessing the user experience, the systems functionality and identifying problems with the system are highlighted as the main motivations (Dix, et al., 2004). A number of evaluation methods used throughout the design process are briefly described.

Expert Based Evaluation

Expert based evaluation comes in a variety of forms, here we will explore just two, cognitive walkthrough and heuristics (Dix, et al., 2004; Lazar, et al., 2009).

A cognitive walkthrough involves a HCI expert to walk through a list of set tasks that have been predefined. Using a specification of the system and an idea of what sort of users will be using the system, the expert will critique the system, highlighting their perceived usability issues.

Heuristics are a set of "rules of thumb" that provide a scheme against which to assess the system. Ideally the expert will be familiar with the heuristics, there are two quite common heuristic set, Shneiderman's golden rules (Shneiderman & Plaisant, 2009) and Nielsen's ten heuristics (Nielsen, 1994).

User Based Evaluation

Just as in the expert based evaluation methods there are a range of user based methods. These include empirical, observational and querying techniques. Although empirical methods are powerful for exploring very specific questions in controlled environments, they are difficult to implement when dealing with the complexities involved in groupware systems (Dix, et al., 2004). Therefore the focus here will be mainly on observational and querying techniques.

Think aloud evaluation (Dix, et al., 2004; Lazar, et al., 2009) is a very simple approach whereby the user talks through what they believe is happening, why they take any particular action and what they wish to do. It can be used very early in the design process and is very cheap and easy to implement.

If resources are limited, Participatory Heuristics evaluation (Muller, et al., 1998) may be used to balance out the need for experts and having a set of participants already. It can be the case in PD, that the users are experts in their work context and that the designer has a good idea of usability issues. Together they use a set of heuristics to explore the systems for usability issues.

Querying techniques of evaluation such as interviews and questionnaires can illicit much more detail about the users experience than can

Table 2. Wood's cognitive dimensions of idea sketches (Wood, 1993)

Delayed Gratification		How much effort and delay is involved in creating a representation. It is sometimes important to get ideas down quickly and conventional media is often better for this.
	transparency	Can the user be unconscious of the system and concentrate on the task? It is important that the interface does not demand cognitive resources. Computers are more opaque than paper!
	richness	Does the representation include many graphical marks, redundant encodings, etc, because it is quick and easy to make it so? Richness facilitates perceptual cueing.
Terseness		Are there few symbols per idea? Terseness allows overview, lower delayed gratification and in turn higher richness. Conventional media seem to favour terseness.
	overview	Can the user perceive much of the representational structure at once? Overview favours accessibility and structurability. Conventional media afford better overview.
	structurability	Is the user's ability to reorganize the structure facilitated by an increase in accessibility and lowering of viscosity which results from terseness?
	visible area	Is there a large display area for the representation? A large visible area, combined with terseness, supports overview and structurability.
Perceptual cues (typographical)		Can the user produce many typographical marks easily? Typographical cues are facilitated by low delayed gratification and help accessibility by providing an access structure.
	Perceptual cues (graphical)	Can the user easily produce graphical marks like clustering, linking, etc? Graphical cues may not be produced on computer due to low richness
Accessibility		Can the user access information with ease? When the idea labels are continuously perceived they help maintain elements in working memory and assist long term memory retrieval.
	location through perceptual cues	Do perceptual cues help the user direct attention to the relevant parts of the representational structure? Computers do not generally allow such rich perceptual access structures.
	facilitation through terseness	Does terseness assist the user in directing attention to the required parts of the representational structure? Conventional media seem to allow this more.
	meaning through perceptual cues	Can perceptual cues be used to carry meaning, or provide context which facilitates the recall of meaning? Conventional media may facilitate recall with perceptual cues more than computer.
Premature commitment		Is the user forced to make choices too early in the task, or can she explore different options fully with the representation? Many idea sketchers use ambiguous notes.
	downsliding	Is the user drawn into fine grained production of grammatical sentences, when they are trying to operate at a more global, exploratory level? Downsliding leads to premature commitment.
	finished character	Does the typographical character of a representation fairly reflect its provisionality, or does its finished looking character mislead the user? Computer text can lead to downsliding.
Viscosity		Does the representation offer high resistance to editing? Computer "cut and paste" should reduce viscosity, but it is not a great problem for conventional methods.
	exhibits evolution	Does the representation display its history, as well as its current state? History is likely to be displayed if deletion is difficult, and may provide context which assists encoding and recall
	temporariness	Is there much investment in the representation, or is it intended to be thrown away shortly after production? Temporariness overcomes viscosity, and discourages premature commitment.
Formalness		Does the representation unambiguously carry meaning for someone with the right background and language, or does it rely heavily on context for interpretation? Idea sketches are informal.
	faithful conveying	Can the representation be used for asynchronous communication with others or the self? Informal idea sketches are often unintelligible outside the context of their production.
	semantic potential	Can the representation mean different things? Semantically potent representations are quicker to produce, terser, avoid premature commitment, and lower viscosity.

be attained from any of the previously mentioned approaches. The power here is that you leave room for the users to present issues that the designer may not have thought of or that lie outside any set of heuristics or task list.

Any number of these evaluation methods may feed into the evolutionary growth phase of Meta-Design. Participatory Heuristics are probably the best solution if this approach is taken, as they involve the user and respect them as experts in their respective domains.

A very brief and limited overview of evaluation methods has been presented here. There are a plethora of other approaches and methods that we would recommend the reader to explore if interested (Dix, et al., 2004; Lazar, et al., 2009).

Participatory Design

Participatory Design (PD) (Muller, 2003) involves the user in the design process at a very early stage. In this regard it embodies elements of cognitive apprenticeship (Farooq, et al., 2005) where the designer is learning from the practitioner and vice versa.

Muller suggests that the environment in which the users are engaged in the design process is important (Muller, 2003). He makes the distinction between the design environment and the work context and how the user may perform differently in either setting. Muller also discusses the idea of a third hybrid space that brings the users and the designer outside their usual working environment. This "third space" provides an environment for creative thinking and dialogue, allowing the participants and designers to tackle the issues outside the usual contexts.

Muller's work highlights workshops as an effective means by which PD may be conducted. Future Technology Workshops (FTW) (Vavoula & Sharples, 2007) provide potential end-users with the opportunity to envision future technologies to help support their current activities. This sort of workshop provides such a "third space" and

creates a good basis for initiating dialogue with the novice researcher community.

Meta-Design (Fischer, 2003; Giaccardi, 2005Giaccardi & Fischer, 2008; Fischer, et al., 2007) is an extension of PD, where the users become active designers themselves and there are a number of steps that are suggested in order to empower the users to get involved within design process. Seeding, evolutionary growth and reseeding are the processes about which meta-design is centred. A seed is an artefact about which work and discussions can take place. The evolutionary growth phase is where the participants focus on a particular issue to solve, using the seed as the resource for work. Reseeding is where the efforts from the evolutionary growth phase may radically alter the original seed.

Synthesis

The preceding sections have explored the research and writing skills needed by novice researchers across scientific disciplines and the pedagogical theories that underlie their acquisition. A number of existing tools and approaches were explored to provide a basis on which to build tools to support academic writing. Finally HCI methods and theories, such as Cognitive Dimensions, were introduced to provide guidelines and techniques with which to tackle the design of tools to support research and writing skills.

The following section explores the implications from the literature on the design of such a tool and develops a set of principles to inform the design of CAWriter. These principles are displayed in a table (Table 3), documenting the four main areas of concern, tool context/pedagogies, supports for higher order thinking skills, functional supports, and cognitive dimension.

The pedagogical theories of CoP and CA, the Holz et al. framework and the work on the acquisition of writing skills all suggest the benefits of an element of collaboration when it comes to training doctoral candidates; one-to-one meeting

Table 3. Initial design principles

Context/Pedagogies	
CA, CoP, Peer Learning	Lave & Wegner, Boud & Lee, Leshem, Hopwood & McAlpine etc.
Supports for Higher Order Skills	
Support	**Literature**
Synthesis	Holz et al., Bloom
Analysis	Holz et al., Bloom
Evaluation	Holz et al., Bloom
Melioration	Holz et al.
Written	Holz et al.
Monitoring	Holz et al.
Cognitive Apprenticeship, Communities of Practice, Peer Learning	Lave & Wegner, Boud & Lee, Leshem, Hopwood & McAlpine etc.
Functional Supports	
Support	**Literature**
Collaboration	CA, CoP, CSCW, Single
Outlining View	iWeaver, Writer's Assitant, Single
Concept/Context View	iWeaver, Writer's Assitant, Sharples, Novak
Drafting View	iWeaver, Writer's Assitant, Single
Interactive Reading	Single
Interactive Note taking	Single
Citable Notes	Single
Long Outline	Single
Referencing system	Single
Revision and drafting	iWeaver, Writer's Assitant, Single, Sharples
Cognitive Dimensions	
Delayed Gratification	Woods, Green
Terseness	Woods
Perceptual Cues	Woods
Accessibility	Woods
Premature Commitment	Woods, Green
Viscosity	Woods, Green
Formalness	Woods

with their supervisor, reading or writing group etc. This paves the way for the introduction of CSW/L tools.

The work on awareness of perspectives in the CSCL/W literature suggests that structured comments, drafts and notes shared amongst collaborators will help elicit a shared understanding, again echoing the work on CoPs. Elements found in the systematic literature process such a review protocols (Brereton, Kitchenham, Budgen, Turner, & Khalil, 2007) may also be included in order to scaffold the review process and aid collaborators in understanding what criteria and metrics are being looked for in the reviewed material. This may be further supported through shared argumentation rules similar to the prompts discussed be Ravenscroft and McAlister (2008).

The "Single System" may be supported through a number of facilities described above. Interactive notes may be augmented through the provision of literature review protocols and argumentation prompts, to promote higher order cognitive processes such as, synthesis, analysis and evaluation as discussed by Holz et al. The integration of citable and interactive notes should be easily facilitated through intelligent interface design, supporting the user in synthesis, evaluation and melioration. Both outlining techniques found in the "Single System" could be supported by something similar to the outlining and concept mapping facilities found in Writer's Assistant and iWeaver, once altered to include a referencing system. Finally support for the "smoothing" process and prompts relating to writing style would be beneficial to any design hoping to support the writing process.

Although both Writer's Assistant and iWeaver provide novel approaches to the writing process, there are not widely used as word processors. However, the outlining views found in Writer's Assitant and iWeaver have been integrated into most modern word processors. The most commonly used word processors today, such as MSWord and OpenOffice, typically offer a linear view of documents and are not explicitly designed to support the free association of ideas, thus promote thinking in a linear manner.

There are a number of online options emerging that allow for collaboration such as Google Docs (http://docs.google.com), Zoho (http://docs.zoho.com) or the open source alternative EtherPad (http://etherpad.org), but these again are limited by a linear focus. As for third party concept mapping tools, they facilitate a freer association of ideas, and even have collaborative features as in KPE, but the majority were not explicitly designed to support the writing process nor do they integrate multiple representations of the document as does Writer's Assitant and iWeaver.

Cognitive Dimensions of idea sketches provide a way to assess the qualities of a design. Wood's dimensions in particular offer an excellent way to assess the concept mapping elements and note taking elements. The specification of guidelines from this approach makes it easier to use than the more broad conceptual approaches of Distributed Cognition and Activity theory. The Delayed gratification, Terseness and Perceptual Cues dimensions provide an excellent motivation for using a concept mapping space. Accessibility and Viscosity promote the idea of tight integration and easy access to notes, quotes and papers throughout the system. Cognitive Dimensions afford a very simple lens through which we can view activities, before and after a prototype has been developed.

The next section shall bring a number of the issues discussed here together in a design example in the form of an ongoing Participatory Action Research project. The project looks at the development of a tool to support computer science doctoral students with their academic writing.

CAWRITER

As has been seen, doctoral candidates often receive little support with their academic writing beyond the one-to-one meetings with their supervisor. It

Figure 1. left: post-graduates writing approach, right: FTW prototype

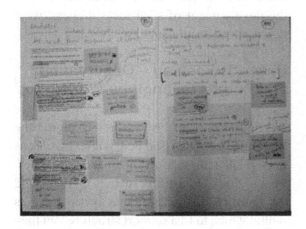 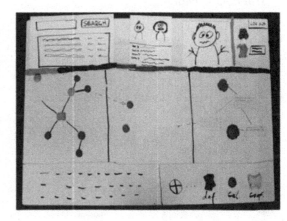

is this issue that lies at the heart of the CAWriter project. This section describes the rational and approaches used in the design of a computer supported collaborative writing tool, CAWriter (Cognitive Apprenticeship/Assistant Writer) (Byrne & Tangney, 2010), which is being developed as part of a larger ongoing Participatory Action Research project concerned with the creation of a virtual research management system to support doctoral candidates.

The Holz et al. framework and the "Single System" act as a theoretical framework for the current iteration of the CAWriter tool, which aims to develop a computer supported collaborative prototype to support writing activities relevant to doctoral candidates. This is being achieved through the development and support of a blended face to face and internet based writing tool.

This work adopts a Participatory Action Research (PAR) methodology (Creswell, 2005; Kemmis & Wilkinson, 1998; Whyte, 1989). The PAR approach promotes an individual from within a community to address an issue found within that same community. As the lead researcher of this project is a computer science doctoral candidate, it is this community that will be the initial focus, with the potential to expand to support doctoral candidates in other scientific disciplines.

The PAR approach is complimented by ideas from Participatory Design (PD) (Muller, 2003) and Meta-Design and involves the implementation of a series of Future Technology Workshops (FTWs) (Vavoula & Sharples, 2007) and participatory design sessions involving doctoral students, supervisors and relevant colleagues. These workshop sessions explore both current and emergent activities within the doctoral education process.

Evaluation is conducted in an iterative fashion, using an array of datasets. Initially FTWs and participatory design sessions explored the community's perceived requirements for future tools in order to inform the initial design. This initial design acts as a "seed" for an evolutionary growth iteration of the prototype, with the aim of "reseeding" again later in the process. The early prototypes are being evaluated using participatory heuristic evaluation (Muller, et al., 1998), talk aloud protocols, interviews and observations. A brief report is made on preliminary finding from these initial heuristic evaluations and design process, involving 5 PhD candidates as participants. This is supplemented by an initial test of the system in legitimate context, highlighting a number of issues that need to be addressed before the tool may be deployed more widely.

As the tools progress, more formal usability tests will be implemented with larger numbers of

Figure 2. MobileCog-0.1 prototype showing "post-it notes" view

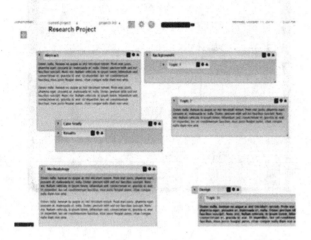

participants ranging from between 15 to 30 users. These tests will be used to explore the users experience and the tools usability within legitimate learning contexts such as supervisory sessions and writing groups. Interviews will be triangulated with prototype usage data and observation notes so that an assessment can be of the tool to see if it is effective in supporting and scaffolding the acquisition and use of the skills, as set out in the Holz framework.

Design Process

The chapter so far has explored a range of issues that can be used to inform the design of tools to support PhD candidates with their academic writing. Although the issues are described here in a coherent manner, they emerged from a dynamic and evolutionary design process. Following the PAR approach of look, think, act, and reacting to participant feedback, new avenues were explored and community issues elucidated. The following section explores the process that led to the development of design principles above and how they were used to inform the design of CAWriter. This should provide the reader with an inside look at the

more practical and chaotic aspects involved in the development of such tools, beyond what theory alone would suggest.

Phase 1: Seeding – Observations and Future Technology Workshops

The initial part of this research explored the literature that discussed pedagogical issues as they related to supporting PhDs candidates. This highlighted aspects such as CoP, CA and the Holz et al. framework as broad theories within which to fit a support structure, but they did not however provide a basis for legitimate practices within the community.

In line with the PAR approach of look, think and act, an initial outreach to the community revealed a post-graduate student, looking to digitize his approach to writing academic papers. The student in question uses conventional media such as sheets of A4 paper and applies printed and "post-it" notes to these sheets (see Figure 1, left). This resembles both Sharple's work on writing as creative design and the notes network of Writer's Assistant. It also reflects similarities to the practice Wood's talks of in his work on Cognitive Dimensions of idea sketches, exemplifying terseness and perceptual cues.

The scope was widened to look at the needs of the PhD candidates specifically. An initial FTW was organised and attended by 12 PhD candidates, the focus was on future supports for the PhD process. During the FTWs participants were asked to produce rough prototypes of their desired technologies to support them with their doctoral work. A number of common themes emerged: communication/collaboration, privacy controls, planning, different views of information and integrated referencing management. One prototype in particular reflected the desire for a system that centres on concept-mapping spaces, with auxiliary functionality built around them (Figure 1, right). Further requirements that emerged from the workshops ranged across a number of themes that are reflected in the literature, these included support for document drafting, advanced referencing, organisation, visualisations, ubiquitous access and collaboration.

An initial prototype, MobileCog-0.1 (Figure 2), was developed with a number of purposes in mind. Firstly it hoped to meet the desires and needs of the participants, as noted from observations and FTWs. Secondly it was developed in order to explore what was possible within the modern browser using Web 2.0 technologies, APIs, JavaScript, CSS, PHP and MySQL. The aim was to use open-source and non-proprietary technologies so as to allow the participants access to a ubiquitous tool that allowed for easy future involvement in the development process, as per the meta-design approach.

The focus of this initial iteration of the prototype was on what Holz et al. refer to as organisational tools and included calendar functionality, task lists, project note spaces, file storage, bibliography management and meeting audio recording. These sort of tools are commonly found in a number of virtual research environments (Carusi & Reimer, 2010).

These tools formed a "mash-up," using existing open source software and the latest in dynamic AJAX technology, thus allowing the user to load everything into a single page, moving away from the traditional web approach of loading a new page for each new resource/tool. The development of this tool provided an insight into the flexibility of the modern browser and the potential for the development of desktop like applications within the browser. From a Meta-Design perspective it would act as a "seed" with which to start the dialogue with the users and community.

Phase 2: Evolutionary Growth – Participatory Heuristics and Talk Aloud

After initial participatory heuristic sessions, with a number of PhD candidates, a number of issues

arose relating to usability. This represented an "evolutionary growth" phase where the participants discussed what needed to be changed and how these changes could be made. One of the main issues was that there was a lack of flow in the task orientated facilities, suggesting that a more rigorous framework and scaffold was needed to structure the activity within the system. In discussions with student support services at our institution, a group that aims to help students enhance their learning and study skills, there were further calls for more explicit focus on writing support, an issue reflected in the Aitchison and Lee's work. This new writing focus also falls in line with support for the written expression skills requested by Holz et al. The combination of this call for writing support and the plethora of existing organizational tools, suggesting that MobileCog-0.1 was not novel in its affordances, a decision was made to shift the focus towards explicit support for the writing process.

CAWriter-0.1 was developed from the need for of a more structured interface as noted from the feedback on MobileCog-0.1 and the need to explicitly support academic writing. CAWriter-0.1 aimed to help novice academic writers collect notes and resources from the literature, construct a draft document and collaborate as they do so. It went beyond the anecdotal evidence used to design MobileCog-0.1, and instead drew heavily on the literature. A non-linear approach to writing was developed from both anecdotal experiences of practice amongst peers, suggestions from the literature (Shibata & Hori, 2008; Sharples, 1999; Sharples, et al., 1989) and requested features from the FTWs. This saw the creation of multiple views that allow the user to move from a brainstorming, concept-map view through to an outline and draft document view (Figures 3 and 4). In terms of cognitive dimensions there was an emphasis on reducing the delayed gratification through the ease at which one can create elements in concept mapping space, the position and linking of elements provide perceptual cues

Figure 3. Mapping of views of iWeaver to CAWriter

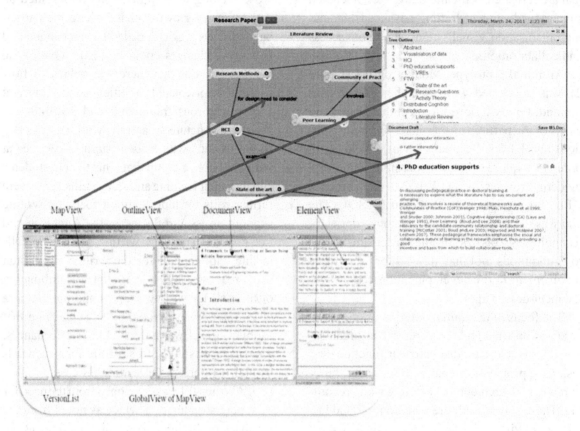

Figure 4. Shows the latest CAWriter prototype. The three views are visible along with the file and referencing systems.

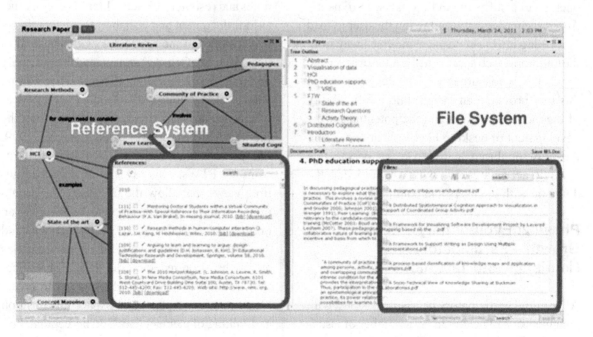

Figure 5. Shows the latest CAWriter prototype. The file view with embedded interactive notes and quote are visible on the left, above their respective document. Within the map view (left) the citable note window may be seen.

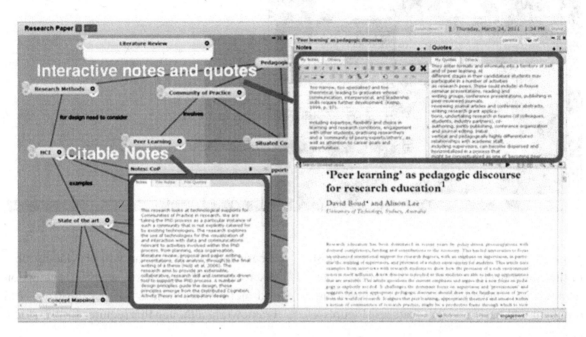

and would provide a terse account of where the user was conceptually.

In supporting the sociocultural perspective, basic collaborative features were added that allowed multiple users to work on a single project. These include basic chat, location awareness in the concept mapping spaces and the ability to co-edit shared content; these were heavily influenced by the CSCW literature.

Following a software engineering rapid application development approach, the CAWriter prototype underwent a number of iterations, following from participatory heuristic feedback. These iterations were developed to further support a number of the specific skills outlined in the framework of Holz et al. and the literature on writing tools (Shibata & Hori, 2008; Sharples, et al., 1989); this saw the integration of support for the early literature review process, note taking and the drafting of a document (Figure 5). These later additions would reduce the viscosity and improve

the accessibility of the system, allowing the user to access their notes and quotes on the relevant topic from any of the views.

Phase 3: Reseeding – Integrating the "Single System"

Further participatory heuristics with PhD candidates showed that there was still a lack of flow within the tasks and did not explicitly support the higher order skills form the Holz et al. framework, suggesting that more scaffolds were necessary. Here the "Single System" argumentation prompts and structured literature review protocols were reviewed as a solution to these issues.

The similarities between the features suggested in Writer's Assistant and iWeaver and the activities found in the "Single System" made it an obvious choice as a scaffold. The project underwent a reseeding phase with the integration of a number of elements of the "Single System" into CAWriter.

Figure 6. Current CAWriter prototype, after visual and layout updates

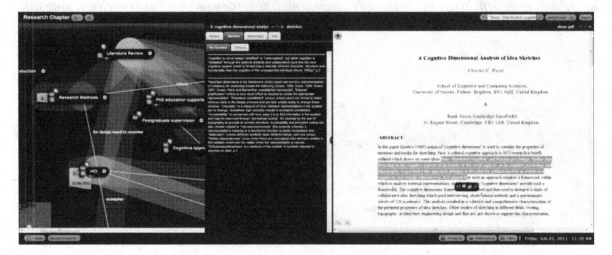

This required relatively minor alterations as most of the components are present; interactive note/quote taking, citable notes collection, referencing, outlining and basic revision features (Figures 4 and 5). The capability of annotating and grabbing quotes and notes from .pdf documents was introduced by converting the .pdf to html and using JavaScript to annotate and collect quotes.

There is still a need for more explicit visual cues and graphics to portray the progress and stage which the user is at. This would allow the user to monitor their writing routine and related activities, supporting a number of the meta-cognitive skills from the Holz et al. framework and the regular writing routine discussed in the "Single System." This could also enhance collaborators awareness of activity in the system, as per the CSCW/L literature.

The argumentation prompts and structured literature protocols, as discussed in the CSCW/L literature, are to be integrated into the interactive note taking fields so as to promote deeper analysis and evaluation on the user's behalf. The combination of more thorough interactive notes and their grouping under user generated themes, as nodes in the concept mapping spaces, will provide the user with easy access to all their content and reduce use viscosity. It is hoped that this ease of access and visual relation will provide a richer environment for synthesis, analysis, evaluation and melioration to occur, as per the Holz et al Framework, although this requires further study.

Preliminary Evaluations

Participatory heuristics sessions were carried out largely with PhD candidates, but time was taken to run a heuristics session with a Web-Design specialist to improve the look and layout of the application. A number of design elements were tweaked for consistency and to help define relationships between elements (Figure 6). This we deemed necessary before the system could be used for a legitimate writing activity.

The preliminary pilot saw CAWriter used in the drafting of this chapter and the preparation of a literature review by another PhD candidate. This may be viewed as a new reseeding stage in the design process. Initial results were promising, although the strength currently lies as the start of the process i.e. literature review and note taking. There is need for greater supports in the drafting elements of the tool. It should be possible to tackle these issues by porting the literature review processes over to the drafting process, providing richer annotation reviews and comments.

There is definitely a need for the "Single System" smoothing process as there is a tendency for the elements in the drafting process to become disjointed and lack flow from section to section.

Four main elements emerged as necessities that were not completely implemented in the system to date: broader range of reference style, ability to add equations, greater support for the drafting process, version and revision management and more export and import formats such as Microsoft Documents, XML and LaTex.

Future Work

The short term will address the issues raised in the preliminary evaluation and the continuation of the heuristic tests on the system going through a number of seeding, evolutionary growth, and reseeding phases. This will ascertain if the system is largely usable and if there are enough scaffolds in place to guide them through the process and support the skills desired.

Once a relatively robust system is in place a more longitudinal study is planned. This entails will entail 3 month study involving a cohort of 20-25 1st year computer science PhD candidates. An integral part will be to start reading and writing groups to promote the "Single System" and the adoption of the prototype. This will provide the community of practice and peer supports beyond what is found in the supervisor-student relationship, as discussed in the literature on pedagogical approaches to doctoral education. This will also provide an opportunity to engage the wider community in a participatory and meta design processes. This will also provide an opportunity to assess the formalness Cognitive Dimension when users collaborate on a document, an issue that will also arise in the candidate-supervisor relationship.

To support the supervisor and candidates in revision work it will be necessary to provide a rich set of annotation and commenting tools to the drafting aspects of the tool. This will involve analysis of current supervisory practice, through observations and interviews. The data collected will be combined with aspects from the literature on writing style and revision techniques (Single & Reis, 2009; Strunk, 2006) to inform how best to integrate the highlighted practices into the system.

When the prototype has been deemed usable from the participatory heuristics, it will be subjected to more standardised usability tests. There are a variety of usability studies to choose from; SUMI, WAMMI, SUS, QUIS (Blecken, Bruggemann, & Marx, 2010; Kirakowski, 1994; Kirakowski & Claridge, 2008). Depending on form the prototype takes an appropriate test will be adopted and administered to 15-25 experienced participants. A number of tasks will be set for the users to complete.

In the final stages of the CAWriter project all data will be collated and analysed, codes and themes will be used to create interview questions that will help explore whether the tools effectively facilitated the acquisition of any research and writing skills and whether the cognitive dimensions used to design the system are actually present in the final system. Once this is achieved the existing prototype will be ready to integrate into a larger virtual research environment that will support the full set of research skills as set out by Holz et al.

CONCLUSION

This chapter has presented current research on skills and pedagogies involved in the doctoral process. As is evident in this literature review, there is a lack of work covering the use of technology in supporting doctoral skills and activities directly, especially when it comes to writing skills.

By exploring a number of existing tools and approaches in designing tools to support human computer interaction and computer support collaborative activities, this chapter provides a base for those interested in the design and use of technologies to support doctoral candidates and other novice researchers in their transition to legitimate members of the academic community, with particular interest in supporting writing skills.

An example of our current work on the computer supported collaborative writing tool, CAWriter and the design rational and approaches taken were presented. This practical example provides a guide or template for those interested in developing technologies to support the novice researcher, with particular emphasis on writing supports. The design process shows that the process is not always straightforward calling for iterative and adaptive design processes in the development of such tools. It also reflects the importance of HCI methods and community involvement in such an endeavour.

CAWriter is a unique piece of software that combines and tightly integrates a number of existing systems into one easy to use package. It takes elements from existing referencing, word-processing, and concept mapping systems. This provides the users with a system that is quick to learn and easy to use, providing them with an instant overview and access to all their work while they draft a document. We do not know of any current tool that provides all of these services in a single tool.

As Leonard and Becker (2008) suggest a lot of work to date on doctoral training does not put the doctoral candidate at the centre of the study. It is the aim of this project to address this shortfall and put the doctoral candidate at the heart of the problem and empowering them to be part of the solution through their involvement in both the Participatory and Meta-Design approaches.

REFERENCES

Aitchison, C., & Lee, A. (2006). Research writing: Problems and pedagogies. *Teaching in Higher Education, 11*(3), 265–278. doi:10.1080/13562510600680574

Blecken, A., Bruggemann, D., & Marx, W. (2010). *Usability evaluation of a learning management system.* Paper presented at the 43rd Hawaii International Conference on Systems Sciences. Hawaii, HI.

Bloom, B. S., Krathwohl, D. R., & Masia, B. B. (1956). *Taxonomy of educational objectives: The classification of educational goals.* New York, NY: Longmans.

Boud, D., & Lee, A. (2005). Peer learning as pedagogic discourse for research education. *Studies in Higher Education, 30*(5), 501–516. doi:10.1080/03075070500249138

Boud, D., & Lee, A. (2008). *Changing practices of doctoral education.* London, UK: Routledge.

Brereton, P., Kitchenham, B. A., Budgen, D., Turner, M., & Khalil, M. (2007). Lessons from applying the systematic literature review process within the software engineering domain. *Journal of Systems and Software, 80*(4), 571–583. doi:10.1016/j.jss.2006.07.009

Brown, J. S., Collins, A., & Duguid, P. (1989). Situated cognition and the culture of learning. *Educational Researcher, 18*(1), 32.

Buder, J., & Bodemer, D. (2008). Supporting controversial CSCL discussions with augmented group awareness tools. *International Journal of Computer-Supported Collaborative Learning, 3*(2), 123–139. doi:10.1007/s11412-008-9037-5

Bush, V. (1945). As we may think. *Atlantic Monthly, 176*(1), 101–108.

Byrne, J. R., & Tangney, B. (2010). *CAWriter: A CSCW/CSCL tool to support research students' academic writing.* Paper presented at the British Computer Society HCI2010. Retrieved from http:// www.scss.tcd.ie/ crite/ publications/ sources/ CAWriter_ ByrneJR.pdf.

Carusi, A., & Reimer, T. (2010). *Virtual research environment collaborative landscape study.* Retrieved from http://www.jisco.com.

Cox, D., & Greenberg, S. (2000). *Supporting collaborative interpretation in distributed groupware.* Paper presented at the CSCW. Philadelphia, PA.

Creswell, J. W. (2005). *Educational research* (2nd ed.). Upper Saddle River, NJ: Pearson Education Inc.

Cumming, J. (2008). *Representing the complexity, diversity and particularity of the doctoral enterprise in Australia.* Sydney, Australia: The Australian National University.

Dix, A., Finlay, J., & Abowd, G. D. (2004). *Human-computer interaction.* Upper Saddle River, NJ: Prentice Hall.

Farooq, U., Merkel, C., Nash, H., Rosson, M., Carroll, J., & Xiao, L. (2005). Participatory design as apprenticeship: Sustainable watershed management as a community computing application. In *Proceedings of the 38th Annual Hawaii International Conference on System Sciences (HICSS 2005).* Hawaii, HI: HICSS Press.

Fischer, G. (2003). *Meta-design: Beyond user-centered and participatory design. Human-Computer Interaction: Theory and Practice* (p. 88). New York, NY: Horwood.

Fischer, G., Rohde, M., & Wulf, V. (2007). Community-based learning: The core competency of residential, research-based universities. *Computer-Supported Collaborative Learning.* Retrieved from http://l3d.cs.colorado.edu/~gerhard/papers/final-iJCSCL07-rhode-wulf.pdf.

Giaccardi, E. (2005). Metadesign as an emergent design culture. *Leonardo, 38*(4), 342–349. doi:10.1162/0024094054762098

Giaccardi, E., & Fischer, G. (2008). Creativity and evolution: A metadesign perspective. *Digital Creativity, 19*(1), 19. doi:10.1080/14626260701847456

Green, T. (1989). Cognitive dimensions of notations: People and computers V. In *Proceedings of the Fifth Conference of the British Computer Society Human-Computer Interaction Specialist Group,* (p. 443). BCS Press.

Green, T., & Blackwell, A. (1998). *Cognitive dimensions of information artefacts: A tutorial.* Paper presented at the BCS HCI Conference. London, UK.

Holz, H. J., Applin, A., Haberman, B., Joyce, D., Purchase, H., & Reed, C. (2006). *Research methods in computing: What are they, and how should we teach them?* Retrieved from http://www.dcs.gla.ac.uk/publications/PAPERS/8445/sigsce-final.pdf.

Hopwood, N., & McAlpine, L. (2007). *Exploring a theoretical framework for understanding doctoral education.* Retrieved from http://ogpr.educ.ubc.ca/Doctoral%20ed/Documents/Hopwood%20&%20%20MacAlpine%20(2007).pdf.

Johnson, C. M. (2001). A survey of current research on online communities of practice. *The Internet and Higher Education, 4*(1), 45–60. doi:10.1016/S1096-7516(01)00047-1

Kemmis, S., & Wilkinson, M. (1998). Participatory action research and the study of practice. *Action Research in Practice: Partnerships for Social Justice in Education,* 21-36.

Kirakowski, J. (1994). *SUMI.* Retrieved Oct, 2010, from http://sumi.ucc.ie/index.html.

Kirakowski, J., & Claridge, N. (2008). *WAMMI.* Retrieved Oct, 2010, from http://www.wammi.com/about.html.

Kosonen, K., Ilomäki, L., & Lakkala, M. (2008). *Developing and applying design principles for knowledge creation practices.* Paper presented at the International Conference for the Learning Sciences. New York, NY.

Lave, J., & Wenger, E. (1991). *Situated learning: Legitimate peripheral participation.* Cambridge, UK: Cambridge University Press.

Lazar, J., Feng, J. H., & Hochheiser, H. (2009). *Research methods in human-computer interaction.* New York, NY: Wiley.

Lee, A., & Aitchison, C. (2009). Writing for the doctorate and beyond. In Boud, D., & Lee, A. (Eds.), *Changing Practices of Doctoral Education* (pp. 87–99). London, UK: Routledge.

Leonard, D., & Becker, R. (2008). Enhancing the doctoral experience at the local level. In Boud, D., & Lee, A. (Eds.), *Changing Practices of Doctoral Education.* London, UK: Routledge.

Leshem, S. (2007). Thinking about conceptual frameworks in a research community of practice: A case of a doctoral programme. *Innovations in Education and Teaching International, 44*(3), 287–299. doi:10.1080/14703290701486696

McCotter, S. S. (2001). The journey of a beginning researcher. *Qualitative Report, 6*(2), 1–22.

Miao, Y., Fleschutz, J. M., & Zentel, P. (1999). Enriching learning contexts to support communities of practice. In *Proceedings of the 1999 Conference on Computer Support for Collaborative Learning, (CSCL 1999).* Stanford, CA: International Society of the Learning Sciences.

Muller, M. J. (2003). Participatory design: The third space. In *Proceedings of HCI,* (pp. 1051-1068). HCI Press.

Muller, M. J., Matheson, L., Page, C., & Gallup, R. (1998). Methods & tools: Participatory heuristic evaluation. *Interaction, 5*(5), 18. doi:10.1145/285213.285219

Nielsen, J. (1994). *Heuristic evaluation. Usability Inspection Methods* (pp. 25–62). New York, NY: Wiley.

Novak, J. D. (1998). *Learning, creating and using knowledge.* New York, NY: Lawrence Erlbaum.

Paré, A., Starke-Meyerring, D., & McAlpine, L. (2009). The dissertation as multi-genre: Many readers, many readings. In C. Bazerman, A. Bonini, & D. Figueiredo (Eds.), *Genre in a Changing World,* (pp. 179-193). Fort Collins, CO: Parlor.

Ravenscroft, A., & McAlister, S. (2008). Investigating and promoting educational argumentation: Towards new digital practices. *International Journal of Research & Method in Education, 31*(3), 317–335. doi:10.1080/17437270802417192

Scardamalia, M., & Bereiter, C. (1987). *The psychology of written composition.* Hillsdale, NJ: Lawrence Erlbaum Associates, Inc.

Sharples, M. (1999). *How we write.* London, UK: Routledge.

Sharples, M., Goodlet, J., & Pemberton, L. (1989). *Developing a writer's assistant. Computers and Writing: Models and Tools* (p. 22). New York, NY: Ablex.

Shibata, H., & Hori, K. (2002). *A framework to support writing as design using multiple representations.* Retrieved from http:// www.ai.rcast.u-tokyo.ac.jp/ ~shibata/ pdf/ Shibata2002d-IW-APCHI.pdf.

Shibata, H., & Hori, K. (2008). Cognitive support for the organization of writing. *New Generation Computing, 26*(2), 97–124. doi:10.1007/s00354-008-0037-9

Shneiderman, B., & Plaisant, C. (2009). *Designing the user interface: Strategies for effective human-computer interaction* (5th ed.). Boston, MA: Addison-Wesley Longman Publishing Co.

Single, P. B., & Reis, R. M. (2009). *Demystifying dissertation writing: A streamlined process from choice of topic to final text.* New York, NY: Stylus Pub Llc.

Strunk, W. Jr. (2006). *The elements of style.* New York, NY: Filiquarian Publishing.

Suthers, D. (2001). Collaborative representations: Supporting face to face and online knowledge-building discourse. In *Proceedings of the 34th Annual Hawaii International Conference on System Sciences (HICSS-34),* (vol 4). Maui, HI: HICSS Press.

Suthers, D. D. (2006). Technology affordances for intersubjective meaning making: A research agenda for CSCL. *International Journal of Computer-Supported Collaborative Learning, 1*(3), 315–337. doi:10.1007/s11412-006-9660-y

Trochim, W. M. K. (1989). An introduction to concept mapping for planning and evaluation. *Evaluation and Program Planning, 12*(1), 1–16. doi:10.1016/0149-7189(89)90016-5

Vavoula, G. N., & Sharples, M. (2007). Future technology workshop: A collaborative method for the design of new learning technologies and activities. *International Journal of Computer-Supported Collaborative Learning, 2*(4), 393–419. doi:10.1007/s11412-007-9026-0

Wenger, E. (1998). Communities of practice: Learning as a social system. *Systems Thinker, 9*(5), 1–5.

Wenger, E. C., & Snyder, W. M. (2000). Communities of practice: The organizational frontier. *Harvard Business Review, 78*(1), 139–146.

Whyte, W. F. (1989). *Advancing scientific knowledge through participatory action research.* Retrieved from http:// intranet.catie.ac.cr/ intranet/ posgrado/ Met%20Cual%20 Inv%20accion/ Semana%204/ Whyte,%20W.%20 Advancing%20 Scientific%20 Knowledge%20 Through.pdf.

Wood, C. C. (1993). A cognitive dimensional analysis of idea sketches. *Cognitive Science Research Paper, 275.* Retrieved from http:// www.cogs.susx.ac.uk/ cgi-bin/ htmlcogsreps? csrp275.

KEY TERMS AND DEFINITIONS

Computer Supported Collaborative Learning: CSCL looks at how computers may support collaborative learning.

Doctoral Candidates: Those studying for a doctorate at a higher education institute.

Higher Education: Third level or tertiary education. Largely occurs at universities: colleges and institutes of technology.

Human-Computer Interaction: The discipline focused on how people interact and utilize computer based technologies.

Participatory Design: A design process that involves the end user in the design process.

Pedagogy: The study of teaching and learning.:

Research Skills: Skills related to academic work.

Writing Skills: skills related to the writing process: from early planning and research to final drafting and editing.

Chapter 10

Collaboration within Multinational Learning Communities:
The Case of the Virtual Community Collaborative Space for Sciences Education European Project

Maria Kordaki
University of the Aegean, Greece

Gabriel Gorghiu
Valahia University Targoviste, Romania

Mihai Bîzoi
Valahia University Targoviste, Romania

Adina Glava
Babes-Bolyai University, Romania

ABSTRACT

This chapter focuses on the investigation of essential features of a multinational virtual community that can promote effective collaboration and research among its members so as to overcome space, time, and language barriers. Specifically, a multinational Virtual Community Collaborative Space for Sciences Education has been formed in the context of the Socrates Comenius 2.1 European Project: "VccSSe – Virtual Community Collaborating Space for Science Education." In this project, researchers from five European countries (Romania, Spain, Poland, Finland, and Greece) participated in a multinational learning community where blended collaborative learning courses were formed in order to train teachers from these countries in the use of Information and Communication Technologies (ICT) in their real

DOI: 10.4018/978-1-4666-0125-3.ch010

teaching practices. Within this framework, a number of specific software and pedagogical tools were formed to support collaboration and learning for the teachers and the researchers who participated in this virtual community. After the end of these courses, the teachers were asked to design their own virtual experiments and lesson plans and then to implement them in their classrooms. The analysis of the data shows that the researchers-partners of VccSSe effectively used various collaborative methods to produce the previously mentioned software and pedagogical tools. It has been also shown that teachers who participated in the VccSSe project were encouraged—by the use of the collaborative tools provided and the aforementioned collaborative blended course—to develop interesting virtual experiments and use them in their classrooms. Finally, it is worth noting that students who participated in those classes provided favourable feedback related to the implementation of virtual experiments in their everyday learning experiences.

INTRODUCTION

How should one define computer-supported collaborative learning? In a nutshell, Computer-Supported Collaborative Learning (CSCL) is focused on how collaborative learning supported by technology can enhance peer interaction and work in groups, and how collaboration and technology facilitate sharing and distributing of knowledge and expertise among community members (Lakkala, Rahikainen, & Hakkarainen, 2001). In the field of CSCL, technology meets psychology, philosophy, and pedagogy. Instructional designers and software developers, educational psychologists, learning theorists, computer scientists, and even sociologists are interested in this area of research.

Recent studies of e-learning have pointed out that involving learners in collaborative learning activities could positively contribute to extending and deepening their learning experiences, test out new ideas, improve learning outcomes and increase learner satisfaction, at the same time decreasing the isolation that can occur in an e-learning setting (Palloff & Pratt, 2004). Furthermore, collaborative learning situations can provide a natural setting for demanding cognitive activities such as explanation, argumentation, inquiry, mutual regulation etc., which can also trigger collaborative learning mechanisms such as knowledge articulation as well as sharing and distributing the cognitive load (Dillenbourg,

1999). Within the context of online collaborative learning, learners could also be provided with opportunities to be motivated to actively construct their knowledge and to enhance their diversity and their understanding of the learning concepts in question as well as to acquire a sense of belonging online (Scardamalia & Bereiter, 1996; Haythornthwaite, Kazmer, Robins, & Shoemaker, 2000). In addition, online learning has provided education with many benefits in terms of flexible opportunities to learn anytime and anywhere as well as to communicate and collaborate virtually throughout the world (Harasim, Hiltz, Teles, & Turoff, 1995). On the whole, CSCL has been recognized as an emerging paradigm of educational technology (Koschmann, 1996).

Appropriately designed educational software can also catalytically affect the changes in the whole learning context in terms of learning content, learning activities and the roles of both teachers and learners (Soloway, 1993; Noss & Hoyles, 1992; Jonassen, Carr, & Yueh, 1998). In particular, computers provide wide opportunities for the construction of various, different, linked and dynamic representation systems such as: texts, images, equations, variables, tables, graphs, animations, simulations of a variety of situations, programming languages and computational objects (Kaput, 1994). The use of Multiple Representation Systems (MRS) is acknowledged as crucial in encouraging the expression of learners' different kind of knowledge regarding the subject to be learned (Dyfour-Janvier, Bednarz, & Belanger, 1987; Janvier, 1987). In addition, multiple and linked representation systems provide learners with opportunities to study how variation in one system can affect another. In this way, each learner can make connections between different aspects of a learning concept and develop broad views about it (Lesh, Mehr, & Post, 1987; Janvier, 1987). In addition, richly endowed computer environments can embody powerful scientific ideas which students can explore and reflect on, giving them also the opportunity to conceptualize, and construct for themselves, scientific concepts that have already been formulated by others. Such computer learning environments can provide opportunities for the learners to actively construct their knowledge as well as to develop their problem solving skills (Dubinsky & Tall, 1991; Jonassen, Carr, & Yueh, 1998). Most importantly, in the context of ICT, modern social and constructivist perspectives of teaching and learning can be realized (Papert, 1980; Balacheff & Kaput, 1996; Noss & Hoyles, 1996; Jonassen, Carr, & Yueh, 1998).

On the whole, the rapid evolution and the achievements of ICT opens up endless possibilities of the design and implementation of innovative teaching and learning models (Looi, Ogata, & Wong, 2010), ranging from conventional personal computer labs to perpetual and ubiquitous learning (Mifsud & Mørch, 2010), authentic and contextualized learning (Wong & Looi 2010), seamless learning (Roschelle, Patton, & Tatar, 2007; Looi, Seow, Zhang, So, Chen, & Wong, 2010), rapid knowledge co-construction (Lin, Liu, & Niramitranon, 2008) and it is acknowledged that we are now at the onset of a digital classroom wave which will bring significant changes to education (Chan, 2010). However, teachers who wish to update and upgrade their teaching and learning designs using new learning technologies have some difficult issues to confront (Laurillard, 2010). In fact, teachers should develop wholly new ways of conducting teaching and learning, should develop

new digital materials and online activities ahead of the start of the course, should build 21st century skills into the curriculum as well as should learn to be ahead of their 'digital native' students even though they have not been trained themselves. Taking into account all the above, the need for training primary and secondary level education teachers in the use of ICT in education is of vital importance not only for their integration into the modern social and educational context created, but also for the integration of ICT into education (European Commission, 1997). The necessity of training teachers in ICT concerns the acquisition of basic technical and pedagogical skills related to the use of ICT so that they will be capable of integrating it into their real teaching practices (Davis & Tearle, 1998).

Blended learning is an approach suitable for teacher training as it aligns learning undertaken in face-to-face sessions with learning opportunities created online (Littlejohn & Pegler, 2006). The aim of blended learning is basically to join the best points of classroom or face-to-face learning with the best points of online learning as well as to compensate the pitfalls and weaknesses of the one type of learning with the benefits of the other type and vice versa. On the one hand the opportunities presented by online learning in terms of flexible opportunities to learn anytime and anywhere as well as to communicate and collaborate virtually throughout the world (Harasim, Hiltz, Teles, & Turoff, 1995; Palloff & Pratt, 2004; Roberts, 2005; Van Eijl & Pilot, 2003) are essential for teacher training because teachers are adults with many constrains in terms of time and space. On the other hand, several constraints of online collaboration such as: not appropriate perceptions about e-learning, negative attitudes, lack of on-line collaborative skills, not appropriate knowledge about the basic technological skills needed for participation in online learning and a sense of difference between online learning and reality (Nel & Wilkinson, 2006) can be eliminated through face-to-face sessions.

Based on the above, a multinational Virtual community collaborative space for positive sciences education was formed in the context of a European project: "VccSSe – Virtual Community Collaborating Space for Science Education," (project number 128989-CP-1-2006-RO-COMENIUS-C21). This project, designed to last for three years, started in October 2006 and was carried out by 9 partner institutions from 5 different European countries (Romania, Spain, Poland, Finland, and Greece). It has as its main purpose to adapt, develop, test, implement and disseminate training modules, teaching methodologies and pedagogical strategies based on the use of well-known educational software, in terms of virtual experiments and tools in teaching and learning of positive Sciences: Mathematics, Physics and Chemistry. Within the context of VccSSe, a blended teacher training framework and a virtual multinational community of teachers and partners were formed. To this end, one of the main targets of this project was to encourage teachers to develop their own Learning Objects (LO) consisting of: (a) specific constructions based on the use of appropriate educational software—henceforth called "Virtual Experiments" (VEs)—and (b) appropriate lesson plans. Then, these teachers were encouraged to implement those LO in their classrooms. To support collaboration among the participants, various software and pedagogical tools were developed. This chapter focuses on the investigation of the essential features of the multinational virtual community - formed within the context of Vcc-SSe - that has promoted effective collaboration among its members, so that to fulfill the aims of this project at the same time overcoming space, time and language barriers. This chapter also focus on the collaboration among the researchers who participated as partners within the context of Vcc-SSe in order to: (a) produce appropriate software and pedagogical tools for teacher education, (b) effectively manipulate the collaboration within the whole VccSSe community including the tutors and the teachers-participants, (c) successfully manage

the teacher-education courses within VccSSe and the implementation of the teachers' products in their classrooms and (d) analyze and evaluate the results of this 3-year study and crystallize best practices for teacher education in order to use Information and Communication Technologies in their real practices. To this end, it is worth noting that, the education reform could be encouraged by putting together the researchers' community and the schools community—including teachers and students—as researchers seek new knowledge and produce new tools while schools ask for new solutions to operational problems (Looi, So, Toh, & Chen, 2010). In fact, this chapter is about Collaborative and Distributed e-research viewed as an ongoing process that takes place together with the real experiment. This is the contribution of this chapter.

This chapter is organized as follows: In the following section the main ideas inspiring the creation of VccSSe and the design of software and pedagogical tools will be presented followed by the description of the project and the tools developed. The results emerged from the implementation of the aforementioned collaborative teacher training course in the said multinational context will be also presented with an emphasis on the collaboration models and tools used. Then, these results will be discussed in terms of the previously mentioned theoretical framework. Finally, the lessons learned from this collaborative experience will be addressed and proposals for future research plans will be drawn.

BASIC IDEAS INSPIRING THE CREATION OF VCCSSE

In 2001, the Education Council of the European Union presented a Report addressed to the Council the EU entitled "The concrete future objectives of education and training systems" (5980/01), where it was indicated—as the first strategic objective for the subsequent 10 years—"to increase the quality and effectiveness of education and training systems in the European Union," In this sense, as a main direction, the document mentioned the necessity of 'ensuring access to ICT's for everyone.' The developing use of ICT within society has meant a revolution in the way that schools, training institutions and other learning centers could work, as indeed it has changed the way in which many people in Europe work. ICT is also of increasing importance in open learning environments and e-learning. "As far as the education and training systems are concerned, the ability to respond to the rapid developments and the need to stay competitive will continue to play an important role. In addition, flexibility will be needed for individuals to acquire ICT skills throughout their lives." (Council the European Union, 2001).

Another direction, specified by the Council the EU, was oriented on the increase of the recruitment in scientific and technical studies': "Europe needing an adequate throughput of mathematics and scientific specialists in order to maintain its competitiveness. In many countries interest in mathematics and science studies is falling or not developing as fast as it should. This can be seen at school, where the uptake of these subjects by pupils is lower than could be expected; in the attitude of young people and parents to these subjects and later in the level of new recruitment to research and related professions." (Council the European Union, 2001).

In respect to the aforementioned directions, 9 institutions from EU coming from 5 different European countries joined their efforts and explored a common interest and urgent need in their countries for innovative ways to provide in-service teacher training in the area of positive Sciences education using ICT. The following institutions participated: (1) Valahia University Targoviste (Romania; the coordinating institution), (2) Centro de Formación del Profesorado e Innovación Educativa Valladolid II (Spain), (3) Centro del Profesorado y de Recursos de Gijón (Spain), (4) Centro de Profesores y Recursos de Zaragoza I (Spain), (5) Politechnika Warszawska (Poland), (6) Regionalny Ośrodek Doskonalenia Nauczycieli "WOM" w Bielsku-Białej (Poland), (7) Joensuun Yliopisto (Finland), (8) Babes Bolyai University Cluj Napoca (Romania), and (9) University of Patras (Greece). Thus, the partnership concluded that one appropriate solution to increase the participation in Mathematics and Science studies should be realized by the promotion of ICT in the teaching and learning of the Sciences in the primary and secondary levels of education. To this end, it was decided to encourage the design and implementation of appropriate Virtual Instruments (VIs) and Virtual Experiments (VEs)—as educational resources—in order to support the in-service education of the teachers, so as to enable them to develop innovative ICT-based teaching methods in their classrooms (Gorghiu, 2009).

It was evident that most of the projects which promoted the use of virtual instrumentation were addressed to University level teachers (especially focused on engineering topics) and few were targeted on Science in-service teacher training. In fact, that was the point of starting the transnational European Socrates Comenius 2.1 project ("VccSSe – Virtual Community Collaborating Space for Science Education"; webpage http://www.vccsse.ssai.valahia.ro [Figure 1], code: 128989-CP-1-2006-1-RO-COMENIUS-C21), its approval (in summer 2006) offering a chance for the partnership to put in practice their ideas and knowledge with the end goal to encourage teachers of the Sciences to exploit the great potential given by ICT—in terms of virtual instruments and virtual experiments—in their real teaching practices.

The design of the activities performed during the project life emerged as a result of: (a) focusing on theoretical ideas—which have been already reported within the framework presented in the "Introduction" section of this paper—concerning constructivist learning, collaboration and the unique role of ICT in the learning process, (b) a thorough analysis of the curriculum in the participating countries, and (c) an analysis of the attitude of the schools—in the aforementioned countries—towards ICT-based teaching and learning.

Analysis of the curriculum: As it was emerged from the partnership investigations, the field of the Sciences in European education comprises of curriculum contents related to the following school subjects: Mathematics, Physics, Chemistry, Biology, and Geology. In a limited number of cases, such as the case of Spain, the area of the Sciences includes integrated school subjects like science, technology and society, a subject aimed to study the social aspect of the science and their impact in the past, in the present, and in the future of our society. All these subjects are included in lower and upper secondary curriculum with a different number of teaching hours at different levels. The curricula vary in different European educational systems in terms of:

- Contents' structure and degree of contents integration
- Types of competences targeted and trained
- Recommended teaching methodologies
- Types of learning experiences to be organized

One of the main objectives of VccSSe was to identify the most suitable and up to date tools that could offer teachers in different European countries the possibility to effectively meet national curriculum requirements, while proposing dynamic and relevant learning situations based on scientific reality experimentation, through the use of well known educational software within an appropriate e-learning collaborative context. Consequently, a thorough analysis of the curriculum requirements was performed, in terms of their aims and objectives, values and attitudes, contents, and typical learning situations. Added to this, the partnership detailed the trends in European countries in teaching of scientific subjects and learning in terms of innovative:

- Teaching methodologies and pedagogical strategies
- Roles for the students

Figure 1. The VccSSe project webpage

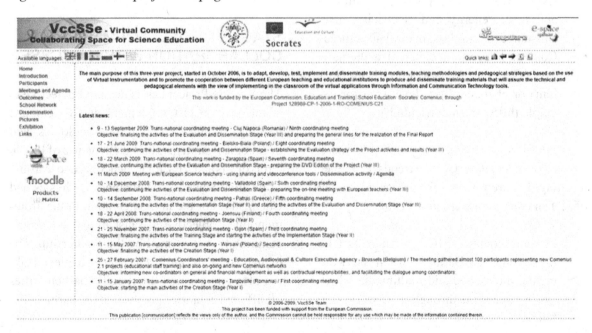

- Ways of evaluation
- Technologies and materials
- Curricular recommendations and trends

At a general analysis of the positive Sciences' curriculum programs, some conclusions were extracted regarding the types of competence desired, types of contents and their organization as well as types of values and attitudes promoted. Specifically, throughout Europe, the curriculum of Science is focused on:

- Systemic acquisition of knowledge
- Training of the main research competences
- Development of a critical attitude towards the effects of science on the technological and social development and of the interest for the environmental protection
- Values such as respect for truth and diversity, respect for individual needs and nature, curiosity and initiative, openness for the opinions of others and disposition to modify own perspectives in the light of new facts
- Exploration of concepts such as: motion and force, energy and electricity, heat, substances around us, natural structures
- Content integration either at a thematic level (see for example Finnish curriculum) or at the abilities level (see for example the Spanish curriculum).

Analysis of the attitude towards ICT-based teaching and learning: Certain trends in Science teaching that are relevant for the actual impact of ICT in education were also visible:

- In some countries, ICT instruments tend to become a routine: virtual environments, interactive and multimedia which can be accessed through a network, e.g. Spain

- There is a need for multi-sensory teaching with a wide use of multimedia and virtual experiments e.g. Poland
- The education process should be widely assisted by new technologies which allow for the common usage of multimedia
- Achievement of educational goals should be assisted by school libraries with updated sources, using Internet, multimedia and other ICT based tools
- E-learning is also recommended to play a more significant role in education, being a component of the traditional teaching and learning (blended learning).

The design of both; the activities and the tools provided by the VccSSe project for the participants and for the teachers was based on the ideas described above. The work done in the project was organized in four project stages (Gorghiu, et al., 2009) which are reported in the next section of this chapter, with a special focus on the collaboration activities performed by the aforementioned community throughout each stage, and on the role of the tools provided for the achievement of the goals of the project.

STAGES OF DEVELOPMENT AND COLLABORATION WITHIN VCCSSE

The VccSSe Project has as declared objective to adapt, develop, test, implement, and disseminate training modules, teaching methodologies, and pedagogical strategies based on the use of ICT in terms of VIs and VEs, for the teaching and learning of positive Sciences: Mathematics, Physics and Chemistry. For the implementation of the aforementioned objective a transnational e-learning community was formed by the partnership. The main goals of the project have been achieved taking also into account the specific particularities of different countries involved in the partnership.

The work done throughout the project was divided into four stages, namely: (1) Creation stage, (2) Training stage, (3) Implementation stage, and (4) Evaluation and Dissemination stage. The project activities have been designed on targeting on the following three groups (Gorghiu, et al., 2009):

- *Leading staff*: local coordinators (who acted also as tutors), tutors, researchers and educational local authorities—even that in the proposal phase of VccSSe—the number of tutors and researchers has been approximated at 27, it reached 32 finally. Along with the 18 representatives of local authorities in education, this group comprised of 50 people.
- *In-service teachers* from primary and secondary schools involved in Sciences teaching areas—the initial target group was estimated at 180 teachers but 363 teachers started the training modules proposed by the project.
- *Pupils* – they participated actively to the lessons proposed by the teachers involved in the project, based on the developed pedagogical methods and strategies. Even the initial number of pupils was approximated around 3500, the final number was under 3000 due to the limited number of pupils which formed a study group during the Sciences lessons (Mathematics, Physics, Chemistry).

The description of the aforementioned stages will be described in the following section with an emphasis on the collaboration realized among the members of the community and the role of tools used.

Creation Stage

The activities performed during this stage were focused on: (a) identifying, analyzing, and selecting a number of suitable virtual instrumentation environments for the development of appropriate VEs for the teaching and learning of concepts related to the positive Sciences, (b) creating training modules appropriate for teacher education about essential issues for the integration of Virtual Instrumentation in the positive Sciences' Education, (c) implementing an e-learning platform to support the teacher training activities, and (d) developing a Virtual experiment space (e-Space)—a repository of VIs and VEs to be used like examples during the teacher training sessions. The aforementioned activities are further described below:

a. *Identifying, analysing and selecting suitable virtual instrumentation environments for positive Sciences education*: As one of the project's objectives targeted at offering in-service Sciences teachers a particular technology that can enhance the learning process in specific Science lessons and laboratories, the partnership designed the training modules "Virtual Instrumentation in Sciences Education," with a duration of 40 hours, consisting of 3 seminars and 3 laboratories. The labs were equipped with the following specific educational software applications for developing virtual educational experiments: *Cabri Geometry, LabVIEW, Crocodile Clips* and *GeoGebra*, each participant expressing his/her interest on using one application, according to the own needs. The selection of these pieces of software performed after face-to-face collaboration among the partnership during a 3-day transnational meeting. The formation of specific seminars and laboratories was performed through asynchronous collaboration. In fact, specific partners took charge for the formation of a first draft regarding these specific seminars and labs and then, the partnership arrived to the agreement of their final form after negotiations and corrections performed through e-mail. All the materials produced for training were initially designed in English and then translated in the partner's national languages: Romanian, Spanish, Polish, Finnish, and Greek.

b. *Creating training modules*: Given the tendencies and needs identified in Sciences teaching at the level of the participating countries, the partnership decided to use the blended learning model for designing and implementing the teacher training course. The reasons for this decision were related to the work of the partnership on one hand, and on the training of teachers, on the other hand. The Moodle open source educational platform was selected to facilitate this course. The partnership came to this decision through face-to-face collaboration during a 3-day transnational meeting. The preparation of the training modules "Virtual Instrumentation in Science Education" was realized in respect of two directions: the first one targeted the creation of the content of the training modules, related training materials and assessment tools; the second one focused on the development and implementation of the VIs and VEs that could effectively support the teacher training (Gorghiu, et al., 2009). The training modules introduced specific concepts of virtual instruments, available educational software packages and web examples, pedagogical methods and also particular and didactical elements for the selected educational software applications. For each selected educational software application, specific video-training materials (in English) were formed and uploaded in the *Outcomes* section of the project webpage. The training modules developed in the frame of this project aimed also to help participating teachers acquire interdisciplinary skills. In addition, the training modules included Internet searching exercises, as well as other different pedagogical activities, such as creating complex evaluation rubrics, or designing different teaching and learning

situations that allowed the use of VIs and VEs (Gorghiu, 2009). The formation of the aforementioned training modules was realized through asynchronous collaboration—among the partnership—as it was described in the previous section. All the materials produced for training were initially designed in English and then translated in the partner's national languages: Romanian, Spanish, Polish, Finnish, and Greek.

c. *Implementing an e-learning platform to support the course activities*: The training activities took place with the support of *Moodle*—open source—course management system. Moodle includes tools to support various educational activities such as content presentation, and evaluation as well as tools for collaborative work for the teachers. Here, it is worth noting that a course was formed as a model in English using the Moodle platform and then this course was translated in the partners' languages and placed in a specific space within Moodle. Thus, the trainee teachers in each institution constituted a specific community within Moodle. All of these communities also constituted the trans-national community of teachers in the context of VccSSe. An example of the organization of the training modules inside the particular space of *Moodle* course management system—dedicated for teachers trained by the Babes-Bolyai University at Cluj Napoca—is presented in Figure 2.

By interacting within Moodle, teachers were also provided with the opportunity to get familiarized with the use of this e-learning platform and, given the fact that most e-learning platforms require similar core technical skills, it is expected that they should be able to transfer the skills acquired in this context, to similar e-learning situations. The *phpGroupWare* platform was also used to appropriately facilitate communication and collaborative work within the project partnership. This platform was chosen due to its flexibility and simplicity and to the fact that it's free of charge (Bîzoi, et al., 2009).

d. *Developing the Virtual experiment space (e-Space)*: Consequently, in the first stage of the project the partnership not only tried to exploit the educational facilities proposed by various software applications but also to create a common space (called *e-Space* – Figure 3) for collaboration among the partnership but also for the teachers who participated in the teacher training course. The *e-Space* specific software was developed with the end goal to help all the participants within the VccSSe community to retrieve the necessary information, and also, to help the project partners to upload the virtual experiment samples. The *e-Space* structure is divided into areas (Mathematics, Physics, Chemistry, and Technology) but

related categories were also included. In addition, a search engine which allows the searching of examples by: description, author, keyword and language—English, Romanian, Spanish, Polish, Finnish, and Greek—was designed (Suduc, Bîzoi, & Gorghiu, 2008).

In fact, e-space can function as a repository of VIs and VEs as examples in the context of teacher training, a database equipped with a specific web interface which can be accessed from the project website. Those tools are used in order to manage the information which is included in the web-site, and particularly in the e-Space. Thus, the e-space can provide a proper environment for posting and discussing the ICT-based applications created by the teachers, and consequently, the trainers could directly and individually supervise the activity of the participants. The most important tools included

Figure 2. The organization of the Moodle space for the training module "virtual instrumentation in science education" (edition 2 – participants from Cluj Napoca, Romania)

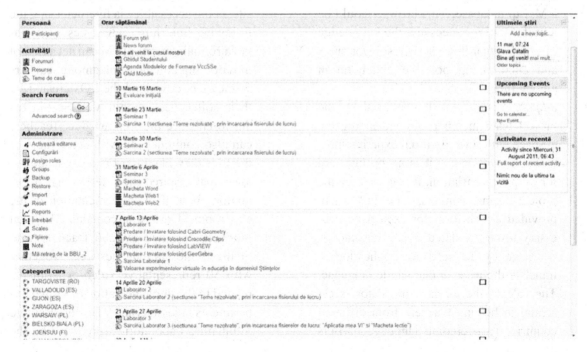

Figure 3. The e-space interface

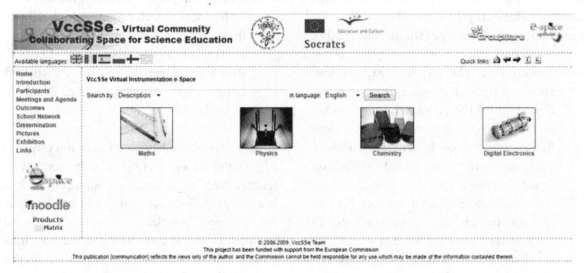

within the aforementioned e-space are presented below:

- *e-Space browser* - it can be used for exploring the space of virtual experiments available on the project web system. This is possible because e-Space stores the experiments in repository files and the information related to those files is recorded in a MySql database. This browser could be a useful tool for accessing the knowledge of others regarding specific subject areas and encouraging possible collaboration among them.
- *e-Space up-loader* - it was used by the project team members for enhancing the e-Space with several virtual experiments.
- *e-Space translator* – it is an on-line tool for e-Space translation. It was used by the project team members. The instrument provided a web-form for each page necessary to be translated. Each translator is restricted by the software application to translate the page in one single language. The role of the e-Space translator is essential in helping teachers from different countries to overcome language barriers

and to effectively participate and collaborate within the VccSSe project.

- *Teachers' Products Matrix* – it is a database where teachers' LO including VEs and lesson plans can be uploaded. Teachers' Products Matrix (TPM) was developed as an open resource tool for all the teachers interested in introducing VEs in their lessons. TPM is included in the *VccSSe* website, being accessible via Internet, using the following link: http://www.vccsse.ssai.valahia.ro/main/matrix. TPM can act as a tool of enforcing collaboration among teachers as they can download the LOs created by their colleagues—within VccSSe—in order to enhance their knowledge. Teachers can also communicate with the authors of the LOs they liked most and exchange the ideas that inspired their design and information about their implementation in the classroom. TPM now contains 218 final products designed by 206 teachers who finalized the training sessions. Together with 50 representative video-experiments related to the implementation of virtual experiments in lessons and 9 On-line/Remote Simulating Laboratories (produced by the project partnership), all of them grouped as VccSSe Exhibition, it closes the open educational space created in the frame of the VccSSe project and dedicated to the promoting of Virtual experiments in European Sciences education (Bîzoi, Suduc, & Gorghiu, 2010).

This educational space, even mainly dedicated to teachers of scientific subjects, is also a space of resources for any person searching for an understanding of different Science concepts. The partnership collaborated synch/asynchronously—in the previously mentioned sense—for the design of the aforementioned *e-Space*.

Training Stage

The main activities in this stage were focused on in-service teacher training using the materials as well as the VIs and VEs developed in the first stage. The face to face meetings allow discussing the possibilities for action at the local level and getting direct feedback for the trainer.

The duration of the training sessions covered an amount of approximately 42 hours, including the evaluation through the projects' web-page. It is worth noting that the face-to-face teaching sessions provided teachers with opportunities to clarify some complicated issues related to the construction of VEs using the selected educational software, to exchange ideas about didactical issues using ICT, to be motivated to construct their own VEs and implement them in their classrooms, and most importantly, to overcome their fears and doubts about the introduction of innovative technology in real educational practices. In fact, these face-to-face sections played a crucial role in the teachers' progress in creating and implementing virtual experiments in their classrooms. Various types of communication also helped teachers to make progress in their work, such as telephone calls to their tutors, e-mails to their tutors and their colleagues as well as asynchronous communica-

tions via forum and synchronous communications via chat.

The course was implemented in two editions and started at different moments, depending on each partner. This offered the opportunity to improve some elements of the course based on the partial evaluation made at the end of the first edition. After they had finished the training course, the teachers implemented the new learned methodologies in the classroom and this activity involving children was also evaluated.

Implementation Stage

The activities related to this stage consisted of the design and implementation of LOs by the teachers in their lessons. Assessment tools for evaluating the quality of the in-service teacher training process were also developed. A number of 363 in-service teachers involved in lower and upper level of secondary education as well as in primary education were trained through the previously mentioned blended learning approach on how to create, use and implement ICT based lessons in their real teaching practices. These in-service teachers were required to choose one of the software environments for understanding its main functions and creating at least one LO (that had to include also at least one VE for students with a significant level of interaction, for specific Sciences disciplines: Mathematics, Physics and Chemistry). Their lesson plans—designed under a specific Template—proposed explanations on the concepts to be learned.

Number of VEs produced: The VccSSe project involved in the two editions of the course Virtual Instrumentation in Science Education a number of 363 teachers of Mathematics, Physics, Chemistry, and integrated sciences that teach in lower and upper secondary schools of the participating countries. As a result of the course, a number of 218 LOs were designed, each of them including a virtual application of a different type (demonstration, experiment or exercise) associated with a specific lesson plan. Data indicating relevant number of products for each discipline/per partner institution and in total is presented in Table 1.

Here, it is worth noting that, teachers designed a variety of types of VEs supporting various learning activities. For example, mathematics teachers designed VEs supporting the following types of learning activities: (1) Forming/verifying conjectures by focusing on the alteration of an interactive geometrical construction using the drag-mode operation; (2) Forming/verifying conjectures by focusing on the numerical data automatically collected during the alteration of a geometrical construction using the drag-mode operation; (3) Verifying a formula by focusing on the numerical data automatically collected during the alteration of a geometrical construction using the drag-mode operation; (4) Multiple Representation-based activities; (5) Constructions simulating real-life problems; (6) Black-box activities; (7) A scenario-based approach emphasizing the formation of networks of learning concepts; (8) Multiple-solution activities. It is also worth noting that, all teachers also took ideas from the VIs and VEs uploaded in the e-Space by the partnership in order to design their own LOs. All teachers also visited the LOs uploaded in the TPM and enhanced their ideas about the design and implementation of VIs and VEs within real classrooms. Some teachers were also motivated to construct their own VEs by their intention to try new ideas in their classrooms as well as to improve their knowledge of modern educational technologies.

Evaluation and Dissemination Stage

The main activities of this stage were oriented on evaluating the project activities and its outputs and also on disseminating the project results through different channels: webpage, posters, scientific articles, exhibition, DVD edition, web / external dissemination, etc.

Evaluation: In order to assess the formative impact of the training materials an experimental design was associated with the training process that included an initial and a final survey based on questionnaire. The questionnaires focused on teachers' understanding and attitude towards the use and efficacy of ICT, specific educational software and virtual instrumentation tools in Science education, as well as on their feedback related to the teacher training course and aspects that made it effective. To this end, a set of assessment tools was created during the different stages of the project.

Table 1. Relevant number of products for each discipline and institution

VccSSe Institutions	Number of LOs				
	Math	Physics	Chemistry	Technology	Total
Valahia University of Targoviste	16	4	4	0	24
Teacher Training and Educational Innovation Centre Valladolid II	0	6	10	3	19
Teachers Training Centre of Gijon	37	33	0	1	71
Teachers Training Centre of Zaragoza 1	0	15	0	0	15
Warsaw University of Technology	2	8	0	3	13
Regional In-service Teacher Training Centre "Wom" in Bielsko-Biala	21	1	0	1	23
University of Joensuu	10	3	0	0	13
Babes-Bolyai University Cluj Napoca	8	11	2	0	21
University of Patras	19	0	0	0	19
Total Number of LOs for Each Discipline	**113**	**81**	**16**	**8**	**218**

The first group of *Assessment Tools* consisted of instruments for the evaluation of the quality of the teacher training process (*Teachers' Initial Evaluation*; *Teachers' Final Evaluation*). A particular topic included in the *Teachers' Initial Evaluation* questionnaire was related to the training needs for teachers, as they were declared in terms of the field of new technologies and of the educational software. While this questionnaire included general questions related to the previously mentioned subjects, the *Teachers' Final Evaluation* questionnaire included more specific items referring to virtual instrumentation in education and its educational value as it is perceived by the teachers.

In the following Stage (*Implementation Stage*), the impact of the *Learning Objects* created during the training process by the teachers was assessed (*Teachers' Impact Questionnaire* and *Pupils' Feedback Questionnaire*). This category of evaluation instruments was dedicated to different phases and target groups involved in the teacher training stage of the project. The questionnaires were composed mainly from multiple choice items, a fact that allowed for a statistical processing of data. With a small number of exceptions, open questions were avoided due to the language barrier in the discourse analysis process (Gorghiu, et al., 2011). The aforementioned questionnaires were translated in all the partnership countries languages using the *e-Space translator* and were delivered online at the initial and final stage of the teacher training course, so that these could be directly accessed by the teachers through the *Moodle* course management system.

The analysis of the data gathered from the aforementioned questionnaires shows that a great number of the teachers regarded virtual instrumentation applications as a source of inspiration for their teaching actions that should be used as an alternative to traditional tools, and as a means for improving students' understanding of abstract concepts. However, teachers did not find direct correlations between use of VIs and improvements in students' learning skills. A part of the Spanish teachers reported that even though the term Virtual Instruments is not very well known to them, they enjoy and find natural to use computer simulations and virtual applications as long as they are motivating for students.

In fact, the best scores were obtained to the feedback item regarding the improvement of students' motivation for learning. Most of the teachers in different countries reported that VI applications and VEs were the most useful for creating and maintaining students' interest for scientific topics as well as in obtaining better results in evaluations. This last aspect correlates with good scores given to improved understanding of concepts. Good scores were registered also in students' interactive learning mediated by Vis and VEs.

As for most of the teachers using virtual science applications in the classroom was one of the first experiences of this type, difficulties were reported in management of the classroom especially in: evaluation of students performance as well as in access to hardware or general management of students.

A number of teachers that work in more structured and less flexible curriculum systems (for example, the Romanian teachers) were concerned with meeting curriculum requirements through such special lessons. Indeed, displaying and working with virtual experiments in teaching and learning may be time consuming in certain school settings, for instance in case of a low number of computers for individual intervention, or in the case of teacher or students' low computer use abilities, or in the case of absence of hands on intervention for all students with consequences for their learning motivation.

Nevertheless, most of the teachers declared that lessons that included VIs and VEs were successful or rather successful and that they would decide to use such educational applications again, provided that they would have better and constant access to computers and would be able to involve students more in the creation and modulation of virtual learning spaces and experiments.

Dissemination: In the knowledge dissemination process, collaboration is the primary function. The dissemination technologies which support collaboration are: World Wide Web, groupware, on-line access, video conferencing, and document management. In the selection of a specific dissemination technology, it is important to consider the particular characteristics of the target group: small or large groups, intermediate or advanced computer skills etc. The selected technology should meet the capabilities of the user and the nature of the use (Gray & Tehtani, 2003). Thus, for reaching as many individuals of the target group as possible, who may have different specific characteristics, it is necessary to combine and use different dissemination methods.

Traditional and web conferencing as a method of disseminating research findings and good practice is expanding each year. Web conferencing is a good tool for information sharing and dissemination. Usually web conferencing software allows, besides visual and audio participation, face-to-face like, shared whiteboards, desktop application sharing (Suduc, Bîzoi, & Filip, 2009), computer access and storage, video recording to keep a permanent record of the knowledge transfer (Gray & Tehtani, 2003). Due to the great advancement in web speed, the last generations of web conferencing software provide high-quality of audio and video connections.

Taking into account the above, various ways were considered for the dissemination of the results of this project, such as: the project webpage, posters, scientific articles, exhibition, DVD edition, web/external dissemination, and web conferencing. *Abobe Connect Pro* was selected for a number of the partners of the project on-line meetings (videoconference) in the last year of the project as well as for the dissemination of the project products. In this dissemination event participated many attendants including project national partners, teachers, researchers and national educational authorities.

Abobe Connect Pro was selected as the specific software suitable to sustain the meeting of 100 persons. Web conferencing may be considered as a project results dissemination method due to its many benefits. Two main benefits, compared with other dissemination methods, are as follows: (1) in comparison with face-to-face dissemination methods, virtual meetings eliminates the physical limitations of distance and the expenses for dissemination meeting organization are lower; (2) unlike the paper material dissemination, the videoconference allows direct interaction with the presenters (e.g. the partnership that developed a project and disseminate the outcomes through a web conference), so the responses to the questions are offered immediately (Suduc, Bîzoi, & Filip, 2009).

DISCUSSION AND CONCLUDING REMARKS

Upon examining the results of the reported 3-year project, it is clear that the main aims of VccSSe project have been adequately met. Specifically, a large number of researchers and educational specialists from different European countries—the partners of VccSSe—collaboratively designed appropriate training materials and Virtual experiments using appropriate Virtual instruments and well known educational software. For the design of these training materials specific characteristics regarding with the Science curricula of each country were taken into account. The partnership collaborated synchronously within face-to-face meetings and asynchronously using e-mails and the phpGroupWare platform for the design of the aforementioned educational materials and tools. This platform helped the partnership to organize their training materials by dedicating a specific space for the materials written in English. Those materials acted as a model for all partners for the development of custom language-specific spaces, where their own materials would be stored.

The *Moodle* collaborative platform played an important role during the teacher training stage as it facilitated the organization of the teacher training course by providing synchronous and asynchronous communication as well as content and assignment delivery. The *e-Space* also played an essential role during this stage in terms of providing appropriate VIs and VEs for teacher training as well as a specific *search engine* for searching within the e-Space contents. In fact, teachers collaborated with their tutors and their colleagues through the Moodle platform as well as through the e-Space. During the implementation stage, teachers collaborated with their colleagues through the use of the Moodle platform as well as through the *TPM*. Teachers collaborated with the members of the partnership, their colleagues and other authorities during the dissemination stage through the use of *videoconferencing*. However, the formation and the work of the trans-national community formed in the frame of VccSSe would be totally impossible without the use of the *Translation tool*. In fact, the existence of this tool helped teachers from different nationalities to overcome language barriers and fully attend the teacher training course delivered online in their own language.

On the whole, the implementation of this trans-national community of researchers, teachers and educational professionals seemed to succeed in its aims due to various ways of collaboration among its participants. This collaboration took place synchronously and asynchronously. Synchronous collaboration has been supported through face to face interaction as well as through the use of chat and videoconferencing tools. Asynchronous collaboration helped most by the use of appropriate tools encouraging translation, searching, sharing and showcasing of educational materials as well as through various means of communication, including e-mail and forums. The organization of this trans-national community in specific sub-communities in each partner institution also helped the participants to conceptualize clearly the aims of VccSSe project and to successfully fulfill them. The

general model of the teacher education course that was formed taking into account essential theoretical issues about modern theories of learning and the use of ICT in education taking also into account the specific characteristics of learning curricula in the partners' countries seemed also appropriate in terms of meeting the participants needs.

This chapter concludes by highlighting some implications regarding the creation of successful collaborative e-learning trans-national communities. The experience gained through this 3-year European project emphasizes the fundamental contribution of collaborative platforms for the support of synchronous/asynchronous activities through the provision of features for document and file sharing and translating, shared desktop access, simultaneous editing and other electronic forms of communication allowing data to be shared, edited and copied during a web meeting by various groups. More work is needed towards an easier integration of videoconferencing facilities in the collaborative work of trans-national communities as well as support of multi-language communication and automatic monitoring of the participants' progress in terms of tasks at hand and project aim fulfillment.

ACKNOWLEDGMENT

This work was funded through the Socrates-Comenius 2.1. European project 128989-CP-1-2006-1-RO-COMENIUS-C21: "VccSSe – Virtual Community Collaborating Space for Science Education." The support offered by the European Commission, Education and Training, School Education: Socrates: Comenius and the Education, Audiovisual and Culture Executive Agency as responsible for the management of EU's programmes in the fields of education, culture and audiovisual, through the project mentioned above, is gratefully acknowledged.

REFERENCES

Balacheff, N., & Kaput, J. (1996). Computer-based learning environments in mathematics. In Bishop, A. J., Klements, K., Keitel, C., Kilpatric, J., & Laborde, C. (Eds.), *International Handbook on Mathematics Education* (pp. 469–501). Dortdrecht, The Netherlands: Kluwer.

Bîzoi, M., Suduc, A. M., & Gorghiu, G. (2010). Teachers' perception on developing and implementing virtual experiments. In *Proceedings of 1st International Multi-Conference on Innovative Developments in ICT (INNOV 2010)*, (pp. 133-136). Science and Technology Publications.

Bîzoi, M., Suduc, A. M., Gorghiu, G., & Gorghiu, L. M. (2009). Analysis of 1000 days of collaborative activities in two multinational educational projects. *WSEAS Transactions on Advances in Engineering Education*, 6(10), 337–346.

Bruner, J. S. (1996). *Culture of education.* Cambridge, MA: Harvard University Press.

Chan, T. W. (2010). How east Asian classrooms may change over the next 20 years. *Journal of Computer Assisted Learning*, 26, 28–52. doi:10.1111/j.1365-2729.2009.00342.x

Council the European Union. (2001). *Report from the education council to the European council: The concrete future objectives of education and training systems*. Retrieved from http://ec.europa.eu/education/policies/2010/doc/rep_fut_obj_en.pdf.

Davis, N., & Tearle, P. (1998). A core curriculum for telematics in teacher training. In *Proceedings of the 15th IFIP World Computer Congress – Teleteaching 1998 Distance Learning, Training and Education*, (vol 1), (pp. 239-248). ACM Press.

Dillenbourg, P. (1999). Introduction: What do you mean by collaborative learning? In Dillenbourg, P. (Ed.), *Collaborative Learning: Cognitive and Computational Approaches* (pp. 1–19). Oxford, UK: Pergamon.

Dubinsky, E., & Tall, D. (1991). Advanced mathematical thinking and the computer. In Tall, D. O. (Ed.), *Advanced Mathematical Thinking* (pp. 231–248). Berlin, Germany: Kluwer.

Dyfour-Janvier, B., Bednarz, N., & Belanger, M. (1987). Pedagogical considerations concerning the problem of representation. In Janvier, C. (Ed.), *Problems of Representation in Teaching and Learning of Mathematics* (pp. 109–122). London, UK: Lawrence Erlbaum Associates.

Engestrom, Y. (1987). *Learning by expanding. An activity-theoretical approach to developmental research*. Helsinki, Finland: Orienta-Konsultit Oy.

European Commission. (1997). *Framework programme: Information society programme for technologies and skills acquisition: Proposal for a research agenda*. Brussels, Belgium: European Commission.

Gorghiu, G. (2009). VccSSe: Virtual community collaborating space for science education - An European project experience under socrates comenius 2.1 action. In Gorghiu, G., Gorghiu, L. M., Glava, A. E., & Glava, C. C. (Eds.), *Education 21* (pp. 7–16). Cluj Napoca, Romania: Casa Cărţii de Ştiinţă Publishing House.

Gorghiu, G., Bîzoi, M., Gorghiu, L. M., & Suduc, A. M. (2011). Promoting the European cooperation with the view of improving the methodologies for science teaching and learning using virtual instrumentation. In Bolte, C., Gräber, W., & Holbrook, J. (Eds.), *Making Science Lessons Popular and Relevant - Examples of Good Practice*. Münster, Germany: Waxmann Verlag.

Gorghiu, G., Gorghiu, L. M., Suduc, A. M., Bîzoi, M., Dumitrescu, C., & Olteanu, R. L. (2009). Related aspects to the pedagogical use of virtual experiments. In *Proceedings of the Fifth International Conference on Multimedia & ICTs in Education*, (pp. 809-813). Lisbon, Portugal: ACM.

Gray, P., & Tehtani, S. (2003). Technologies for disseminating knowledge. In Holsapple, C. (Ed.), *Handbook on Knowledge Management - Knowledge Matters* (pp. 109–127). Berlin, Germany: Springer-Verlang.

Häkkinen, P., & Jarvela, S. (2006). Sharing and constructing perspectives in web-based conferencing. *Computers & Education*, *47*, 433–447. doi:10.1016/j.compedu.2004.10.015

Harasim, L., Hiltz, S. R., Teles, L., & Turoff, M. (1995). *Learning networks: A field guide to teaching and learning online*. Cambridge, MA: MIT Press.

Haythornthwaite, C., Kazmer, M. M., Robins, J., & Shoemaker, S. (2000). Community development among distance learners: Temporal and technological dimensions. *Journal of Computer-Mediated Communication*, *6*(1). Retrieved from http://www.ascusc.org/jcmc/vol6/issue1/haythornthwaite.html

Janvier, C. (1987). Representation and understanding: The notion of function as an example. In Janvier, C. (Ed.), *Problems of Representation in Teaching and Learning of Mathematics* (pp. 67–72). London: Lawrence Erlbaum Associates.

Jonassen, D. H., Carr, C., & Yueh, H.-P. (1998). Computers as mindtools for engaging learners in critical thinking. *TechTrends*, *43*(2), 24–32. doi:10.1007/BF02818172

Kaput, J. J. (1994). The representational roles of technology in connecting μathematics with authentic experience. In R. Biehler, R. W. Scholz, R. Strasser, & B., Winkelman (Eds.), *Didactics of Mathematics as a Scientific Discipline: The State of the Art,* (pp. 379- 397). Dordrecht, The Netherlands: Kluwer Academic Publishers.

Koschmann, T. (1996). Paradigm shifts and instructional technology: An introduction. In Koschmann, T. (Ed.), *CSCL: Theory and Practice of an Emerging Paradigm* (pp. 1–23). Mahwah, NJ: Lawrence Erlbaum Associates.

Lakkala, M., Rahikainen, M., & Hakkarainen, K. (2001). *Perspectives of CSCL in Europe: A review*. Retrieved from http://www.euro-cscl.org/site/itcole/D2_1_review_of_cscl.pdf.

Laurillard. (2010). Supporting teacher development of competencies in the use of learning technologies. In *Proceedings of the International Conference on ICT in Teacher Education: Policy, open Educational Resources and Partnership*, (pp. 63-74). St. Petersburg, Russia: ACM.

Lesh, R., Mehr, M., & Post, T. (1987). Rational number relations and proportions. In Janvier, C. (Ed.), *Problems of Representation in Teaching and Learning of Mathematics* (pp. 41–58). London: Lawrence Erlbaum Associates.

Lin, C.-P., Liu, K.-P., & Niramitranon, J. (2008). Tablet PC to support collaborative learning: An empirical study of English vocabulary learning. In *Proceedings of IEEE International Conference on Wireless, Mobile, and Ubiquitous Technology in Education 2008*, (pp. 47–51). Beijing, China: IEEE Press.

Lipponen, L. (2002). Exploring foundations for computer-supported collaborative learning. In Stahl, G. (Ed.), *Computer Support for Collaborative Learning: Foundations for a CSCL Community* (pp. 72–81). Hillsdale, NJ: Erlbaum.

Littlejohn, A., & Pegler, C. (2006). *Preparing for blended e-learning: Understanding blended and online learning*. London: Routledge.

Looi, C.-K., Ogata, H., & Wong, L.-H. (2010). Technology-transformed learning: Going beyond the one-to-one model? In *Proceedings of the 18th International Conference on Computers in Education*, (pp. 175–176). Putrajaya, Malaysia: ACM.

Looi, C.-K., Seow, P., Zhang, B., So, H.-J., Chen, W., & Wong, L.-H. (2010). Leveraging mobile technology for sustainable seamless learning: A research agenda. *British Journal of Educational Technology*, *41*, 154–169.doi:10.1111/j.1467-8535.2008.00912.x

Looi, C.-K., So, H.-J., Toh, Y., & Chen, W. (2010). The Singapore experience: Synergy of national policy, classroom practice and design research. *Computer-Supported Collaborative Learning, 6*(1).

Mifsud, L., & Mørch, A. I. (2010). Reconsidering off-task: A comparative study of PDA-mediated activities in four classrooms. *Computer Assisted Learning, 26*, 190–201.doi:10.1111/j.1365-2729.2010.00346.x

Noss, R., & Hoyles, C. (1992). Looking back and looking forward. In Hoyles, C., & Noss, R. (Eds.), *Learning Mathematics and Logo* (pp. 431–470). Cambridge, MA: MIT Press.

Noss, R., & Hoyles, C. (1996). *Windows on mathematical meanings: Learning cultures and computers*. Dordrecht, The Netherlands: Kluwer Academic Publishers.

Palloff, M. R., & Pratt, K. (2004). Learning together in community: Collaboration online. In *Proceedings of the 20th Annual Conference on Distance Teaching and Learning*. Retrieved on September 30, 2009, from http://www.uwex.edu/disted/ conference/ Resource_library/proceedings/04_1127.pdf.

Papert, S. (1980). *Mindstorms: Children, computers, and powerful ideas*. New York, NY: Basic Books.

Roberts, T. S. (2005). Computer-supported collaborative learning in higher education: An introduction. In Roberts, T. S. (Ed.), *Computer-Supported Collaborative Learning in Higher Education* (pp. 1–18). Hershey, PA: IGI Global.

Roschelle, J., Patton, C., & Tatar, D. (2007). Designing networked handheld devices to enhance school learning. *Advances in Computers*, *70*, 1–60. doi:10.1016/S0065-2458(06)70001-8

Scardamalia, M., & Bereiter, C. (1996). Computer support for knowledge-building communities. In Koschmann, T. (Ed.), *CSCL: Theory and Practice of an Emerging Paradigm* (pp. 249–268). Mahwah, NJ: Erlbaum.

Soloway, E. (1993). Reading and writing in the 21st century. *Communications of the ACM, 36*(5). doi:10.1145/155049.155052

Suduc, A. M., Bîzoi, M., & Filip, F. G. (2009). Exploring multimedia Web conferencing. *Informatica Economică, 13*(3), 5–17.

Suduc, A. M., Bîzoi, M., & Gorghiu, G. (2008). Virtual instrumentation environment used in the VccSSe project. In *Postępy Eedukacji* (pp. 364–370). Warsaw, Poland: Praca Zbiorowa Pod Redakcją Zespołu Ośrodka Kształcenia Na Odległość OKNO PW.

Tomasello, M. (1999). *The cultural origins of human cognition*. Cambridge, MA: Harvard University Press.

Van Eijl, P., & Pilot, A. (2003). Using a virtual learning environment in collaborative learning: Criteria for success. *Educational Technology, 43*(2), 54–56.

Vygotsky, L. S. (1962). *Thought and language*. Cambridge, MA: MIT Press.

Wong, L.-H., & Looi, C.-K. (2010). Vocabulary learning by mobile-assisted authentic content creation and social meaning making: two case studies. *Journal of Computer Assisted Learning, 26*, 421–433.doi:10.1111/j.1365-2729.2010.00357.x

ADDITIONAL READING

Dillenbourg, P. (2002). Over-scripting CSCL: The risks of blending collaborative learning with instructional design. In Kirschner, P. A. (Ed.), *Three Worlds of CSCL: Can We Support CSCL* (pp. 61–91). Heerlen, The Netherlands: Open Universiteit Nederlands.

Goodyear, P. (2005). Educational design and networked learning: Patterns, pattern languages and design practice. *Australasian Journal of Educational Technology, 2*(1), 82–101.

Johnson, D. W., & Johnson, R. T. (1999). *Learning together and alone: Cooperative, competitive and individualistic learning* (5th ed.). Needham Heights, MA: Allyn and Bacon.

Kagan, S. (1994). *Cooperative learning.* San Clemente, CA: Kagan Publishing.

Kordaki, M., Papadakis, S., & Hadzilacos, T. (2007b). Providing tools for the development of cognitive skills in the context of learning design-based e-learning environments. In T. Bastiaens & S. Carliner (Eds.), *Proceedings of World Conference on E-Learning in Corporate, Government, Healthcare & Higher Education (E-Learn 2007),* (pp. 1642-1649). Chesapeake, VA: AACE.

Kordaki, M., & Siempos, H. (2009b). Encouraging collaboration within learning design-based open source e-learning systems. In J. Dron, T Bastiaens, & C. Xin (Eds.), *Proceedings of World Conference on E-Learning in Corporate, Government, Healthcare & Higher Education (E-Learn 2009),* (pp. 1716-1723). Chesapeake, VA: AACE

Kordaki, M., Siempos, H., & Daradoumis, T. (2009). Collaborative learning design within open source e-learning systems: Lessons learned from an empirical study. In Magoulas, G. (Ed.), *E-Infrastructures and Technologies for Lifelong Learning: Next Generation Environments.* Hershey, PA: IGI Global.

Lehtinen, E. (2003). Computer-supported collaborative learning: an approach to powerful learning environments. In de Corte, E., Verschaffel, L., Entwistle, N., & van Merrieboer, J. (Eds.), *Powerful Learning Environments: Unravelling Basic Components and Dimensions* (pp. 35–54). Amsterdam, The Netherlands: Pergamon.

Lipponen, L. (2002). Exploring foundations for computer-supported collaborative learning. In Stahl, G. (Ed.), *Computer Support for Collaborative Learning: Foundations for a CSCL Community* (pp. 72–81). Hillsdale, NJ: Erlbaum. doi:10.3115/1658616.1658627

Lloyd, G., & Wilson, M. (2001). Offering prospective teachers tools to connect theory and practice: Hypermedia in mathematics teacher education. *Journal of Technology and Teacher Education, 9*(4), 497–518.

Scardamalia, M., & Bereiter, C. (1996). Computer support for knowledge-building communities. In Koschmann, T. (Ed.), *CSCL: Theory and Practice of an Emerging Paradigm* (pp. 249–268). Mahwah, NJ: Erlbaum.

Slavin, R. E. (1990). *Cooperative learning: Theory, research, and practice.* Englewood Cliffs, NJ: Prentice Hall.

Strijbos, J. W., Martens, R. L., & Jochems, W. M. G. (2004). Designing for interaction: Six steps to designing computer-supported group-based learning. *Computers & Education, 42*(4), 403–424. doi:10.1016/j.compedu.2003.10.004

KEY TERMS AND DEFINITIONS

Blended Learning: Face to face learning in combination with online learning settings.

Innovative Teaching Methods: Teaching methods emphasizing modern social and constructivist learning theories as well as the appropriate use of digital technologies.

In-Service Teachers: Teachers who are active members of an educational system and teach in real classrooms.

Learning Object: A set consisting of a lesson plan and appropriate Virtual experiments and Virtual Instruments.

Virtual Community: A community of people who collaborate online synchronously and asynchronously, to achieve specific goals.

Virtual Experiments: Specific interactive constructions -formed using specific pieces of educational software- which can assist students' experimentation and active participation in their learning of a specific subject matter.

Virtual Instruments: Computer based istruments that can be used by the students to perform scientific experiments.

Chapter 11
E–Mentoring:
Issues and Experiences in Starting e–Research Collaborations in Graduate Programs

Javier Faulin
Public University of Navarre, Spain

Angel A. Juan
Open University of Catalonia, Spain

Fernando Lera
Public University of Navarre, Spain

Barry B. Barrios
Northwestern University, USA

Alex Forcada
University of Zaragoza, Spain

ABSTRACT

This chapter introduces the interrelated concepts of e-Research and e-Mentoring, reviews some recent works related to them, and discusses their importance in a global, Internet-based world. In this chapter, a conceptual framework is proposed to distinguish among the concepts of e-Research, e-Science, and Cyberinfrastructure, which are frequently used synonymously in the existing literature. Then, some issues related to e-Mentoring are discussed, including its characteristics, benefits, challenges, and a review of different Web 2.0 tools that can facilitate and promote e-Mentoring practices in most research organizations. Some personal experiences in e-Mentoring are then related. These experiences involve different universities and international programs, and their study points out several key factors of a successful e-Mentoring collaboration.

DOI: 10.4018/978-1-4666-0125-3.ch011

INTRODUCTION

In the last decades, the proper training of new researchers has been gaining increasing interest, both in academic and industrial environments. This might be due to several factors, such as globalization and the emergence of new computing, information, and communication technologies. Nowadays, most noticeable research projects are being developed through joined collaboration among researchers from different institutions or even from different countries. These collaborations have been greatly facilitated by the continuous appearance of new Internet-based software tools as well as hardware infrastructures, which are modeling the concept of e-Research, i.e. the use of online or Web-based tools to support collaborative research (Anandarajan & Anandarajan, 2010). As a result, this technology has allowed two decades of 'remote' or geographically-distributed cooperation to reach major research breakthroughs without requesting physical presence of the researchers in a single geographical point (Borgman, 2006; Dutton & Meyer, 2009), and even without having to necessarily follow a synchronous model for developing research.

The main goal of this chapter is to analyze how e-Research technologies and methodologies can be successfully employed to perform the instruction and guidance processes of new young researchers. These formative processes usually require the assistance of university professors, or more experienced researchers, who serve as mentors for the would-be investigators. The role of mentors in the formation of new capable researchers is revealed as essential in the performance of the PhD and Master students (Erhut & Mokros, 1984). In fact, mentoring can be seen as a process by which experienced researchers instruct, counsel, guide, and facilitate the intellectual or career development of persons identified as protégés (Blackwell, 1989). Thus, mentorship is a bonded reciprocal developmental relationship aimed at helping an emergent researcher to be trained (Packard,

2003). Some of the mentorship characteristics are featured by long duration, great reciprocity, clear presence of both career and psychosocial functions, and a focus on the transformation of the protégé's identity (Johnson, 2007). When most of this counseling relationship is performed online, we are developing e-Mentoring, which allows a more continuous, and sometimes more perdurable, research link between the mentor and the protégée.

The chapter is structured as follows: the next section reviews the concepts of e-Research, e-Science, and Cyberinfrastructure, performing a literature review on these subjects and proposing a new conceptual model that establishes some differences among them. Afterwards, we analyze in more detail the mentoring process and discuss how the introduction of e-Research technologies and methodologies are facilitating the emergence of e-Mentoring. Subsequently, several benefits and challenges of e-Mentoring are examined, and we review some of the currently existing software that can be useful when developing e-Mentoring and e-Research practices. At that point, three different e-Mentoring experiences are described. From these experiences, some best practices and key factors of a successful e-Mentoring activity are extracted. Finally, a conclusion section summarizes the most important findings and results of this chapter.

E-RESEARCH, E-SCIENCE, AND CYBERINFRASTRUCTURE

The terms e-Research, e-Science, and Cyberinfrastructure have been sometimes used in the literature as interchangeable concepts. However, although they are strongly related, we prefer to establish some differences among them. First of all, the term Cyberinfrastructure has a more technical meaning. It focuses on the technological infrastructure, software, and hardware necessary to communicate and develop research throughout the Internet. This infrastructure includes high technology such as Grids, Cloud Computing, Web 2.0, etc. Secondly, the term e-Science seems to focus more on the scientific aspects of this collaborative research, i.e. on how to generate new scientific results by combining the computing infrastructure, remote labs, huge amounts of shared data, and the use of advanced simulation and data analysis techniques. Notice that the term e-Science was originally related to experiments in classical scientific and engineering disciplines, i.e. Physics, Computer Science, Meteorology, Chemistry, Mathematics, Bioinformatics, etc. Therefore, we could see Cyberinfrastructure as a fundamental support over which e-Science builds upon. To put it another way, we could see Cyberinfrastructure as a fundamental part (subset) of e-Science, although most of the times both terms are used synonymously in the literature. Finally, we see e-Research as a more general concept which includes both e-Science and Cyberinfrastructure. As a matter of fact, e-Research would be concerned with any kind of collaborative research activity throughout the Internet, in any academic discipline and fields (not only Science and Engineering), and would include also the design and development of Internet-based environments designed to facilitate this research. Additional issues, related to online collaboration, teams management, inter- or multi-disciplinary approaches, research globalization, etc. must also be considered in e-Research. Figure 1 represents these ideas and shows how these terms are conceptually related.

While the number of articles published on e-Science and Cyberinfrastructure has been increasing quickly during the last decade, scientific articles on how Internet and, in particular, the World Wide Web are changing the way we do research in a globally interconnected world are just starting to emerge. Next, we give a chronological and non-extensive overview of different works related to these concepts.

On the one hand, in regard to technical aspects of e-Research, we can start our overview with Pham et al. (2006), which presented a case study concerning the use of a collaborative e-Science platform. The author discussed how the collaboration in e-Science and e-Research depends on the exchange of huge volume of data and the sharing of high-tech computational resources amongst scientist from different disciplines. Also, Yang and Allan (2006) recognized the urgency for building up Virtual Research Environments and presented their own platform based on the well-known Sakai Virtual Learning Environment. In Fox et al. (2007), the impact of Web 2.0 technology to e-Science was examined, and a hybrid approach, combining both Web 2.0 and Web Service systems was proposed. Atkinson et al. (2007) brought in an infrastructure for remote access to different data sources and research instruments. Quite recently, Khatibi & Montazer (2009) described e-Research as an activity which "… encompasses how the information technologies, such as Internet, changes, evolves, improves and yet often complicates the research process." They also recommended a framework, based on web-services, for developing e-Research processes. Razum et al. (2009) introduced eSciDoc, an open-source framework to develop e-Research. Moreover, they analyzed some technical and management challenges associated with e-Research infrastructures and offered several pieces of advice aimed to solve them. Riedel and Terstyanszky (2009) defined e-Science as a "… research field that focus on collaboration in key areas of science using next generation computing infrastructures such as Grids to extend the potential of scientific computing." In Memon et al. (2010), a case study regarding the application of multiple e-Research infrastructures to e-health was exposed. In De Roure (2010), a long-term experience in e-Research was depicted, and Web 2.0 was identified as the "technology of choice for rapid application development" in the e-Research arena. Augustine and Robinson (2010) proposed the use of virtual machines as an efficient way to develop e-Research. Another technical case study can be found in Gao (2010), who related the development and use of a web-

Figure 1. Relationship among the e-research, e-science, and cyberinfrastructure concepts

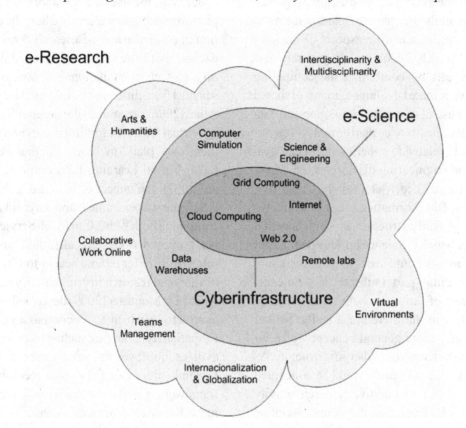

based collaborative research environment in a multi-disciplinary and multi-institute scenario. Finally, De Roure (2010) gave an overview on the evolution of e-Research.

On the other hand, in relation to social and management aspects of e-Research, one of the first references is that of Herron & Young (2000) who recognized the importance of e-Research and defined it as "the use of the Web to disseminate research materials to subjects, manipulate constructs, and capture empirical data." In Egan et al. (2005), authors presented the Australian National Neuroscience Facility, which provides Australian neuroscientists with access to networks of laboratories. Borgman (2006) discussed different key aspects of collaboration in e-Research, and concluded that more studies were needed in order to understand how e-Research facilitates collaboration through distributed access to con-

tent, tools, and services. In Hey and Hey (2006), authors pointed out the fact that the "next generation of scientific problems" required collaboration among multi-disciplinary and distributed teams of researchers. Jirotka et al. (2006) discussed collaboration issues in e-Research, including some of the benefits, concerns, and challenges it raises. Also in that year, Lawrence (2006) described a case study regarding a large e-Research project and discussed issues related to multi-disciplinary research, management of geographically-distributed teams, etc. The author argued that some of the most significant challenges in e-Research practice are not technological but socio-cultural instead. David et al. (2006) analyzed the differences between e-Science and Open Science and concluded that the development of the former does not necessarily promote the development of the latter. In Blanke et al. (2007), the authors explained the role of Arts and Humanities in the UK e-Science Initiative. Bravo and Alvite (2007) discussed the role of science repositories in the development of e-science, and gave an overview of available open access repositories in Spain. Osswald (2008) defined e-Science as a research activity "…based on distributed networks providing the software and computer power necessary to process large sets of data, by interconnecting computers and tools wherever they are available." Pierson et al. (2009) proposed a distributed collaborative research model and discussed how newly emerging web-based collaborative tools facilitate the raising of distributed collaboration. As they stated in this recent work, "the timing for distributed collaborative research is ideal." In Fry et al. (2009), the authors concluded that current e-Science is still far from being the same as Open Science. Meyer and Schroeder (2009) recognized e-Research as a "… rapidly growing area in many fields of scholarship, from the natural sciences to the humanities, as research moves online and becomes increasingly distributed across larger-scale and multi-institutional collaborations." They also analyzed how scientific publications on e-Research have been increasing and evolving during the last years. In Faily and Flechais (2010), the authors identified some key factors affecting security in multi-organizational systems and proposed a model of security culture for developing e-Science. Fitzgerald et al. (2010) described a case study regarding online collaborative research. They pointed out some of the benefits that collaborative research can provide to researchers and research groups and provided some advice based on their experience. Finally, Ribes and Lee (2010) recently defined e-Science (also Cyberinfrastructure or eInfrastructure for them) as "networked information technologies supporting scientific research activities such as collaboration, data sharing and dissemination of findings."

From the previous overview, it is possible to say that e-Research is an emerging, tech- and social-based, multi-disciplinary, and continuously evolving area of interest for researchers worldwide. With the currently available information, communication, and computing technologies, it is reasonable to expect that an important part of the next-decade research will be developed by multi-disciplinary and international teams, sharing and analyzing vast amounts of data, performing simulations over distributed computing systems, and using Web-based environments to communicate and collaborate online. If we also consider the rate at which the aforementioned technologies have been evolving during the last decade, and expecting a similar evolution for the following years, we can only say that the best is yet to come.

FROM MENTORSHIP TO E-MENTORSHIP

As it was stated in the Introduction section, one of the main goals of this chapter is to analyze how e-Research technologies and methodologies can be successfully employed to perform the instruction and guidance processes of new young researchers, i.e. to analyze e-Mentorship processes and their related issues. To start with, it is worthy to summarize the main characteristic features of a mentoring relationship (Johnson, 2007): (a) mentorship is an enduring personal relationship; (b) it involves reciprocal liaisons; (c) mentors demonstrate greater achievement and experience; (d) they provide protégés with direct career assistance; (e) they also provide protégés with social and emotional support; (f) mentors serve as models; (g) mentoring results in an identity transformation; (h) mentorship offers a safe harbor for self-exploration. The previous list of traits depicts a good profile of the characteristics expected from a good mentor. Of these characteristics, and according to Haggard et al. (2011), the core attributes of a mentoring process include a reciprocal relationship with variety of forms and interactions, and a regular and consistent interaction between the mentor and the protégé. Moreover, mentorship goes beyond classical instruction or academic advising. In effect, the advisor is usually a faculty member whose greatest responsibility is to guide the advisee through the educational program. Thus, following Schlosser et al. (2003) we could say that mentoring usually refers to a positive relationship focused on the faculty member's strong commitment to the protégé's development and success, while advising refers to a relationship that may be positive, negative, or indifferent and that may or may not include guidance and skill maturity.

Concerning the mentoring process, there are different ways to face it: (a) individual mentoring, establishing links between one mentor and one protégé only; (b) secondary mentoring, when more than one mentor is considered by a protégé; (c) peer mentoring, when the role of mentor is played by a senior student; (d) team mentoring, when the mentoring tasks are performed by mentors in group activities; and (e) e-Mentoring, when most of the mentoring activities are performed on-line with the help of a computer. Thus, e-Mentoring is a new variant of the traditional mentoring process, which has to be developed in a parallel way. The e-Mentoring activity may occur when a faculty member offers some mentor functions using Internet-based tools, e.g. video-conference, e-mail, virtual environments, groupware, etc. Bierema and Merriam (2002) defined e-Mentoring as "a computer-mediated, mutually beneficial relationship between a mentor and a protégé which provides learning, advising, encouraging, and promoting." Similarly, Ensher and Murphy (2007) defined e-Mentoring as "a mutually beneficial relationship between a mentor and a protégé, which provides new learning as well as career and emotional support, primarily through electronic means or use electronic methods of communication to supplement face-to-face mentoring." Thompson et al. (2010) defined it as "a relationship that is established between a more senior and/or experienced individual (mentor) and a lesser skilled or experienced individual (mentee or protégé), primarily using electronic communications, and is intended to develop and grow the skills, knowledge, confidence, and cultural understanding of the protégé to help him or her succeed." Therefore, it is implied that e-Mentoring has to be combined with traditional mentoring to give a suitable support to the student.

Traditionally, the mentoring process has been applied to the academic field, but in the last thirty years, mentorship has drastically changed. For example, mentorship has been applied within the workforce, providing greater job satisfaction, higher salary, and more promotions for protégés (Perren, 2003), not to mention progress in the integration of disabled and specific social groups, such as women and diverse groups (Headlamwells, et al., 2005). Thus, the literature review (Haggard, et al., 2011) has emphasized that there is a wide range of mentoring definitions and that the word 'mentor' could mean different things to different people (Kram, 1985). In fact, although the general concept of mentoring might be understood relatively consistently as a mentor (senior person) who provides various kinds of personal and career assistance to a protégé or mentee (a less senior or experienced person), different studies have been developed to analyze and define the mentoring functions (Haggard, et al., 2011). As Khalil (2008) suggested, in the educational context, a mentoring system should provide direct assistance with protégés' careers and professional development, encourage and motivate students with their involvement in learning and giving them new opportunities for research, provide emotional support for students and researchers who have less confidence, and also improve students' academic and research achievements. Likewise, and following Haggard et al. (2011), mentor functions are generally classified into three broad categories: (a) career functions (sponsorship, exposure and visibility, challenging assignments, etc.); (b) psychosocial functions (counseling, friendship, acceptance, emotional support, etc.); and (c) role-modeling (demonstration of the mentor appropriate behavior either implicitly or explicitly). Traditionally, career functions have been the most prevalent and the most important aspect of the mentoring process.

Regarding the e-Mentoring process, it could be developed in three different levels: (a) mentor and protégé communicate only electronically; (b) communications primarily through electronic means; and (c) use of electronic methods as a supplement of the face-to-face mentorship. Moreover, according to Hamilton and Scandura (2003) and Kram (1985), the e-Mentoring process should be developed in four different phases, as illustrated in Table 1. The Initiation phase involves the creation of atmosphere of acceptance and trust between the mentor and the protégé. This Initiation phase should be the moment to provide them with a computer network infrastructure, the generation of program guidelines and evaluation procedures. As the relationship is initiated and cultivated it should be expected to reap mutual benefits for both agents and to develop a supportive atmosphere of open communication. This Cultivation phase is the heart of the mentoring relationship (Headlam-Wells, et al., 2006). As the relationship goes on and both feel that the protégé's career improves and they are not getting much out of the e-Mentoring process then we reach the third phase, Separation or Termination, and it could end with a Redefinition of the relationship between the mentor and the protégé. It should be noticed that other authors (Salmon, 2004) suggests five stages in the e-Mentoring process: (1) access and motivation; (2) online socialization; (3) information exchange; (4) knowledge construction (the heart of the process); and (5) development of the relationship.

BENEFITS OF E-MENTORING

Similarly to what happens with e-Learning in general, e-Mentoring programs and technologies can offer relevant benefits to online students. Two

clear benefits for them are: (a) relief from the constraints imposed by having to attend frequent on-campus meetings at scheduled times; and (b) contribution to the development of technical skills. Regarding the latter benefit, it seems clear that the student's technical skills and competencies may be significantly improved by having to interact with collaborative software, communicate with instructors and/or other students using computing, information, and collaboration technologies (e.g. voice over IP, e-mail, chats, etc.), and develop collaborative projects via web-based platforms (e.g. Moodle, Sakai, BSCW, etc.). Of course, these social and technical experiences can be very valuable for the student's future career in a global world. Another important benefit for students might be the possibility of interacting with world-class specialists and co-advisors, or even the possibility of completing part of their PhD online at universities from other regions or countries. According to Leppisaari and Vainio (2009), e-Mentoring appears to be specifically applicable to the kind

Table 1. Encouraging e-mentoring development

E-Mentoring practice	E-Mentoring phase
Computer network infrastructure	*Initiation*
Program guidelines	
Program evaluation procedures	
Posting resumes and biographies	
Responsibility and expectations of parties	
Opportunity to meet face-to-face	
Mentoring training	*Cultivation*
Internet social protocol trainings	
Systems administrator support	
Program recognition	
Celebrate successes	
Opportunity to face-to-face interactions	
Acknowledging comments	*Separation/ Termination*
Personal communication	*Redefinition*

Source: Hamilton and Scandura (2003).

of mentoring which includes articulated learning and developmental objectives with the purpose of sharing and developing expertise within a specific and restricted area, such as the e-Research and e-Learning context. In this context, the efficient use of time is the most preferential reason for e-Mentoring adoption (Tesone & Gibson, 2001). Also, e-Mentoring could facilitate synchronous as well as asynchronous communication, helping to a more reflective learning atmosphere, where mentors and protégées could work at their own pace in a more flexible and more free way without the need of an immediate response, as it would be the case in a face-to-face mentoring system (Mueller, 2004; Headlam-Wells, et al., 2006).

Besides, in the learning process, the e-Mentoring system enables the mentees to take responsibility for initiating contact and to play an active role in the e-Mentoring process. Also, e-Mentoring offers the opportunity to set up dynamics two-way learning networks and the development of team online mentoring process using the networks in a multidimensional way rather than one-individual-to other individual. As Gareis and Nussbaum-Beach (2007) mention, that could imply the development of "a community of learners": a group of professionals constructively and collectively engaging with each other to identify and address areas in which individual careers and the whole group may be improved. A relatively new phenomenon in the mentoring process is what is called "reverse mentoring" (Greengard, 2002). It implies that the protégé provide developmental assistance to the mentor, usually involving the sharing of information and knowledge or the use of technology. In a similar way, the peer e-Mentoring or co-mentoring as a two-way, non hierarchical process of equality making mentoring reciprocal and mutual, can promote learning, mutual exchange of ideas, and construction of knowledge (Leppisaari & Tenhunen, 2009). In the educational context, and particularly in the research field, both of these phenomena could

positively boost the successful adoption of the e-Mentoring system.

Thus, benefits of e-Mentoring include flexibility and greater access, no costly meetings, less time scheduling and holding meetings, a more egalitarian connection between parties, access to a greater number of mentors and a large amount of information, and reduction of demographic and personality barriers in traditional mentoring such as gender, race, power, status and other barriers (Ensher & Murphy, 2007; Hamilton & Scandura, 2003; Tesone & Gibson, 2001). Additionally, e-mentorship is presumed to reduce the amount of time needed to manage a traditional mentoring relationship (Hamilton & Scandura, 2003). More than that, e-Mentoring supports the development of team-mentoring beyond the traditional one-to-one relationship, making it more practical and flexible. Further benefit of adopting e-Mentoring is the construction of records of the interaction process, making easy an immediate response on behalf of the mentors. This quick feedback is much more difficult in the face-to-face mentoring. The existence of records allows us to develop evaluations of the e-Mentoring system and its outcomes. Finally, as some practical experiences have shown, the e-Mentoring process not only has an effect on personal and career development but also promotes the development of specific skills and helps to gain inspiration (Headlam-Wells, et al., 2006). Table 2 shows some of the most important e-Mentoring strengths.

E-Mentoring programs also offer several benefits to instructors, mentors and institutions, in particular: the opportunity to develop networked teams of instructors, who can collaborate online as co-advisors in a PhD or Master program; the possibility of offering education in several languages to students from different countries or regions; and the opportunity to improve formation methodologies and shared resources—computer resources, article databases, benchmarks and experimental data, etc. Furthermore, in the context of the European Area of Higher Education, e-

Mentoring offers the opportunity of sharing materials, methodologies and experiences among universities in order to ensure compatibility of curricula and assessment of theoretical, practical and transversal competencies and capabilities. Going one step further, one can foresee the possibility to offer joint PhD and Master programs in conjunction with other universities, e.g. each university could specialize in a knowledge area and offer the corresponding part of the program, thus offering an interdisciplinary and international formation in research.

Table 2. E-mentoring strengths

Barrier	E-Mentoring advantage
Organizational structure	Not geographically bound
	Lack of status cues and reduction of the impact of status differences
	Enables international mentoring contacts
	Enables team-mentoring and learning communities
	Increased number of available mentors
Individual and interpersonal factors	Face-to-face relationship not required
	Increase diversity of participating mentors
	Increased number of available mentors
	Less social information present and reduction of the impact of status differences
Flexible/alternative work arrangements	Not time constrained (flexibly available and affordable)
	Not geographically bound
	Face-to-face relationship not required
	Develops working life skills such as team work, web-based writing and communication)
	Enables continual professional development

Source: Author elaboration from Hamilton and Scandura (2003) and Leppisaari and Tenhunen (2009).

DISADVANTAGES AND CHALLENGES OF E-MENTORING

Together with the benefits, there are also disadvantages of using e-Mentoring instead of traditional mentoring, such as miscommunication, misinterpretation, delays in relationship development (e-Mentoring lacks the social and non-verbal richness of face-to-face interactions), and cold relationship which might diminish the strength of the mentorship connection. Lack of face-to-face interaction is a relevant challenge, since many research activities, especially those requiring discussions of research details, benefit from the face-to-face interaction among the advisor/mentor and the student. Obviously, in an online environment this kind of interaction is not possible and, therefore, sporadic face-to-face meetings as well as other interaction methodologies—e.g. videoconferences, online blackboards, etc.—must be introduced in order to compensate this deficiency as much as possible. Thus, if the e-communication is the predominant mode of interaction, slower development of relationships (developing trust and confidence could be a time demanding process), discomfort with technology and variability in written communication skills. Furthermore, e-Mentoring could require a high level of computer literacy and written communication skills as well as trust in the privacy protection mechanisms inherent in the technology used (Spitzmüller, et al., 2008). Therefore, it is implied that e-Mentoring has to be combined with traditional mentoring to give a suitable support to the student and to avoid the less psychosocial and career support received through e-mentorship compared to mentorship in some empirical studies (Smith-Jentsch, et al., 2008). Financial considerations provide both advantages and disadvantages, as there are high start-up costs in implementing an e-Mentoring system, but once established the operational or running costs are relatively low (Headlam-Wells, et al., 2006). In effect, e-Mentoring can be a costly method for the institution when offering PhD and Master programs. The start-up and ongoing costs of online programs are significant, due in part to: (a) the cost of communication technology—dedicated servers, telecommunication lines, etc.—and specialized staff who must support it; (b) licensed software—web platforms, operating systems, database managers, utilities, etc.; (c) formative courses and programs for faculty and administration staff, both at the methodological and technical levels; and (d) sporadic travels of advisors, mentors, or PhD students to engage in face-to-face meetings.

On top of that, it is important to notice that any type of distance education and research presents higher dropout rates than traditional programs: the nature of distance education/research can create a sense of isolation in PhD students, who might feel disconnected from the instructor, from the rest of the students in the program, and even from the institution. It is necessary, then, that instructors/advisors provide just-in-time guidance to a student's research activities and also that they provide regular—almost daily—feedback on these activities. This fact suggests that communication among different online PhD students should also be facilitated and promoted by advisors and mentors, as well as by the institution—which should provide an easily usable and efficient web platform that could be used as an online virtual campus for doing e-Research.

On the advisor or mentor side, one important challenge can be the time required to design the research program and, once it has started, to effectively provide guidance and support to the PhD or Master students. Being online advisor/mentor presents continual demands for faculty training on the use of ITs and professional development. Therefore, universities must provide their faculty with up-to-date courses and efficient technological tools oriented to facilitate the design and development of online Masters and PhD projects.

SOFTWARE FOR E-MENTORING AND E-RESEARCH

One of the key factors that facilitates and promotes e-Research activities and, in particular, e-Mentoring processes is the existence of Web 2.0 tools. Nowadays, there exists a wide variety of free and open-source software which allows synchronous and asynchronous communication among people in a global world. Among the different types of communication software that might be used to enhance the e-Mentoring processes, it is possible to cite the following ones: (a) e-mail and joined calendars; (b) chat, voice, and videoconference; (c) Internet-based repositories to store and share data and documents; (d) learning management systems and content management systems; and (e) remote-access software. In this section, some specific examples of each of these types of software have been reviewed, illustrating how they can be used to develop efficient e-Mentoring and e-Research processes (Figure 2). To begin with, one of the basic tools that researchers have been using during the last decades is the e-mail. Web-based solutions such as Gmail, Hotmail, etc. facilitate not only asynchronous communication but also synchronous communication since they also integrate chat options as well as user-availability monitoring tools. Other collaborative tools integrated with this enhanced web-based e-mails are joined calendars and shared online documents that can be edited online. Another frequently used tool in synchronous voice communication is Skype or, alternatively, Google Talk or MS Messenger. These solutions allow two or even more distant researchers to communicate by voice without incurring in prohibitive costs, which contribute to significantly enhance the e-monitoring processes. A third group of useful tools is that represented by DropBox (and similar solutions like Subversion) or browser-based desktops, which allow sharing folders and documents online with different researchers. Thus, for instance, one of the most useful characteristics of DropBox is the fact that all users of a folder keep always the most recent version of any shared document, since their local folders are synchronized with a cloud folder anytime they connect to the Internet. Another group of useful tools are those represented by online platforms such as Moodle, Sakai, or BSCW. These tools are designed to promote online collaboration and some of them are designed for offering e-learning programs. Other web-based platforms are those like Joomla, Drupal, or WordPress, which allow to easily post and share multi-media contents on-line, including pictures, powerpoints, and videos. Finally, tools like TeamViewer allows one user A (e.g. the advisor or mentor) to remotely access user's B computer (e.g. the student's computer). Then, user at computer A can interact with the remote computer B as if A was just in front of B, showing users at B how to complete a specific task or action. Similarly, using TeamViewer (or a similar software) several students could remotely access their advisor/mentor computer and then follow the explanations he/she performs on his/her computer. All in all, an intelligent combination of the aforementioned tools makes possible to

significantly reduce (but not completely eliminate) most of the problems generated by the absence of a face-to-face communication.

SOME EXPERIENCES IN E-MENTORSHIP PROCESSES

The development of e-Research in different arenas needs the involvement of people, who are prone to mutual collaboration (David, 2006; Carusi & Reimer, 2010). It is difficult to make this mutual collaboration if they have not had a previous physical and real communication (Jankowski, 2009). Nevertheless, if that real communication has been performed, the collaborative networks associated with e-Research allow an interesting success of the e-Research activities. Likewise, the mentoring and e-Mentoring processes are important factors, which are needed for a positive interaction, thus allowing the advancement of e-Research. Therefore, mentoring and e-Mentoring are revealed as catalysts or crucibles of the collaborative e-Research activities. According to Barjak

Figure 2. Web 2.0 tools that facilitate efficient e-mentoring processes

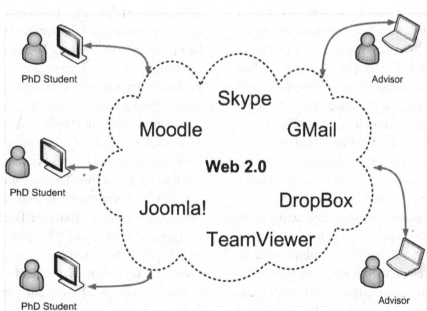

et al (2009), the description of suitable cases of e-Research based previously on mentoring activities can help to understand better this process. In this section, the authors of this chapter describe some personal experiences as either e-mentors or e-protégés. In fact, the potential experiences explained here are connected to Internet-based courses and research projects offered at the G9 Virtual Campus (www.uni-g9.net), the Open University of Catalonia (www.uoc.edu), and the MIT-Spain program (http://web.mit.edu/misti/mit-spain/).

The G9 Case in Spain

The G9-Spanish University Group (www.uni-g9.net) is a non-profit organization integrated by nine Spanish public universities since May 1997: Cantabria, Castilla La Mancha, Extremadura, Islas Baleares, La Rioja, Navarra, Oviedo, País Vasco and Zaragoza. The common goal of the group is to collaborate together in teaching and doing research activities regarding management and services. Thus, a virtual campus was created, where 89 different courses were offered during the academic course 2010-2011. Furthermore, these courses are clustered into thematic groups, which in turn provide an additional degree. It is then a good opportunity for students to extend their studies within the G9 Virtual Campus. Although the G9 was not widely known among students a few years ago, its ever-increasing course portfolio and the differences with face-to-face classes turned it into a very popular complementary educational system. Students involved in the G9 not only learn to apply the new technologies into an educational framework, but also to become familiar with the different ways of teaching and learning. Students gained additional knowledge and experience through e-learning: new directions to tackle the problems, new structure of the subject and its deadlines and requirements, new people from the rest of the country interconnected by forum online tools and, in general, the opportunity to meet and

face different cultures, points of view and share knowledge. Moreover, the wide offer of courses favors students to expand their professional field, e.g. an Engineering student can study Enterprises Management and Finances.

The e-learning system also involves the professors. The professors who are responsible of the course can participate as much as they want in generating different environments in e-teaching. However, what they all have in common is the need to use different techniques from their daily attended classes. This makes the teachers get experienced with new methods and modify them, according to direct and indirect feedback received from the students. Direct feedback comes from a survey made by the students after the course. Indirect feedback comes from the results of the weekly assignments and the activity of the students registered in the online platform. Therefore, a two-way learning network arises (Headlam-Wells, et al., 2006). These applied techniques, added to a better knowledge of the new possibilities in the e-education engendered by the current technologies, give the teachers new chances to meet potential future researchers and developers to work with. There are different mentor-mentee relationships depending on the different status of each part of the tandem. At this point, both parts do not nearly know each other, so high technical skills cannot be proven by the student. Therefore, soft skills are better judged as technical ones. Motivation, interest and hardworking are features which will potentially develop into a great capability to work in a team and contribute to do research. Nevertheless, not all the students with these soft skills are to become necessarily future researchers. It is in this environment how instructor/mentor and protégé knew each other using the on-line communication tools in the course "Toma de Decisiones en la e-Empresa" (Decision Making in e-Companies) (see Figure 3) taught in the Public University of Navarre. This course is a subject about decision making in virtual and real companies which is completely integrated in the studies of the Schools of Civil Engineering and Business for all participating Universities. The protégé is usually a student of those schools belonging to one of the nine universities comprising the G9. The course is still offered and it is an introduction to Operations Research methodology with applications to real decision making problems in e-companies. The protégé's interest in the subject and the feedback he receives from his/her instructor/mentor, makes the former usually to continue in his/her studies following subjects related to Operations Research in the following semester, in their local universities.

More precisely, this course entitled "Toma de Decisiones en la e-Empresa" (Decision Making in e-Companies) offered in the G9 Group starts in February and finishes in June of each academic year, with an extension to July for those who want to delay their last assignment or do not pass the one handled in June. Thus, the typical first personal contact between instructor/mentor and protégé usually starts in March/April through the online platform of the course or other on-line

tools (Skype, Dropbox, etc.). Some protégés admit that initially they were not really interested in research and collaboration. However, this possibility became more interesting as the protégé is introduced deeper into the subject matter. Thus, there exist three possibilities to collaborate between mentor and protégé. The first one is the online collaboration in order to help the protégé to develop a specific task or assignment (for instance, the final studies project). Secondly, short internships are also possible solutions for research which have begun in the use of online tools. Normally, these internships are not carried out online, but they might exist thanks to the virtual campus and previous e-Mentoring. The third way can be achieved by writing research papers in a collaborative way. However, e-Mentoring was in this case the prelude to future collaboration. Likewise, e-learning was the prelude to mentoring. The e-mail has been the most useful tool in this mentor-protégé relationship (Figure 3). Thus, the answer can be carefully thought and relayed to the appropriate moment. It also allows attaching

Figure 3. Keeping in touch between mentor and protégé on the G9 group scenario

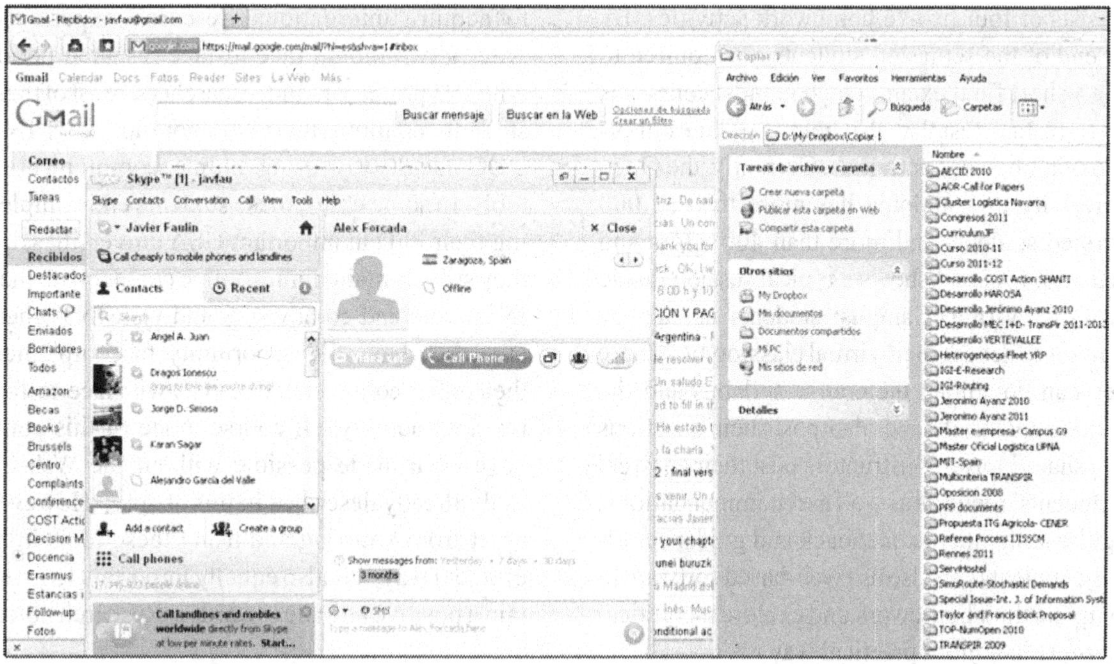

documents as personal studies or presentations and links to other internet sites as well. Nevertheless, other online tools, such as videoconferences, are also very popular in e-Mentoring.

The Open University of Catalonia Case in Spain

In this subsection, we will discuss the insight gathered from our experiences in developing e-Mentoring processes at the Open University of Catalonia (UOC). The UOC (www.uoc.edu) is a purely-online university located in Barcelona, Spain, that has offered undergraduate and graduate degrees since 1995. For undergraduate students, the UOC mainly uses an asynchronous learning model: at the beginning of the semester, students access the course's online classroom and, following the recommendations provided by their instructors, download a complete syllabus of the course along with all associated learning materials and resources. Throughout the course, students are encouraged to participate actively in discussion forums, to develop collaborative learning projects and, especially, to follow a scheduled continuous assessment process, which typically consists of four or five homework activities. By the end of the semester, students are required to take a short final exam, which in most courses is a face-to-face test that also helps validate authorship of homework activities. Currently, the Open University of Catalonia has more than 37,000 enrolled students and more than 400 tutors and lecturers. Figure 4 shows a typical session inside the UOC Virtual Campus: students use a web browser to access their virtual classrooms, where they can download the course syllabus and the learning materials and also post their questions on a shared forum. Instructors post their answers to students' requests as well as recommendations, regular assignments, feedback and guidance. Finally, students can also use web-based software to complete their homework and explore theoretical concepts in a more practical way.

In the case of PhD and Master students, the UOC combines the aforementioned model with synchronous online communication and, whenever possible, also with face-to-face meetings between students and their advisors. In this scenario, the use of Web 2.0 tools such as the ones described in the previous section is not only convenient but even necessary in order to improve the quality of the e-Mentoring process. UOC's Internet Interdisciplinary Institute or simply IN3 (http://in3.uoc.edu), is visited each year by several dozens of invited professors, researchers, and PhD students who, in most cases, belong to foreign countries and can only spend some weeks or months during the year at the IN3 facilities. Most of the research activity developed by IN3 visitors is according to a blended model, meaning that online activity usually last for the entire year and it is complemented with face-to-face activity during the periods (some weeks or some months) these researchers visit the IN3 facilities, which are located in Barcelona, Spain. An interesting experience of the IN3 blended model is the MIT-Spain program (http://web.mit.edu/misti/mit-spain), which every year sends to Spain some promising MIT students and young researchers to acquire international research experience. After a two-month face-to-face research period with IN3 professors and researchers, most of these students continue their collaboration with IN3-UOC faculty by using online communication tools. In some cases, these students end completing their PhD in important USA universities, but they still are maintaining online contact with their IN3 tutors and co-advisors and visit IN3 whenever they have the opportunity to complement their online collaboration activity with face-to-face research activity. Of course, none of this could have been made possible without the Web 2.0 tools already described in this chapter. However, apart from knowing and using these tools in an efficient way, it is also equally important to maintain a positive attitude towards e-Research poten-

Figure 4. A typical session in the UOC virtual campus

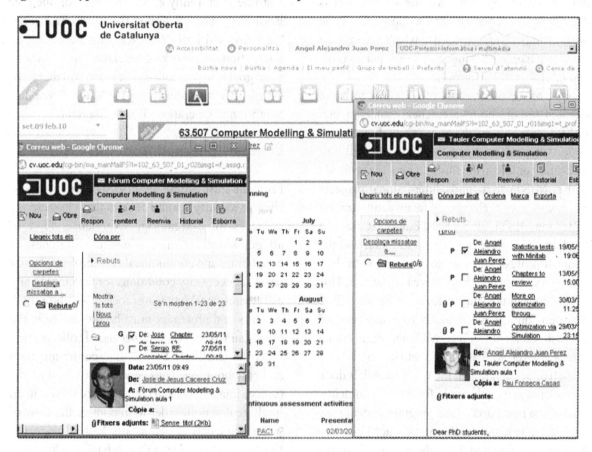

tial and be aware of the possibilities it offers the researchers of the twenty-first century.

The MIT Case in USA

The MIT International Science and Technology Initiatives—better known as MISTI—connects MIT students with research and innovation around the world. MISTI is a well-organized and resourceful program that gives students a chance of grasping the concept of globalization. There are currently 10 different host countries in MISTI: Brazil, China, France, Germany, India, Israel, Italy, Japan, Mexico, Spain and Africa. The MIT-Spain program, in particular, is about a four-year-old program and its main objective is to increase the flow of MIT students to Spain, which includes undergraduate and graduate students, as well as recent alumni.

MIT, as most people know, is a talent magnet, attracting some of the most outstanding international students to MIT. The MIT-Spain program's goal is to reverse this flow, and to allow MIT students to go outside of MIT and do internships in Spain. The internships can either be done in a university or in a company. The MIT-Spain program allows one to experience first-hand what it means to work and collaborate on a global scale. It is a program that not many schools have the privilege of offering to their students.

MISTI allowed students to integrate their expertise in science with their knowledge of the host country's language and culture. Students are immersed in the host country's life academically, socially, culturally, and linguistically. The atmosphere, the interactions, the way of doing things present the students with new environments that delved into the appreciation of the way research is done in another country. On the opposite end, the host institutions are exposed to what an American student is like, who brings a different perspective and educational background.

One of the other goals of MISTI is to bring talented foreign-born researchers, students, etc. to MIT and engage them in research activities with MIT professors, so that they can still collaborating online in the future. There is a program within MISTI that funds international projects and encourages exchanges of faculty and students called the MISTI Global Seed Funds. At the seed fund, an MIT professor can go to Spain and the Spanish professor can go to MIT and both do a research stage at their respective institutions. This is also done at the student level. In the seed fund program, one of the goals is to bring talented Spanish students to go to MIT and do research stages at MIT so that both countries can have a mutual understanding of the way research is done abroad, not just exclusively for the MIT students. One of the best parts of the program is that, usually, these research collaboration activities are continued online and throughout time by means of Web 2.0 tools.

The progression throughout the three years we have been with the MIT-Spain program has been exemplary. We have been very productive in terms of research development due to the MISTI program. For example, we have increased the number of MIT students who every year arrive at the Internet Interdisciplinary Institute (http://in3.uoc.edu) and have worked on different research projects that can be reasonably done in a short-time visiting period and complemented with a long-time period of online collaboration. From the perspective of the Spanish Professors, they were able to collaborate in research projects with MIT faculty, in our particular case, at the MIT Center for Transportation and Logistics.

Following these trends, and in collaboration with the MISTI program, the HAROSA Knowledge Community at the Internet Interdisciplinary Institute is currently expanding their online collaboration network among the European Union, the USA, and Latin America, thus becoming an international network of research groups whose main goal is to promote and develop collaborative e-Research on specific topics in the Computer Science and Operations Research arenas.

Lessons Learned from Case Studies

From the Case Studies described before, it is possible to identify several factors that characterize a successful e-Mentoring experience. First of all, good levels of motivation and willingness to collaborate and communicate online on a regular basis are necessary conditions for developing any e-Research or e-Mentoring process. Secondly, both mentors and protégées must be pro-active in the testing and use of new Internet-based collaboration tools that facilitate both online communication and collaboration. Thus, several tools and media (voice, image, and text) must be combined in an intelligent way in order to maximize the flow of information between both parts. In third place, it is fundamental to select a research topic which perfectly fits the shared interest of both the protégée(s) and the mentor. Finally, it is worthy to remember that efficient online collaboration can significantly diminish the amount of the inconvenience of a lack of face-to-face collaboration brings. However, and according to our experience, it cannot substitute direct, face-to-face, contact between the agents involved in the e-Mentoring process. As a consequence, sporadic face-to-face meetings –and, whenever possible, several-day visiting stages– are strongly recommended to complement online meetings and communication activity.

CONCLUSION

Internet-based tools offer new possibilities of collaboration among researchers in a global world. Among those, e-Mentoring processes might become a usual practice both in academics and industries, as more institutions understand their potential benefits and overcome their challenges. Thus, e-Research and e-Mentoring are emerging issues which are greatly promoted and facilitated by recent advances in Web 2.0 tools and also by the arising of new international research networks and knowledge communities. Among the main benefits provided by e-Mentoring are the possibility of collaborating with experts from different countries and the possibility of offering joined international Master and PhD programs. Probably the main challenge of e-Mentoring is the lack of face-to-face interaction, which might affect the richness of the communication and collaboration processes. Fortunately, current technology is able to partially solve this problem, allowing a much richer communication than it was possible just some years ago. In any case, sporadic face-to-face interaction is still a necessary factor for developing successful e-Mentoring experiences. All in all, we expect in the next decade to see the emergence and dissemination of e-Mentoring and e-Research practices in a similar way the last decade can be recognized by the emergence and dissemination of e-Learning practices.

ACKNOWLEDGMENT

This work has been partially supported by the Spanish Ministry of Science and Innovation (grants MTM2008-06695-C03-03, TRA2010-21644-C03, and ECO2009-11307), by the Working Community of the Pyrenees (grants IIQ13172.R11-CTP09-R2 and CTP09-00007), by the CYTED-IN3-HAROSA network (http://dpcs.uoc.edu) and by the Sustainable TransMET network (Jerónimo de Ayanz Program, Government of Navarre, Spain).

REFERENCES

Anandarajan, M., & Anandarajan, M. (2010). *E-research collaboration: Theory, techniques and challenges*. Berlin, Germany: Springer.

Atkinson, I. M., du Boulay, D., Chee, C., Chiu, K., Coddington, P., & Gerson, A. … Zhang, D. (2007). Developing CIMA-based cyberinfrastructure for remote access to scientific instruments and collaborative e-research. In *Proceedings of the Australasian Symposium on Grid Computing and Research (AusGrid)*, (vol 68), (pp. 3-10). Ballarat, Australia: IEEE Press.

Augustine, V., & Robinson, D. (2010). Using virtual machines for collaborative research. In *Proceedings of the ESEM, 2010*, 1–4. doi:10.1145/1852786.1852836

Barjak, F., Lane, J., Kertcher, Z., Poschen, M., Procter, R., & Robinson, S. (2009). Case studies of e-infrastructure adoption. *Social Science Computer Review*, *27*(4), 583–600. doi:10.1177/0894439309332310

Bierema, L. L., & Merriam, S. B. (2002). E-mentoring: Using computer mediated communication to enhance the mentoring process. *Innovative Higher Education*, *26*, 211–227. doi:10.1023/A:1017921023103

Blackwell, J. E. (1989). Mentoring: An action strategy for increasing minority faculty. *Academe*, *75*, 8–14. doi:10.2307/40249734

Blanke, T., Dunn, S., & Hedges, M. (2007). *Arts and humanities e-science - From ad hoc experimentation to systematic investigation*. Paper presented at the Third IEEE International Conference on e-Science and Grid Computing. New York, NY.

Borgman, C. (2006). What can studies of e-learning teach us about collaboration in e-Research? Some findings from digital library studies. *Computer Supported Cooperative Work, 15*(4), 359–383. doi:10.1007/s10606-006-9024-1

Bravo, B. R., & Alvite, M. L. (2007). E-science and open access repositories in Spain. *OCLC Systems & Services, 23*(4), 363–371. doi:10.1108/10650750710831501

Carusi, A., & Reimer, T. (2010). Virtual research environment: Collaborative landscape study. *JISC*. Retrieved from http:// www.jisc.ac.uk/ media/ documents/ publications/ vrelandscapereport.pdf.

David, P. A. (2006). Towards a cyber-infrastructure for enhanced scientific collaboration: Providing its 'soft' foundations may be the hardest part. In Kahin, B., & Foray, D. (Eds.), *Advancing Knowledge and the Knowledge Economy* (pp. 431–454). Cambridge, MA: MIT Press.

David, P. A., den Besten, M., & Schroeder, R. (2006). How open is e-science? In *Proceedings of the Second IEEE International Conference on e-Science and Grid Computing (e-Science 2006)*, (pp. 1-8). IEEE Press.

De Roure, D. (2010). *Semantic grid and sensor grid: Insights into the e-research ecosystem.* Paper presented at the 4th IEEE International Conference on Digital Ecosystems and Technologies (IEEE DEST 2010). New York, NY.

Dutton, W. H., & Meyer, E. T. (2009). Experience with new tools and infrastructures of research: An exploratory study of distance from, and attitudes toward, e-research. *Prometheus, 27*(3), 223–238. doi:10.1080/08109020903127802

Egan, G. F., Liu, W., Soh, W.-S., Hang, D., Wang, L., Chen, K., & Ong, Y. S. (2005). *Australian neuroinformatics research grid computing and e-research.* Paper presented at ICNC 2005, (pp. 1057-1064). ICNC Press.

Ensher, E. A., Heun, C., & Blanchard, A. (2003). Online mentoring and computer-mediated communication: New directions in research. *Journal of Vocational Behavior, 63*, 264–288. doi:10.1016/S0001-8791(03)00044-7

Erhut, S., & Mokros, J. R. (1984). Professors as models and mentors for college students. *American Educational Research Journal, 21*, 399–417.

Faily, S., & Flechais, I. (2010). Designing and aligning e-science security culture with design. *Information Management & Computer Security, 18*(5), 339–349. doi:10.1108/09685221011095254

Fitzgerald, S., Hanks, B., & McCauley, R. (2010). Collaborative research in computer science education: A case study. In *Proceedings of SIGCSE, 2010*, 305–309.

Fox, G. C., Pierce, M. E., Mustacoglu, A. F., & Topcu, A. E. (2007). Web 2.0 for e-science environments. In *Proceedings of the Third International Conference on Semantics, Knowledge and Grid*, (pp. 1-6). IEEE Press.

Fry, J., Schroeder, R., & den Besten, M. (2009). Open science in e-science: Contingency or policy? *The Journal of Documentation, 65*(1), 6–32. doi:10.1108/00220410910926103

Gao, J. (2010). Developing a web-based collaborative research environment for undergraduates. *Journal of Computing Sciences in Colleges, 26*(2), 39–46.

Gareis, C., & Nussbaum-Beach, S. (2007). Electronically mentoring to develop accomplished professional teachers. *Journal of Personnel Evaluation in Education, 20*, 227–246. doi:10.1007/s11092-008-9060-0

Greengard, S. (2002). Moving forward with reverse mentoring. *Workforce, 81*, 15.

Haggard, D., Dougherty, T., Turban, D., & Wilbanks, J. (2011). Who is a mentor? A review of evolving definitions and implications for research. *Journal of Management*, *37*(1), 280–304. doi:10.1177/0149206310386227

Hamilton, B., & Scandura, T. (2003). E-mentoring: Implications for organizational learning and development in a wired world. *Organizational Dynamics*, *31*(4), 388–402. doi:10.1016/S0090-2616(02)00128-6

Headlamwells, J., Gosland, J., & Craig, J. (2006). Beyond the organization: The design and management of e-mentoring systems. *International Journal of Information Management*, *26*, 372–385. doi:10.1016/j.ijinfomgt.2006.04.001

Herron, T. L., & Young, G. R. (2000). E-research moving behavioral accounting research into cyberspace. *Advances in Accounting Behavioral Research*, *3*, 265–280. doi:10.1016/S1474-7979(00)03035-0

Hey, T., & Hey, J. (2006). e-Science and its implications for the library community. *Library Hi Tech*, *24*(4), 515–528. doi:10.1108/07378830610715383

Jankowski, N. (Ed.). (2009). *E-research: Transformation in scholarly practice*. New York, NY: Routledge.

Jirotka, M., Procter, R., Rodden, T., & Bowker, G. C. (2006). Collaboration in e-research. *Computer Supported Cooperative Work*, *15*, 251–255. doi:10.1007/s10606-006-9028-x

Johnson, W. B. (2007). *On being a mentor: A guide for higher education faculty*. New York, NY: Lawrence Erlbaum Associates.

Khalil, M. (2008). Promoting success: Mentoring students with disabilities using new technologies in higher education. *Library Hi Tech News*, *25*(1), 8–12. doi:10.1108/07419050810877490

Khatibi, V., & Montazer, G. A. (2009). *Study the role of web services in adoption of e-resarch process*. Paper presented at the International Conference on Engineering Education (ICEED 2009). Kuala Lumpur, Malaysia.

Kram, K. E. (1985). *Mentoring at work: Developmental relationships in organizational life*. Glenview, IL: Scott Foresman.

Lawrence, K. (2006). Walking the tightrope: The balancing acts of a large e-research project. *Computer Supported Cooperative Work*, *15*(4), 385–411. doi:10.1007/s10606-006-9025-0

Leppisaari, I., & Tenhunen, M. (2009). Searching for e-mentoring practices for SME staff development. *Service Business*, *3*, 189–207. doi:10.1007/s11628-008-0060-4

Memon, M. S., Memon, A. S., Streit, A., Riedel, M., Schuller, B., & Rambadt, M. … Kranzlm, D. (2010). Exploring the potential of using multiple e-science infrastructures with emerging open standards-based e-health research tools. In *Proceedings of the 10th IEEE/ACM International Conference on Cluster, Cloud and Grid Computing*, (pp. 341-348). IEEE Press.

Meyer, E. T., & Schroeder, R. (2009). Untangling the web of e-research: Towards a sociology of online knowledge. *Journal of Informetrics*, *3*, 246–260. doi:10.1016/j.joi.2009.03.006

Mueller, S. (2004). Electronic mentoring as an example for the use of information and communication technology in engineering education. *European Journal of Engineering Education*, *29*(1), 53–63. doi:10.1080/0304379032000129304

Osswald, A. (2008). E-science and information services: a missing link in the context of digital libraries. *Online Information Review*, *32*(4), 516–523. doi:10.1108/14684520810897395

Packard, B. W. L. (2003). Student training promotes mentoring awareness and action. *The Career Development Quarterly*, *51*, 335–345. doi:10.1002/j.2161-0045.2003.tb00614.x

Perren, L. (2003). The role of e-mentoring in entrepreneurial education and support: A meta-review of academic literature. *Education + Training, 45*(8/9), 517-525.

Pham, T. V., Dew, P. M., & Lau, L. M. (2006). Enabling e-research in combustion research community. In *Proceedings of the Second IEEE International Conference on e-Science and Grid Computing.* IEEE Press.

Pierson, M., Shepard, M., & Leneway, R. (2009). Distributed collaborative research model: Meaningful and responsive inquiry in technology and teacher education. *Journal of Computing in Teacher Education, 25*(4), 127–133.

Razum, M., Schwichtenberg, F., Wagner, S., Hoppe, M., Agosti, M., et al. (2009). eSciDoc infrastructure: A fedora-based e-research framework. In *Proceedings of ECDL 2009*, (pp. 227-238). ECDL Press.

Ribes, D., & Lee, C. P. (2010). Sociotechnical studies of cyberinfrastructure and e-research: Current themes and future trajectories. *Computer Supported Cooperative Work, 19*, 231–244. doi:10.1007/s10606-010-9120-0

Riedel, M., & Terstyanszky, G. (2009). Grid interoperability for e-research. *Journal of Grid Computing, 7*, 285–286. doi:10.1007/s10723-009-9138-z

Salmon, G. (2004). *E-moderating: The key to teaching and learning online* (2nd ed.). London, UK: Routledge.

Schlosser, L. Z., Knox, S., Moskovitz, A. R., & Hill, C. E. (2003). A qualitative examination of graduate advising relationships: The advisee perspective. *Journal of Counseling Psychology, 50*, 178–188. doi:10.1037/0022-0167.50.2.178

Smith-Jentsch, K., Scielzo, S., Yarborough, C., & Rosopa, P. (2008). A comparison of face-to-face and electronic peer-mentoring: Interactions with mentor gender. *Journal of Vocational Behavior, 72*, 193–206. doi:10.1016/j.jvb.2007.11.004

Spitzmüller, C., Neumman, E., Spitzmüller, M., Rubino, C., Keeton, K., Sutton, M., & Manzey, D. (2008). Assessing the influence of psychosocial and career mentoring on organizational attractiveness. *International Journal of Selection and Assessment, 16*(4), 403–415. doi:10.1111/j.1468-2389.2008.00444.x

Tesone, D., & Gibson, J. (2001). E-mentoring for professional growth. In *Proceedings IEEE International Professional Communication Conference.* IEEE Press.

Thompson, L., Jeffries, M., & Topping, K. (2010). E-mentoring for e-learning development. *Innovations in Education and Teaching International, 47*(3), 305–315. doi:10.1080/14703297.2010.498182

Yang, X., & Allan, R. (2006). Web-based virtual research environments (VRE): Support collaboration in e-science. In *Proceedings of the 2006 IEEE/WIC/ACM International Conference on Web Intelligence and Intelligent Agent Technology*, (pp. 1-4). IEEE Press.

Chapter 12
Addressing Conflicting Cognitive Models in Collaborative E–Research:
A Case Study in Exploration Geophysics

Paolo Diviacco
Istituto Nazionale di Oceanografia e di Geofisica Sperimentale, Italy

ABSTRACT

A certain number of disciplinary fields are characterized by the intersection of "soft" and "hard" sciences, resulting in the coexistence of quasi-hermeneutic and nomological approaches. Among the many that correspond to this description, such as medicine or archeology, the author focused on the geo-sciences and in particular on exploration geophysics. Here the inductive/deductive method that characterizes physics meets the abductive approach of geology, creating a very fertile ground for researchers to develop concurrent cognitive models for the same issue. These contrasting visions tend to isolate themselves, thus developing specific knowledge and practices that subsequently make them incompatible. Collaborative research intending to bridge these communities of practices can therefore prove to be problematic, so a form of mediator becomes necessary.

Most existing collaborative tools assume that partners share the same perspective on the entities they are working on and therefore these solutions cannot be applied directly to the types of cases this chapter addresses. By exploring geophysics and its peculiarities, one understands its inner dynamics, so that possible solutions can be proposed. These rely on the creation of "boundary objects" capable of bridging different cognitive models. These solutions are based on the integration of diagrams, where concepts and their relations are expressed at an optimal granularity and shared spaces where information can be made available to all partners. These ideas have been implemented in a Web-based Computer-Supported Collaborative Research (CSCR) system that is currently successfully used within many international research projects in this disciplinary field.

DOI: 10.4018/978-1-4666-0125-3.ch012

INTRODUCTION

Scientific research covers a wide area of human activities that span several fields and that, following the introduction of Information Technologies (IT) and Internet, are moving radically towards e-research: a perspective where the life of researchers will be augmented through on-line interaction, communities, and knowledge.

The exciting opportunities that this moment offers also entail the risk that if these changes are driven only by technology, the real needs of scientific research could be overlooked. It is, therefore, very important to consider first the needs, and only then devise the technology that could support them (Beyer & Holtzblatt, 1998).

The traditional view states that scientific research in all disciplines should be built upon the common perspective of the scientific method, which in the perspective of e-research and Computer-Supported Collaborative Research (CSCR) would reflect in the possibility of following a common approach.

We claim that this is not the case, since the existence of a single scientific method is only a myth (Galison & Stump, 1996; Feyerabend, 1975; Latour & Woolgar 1979), as scientific disciplines have rather different approaches and peculiarities that make them diverge from a common perspective.

This is particularly true in the case where a discipline studies complex systems where experiments are reproducible only with difficulty, and where, therefore, the hinge of the scientific method itself can be questionable.

Medicine, history, physical astronomy, geology, palaeontology, archaeology, to mention but a few, are based on clues, so that for example, Ginzburg (1989) groups them under the definition of *"symptomatological sciences."*

Symptoms are subjective, so that more than observations or measurements can be considered signs, and signs need to be interpreted through reference to an explanation, a theory, a vision.

This duality, clue/interpretation, is typical of these scientific domains so that even Leibnitz, in his time, referring to medicine, highlighted the fact that the discipline is based on a *"Duplex methodus tractandi morbos: una Analytica per symptomata, altera Syntetica per causas"* (Pasini, 1997).

Modern epistemology teaches us that visions bias clues, so that researchers can become detached from facts, which leads them to becoming isolated in communities that speciate and diverge even within the same disciplinary field. In addition, scientific research is increasingly multi-disciplinary, so that the same issue is studied from different perspectives and by researchers with different backgrounds.

Coupling distant visions and disciplinary backgrounds with difficulties to refer to solid facts creates a complicated situation that needs to be carefully considered in the perspective of collaborative e-research. In this area, there is a rather long-standing tradition and a vast amount of literature in many disciplinary fields that span from physical sciences to health or environmental research (see for example Olson, et al., 2008, for a large collection of case studies). These studies are generally more focused on large scientific instruments and resource sharing e-science, for example Olson et al. (2008) show that physical sciences are fundamentally "physical" so that, researchers, there, are mainly aiming at making expensive devices available widely and remotely. In other fields, the goal is to link together resources creating powerful computing environments (Foster & Kesselman 1998), see for example Dove and de Leeuw (2005) for molecular simulation.

However, not so much research has been done in distributed scientific collaboration directly between peers in communities (Farooq, et al., 2007) and, in particular, in shared spaces characterized by the risk of cognitive model incompatibility.

It is exactly this area that we would like to explore in this chapter and from this perspective research fields such as medicine, archeology or earth sciences are perfect subjects for dissection.

Since a deep analysis of all of them is impossible, we will focus on geophysics, which is a particularly rich environment from the point of view of blurred facts and clashing visions, where most of the research is carried out in multidisciplinary teams and where a lively community is starting to bridge intra-disciplinary "tribal areas" and to demand proper technological support for its collaborative activities.

Outline of the Chapter

In this chapter, we start by analysing the reasons and the conditions for the above mentioned dynamics to emerge. We describe what exploration geophysics is, and analyse the peculiarities of reasoning in this field. We will show that it is primarily an abductive process mirrored in a complex, context-dependent, connotative coding system.

Starting from the fact that abductive reasoning allows multiple and concurrent explanations for the same phenomenon to coexist, we address the problem of how scientists bias one hypothesis over another not only on strictly logical but also on sociological motivations. Following a vision, scientists tend to evolve and isolate themselves from other scientists creating communities characterized by different cognitive models, so that after some time these become incompatible and scientists stop understanding each other. This creates serious practical problems in collaborative e-research since the lack of overlap among different mental frameworks would create problems in organizing information.

We address these problems as a communication issue so that the classic distinction into three levels (syntactic, semantic, and pragmatic) can be used.

At the syntactic level, we highlight non-technical obstacles that condition interoperability and data availability and transparency. At the semantic level, possible incompatibilities of cognitive models are particularly evident, so that by using ontologies, cross-domain reconciliation needs to be applied, which is a very difficult task to perform

since the projection of knowledge by scientists, in the designated community, is political and thus can create a lot of tension. The strategy we propose to overcome these issues pertains to pragmatics, in the sense that it is intended to acknowledge the cultural and personal factors each partner brings into the collaboration and is based on the idea that meaning should remain a flexible and contingent representation of possibly divergent views. This can be achieved through the introduction of boundary objects (Star & Griesemer, 1989) that are weakly structured in common use while strongly structured in individual use. In our experience, these are very effective in coordinating collaborative work, creating a map of activities, tasks, concepts or events that can be used to drive through the collaborative space in order to locate information. The collaborative work itself, populating this space with information, will build the contingent meaning of the represented features. We report on the use of several types of maps, from geographical maps that are inborn in the geosciences, to mind maps, event bushes and workflows, and we describe then how this space can be populated through messaging and data upload, access and analysis.

In the last section, we present a Web-based, e-research system (COLLA) we developed to test the pragmatic approach we propose. This is used within several collaborative e-research projects ranging from large European-scale initiatives to smaller internal activities. Practical experiences confirm the usefulness of the approach while some limitations have also been noticed. Improvements and extensions are currently under development and will be soon tested within the designated community.

BACKGROUND

The Dissection

The existence of a single scientific method has been questioned by many (Galison & Stump, 1996;

Latour & Woolgar 1979; Feyerabend, 1975). Can we refer to any notion, to understand what distinguishes one scientific discipline from another, with particular attention to the implications related to collaboration and e-research? We will address these issues in this section by discussing:

1. The role of the scientific experiment and its reproducibility in cases where observations can be difficult or subjective.
2. The role of the various possible practices in scientific reasoning, with particular emphasis on abduction, that is a type of reasoning that allows clues to be reconstructed in the light of an interpretation.
3. The case of exploration geophysics, where, in order to overcome the limitations in observations, abductive reasoning practices are adopted.

Reproducibility of the Scientific Experiment

The scientific method prescribes that scientific laws are founded on observations that should be reproducible experimentally at any time. The problem many scientists have to deal with is that natural processes involve complex interactions over a range of spatial and temporal scales that are difficult to break down into elementary processes, as is done, for example, in physics and chemistry. For example, environmental sciences are well known to be a breeding ground for "butterfly effects" where small changes in non linear systems can turn into large differences at later states. In epidemiology, very often, hindsight confirms that correlation does not imply causation, highlighting the role of an underestimated parameter (Lawlor, Davey Smith & Ebrahim, 2004).

Besides, laws must be set up from a relatively limited number of cases that generally vary so much in detail that it can be difficult to recognize analogies in manifestations of the same phenomenon (Engelhardt & Zimmerman, 1982). Meteorite impacts, for example, are luckily not frequent and not bookable.

Following Popper (1963), positive outcomes of experiments cannot confirm a scientific theory, but a single counter-example can demolish it. If this makes sense in the case of physics or chemistry, applying the criterion where there are objective difficulties in handling observations raises problems for devising any *experimentum crucis*.

Scientific Reasoning and the Importance of Abduction

Following Salmon (1990), a complete, scientific explanation consists in the logical connection between three components, namely: statements describing the controlling (initial) state of affairs (A), statements of law (L) and statements describing the resulting affairs (B). As noted by Peirce (1931), the fundamental issue is that we do not, in the first instance, have all three components of inference at our disposal. Three initial situations can be distinguished, each involving a different procedure for setting up an explanation:

Induction: where the controlling states of affairs (A) and the resulting states of affair (B) are known, while a law (L) is sought.

Deduction: where the controlling state of affairs (A) and the law (L) are known, while the resulting state of affairs is sought

Abduction: where the resulting state of affairs (B) and the law (L) is known, while the controlling state of affairs is sought.

In *sensu stricto*, only the process of deduction yields a logic inference.

Abduction is a method of reasoning to explore a context which is uncertain in order to come up with new ideas. Umberto Eco (1981) highlighted its power for drawing conclusions from an array of seemingly disparate and unconnected facts and observations, taking as an example Conan Doyle's fictional hero Sherlock Holmes, who, by the way, innocently refers to his reasoning as deductive.

Abductive inferences, going from the resulting state of affairs (B) to the controlling state of affairs (A), cannot be considered definitive since the same result (B) could be produced also by other premises (A'). The only case when abduction produces a definitive conclusion is that of a biconditional law, that is when a controlling state of affairs A produces a result B that can be produced if and only in the case of that specific controlling state A. Therefore, quoting Peirce (1931):

"Abduction merely suggests that something may be."

Coming in defense of Abduction, it must be said that the limits of deduction and induction are also well known. Deduction works within a closed system, it is basically a tautology, it simply changes the configuration of knowledge, therefore it cannot discover anything new. Induction has a considerable opponent literature, from the ancient Skeptics through Hume [1748] (1910) to Popper (1979), which questions its logical foundation, since the truth of the premises does not guarantee the truth of its conclusions. Inductive inference proceeds from statements about a known phenomenon to amplified statements about phenomena that resemble the known

Exploration Geophysics

Albeit very interesting, it would be well beyond the possibilities of this work to explore all the possible scientific research fields that rely on Abduction (see for example Patel et al [2004] for the case of medicine or Shelley [1996] for the case of archeology or Kovács and Spens [2005] for the case of logistics) and in particular, to consider the role abduction has in those disciplines in the perspective of collaborative research. We will therefore concentrate on the case of exploration geophysics, which is a very fertile ground from this point of view and a disciplinary area we have

had the chance to study in depth from inside, referring, where useful, to other experiences in different disciplinary fields.

Exploration geophysics is a multidisciplinary branch of the geo-sciences where the Earth is studied using mainly seismic, but also magnetic, gravimetric, and other methods (Sheriff, 1973). These methods are widely used for oil and gas prospecting, for environmental protection, for hazard mitigation and for general studies on the structure of the lithosphere (from the surface to depths of tens of kms). Seismic prospecting, not to be confused with earthquake seismology, involves recording the propagating wave field, induced by a set of artificial "Earthquakes" near the surface. In geophysics, as in other natural sciences, recorded data cannot be read in a straightforward manner, but need to be processed and interpreted.

Using the terminology proposed by Becher and Trowler (2001), exploration geophysics can be described as built of a matrix of hard, pure and applied sciences saturated with a pervasive "soft" interpretive fluid. It is a field where two "forma mentis" coexist, often causing quite a headache for geophysicists. This schizophrenic perspective comes from the overlap of two forms of reasoning, borrowed on the one hand from physics and chemistry and on the other from geology. These are very different and, although a degree of osmotic flow exists between them, they generally remain separate. This gap is mainly due to the incompatibility of the quasi-hermeneutic approach of geology with the nomological necessity common in physics.

Reasoning in Geophysics (What is so Special?)

Peirce himself pointed out that the main difference between physics/chemistry and geology is that while the former rely mainly on induction and deduction, the latter relies heavily on abduction (Peirce, 1931). Earth science investigates and explains causation in the natural word, much as historians of human history investigate and explain the development of mankind. These historical enterprises are analogous in that both deal with abductive reconstruction of unique, often non-reproducible, and contingent processes of the past. They differ in that the explanation of geo-historic processes must have recourse solely to the laws of nature (Engelhardt & Zimmerman, 1982).

Another aspect to consider in geo-reasoning is the temporal relationship among the elements of the inference. We speak of prediction when the inferred state takes place after the initial state, of retrodiction when the inferred state happens before the starting point, and of codiction when the inferred and starting points are simultaneous. This implies that predictions must be deductive, retrodictions abductive, while codictions can be either.

Abductive codiction infers the existence of a state of affairs not accessible to observation; however, as the controlling state, this can become the basis of a deductive codiction inferring the existence of a resulting state that can be confirmed by observation. By deducing observable consequences (different from the initial state of abduction), deductive codiction may help solidify the corresponding abductive codiction (Engelhardt & Zimmerman, 1982). An example of this is the use of geophysical prospecting to search for oil and gas. When using seismic sections it is possible to reconstruct the structural geological setting of an area, for example the existence of a salt dome (abductive codiction). Current geological models predict that, in these cases, it is common to find low permeability layers sealing hydrocarbon reservoirs, so that the oil geologist may therefore take the risk and drill alongside the salt dome (deductive codiction). However, even in highly explored areas such as the North Atlantic margin of the UK, only one in five wells may be successful (Loizou, 2002).

Another common kind of reasoning in the geo-sciences is abductive retrodiction followed by deductive prediction. The idea is that retrodic-

tion (abductively) builds a past state of affairs (A) that can then be used as a basis to predict (deductively) an observable present state of affairs (B). If B is confirmed from real observations, the process is deemed likely to have occurred, although doubts may remain due mainly to the assumptions imposed during retrodiction (in the case of non-biconditional laws). An example of this common kind of reasoning is found in Diviacco et al. (2006), who presented evidence, from Seismic data reprocessing, of a submarine mega-debris-flow deposit on the continental rise of the Pacific margin of the Antarctic Peninsula. The authors sought to explain, inter alia, the huge dimension of the deposit and suggested that the deposit could be linked to an exceptional event such as an asteroid impact (abductive retrodiction). In this case, a mega-tsunami generated by the asteroid impact could have triggered a unique failure of the continental margin that gave birth to the mega-debris flow deposit. If this had happened, geochemical evidence, in the form of an iridium anomaly, should be present (deductive prediction). This is in fact the case, and during the late Pliocene, an asteroid 1 to 4 km in diameter is thought to have impacted into the deep ocean in the Bellinghausen Sea about 1000 km west of Cape Horn and some 1300 km from the area of the deposit (Margolis, et al., 1991). This event, called the Eltanin asteroid impact, turned up in sea-floor morphological and sedimentological evidence as well as in an iridium anomaly, which corroborates the thesis of a mega-debris flow triggered by an asteroid impact.

Of course, the asteroid impact is and will remain a suggestion supported by evidence, since nobody will ever have the possibility of witnessing it directly.

The convergence of circumstantial evidence may convince a jury that the Eltanin asteroid is guilty of causing the mega-debris flow deposit but, as in many detective stories, other plausible explanations can undermine the apparent consistency of available clues. This is the problem of the excessive number of possible configurations of controlling states (A, A', A"...) involved in abduction, an issue which does not help mitigate the Cartesian anxiety experienced by the public, by the jury and by the researchers themselves.

MAIN FOCUS OF THE CHAPTER

Logic or Socio-Logic?

If abductive reasoning allows multiple and concurrent explanations for the same phenomenon, researchers have the possibility of trusting each model to a greater or lesser degree, so that a question arises about how these choices are made. These decisions are not only based on strict and cold logical mechanisms, but also on "warmer" socio-logic motivations. Contemporary epistemology and sociology of science describe researchers as members of tribes that evolve and diverge in their visions and practices up to a point where they cannot understand each other any more.In this section we will discuss:

- How abductive reasoning induces researchers to reduce the complexity of cognitive models
- The motivations that can guide researchers in doing so and the consequences that this has in the designated community, in creating isolated communities of practice.
- The issue of mutual understanding among members of different communities of practice.

Bias

The problem of an excessive number of possible causes of a phenomenon is a rather serious inconvenience for researchers. However, if they were able to focus on the more likely causes of a phenomenon and exclude others, they could relax and leave the more relativistic and anxious

world of contemporary detective stories in favour of the good old days of Sherlock Holmes where everything was "elementary."

How can this be done? How can a researcher decide to exclude possible controlling states?

Let us reverse the perspective. The mirror image of confidence is uncertainty, which is a hot topic in the geo-sciences, especially considering its possible implications in cases of hazard mitigation or of oil prospecting. Following Woo (1999), conceptual (epistemic) and aleatory uncertainties may be distinguished. Epistemic uncertainty is rooted in knowledge itself, while aleatory uncertainty is rooted in the belief in knowledge. Every model has its own intrinsic approximation and associated uncertainty (epistemic), but at the same time every researcher may trust each model to a greater or lesser degree (aleatory uncertainty). This degree of trust is called, in an uncertainty assessment in the geo-sciences, the researcher's "bias," and it is something we are not generally able to handle. Following Popper (1963), we cannot avoid or suppress our theories or prevent them from influencing our observations, yet we can try to recognize them as hypotheses and formulate them explicitly so that they may be criticized. Following Pshenichny (2004), bias should be explicitly formulated and included in theories. He notes that logic may provide a means to assess probability of knowledge on absolutely strict foundations, but he also acknowledges that this is not easy to achieve in practice.

Bias is at the heart of geo-reasoning. It may have a negative connotation, but also a positive one: the capacity of focusing on the more likely causes of a phenomenon. In medicine, expert physicians are those able to selectively attend to relevant information and to narrow the set of diagnostic possibilities (Patel, et al., 2004). In Frodeman (1995) bias is considered a virtue of the "interpretive" sciences. It is a predisposition of the mind that resembles the "Ars inveniendi" of Leibniz, where a "combinatory" spirit is able to connect and link distant entities to allow new knowledge to arise (Pasini, 1997).

This of course works at the level of the individual, but we cannot stop here as, quoting Bloor (1976):

"Science is a social construct."

The Social Aspects of Bias

Researchers are individuals rooted in different traditions, schools, cultures, and some may say generations. Their myths and models about scientific research do not necessarily correspond to their "normal" scientific life, and many of them are not even aware that this may be the case.

Following Kuhn (1962), scientists live within paradigms, a philosophical or theoretical framework, a tradition or school that conditions their way of thinking. Different, concurrent, and incommensurable paradigms exist within any discipline.

After Lakatos (1970), theories or paradigms can shield their core from attempts at falsification by changing a set of auxiliary and peripheral hypotheses (the protective belt) while leaving essentially unaltered the kernel of the theory. This is postulated to happen in any scientific discipline. However, while in the case of Physics or Chemistry the role of the scientific experiment (or the simple existence of analgesics or of mp3 readers) can be used to defend the traditional myth of the scientific method, the distance of the geo-sciences from nomological necessity creates a peculiar no-man's land where everything is more complex. It would be interesting to know whether the average oil and gas Exploration and Production (E&P) manager is aware of the thesis of Popper or Lakatos. The fact is that, notwithstanding the seemingly poor results from drilling salt domes, they keep on drilling those geological settings, and we all keep on driving our cars.

Bond et al. (2008) surveyed a representative sample of geophysicists to analyze how they tend to build a geological model out of seismic data,

highlighting the role of previous experiences and preconceived notions that stem from their personal backgrounds. Baddeley et al. (2004) reported on the phenomenon of opinion shaping and herding, while suggesting paths to interrogate experts through elicitation.

Paradigm anchoring and protective belts drive scientists to gather in communities that, following Becher and Trowler (2001), resemble "tribes" that evolve separately, and eventually cannot understand each other. Here, social and institutional characteristics of knowledge communities matter for the epistemological properties of the knowledge they produce (their territories). Conditions and circumstances that are external, such as how universities, faculties and departments are organized, or the control over facilities, as in Whitley (2000), can and do make a difference to disciplinary status and identity.

Starting from the idea that "Science is a social construct," Latour and Woolgar (1979) took this vision to the extremes by saying that bias is conditioned by the network of allies and by the strategic positioning that the researcher is able to maintain in the community.

In this perspective, Pshenichny (2004) was absolutely right, we cannot refuse Bias, nor reduce it. On the contrary, at least in the geo-sciences, it is mandatory to consider it an important part of the process of scientific inquiry, so that any system intended to support scientific research in this field should be tailored to such a perspective.

Practical Issues Related to Bias

After Frege (1892) there is a clear distinction between the sense *(sinn)* and the reference *(bedeutung)* of a concept. Carnap (1947) developed this vision, associating an "intension" to any given expression, a sort of list of all pertinent attributes, and an "extension," or the set of all individuals that match the intension. The model is based on the assumption that it is the intension that determines the extension, which means that only once we have defined the set of properties of a concept "A" can we realize if an entity is "A." The problem is that, following this vision, a change in the intension will change the contents of the set of related entities (Putnam, 1975).

If we accept ideas such as paradigm anchoring, bias, protective belts or tribes, we are driven to think that some view of a concept or of an activity may include a specific entity, while other views may exclude it.

This has consequences for all the activities of a collaborative research project. Collaboration among scientists from different backgrounds and visions may involve the gathering of data and information in different ways, so that the imposition of a "filter" by one of the partners could hide useful information to other partners, lowering the possible "combinatory" outcomes. In fact, information can be, and often is, organized and stored within frameworks that reflect mental representations, so that the pursuit introduces the need to consider, in each and every case, the context in which these representations were defined. This adds a connotative level that makes information management a process that cannot be easily coded and shared among researchers.

Communication

Conflicting cognitive models mirroring in difficulties in the very basic collaborative activity of handling information among partners is a communication problem that can be analyzed using the traditional distinction in syntactics, semantics, and pragmatics (Morris, 1971).

In the traditional syntactic/technical approach of Shannon and Weaver (1949), which is very close to the statistical-mathematical information theory, establishing a shared and stable syntax/technology could ensure accurate communication between sender and receiver across a boundary and solve communication or information processing problems.

Semantic interoperability is a higher level goal where, besides the ability to exchange information, the focus is on the use of information, introducing the need to consider terms denoting concepts with possibly concurrent uses.

Pragmatics is related to the significance of information referring also to the state of the surrounding world excluded from the utterance, including cultural and personal factors.

The progression from syntactics to pragmatics is often seen as mirroring a progression from tangible to abstract objects. A tangible entity, for example, being the output of a sensor and an abstract entity being a geological model, so that addressing the former should be less complex than addressing the latter since the first case is supposed to offer only limited headroom for theorization while the second case relies heavily on visions, theories, backgrounds, cognitive models, schools and other "human" factors. In reality, things are more complicated.

Syntactics

The syntactic approach is traditionally concerned with low-level interoperability that can be achieved by making data structures, formats, or even hardware consistent across systems.

For example, in the case of the BIRN (www.birncommunity.org) biomedical research initiative, multi-site clinical trials are supported from packaging and shipping of hardware racks, up to software tools tailored to address specific problems as the calibration of magnetic resonance data.

This level should not consider conflicting cognitive models because it is supposed to stop well before theories or visions, and it should neglect the existence of interpretation that arises whenever someone is creating or using information. However, Hanson (1971) postulated the existence of a "shadow" of theorization at this level as well; David and Bunn (1988) have also shown that there are substantive economic interests that can interfere with the quest for interoperability.

In exploration geophysics, syntactic interoperability has been traditionally driven by the oil and gas Exploration and Production industries (E&P) and by their interest in selling and buying data without leakage of knowledge that might give advantages to competitors. The E&P industry coded strict practices for data purchase and exploitation, and data brokering is an important commercial activity. Web based commercial data discovery systems are available (see for example Diskos [www.landmarkvspace.com/nocs/] or UKDEAL [www.ukdeal.co.uk]), but once the transaction is done, activities generally remain within the scope of the company, following prescriptive "best practices" and homogeneous and vertical software environments. At the same time, software companies tend to create brand-specific standards in order to keep customers within sight.

All this resolves in a trend to limit technical interoperability to the very basic information, as can be demonstrated by the fact that, notwithstanding the fact that this discipline experienced an incredible increase of complexity, the standard for seismic data sharing, the SEG-Y format (Barry, et al., 1975), was published in 1975 and is still widely accepted and used in both industrial and scientific contexts, revealing then, in both cases, concern for information sharing.

We see then that the obstacles to technical interoperability are not only technical.

Non-Technical Obstacles to Syntactic Communication in Scientific Research

Researchers are committed to the development and successful strategic positioning, in the community, of their visions and of themselves as an obligatory passage point (Latour & Woolgar, 1979) in order to grant control over the evolution of their idea and the possibility of entering new research projects. In this perspective, collaboration means also trying to balance at the same time:

- the need to preserve the scientist's original position,
- the need to be at the cutting edge of innovation and
- the need for other partners and their resources.

This is a very complex task, where the control of data is extremely important, so that its availability and transparency (meaning the possibility to access the work of the data provider) has to be modulated also upon the desired "social" result. In the absence of a solution that can support such activities, data owners generally prefer to secure their assets leaving the community without important primary sources of research.

Data availability/transparency as a function of the role and expectations of a researcher in a community, is a general issue. In the case of medicine, concerns about releasing data within large collaborative initiatives have been reported by Olson et al. (2008). Pratt et al. (2004) highlighted the different sharing attitude of junior and senior, or higher rank physicians. Nentwich (2003) reports concern for data transparency in fields that are close to economic applications and Kötter (2001) highlights the economic interests of private companies in molecular biology. Orlowski (1992) highlighted the strong need for motivation in data sharing which, in the case of scientific research, means essentially the possibility of publishing; for example, in the case of high energy physics, Birnholtz (2006) reports on the practice of acknowledging all participants of a project as authors in publications. Ribes and Bowker (2009) report on the possibility that scientists can be ashamed of the quality of their data and thus unwilling to share it with their peers, and, on top of all this, legal issues have to be considered also, as mining exploration licensing regulation in the case of seismic data or privacy in biomedical research as, for example, in the U.S. with the HIPAA federal regulation.

As can be seen, things are not as easy as one would suppose. Interoperability at the syntactic level is not only a matter of agreeing on a format, but it also needs to consider an intermingling layer of social relations among actors. In the field of exploration geophysics, issues related to data transparency have been addressed in Diviacco (2005) and Diviacco (2011), where Web-based collaborative systems have been developed that allow partners to access and analyze seismic data without the need to move them outside the controlled scope of the web site of the data owner, and therefore relieving these latter from the fear of losing control of their data.

Various international initiatives aim at fostering a collaborative attitude in the scientific community through data sharing and, therefore, harmonization at technical level. All these need to consider the above mentioned issues, otherwise the risk is that they can become wonderful boxes but absolutely empty. In the field of exploration geophysics, within the EU 7th framework project Geo-Seas (www.geo-seas.eu), these issues were carefully considered (Diviacco, 2011) providing, at the same time (1), solutions to relieve the concerns of data owners and (2) forums to discuss technical issues and grow consensus on the harmonization process.

Semantics

We are going through a period of important innovations and enthusiasm in information technology which, considering its ubiquity, is reflected in every aspect of our lives and, of course, of science. Following the vision of Tim Berners-Lee (2001), structured collections of information and sets of inference rules can be used to conduct automated reasoning. This enables machines to comprehend semantic documents and data.

In many disciplinary fields this enthusiasm fosters a large number of very interesting initiatives as for example, to mention only a few, in the case of medicine, the Unified Medical Language System, the OBI consortium, or in the case of earth sciences the Open GIS consortium, the GeoN network or the GeoSciML initiative.

In this vision, the semantic information is embedded in declarative sentences about an issue. The probability of a sentence is inversely proportional to its information (Meriluoto, 2003), so that if we can code all aspects of what we want to analyze, then we should come close to the truth.

In fact, this works pretty well when considering computers understanding each other, but is not easy to apply when considering human beings. The problem here again is that from an epistemological and sociological perspective, in scientific research, at least in the area we are focusing on, we are not addressing "one single truth."

Considering the abductive and connotative aspects of scientific research in the field of geophysics, can the ease with which semantic agents are able to organize our next holiday or compare prices for our next TV set also be applied here? Can we rely on them to organize our scientific projects or even to seek data and information?

Controlled Vocabularies

A Controlled Vocabulary (CV) is a method for organizing knowledge into lists of predefined and authorized terms. Examples of CVs are, the General Multilingual Environmental Thesaurus (GEMET) in environmental sciences, the NASA Thesaurus in aereonautics and space science, the CBD in biological diversity or UMLS in medicine.

Building CVs in large scientific environments can be very difficult (Kelso, et al., 2003). In the case of the geo-sciences, the development of a CV in a large community of researchers (Diviacco, et al., 2011b; Lowry, et al., 2006) reveals that even in the case of tangible objects as scientific instrumentation, different visions might clash. Reported problems span from authorization of terms to convergence on definitions. In the first case, the need to decide which term to use, brings to light possible incompatibilities in the use of software or practices so that, ironically, the very actors who are less advanced in internal standardization have less problems and often contribute more freely to the discussion.

Vocabulary governance can be a difficult activity that leads to endless discussions on the definition of a term that can eventually be solved only by the firm imposition of a very authoritative personality. This, of course, can trigger a "meltdown" problem (Ackerman, 2000), where part of the community could decide not to conform and develop its own dialect instead. Diviacco et al. (2011b) highlighted the importance for confrontations to be made public in a collaborative tool tuned for the purpose. By putting enough efforts into maintaining high levels of awareness and participation among partners, there are good chances of avoiding defections and obtaining a good mental habit from the partners.

Ontologies

An ontology is a specification of a conceptualization (Gruber, 1995). Practical applications of ontologies should allow the representation of knowledge in the form of meaning-based relations linking heterogeneous entities in order to facilitate across-discipline communication.

A key point in building an ontology in scientific research is the capture of knowledge through expert elicitation, which opens the door to the plethora of epistemological and sociological issues we already mentioned above.

Knowledge is embedded in practice and accumulated in the experiences and know-how of individuals engaged in a given practice (Taylor, 1992; Harper, 1987), and therefore it is hard to articulate or recall. Knowledge is also embedded in the technologies, methods and rules of thumb used by individuals in a given practice. For example Ribes and Bowker (2009) reported on a heated discussion during a trial to converge on a common use of the color red in geological maps that traced back to specific representation conventions tied to the different nationality and academic background of the participants.

In emphasizing that knowledge is embedded, we mean that often knowledge might be difficult to be put explicitly because, as stressed by Polanyi (1966):

"We know more than we can tell"

Moreover, even if it were possible to analyze all this in depth, we need to consider sociological issues that can scramble the whole picture as well. Scientists' projection of knowledge in the designated community is political and, in fact, the development of ontologies can be a catalyst or can create a lot of tension in a community (Ribes & Bowker, 2009).

Strategies Towards Harmonization

When scientific domains are difficult to reconcile, strategies have to be devised in order to overcome the impasse (Hameed, et al., 2003).

The simplest approach is mapping among individual ontologies of different domains. This method has the disadvantages that (1) it provides no general organizing principle at work (no attempt to identify common conceptualizations across the individual ontologies) and (2) it determines an excessive increase in the sets of mappings required when many ontologies need to be reconciled.

A different approach is to develop a new ontology based on manual categorization of semantic relationships among different concepts from different domains. This generally reverts to modifying the granularity of the original ontologies, since normally the only way to achieve consensus is to reconcile mismatched concepts in a more abstract or general superclass (Weng, et al., 2007).

Then the choice is between losing the structure by focusing on details or blurring these latter to get a structure.

Multi-faceted ontology is an attempt to achieve both at the same time, relying on the definition of a single ontology for the issue addressed and on the creation of windows to access the ontology, following specific perspectives. Each window is a facet while the ontology becomes in this sense multi-faceted. The philosophy behind this method implies that formal knowledge can only be achieved by representing the complete conceptual universe, which, in the case of scientific research is very unlikely to be possible. Moreover, this technique neglects the human aspects, like the possibility that knowledge could be manipulated.

So to sum up, when concurrent visions clash in collaborative scientific research, since (1) it is not possible to obtain structure and detail at the same time and (2) mapping, although appealing for its ease, cannot scale up to the complexity of scientific problems, it seems advisable to prefer the manual categorization of semantic relationships with a reduction of detail.

In other words, if convergence is not possible, the only possibility of meeting the expectations of all the partners is to reduce the semantic content, to get what in the seminal work of Star and Griesemer (1989) is called the lowest common denominator and defined as:

"What satisfies the minimal demands of each world by capturing properties that fall within the minimum acceptable range of all concerned worlds."

Practical experiences on semantic harmonization in scientific research can be found, for example, in the field of biomedical informatics in Weng et al (2007), who report on semantic harmonization strategies that were put in place within the BRIDG (www.bridgmodel.org) project and on the practice of stewardship used by them to ease knowledge elicitation during harmonization meetings.

In the case of the geo-sciences, Ribes and Bowker (2009) report similar experiences while focusing on reapprehension: a double movement of the domain specialists reflecting on their own knowledge and of the IT experts establishing a sufficient familiarity with the domain knowledge.

Pragmatics (Semiotics)

The problem of context is a major issue that has concerned many philosophers, so that even Frege, as reported by Dummet (1993), acknowledged that a word has meaning only in a context. Similarly, the later Wittgenstein claimed that thoughts are not pictures of how things are in the world, rather, meaning stands in the use of a word, and in Russell (1905), the notion of scope also heads in the same direction. In a perspective of collaboration among researchers with different backgrounds and visions, all this seems to lead to a dead end.

A major step forward was made by Kripke (1972) with the introduction of the notion of rigid designator, where a name refers to an object by virtue of a causal connection with the object as mediated through communities of speakers. Thus, even if it is not possible, to converge on a shared model of a concept, this does not mean that concepts cannot be used anyway. Different communities can refer to concepts through common signs, since sign-users will invest them with the meaning pertinent to their context or domain. Since all this deals with (1) facts about the objective facts, (2) facts about the speaker's intentions, (3) facts about beliefs, and (4) facts about relevant social institutions involved, following Korta et al. (2011), the study of how communication can take place among communities with different visions and backgrounds falls within the scope of pragmatics, or as other authors prefer to call it semiotics (Nadin, 1987). We will explore two methods: Social tagging and boundary objects that match the requirements of pragmatics/semiotics.

Social Tagging

Social tagging, also known as folksonomy is a very popular practice, whose appeal is mainly derived from being a bottom-up classification, an implicit user-generated taxonomy that generally does not rely on a controlled vocabulary. By avoiding formal representation, social tagging allows the coexistence of multiple cognitive models (Steels, 2006; Jäschke, et al., 2008). Data is associated with an abstraction labeled to connote a concept or an activity, but not to an already existing framework. The framework itself is built at the end, then no structure exists but a contingent gathering of information is available on the basis of user-created tagging.

Is it possible to imagine social tagging as a method to help us handle multiple cognitive models in collaborative e-science? A possibility would be to provide users with tools to tag the information stored in the collaborative system, similarly to what happens in Flickr (www.flickr. com). To request all partners to comment on each entity could be quite time consuming, but theoretically possible. This way tags can provide the path to follow backwards, the concurrent cognitive models that converged in the tagged object.

Social tagging is very flexible but also rather difficult to "capture": it is easy to generate a proliferation of tags that eventually makes the framework very difficult to use. Social tagging has several limitations, among which are ambiguity, synonymy and discrepancies in granularity (Golder & Huberman, 2005). To solve these problems, many authors have tended to apply semantics to collaborative tagging, or to extract semantics from contexts where this is used (Specia & Motta, 2007). This introduces the need for further work such as cleaning up of tags, disambiguation or analysis of co-occurrence that can impose biases and drifts. For example, if a controlled vocabulary was employed, the usability would definitely improve but mainly because the clashing problems would be moved to the vocabulary itself.

Besides, social tagging is a way to build only taxonomies, which only partially address the activities of collaborative work; in fact, workflows, or causal relations between entities cannot be expressed here and if needed, should be made available by using different means.

Boundary Objects

In line with the view that diverging communities can collaborate even without a shared cognitive model, Star and Griesemer (1989) introduced the concept of "boundary objects."

Full consensus is not necessary neither for cooperation nor for the successful conduct of work. Boundary objects are weakly structured in common use, and become strongly structured in individual use. They contain sufficient detail to be understood by one partner, although it is not necessary that he/she understands the context in which the other partners use it. They are artifacts related to sets of information, conversations, interests, rules, or plans, and are at the centre of communities of practices.

The original work of Star and Griesemer (1989) focused indeed on scientific research. They observed the fact that in spite of the deep differences between scientists in various disciplines, they were nevertheless often very successful in cooperating to create *"good science."* At the same time, they claimed that:

"Because of the heterogeneous character of scientific work and its requirement for cooperation, the management of this diversity cannot be achieved via a simple pluralism or a laissez-faire solution."

A passive attitude is not the solution in their view. The creation of boundary objects is an active way of allowing findings that incorporate different meanings to become coherent.

Boundary Objects in Collaborative E-Research

The use of boundary objects in collaborative research is more common than can be seen in the literature. In almost all cases boundary objects are simply "used" without recognizing them as such (see the case of GIS systems) while, interestingly, they are often explicitly mentioned in knowledge elicitation activities (Paay, et al., 2009).

Boundary objects are artifacts that aim to bridge concurrent cognitive models through abstraction from all the domains of the partners. Therefore one can foresee their application mainly in the coordination rather than in the actual working activities.

The coordination of scientific research is an issue unto itself that cannot be addressed here, except to recall the importance of flexibility and serendipity in scientific research (for an interesting discussion on organizational typologies in scientific research see Chompalov, et al. [2002]).

Boundary objects should be artifacts characterized by flexibility and coarse granularity, that can be used to coordinate activities in a similar fashion to what Suchman (1987) names a "map": a formal construction that can, but not necessarily does, control activities, as a traveler's map: *"does not control the traveler's movements through the world,"* rather describes how to go from one place to another. This can be put into practice following the various approaches described below.

Spatial Frameworks/Atlases

Following Star and Griesemer, spatial frameworks/atlases are boundary objects that arise in the presence of different means of aggregating data as, for example, when different disciplines in geo-sciences produce different artifacts related to the same geographical area.

The result is that work in different sites and with different perspectives can be conducted autonomously while cooperating parties share a common referent, with the advantage of being able to achieve different goals.

The case of geographical maps is rather inborn in the geo-scientific community. They have been traditionally used as boundary objects well before Star and Griesemer's work, and very likely since Paleolithic cave painting. Their use in IT systems is of course not new, but not common in collaborative systems, and not understood as boundary objects. Only recently (Xu, et al., 2011) have Geographic Information Systems (GIS) been recognized as spaces where cross-disciplinary collaboration can take place, while web-based implementation of such a perspective is still rather far away.

Tangible entities, such as outcrops or seismic sections or wells, can be clearly located so that each partner can refer to them and use them in their work. The position of each entity in relation to the others will define the use of the entity itself. Partners with different backgrounds, as for example stratigraphers or seismic data analysts, will of course use the same entity in different ways, but eventually, referring to the map, they will be able to collaborate.

Spatial frameworks can be used to bridge even wider gaps as among geo-scientists, biologists, historians, epidemiologists, or even policy makers. For example, the same geographical extent, as for instance an exclusive economic zone (i.e., the one where the coastal nation has sole exploitation rights over all natural resources) can be used for scientific research, exploration and production and at the same time also for administrative issues.

Spatial frameworks do not need to be necessarily only geographical. A very interesting application for this approach, for example, took place within the Mouse BIRN project in the field of biomedical research (Olson, et al., 2008; Martone, et al., 2004). Here, although many of the neuroscientists working at the project came from the same field, they had serious differences in the culture of their subfields. To overcome these problems, the SmartAtlas tool was developed, which allows them to integrate data within a common spatial framework. The SmartAtlas makes use of a common coordinate system to bring together multi-scale imaging of data on the mouse brain stored at each of the BIRN sites, so that scientists can issue spatial queries on anatomical features.

Diagrams

Maps, in a wide sense, can represent non spatial features, such as processes or concepts, but in this case, the problem of granularity becomes relevant in avoiding clashing concurrent visions.

A location in a geographical map is denoted by latitude and longitude or by a name. The name of a place can fuel common emotions, but generally allows each one of us to have his/her own memories and sensations or even no memory and no sensation. The name of a place is essentially a label to which we attach our specific visions.

Labels behave like the demonstrative pronouns 'this,' 'that,' 'these,' and 'those,' which refer to an entity even if depending on different contexts (Di Francesco, 1994). These entities can be anything, from existing objects to "something happening" to concepts or ideas.

There is no specific rule for the use of labels. They can have any form, so that we can use terms, sentences, or even images, but all these need to be devised at the correct granularity to avoid concurrent visions clashes.

The diagram itself can be of many types, from very simple sketches to workflows, mind maps or more formal and computational formalizations. We cannot explore all the possible flavours of diagrams that can be used in collaborative work so that we will mention a few that, in our experience, turned out to be easy to use and helpful. Below, in section five, we will describe a general method for the use of diagrams that allows other possibilities to be explored.

Mind/Concept Maps

Mind maps are diagrams used to represent concepts around a central idea. They have a long tradition, and recently gained a lot of consideration in many fields since Web-based technologies enabled their collaborative building. Compared to mind maps, concept maps are diagrams that show the relations among concepts but in a hierarchical structure and without being concentrated on one single central topic.

These methods generally have difficulties in intersecting different visions, but since they do not impose the level of detail can have the vagueness necessary to achieve a sufficient grasp of the issue or of the entity under collaborative examination without triggering conflicts among different cognitive models.

Event Bushes

An interesting alternative method that can intersect different visions within the same diagram is the 'event bush' (Pshenichny, 2002, 2004, Pshenichny, et al., 2009). This intends to give a strict display of an area of reality and the corresponding domain of knowledge by means of the interaction of events in causal relations. This method can describe both natural phenomena and human activities, and is rather powerful in plotting, graphically, concurrent explications for the same phenomenon or observation. In fact, one "overlying" network can find its way through using some of the nodes and arcs of another network, each network corresponding to a different vision of the problem considered.

Using the same example given above in Diviacco et al. (2006), the mega debris flow seen in the Alexander channel (D) could be considered caused by the Eltanin asteroid event (E) or for example the consequence of margin instability due to the shallow level of gas hydrates (G) caused by a phase of global warming (W). These two explanations can coexist in the same diagram without the need to mention if one is true or false (or maybe both false or both true), while the node associated with the debris flow will be just one (D) and referred to by both explanations.

This promising approach has also the advantage of having a computable translation into Bayesian networks that could be very useful for example in hazard assessment (Pshenichny, et al., 2009). Bayesian networks need quantitative input from qualitative expertise of various scientists. Means to support this activity in CSCR using event bushes, have been reported by Diviacco and Pshenichny (2010, 2011).

Workflows

Another interesting class of diagrams that could help researchers during collaboration and that can play the part of a boundary object is that of workflows. Here nodes represent activities/tasks that need to be done in a specific order and timing. Human resources are assigned to activities/task and once their duties are accomplished the focus can shift to another activity. This type of diagram, in the perspective of pragmatics, is interesting and problematic at the same time because workflows are intended generally in a prescriptive sense and, therefore, when incompatible practices meet, balancing granularity is not an easy task.

From the Map to the Actual Work

Maps are means for coordinating collaboration. Leveraging the reduction of semantic content implied in considering nodes as labels, they allow concurrent cognitive models to project their vision on the work, overcoming the problem of meaning, which, as we saw above, can create large problems in the very basic activity of information sharing among partners.

To get closer to the actual work of collaboration, we need to enter the nodes and see what they can refer to or, considering them as containers, what can take place inside them.

The simplest approach would be to use them to isolate homogeneous work. In this sense partners with different paradigmatic knowledge would control their own nodes and, by avoiding those of the other partners, virtually avoid conflicts. In a broad sense, this can be considered collaborative work, but it is rather evident that in this perspective people actually work side by side; they are neighbours. Besides, this approach assumes that the collaboration can be split by a knowledge paradigm or disciplinary field in homogeneous areas, which is not always possible.

In the case of exploration geophysics, within the E&P industry, homogeneous and well defined areas can be isolated when "best practices" are used. These are standardized and prescriptive workflows that allow the assignment of employees upon their specific knowledge. Here, the possibility of referring to highly detailed definitions of the activities is very helpful in producing standardized outcomes. In fact, standardization is the key point, so that when a situation is not coded, things get complicated and paradigmatic conflicts might arise. We are moving to scientific research, where prescriptive flows and the assumption of nodes with homogeneous paradigmatic knowledge cannot hold. For example, large-scale international research projects often unite several research institutions that will provide the community individuals with a similar disciplinary scope, but with different views and traditions. Nodes cannot host homogeneous visions and therefore cannot be detailed.

In the Actor Network Theory (ANT) (see Law & Hassard, 1999; Callon, 1986), the concept of translation denotes what is put into action by the partners when positioning themselves in a community. The translation depends on the capability of building a network of allies through negotiation, which, besides personal skills, in practice requests the possibility to (1) discuss issues (2) referring to data.

Discussions must be as free and medium-agnostic as possible in order to avoid partners perceiving contributions as unbalanced, which can induce disaffection.

Asynchronous messaging systems, even in highly convoluted implementations, resemble the simple e-mail so that it is difficult to imagine researchers feeling manipulated by the medium. Discussions can be a purely abstract exchange of text or can also refer to tangible objects such as scientific data, files, images, or documents, so that both, (discussions and files) can be considered information pertaining to the specific issue currently under discussion. As in the example of a bookshop, where books are not simply dumped in a single room, but arranged in places that make sense, so that travel guides are all on the same shelves, and cookbooks on others, similarly, in the case of a system supporting collaborative e-research, information should also be accessible in ways that make sense, associating it to the topics, the issues, the tasks, or the concepts collaboratively addressed. In this perspective, labels in the map allow us to locate the "bookstore shelf" where information is stored.

This way the map becomes one of the faces of an imaginary, three-dimensional volume where information is located (Figure 1). Partners use the diagram to move through the collaborative space, find the labeled entity they are interested in, and by "entering" the latter they find all the information associated to it.

An interesting possibility offered by this perspective is to use multiple diagrams, simultaneously for the same information space, provided that the entities, or at least some of them, can be shared among them. An example of this could be having a mind map describing a research project on one face of the three dimensional volume and a workflow that would schedule its activities on another (Figure 2).

Synchronous systems, from traditional remote conferencing to those based on the metaphor of the shared desktop, generally, focus more on "brainstorming," which is the specific characteristic and aim of such systems, so that the problem

Figure 1. Joining the diagram and the messaging and storage facility, we create a three dimensional space where information becomes the third dimension of the diagram. Users follow the diagram to find the issue they are interested in and then by entering the corresponding node they can access the corresponding messages and files.

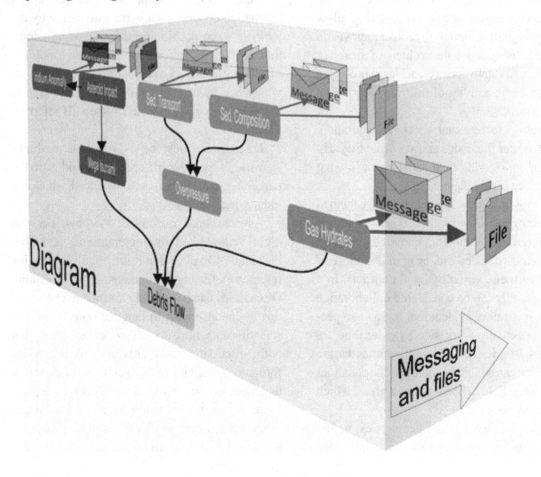

of possible conflicts of concurrent cognitive models is often overlooked. Following Star and Griesemer, a "laissez-faire" approach is not advisable; boundary objects (the maps) could be integrated into the systems to provide support for collaboration. This can be done in two ways: (1) partitioning the discussion into segments that can take place within homogeneous nodes, or (2) moving the discussion above the map while using the map as an agenda for the free discussion and as a help in locating data.

Requirements for a Possible Tool

We can try, at this point, to summarize the requirements of a tool aiming at supporting collaborative e-research activities in the light of what has been discussed so far.

- This tool should offer means to coordinate the activities using boundary objects as spatial/mind/concept maps or diagrams.
- These maps or diagrams should be built upon labels enabled to refer to an entity or concept even if it depends on different contexts.
- The tool should offer means to support negotiation among partners through:
  ○ remote interactivity, such as, for example, messaging services
  ○ data access, taking into account issues related to data transparency.

Figure 2. The same three-dimensional space of Figure 1 can be accessed from two different faces representing different diagrams but referring to the same subset of information

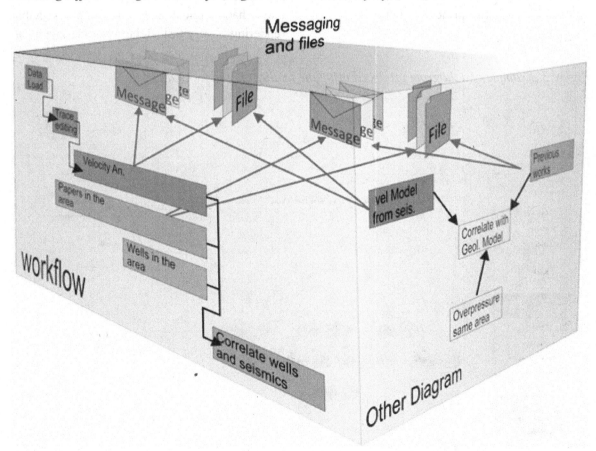

- Maps and diagrams should be linked to the messaging and data access systems through the use of labels as containers

Implementation

To test the above-mentioned ideas and to tune them to the outcomes of real working experiences, we decided to develop a system that we named COLLA. Colla in Italian means glue, and in fact, it is supposed to keep researchers together.

COLLA is a remote (Web-based), asynchronous (we are currently developing a syncronous extension) system that integrates the above-mentioned idea of maps as boundary objects with messaging, file management, and geophysical data visualization tools.

COLLA offers an internal facility for the creation of very simple and flexible diagrams with nodes and arcs that can be used to sketch different kinds of collaborative projects (Figure 3).

This method is very basic and cannot offer the richness of mind maps, or other more evolved diagrams, but has the advantage of offering a very quick and rough way of producing a diagram to start to work immediately. Its force lies in its simplicity, and its flexibility makes it match most of the practical cases seen so far. For example, it was used for controlled vocabulary building (Diviacco, et al., 2011b), in following the various steps of data processing for many geophysical research projects (Diviacco, 2007) or in building "ad hoc" scientific file repositories for many research projects. If no computation is expected from it, the built-in facility plots workflows too. It was also used in rather unexpected ways to manage several administrative issues and as an open forum to discuss workers union's policies.

Maps are available both as bitmaps with active areas, or, in the version we prefer and encourage, as Scalable Vector Graphics (SVG). SVG allows one to handle client-side vector graphics so that rendering is very fast. Being vectors, objects do

Figure 3. Example of a diagram produced using the facility offered by COLLA

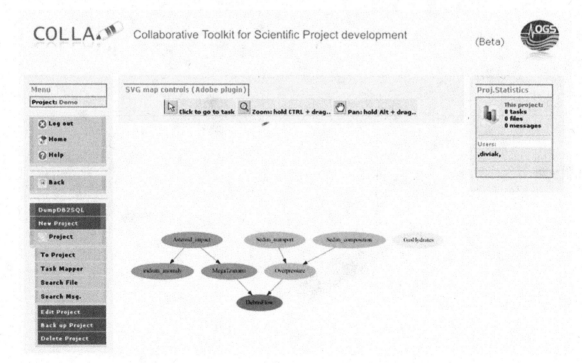

not show pixilation upon zooming (Figure 4). Each object behaves independently from the others and can embed functionalities as for example hyper-linking or scripting.

In the past, there have been concerns regarding the use of SVG (www.w3.org/Graphics/SVG) due to the lack of support by some web browsers. This introduced the need for a specific plug-in that was not available for all operating systems. This limitation has been lifted by the introduction of Batik (xmlgraphics.apache.org/batik), which allows java applets to be embedded in the web pages that can visualize SVG graphics, on any browser and on any operating system.

The internal diagram drawing facility offered by COLLA, upon creation of a new node, allocates a messaging and file management space that is made available and usable immediately by clicking on the node itself. Following the pragmatic (semiotic) approach described above, nodes are just labels for concepts, issues or activities, it

is the population of this space with information that builds its contingent meaning. Upon entering the node, partners can upload files, documents or scientific data and refer to them within COLLA's messaging system. The latter is a very simple e-mail-like tool that sends messages to all the partners enrolled in the project (Figure 5). Messages are stored in the database, listed on the web pages that correspond to each node, and at the same time forwarded to all partners via e-mail, with a specific format of the sender field that allows partners to easily sort out the received messages on their own mailing system, as they prefer. The message text contains a "magic link" (a Web link containing several parameters and keys to log in automatically) that allows the user to be driven inside the discussion thread directly from his mailing system, without the fuss of login and topic search.

Aside of the messaging facility, COLLA offers also uploading and versioning functionalities for

Figure 4. SVG-based diagrams allow to zoom without pixilation

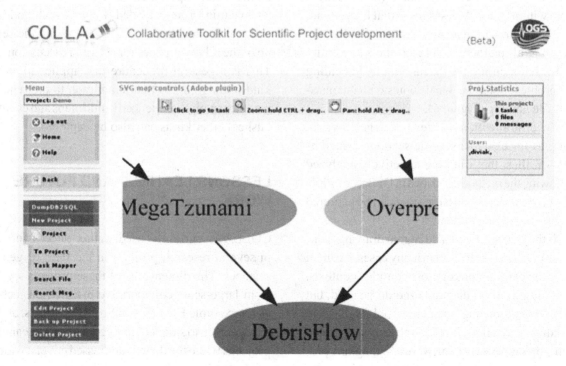

Figure 5. Messaging facility offered by COLLA

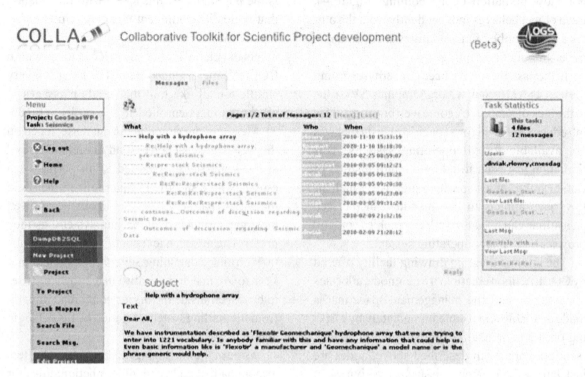

documents, images, geophysical data or files in general within the nodes. Once these are uploaded, they can be easily linked (not attached) from within COLLA messages so that files remain on the central system and are not duplicated, enabling all partners to refer to the same entity and version during the discussion, and avoiding the problem of having local copies with inconsistent file naming (Figure 6).

Specific attention was devoted to geophysical data, as for example seismic sections loaded as SEG-Y files, that can be interactively analyzed following the method described in Diviacco (2005, 2011) triggering discussions that can be captured by the messaging system.

If the "basic," internal, diagram drawing facility of COLLA is sufficient in many cases, it cannot meet the expectations of more complex contexts. Here, higher-level diagrams should be used, but instead of producing yet another tool for diagram building, we decided to rely on already well-tested and popular external software for diagram pro-

duction, while developing, within COLLA, the functionalities to ingest them and automatically set up the system upon their structure. For example, when a mind map is loaded (Figure 7), all nodes and arcs are handled as labels, triggering the set up of the relative spaces for files and discussions. This is a general procedure that applies to any kind of diagram, so that in addition to the types we extensively experienced (mind maps and event bushes) other kinds can also be explored.

LESSONS LEARNED AND FUTURE WORK

COLLA is currently used, rather successfully, in several research projects in the field of geosciences. The dimensions of these projects span from large-scale collaborative research projects as for example EU FP7 GeoSeas, Eurofleets, and CO2geoNet, to smaller scale geophysical research projects, while the themes addressed cover a wide

Figure 6. Data access and visualization within COLLA

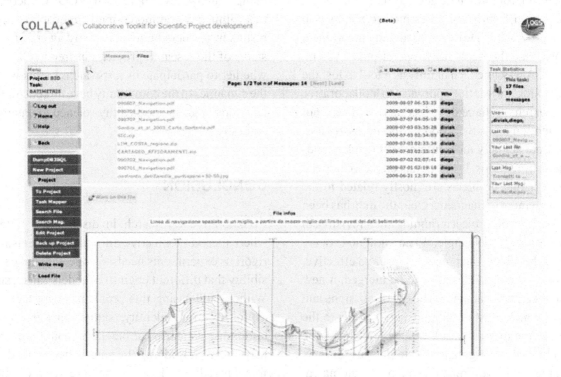

Figure 7. Integration, within COLLA, of a mind map generated with external software. It is possible to access the corresponding discussion and data upload space from each node.

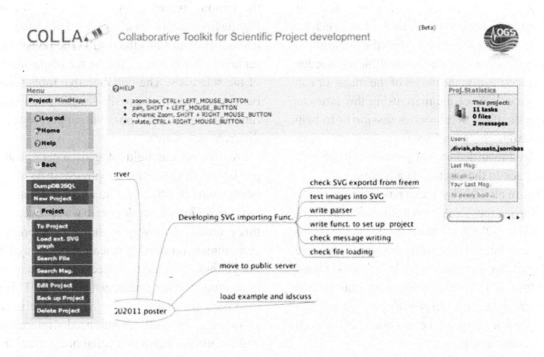

spectrum from structural geology to technological innovation, from hazard assessment to geophysical data processing. However, as already mentioned, more than being a fully operational system, COLLA was intended mainly as a tool to test the pragmatic (semiotic) approach to collaborative e-research we have described above. Then, not to mention our satisfaction for its successful use, we were actually more interested in understanding its limitations. In this perspective, we noticed that existing problems are mostly related to the management of diagrams. Once the map has been created and the project is running, their revision, in fact, is not always simple. When a new node or arc has to be added, the process is fast and effective. If two existing nodes have to be merged, a new one is created that inherits all the discussions and files, which most of the time corresponds to the will of the users. Instead, when a node has to be subdivided things get complicated because the new location of the information cannot be automated.

We are currently considering the extension of the discussion tool, from the current asynchronous modality so as to be able to provide spaces for synchronous collaboration. These discussions can be separated topic by topic, with the assumption of homogeneous or at least compatible knowledge and located within the nodes of the maps, or can take place "above" the map, using this latter as an agenda of the synchronous session or to help to locate data and files. Synchronous sessions can be logged/recorded so that partners will be able to get back to the discussion anytime.

We are also currently extending the possibilities of the geophysical data visualization facilities offered by COLLA to embed the possibility to directly annotate data using this as a map to organize further discussions. For example, interesting areas or features on a seismic section can be labeled and therefore linked to a "deeper" discussion and data management space as the seismic section itself can become a map.

User acceptance of COLLA has always been good, because it does not impose learning new

complicated software and mirrors COLLA activities within any common e-mail application. This results in partners being constantly aware of the status of the research project, but free to choose whether to participate or just watch. In this way, the dynamics of the community have no constraint and allow a good and healthy science to emerge naturally.

CONCLUSION

Collaborative e-research in disciplinary fields where there are objective difficulties in devising rigorous experiments needs to cope with the possibility that different cognitive models can clash. Without addressing this problem, many factors as for example identity, status, backgrounds, traditions, standards, or practices would prevent partners from bridging the gaps between the different paradigms. Even worse, researchers could be left at the mercy of a technology that could severely condition their will. This would reverse the famous quotation that it must be "the end that justifies the means," as we would have here a tool that conditions the result. The power must remain in the hands of and be the responsibility of the scientists. The collaborative tools should be as transparent as possible while at the same time providing all the possible support to bridge different paradigms.

Analyzing the field of geosciences, and in particular of exploration geophysics in depth, and being stimulated by a vast literature in epistemology and sociology, we devised a way to overcome this problem. This way is shown by supporting communication among researchers through the integration of boundary objects as diagrams and messaging and data management tools. This allows partners to move through representations of knowledge, find and access the needed information and discuss the status of a collaborative research.

This perspective was implemented in a Web-based system (COLLA) that is currently used within several international collaborative research initiatives, where it has allowed collaborative research to emerge naturally.

AKNOWLEDGMENT

Alessandro Busato, Daniel Praeg, Vesna Pahor, Živa Pahor, Jaren Diviacco, Ilija Diviacco.

REFERENCES

Ackerman, M. (2000). The intellectual challenge of CSCW: The gap between social requirements and technical feasibility. *Human-Computer Interaction*, *15*, 179–203. doi:10.1207/S15327051HCI1523_5

Baddeley, M. C., Curtis, A., & Wood, R. (2004). An introduction to prior information derived from probabilistic judgments: Elicitation of knowledge, cognitive bias and herding. *Geological Society*, *239*, 15-27.

Barry, K. M., Cavers, D. A., & Kneale, C. W. (1975). Recommended standards for digital tape formats. *Geophysics*, *40*(2), 344–35. doi:10.1190/1.1440530

Becher, T., & Trowler, P. R. (2001). *Academic tribes and territories intellectual enquiry and culture of disciplines*. Buckingham, UK: The Society for Research into Higher Education and Open University Press.

Berners-Lee, T., Hendler, J., & Lassila, O. (2001). The semantic web. *Scientific American Magazine*. Retrieved from http://www.scientificamerican.com.

Beyer, H., & Holtzblatt, K. (1998). *Contextual design: Defining customer centered systems*. New York, NY: Academic Press.

Birnholtz, J. P. (2006). What does it mean to be an author? The intersection of credit, contribution, and collaboration in science. *Journal of the American Society for Information Science and Technology*, *57*(13), 1758–1770. doi:10.1002/asi.20380

Bloor, D. (1976). *Knowledge and social imagery*. London, UK: Routledge.

Bond, C. E., Shipton, Z. K., Gibbs, A. D., & Jones, S. (2008). Structural models: Optimizing risk analysis by understanding conceptual uncertainty. *First Break*, *26*, 65–71.

Callon, M. (1986). Some elements of a sociology of translation: Domestication of the scallops and the fishermen of St. Brieuc Bay. In *Power, Action and Belief: A New Sociology of Knowledge* (pp. 196–233). London: Routledge & Kegan Paul.

Carnap, R. (1947). *Meaning and necessity*. Chicago, IL: The University of Chicago Press.

Chompalov, I., Genuth, J., & Shrum. (2002). The organization of scientific collaborations. *Research Policy*, *31*, 749–767. doi:10.1016/S0048-7333(01)00145-7

David, P. A., & Bunn, J. A. (1988). The economics of gateway technologies and network evolution. *Information Economics and Policy*, *3*, 165–202. doi:10.1016/0167-6245(88)90024-8

Diviacco, P. (2005). An open source, web based, simple solution for seismic data dissemination, and collaborative research. *Computers & Geosciences*, *31*(5), 599–605. doi:10.1016/j.cageo.2004.11.008

Diviacco, P. (2007). *Perspective in distributed, web based seismic data handling for collaborative scientific research*. Paper presented at the 69th EAGE International Conference. London, UK.

Diviacco, P. (2011). *Towards a collaborative research data space in Geophysics*. Mediterranean Marine Sciences.

Diviacco, P., Lowry, R., & Leadbetter, A. (2011b). Collaborative work and tools towards wide scientific community driven metadata model and vocabulary building. In *Geophysical Research Abstracts* (*Vol. 12*). Vienna, Austria: EGU.

Diviacco, P., & Pshenichny, C. A. (2010). Concept-referenced spaces in computer-supported collaborative work. In *Geophysical Research Abstracts* (*Vol. 12*). Vienna, Austria: EGU.

Diviacco, P., & Pshenichny, C. A. (2011). A case study on the use of event bushes as a formal representation for computer supported collaborative work in the geosciences. In *Geophysical Research Abstracts* (*Vol. 12*). Vienna, Austria: EGU.

Diviacco, P., Rebesco, M., & Camerlenghi, A. (2006). Late pliocene mega debris flow deposit and related fluid escapes identified on the antarctic peninsula continental margin by seismic reflection data analysis. *Marine Geophysical Researches*, *27*(2), 109–128. doi:10.1007/s11001-005-3136-8

Dove, M. T., & de Leeuw, N. H. (2005). Grid computing and molecular simulations: The vision of the eMinerals project. *Molecular Simulation*, *31*(5), 297–301. doi:10.1080/08927020500065801

Dummet, M. (1993). *Origins of analytical philosophy*. London, UK: Duckworth.

Eco, U. (1981). Guessing: From Aristotle to Sherlock Holmes. *Versus, 30*.

Engelhardt, W., & Zimmerman, J. (1982). *Theory of earth science*. Cambridge, UK: Cambridge University Press.

Farooq, U., Ganoe, C., Carroll, J., & Giles, L. (2007). Supporting distributed scientific collaboration: Implications for designing the CiteSeer collaboratory. In *Proceedings of the 40th Annual Hawaii International Conference on System Sciences (HICSS 2007)*. IEEE Computer Society.

Feyerabend, P. (1975). *Against method*. London, UK: Verso.

Foster, I., & Kesselman, C. (1998). *The grid: Blueprint for a new computing infrastructure*. New York, NY: Morgan-Kaufman.

Francesco, D. (1994). *Aspetti logico-linguisitici dell'impresa scientifica*. Paper presented at Introduzione alla Filosofia della Scienza. Bompiani, Italy.

Frege, G. (1892). *Über sinn und bedeutung*. Milano, Italy: Bompiani.

Frodeman, R. (1995). Geological reasoning: Geology as an interpretive and historical science. *Bulletin of the Geological Society of America, 107*, 960–968. doi:10.1130/0016-7606(1995)107<0960:GRGAAI>2.3.CO;2

Galison, P. L., & Stump, J. D. (1996). *The disunity of science: Boundaries, context and power*. Palo Alto, CA: Stanford University Press.

Ginzburg, C. (1989). *Clues, myths and the historical method*. Baltimore, MD: Johns Hopkins University Press.

Golder, S., & Huberman, B. A. (2005). The structure of collaborative tagging systems. *HP Labs Technical Report*. Retrieved august 2011 from http://www.hpl.hp.com/research/idl/papaers/tags.

Gruber, T. R. (1995). Toward principles for the design of ontologies used for knowledge sharing. *International Journal of Human-Computer Studies, 43*(4-5), 907–928. doi:10.1006/ijhc.1995.1081

Hameed, A., Preece, A., & Sleeman, D. (2003). Ontology reconciliation. In Staab, S., & Studer, R. (Eds.), *Handbook on Ontologies in Information Systems* (pp. 231–250). Berlin, Germany: Springer Verlag.

Hanson, N. R. (1971). *Observation and explanation: A guide to philosophy of science*. New York, NY: Harper & Row.

Harper, D. (1987). *The nature of work: Working knowledge*. Chicago, IL: University of Chicago.

Hume, D. (1910). *An enquiry concerning human understanding*. New York, NY: P. F. Collier & Son.

Jäschke, R., Hotho, A., Schmidtz, C., Ganter, B., & Stumme, G. (2008). Discovering shared conceptualizations in folksonomies. *Web Semantics Science Services and Agents on the World Wide Web, 6*(1), 38–53. doi:10.1016/j.websem.2007.11.004

Kelso, J. (2003). eVOC: A controlled vocabulary for unifying gene expression data. *Genome Research, 13*, 1222–1230. doi:10.1101/gr.985203

Korta, Kepa, & Perry, J. (2011). Pragmatics. In E. N. Zalta (Ed.), *The Stanford Encyclopedia of Philosophy*. Palo Alto, CA: Stanford University.

Kötter, R. (2001). Neuroscience databases: Tools for exploring brain structure-function relationships. *Philosophical Transactions of the Royal Society B, 356*, 1111–1120. doi:10.1098/rstb.2001.0902

Kovács, G., & Spens, K. M. (2005). Abductive reasoning in logistics research. *International Journal of Physical Distribution and Logistics Management, 35*(2), 132–144. doi:10.1108/09600030510590318

Kripke, S. A. (1972). Naming and necessity. In Davidson, D., & Harman, G. (Eds.), *Semantics of Natural Language*. Dordrecht, The Netherlands: Reidel. doi:10.1007/978-94-010-2557-7_9

Kuhn, T. S. (1962). *The structure of scientific revolutions*. Chicago, IL: University of Chicago Press.

Lakatos, I. (1970). Falsification and the methodology of scientific research programmes. In Lakatos & Musgrave (Eds.), *Criticism and the Growth of Knowledge*. Cambridge, UK: Cambridge University Press.

Latour, B., & Woolgar, S. (1979). *Laboratory life: The construction of scientific facts*. Princeton, NJ: Princeton University Press.

Law, J., & Hassard, J. (1999). *The actor network theory*. Oxford, UK: Blackwell Publishing.

Lawlor, D. A., Davey Smith, G., & Ebrahim, S. (2004). Commentary: The hormone replacement-coronary heart disease conundrum: Is this the death of observational epidemiology? *International Journal of Epidemiology, 33*(3), 464–467. doi:10.1093/ije/dyh124

Loizou, N. (2002). A post-well analysis of recent years exploration drilling in the Atlantic Margin. In *Sharp IOR E-Newsletter, no. 3*. London, UK: DTI Oil and Gas Directorate.

Lowry, R., Bermudez, L., & Graybeal, J. (2006). *Semantic interoperability: A goal for marine data management*. Paper presented at ICES CM 2006: Environmental and Fisheries Data Management, Access, and Integration. Maastricht, The Netherlands.

Margolis, S. V., Claeys, P. F., & Kyte, F. T. (1991). Microtektites, mictokrystites and spinels from a late pliocene asteroid impact in the southern ocean. *Science, 251*, 1594–1597. doi:10.1126/science.251.5001.1594

Martone, M. E., Gupta, A., & Ellisman, H. (2004). e-Neurosceince: Challenges and thìriumphs in integrating distributed data from molecules to brains. *Nature Neuroscience, 7*, 467–472. doi:10.1038/nn1229

Meriluoto, J. (2003). *Knowledge management and information system*. Paper presented at ICE 2003 Conference. Helsinki, Finland.

Morris, C. (1971). *Foundations of the theory of signs*. Chicago, IL: University of Chicago Press.

Nadin, M. (1987). Pragmatics in the semiotic frame. In Stachowiak, H. (Ed.), *Pragmatik: Handbuch pragmatischen denkens* (pp. 148–170). Hamburg, Germany: Felix Meiner.

Nentwich, M. (2003). *Cyberscience: Research in the age of the internet*. Vienna, Austria: Austrian Academy of Science.

Olson, J. S., Ellisman, M., James, M., Grethe, J. S., & Puetz, M. (2008). Biomedical informatics research network (BIRN). In Olson, G. M., Zimmerman, A., & Bos, N. (Eds.), *Scientific Collaboration on the Internet*. Cambridge, MA: MIT Press.

Orlowski, W. (1992). Learning from notes: Organizational issues in groupware implementation. In *Proceedings of CSCW 1992*. CSCW Press.

Paay, J., Sterling, L., Vetere, F., Howard, S. T., & Boettcher, A. (2009). Enginering the social: The role of shared artifacts. *International Journal of Human-Computer Studies*, *67*, 437–454. doi:10.1016/j.ijhcs.2008.12.002

Pasini, E. (1997). Arcanum artis inveniendi: Leibniz and analysis. In *Analysis and Synthesis in Mathematics*. Dordrecht, The Netherlands: Kluwer. doi:10.1007/978-94-011-3977-9_2

Patel, V. L., Arocha, J. F., & Zhang, J. (2004). Thinking and reasoning in medicine. In Holyoak, K. (Ed.), *Cambridge Handbook of Thinking and Reasoning*. Cambridge, UK: Cambridge University Press.

Peirce, C. S. (1931). *Collected papers*. Cambridge, MA: Harvard University Press.

Polanyi, M. (1966). *The tacit dimension*. New York, NY: Anchor Day Books.

Popper, K. (1963). *Conjectures and refutations*. London, UK: Routledge.

Popper, K. (1979). *Die beiden grundprobleme der erkenntnistheorie*. Milano, Italy: Il Saggiatore.

Pratt, W., Reddy, M. C., McDonald, D. W., Tarczy-Hornoch, P., & Gennari, J. H. (2004). Incorporating ideas from computer-supported cooperative work. *Journal of Biomedical Informatics*, *37*(2), 128–137. doi:10.1016/j.jbi.2004.04.001

Pshenichny, C. A. (2002). Investigation of geological reasoning as a new objective of geosciences. *Earth Science Computer Applications*, *17*(11), 1–3.

Pshenichny, C. A. (2004). Classical logic and the problem of uncertainty. *Geological Society, 239*, 111-126.

Pshenichny, C. A. (2009). The event bush as a semantic-based numerical approach to natural hazard assessment (exemplified by volcanology) 2009. *Computer and GeoSciences*, *35*(5), 1017–1034. doi:10.1016/j.cageo.2008.01.009

Putnam, H. (1975). *Mind, language and reality: Philosophical papers (Vol. 2)*. Cambridge, UK: Cambridge University Press. doi:10.1017/CBO9780511625251

Ribes, D., & Bowker, G. (2009). Between meaning and machine: Learning to represent the knowledge of communities. *Information and Organization*. Retrieved from http://www.sis.pitt.edu/~gbowker/publications/Ribes%20Bowker%20-%20Between%20Meaning%20and%20Machine.pdf.

Russell, B. (1905). *On denoting: Mind (Vol. 14)*. Oxford, UK: Basil Blackwell.

Salmon, W. C. (1990). *Four decades of scientific explanation*. Minneapolis, MN: The University of Minnesota Press.

Shannon, C. E., & Weaver, W. (1949). *A mathematical model of communication*. Chicago, IL: University of Illinois Press.

Shelley, C. (1996). Visual abductive reasoning in archaeology. *Philosophy of Science*, *63*(2), 278–301. doi:10.1086/289913

Sheriff, R. E. (1973). *Encyclopedic dictionary of exploration geophysics*. Tulsa, OK: The Society of Exploration Geophysics.

Specia, L., & Motta, E. (2007). Integrating folksonomies with the semantic web. In *Proceedings of the European Semantic Web Conference*. ESWC Press.

Star, S. L., & Griesemer, J. R. (1989). Institutional ecology, translations and boundary objects: Amateurs and professionals in Berkeley s museum of vertebrate zoology. *Social Studies of Science*, *19*(4), 387–420. doi:10.1177/030631289019003001

Steels, L. (2006). Collaborative tagging as distributed cognition. *Pragmatics & Cognition, 14*(2), 275–285. doi:10.1075/pc.14.2.09ste

Suchman, L. A. (1987). *Plans and situated actions: The problem of human-machine communication.* Cambridge, UK: Cambridge University Press.

Taylor, C. (1992). *To follow a rule in critical perspectives.* Chicago, IL: University of Chicago Press.

Weng, C., Gennari, J. H., & Fridsma, D. B. (2007). User-centered semantic harmonization: A case study. *Journal of Biomedical Informatics, 40*(3), 353–364. doi:10.1016/j.jbi.2007.03.004

Whitley, R. (2000). *The intellectual and social organization of the sciences.* Oxford, UK: Clarendon Press.

Woo, G. (1999). *The mathematics of natural catastrophes.* London, UK: Imperial College Press. doi:10.1142/9781860943867

Xu, B., Lin, H., Chiu, L., Hu, Y., Zhu, J., Hu, M., & Cui, W. (2011). Collaborative virtual geographic environments: A case study of air pollution simulation. *Information Sciences, 181,* 2231–2246. doi:10.1016/j.ins.2011.01.017

Chapter 13

Effects of the Drewlite CSCL Platform on Students' Learning Outcomes

Omid Noroozi
Wageningen University, The Netherlands

Martin Mulder
Wageningen University, The Netherlands

Harm Biemans
Wageningen University, The Netherlands

Vitaliy Popov
Wageningen University, The Netherlands

Maria C. Busstra
Wageningen University, The Netherlands

Mohammad Chizari
Tarbiat Modares University, Iran

ABSTRACT

This chapter presents a case study of Computer Supported Collaborative Learning (CSCL) in the field of human nutrition and health at Wageningen University in the Netherlands. More specifically, this study investigates the effect of the type of collaboration (personal discussion in front of a shared computer vs. online discussion) in CSCL on students' learning outcomes. A pre-test, post-test design was used. Eighty-two students were asked (as an individual pre-test) to design and analyze a study which evaluates a certain dietary assessment method. Subsequently, they were asked to discuss their evaluation studies in randomized pairs. The pairs in one group discussed their task results online and the pairs in the other group discussed their results face-to-face while sharing one computer, in both cases using the CSCL platform Drewlite. As an individual post-test, students had to re-design and re-analyze the same evaluation study. Learning outcomes were measured based on the results of teachers' regular evaluation of students' achievements as well as on the quality of the students' knowledge construction. The results showed that both teachers' marks and the quality of knowledge construction of all students improved significantly from pre-test to post-test. However, the type of collaboration had no significantly different effect. Furthermore, the scores on knowledge construction were consistent with exam results as obtained by teachers' evaluations.

DOI: 10.4018/978-1-4666-0125-3.ch013

INTRODUCTION

With the arrival of the knowledge-based era, the swift growth of information and communication technology, and the rapid growth and widespread accessibility of the World Wide Web, it is inevitable that professionals in all fields will be confronted with rapidly changing global problems and complex issues. These complexities call for appropriate action. In the field of education, it is believed that proper educational designs have the potential to prepare and train students to become capable and qualified professionals, who can analyze, conceptualize, synthesize, and cope with complex and authentic problems (Jacobson & Wilensky, 2006).

The use of new collaborative technologies as teaching and learning tools is now quickly increasing in education. According to many scholars in the field of learning science, collaborative online learning environments prepare learners to adjust to and cope with today's complex issues. Platforms for online learning environments have evolved to increase deep learning and student knowledge construction. They can also encourage students to discuss their ideas, concepts, and problems from different perspectives and viewpoints in order to re-construct and co-construct knowledge while solving authentic and complex problems (Noroozi, Biemans, Busstra, Mulder, & Chizari, 2011; Veldhuis-Diermanse, Biemans, Mulder, & Mahdizadeh, 2006). In collaborative online learning environments, knowledge can be constructed through structuring, elaborating, and evaluating concepts and ideas, eliciting and summarizing information, as well as connecting concepts, facts, and ideas about the topic (Veldhuis-Diermanse, et al., 2006). That is why some theoretical and empirical evidence favors more online instructional settings than traditional (face to-face) settings with respect to knowledge construction processes and outcomes (Andriessen, Baker, & Suthers, 2003; Joiner & Jones, 2003; Kanselaar, De Jong, Andriessen, & Goodyear, 2000; Kirschner, Buckingham-Shum, & Carr, 2003).

However, simply putting learners in a group to work together on an authentic and complex problem in an online learning environment is not always beneficial for learning, knowledge construction or problem solving (Kirschner, Beers, Boshuizen, & Gijselaers, 2008; Kreijns, Kirschner, & Jochems, 2003; Slof, Erkens, Kirschner, Jaspers, & Janssen, 2010). Empirical findings show that online collaborative learners generally encounter communication and coordination problems (Doerry, 1996; Janssen, Erkens, Kanselaar, & Jaspers, 2007) due to the reduced bandwidth or available modes of interaction associated with online learning, resulting in degradation of problem solving performance and knowledge construction (Baltes, Dickson, Sherman, Bauer, & LaGanke, 2002; Doerry, 1996). In response to this, a variety of instructional approaches (e.g. shared workspaces, game-based learning, awareness features, knowledge representations, scripts) has been developed to promote learning performance in online collaborative learning environments. These types of learning arrangements have collectively been named Computer Supported Collaborative Learning (CSCL), which is seen as a promising context in which to facilitate and foster student knowledge construction (Andriessen, et al., 2003; Stegmann, Weinberger & Fischer, 2007; Veerman, 2000). CSCL has recently been recognized as an important and achievable instructional strategy to support learning and thereby help learners achieve a deeper understanding. In today's information and communication era, CSCL is gradually moving into the mainstream of educational designs, as it is currently receiving enormous attention in universities and schools throughout the world (Noroozi, Mulder, Biemans, & Chizari, 2009; Weinberger, Ertl, Fischer, & Mandl, 2005; Weinberger, Stegmann, Fischer, & Mandl, 2007). When students are expected to solve authentic and complex problems and reach a deeper understanding, CSCL provides a fruitful environment in which to integrate different perspectives, theories and ideas with their own arguments, counter-arguments, clarifications, and discussions (Noroozi & Busstra, et al., in press; Noroozi & Weinberger, et al., in press; Noroozi, Biemans, Weinberger, Mulder, Popov, & Chizari, 2011; Van Bruggen, 2003).

BENEFITS OF ONLINE PLATFORMS FOR COLLABORATIVE LEARNING IN EDUCATIONAL RESEARCH

Researchers have used various forms of online platforms to support collaborative learning in educational research. Collaborative online or e-learning platforms such as CSCL provide various opportunities for researchers, including the following:

Researchers and scholars in the field of educational research can use various sorts of e-learning and online platforms to promote collaborative learning. They created, for example, asynchronous modes of communication (e.g. ALLAIRE FORUM, KNOWLEDGE FORUM, COLLABORATORY NOTEBOOK, DUNES) to engage learners in high-quality argumentative processes (Clark, D'Angelo, & Menekse, 2009; Clark, Sampson, Weinberger, & Erkens, 2007), and to promote individual knowledge construction (Schellens & Valcke, 2006). They created synchronous modes of communication (e.g. TC3, SENSEMAKER, VCRI, DUNES, DIGALO, DREW, BELVEDERE, NETMEETING, DREWLITE) for coordinating and facilitating task-oriented activities (Janssen, et al., 2007), as well as engaging learners in deep and elaborated discussions (Munneke, Andriessen, Kanselaar, & Kirschner 2007).

Using collaborative online and e-learning platforms enables researchers and scholars to include enriched learning materials in the learning environment remotely without physical interaction. For example, technology-enhanced learning environments provide enriched access to information that instructs learners in how to deal properly with the learning task as well as other materials that boost the authenticity of the learning. Researchers have

the opportunity to embed various sorts of information and internet-based sources such as structured knowledge bases, unstructured knowledge bases, media-rich representations, and visualizations to provide learners with rich data to support successful interactions.

Using collaborative online and e-learning platforms enables researchers and scholars with similar interests to run simultaneous educational projects in institutional settings. In the scientific literature we can see many international projects that have been conducted in educational settings using collaborative online and e-learning platforms.

Researchers and scholars with similar interests in the field of educational research can collaboratively create various sorts of e-learning and online platforms, implement them simultaneously in their institutional settings, monitor the processes, evaluate, and if necessary modify them for future joint collaboration without a need for physical presence and interaction.

Using collaborative online and e-learning platforms facilitates quantitative and qualitative data analysis for researchers and scholars with similar interests in educational research. All researchers with similar interests can actively participate and contribute in the processes of the data analysis using technology-enhanced environments. Furthermore, the data in an online platform can be analyzed much faster than in traditional platforms using computerized systems.

Despite all the befits of online learning platforms, it is assumed that the lack of physical, mental and psychological signs and the absence of nonverbal communication in these environments may hamper the communication process (Kreijns, et al., 2003; O'Conaill & Whittaker, 1997), which in turn might limit the effectiveness of the learning processes and outcomes (Van Amelsvoort, 2006; Kiesler, 1986; Coffin & O'Halloran, 2009). Furthermore, social interaction could be missing to a large extent in CSCL (Kreijns, et al., 2003), while it is perceived as being important in learning processes and outcomes (Van Amelsvoort, 2006). This study thus investigates the effect of type of collaboration (Personal Discussion "PD" in front of a shared computer vs. Online Discussion "OD") in CSCL on students' learning outcomes. The main research question for this study is: Does type of collaboration (PD vs. OD) in CSCL with Drewlite platform affect students' exam marks as assessed by teachers, regular evaluation and students' quality of knowledge construction in a real educational setting?

METHOD

The study took place in an international university in The Netherlands with a student body encompassing over 100 nationalities, namely Wageningen University. About a third of the MSc students and one half of the PhD students come from abroad. This university offers a broad range of research activities and a unique combination of academic and professional education that is embedded in a coherent system of bachelor, master and PhD programs. With its central focus on "healthy food and a healthy living environment," the university stimulates students to combine the natural and social sciences; from plant sciences to economics and from food ingredients technology to sociology. Participants in this study were eighty-two (82) students enrolled in the 168-hour course "Exposure assessment in nutrition and health research" organized by the division of human nutrition. In this 6 ECTS course, students acquire insight into the methodology of assessing food and nutrient intake. The main focus of this course is on knowledge and skills related to the design, analysis and interpretation of validation and reproducibility studies. Of the 82 course participants about 50% were third-year bachelor students and the other 50% were first-year master students, both from the Nutrition and Health program. The number of master and bachelor students was about equal

in the PD and OD groups, as was the number of Dutch and foreign (i.e. non-Dutch) students.

The Drewlite platform was used as the CSCL platform for this study. The Drewlite platform is a simplified version of Drew, which was developed within the Scale project to support argumentative CSCL (Corbel, Jaillon, Serpaggi, Baker, Quignard, Lund, & Séjourné, 2002). The 'lite' version is less elaborate in managing sessions and traces, which were irrelevant in our study. The platform comprises various tools for communication, collaboration, and argumentation such as chat, graph, text board, view board, and multi modules. The modules can be used both individually and collectively. For the present study both individual and collaborative versions were used. With respect to the individual version, the graph module was used. With the graph module, the student could build boxes and draw arrows between the boxes in a diagram, in this case to construct a representation of key factors for the given assessment. Every box and arrow could be filled with text. The student could also add comments and express his or her opinion in favor of or against given arguments.

In this study, the dependent variable was learning outcomes in terms of teachers' regular evaluation of students' achievements as well as quality of knowledge construction. To investigate the effect of different modes of collaboration on knowledge construction a pre-test, post-test design was used. After receiving guidelines and instructions, students were given a 20-minute introduction on working with the CSCL platform. As a pre-test (45 minutes), students were asked to individually design and analyze the essential aspects of an evaluation study which aimed to evaluate a certain dietary assessment method (a 24-h recall) that was used to assess protein intake in a population of immigrants in the Netherlands. The students were then randomly assigned to pairs to discuss their results under either the Personal Discussion (PD) or Online Discussion (OD) condition using the CSCL platform. The two students in each pair discussed the essential aspects of the evaluation studies they had developed individually during the pre-test. The discussions took 90 minutes, during which the CSCL platform was used. Students within the OD condition used the chat tool in the CSCL platform as the discussion platform. Students within the PD condition viewed the screens of the evaluation studies they designed in the CSCL platform on a desktop computer in front of them. The OD students did not have personal (face-to-face) contact, whereas the PD students were sitting together behind the same computer. The pairs of students in the OD condition were separated in two different laboratory rooms to prevent personal contact.

Finally, a post-test took place in which students were asked to re-design and re-analyze the same evaluation study individually (45 minutes) based on what they had learned during the collaboration. In our study, pairs of students in both OD and PD conditions did not know each other in advance and we did not try to homogenize the pair composition with respect to knowledge awareness. Pairs of students in the OD condition could introduce themselves to one another through online chatting and pairs of students in the PD condition could introduce themselves in person when they were sitting behind the same computer to discuss their own individually made graphs. Furthermore, as the student group was relatively large, and the students were randomly divided over the different conditions, we assumed that possible differences in awareness would be equally distributed.

Learning outcomes were measured based on the results of teachers' regular evaluation of students' achievements as well as their quality of knowledge construction using a developed coding scheme. First, an overall mark was given by teachers to determine which students passed or failed the interim exam in the same way that teachers usually assess their students. Then, using teachers' regular evaluation of students' performances, each student received a score from 1 to 10 both for the pre-test and post-test. Subsequently, the mean quality scores for students' performances were calculated for each individual student by measuring the difference in mean quality score from pre-test to post-test $(M = t2-t1)$. Teachers were not aware of the learning conditions nor of the characteristics of the students during the assessment.

A validated analysis scheme (Veldhuis-Diermanse, 2002) was used to assess the quality of students' knowledge construction which is an elaborated version of the SOLO taxonomy (Biggs & Collis, 1982). SOLO stands for the Structure of the Observed Learning Outcome and is a way of classifying learning outcomes in terms of their complexity. The SOLO taxonomy aims to analyze the quality of students' contributions to reflect their quality of knowledge construction regardless of the content area (Biggs & Collis, 1982). It provides a systematic way of unfolding how a student's quality of knowledge construction develops in complexity when handling complex tasks, particularly the sort of tasks undertaken in school. As students proceed in their learning process, the outcomes of their learning display comparable stages of increasing structural complexity. Since the SOLO levels are not context dependent, the taxonomy can be applied across a range of disciplines. The coding scheme of Veldhuis-Diermanse provided a series of categories for ranking the complexity of students' contributions as a proxy of their level of knowledge construction when performing learning tasks in online environments. This coding scheme categorizes the contributions of students into five hierarchical levels, and within each level into one or more subcategories that characterize the nature of the response:

- Level A: Extended Abstract
  Subcategories: Reflect/conclude/generalize/
      theorize/hypothesize
- Level B: Relational
  Subcategories: Explain, relate/combine,
      compare/contrast

- Level C: Multi-Structural
  Subcategories: List/enumerate/number, describe/organize, classify
- Level D: Uni-Structural
  Subcategories: Identify/define
- Level E: Pre-Structural (no subcategories), i.e. irrelevant answers.

To assess the quality of the learning outcomes, the contributions of students (both in pre-test and post-test) were segmented into meaningful units. Each unit was scored according to the coding scheme. Student contributions were given points according to their level in the coding scheme: 1 point for category E contributions, 2 points for D, 3 for C, 4 for B, and 5 for A-level contributions. Subsequently, the points for the contributions of each student were added together and this number was then divided by the number of meaningful units, which resulted in an individual mean score for the quality of knowledge construction in the pre-test and a mean quality score for the post-test (see Busstra, Geelen, Noroozi, Biemans, De Vries, & van 't Veer, 2010; Mahdizadeh, 2007; Noroozi, Biemans, Mulder, & Chizari, 2010a, 2010b; Noroozi, et al., 2011; Veldhuis-Diermanse, et al., 2006 for more information and examples on data analysis). Each student could thus get a score from 1 to 5 both for the pre-test and post-test for the quality of knowledge construction. Finally, a mean quality score for knowledge gain was calculated for each student by measuring the difference in mean quality score from pre-test to post-test ($M = t2\text{-}t1$). Scores of two inactive students were excluded from the analysis due to the limited number of their contributions, which means that for the data analysis 80 students were included in the study.

Two coders analyzed the contributions using the coding scheme described above. They were not aware of the learning conditions or of the characteristics of the students. The teachers of the course helped coders to get in-depth insight into the content-related topics of the learning tasks (on exposure assessment in nutrition and health research). The main teacher of the course and her assistant evaluated students' contributions to give marks to students and determine which students passed or failed the post-test in the same way that teachers usually assess their students. Both intra-analyses and the reliability were calculated for various signifiers and levels of knowledge construction. Cohen's kappa was employed as a reliability index of inter-rater agreement, which was 0.78 for pre-test and 0.81 for post-test. Moreover, intra-coder test-retest reliability was calculated for 20% of the contributions. This resulted in identical scores in 85% of the contributions. For both inter- and intra-analyses, the reliability was deemed sufficient. ANOVA was used to assess the prior knowledge of students in both conditions (OD and PD) in terms of quality of knowledge construction and students' regular marks by teachers as measured by the pre-test. The ANOVA test for repeated measurement was used to assess the effects of the two collaborative learning conditions on the quality improvement of knowledge construction and students' regular marks by teachers as measured by pre-test-post-test.

RESULTS

Students in the OD and PD conditions did not differ significantly with respect to their pre-test scores ($F = 0.93$; $p = .34$ based on teachers' marks; $F = 0.009$; $p = .92$ based on Veldhuis-Diermanse coding scheme): there thus appeared to be no significant differences with respect to prior knowledge between students in the OD condition ($M = 5.91$; $SD = 1.60$ based on teachers' marks; $M = 3.00$; $SD = 0.48$ based on Veldhuis-Diermanse coding scheme) and students in the PD condition ($M = 5.61$; $SD = 1.21$ based on teachers' marks; $M = 2.99$; $SD = 0.35$ based on Veldhuis-Diermanse coding scheme).

Both the teachers' marks and the quality of knowledge construction of all students improved significantly (F = 82.19; p < .01; MT1 = 5.76; MT2 = 6.83 based on teachers' marks; F = 4.40; p < .05; MT1 = 3.00; MT2 = 3.09 based on Veldhuis-Diermanse coding scheme) from pre-test to post-test. The improvement of students' performance based on the teachers' marks was about equal under the OD condition (MT1 = 5.91; MT2 = 6.98) compared to students under the PD condition (MT1 = 5.61; MT2 = 6.68) (F = 0.004; p = .95) (see Figure 1 for a graphical representation of this result).

The knowledge construction quality improvement of students based on the Veldhuis-Diermanse coding scheme under the OD condition (MT1 = 3.00; MT2 = 3.16) was also about equal to that of students under the PD condition (MT1 = 2.99; MT2 = 3.01) (F = 2.81; p = .10). (Figure 2 shows a graphical representation of this result). In other words, both types of collaborative learning facilitated improvement in students' scores both in terms of teachers' marks and the Veldhuis-Diermanse coding scheme for knowledge construction. In the latter category, the quality improvement was somewhat larger under the OD condition than under the PD condition, but the difference was not statistically significant.

CONCLUSION AND DISCUSSION

This study revealed that a particular synchronous CSCL platform, Drewlite, has the capability to promote learning regardless of type of collaboration. Other researchers, e.g. Clark et al. (2007), have also confirmed that synchronous modes of communication provide learners with an equal opportunity to participate in the learning process with a high degree of integration. Furthermore, other sorts of synchronous platforms (e.g. NetMeeting and Belvédère) have also been found to promote argumentative learning (Veerman, 2000). This is why many researchers now use these platforms in their educational settings. We found that both the students' scores based on teachers' marks and their quality of knowledge construction improved significantly over time under collaborative learning conditions, both through Online Discussions (OD) within the CSCL platform and through per-

Figure 1. Mean scores of students evaluation based on teachers' marks on pre-test and post-test by collaboration type (OD=online discussion; PD=personal discussion)

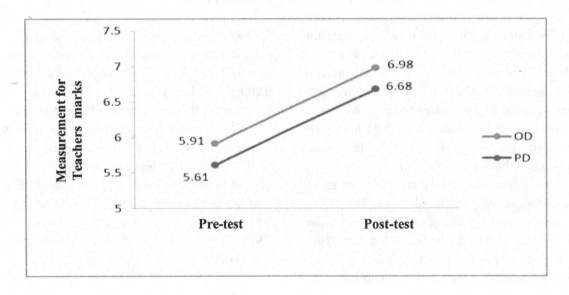

sonal face-to-face-discussions (PD) in front of a computer during which they could use the CSCL platform. This result is in line with conclusive findings in research on CSCL showing various added values and benefits of collaboration in CSCL (Ertl, Kopp, & Mandl, 2008; Suthers & Hundhausen, 2003; Weinberger, et al., 2005, 2007). In CSCL with various forms of collaboration, students can discuss their ideas and conceptions from different perspectives in order to re-construct and co-construct (new) knowledge while solving authentic and complex problems (Veldhuis-Diermanse, et al., 2006; Weinberger & Fischer, 2006). Furthermore, in CSCL environments, students can re-construct their thoughts while formulating and organizing ideas and opinions and they can also re-read posted notes by looking at the conversation history. Writing notes and re-reading and re-thinking those notes are regarded as important tools for learning and knowledge construction in CSCL (e.g. De Jong, Veldhuis-Diermanse, & Lutgens, 2002; Veerman, 2000).

There was no significant difference between students under the OD condition compared to students under the PD condition both in terms of teachers' marks and the Veldhuis-Diermanse coding scheme for knowledge construction. This result is in line with inconclusive findings in research on online learning environments. Various studies point to positive effects of online collaboration (e.g. Andriessen, et al., 2003; Kanselaar, et al., 2000; Kirschner, et al., 2003), while some theoretical and empirical evidence also demonstrates various downsides of online collaboration (e.g. Doerry, 1996; Janssen, et al., 2007; Olson & Olson, 1997). Despite the fact that Personal Discussion (PD) in front of a shared computer provides students with various forms of social interaction, nonverbal communication, and physical, mental and psychological signs which can facilitate turn-taking, giving feedback, mutual understanding, etc. (e.g. Kiesler, 1986; Kreijns, et al., 2003; Van Amelsvoort, 2006), learners can compensate for and even benefit from restricted interactive environments (e.g. Fischer & Mandl, 2005) using support techniques (Engelmann, Dehler, Bodemer, & Buder, 2009), and factors that are extrinsic to the technology itself (Walther, 1994).

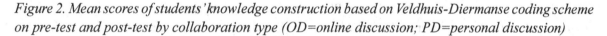

Figure 2. Mean scores of students' knowledge construction based on Veldhuis-Diermanse coding scheme on pre-test and post-test by collaboration type (OD=online discussion; PD=personal discussion)

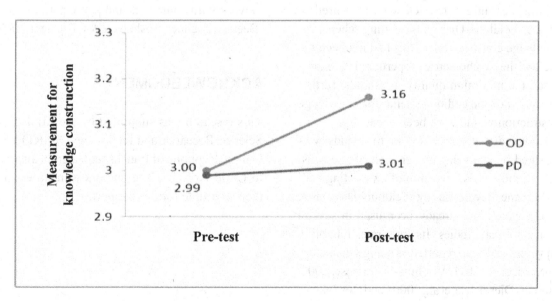

Students in the OD condition can also compensate for the restricted interaction by writing notes, and re-reading and re-thinking those notes, which are important tools for learning and knowledge construction in CSCL (Veerman, 2000). Based on our study, we conclude that online discussions within a CSCL platform as well as personal discussions using the CSCL platform can support the process of knowledge construction and this can also be reflected in students' course exam results. The similar performance shown by participants in the two experimental conditions, both in terms of knowledge acquisition and teachers' assessment could indeed be attributed to the fact that in both conditions knowledge was represented in artificial deposits within the same Drewlite CSCL platform.

We found that the scores on knowledge construction as obtained by the Veldhuis-Diermanse coding scheme were consistent with exam results as obtained by teachers' regular evaluations. There was thus a relationship between students' course exam results and knowledge construction. When teachers' marks were used to analyze students' learning outcomes, the scores of all students improved significantly but no significant difference was reported for quality improvement of their scores between students under the OD and PD conditions. Identical results were achieved when students' learning outcomes were measured in terms of Veldhuis-Diermanse coding scheme for knowledge construction. If this had not been the case, and the psychometric properties of the exams passed the minimum quality thresholds, further calibration of the coding scheme for knowledge construction would have been necessary.

Knowledge construction in this study was measured by analyzing student contributions using a slightly revised version of an existing coding scheme developed by Veldhuis-Diermanse (2002), which had already been used in several other empirical studies. Its inter-rater reliability and values had been reported as being satisfactory (Noroozi, et al., 2011; Veldhuis-Diermanse, 2002; Veldhuis-Diermanse, et al., 2006), and these values were even higher in the present study. Furthermore, using existing coding schemes is advocated in the literature (Stacey & Gerbic, 2003). This form of content analysis is very time consuming, but there is hardly any alternative in this research context. It is therefore not surprising that this type of analysis is most frequently used when analyzing written notes and transcripts of discourse corpora in CSCL environments. In our case, meaningful parts within the contributions were coded with a slight variation of an existing five-tier scheme. The codes were seen as proxies for the achievement of learning outcomes. This study was embedded in an existing course with its own dynamics. This means that there is a high level of ecological validity of the study, and therefore we assert that the findings are quite robust. However, this context constrains the possibilities to experiment. Now that we know that using the Drewlite CSCL platform affects learning outcomes in real courses, we suggest proceeding with controlled experiments in which student learning processes are intensively monitored and learning results more elaborately tested. Factors which we suggest should be taken into account are the nature of learning tasks (Veerman, 2000) and student characteristics, including personal character (Rummel & Spada, 2005), communication skills (Weinberger, 2003), and interest in and willingness to work with computers and participate in CSCL (Beers, Kirschner, Boshuizen, & Gijselaers, 2007).

ACKNOWLEDGMENT

This research was supported by the Ministry of Science, Research, and Technology (MSRT) of the Islamic Republic of Iran through a grant awarded to Omid Noroozi. The authors want to express their gratitude for this support.

REFERENCES

Andriessen, J., Baker, M., & Suthers, D. (2003). *Arguing to learn: Confronting cognitions in computer-supported collaborative learning environments*. Dordrecht, The Netherlands: Kluwer.

Baltes, B. B., Dickson, M. W., Sherman, M. P., Bauer, C. C., & LaGanke, J. (2002). Computer-mediated communication and group decision making: A metaanalysis. *Organizational Behavior and Human Decision Processes*, *87*(1), 156–179. doi:10.1006/obhd.2001.2961

Beers, P. J., Kirschner, P. A., Boshuizen, H. P. A., & Gijselaers, W. H. (2007). ICT-support for grounding in the classroom. *Instructional Science*, *35*(4), 535–556. doi:10.1007/s11251-007-9018-5

Biggs, J. B., & Collis, K. F. (1982). *Evaluating the quality of learning: The SOLO taxonomy*. New York, NY: Academic Press.

Busstra, M. C., Geelen, A., Noroozi, O., Biemans, H. J. A., De Vries, J. H. M., & van 't Veer, P. (2010). Timing of information presentation in interactive digital learning material affects student's learning outcomes and appreciation of the material: a pilot study in the domain of nutritional research education. In *Proceedings of World Conference on Educational Multimedia, Hypermedia and Telecommunications 2010,* (pp. 3091-3100). Chesapeake, VA: AACE.

Clark, D. B., D'Angelo, C. M., & Menekse, M. (2009). Initial structuring of online discussions to improve learning and argumentation: Incorporating students' own explanations as seed comments versus an augmented-preset approach to seeding discussions. *Journal of Science Education and Technology*, *18*(4), 321–333. doi:10.1007/s10956-009-9159-1

Clark, D. B., Sampson, V., Weinberger, A., & Erkens, G. (2007). Analytic frameworks for assessing dialogic argumentation in online learning environments. *Educational Psychology Review*, *19*(3), 343–374. doi:10.1007/s10648-007-9050-7

Coffin, C., & O'Halloran, A. K. (2009). Argument reconceived. *Educational Review*, *61*(3), 301–313. doi:10.1080/00131910903045948

Corbel, A., Jaillon, P., Serpaggi, X., Baker, M., Quignard, M., Lund, K., & Séjourné, A. (2002). DREW: Un outil internet pour créer situations d'appretissage coopérant. (DREW: An internet tool for creating cooperative learning situations) In Desmoulins, C., Marquet, P., & Bouhineau, D. (Eds.), *EIAH2003 Environnements Informatique pour l'Apprentissage Humains* (pp. 109–113). Paris, France: INRP.

De Jong, F. P. C. M., Veldhuis-Diermanse, A. E., & Lutgens, G. (2002). Computer-supported learning in university and vocational education. In Koschman, T., Hall, R., & Miyake, N. (Eds.), *CSCL 2: Carrying Forward the Conversation* (pp. 111–128). Hillsdale, NJ: Erlbaum.

Doerry, E. (1996). *An empirical comparison of co-present and technologically-mediated interaction based on communicative breakdown*. PhD Dissertation. Eugene, OR: University of Oregon.

Engelmann, T., Dehler, J., Bodemer, D., & Buder, J. (2009). Knowledge awareness in CSCL: A psychological perspective. *Computers in Human Behavior*, *25*(4), 949–960. doi:10.1016/j.chb.2009.04.004

Ertl, B., Kopp, B., & Mandl, H. (2008). Supporting learning using external representations. *Computers & Education*, *51*(4), 1599–1608. doi:10.1016/j.compedu.2008.03.001

Fischer, F., & Mandl, H. (2005). Knowledge convergence in computer-supported collaborative learning: The role of external representation tools. *Journal of the Learning Sciences*, *14*(3), 405–441. doi:10.1207/s15327809jls1403_3

Jacobson, M. J., & Wilensky, U. (2006). Complex systems in education: Scientific and educational importance and implications for the learning sciences. *Journal of the Learning Sciences*, *15*(1), 11–34. doi:10.1207/s15327809jls1501_4

Janssen, J., Erkens, G., Kanselaar, G., & Jaspers, J. (2007). Visualization of participation: Does it contribute to successful computer-supported collaborative learning? *Computers & Education, 49*(4), 1037–1065. doi:10.1016/j.compedu.2006.01.004

Joiner, R., & Jones, S. (2003). The effects of communication medium on argumentation and the development of critical thinking. *International Journal of Educational Research, 39*(8), 861–971. doi:10.1016/j.ijer.2004.11.008

Kanselaar, G., De Jong, T., Andriessen, J., & Goodyear, P. (2000). New technologies. In P. J. R. Simons., J. L. Van der Linden., & T. Duffy (Eds.), *New Learning,* (pp. 55-82). Dordrecht, The Netherlands: Kluwer Academic Publishers.

Kiesler, S. (1986). The hidden messages in computer networks. *Harvard Business Review, 64*(1), 46–60.

Kirschner, P. A., Beers, P. J., Boshuizen, H. P. A., & Gijselaers, W. H. (2008). Coercing shared knowledge in collaborative learning environments. *Computers in Human Behavior, 24*(2), 403–420. doi:10.1016/j.chb.2007.01.028

Kirschner, P. A., Buckingham-Shum, S. J., & Carr, C. S. (Eds.). (2003). *Visualizing argumentation: Software tools for collaborative and educational sense making.* Dordrecht, The Netherlands: Kluwer.

Kreijns, K., Kirschner, P. A., & Jochems, W. (2003). Identifying the pitfalls for social interaction in computer-supported collaborative learning environments: A review of the research. *Computers in Human Behavior, 19*(3), 335–353. doi:10.1016/S0747-5632(02)00057-2

Munneke, L., Andriessen, J., Kanselaar, G., & Kirschner, P. (2007). Supporting interactive argumentation: Influence of representational tools on discussing a wicked problem. *Computers in Human Behavior, 23*(3), 1072–1088. doi:10.1016/j.chb.2006.10.003

Noroozi, O., Biemans, H. J. A., Busstra, M. C., Mulder, M., & Chizari, M. (2011). Differences in learning processes between successful and less successful students in computer-supported collaborative learning in the field of human nutrition and health. *Computers in Human Behavior, 27*(1), 309–318. doi:10.1016/j.chb.2010.08.009

Noroozi, O., Biemans, H. J. A., Mulder, M., & Chizari, M. (2010a). Analyzing learning processes and outcomes in computer-supported collaborative learning in the domain of nutritional research methodology education. In J. Baralt, N. Callaos, W. Lesso, A. Tremante, & F. Welsch (Eds.). *Proceedings of the International Conference on Society and Information Technologies,* (pp. 55-60). Orlando, FL: IEEE.

Noroozi, O., Biemans, H. J. A., Mulder, M., & Chizari, M. (2010b). Students' knowledge construction in computer-supported learning environments: A comparative study in the domain of nutritional research methodology education. In D. Gibson & B, Dodge (Eds.). *SITE Book of Abstracts: 21st International Conference on Society for Information Technology & Teacher Education,* (p. 83). San Diego, CA: ACM.

Noroozi, O., Biemans, H. J. A., Weinberger, A., Mulder, M., Popov, V., & Chizari, M. (2011). Supporting computer-supported argumentative knowledge construction in multidisciplinary groups of learners. In L. Gómez Chova, D. Martí Belenguer, & A. López Martínez (Eds.), *Proceedings of the 3rd International Conference on Education and New Learning Technologies,* (pp. 1937-1945). Barcelona, Spain: ACM.

Noroozi, O., Busstra, M. C., Mulder, M., Biemans, H. J. A., Geelen, M. M. E. E., van't Veer, P. & Chizari, M. (in press). Online discussion compensates for suboptimal timing of supportive information presentation in a digitally supported learning environment. *Educational Technology Research & Development.* doi: 10.1007/s11423-011-9217-2.

Noroozi, O., Mulder, M., Biemans, H. J. A., & Chizari, M. (2009). Factors influencing argumentative computer supported collaborative learning (ACSCL). In F. Salajan (Ed.), *Proceedings of the 4th International Conference on E-Learning*, (pp. 394-403). Toronto, Canada: ACM.

Noroozi, O., Weinberger., Biemans, H. J. A., Mulder, M., & Chizari, M. (in press). Argumentation-based computer supported collaborative learning (ABCSCL). A systematic review and synthesis of fifteen years of research. *Educational Research Review*. doi: 10.1016/j.edurev.2011.11.006.

O'Conaill, B., & Whittaker, S. (1997). Characterizing, predicting, and measuring video-mediated communication: A conversational approach. In Finn, K. E., Sellen, A. J., & Wilbur, S. B. (Eds.), *Video-Mediated Communication* (pp. 107–132). Mahwah, NJ: Lawrence Erlbaum Associates, Inc.

Olson, G. M., & Olson, J. S. (1997). Research on computer-supported cooperative work. In Helander, M., Landauer, T. K., & Prabhu, P. (Eds.), *Handbook of Human-Computer Interaction* (2nd ed.). Amsterdam, The Netherlands: Elsevier.

Rummel, N., & Spada, H. (2005). Learning to collaborate: An instructional approach to promoting collaborative problem solving in computer-mediated settings. *Journal of the Learning Sciences, 14*(2), 201–241. doi:10.1207/s15327809jls1402_2

Schellens, T., & Valcke, M. (2006). Fostering knowledge construction in university students through asynchronous discussion groups. *Computers & Education, 46*(4), 349–370. doi:10.1016/j.compedu.2004.07.010

Slof, B., Erkens, G., Kirschner, P. A., Jaspers, J. G. M., & Janssen, J. (2010). Guiding students' online complex learning-task behavior through representational scripting. *Computers in Human Behavior, 26*(5), 927–939. doi:10.1016/j.chb.2010.02.007

Stacey, E., & Gerbic, P. (2003). Investigating the impact of computer conferencing: Content analysis as a manageable research tool. In G. Crisp., D. Thiele., I. Scholten., S. Barker., & J. Baron (Eds.), *Interact, Integrate, Impact: Proceedings of the 20th Annual Conference of the Australasian Society for Computers in Learning in Tertiary Education*. ASCLTE Press.

Stegmann, K., Weinberger, A., & Fischer, F. (2007). Facilitating argumentative knowledge construction with computer-supported collaboration scripts. *International Journal of Computer-Supported Collaborative Learning, 2*(4), 421–447. doi:10.1007/s11412-007-9028-y

Suthers, D. D., & Hundhausen, C. D. (2003). An experimental study of the effects of representational guidance on collaborative learning processes. *Journal of the Learning Sciences, 12*(2), 183–219. doi:10.1207/S15327809JLS1202_2

Van Amelsvoort, M. (2006). *A space for debate: How diagrams support collaborative argumentation-based learning*. Dissertation. Utrecht, The Netherlands: Utrecht University.

Veerman, A. L. (2000). *Computer supported collaborative learning through argumentation*. PhD Dissertation. Utrecht, The Netherlands: Utrecht University.

Veldhuis-Diermanse, A. E. (2002). *CSCLearning? Participation, learning activities and knowledge construction in computer-supported collaborative learning in higher education*. PhD dissertation. Wageningen, The Netherlands: Wageningen University.

Veldhuis-Diermanse, A. E., Biemans, H., Mulder, M., & Mahdizadeh, H. (2006). Analysing learning processes and quality of knowledge construction in networked learning. *Journal of Agricultural Education and Extension, 12*(1), 41–58. doi:10.1080/13892240600740894

Walther, J. B. (1994). Anticipated ongoing interaction versus channel effects on relational communication in computer mediated interaction. *Human Communication Research, 20*(4), 473–501. doi:10.1111/j.1468-2958.1994.tb00332.x

Weinberger, A. (2003). *Scripts for computer-supported collaborative learning effects of social and epistemic cooperation scripts on collaborative knowledge construction*. PhD Dissertation. München, Germany: München University.

Weinberger, A., Ertl, B., Fischer, F., & Mandl, H. (2005). Epistemic and social scripts in computer-supported collaborative learning. *Instructional Science, 33*(1), 1–30. doi:10.1007/s11251-004-2322-4

Weinberger, A., & Fischer, F. (2006). A framework to analyze argumentative knowledge construction in computer-supported collaborative learning. *Computers & Education, 46*(1), 71–95. doi:10.1016/j.compedu.2005.04.003

Weinberger, A., Stegmann, K., Fischer, F., & Mandl, H. (2007). Scripting argumentative knowledge construction in computer-supported learning environments. In F. Fischer., H. Mandl., J. Haake., & I. Kollar (Eds.), *Scripting Computer-Supported Communication of Knowledge - Cognitive, Computational and Educational Perspectives,* (pp. 191-211). New York, NY: Springer.

ADDITIONAL READING

Baker, M., & Lund, K. (1997). Promoting reflective interactions in a CSCL environment. *Journal of Computer Assisted Learning, 13*(3), 175–193. doi:10.1046/j.1365-2729.1997.00019.x

De Laat, M., Lally, V., Lipponen, L., & Simons, R. J. (2007). Online teaching in networked learning communities: A multi-method approach to studying the role of the teacher. *Instructional Science, 35*(3), 257–286. doi:10.1007/s11251-006-9007-0

De Vries, E., Lund, K., & Baker, M. (2002). Computer-mediated epistemic dialogue: Explanation and argumentation as vehicles for understanding scientific notions. *Journal of the Learning Sciences, 11*(1), 63–103. doi:10.1207/S15327809JLS1101_3

Erkens, G., Jaspers, J., Prangsma, M., & Kanselaar, G. (2005). Coordination processes in computer supported collaborative writing. *Computers in Human Behavior, 21*(3), 463–486. doi:10.1016/j.chb.2004.10.038

Ertl, B., Kopp, B., & Mandl, H. (2006). Fostering collaborative knowledge construction in case-based learning scenarios in videoconferencing. *Educational Computing Research, 35*(4), 377–397. doi:10.2190/A0LP-482N-0063-J480

Fischer, F., Bruhn, J., Gräsel, C., & Mandl, H. (2002). Fostering collaborative knowledge construction with visualization tools. *Learning and Instruction, 12*(2), 213–232. doi:10.1016/S0959-4752(01)00005-6

Rourke, L., & Kanuka, H. (2007). Barriers to online critical discourse. *International Journal of Computer-Supported Collaborative Learning, 2*(1), 105–126. doi:10.1007/s11412-007-9007-3

Schellens, T., & Valcke, M. (2005). Collaborative learning in asynchronous discussion groups: What about the impact on cognitive processing? *Computers in Human Behavior, 21*(6), 957–975. doi:10.1016/j.chb.2004.02.025

Suthers, D. (2001). Towards a systematic study of representational guidance for collaborative learning discourse. *Journal of Universal Computer Science, 7*(3), 254–277.

Veerman, A. L. (2003). Constructive discussions through electronic dialogue. In Andriessen, J., Baker, M., & Suthers, D. (Eds.), *Arguing to Learn: Confronting Cognitions in Computer-Supported Collaborative Learning Environments* (pp. 117–143). Amsterdam, The Netherlands: Kluwer.

Veerman, A. L., Andriessen, J. E. B., & Kanselaar, G. (2000). Learning through synchronous electronic discussion. *Computers & Education, 34*(3-4), 269–290. doi:10.1016/S0360-1315(99)00050-0

KEY TERMS AND DEFINITIONS

Asynchronous Platform: A platform that provides learners with the opportunity to participate and communicate at different times.

Computer-Supported Collaborative Learning: A type of learning arrangement that allows researchers, educational designers and planners to scaffold learning in an educational setting using external representations.

Knowledge Construction: Elaborating, evaluating, and linking different facts and ideas that could contribute to the problem solutions. **Online Discussion:** Non-verbal discussion between learners by means of a textual chat.

Personal discussion in Front of Computer: Verbal discussion between learners using spoken language in front of computer.

SOLO: Structure of the Observed Learning Outcome that classifies the complexity of learning outcomes.

Synchronous Platform: A platform that provides learners with the opportunity to participate and communicate at the same time.

Chapter 14
Social Network Analysis Tools to Understand How Research Groups Interact:
A Case Study

Mayte López-Ferrer
Polytechnic University of Valencia, Spain

ABSTRACT

This research is within the frame of sociometric studies of science, particularly the application of social networks to co-authorship, and patterns of citations among researchers in Psychiatry and Neurosciences, General Psychology, and Experimental Psychology. This chapter applies Social Network Analysis to information retrieval from a multidisciplinary database; subject headings lists are not considered sufficient or sufficiently flexible to describe relationships between the sciences. The aim is also to identify similarities and differences among these areas according to bibliometric and network indicators. Social Network Analysis used to select scientific articles within a discipline overcomes the rigidity of information retrieval based on a preselected set of topics. Network graphs can be used to show working groups that otherwise would remain hidden. It is useful, also, to overlap networks of co-authorship (explicit relations) and patterns of cited references (implicit relations), which allow comparison between individual author or groups and the whole group. Finally, the author highlights the need to adapt assessment indicators from different scientific areas to allow consideration of the characteristics of diverse disciplines, based not only on the productivity of individual authors, but also their capacity to mediate with other actors and works within the research system.

DOI: 10.4018/978-1-4666-0125-3.ch014

INTRODUCTION

Social Network Analysis (SNA) represents a revolution in bibliometric studies of scientific activity. The term bibliometrics is used in the statistical literature to conceptualize the application of statistical and mathematical methods to scientific publications to explain the development of scientific disciplines, primarily by counting and analyzing elements (Pritchard, 1969). Following this, other lexical terms have been coined, such as scientometrics, informetrics, cybermetrics, etc. with related clarifications and expansions of and restrictions to their meanings, to expand the scope of and include other elements of scientific communication that might explain scientific enterprise. In this chapter we use the term bibliometrics or bibliometric studies, which are the most popular terms in international science (Jiménez Contreras, 2000).

SNA studies the relationships among elements in a given environment (Wasserman, 1994). Both elements and their relationships can be applied to any of the fields in which they interact. Traditional social analysis studies elements, classified or grouped according to their characteristics (social class stratification, gender, age group, geographic location, etc.); SNA is based on the idea that the structure of the relationships among elements better explains the set, social surroundings and the individual elements than each of these attributes individually.

Bibliometric studies have been transformed by the introduction of SNA. They are less concerned with the scientific production of institutions, than with these institutions' collaborative networks. Similarly, the study of publication quality, based on citations, now focuses on the meaning of citation flows and how they explain the interactions among scientific disciplines. Visualizations provided by SNA have changed bibliometrics based on their power to communicate phenomena whose explanation is difficult using only data.

BACKGROUND

SNA has made a major contribution to the level of analysis of scientific research; it allows meso level examination (groups of researchers as the unit of analysis) even when working with large volumes of data, such as national scientific production (He, Ding & Ni, 2011).

The most widespread applications of bibliometrics to SNA are mapping of science, that is, thematic networks typically built from citations (Boyack, Klavans & Borner, 2005; Iñiguez, Muñoz Justicia, Peñaranda & Martínez, 2006; Leydesdorff, 2004; Leydesdorff & Rafols, 2009; Moya-Anegón, Vargas-Quesada, Herrero-Solana, Chinchilla-Rodriguez, Corera-Alvarez, Munoz-Fernandez, 2004), and studies of scientific collaboration, based on personal networks built from co-authorship of papers (Acedo, Barroso, Casanueva, Galan, 2006; Bozeman & Corley, 2004; Olmeda-Gómez, et al, 2009a; Perianes-Rodríguez, Olmeda-Gomez, Moya-Anegon, 2010). Personal networks based on copresence on dissertation committees (Martín, del Olmo Martínez, Gutiérrez, 2006; Casanueva Roche, Escobar Pérez, Larrinaga González, 2007; Delgado López-Cózar, Torres-Salinas, Jiménez-Contreras & Ruiz-Pérez, 2006; Olmeda-Gómez, et al, 2009b), or competitive examinations panels (Sierra, 2003) are also examined. However, its application to many other information sources are still unexplored.

A visual representation of a network provides the opportunity to analyze its structural properties: "By mapping the structure of interactions, a researcher can identify the channels through which information flows from one node to another and the potential for a corresponding influence of one over another" (Schultz-Jones, 2009, p. 595).

Visualization is the most frequent approach in the literature. In general, most studies in the literature are descriptive their intention is to apply the knowledge generated in science policy to particular scientific areas (Rosas, et al, 2011; Valenciano Valcarcel, Devis-Devis, Villamon,

Peiro-Velert, 2010; Racherla & Hu 2010; Tonta & Darvish 2010, Sun & Jiang 2009; Cantner & Rake 2011), conferences or institutions (Erman & Todorovski, 2010; Perianes-Rodríguez, et al, 2010; Reijers, et al, 2009; Perianes-Rodríguez, et al, 2009; Olmeda-Gómez, et al, 2009a, Boardman & Corley 2008), regions or countries (Neto, et al, 2010; Shapiro, et al, 2010; Yan, Ding & Zhu, 2010; Sun & Jiang, 2009; Morel, et al, 2009).

Network analysis when applied to science policy provides the dual advantage of what Molina (2009) describes as a weak reduction in the observed reality, and a simultaneous strong operationalization of the representations and its properties. It is a weak reduction because visualizations of the studied phenomenon are easily recognizable by the actors, and they allow the incorporation of many attributional variables which qualify the observations—often derived from perception of the event by its actors. A strong operationalization because the mathematical properties of graphs provide parameters to measure, compare and even experiment, with individuals and team structures.

Bibliometrics takes the individual researcher as the unit of analysis in assessing science and bibliometric indicators are designed to compare researchers. In bibliometric analyses that include examination of group, country, university, etc. performance, based their comparisons on the indicators relating to individual researchers with these groups, countries, or universities. For example, in competition for research funding, projects with teams whose individual members are ranked highly for excellence of research will have more chance of receiving an award. However, the 'value' of the group as a whole team is unknown, because there are no tools available to assess this. To evaluate groups, we require a new system that includes descriptions of the various work organizations and systems of academic achievement in every field of knowledge.

SNA enables a focus on both the individuals and their organizational and other contexts. New indicators of scientific performance based on this perspective will have applications in science policy since they assess the structure not just the individual.

Some work in applied economics and science policy uses tests to evaluate the efficiency of the research groups based on criteria for efficiency in the use of human and economic resources and their outputs. Papers and patents are seen as scientific output, PhD staff and dissertations as academic output, and bilateral contracts with companies as socioeconomic output. It has been observed that different research groups adopt particular trajectories and aim at different types of bibliometric outputs. Therefore, a dynamic analysis of the efficiencies offered by each group is required in order to design policy that is more appropriate for the needs of different types of groups (Jiménez, et al, 2007). SNA allows consideration of different elements in efficiency analyses. The organizational culture of different groups, the size, structure, composition and openness to new members all could have an influence on achievement and would allow policy makers to design initiatives to encourage more efficient group behavior.

In the wider context, scientific and technical human capital is defined as the sum of the relations of researchers within their professional networks, their expertise and the available resources (Bozeman & Corley 2004). A wide range of studies tracks the incidence of co-authored articles and uses this as a proxy for collaboration (Birnholtz, 2007). Using the social networks built from co-authorship in scientific publications, we can take clusters of authors as bibliometric footprints to measure the collective production of knowledge (Velden, Haque, Lagoze & 2010). The research group is the unit of knowledge production, and co-authorship networks enable them to be studied, analyzed and visualized in terms of scientific collaboration (Lee, Kwon & Kim, 2011; Sorensen, Seary & Riopelle, 2010).

There are many reasons for co-authorship. Lassi & Sonnenwald (2010) refer to several benefits of scientific collaboration including that:

the works with several authors are more often cited and are cited over longer periods of time; research funding agencies encourage collaborative research; collaboration increases efficiency through better use of existing resources; larger research groups can take on larger projects; collaborative working enables transfers of learning; and being a member of a research community brings prestige. Smykla & Zippel (2010) add that building international reputation can play a major role in achieving promotions, hence the growing importance of international mobility for advancing research careers.

At the same time, SNA provides its own indicators, obtained from network structure and node position which complete and supplement at micro-level the most widespread bibliometric indicators in science policy, that is, productivity and impact (Sharma & Urs, 2008).

Analysis of co-authorship is essential for an analysis of fractional scientific productivity. Lee & Bozeman (2005) examine the effects of collaboration on scientific productivity. Exploiting co-authorship analysis he compares two measures of scientific productivity, productivity as number of publications, and fractional productivity ("fractional count"), productivity of an individual authors divided by the number of co-authors. The regression models in Lee & Bozeman (2005) confirm that among all possible alternative explanations of productivity, such as, job satisfaction, academic rank, age, gender, nationality, and collaboration strategy, number of collaborators, or co-authors is the best indicator of productivity, measured as direct or fractional productivity.

Therefore, scientific collaboration is seen as a virtue, and various public policies actively promote scientific collaboration among individuals and institutions. Some studies suggest that the leaders of potential research teams as well as policy makers, should take account of scientific studies that show a relation between collaboration and productivity, when deciding about the composition of teams, and exploiting the qualities that will

bring benefits to the whole team and the project (Barjak, 2006)

There are some comparative studies that try to find some correspondence among different measures of centrality (Freeman, 1979) and productivity (López-Ferrer, 2008; Sun & Jiang 2009) or impact factors (Yan & Ding 2009; Yan, Ding & Zhu, 2010). Other lines of research are the visualization of research teams by applying SNA to scientific communication platforms, such as email, discussion forums, social networks, etc. (Harrer, Zeini & Ziebarth, 2009)

In this study, we consider also that the diachronic view of emergence, consolidation and maturation of research groups to enable an organic view of innovation systems and production in knowledge-based economies (López-Ferrer, Velasco Arroyo, Osca-Lluch, 2009; Berlingerio, et al, 2010; Sun & Jiang 2009)

This paper follows the approach in Klenk, Hickey & MacLellan (2010). It focuses on the bounded subject of knowledge, that is, Psychology, a geographic area, that is, Spain, and combines bibliometrics and SNA. There are also similarities with Velden, Haque & Lagoze (2010), who compare three sub-areas of research within a large discipline, that is, chemistry.

The present work is framed in sociometric studies in the scientific literature. It applies SNA to three aspects of literature studies: the first is the definition of scientific areas; the second involves co-authorship, and third deals with citation patterns among authors. The paper has three main objectives:

- to apply SNA to delimit independent, but close and related areas of knowledge, to study them in parallel, observing similarities and differences;
- to use bibliometrics complemented by SNA techniques to study co-authorship and citation patterns among researchers;
- to study the similarities and differences resulting from the first objective, in relation to

the three areas of knowledge of Psychiatry and Neurosciences, General Psychology, and Experimental Psychology.

The objective is to provide a picture of the research groups in these three disciplines, their distribution, their prominence, and their interactions or lack of them. The study sample was unknown a priori, although its selection is highly objective since it is retrieved from publicly accessible databases though repetitive information retrieval based on existing bibliographic sources. This overcomes one of the limitations of applying SNA to data collected by researchers, that is, that data collection is partial due to the complexities of direct observation.

The limitations represented by the capacity of social network software to work with only a few thousand vertices, is overcome by combining use of relational variables with attributive variables of scientific production. This justifies the elimination of some less productive actors in order to make the study more comprehensible (Lotka, 1926).

However, there are two other limitations that need to be considered: First, the suitability of authorship as an indicator of scientific collaboration. Katz & Martin (1997) argue that although collaboration is conventionally measured through coauthorship, it is only a partial indicator and should be treated with caution since what can and cannot be considered collaboration among scientists varies according to the social conventions of different institutions, disciplines and countries, and changes as a result of funding agencies' and government policies to stimulate collaboration.

There are some limitations to the use of co-authorship as an indicator of scientific collaboration. Six types of research collaborations with different patterns of rewards are identified in Laudel (2002). Half the partnerships are invisible through the formal communication channels of scientific publications, because they are not rewarded, and some one are recognized only in the acknowledgments section, which does not count in evaluating

experience. These six types of collaboration are: Collaboration involving division of labor, Service collaboration, Transmission of know-how, Provision of access to research equipment, Trusted assessorship, and Mutual stimulation. Of these, only in cooperation through division of labor is there a strong relationship between participation and recognition through co-authorship. This type can be measured fairly accurately through co-authorship. For other types of collaborations the rules are less clear. Provision of services, providing access to research teams and transmission of know-how are commonly used by scientists to test methods or to validate results, all of which are measured poorly by formal communication, that is, co-authorship of scientific publications. Trusted assessorship and mutual stimulation are common types of intraorganizational collaboration which never result in co-authorship.

On the other hand, we should consider also what a citation or absence of a citation between authors means. According to Vinkler (1987) there are two reasons for citing work: professional and social reasons. The first is related to the theoretical and practical aspects of research; the second is related to the influence of factors that are personal or external to the research. There are also reasons why authors do not cite certain works, including ignorance of their existence and inaccessibility due to the paper being published in another language (Romera Iruela, 1996). Authors who have collaborated previously should not have reasons not to cite their coauthored work. It is somewhat surprising that groups within the same scientific discipline do not use common bibliographies. The reasons for this could be investigated by studying the lines of research engaged in by various groups. thus, the absence of cross citations among members of different groups seems to be due to factors that are personal, social or external to the research.

Citations are used to measure the influence of the current work on successive studies, but personal collaboration also constitutes a privileged channel of influence (Molina, Muñoz Justicia & Domènech Argemí, 2002). The contribute of this paper is that it analyzes and compares these two types of networks, coauthorship and citation patterns obtained from the same sets of actors, to identify the establishment or not of links and to try to understand why structural holes emerge.

METHODS AND MATERIALS

The sources of information for this study are Thomson Reuters' Social Sciences Citation Index® (SSCI), and the Journal Citation Reports® (JCR), Social Sciences Edition. These sources were chosen for their multidisciplinarity and broad coverage of the social sciences. Their choice is justified by certain particularities compared to other databases: as well as bibliographic information (authors, place of work, title, journal, date, etc.), each record also includes other essential information: that is, the references cited in the bibliography of the article, which is invaluable information for our study of the relationships among research groups.

Thematic classification of SSCI records is problematic, however, since topics do not come from any scientific classification and there is no use of controlled indexing language. The description fields are reduced to key words and subject categories assigned to the journals and their articles, derived from the JCR.

The JCR is a directory of scientific journals and provides information on the full and abbreviated journal title, its ISSN, frequency, language, and details of publication such as publisher and country. Of particular interest for this study is that it provides a classification according to a list of topics and subject categories that is produced by the JCR and is explained and updated. It allows users to search, sort and compare journals by internationally recognized bibliometric indicators such as, Total Cites, Impact factor, 5-Year Impact Factor, Immediacy Index, Articles, and Cited Half-life.

The JCR includes a selection of the journals in the SSCI and classifies journals within a limited number of topics, and subject categories. We assume that the papers contained in a journal can be classified under the topic that describes the source.

We searched on the text string Spain in the *Address* field, for the period 1992-2001 and recovered a total of 9,229 records summarizing Spanish scientific production in the area of Social Science. The information for citation analysis is drawn from the field Cited references in the SSCI records.

The database can be categorized according to the topics within which journals are classified, which is relatively small and manageable. However, there is a stronger thematic proximity between some subject categories indicating a higher level of relationship underlying the overall classification; we call this generic level Areas. For example, in the SSCI the same journal can be included under several different subjects. This implies a link among subject categories, a relationship, a proximity issue, and an area of interdisciplinary knowledge.

The network metaphor is widely used by sociologists to explain in a more sensitive and realistic way the existence of several thematic areas entwined within different theoretical approaches, methodologies and disciplines. The software used to process the matrices and graphs is UCINET and Netdraw. The table relating journals to subjects is transformed in a symmetric weighted matrix where the actors are the subjects and the links are the journals matched to them. The resulting graph is depicted in Figure 1. The size of the nodes represents the number of articles in journals categorized under those subjects and the thickness of the links represents the number of journals that are categorized in both subjects. (For convenience, Figure 1 just shows labels only for the nodes that represent the thematic categories of interest in this study.)

Figure 1. SSCI areas

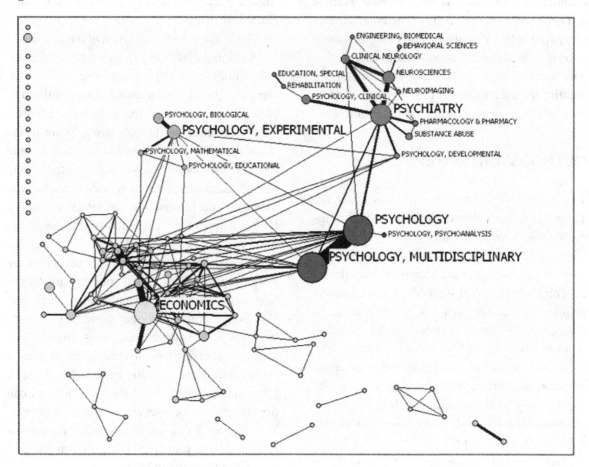

This method of selecting scientific papers in different thematic areas reduces the rigidity related to selection according to exact topic groups, which does not take account of overlaps among them or restrict related areas, and provides no information about emerging relationships (López-Ferrer, & Osca-Lluch, 2009).

Table 1 summarizes the main areas of total Spanish scientific output in Social Sciences and Humanities by weight.

We focus on the areas of Psychiatry, General Psychology and Experimental Psychology Whose weight in total Spanish scientific production in the area of social sciences and humanities collected in SSCI is 48%, and to enable capture of similarities and differences among closely related research areas.

There are numerous bibliometric studies in psychology. After medicine, psychology is the most frequent user of this method of study (Delgado López-Cózar, et al, 2006). The information retrieval strategies applied in previous bibliometric studies on psychology (Osca, et al, 2005), show

Table 1. Co-authorship indicators

Area	Topics	Journals	Papers	
Psychiatry and Neuroscience	12	98	1651	20%
General Psychology	3	31	1555	19%
Economics	5	93	1262	14%
Experimental Psychology	4	48	725	9%
Others	68	275	3156	38%

that in order to collect all the publications related to this discipline, the search cannot be restricted exclusively to the work listed under this topic in the databases. It is necessary to expand the search to include journals from other disciplines, and databases beyond psychology. For example, in the Spanish National Research Council (CSIC) databases, ISOC – Social Sciences and Humanities database includes the topic psychology, and IME includes Biomedicine, psychiatry and clinical psychology which are included and finally closely related to psychiatry and experimental psychology, psychopharmacology and biological psychology, which in their turn are included in the ICYT – Science and Technology database.

Knowledge, rather than the juxtaposition of fields, is a continuous space in which different scientific disciplines are scattered; some are closely related and these relationships can be represented in a network. This is an innovation in terms of delimiting the boundaries between scientific fields that might be comparable.

RESULTS

The results for the three subject areas studied are detailed below. Psychiatry and Neuroscience includes researches in medicine that deals with mental illness and the nervous system. Their methodologies and methods of diagnosis are in part based on engineering and medical informatics; drug treatments and combination of psychological and clinical therapies; rehabilitation of patients; specialization in different age groups; and social aspects of mental illness, especially those related to addictions.

General Psychology includes research in psychology with a general or interdisciplinary approach to the field, and also philosophical psychology, psychoanalysis, and history of psychology. The subject categories in this area are from several different classes and are called by different names. This is common in classifications,

and requires continuous updating of the scientific activity studies. The dynamism of the classification method system proposed increases the value of thematic clustering, a methodology that considers the relationships among different categories and takes account of the changes that occur.

Finally, Experimental Psychology focuses on the processes of consciousness, cognition, memory, and perception (visual, auditory, speech, etc.) and their biological bases; it includes biopsychology, psychophysiology, psychopharmacology, and comparative psychology, and also animal psychology. It also includes the methodology and instrumentation of psychology—multivariate methods, statistical treatment and research strategies—and is widely related to statistics, educational psychology, and school and learning tests and creative behavior.

CO-AUTHORSHIP NETWORKS

We use the scientific output of the authors as an attributive variable, that is, the number of published articles. This allows the exclusion of some actors. In all cases, and in order to enable comparison, only those authors with 25% of their scientific production in the discipline are retained.

There are 3,560 authors publishing in Psychiatry, but the selected group of great producers, those who accumulate 25% of total production in a discipline, includes just 146 authors, i.e. 4.10% of all authors. To belong to this selected group they must have published 9 or more papers during the studied period.

In General Psychology, there are 2,480 authors, 202 of them are great producers, i.e. 8.15% of all of them, and published 4 or more papers during the studied period.

There are 1,139 authors publishing in Experimental Psychology, but the selected group of great producers is just 58, i.e. 5.09% of all authors, and are responsible for at least 7 papers during the studied period.

The transitivity index, percentage of occasional authors (i.e., those who authored only 1 paper) compared with total authors, is significantly lower in Psychiatry than in the other two areas, that is, 43.54%. General Psychology and Experimental Psychology share a very high transitivity index of around 70%.

The co-authorship index in scientific publications is a scientific collaboration indicator. The highest average of number of coauthors is in Psychiatry with 4.1, followed by Experimental Psychology, 3.1, and General Psychology 2.7.

The density and inclusion indexes in network analysis are estimated on the overall social environment, thus, they include all the components even isolated nodes. Therefore, they are indexes for comparison between the graphs representing different social environments. Both measures presented in Table 2 correspond to the graphs for collaboration among the most productive authors in each discipline.

The density index measures the number of ties between the nodes in a given environment, expressed as a percentage of possible links divided by total links. The graph would be complete were all nodes in a given environment related to other nodes; however, this is unlikely in the real world. The inclusion index is the percentage of nodes that are connected, over the total number of nodes in the graph. The lower the number of isolated nodes, the greater degree of inclusion in the graph.

Figures 2 to 4 show first that Experimental Psychology is smaller than General Psychiatry or Psychology.

Comparison of centralization indicators between Psychiatry and Neurosciences, General Psychology and Experimental Psychology shows important differences in collaboration. Density and inclusion indicators show high rates for Psychiatry and low rates for General Psychology, which corresponds to the relevant co-authorship rates: 1.4 points difference between Psychiatry and General Psychology.

Table 2. Co-authorship indicators

	Psychiatry and Neurosciences	General Psychology	Experimental Psychology
Bibliometric indicators			
Transitivity index (%)	43.54	67.78	66.99
Average authors per paper	4.1	2.7	3.1

Figure 2 shows a topic area with a large number of authors and numerous relations among them. Among the different shapes of association of the nodes, the simplest is the component. The component is the largest possible subset of nodes and links in which all the nodes that integrate it are connected at least to one other node in the subset. This allows us to go from any node to some other, within the component, following the ties. Figure 2 shows the social environment of collaboration for the most productive Spanish researchers in Psychiatry and Neuroscience. Almost all are integrated into one component, which has the highest density of the three subject areas studied, 15.49%. Alongside this main component, we can distinguish two other structures that can be considered clusters because there is a high density of links between their nodes (Herrero, 2000) due to the multilateral nature of their relationships.

The inclusion index is higher in Psychiatry and lower in General Psychology. This indicator reveals that about 20% of the main researchers and largest producers in General Psychology are completely isolated from other researchers, throughout the period. This measure is only 7% for Psychiatry.

Figure 3 shows collaboration in General Psychology. In contrast to Psychiatry and Neuroscience, there are many different components, which represent many small collaborative workgroups, that are very knit, but totally isolated from each other, so the density of the graph is very low, 3.57%.

In most cases, the most prolific authors belong to different components which do not collaborate.

Figure 2. Psychiatry and neurosciences co-authorship

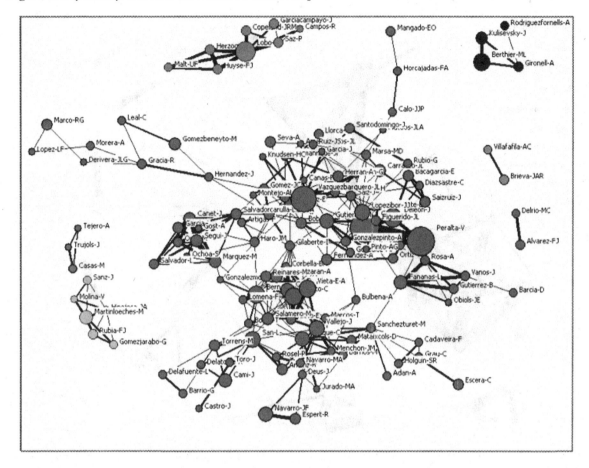

This indicates a high level of competition between them. When there are several highly productive authors in the same component they tend to establish stronger links with scientific authors that are less productive, showing that sub-working groups remain more or less independent inside the main component.

Experimental Psychology presents intermediate values for the average number of co-authors, 3.1, and the transitivity index, 66.99%. Similar to General Psychology it has many components that are completely isolated from each other, but much higher density, 24.74%. Rate of co-authorship, higher in Experimental Psychology than in General Psychology, leads to larger components. Also, the universe of authors available to collaborate with is more limited, and the relationships are more often

repeated. Both aspects have a positive effect on the higher density of the graph.

In relation to the Inclusion Index, 15% of authors in Experimental Psychology are disconnected from their environment, which is a lower percentage than in General Psychology where it reaches 20%.

CITATION NETWORKS

Articles have over 30 citations on average. This makes analysis of citations very complex, and does not allow firm conclusions to be drawn. Each reference includes in one text string the author's name, year of publication, journal that published the paper, length and starting page number of the

Figure 4. Experimental psychology co-authorship

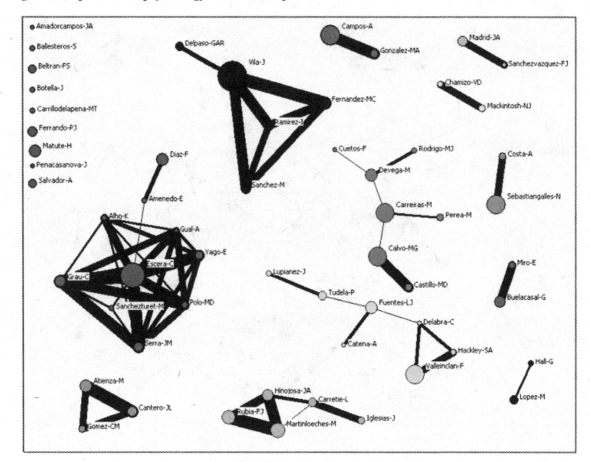

article. Papers on citation patterns require authors to be treated as individuals, not in scattered citations to different studies. We standardized the data by grouping together all the citations to an author, regardless of the particular item cited.

As already mentioned, application of SNA to citations would show the relationships among research groups. The three areas studied rely on foreign publications, primarily European and American. For example, about a half of the papers published in Psychology are translated from other languages (Prieto, Fernández-Ballesteros & Carpintero, 1994). However, for this study, the network analysis matrix is built to include only the most prolific (mostly Spanish) authors in each subject area.

The average number of references attached to articles differs across the three areas (Table 3). Psychiatry has the highest number of citations—an average of 34 per paper. Experimental Psychology has and average of 25, and Psychology has an average of 21.

Comparison of centralization indicators from the graphs representing network citations in the

Table 3. Citation networks indicators

	Psychiatry and Neurosciences	General Psychology	Experimental Psychology
Bibliometric Indicators			
Average no. of references per paper	34	21	25

Figure 3. General psychology co-authorship

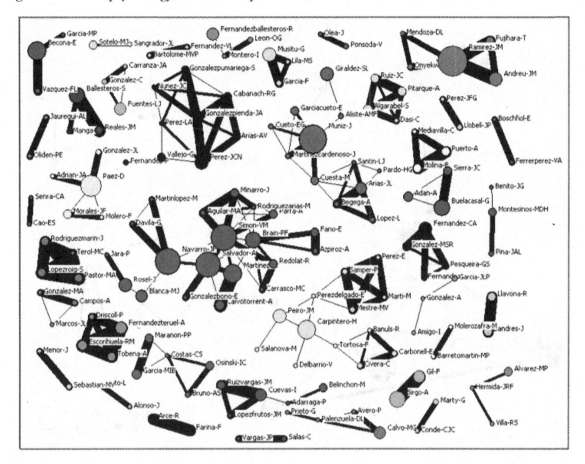

three studied areas shows that the pattern is similar for the psychologies and remarkably different to the pattern in psychiatry. Citation patterns in Psychology and Experimental Psychology range over collaborations in many components that are disconnected from each other, emphasizing the cohesion of one compared to the rest. In Psychiatry almost all members are connected to the same component, although the frequency and flow of their links allow us to distinguish two distinct allegiances that support every citation pattern.

In Figures 5, 6, and 7, the size of the nodes indicates the total number of citations to an author, including self-citations. The ties and their arrows indicate which authors are responsible for the citations and the thickness of the tie lines indicates the amount, consequently, the prestige of

the author not measured just by the absolute size of the node, but also by the number and thickness of the lines pointing him or her.

In Psychiatry and Neuroscience, 32.78% of all possible relationships among the nodes in the graph are established, which is a very high density compared to the psychologies. In addition, up to 85.71% of the nodes establish relations with other members in the area, which means a high inclusion rate.

In Psychiatry and Neuroscience (see Figure 5), there are two completely separate subgroups that mark the citation patterns in the discipline. Most of the authors in each subgroup cite other members of their group, and remain isolated from the other subgroup. However, we cannot comment on independent components because one author

Figure 5. Psychiatry and neurosciences citation patterns network

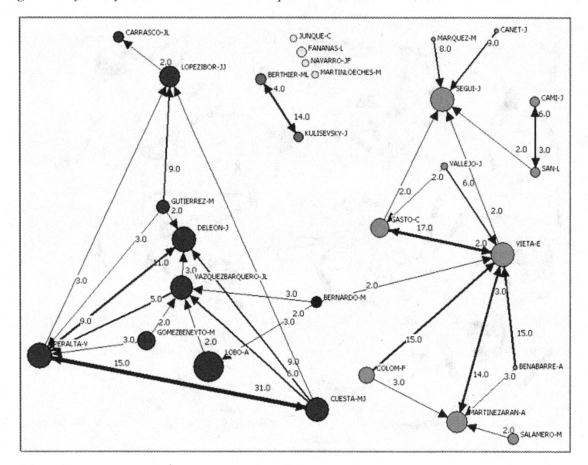

collaborates with members from both subgroups. This particular author is not cited by any other authors from those subgroups.

The thickest linkage in the graph shows a relationship based on mutual citations; it is between the two most prolific authors in the area, who are also members of the same research group, and are structurally equivalent authors.

Apart from these two subgroups there is another group whose members cite only other members of the same group. If we overlay the co-authorship network with the citation pattern network we see that, in all cases, members of the same team are involved.

In General Psychology and Experimental Psychology the centralization indicators are similar, 56.25% and 57.14% inclusion, respectively,

which means that over 40% of the researchers are outside the citation environment. The density index for General Psychology is 8.69%, and for Experimental Psychology is 12.24%.

In General Psychology, the citation pattern is one of many components disconnected from each other, which stresses the tight cohesion of the network.

In all cases, the nodes comprising a component in the citation network are integrated with the same component in the co-authorship network. This means that researchers cite other members of their working teams and also remain isolated from the rest, i.e. they do not cite researchers from other groups.

Excluding the main component in Figure 6, the remaining components are pairs where just one

Figure 6. General psychology citation patterns network

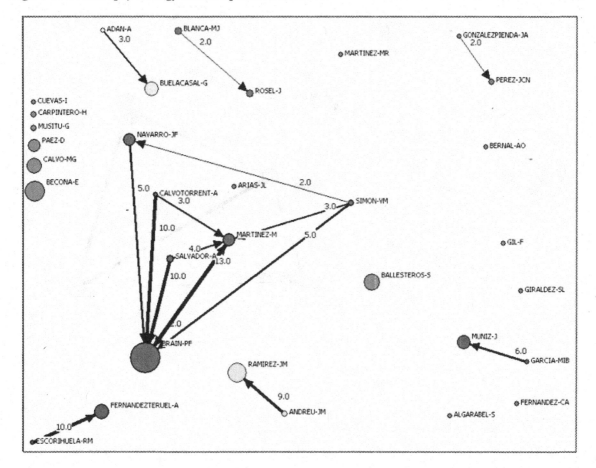

of the nodes receives citations. These receptors are (see co-authorship graphs) leaders of their respective teams.

The citation flows for Experimental Psychology are similar to those for General Psychology. The main component consists of authors who are members of same component (see Figure 4). In the other components leadership changes according to the intensive of production. However, we can identify some differences in the patterns seen so far. There is a node in the main component that receives citations from other members of the component. But if the co-authorship network and the citation network are overlapping, this node integrates a different team. This behavior of citing an author from another is noticeable.

CONCLUSION

The findings of this research are as follows.

1. SNA applied to the classification systems in the databases is useful to delimit universes of knowledge, because these environments go beyond the simplistic classifications, which tend to differ from the reality. The one-dimensional list of subjects used by each database to classify journals or records, are not flexible enough to represent the relationships established between scientific disciplines.

This study shows that the relationships established between some topics and subject categories which are used to categorize journal titles. On the one hand, Behavioral Sciences, Clinical Neurology, Special Educa-

Figure 7. Experimental psychology citation patterns network

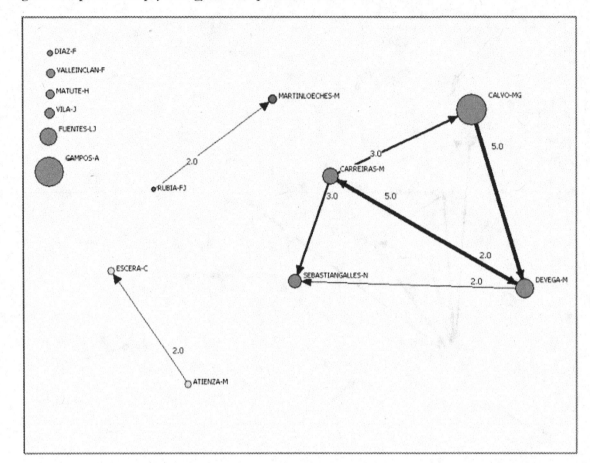

tion, Biomedical Engineering, Neuroimaging, Neurosciences, Pharmacology and Pharmacy, Psychiatry, Clinical Psychology; Developmental Psychology, Rehabilitation, and Substance Abuse are included in the subject area of Psychiatry and Neuroscience. On the other hand, Psychology, and Multidisciplinary Psychology configured General Psychology. And finally, Biological Psychology, Educational Psychology, Experimental Psychology, and Mathematical Psychology are part of the Experimental Psychology area.

2. In this research, complementary use of bibliometrics and SNA is more constructive than using these methods separately. The network figures show working groups that otherwise would be difficult to identify. Delimiting a work

team is important in order to show existing relationships as well as structural holes in the network, i.e. areas where there are no relationships. We show this by showing the overlap among co-authorship networks and citation networks. The former represent explicit relationships and the latter implicit relationships; both serve to position groups and authors.

Scientific production, a well established indicator for research evaluation, is used to justify the elimination of some actors with the lowest production, in order to make graphs more readable. Scientific production is also used as the attribute variable of the nodes, which helps to identify equivalent positions, that is, authors who occupy the same roles (such as team leader) in different teams.

3. We support the finding in social sciences and the humanities of the need for flexibility in assessment of different scientific fields. Assessments should take account of the nuances and unique characteristics of diverse disciplines which institutionally and conceptually are integrated in scientific macrocategories that overlook interdisciplinarity. SNA provides a valuable tool for more useful analysis.

In relation to the scientific areas discussed in this paper we show that the universes are completely different in size and configuration. Experimental Psychology is very different from the two other fields studied. There are different patterns in the configuration of co-authorship and citation networks, with one for psychiatry and another for the two psychologies.

In psychiatry, almost all researchers are included in a working group, and most are connected in a single structure through coauthorship. Citation patterns also show an environment where most of members recognize the contributions made by others, although different allegiances can be distinguished by the frequency and flow of links.

In General Psychology, up to one-fifth of the largest and most productive researchers are isolated, outside of the collaborative networks, and the environment is one of numerous teams, whose members work closely with each other within teams, but are isolated from the other teams. This disconnection between the different groups is even more marked by citation patterns, there is no recognition, outside members of a group, and researcher roles are much more marked: the direction of citations reinforces the role of just one of the nodes in the component. In the co-authorship graphs the most productive author and group leader are the same.

FUTURE RESEARCH DIRECTIONS

Application of SNA to sociometric studies of scientific activity that goes beyond new forms of data representation could result in new, more accurate and detailed assessment systems. It could be adapted to the specificities of different topic areas, geographic differences and scientific cultures. Large scale descriptive and comparative studies are required to confirm this. The present work is a first attempt. Some of the questions to be addressed include whether the research group structure determines its outputs and whether it highlights a particular configuration as being the most suitable.

We should question the use of coauthorship and citation in assessments of scientific production. Perhaps it would be appropriate to complement these data with surveys of researchers. Researchers adapt their conduct to score higher in the relevant science evaluation system; however, some scientific areas have always been disadvantaged compared to others. We need richer and different data to link scientific performance to resources.

REFERENCES

Acedo, F. J., Barroso, C., Casanueva, C., & Galan, J. L. (2006). Co-authorship in management and organizational studies: An empirical and network analysis. *Journal of Management Studies, 43*(5), 957–983. doi:10.1111/j.1467-6486.2006.00625.x

Barjak, F., & für Wirtschaft, H. (2006). *Team diversity and research collaboration in life sciences teams: Does a combination of research cultures pay off?*. Fachhochschule, Nordwestschweiz: Hochschule für Wirtschaft.

Berlingerio, M., Coscia, M., Giannotti, F., Monreale, A., & Pedreschi, D. (2010). As time goes by: Discovering eras in evolving social networks. In *Proceedings of Advances in Knowledge Discovery and Data Mining* (pp. 81–90). ACM. doi:10.1007/978-3-642-13657-3_11

Birnholtz, J. P. (2007). When do researchers collaborate? Toward a model of collaboration propensity. *Journal of the American Society for Information Science and Technology, 58*(14), 2226–2239. doi:10.1002/asi.20684

Boardman, P. C., & Corley, E. A. (2008). University research centers and the composition of research collaborations. *Research Policy, 37*(5), 900–913. doi:10.1016/j.respol.2008.01.012

Boyack, K. W., Klavans, R., & Borner, K. (2005). Mapping the backbone of science. *Scientometrics, 64*(3), 351–374. doi:10.1007/s11192-005-0255-6

Bozeman, B., & Corley, E. (2004). Scientists' collaboration strategies: Implications for scientific and technical human capital. *Research Policy, 33*(4), 599–616. doi:10.1016/j.respol.2004.01.008

Cantner, U., & Rake, B. (2011). *International research networks in pharmaceuticals: Structure and dynamics*. Paper presented at the Mannheim. New York, NY.

Casanueva Roche, C., Escobar Pérez, B., & Larrinaga González, C. (2007). Red social de contabilidad en españa a partir de los tribunales de tesis. *Revista Española De Financiación y Contabilidad, 136*, 707–726.

Delgado López-Cózar, E., Torres-Salinas, D., Jiménez-Contreras, E., & Ruiz-Pérez, R. (2006). Análisis bibliométrico y de redes sociales aplicado a las tesis bibliométricas defendidas en españa (1976-2002): Temas, escuelas científicas y redes académicas. *Revista Espanola la de Documentacion Cientifica, 29*(4).

Erman, N., & Todorovski, L. (2010). Analyzing the structure of the EGOV conference community. *Electronic Government*, 73-84.

Freeman, L. C. (1979). Centrality in social networks conceptual clarification. *Social Networks, 1*(3), 215–239. doi:10.1016/0378-8733(78)90021-7

Harrer, A., Zeini, S., & Ziebarth, S. (2009). *Integrated representation and visualisation of the dynamics in computer-mediated social networks*. Paper presented at 2009 International Conference on Advances in Social Network Analysis and Mining. Athens, Greece.

He, B., Ding, Y., & Ni, C. (2011). Mining enriched contextual information of scientific collaboration: A meso perspective. *Journal of the American Society for Information Science and Technology, 62*(5), 831–845. doi:10.1002/asi.21510

Herrero, R. S. H. (2000). La terminología del análisis de redes problemas de definición y de traducción. *Politica y Sociedad, 33*, 199.

Iñiguez, L., Muñoz Justicia, J., Peñaranda, M. C., & Martínez, L. M. (2006). La psicología social en españa: Estructuras de comunidades. *Redes: Revista Hispana Para El Análisis De Redes Sociales, 10*.

Jiménez, F., Zabala-Iturriagagoitia, J. M., & Zofío, J. L. (2007). Efficiency in public research centers: Evaluating the spanish food technology program. *Working Papers in Economic Theory*. Retrieved from http:// ideas.repec.org/ p/ uam/ wpaper/ 200704.html.

Jiménez Contreras, E. (2000). Los métodos bibliométricos aplicaciones y estado de la cuestión. *Cuadernos De Documentación Multimedia, 10*, 4.

Katz, J. S., & Martin, B. R. (1997). What is research collaboration? *Research Policy, 26*(1), 1–18. doi:10.1016/S0048-7333(96)00917-1

Klenk, N. L., Hickey, G. M., & MacLellan, J. I. (2010). Evaluating the social capital accrued in large research networks: The case of the sustainable forest management network (1995-2009). *Social Studies of Science, 40*(6), 931–960. doi:10.1177/0306312710374130

Lassi, M., & Sonnenwald, D. H. (2010). *Identifying factors that may impact the adoption and use of a social science collaboratory: A synthesis of previous research*. Retrieved from http:// informationr. net/ ir/ 15-3/ colis7/ colis710.html.

Laudel, G. (2002). What do we measure by co-authorships? *Research Evaluation, 11*(1), 3–15. doi:10.3152/147154402781776961

Lee, B., Kwon, O., & Kim, H. (2011). Identification of dependency patterns in research collaboration environments through cluster analysis. *Journal of Information Science, 37*(1), 67–85. doi:10.1177/0165551510392147

Lee, S., & Bozeman, B. (2005). The impact of research collaboration on scientific productivity. *Social Studies of Science, 35*(5), 673. doi:10.1177/0306312705052359

Leydesdorff, L. (2004). Clusters and maps of science journals based on bi-connected graphs in journal citation reports. *The Journal of Documentation, 60*(4), 371–427. doi:10.1108/00220410410548144

Leydesdorff, L., & Rafols, I. (2009). A global map of science based on the ISI subject categories. *Journal of the American Society for Information Science and Technology, 60*(2), 348–362. doi:10.1002/asi.20967

López-Ferrer, M. (2008). *Aplicación del análisis de redes a un estudio bibliométrico sobre psiquiatría, psicología general y psicología experimental.* València, Spain: Universitat de València.

López-Ferrer, M., & Osca Lluch, J. (2009). Una aproximación a la psicología en españa desde el análisis de redes sociales. *Revista de Historia de la Psicología, 30*(4), 55–73.

López-Ferrer, M., Velasco Arroyo, E., & Osca-Lluch, J. (2009). Spanish research groups in economy and management: A network analysis approach. *International Journal of Competitive Intelligence, Strategic. Scientific and Technology Watch, 2*(1), 45–59.

Lotka, A. J. (1926). The frequency distribution of scientific productivity. *Journal of the Washington Academy of Sciences, 16*(12), 317–323.

Martín, J. I. S., del Olmo Martínez, R., & Gutiérrez, J. P. (2006). Estudio de la red de participaciones en tribunales de tesis doctorales de organización y gestión de empresas en españa. In *Actas del X Congreso de Ingeniería de Organizción,* (pp.183-184). Valencia, Spain: University of Valencia

Molina, J. L. (2009). Panorama de la investigación en redes. *Redes: Revista Hispana Para El Análisis De Redes Sociales, 17*, 11.

Molina, J. L., Muñoz Justicia, J., & Domènech Argemí, M. (2002). Redes de publicaciones científicas un análisis de la estructura de coautorías. *Redes, 1*, 3.

Morel, C. M., Serruya, S. J., Penna, G. O., & Guimaraes, R. (2009). Co-authorship network analysis: A powerful tool for strategic planning of research, development and capacity building programs on neglected diseases. *PLoS Neglected Tropical Diseases, 3*(8), e501. doi:10.1371/journal.pntd.0000501

Moya-Anegón, F., Vargas-Quesada, B., Herrero-Solana, V., Chinchilla-Rodriguez, Z., Corera-Alvarez, E., & Munoz-Fernandez, F. J. (2004). A new technique for building maps of large scientific domains based on the cocitation of classes and categories. *Scientometrics, 61*(1), 129–145. doi:10.1023/B:SCIE.0000037368.31217.34

Neto, M., Fernandes, C., Ferreira, A. S., & Fernandes, L. M. (2010). Enterprise information portals: potential for evaluating research for knowledge management and human capital assets using social network analysis. In *Proceedings of the 11th European Conference on Knowledge Management.* Portugal: ECKM Press.

Olmeda-Gómez, C., Perianes-Rodriguez, A., Ovalle-Perandones, M. A., Guerrero-Bote, V. P., & de Moya Anegon, F. (2009a). Visualization of scientific co-authorship in spanish universities from regionalization to internationalization. *Aslib Proceedings, 61*(1), 83–100. doi:10.1108/00012530910932302

Olmeda-Gómez, C., Perianes-Rodríguez, A., Ovalle-Perandones, M. A., & de Moya-Anegón, F. (2009b). Colegios visibles: Estructuras de coparticipación en tribunales de tesis doctorales de biblioteconomía y documentación en españa. *El Profesional De La Informacion, 18*(1), 41–49. doi:10.3145/epi.2009.ene.06

Osca, J., Civera, C., Tortosa, F., Vidal, Q., Ortega, P., García, L., & José, J. (2005). *Difusión de las revistas españolas de psicología en bases de datos nacionales e internacionales*. Retrieved from http:// biblioteca.universia.net/ html_bura/ ficha/ params/ title/ difusion-revistas-españolas-psicologia-bases-datos-nacionales-internacionales/ id/ 1198502. html.

Perianes-Rodríguez, A., Chinchilla-Rodriguez, Z., Vargas-Quesada, B., Olmeda-Gomez, C., & Moya-Anegon, F. (2009). Synthetic hybrid indicators based on scientific collaboration to quantify and evaluate individual research results. *Journal of Informetrics*, *3*(2), 91–101. doi:10.1016/j. joi.2008.12.001

Perianes-Rodríguez, A., Olmeda-Gomez, C., & Moya-Anegon, F. (2010). Detecting, identifying and visualizing research groups in co-authorship networks. *Scientometrics*, *82*(2), 307–319. doi:10.1007/s11192-009-0040-z

Prieto, J., Fernández-Ballesteros, R., & Carpintero, H. (1994). Contemporary psychology in Spain. *Annual Review of Psychology*, *45*(1), 51–78. doi:10.1146/annurev.ps.45.020194.000411

Pritchard, A. (1969). Statistical bibliography or bibliometrics. *The Journal of Documentation*, *25*, 348.

Racherla, P., & Hu, C. (2010). A social network perspective of tourism research collaborations. *Annals of Tourism Research*, *37*(4), 1012–1034. doi:10.1016/j.annals.2010.03.008

Reijers, H. A., Song, M., Romero, H., Dayal, U., Eder, J., & Koehler, J. (2009). A collaboration and productiveness analysis of the BPM community. *Business Process Management. Proceedings*, *5701*, 1–14.

Romera Iruela, M. J. (1996). Citas y referencias bibliográficas en el sistema de comunicación científica. *Revista Complutense De Educación*, *7*(1), 243–270.

Rosas, S. R., Kagan, J. M., Schouten, J. T., Slack, P. A., & Trochim, W. M. K. (2011). Evaluating research and impact: A bibliometric analysis of research by the NIH/NIAID HIV/AIDS clinical trials networks. *PLoS ONE*, *6*(3). doi:10.1371/ journal.pone.0017428

Schultz-Jones, B. (2009). Examining information behavior through social networks: An interdisciplinary review. *The Journal of Documentation*, *65*(4), 592–631. doi:10.1108/00220410910970276

Shapiro, M. A., So, M., & Park, H. (2010). Quantifying the national innovation system: Inter-regional collaboration networks in South Korea. *Technology Analysis and Strategic Management*, *22*(7), 845–857. doi:10.1080/0953732 5.2010.511158

Sharma, M., & Urs, S. R. (2008). Network of scholarship: Uncovering the structure of digital library author community. *Digital Libraries: Universal and Ubiquitous Access to Information*, *5362*, 363–366. doi:10.1007/978-3-540-89533-6_45

Sierra, G. (2003). Deconstrucción de los tribunales del CSIC en el período 1985-2002: Profesores de investigación en el área de física. *Apuntes De Ciencia y Tecnología*, *7*, 30–38.

Smykla, E., & Zippel, K. (2010). Literature review: Gender and international research collaboration. *OISE*, *936970*. Retrieved from http:// www.archive.org/ stream/ logarithmischtr0 0bremgoog/ logarithmischtr0 0bremgoog_ djvu.txt.

Sorensen, A. A., Seary, A., & Riopelle, K. (2010). Alzheimer's disease research: A COIN study using co-authorship network analytics. In *Proceedings of the 1st Collaborative Innovation Networks Conference (Coins2009)*, (pp. 6582-6586). COINS Press.

Sun, W.-J., & Jiang, A.-X. (2009). *The collaboration network in china's management science*. Paper presented at the Management Science and Engineering Conference. Moscow, Russia.

Tonta, Y., & Darvish, H. R. (2010). Diffusion of latent semantic analysis as a research tool: A social network analysis approach. *Journal of Informetrics*, *4*(2), 166–174. doi:10.1016/j.joi.2009.11.003

Valenciano Valcarcel, J., Devis-Devis, J., Villamon, M., & Peiro-Velert, C. (2010). Scientific cooperation in the field of physical activity and sport science in Spain. *Revista Espanola la de Documentacion Cientifica*, *33*(1), 90–105.

Velden, T., Haque, A., & Lagoze, C. (2010). A new approach to analyzing patterns of collaboration in co-authorship networks: Mesoscopic analysis and interpretation. *Scientometrics*, *85*(1), 219–242. doi:10.1007/s11192-010-0224-6

Vinkler, P. (1987). A quasi-quantitative citation model. *Scientometrics*, *12*(1), 47–72. doi:10.1007/BF02016689

Wasserman, S. (1994). *Social network analysis: Methods and applications*. Cambridge, UK: Cambridge University Press.

Yan, E., & Ding, Y. (2009). Applying centrality measures to impact analysis: A coauthorship network analysis. *Journal of the American Society for Information Science and Technology*, *60*(10), 2107–2118. doi:10.1002/asi.21128

Yan, E., Ding, Y., & Zhu, Q. (2010). Mapping library and information science in China: A coauthorship network analysis. *Scientometrics*, *83*(1), 115–131. doi:10.1007/s11192-009-0027-9

Chapter 15
Collaborative and Distributed Innovation and Research in Business Activity

Rob Allan
Science and Technology Facilities Council, UK

Rob Crouchley
Lancaster University, UK

Alastair Robertson
Lancaster University, UK

ABSTRACT

This chapter describes how Value Networks (VNs) can be applied in multi-stakeholder business and research environments to characterise different approaches to collaboration. In an attempt to highlight some of the issues, the authors compare a couple of communities that adopt different approaches to Knowledge Exchange (KE) and resource discovery. A collaboration framework is used by one of the communities for on-line discussion, chat, and Web conferencing to supplement KE between fairly regular in-person meetings. The other community applies more traditional collaboration tools such as e-mail to supplement face-to-face meetings. One of the research objectives was to establish the extent of multi-dimensional KE, i.e. from academic to business sector, business sector to business sector, and government to business sector. Conditional on successful e-facilitation, a quickening in KE was apparent in the community that used the collaboration framework. This was observed to a lesser or greater extent across all stakeholder groups. E-facilitators are those that engage stakeholders into making on-line submissions. The authors discuss the importance of satisfactory levels of support for collaboration frameworks in community projects. They compare the role of the e-facilitator with a more traditional "business broker" and compare the behaviour of the communities with and without particular collaboration tools. The authors conclude that VNs helped provide a useful characterisation of the roles that the various contributing community elements play and the types of interaction between them.

DOI: 10.4018/978-1-4666-0125-3.ch015

INTRODUCTION

This chapter will describe how we used an approach based on Value Networks (VNs) to characterise two different communities, both of which try to join up research and business activity. A collaboration framework is used by one of the communities, but a mix of more traditional tools such as e-mail and face-to-face (F2F) meetings are used by the other. We also describe some of our experiences of adapting the tools designed for collaborative learning and research to meet the evolving needs of the community that used the collaboration framework.

Using ICT to manage and provide tools for a distributed community enables us to capture information about that community. There is nothing new in this, it is going on all around us and sometimes referred to as "Reality Mining." Indeed the use of data to understand the world around us has been referred to as the "Fourth Paradigm" (e.g. by Bell, et al., 2009). Understanding and modelling such a community in the form of a Value Network (VN) can take us a step beyond the Enterprise and the Supply Chain. Much of the work on Value Network analysis has been done by Allee (2008). We describe the VN perspective, this is the approach we use to help us understand the complex sets of social and technical resources and relations that create business, economic and social value in our two communities. The VN literature says "Value networks are complex sets of social and technical resources that create business, economic and social value." We use the VN concept to help us understand the role of the Sakai collaboration environment (technical resources) in knowledge exchange in a range of contexts. Sakai is a community source Collaboration and Learning Environment (CLE), see Sakai (2011) which is introduced later on as our preferred collaboration platform.

A Value Network is a business analysis perspective that describes social and technical resources within and between businesses. Its nodes, depending on the scale, can represent people, groups, companies or roles. Multi-level or layered value networks may be required to capture the salient features of the process of interest. The nodes are connected by interactions that represent tangible deliverables (e.g. contracts, payment) and intangible ones (e.g. benefits that build relationships, favours). Whilst more abstract in concept and by the way it is usually applied, we will attempt to show that Value Network Analysis can replace Enterprise Modelling as a way to represent a distributed community. Understanding the network can help us understand the role each partner is playing, how and where new partners might be added, and how to improve the efficiency of business processes to the mutual benefit of the whole. Value Networks also evolve over time (e.g. Allee & Schwabe, 2009). In a similar way we have found that the requirements of an on-line community also evolve over time as they work together and their understanding of the tools matures. Key to this is to provide a platform that allows multi-directional Knowledge Exchange (KE) and new *ad hoc* communities of interest to form and old ones to wither when they become inactive. The benefit to stakeholders is rapid generation of solutions to problems. A requirement of the groups we worked with is that the software tool set evolves with their need. A key discussion point of this research is that open source collaboration software provides this flexibility and can also be applied to develop 'private Cloud' access to shared resources. As we discuss, this provides research centres with the flexibility to develop software that solves communication problems for their research groups and remains in tune to local data protection legislation.

This chapter presents the case for developing new research collaborations involving business and academia where the functional activities are centred about e-research tools required by the users. We start by discussing some examples of commercial cloud based tools for business, before moving to discuss Sakai, a community/

open source software collaboration framework. We use two case studies to help illustrate the issues involved in deploying Sakai to the interface between business and academia. We note that, to improve the chance of success, users should be evaluated at the outset to determine anticipated needs and stakeholder computer competency. We also discuss the importance of e-facilitation to enhance the likelihood that a research group will succeed on-line. We then discuss the importance of training those that use the tools to ensure that they are applied to best effect and highlight the need to endogenise technology deployment so that it is used as part of everyday routine.

CLOUD BASED TOOLS

Although this chapter eventually looks at the application of a specific technology in its application to research, it is important to understand the role of law that may limit software deployment choices. This backcloth can be different in different countries, e.g. the UK and the USA. The European Network and Information Security Agency (ENISA) carried out an analysis of the benefits and risks and made recommendations for information security in cloud computing (Catteddu & Hogben, 2009). They considered the division of responsibility for security related factors between customer and suppliers. Two independent studies commissioned by the Joint Information Systems Committee (JISC) in the UK have also drawn conclusions from investigating the use of clouds for research (Hammond, et al., 2010; Wills, et al., 2010). These investigated using the Cloud for actually doing research, rather than broader research support activities. The key concern derived from these reports is that the UK Data Protection Act 1998 (DPA) applies to all personal data, i.e. about a living identified or identifiable individual, which cannot easily be upheld in cloud environments. There are similar principles under comparable European Law. For any cloud computing applica-

tion relevant to a UK based organisation, the Act will apply because that organisation is responsible for processing personal information. This applies even if the actual processing takes place in another country, or indeed in several countries, some of which may or may not be known, as is typical for Cloud and Web 2.0 applications.

The Act imposes obligations on the data controller (a legal term which means the organisation collecting or using the data) and on any sub-contractor used by the data controller, i.e. the service provider. It is a breach of the Act if the organisation fails to fulfill its obligations, or if the organisation fails to impose those obligations on its sub-contractors. This will almost certainly result in complex contractual arrangements if the data is not fully under control of the main organisation. Partnership agreements should reflect this, and indeed under UK Law the DPA is automatically applied to them.

Personal data handled by organisations in a research context include material on staff, students, research associates, individuals who happen to be the subject of a research project and individual contractors, suppliers and partners—all part of the value network. The data can range from the most innocuous (e.g. authors' names in a bibliography of a research report, the name of the research associate responsible for particular actions, or the web pages of members of staff) through to moderately sensitive (such as e-mails sent and received in connection with the research), through to highly sensitive (such as financial and medical details of individuals, or details of a major research study of law breaking or drug abuse where respondents, who are identifiable, have been assured anonymity). It cannot be stressed too strongly that the degree of sensitivity of the data is irrelevant—all personal data are subject to the Act—but the risk of damage and bad publicity increases with the sensitivity of the data if there is any breach of the Act.

We consider there to be a major difference between public cloud based and privately hosted (partner) services. Some of the conclusions from the above reports are synthesised in Allan (2011). Some examples of public cloud based technologies are now presented as background information.

Huddle

Huddle is a UK based company established in London in 2006, see Huddle (2011). The product is a hosted site for collaboration in business. Huddle is now used by world-wide companies, and the Web site contains case studies from The Post Office, the Belgian FPS Social Security, Kerry Foods, Boots, Aggie-Lance, and Firefly. Huddle also has offices in San Francisco and has recently established a partnership with Hewlett-Packard (HP). Huddle interfaces with Microsoft SharePoint.

The Huddle interface looks like a Web portal. It has a dashboard providing access to the main features: tasks, files, calendar (with iCal interface), notifications and news. Additional features of project work spaces include meeting setup, Web conferencing (including shared desktop), discussions, whiteboard, teams (with contact details), search, social networks (e.g. LinkedIn), apps, and Microsoft Office plug-in. Workflows can be implemented to manage processes.

CoP

Communities of Practice (CoP) for UK Local Government is a hosted site provided by Local Government Improvement and Development, part of the Local Government Association (LGA) Group. CoP Platform is a community platform which supports professional social networking, collaboration and the sharing of information and ideas across local government, the public sector and those working in public service improvement in the UK. As an example see CoP (2011). A collection of on-line facilities and services is provided including discussion forums, blogs, wikis, news feeds and a search facility (known as People Finder) allowing users who have registered to use the CoP Platform to search for and contact peers, advisers and other practitioners who are also users.

Terms and conditions include the following recommendation that could apply to most hosted solutions. "We will use reasonable endeavours to ensure that the CoP Platform is accessible 24 hours per day but the CoP Platform is provided on an 'as is' and 'as available' basis, and we give no warranties or guarantees that the CoP Platform will meet particular levels of availability or functionality. Therefore, we strongly recommend that you do not post any business critical information or material on the CoP Platform and that you keep copies of all information and content you post on the CoP Platform in accordance with your employer's policies and processes."

TSB Connect

TSB, the UK's Technology Strategy Board (part of the government Department of Business Innovation and Skills), hosts a LifeRay portal specifically aimed at open innovation and used as a social network. It has searchable lists of people and networks (TSB, 2011).

People have icons, profiles, and personal blogs and document libraries; there are currently 5,859 registered members. Networks can be sub-divided into groups and sub-groups. They have News, Articles, Priority Areas, Groups, Events, Funding, Members, and Document Library.

TSB has featured networks and ratings to incentivise participants. There is some aggregation of content on the home pages and a keyword search engine which works across either networks or people. Much of the content is publicly viewable, but log-in is required for the sensitive information.

Microsoft and Apple also provides ranges of solutions for business, see for example: Microsoft (2011) and Apple (2011).

Although the technologies described above may be applied in the UK context for research and are often DPA assured (unlike Google Wave or Facebook groups due to their inherent privacy issues), they lack flexibility to be deployed as the research groups would like. For example, some research groups may have heritage tools that users are familiar with and happy to use. It is unlikely that one of the above services could provide integration services for the organisation that would embody existing tools. It is common among larger enterprises to develop and deploy technologies in a bespoke way by tailoring tools to meet the need of the enterprise. SAP is a private company that provides e-business tool integration services, but it is prohibitively expensive for any except the largest of organisations. Off the shelf cloud platforms do not allow the level of flexibility needed by enterprise as the programming code (i.e. the source code) is kept in-house by the service supplier. Although the tool sets described meet the needs of the Act, they may not be flexible enough to meet the needs of the research organisation. To overcome this limitation we have sought to apply Open Source (OS) tools. In Open Source, the programming code is available to all and may be used and modified without reasonable limitation (subject to the adopted license). A key advantage is that users can build their own private/ partner Cloud services from the freely available code. As importantly, tools can be tailored and integrated based on existing ways of working that would better meet their community's needs.

In terms of collaboration tools, up until 2005-2006 few OS technologies existed that could compete with commercial offerings. Since this time however, two OS Learning Management Systems (LMS) have been developed (Moodle and Sakai), these were designed around lecturer-student on-line collaboration. The deployment of OS LMS in the business context is not new, see e.g. the book by Cole et al. (2011) on Moodle in business. However, in what follows we concentrate on Sakai as it has been used in projects funded by JISC to develop Virtual Research Environments for a number of academic research domains.

Sakai

Sakai was developed, starting at University of Michigan, as an OS collaboration tool for teaching and learning. It is also used to support e-Research activities. A guiding principle of Sakai developers is that "if your business depends on it, you need to have the capability to modify, develop and maintain it in house" (after Severance, et al., 2007). Sakai is now one of the world's largest OS portal projects, managed by the Sakai Foundation with over 340 production installations including Universities of Oxford, see Oxford (2011) and Cambridge (2011) in the UK; see also Sakai (2011). Sakai is a pluggable Java framework and is downloaded and installed using the Tomcat Web server and a database such as mySQL. It is distributed under the Educational Community License which gives the freedom to modify the source and use it in a variety of purposes. The Foundation encourages developers to contribute modifications and additions back for other developers thus creating a vibrant community.

Authentication is built into Sakai as a core functionality. There is internally a strong role based security model with the capability to have moderated or joinable work sites and individual roles of senior site members granting permissions in them (Allan & Yang, 2008). A number of projects in the UK have developed additional tools to plug into Sakai to enable it to be used as a Virtual Research Environment (Allan, 2009). These can connect to Grids and Clouds for computational and data storage resources.

Figure 1 considers work contexts along two dimensions: first, whether collaboration is co-located or geographically distributed, and second, whether individuals collaborate synchronously (same time) or asynchronously (not depending on others to be around at the same time). Sakai has a comprehensive suite of collaboration tools available 'out of the box.' This suite is being augmented by plugging in bespoke tools written in Java, either following the Sakai API development guidelines (tightly coupled tools) or using the JSR-168 portlet API (loosely coupled tools). All the tools can be located on the CSCW matrix, in fact in previous work (Severance, et al., 2007) we identified the need for an audio-visual conferencing tool in this way. The idea is to create an integrated Web 2.0 like environment with everything in one place and single sign on. Back office data is stored in a database which could potentially be used for monitoring and to gather usage statistics.

There is a very large range of tools provided with Sakai which can be configured to appear as portlets on pages belonging to project work sites. The tools we have at our disposal for collaboration and research comprise of the following: home page (information), announcements, calendar, chat room, clog (a blog tool), discussions, drop box, e-mail and archive, forums, glossary, mail-

tool, meetings (BigBlueButton video conferencing), messages, news (RSS reader), people, podcasts, polls, resources, search, site admin, site stats, user generator, video material, web content (iFrame), wiki. Many of these are described in greater detail below.

There are additional tools that can be deployed although they are mostly applied in the e-learning context. There are Learning Tools Interoperability (LTI), evaluations (Open Source Portfolio), forms, learning log, lessons, sessions, link tool, markbook, matrices (OSP), portfolio (OSPI), syllabus, tests and quizzes, wizards (OSP). Some of these could be useful for professional training purposes. There are many more tools developed for educational purposes and there is a well documented procedure for developing and adding other tools. The international community is

Figure 1. CSCW matrix (source: Wikipedia, under Creative Commons Public Domain)

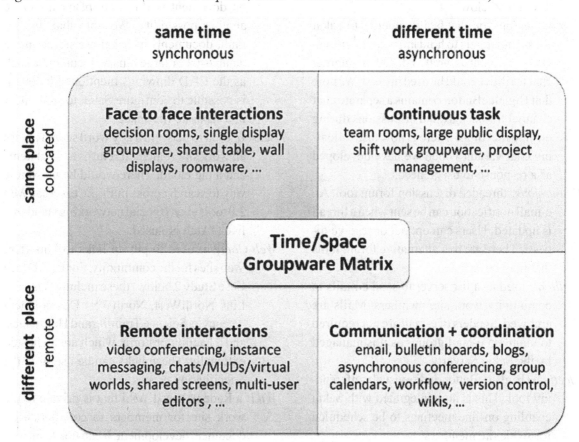

rapidly developing Sakai-3, now known as the Open Academic Environment (OAE), which will have many more social networking features, apps, workflow, and content management capabilities. Note also that users have a 'synoptic' view of some of these tools as they log in (in a site called MyWorkspace), in other words they have a dashboard showing information gathered from all the work sites of which they are a member. MyWorkspace also contains important tools like account, membership and profile. The latter is being extended for social networking activities using open standards. Below is a list of tools and their application to e-collaboration as used by the groups we have worked with.

Announcement: used to post announcements to work site members. An e-mail notification can be sent. An e-mail list server could be used as an alternative to this and the Mailtool described below.

Chat Room: on-line chat facility internal to Sakai for site members to hold impromptu discussions. Content is archived. Other internet chat facilities could be used instead. We note that BigBlueButton contains a separate chat channel for background discussions during on-line meetings. There is now also a floating chat variant which we have developed as a response to users' needs.

Discussions: threaded discussion forum tool. An e-mail notification can be sent when a thread is updated. Users can opt out or receive digests. There are two alternative forum tools that may be selected.

Mailtool: used as a list server to send e-mails to community work site members. Mails are archived. Senders of e-mail are not required to maintain e-mail groups as it is managed by the Sakai Server

Meetings: BigBlueButton audio-visual conferencing tool. This is now integrated with Sakai enabling on-line meetings to be scheduled for work site members.

Profile: used to publish information about yourself, both work related and personal. Users can control which information is visible to other users. They can search by interest and connect to people across all Sakai sites to form networks.

People: used for sharing information between community members. Shows all people on a work site and links to their published profiles, it also provides a quick way to find how to contact people directly.

Resources: shared folders for work site members to post documents and links. An e-mail notification can be sent when a resource is added or changed. Whilst there are public Web 2.0 sites for sharing specific resources like photos (Flickr) and video material (YouTube) we have found few usable alternatives to the general purpose Sakai Resources tool. Google Docs can be used to collaborate on document writing. DropBox might be another possibility. We note that, by default, documents in Sakai are stored in the database. For large binary documents, such as the CAD drawings mentioned below, it is possible to configure Sakai to store them in a separate file space.

Search: used to perform a key word search across all work site content. It returns a list of items and a tag cloud. There would be no simple way to search across multiple external Web 2.0 tools even if social networking standards like OAuth are used.

Web Content: used to put up links to important Web sites for the community. For LEAD (see Case Study 2 below) these include Business Link NorthWest, NorthWest Development Agency, e-Science Training and Help pages, and a Facilitator Form, which are all hosted externally. These links can be useful in the e-facilitation process.

Wiki: a Radeox based Wiki that is private to the work site for members to collaborate on document development. It can link to images and documents in Resources. Wiki is also widely used to record meetings, monitoring development status, etc. There are many external Wiki tools maintained for different purposes—there is even a book on the subject (Klobas, 2006).

Thus far, this chapter has highlighted why Sakai was selected to support research, but it also provides the flexibility to design the platform around the interface of business and academia's needs. We now present two case studies that illustrate individual research scenarios. These are described in terms of Value Network principles. Both case studies support business activities, although the research centers are funded (mostly) by UK's central government.

TWO ILLUSTRATIVE CASE STUDIES

We use two case studies to help us illustrate the issues that arise in deploying and supporting some collaborative technology to the interface between academia and business. In what follows we are not attempting to scientifically understand this process nor attempt to describe current UK practice. Obtaining a representative sample of business and academic practices in the UK is very difficult. First of all, the most appropriate contact details for this list are not publically accessible. Furthermore, to undertake any statistically valid analysis we would need to allow for informative sample selection and for informative technology adoption. Its well known that the reasons why organisations participate in surveys tends to be informative about why they do or don't use particular technologies. The informative nature of the likely sample data and the responses of interest cannot be ignored. A further complication that would apply in a quantitative analysis is that we would also need to know why some businesses want to work with academic institutions and others don't, and *vice versa*. For a very thorough book

length treatment of the issue of missing data, see Little and Rubin (1987). Cross classified tables using the observed data, for example, on the type of collaboration technology by type of firm (sector) by size (employment) can only be descriptive at best, at worst they could be misleading. To be analytical, the statistical procedures applied to this table would need to allow for the correlations in the unobserved effects that affect the observed behaviours as well as their actual inclusion in the sample. The data on this do not exist, e.g. firms are reluctant to provide any insight to the reasons for why they do or don't do things. Our findings can only be suggestive of the issues, we do not claim they are scientifically valid. It is up to the reader to put our case studies into their own context. There is no one way to do this and no one best interpretation.

Case Study 1: The Virtual Engineering Centre

Our first case study of the Virtual Engineering Centre (VEC) illustrates a traditional approach to managing a large collaborative research projects combining both academic and business partners, see VEC (2011). The VEC is a University of Liverpool project partially funded by the North West Regional Development Agency (NWDA) and the European Regional Development Fund (ERDF). It is located at the Daresbury Science and Innovation Campus. It was established to assist the North West UK aerospace sector and wider industry by providing a focal point for world class virtual engineering technology, research, education and best practice with the aim of improving business performance throughout the supply chain.

The VEC was thus set up to help both small companies and larger organisations embrace ICT in the rapid design life cycle. The intention being that companies bringing their expertise together and using computational modelling would reduce the time taken from idea to product. The manufacturing process and test phases can be modelled prior to implementation and some validation carried out *in silico* to avoid expensive and time consuming prototyping and testing. The use of high definition 3D visualisation is a key element to share information and allow parties to walk through all the stages in the process. On-line access to simulation tools and a document store (which can contain Computer Aided Design [CAD] images among other things) are also required. The key here is to bring together various problem solvers (i.e. programmers, technical specialists, designers, and general users) and to provide them various computational resources that can be applied to develop an idea into a final consumable product.

Another example of this emerging usage model is from the JISC funded National e-Infrastructure for Social Simulation (NeISS) project. In this project, simulations are undertaken to illustrate the impact of decision making on urban environments with a realistic population model over a 30 year period. The results of various scenarios are shown on maps available to the general public and partly result from surveys on topics of interest. This ultimately gives public awareness of and participation in the planning process. The project is described in NeISS (2011), and some of the tools are illustrated. Urban planners wishing for instance to look at the impact of a new road on surrounding existing infrastructure and evolving population would require the skills of programmers to develop software to enact various scenarios. Multiple assumption based runs can be made on a computational Grid to determine whether a new road is likely to impact positively and under which assumptions do problems occur. Typically, users in this space (i.e. the urban planners) will be domain specialists able to input realistic data to the system and analyse the outputs, once the simulation tools have been set up by the programmers. The computational specialists, although not urban planners, understand the complexity of developing and running computationally intensive algorithms and can create the visual outputs (e.g. a map) that the urban planning

specialists can use. Outputs may also be required to be accessible by less technical users such as policy makers or residents in the area, and software is being simplified and provided in a Web based portal to accommodate this type of user. The Taverna-2 workflow system, see Taverna-2 (2011), is used to lead the user through various steps in the simulation and ensure the results are consistent across computational runs.

To accomplish its goals, the VEC currently plays multiple roles and is pivotal to successful collaboration and the uptake of the virtual engineering methodology. It negotiates and provides a suite of licensed software running on top end computational (NW-GRID) and visualisation resources thus providing a facility that small firms can access. It provides consultancy through its in-house researchers and software experts, plus it can call upon other experts at universities (e.g. automotive and aerospace), the Daresbury Laboratory and other companies on the Campus. It also acts as a business broker, potentially bringing partners together as driven by the needs of the various industries it supports. Whilst Web sites are used by the VEC and North West Aerospace Alliance as shop windows on their support activities, they currently do not use on-line collaboration. Thus the role of broker is key to their success using face-to-face meetings, telephone and e-mail to share information. For the purposes of this chapter we refer to this as traditional communication methods. A VN characterisation of the VEC is given in Figure 2.

The network diagram in Figure 2 illustrates the initial phase of the Virtual Engineering Centre with just one node labelled "Enterprise Partners," the latter including both Small and Medium Enterprises (SMEs) and larger companies who use the VEC facilities and get support. There is no clear centre to this network diagram. Centrality could be provided by the application of portal software to integrate project resources under single sign-on authentication. This could raise efficiency and simplifies access for various users.

Figure 2. Value network for the virtual engineering centre and its stakeholders

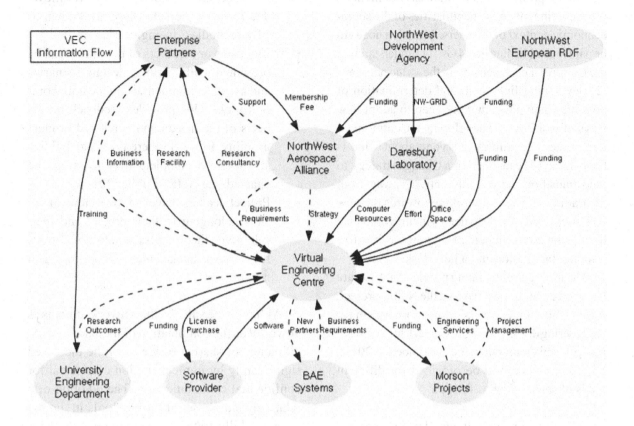

In the VEC's present traditional communication system, project resources must be managed by each user at their local machine (e.g. save attachments into their local file stores). For example, outputs from CAD software can be viewed by the design specialists but if other less technical specialists or potential customers require outputs the designers would need to make this information available in a more accessible form. Typically images can be circulated as attachment via e-mail and face-to-face meetings can make use of the 3D visualisation facility. There are, however, problems with circulating potentially sensitive business information by e-mail (security, spam, etc.). Multiple e-mail threads may be appropriate for general messages that people now receive on a day-to-day basis, but a more secure and managed project space is required for sharing data.

Some partners are now beginning to use Sakai to assist in the management of projects and have expressed an interest in using it to provide support to their own 'customers' as part of the overall supply chain. The use of Sakai has been discussed generically above, and will be further addressed in the second case study. In VEC, Sakai will enable on-line collaboration among designers and manufacturers and also enable feedback from end users of engineering products. We envisage the provision of a small number of tools to enable end users to test small changes to the design specification, run simulations on a computational Grid using pre-defined workflows and visualise the results of their changes. In this way they can participate in the overall process and better understand the reason for some of the final design choices.

The adoption of collaboration environments is often contingent on the peculiarities of the socio-economic context of the users. Attention needs to be paid to establishing the '4 Cs': (1) understanding the Culture of each activity in the value network; (2) developing links with and determination of possible Champions that are keen to adopt new ways of working; (3) developing a Communication strategy to inform everyone about what is happening; (4) establishing a Change strategy to help transition the existing activity away from the traditional ways of working towards the new ICT supported VN. Any deployment would also require the establishment of support services like training, facilitation and a help desk.

The tools currently being provided in VEC are based on development work in the NeISS project. A trial is also under way of a workflow system for engineering design using the CenterLink software from Phoenix Integration Inc., see Phoenix (2011). Different tools are to be provided for different kinds of stakeholder as follows:

- Experts or consultants develop simulation tools with access to the best available data, Grid based computational resources and open source (or commercial) applications. The simulations can be validated in depth and used as design modelling tools. These tools are made available in a portal "Simulation" or "Analysis" work site with separate portlet interfaces for each tool and an accompanying set of collaboration tools. A separate work site is provided for each design project.

- Experts compose the tools and data into a workflow. This will enable others who are less familiar with the computational aspects to vary a small number of parameters and re-run the complete design simulation to see the results, potentially in a visual format such as a map or artefact view. Various design scenarios can then be tested and their impact analysed. Again, collabora-

tion tools are provided with a "Workflow" site for each project. These are known as "Trade Studies" in engineering design.

- End users or members of the public can be presented with various design scenarios and asked to comment using the collaboration tools. This provides feedback on aspects of the design and perceived product usability. In NeISS there is also a "Public" site where a complete workflows can be enacted, see NeISS Public (2011).

- Project leaders have an overview of all sites belonging to their project and their role gives them access to additional tools for project management, reporting, and monitoring.

Although the value of the network remains as powerful as the combination of its stakeholders, efficiency of sharing of ideas can be increased significantly by implementation of a portal for confidential communication. The addition of a relatively simple set of on-line tools in the usage model illustrated above provides access for multiple user types and makes sharing and use of design data more efficient. It is useful to consider how business processes may be affected had the VEC considered employing a more centralised approach to managing resources via the application of intranet and extranet functions that portals can provide and how this would affect their value network. A VN characterisation of how the collaboration environment (Sakai) could be deployed by Enterprise Partners is given in Figure 3.

The VEC case study shows how existing projects are beginning to adopt portals to support project communications in various ways combining collaboration and design and simulation tools. The thrust of the argument posed here is that any new research and development centre should use ICT to support workloads endogenously, rather than adding disparate components without full consideration of the capabilities of the various

Figure 3. Value network showing the central role of Sakai for an enterprise partner

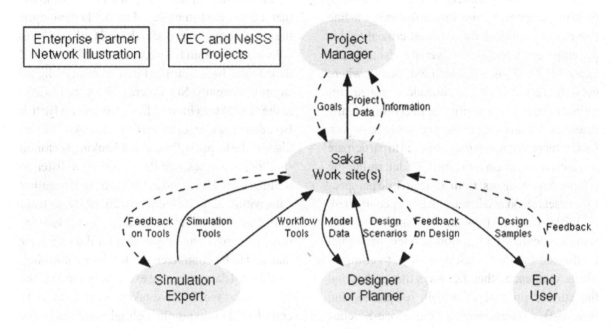

users. The second case study exemplifies where this has occurred.

Case Study 2: LEAD and CRIB

Our second case study arises from a relatively small project called Collaborative Research in Business (CRIB). It is another JISC funded project, this time examining KE conduits between government agencies, entrepreneurs of Small and Medium sized Enterprises (SMEs) and academics. Central to the CRIB project was to build web based social networking tools into the existing Sakai Collaboration and Learning Environment; to harness the power of social networking but minimizing the risk associated with public social nets such as Facebook. Prior to CRIB, Sakai provided managers of communities (e.g. research, learning or communities of practice) with secure on-line spaces called worksites where asynchronous communication tools are provided as described above.

It is useful to visualise the case where technology had not been implemented for leadership in SMEs (LEAD). Lancaster University, Institute

of Entrepreneurship and Enterprise Development (IEED) LEAD programme began in 2002 and for early cohorts communication was managed by face-to-face interaction, letters, telephone and e-mail. This implies that the N-dimensional on-line communication we seek was unavailable, except via e-mail lists and face-to-face interaction. The Director of LEAD sought novel technological approaches to support enhanced communication between meetings, so that interest in various leadership matters could be maintained. An issue surrounding the use of e-mail is the problem of un-workable multi-dimensional mail shots becoming lost in the time line of receipt. To address this problem LEAD initially selected various PHPBB forums and tested their use on LEAD delegates. A key feature they sought was to foster e-community engagement so that the overhead of traditional communication methods could be reduced. For example, if most participants could be encouraged to communicate on-line, the management team felt that it would reduce the need for mail lists, physical mail shots and also provide delegates with a searchable database of past communication threads on various matters. From a knowledge growth perspective, the move towards on-line community building was deemed crucial to this development. Lancaster University Management School (LUMS) is a research led faculty where most interactions with the 'outside world' are required to have some positive impact on academic research. To this end, those that study at or join Lancaster programmes may be asked to participate in research from time to time. To determine the feature requirements, from an academic perspective, research on academic needs was conducted.

Initial findings from surveys and interviews with academics and public service personnel confirmed that they seek new ways to communicate with each other, i.e. ways that go beyond the current practice of e-mail, telephone, and face-to-face. The Lancaster Centre for e-Science began working with LEAD to provide worksites that support on-line communication between Owner-Managers (OMs) of SMEs and the IEED in order to support the delivery of LEAD. Sakai provides an on-line space where OMs can communicate between monthly face-to-face meetings. A LEAD cohort consists of approximately 25 OMs and a number of e-facilitators. The latter guide on-line conversations within each cohort setting. For example, e-facilitators continue to encourage on-line activity between meetings by asking delegates about news items of the day that should be of interest to others. This approach quickens KE as forum responses to questions like this tend to be quicker than by conducting telephone interviews and is less costly. It is also used by OMs to ask other OMs questions that relate to their business. Many OMs of smaller enterprises report that they have few business support mechanisms available, but that LEAD provides them with a space where they can bounce ideas around other OMs. An additional value of using forums for this type of activity is that they are searchable later on, in this sense, tacit knowledge held by individuals become explicit within the worksite.

From time to time, e-facilitators ask questions that are relevant to policy. The IEED developed the e-facilitation approach adopted for LEAD that culminates in rapid KE between e-facilitators and their OMs; based on trust and enduring 'digital capital.' Recently, Sue Peters (Director of LEAD at the IEED) was invited for interview on British Broadcasting Corporation (BBC) Breakfast TV to discuss the impact of the ailing banking sector on smaller businesses, see Peters (2009) to listen to the interview. Using Sakai LEAD forums to gather data, within 12 hours more than 20 responses from a diverse base of approximately 60 OMs were received, providing ample data for the interview that was to be conducted the following morning. Traditional data gathering exercises looking at the same issues would have taken several weeks to complete. This example highlights the value that can be derived from managing large numbers of OMs to become part of a self supporting cohesive e-community of business leaders advising public sector on urgent matters of the day, quickly, securely and efficiently; but also becoming a potent and cohesive voice for smaller businesses. In this sense, the value network shows how KE occurs faster between smaller business owners and the public sector and crucially, how knowledge from academic and the public sector diffuses to smaller companies.

An additional value of LEAD has been to link a first-hand perspective on the user needs of OMs and the e-facilitators and to develop Sakai tools based on their needs. Early on, it quickly became apparent that OMs are more comfortable using the platform if they can identify those people that they are communicating with. To accommodate this, a profiling system was designed that linked into a newly designed forum tool, this allows users to read profiles while browsing forum posts. In fact, this approach is applied today and is how CRIB became a reality. For a review of LEAD see LEAD (2008).

During 2009, LEAD was extended across the North West England and Welsh regions via a network of 15 institutions, which are a mix of universities, higher education institutions and private training organisations. The LEAD project is funded by the North West Regional Development Agency (NWDA) and Welsh Assembly and the development of on-line tools is funded by JISC. There are presently 6 stakeholders in the project that include the 3 funding agencies, IEED, Lancaster Centre for e-Science and the OMs. Lancaster University Management School and the parent Lancaster University may also be considered independent stakeholders as they are cost centres and their policies are independently operated. To date, the Lancaster Centre for e-Science has managed approximately 1,500 OMs on-line across 50 cohorts. CRIB was designed to provide the software that would enable a self supporting community of businesses and includes better identification and contact support; but it also helps to make knowledge permeate between the stakeholders. A key takeaway message from this work was that to obtain any large scale adoption by all key stakeholders (IEED, NWDA, and OMs) we need to endogenise the technology into the programme, so that the use of the portal becomes a day to day expectation rather than something "we might need to do."

In Figure 4, the arrows highlight the permeability of knowledge and other assets between the main stakeholders. The academics at business schools need continuous contact with SMEs for various reasons, including the validation of new theories of business practice as well as learning how to improve business performance by developing new and relevant programmes for Owner-Managers (OMs) and their staff. Crucially, entrepreneurs participate in the network in order to become attached to other entrepreneurs that form a business support network. To provide a link between entrepreneurs and government, entrepreneurs must be engaged in such a way as to feel confident about the supply of information to academics and government. When trust emerges (e.g. via the use of e-facilitation techniques designed to engage with entrepreneurs) and is supported via an on-line collaboration platform, knowledge exchange quickens because of the use of Web 2.0 tools such as discussion forum, chat, wiki, blog, announcements, mail, and a document store, all of which are found in the Sakai Collaboration and Learning Environment.

Figure 4 characterises the Lancaster Value Network. The other VNs are obtained by replacing Lancaster University Management School with the provider's name and dropping the e-Science Lancaster, CRIB and JISC sub-graph. Sakai is used to provide secure communication work sites to project groups, learning groups and other communities. During the summer of 2010, Sakai 2.7 was released and an enhanced range of communication tools including social networking tools and Web conferencing were deployed.

External Web resources and tools are being added as required. Hierarchical role based security is embedded in the framework so that a single Sakai instance can manage many independent collaboration sites for which membership is moderated (i.e. people are added and their roles defined by the Sakai administrators, thus protecting the data and other on-line assets). The main advantage of using a secure collaboration environment is that entrepreneurs get to know academic staff (often their e-facilitators) and develop the 'digital capital' required to engage with other entrepreneurs successfully (see Tapscott, Ticol, & Lowy, 2000). This means that academic staff become respected by their delegates in a unique way and to the extent that OMs are highly likely to respond to information requests from academics. Making the social network private (i.e. hosted by one of the partners) rather than in the cloud means that we can respond to the legal requirements and adapt the framework in an agile manner to meet the needs of the community (Allan, 2011). It also means that government can take advantage of the on-line linkages forged by academics via the e-facilitators as such information can be captured (subject to prior agreement). Note that this activ-

Figure 4. Value network for LEAD and CRIB project stakeholders

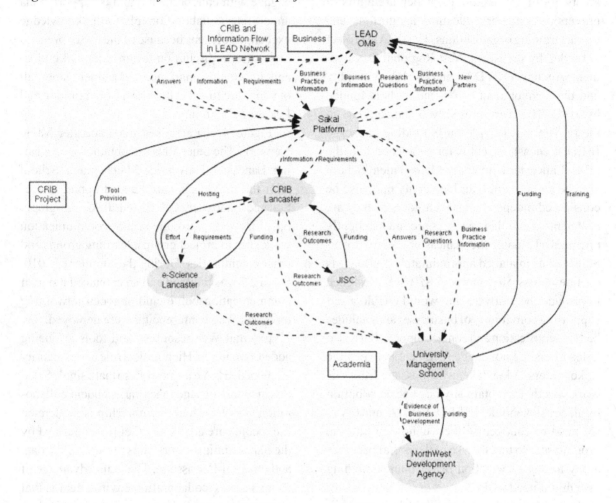

ity is different to 'crowd sourcing' as it targets a specific set of questions at an expert community and if often more useful for research.

KE is also heterogeneous among groups. For example, KE between academia and business enterprises can be in the form of student placements or academics supporting enterprise activities via training. An example of knowledge transferred from business to university and then onto business occurred when Lancaster Master of Business Administration (MBA) students contacted entrepreneurs via e-facilitators for a project sponsored by Price Waterhouse Coopers requesting face-to-face interviews and completion of an on-line survey. This resulted in 13 inter-

views being completed and a 33% response rate to the survey. More typically, mail surveys yield response rates of around 10 to 15%. Knowledge transfers from business to university can occur also. More usually, entrepreneurs are notoriously difficult to engage in research but the application of the Sakai work sites via e-facilitated groups of entrepreneurs increased participation rates. During recent evaluations conducted on 80 entrepreneurs, a questionnaire was deployed within Sakai. With encouragement from e-facilitators via forums, a response rate of nearly 100% was achieved. These successful KE activities highlight the desire of the OMs to voluntarily engage with public sector researchers and it is likely that the development of a larger e-community of SMEs based on the e-facilitation principle will provide us the platform to understand business practice better and to inform policy. Moreover, it provides the public sector with a conduit to pass information to sizable numbers of entrepreneurs. Crucially, the work sites provide a safe space where OMs can communicate among themselves which is a further conduit for KE. For example, delegates can ask each other questions relating to their businesses practices.

PROBLEMS IN DEPLOYMENT ACROSS CASE DOMAINS

We now summarise deployment lessons learnt under the headings of e-facilitation, software training, and endogenising technology deployment.

Importance of e-Facilitation

There are several books on community building that help describe many of the issues that arise in e-facilitation, see e.g. Kim (2000), Wenger et al. (2002, 2009), and Bacon (2009). It was mentioned during the second case study that the role of e-facilitation is to engage users into communicating on-line. However, we maintain that the importance of e-facilitation in the uptake of technology offerings is poorly understood and is often under estimated by the academic and business communities. Of the 15 providers that deliver LEAD, many had e-facilitation skills that were un-satisfactory. For some the problem lay with their ability or desire to use computers generally, for others shyness of being on-line was a problem. For those institutions that e-facilitated well, they could expect forum posts in excess of 300 per cohort plus regular chat sessions. Eight institutions are considered to have e-facilitated well using a blend of announcements, forum posting and chats. Different e-facilitators applied the tools in different ways; the impact of this heterogeneity is worthy of further investigation.

A further lesson learnt is that good e-facilitators are quite a rare breed. LEAD has placed us in contact with more than 100 e-facilitators, some excellent, some bad. Overall, good facilitators tend to be good social networkers generally and enjoy communicating with people and finding out how they 'tick.' By doing so, they are able to engage others into communication about specific issues. Even academics and trainers that provide excellent face-to-face facilitation may not be very good at e-facilitation. Good e-facilitation requires the person to be strongly motivated to communicate on-line. This may be evidenced by the degree to which they are attached to on-line social networks such as LinkedIn or Facebook. It is also of benefit if they are mentally attached to the community in question. When managing OMs, knowledge of news items important to OMs is useful, so that conversations about the issues can be stimulated. If the e-facilitator is not attached to the community in this way, they may find it difficult to keep conversations moving forward. Generally, as soon as the e-facilitation stops, so does the conversation.

Importance of Software Training

Software training is particularly important in the case of deploying new technologies with which no one in the client community is familiar. This is emphasised even more in the case of a framework like Sakai, which has a plethora of tools requiring some knowledge, planning and organisation. In our studies we have found that each community has a different preferred selection of tools and a different way of using them. It is very easy for senior project leaders to assume that technology can be learnt easily by the e-facilitators. For example, to reduce costs for the LEAD project, one training session was provided to e-facilitators with on-line support provided thereafter. This was not sufficient, given that the e-facilitators were expected to also train delegates on use of Sakai. During the early stages of deployment, insufficient training led to frustration which then led to low adoption by the OMs. In one extreme case, the provider failed to use the on-line tool set in any way. The academic institutions that sought further training at their own expense did considerably better in e-facilitation terms than those without. The recommendation from this finding is to ensure that each project has sufficient training resources to maximise returns from the community.

This is an additional problem for people who are members of more than one on-line community. Many who are active may need to log onto between 5 and 10 different portals to access information during their working day—some of these portals are associated with the administrative procedures of their own organisation, some for research and some for collaboration. Typically the interfaces are different, the exact tool functionality and usage varies and there is often no way to export data from one portal to another, let alone obtain access through single sign on. A personal 'dashboard' giving an overall picture of what new information is available from each portal would be useful. One reason why the telephone and basic e-mail continue to be used is that they are always present in the work environment, they function seamlessly and they are in common practice.

Importance of Endogenising Technology Deployment

Although tool sets can be applied 'around' the problem, they are usually better embedded within it. For example, at the development stage of the LEAD project, less training budget was allocated than was recommended (also see under the heading "Importance of Software Training" for further information). The mistaken assumption by our project designers was that people will 'learn by doing' and that most collaboration technologies are of this type. Although the technology part of the project team (the experts) made the case for better levels of training this recommendation was discounted by senior project staff to keep costs

down. For some communities this approach may work, but a number of factors need to be considered. For instance, the age group of the expected community will give you a general understanding of their pre-disposition to computer-based communication. For older age groups, if you fail to provide sufficient training resources you place the problem squarely at the feet the e-facilitators who then need to take on the role of computer trainer as well as e-facilitator. There is no reason to expect an excellent e-facilitator to be a good software trainer.

The VEC had planned in its design phase to have a portal to facilitate, manage, and monitor interactions between its partners and clients. However this seems to have been an aspiration with the idea of building a system from scratch. Sakai was demonstrated to some of the project partners, and they said that with some additional tools and data search facilities it would meet their requirements. However, with newly imposed financial constraints, this has not been taken further.

Age of cohort is usually a good indication of the level of training required. In the case of LEAD, the average age of cohort members is approximately 50. This particular age group is difficult to reach and interact with technologically. Many are far from digitally native, although all tend to use e-mail to various degrees. Many struggle with the computer or on-line world, or simply don't see the value of it in their lives. Some useful statistics exemplify the point. From LEAD cohorts, all use e-mail but only 15 to 20% use Facebook or Linke-dIn. Compare this to 20 to 25 year olds who only use e-mail for work, learning or to communicate with older generations (parents, workers, and lecturers), 98% of this age group have Facebook and LinkedIn accounts. Our digitally native younger generations prefer Facebook communication to e-mail and this type of service provides users with 'ground training' for their ability or desire to share information on-line. We find in applying Sakai as an e-learning platform, that students require little or no training to use on-line services;

older lectures can be a different story however. This implies that, if your intended community is of the younger generation, less planning for training is required although e-facilitators will more than likely need some initial assistance. Breaking old habits is hard, unless the value of doing so is perceived to exceed the pain of switching over to the new ways of working.

CONCLUSION AND FURTHER RESEARCH DIRECTIONS

For reasons explained in connection with extensibility and data protection, we chose to host an on-line Web 2.0 style platform for our research and business partners. We used Sakai for this work because it met our requirements—we were familiar with the environment and with an experienced developer skill base we were able to adapt existing tools and develop new tools as the need arose. This enabled us to add value to the network and differentiate it from publicly available cloud platforms, even those that conform to the Data Protection Act. Sakai meets our needs for a modular and secure CSCW groupware environment. Development of the Profile and People tools for social networking and integration was an important research objective for the Lancaster group in the CRIB project. This arose as a response to requirements from stakeholders in government funded projects as described above.

The next major release of Sakai is known as the Open Academic Environment (OAE). An online demonstration of this shows its use for the ATLAS Network pilot at New York University, see NYU (2011). Sakai OAE is innovative in its ability to provide a combination of networking, content authoring and management with internal group structures replacing the current work site arrangement. Its networking functionality allows participants to work together in courses, research groups, administration and other activities. It has a single dashboard and searchable profile space.

In all the work we have carried out we have realised the importance of e-facilitation. This includes training, particularly for people new to Web based technology, and leadership in bringing cohorts together for useful interactions. Once sufficient network members are active, social dynamics can lead to the self organisation and sustainability of the on-line community.

Using the language of value networks has given us an insight into the processes and requirements involved in deploying technology. This work can be extended, e.g. by placing values on the linkages of the value network to help provide more detail. Using on-line support tools where information is captured may also give us a way to quantify the interactions and study their evolution. Using this information may help provide further insight into how innovation can be stimulated in such networks thus enhancing the uptake of research outputs in small businesses.

ACKNOWLEDGMENT

We would like to thank: the JISC for funding Sakai Evaluation, Sakai Demonstrator, the CRIB project and NeISS; the NWDA for funding LEAD and NW-GRID; the UK's Engineering and Physical Sciences Research Council (EPSRC) for supporting background work on distributed and high performance computing under its service level agreement (SLA) with Daresbury Laboratory. We would also like to thank Mark Baker (University of Reading) and others participating in the Research3 Theme "The Influence and Impact of Web 2.0 on e-Research Infrastructure, Applications and Users," see Baker (2010). Our thanks also go to Chuck Severance and Ian Dolphin of the Sakai Foundation for continuing to provide support and advice; Adrian Fish (Lancaster), Dan Robinson (Lancaster) and Steve Swinsburg (Australia's National University) for technical support; John Bancroft and Michael Gleaves (STFC Innovations Ltd.) for discussions about business outreach and innovation, as well as other members of the CRIB project at Universities of Hull and Lancaster. Finally, thanks to members of the NeISS project for stimulating discussions and for providing a new rich set of open source portlet based tools for use in Sakai and other portal frameworks and to Gillan Murray and Tony Robotham of the Virtual Engineering Centre.

REFERENCES

Allan, R. J. (2009). *Virtual research environments: From portals to science gateways*. Oxford, UK: Chandos Publishing.

Allan, R. J. (2011). Clouds and Web 2.0 services supporting research. *Daresbury Laboratory*. Retrieved 1 September 2011 from http:// 193.62.125.70/ NWGrid/ Clouds/.

Allan, R. J., & Yang, X. (2008). Using role based Access Control in the Sakai Collaborative Framework. *Daresbury Laboratory*. Retrieved 1 September 2011 from http:// epubs.cclrc.ac.uk/ work-details? w=50402.

Allee, V. (2008). Value network analysis and value conversion of tangible and intangible assets. *Journal of Intellectual Capital, 9*(1), 5–24. doi:10.1108/14691930810845777

Allee, V., & Schwabe, O. (2009). *Measuring the impact of research networks in the EU: Value networks and intellectual capital formation*. Paper presented at the European Conference on Intellectual Capital. Haarlem, The Netherlands.

Apple. (2011). *Apple's web page for business*. Retrieved 1 September 2011 from http:// www.apple. com/ uk/ business/ solutions/.

Bacon, J. (2009). *The art of community: Building the new age of participation*. Sebastopol, CA: O'Reilly Media.

Baker. (2010). *The influence and impact of Web 2.0 on e-research infrastructure, applications and users*. Retrieved 1 September 2011 from http:// www.research3.org.

Bell, G., Hey, T., & Szalay, A. (2009). Computer science: Beyond the data deluge. *Science, 323*(5919), 1297–1298. doi:10.1126/science.1170411

Cambridge. (2011). *The University of Cambridge VLE home page*. Retrieved 1 September 2011 from http://camtools.caret.cam.ac.uk.

Catteddu, D., & Hogben, G. (2009). *Cloud computing - Benefits, risks and recommendations for information security*. Retrieved 1 September 2011 from http:// www.enisa.europa.eu/ act/ rm/ files/ deliverables/ cloud-computing-risk-assessment.

Cole, J., Henrick, G., & Cole, J. (2011). *Moodle 2.0 for business: Beginner's guide*. Birmingham, UK: Packt Publishing.

CoP. (2011). *The communities of practice web site*. Retrieved 1 September 2011 from http://www. communities.dl.ac.uk.

Hammond, M., Hawtin, R., Gillam, L., & Oppenheim, C. (2010). *Cloud computing for research: Report to JISC*. Retrieved 1 September 2011 from http:// www.jisc.ac.uk/ whatwedo/ programmes/ researchinfrastructure/ usingcloudcomp.aspx.

Huddle. (2011). *Huddle's web site*. Retrieved 1 September 2011 from http://www.huddle.com.

Kim, A. J. (2000). *Community building on the Web*. Berkley, CA: Peachpit Press.

Klobas, J. (2006). *Wikis: Tools for information, work and collaboration*. Oxford, UK: Chandos Publishing.

LEAD. (2008). *Lead evaluation report*. Retrieved 1 September 2011 from http:// www.lums.lancs. ac.uk/ files/ evaluation.pdf.

Little, R. J. A., & Rubin, D. B. (1987). *Statistical analysis with missing data*. New York, NY: Wiley.

Microsoft. (2011). *Microsoft's web page for business*. Retrieved 1 September 2011 from http:// www.microsoft.com/ business/ en-gb/ Pages/ default.aspx.

NeISS. (2011). *National e-infrastructure for social simulation web site*. Retrieved 1 September 2011 from http://www.neiss.org.uk.

NeISS Public. (2011). *The NeISS public web site*. Retrieved 1 September 2011 from http:// weaver. dl.ac.uk:8080/ portal/ site/ neiss_public.

NYU. (2011). *The ATLAS network pilot at New York University*. Retrieved 1 September 2011 from http:// www.nyu.edu/ its/ connect/ w11/ atlas.html.

Oxford. (2011). *WebLearn VLE home page*. Retrieved 1 September 2011 from http://weblearn. ox.ac.uk.

Peters, S. (2009). *BBC Radio 4 interview*. Retrieved 1 September 2011 from http:// www.lums. lancs. ac.uk/ news/ 17271/ sue-peters-bbc/.

Phoenix. (2011). *The Phoenix integration web site*. Retrieved 1 September 2011 from http:// www.phoenix-int.com.

Sakai. (2011). The Sakai project web site. Retrieved 1 September 2011 from http://sakaiproject. org/.

Severance, C., Hardin, J., Golden, G., Crouchley, R., Fish, A., & Finholt, T. (2007). Using the Sakai collaborative toolkit in e-research applications. *Concurrency and Computation, 19*(12), 1643–1652. doi:10.1002/cpe.1115

Tapscott, D., Ticol, D., & Lowy, A. (2000). *Digital capital: Harnessing the power of business webs*. Cambridge, MA: Harvard Business School Press.

Taverna-2. (2011). *The Taverna-2 web site*. Retrieved 1 September 2011 from http:// www. taverna.org.uk/ documentation/ taverna-2-x/.

TSB. (2011). *The TSB connect web site*. Retrieved 1 September 2011 from https:// ktn.innovateuk. org/ web/ guest.

VEC. (2011). *The VEC web site*. Retrieved 1 September 2011 from http:// www.stfc.ac.uk/ News+ and+ Events/ 13880.aspx.

Wenger, E., McDermott, R., & Snyder, W. (2002). *Cultivating communities of practice: A guide to managing knowledge*. Cambridge, MA: Harvard Business School Press.

Wenger, E., White, N., & Smith, J. D. (2009). *Digital habitats: Stewarding technology for communities*. Portland, OR: Cpsquare.

Wills, G., Gilbert, L., Chen, X., & Bacigalupo, D. (2010). Technical review of using cloud for research (TeciRes). *Report to JISC*. Retrieved 1 September 2011 from http:// www.jisc.ac.uk/ whatwedo/ programmes/ researchinfrastructure/ cloudcomptechreview.aspx.

ADDITIONAL READING

Berg, A., & Korcuska, M. (2009). *Sakai courseware management - the official guide*. Birmingham, UK: Packt Publishing.

CSCW. (2011). *Wikipedia article on computer supported cooperative work*. Retrieved 1 September 2011 from http:// en.wikipedia.org/ wiki/ CSCW.

Open Innovation. (2011). *Wikipedia article on open innovation*. Retrieved 1 September 2011 from http:// en.wikipedia.org/ wiki/ Open_innovation.

Sakai Overview. (2006). *Sakai overview on YouTube*. Retrieved 1 September 2011 from http:// www.youtube.com/ watch?v=_SkGi_tKBL4& feature= related.

Value Network Analysis. (2011). *Wikipedia article on value network analysis*. Retrieved 1 September 2011 from http:// en.wikipedia.org/ wiki/ Value_ network_ analysis.

Value Networks. (2011). *Wikipedia article on value networks*. Retrieved 1 September 2011 from http:// en.wikipedia.org/ wiki/ Value_ network.

Chapter 16
E–Research Collaboration of International Scope in Social and Political Sciences:
Scale and Complexity Linkage with the Requirement of Physical Encounters

Mayo Fuster Morell
Berkman Center for Internet & Society, Harvard University, USA

ABSTRACT

This chapter presents a comparative analysis of three case studies (all from the field of social and political science) on global e-research collaboration, describing how Information and Communication Technologies (ICTs) are facilitating the overcoming of geographical barriers. Previous research points out that physical e-research collaboration meetings play a relevant role. This chapter explores whether this requirement of physical meetings in e-research collaboration is independent of the scale and complexity of the collaboration established. The findings suggest that high complexity can be achieved using communication tools if the scale of the group is small, while very large groups can collaborate using communication tools if their target is a loose collaboration. However, if the collaboration involves both a large group and a considered complexity of collaboration, establishing a balance between communication tools with the requirement of physical meetings becomes a relevant issue.

INTRODUCTION AND BACKGROUND

In 1963, Price noted that since the beginning of the 20th century, a more rapid increase of scientific collaboration has taken place. Over the last decades, several authors have agreed that the

DOI: 10.4018/978-1-4666-0125-3.ch016

adoption of ICTs has provided a strong impetus on growth in collaborative research (Anandarajan & Anandarajan, 2010; Hackett, 2005). However, ICTs not only quantitatively increase research collaboration, but also transform the way collaboration is carried out. Research has always depended on the dominant media matrix (Johns,

Chen, & Hall, 2004) and has changed over time, depending on the communicational capacities of each conjuncture. The adoption of ICTs represents the latest stage in this development and transformation.

The term "collaboration" originates from the Latin word *collaborare*, which means to work together. Hagstrom defined scientific or research collaboration as a group of intellectual peers working together over a period of time to solve a research question (Hagstrom, 1965). Research collaboration can take many forms. Several questions emerge from Hagstrom's characterisation: 1) Who are those peers? (peers from the same institution or diverse institutions; peers from the same discipline or from several disciplines; academic peers only or also collaboration amongst academics and non-academics); 2) How many peers will be involved? (i.e. collaboration amongst two researchers or small- and large-scale groups); 3) How long will they have to work together? 4) How closely will researchers have to work together? (in physical terms or in terms of regular contact); and, 5) Which type of common goal or question do they have or address together in order to constitute collaboration? More importantly, is the adoption of ICTs in research changing research in some of these parameters? Several authors agree that with the advancement of ICTs, scientific collaboration has evolved into new forms of social network and interaction mediated through computers, known as e-research collaboration (Anandarajan & Anandarajan, 2010; Jankowski, 2009; Jirotka, Procter, Rodden, & Bowker, 2006; Ribes & Lee, 2010) or e-science (Hine, 2006).

Apart from the initial theoretical conceptualisation and the prospects of ICTs' potential for research, empirical analysis of cases of e-research collaboration has already been developed (Dutton & Jeffreys, 2010). Initiated in the field of science and technology research, it has more recently expanded to humanities and social and political science research (Anandarajan & Anandarajan, 2010). However, even if empirical research on a specific case has already been developed, little empirical research is based on a comparative analysis of different types of e-research collaborations. Consequently, the following chapter aims to analyse and compare emerging forms of e-research collaboration in the field of social and political science.

Furthermore, the analysis will be developed on a global or international scope, that is, collaboration that involves research in different regions of the world. Edge (1979) and Stokes and Harley (1989) found that most collaborations start informally. In addition, the spread of ICTs' spatial proximity seems to have encouraged collaboration in the past, since it tends to encourage informal communication—communication that is dependent on physical meetings (Hagstrom, 1965). Hence, the following chapter will address the question: How do ICTs facilitate the overcoming of geographical distance barriers and facilitated e-research collaboration of global scope? Since Siemens (2010) highlighted the importance of not being over-reliant on e-research tools, and that a balance between e-research tools and face-to-face meetings is needed in order to strengthen collaboration, this chapter aims more specifically to explore and compare how this balance is established within collaborations that involve diverse scale and complexity.

This chapter will analyse the links to physical encounters of diverse cases of e-research collaboration in terms of scale, specification and complexity of the collaboration. Scale refers to the number of researchers involved in the collaboration. Specification and complexity of the collaboration refer to the level of definition of the common goal (if the common goal is clearly defined around a specific common target *versus* if the collaboration is left open to what emerges from the interaction around common interests) and the level of interaction that is involved (from developing a final outcome together versus sharing a space). Links to physical encounters refers to the frequency and type of physical meetings as part of the collaboration process.

The chapter will proceed by providing an overview of e-research collaboration in social and political science of global scope, after which three cases of emerging forms of e-research collaboration will be presented. Comparison of the cases will be developed in terms of the dynamics of interaction and collaboration and by analysing how the differences in scale and complexity of the collaboration might relate to the requirements that allow the organization of physical encounters. The ICT methods used in each case will also be presented. Consequently, the chapter aims to contribute to two main areas: ICTs in research collaboration (Anandarajan & Anandarajan, 2010; Jankowski, 2009; Jirotka, Procter, Rodden, & Bowker, 2006; Ribes & Lee, 2010) and ICT in research methods (Hine, 2000, 2005; Rogers, 2009). Finally, potential future trends in e-research collaboration will be presented.

CONTEXTUALISATION: OVERVIEW OF E-RESEARCH IN SOCIAL AND POLITICAL SCIENCES

In order to contextualise the analysis and limit the possibility of generalisation in the findings, it is useful to provide some background on the adoption of ICTs by researchers involved in the field of social and political sciences.

Researchers with a background in social and political science do not possess a more advanced context in which to adopt ICTs; that could initially limit their capacity to incorporate ICTs into their research processes. Analyses of other fields with more advanced ICT capacities may arrive at other conclusions about how ICTs are reshaping the organisation of research collaboration.

On the one hand, social and political science is not a technologically intensive discipline (unlike research on computer sciences or information sciences). This limits the possibility for the use of technology in the field. Firstly, social scientists are not generally trained in the use of technological

tools. Secondly, universities are not adapted to respond to researchers' technological needs. It is either difficult to find funding for technological support or it is not included in competitive research funds. Furthermore, there are no references or institutional facilities to build partnerships with other disciplines that have more advanced technological training. The current situation in most departments is that only the researchers who have double training (in social science and computer science) or access to technological skills through their own costs and risks are in a competitive position. In other words, the technological training required to approach the potential opened up by ICTs to develop research is being determined by researchers' personal capacities. Hence, more institutional support is required to consolidate and advance the use of ICTs in social and political science.

In terms of the general spread of the use of ICT in the field of social and political sciences, the adoption of ICTs varies substantially, depending on the university. Generally, however, rates tend to be *low*. For example, the community of researchers at the Social and Political Science Department of the European University Institute (an international postgraduate and post-doctoral teaching and research institute based in Florence) uses e-mail as a communication channel (not mailing lists), a static-expositive website and a limited Intranet. Another aspect contributes to shedding light on the low level of awareness and capacity to adopt ICTs: While funding is available to support PhD travel to international conferences, applications to obtain technical support for PhD development are not considered[1]. The same can be said of the Institute of Government and Political Science of the Autonomous University of Barcelona[2]. Generally, universities or centres specialising in ICT research and those with a more plural interdisciplinary character adopt more developed sets of tools amongst their communities. For example, the School of Information at the University of California, Berkeley (a graduate school offering both professional master's degree programs and a research-oriented PhD), in addition to the tools mentioned in the previous cases, provides researchers with e-lists, an elaborate Intranet and technical support, as do the Internet Interdisciplinary Institute (the research body of the Open University of Catalonia, a private Internet-centred open university based in Barcelona, Spain) and the Berkman Centre of Internet and Society (a research centre at Harvard University that focuses on the study of cyberspace[3].)

Finally, in terms of the limitations or challenges within e-research, the potential for collaboration amongst researchers and greater access and diffusion of scientific production, as opened up by the ICTs, is being wasted and limited by a frame predominant in academia (through the intellectual property regulation and system of merits) that privileges individualism and non-collaboration. According to an analysis of 50 cases, the online settings based on free licenses (such as copyleft or Creative Commons licenses) hosted and raised more collaboration than the online settings based on copyright (Fuster Morell, 2010). This finding suggests that a redefinition of the academic career towards a system of merits that would privilege collective research and collaboration and a transition towards open access policies might increase e-research collaboration.

Even if this background does not seem to be the more favourable one in terms of e-research collaboration of global scope, several types of international interactions and group collaborations that have emerged as a result of the new windows being opened can already be distinguished. For example, ICTs have facilitated the emergence of very lively mailing lists around common research topics. This is the case in the example of the International Forum for Discussion and Information on Social Movements (social movements mailing list[4]), with a total of 357 subscribers and a mean number of 2 messages per week of traffic publications or calls for papers and conferences. Professor Laurence Cox started it in 1998 as an

individual initiative, and it is mainly used to post bibliographical questions, debates on concepts or research problems, and announcements of new facilities opened up by ICTs. It builds on the personal network of the mailing list's founder and the network of people researching social movements. Similar mailing lists have been created around other international research associations and conferences (such as the Informational Technology and Politics of the American Political Science Association or the Standing Group of Internet and Politics of the European Consortium of Political Research[5]). Other particular types of mailing lists have a "solidarity" character. This is the case for the Get Article mailing lists[6]. The goal of this mailing list is to provide researchers with access to articles in poor countries or universities with meagre resources that do not have much access to scientific publications compared to high-resource universities.

Another set of "windows" for research collaborations is linked to blogs as arenas for online debate. These could be individual blogs, such as Danna Boyd's blog on youth culture and social media[7], or a blog by a set of several authors around a particular discipline such as organisational theory[8].

As there is increased contact and information exchange in society through networking platforms, so is the case amongst researchers. The more popular interactive platforms tend to host groups dedicated to topics or international research associations. This is the case for Facebook. More recently, since 2010, www.academia.edu, a networking site specifically for academics and researchers, has become more popular.

There is also a set of online resources linked to academic literature, with various formats such as communities of collaboration for the exchange and systematisation of bibliographic references (such as the Zotero program) or the promotion of open access publishing (such as the Public Library of Science[9]).

Linked to ICTs and the capacity to spread information and coordinate groups, as well as the decrease of transportation costs and the processes of political regionalisation (such as the creation and promotion of the European Union), there has been an increase in international associations around disciplines or specific topics. In addition, there has been a proliferation of international meetings associated with these, such as the European Consortium of Political Research.

In terms of e-research grouping collaboration of global scope, three typologies can be distinguished: groups around a specific research project, large networks, and communities of researchers building or sharing a common goal. These three typologies of research collaboration will be presented in more detail in the next section as part of the empirical analysis.

METHODOLOGY

The analysis is based on three case studies with international scope, (as they involve researchers and research centres placed in various regions).

The case selection is driven by aiming to achieve diversity in terms of scale of the case: a small, middle and very large size case. It also considers diversity in terms of the three degrees of complexity of the collaboration. The indicators of the complexity and specificity of the collaboration were obtained from the presentations of each project goal and were dependent on the specification of the common target and the level of interaction between the case members required by the goal (from an interaction that involve all the members and the collective building of a final outcome, to forms that do not involve the interaction of all the members and are mainly based on sharing a space without a collective final outcome).

The three cases were a small group centred around a specific research project (the research project on "Dynamics of Online Interactions and Behaviour" developed in partnership between the Berkman Centre of Internet and Society at Harvard University and Sciences Po), a large international network that builds connections around common interests (the Networked Politics collaborative network), and finally, a large community building and sharing a research commons, that is to say, a community (composed of a galaxy of individuals and research groups) that collaboratively builds and shares a common resource (Wikipedia research commons).

Concerning empirical data, the use of "organic data" was privileged. "Organic data" refers to a collection of digital threads available online, or the observation of the public practices and discussions that the cases generate in their daily on and offline lives without the researcher's external intervention. In using "organic data," the *digital* methods approach, which was based on "following the medium," was followed (Rogers, 2009). This contradicts the virtual method approach of trying to adapt already known methods of the study of online practices and methods, requiring the "creation" of data rather than the use of available data (Hine, 2000).

The methods used were virtual ethnography and participative observation. Field notes were kept during the data collection. The researcher's experience as a researcher participant in the three cases was also used as data for the analysis. Additionally, unstructured interview and content analysis were developed in two of the cases (Networked Politics international network and Wikipedia Commons), due to their larger dimension and fact that they were more complex in contrast to the research project case. In these two cases, five people were interviewed (in an informal setting) amongst the main promoters or participants in the projects. The Networked Politics international network was observed from 2005 to 2008, online behaviour research project from November 2009 to July 2010, and Wikipedia Commons from 2007 to 2011[10].

Finally, the analysis was based on the systematisation of the experiences approach (Capó, et al., 2010).

CASE STUDIES DESCRIPTION AND QUALITATIVE ANALYSIS

In this section, each case study will first be presented and then analysed in light of the linkage between its scale and the specificity of its collaboration, and in terms of the balance between communication tools and physical encounters.

The differences between the cases are also exposed in Table 1.

First Case Study: Research Project Partnership between Berkman Center and Sciences Po based on Large-Scale Digital Methods[11]

This case is based on a small group of researchers from different universities that established collaboration for the development of a specific and time-limited research project.

Table 1. Comparison characteristics of case studies

	Research project partnership	Networked Politics collaborative network	Wikipedia research commons
Type of group	Small research group based on a partnership between Universities	Large network of researchers and specialists with an international promotional group	Very large ecosystem of individuals and research groups around common resources with multiple centres
Scale: Number of members	4	Around 300 people involved at different levels: 3 heavily involved; 10 medium involved; 200 contributors; 100 weak contributors	More than 500
Collaboration goal	Development of a specific research project	Exchange on a set of questions of common interest	Build and share a common resource
Outcomes	Articles	Books and online repositories	Online bibliographic repositories and forums
Research methods	Online experimental games	Focus groups, case studies, interviews, and e-mail surveys	Online surveys and wiki compilations
Time frame	From October 2010 to October 2011	From 2006 to 2010	From 2005 to present
Communicational tools	E-mail & chat	Mailing lists, website, chat, e-mail, phone	Wiki pages and mailing lists
Celebration of physical encounters	None	Seminars, meetings of the promoter group and coincidentally in larger audience conferences	Coincidence of some of community members in larger audience conferences
Linkage with physical encounters	No need for physical encounters when there is a clear research goal for a small research group (and previous trust built amongst the research group's members).	* For loose networks with elaborated outcomes, physical encounters played an important role. * Once the network stopped its physical activity, the maintenance of the network's production became problematic.	No physical meeting place for all the community where there is not a specific goal framing the whole interaction.
Lessons in terms of ICTs methods used	Digital methods might require more time than expected. Building trust with research subject required time.	Difficult technological transitions. Interactive website required high levels of facilitation.	* Risk of informational overwhelming. * Wiki facilitates the *know-how* transfer without the need for coordinators.

Source: author elaboration

In 2009, the members of one of the three universities applied for research funding and wanted to involve the research members from the other two universities in order to complete and enrich the expertise and skills needed for research development. The group was comprised of four individuals: two professors, a post-doctoral researcher and a PhD candidate. A programmer also provided technical support. The group was international: Two of the research members (and the technical programmer) lived in Paris, another researcher in Boston, and a fourth one in Barcelona.

Some previous connections between the members were present on the basis of previous encounters or activities. However, not all the members knew one another, and no physical meetings took place during the research project.

At the beginning, very intensive and rapid e-mail exchanges were observed, and chat meetings were arranged in order for the members to get to know each other and establish the research goals and procedures. The research project was then developed through e-mail exchanges and occasional chats.

The research group had a specified research goal and limited time frame. The group's collaborative time frame was one year and was set by the research funding. The project outcomes were articles in scientific journals.

The methodology for the empirical research was experimental and ICT-intensive. There were also no physical encounters with informants. It was a large-scale research project addressed to online users, and in particular, Wikipedians. In order to research their online behaviour and dynamics, informants were asked to participate in an experimental game. The most difficult part involved defining a subject recruitment strategy (that is, a method of mass message delivery to request participation in the survey) and establishing trust with the community when forming the subject of the research; there was the risk that the call would be considered intrusive or mistaken as spam. Another problem associated with this method concerned the difficulty of controlling the representativeness of the sample and the low response rate. Beyond the need to know the online community target netiquette and community rules, highly developed technical skills and knowledge of the technical platform of the community were also needed in order to use programs to spread the call, which required several instances of time rescheduling. In total, understanding (technically and socially) the target community and building trust are required elements when using digital methods; this opens up possibilities for large-scale data analysis, but might require more time than expected.

Scale and Specificity Collaboration and Balance between Communication Tools and Physical Meetings

Apart from the fact that two of the members were from the same institution, the small dimension of the entire group and the clear objective or target and time frame of the collaboration (as well as the trust amongst the researchers on the basis of previous relationships amongst some of them and their research reputation) seems to be the basis for the group's managing to function entirely using communication tools and without requiring any physical encounters. Additionally, the research methodology (based on an experimental game for online users) did not require any physical encounters between the researchers collaborating or between the researchers and informants. This case suggests that under certain scale and specific collaboration conditions, e-research collaboration of global scope can take place without the requirement of physical encounter.

Second Case Study: Networked Politics Collaborative Network[12]

This case is based on a large network of researchers interacting around common research questions.

In 2004, a group of three researchers from different European countries who held similar research, activist and personal interests, and who met regularly at events and conferences, decided to set up a network of researchers and practitioners. They specialised in a set of research questions of common interest (linked to questions about how ICTs are reshaping political organising).

The collaboration was more problem-oriented than funding- or career-oriented, in the sense that the researchers involved were highly committed to increasing their common understanding of the research questions without a clear timetable or funding framework to establish the collaboration. The organisation of several seminars resulted from the collaboration, built from two online repositories and the publication of books in several languages (based on individual authorship or collective authorship by the network).

The first activities were based on organising panels and discussions held at larger events and conferences, after which a set of seminars (one or two per year) were organised. Seminars took place in different parts of Europe (Germany, Spain, Italy, and Great Britain), Latin America (Venezuela and Brazil), Kenya, and the United States. After the first encounter, the network set up mailing lists and then built a website. 300 people were involved in the network at different levels: 3 were heavily involved (promoters); 10 were involved at medium levels (organisational support); 200 were contributors (to mailing lists, book contributors, attending seminars, etc.); and 100 were weak contributors (basically receiving the mailing lists). The promoters played a leadership role in the process, defining the agenda and the boundaries of the network membership, and they managed the organisational matters.

The collaboration between seminars was sustained through the mailing lists, which became highly international and lively. Participation in the mailing lists was connected to the organisation of the upcoming seminar. An online repository and collaborative tool was designed. However, it became difficult to migrate the activity from the mailing lists to the web tool. The web tool was mainly used to present and document the research project, to provide practical information, as a directory of the network members, and to provide access to the research outcomes. However, its collaborative features were poorly employed. A digital library was then designed in order to collect, spread and share the literature and materials related to the research question.

The research methodology to address the common questions was an adaptation of the *focus group* method utilised during the seminars, surveys conducted by e-mail, and commissioning case studies. The surveys were a set of questions distributed via e-mail. Participants reported that it was difficult to obtain answers from informants without previous relationships being in place. However, the active character of the research increased their willingness to participate or facilitated the establishment of contacts and trust. Following this, the results of the research conducted by network members were also discussed. Seminars were designed in detail following an adaptation of a *focus group* method. They involved no more than 30 participants (selected on the basis of equilibrium between approaches and backgrounds to ensure diversity in the discussion), and were very participative and discussion-focused (not based on panel presentations). The discussions at the seminars were then transcribed (collaboratively edited through the website tool), elaborated and adapted, and used as material to build upon and further the discussion, as well as content for the publications.

The collaboration was quite active and productive for a number of years (from 2005 to 2010, even though it took more than one year to achieve a more collaborative dynamic amongst the research members). However, for this loose and middle-site network, physical encounters played an important role in fostering and keeping the process alive. With the economic crisis in 2008, it became more difficult to find funding for organising the seminars, and the network gradually ceased its activities. Promoters also reported that it became difficult to encourage organisational willingness from other members who were not the initial promoters and to rotate the organisational effort and leadership. The collaboration between many of the network members endured over time, but in other projects or through other frameworks. This case suggests that the network ceased its activity in terms of physical encounters when the maintenance of the network's production and memory on the web tool and mailing list archive became problematic.

Scale and Specificity Collaboration and Balance between Communication Tools and Physical Meetings

In terms of scale, this network was made up of 300 people spread around the world who had several degrees and diverse methods of involvement. The collaboration was not specified in terms of a time frame or specific target, even if the network could be considered highly productive on the basis of its resulting outcomes. Communication tools such as the mailing list were important to maintain the connection between one physical encounter and the other, and the online repositories helped to systematise the results of the process and coordinate the network. However, the network dynamics were very much physical encounters, both driven and dependent. The physical meetings between the small groups of promoters were also developed in order to organise the larger seminars. Once the physical encounter stopped taking place, the network stopped being active. Overall, this case suggests that in the development of specific and collective outcomes amongst a relatively large network, physical encounters amongst the network members and amongst a small group of promoters play an important role to foster and keep the process alive.

Third Case Study: Wikipedia Research Commons

This case examines the interaction and collaboration of a very large community of researchers and non-researchers, based on a set of common interest via a plurality of online channels and repositories in order to exchange expertise and build and share diverse informational pools.

Wikipedia research commons, in contrast to the other two cases, is neither small nor time-constrained, and there is no structured goal around a specific research project (as in the first case). In addition, it is even larger, of much more permeable membership (practically open to any person willing and with the skills to contribute), and more fluid in its organisation than the international network in the second case. Furthermore, and again, unlike the second case, it does not have a core-promotional centre and moments of congregation of the entire community, but rather multiple pulses and several processes and networks feeding into it.

Wikipedia research commons is a very large (more than 500 collaborators) global, and multi-centred network of sub-networks composed of individuals (researchers, experts, or Wikipedians) and research groups (national or international research groups performing research projects in universities and research committees and other research groups linked to the Wikimedia Foundation or other wiki-related initiatives and foundations) that communicate, collaborate and interact in several online channels (mailing lists, wiki pages, real-time Internet text messaging [IRCs], without clear coherence and sometimes overlapping amongst those channels). The goal is to become a node and resource of expertise (from the most plural of perspectives and disciplines) and to build, maintain, update, share and provide (as a public resource) a set of diverse research resources (including a compilation, systematisation and review of bibliographies, directory of researchers and experts, list of on-going research projects, access to research data, methodological guides and manuals, amongst others[13]). This community interaction takes place without a predefined plan or centre of coordination, even if the Wikimedia Foundation, which is based in San Francisco, is in charge of maintaining the infrastructure that sustains this community interaction.

It is worth highlighting that in 2011, more than 2,100 peer-reviewed articles and 38 doctoral dissertations were dedicated to Wikipedia[14]. This constitutes a substantial amount of research on Wikipedia—even more so if one considers that Wikipedia started in 2001 and the academic research on it has substantially increased only since 2005[15].

Wikipedia itself (through wiki pages and other communicational channels) provides an environment and framework for collaboration within this community, even if some collaboration takes place outside Wikipedia (in conference panels or external digital resources). In terms of physical encounters, non-physical encounters are planned amongst all the community of people interacting around the project. However, some of its members meet in conferences or during the annual meeting of Wikipedians (called Wikimania). Actually, this collaboration amongst the Wikipedia research community takes place as part of the overall Wikimedia ecosystem of projects. As with any other wiki collaboration, wiki facilitates the *know-how* transfer without the need for "coordinators," and it promotes the generation of a community more than a centralised core that plans and coordinates collaboration.

The fact that the collaborative community has grown inside Wikipedia makes it less of a protagonist or visible from certain perspectives compared to other international academic associations. However, as a collaborative research community, it is relatively productive and builds useful research resources, even though this research community might be difficult to evaluate in terms of traditional academic indicators (such as academic publications), and even if community members are amongst the more academically recognised researchers in the area.

The network of wiki pages and communicational channels that synthesise and concentrate the up-to-date scientific knowledge and expertise conducted within Wikipedia and its sister projects conforms to the structure of a sort of common community of Wikipedia researchers. The free license used to preserve the resources facilitates collaboration, and it allows reuse and derivative work. As it is referred to in one of its wikis, it exists to "wiki-organize all individuals engaged in Wikipedia research[16]." Benkler (2006) refers to common-based peer production to point out this type of collaborative production amongst individuals, suggesting the growing importance of this type of production in the digital environment. The commons becomes a valuable resource (to identify literature or obtain methodological advice) for conducting research on Wikipedia; furthermore, researchers have incentives to maintain the commons and contribute to it in order to distribute their own research and achieve community recognition. Research groups or individual researchers at universities and academic institutions then use this commons to feed and gain input in order to define their research projects.

Finally, a limitation of this type of format is the risk of information overload. For example, a search on Wikipedia is easy to carry out and allows access to the available literature on Wikipedia. However, the researcher would experience difficulties if he or she aimed to manage or read it all. It is practically impossible for a single researcher to read all of the material and literature already available on the matter. Interestingly, this is leading to the creation of collaborative groups to develop reviews of parts of Wikipedia literature.

Scale and Specificity Collaboration and Balance between Communication Tools and Physical Meetings

This case involves a very large community of collaborators sharing online communications tools and repositories around a set of common research questions. Although the community does not have a centre, the interaction is distributed through several online channels. It has neither a structured plan nor goal beyond sharing a space, and it does not exchange expertise or communally systematise informational resources. Non-physical meetings are planned, even if community members meet each other on a larger scale at conferences. The Wikimedia Foundation, a formal foundation based in San Francisco, maintains the online infrastructure. In summary, this case suggests that collaboration based on a loose and open interaction without a centralised outcome, specific time frame, and planning framework, even if it involves a very large community, does not require physical encounters between the community members.

FUTURE RESEARCH DIRECTIONS

Several current and future trends in ICTs and collaborative research can be highlighted: internationalisation, multi-belonging formats, transdisciplinary groups, the use of organic data, and "interactivity" in the methodology and results.

As this chapter discussed, ICTs facilitate the formation of different types of international research groups. Furthermore, another characteristic observed from the cases presented is the increase of single researchers' multiple belongings, that is, single researchers who are linked to several universities or research groups (even in different countries).

Additionally, several aspects suggest that the use of ICTs in research will lead to increased multi-disciplinary research (Anandarajan & Anandarajan, 2010). First, the design of ICTs as a research tool requires a variety of skills. Researchers need to not only know how to use research methods, but also have the skills and capabilities to design technical tools. Consequently, the use of ICTs to investigate the formation of research groups with several profiles (data analytics, designers, and engineers) is frequent (Rogers, 2009). In order to

profit from this frontier, it is useful for research centres and departments to build alliances and create the conditions for the technological support of research. However, the need to find solutions for social scientists and engineers to work together in cross-disciplinary groups is probably one of the greatest challenges in the field, as the authors have reported the difficulties encountered in these types of groups (Lampe, 2010).

Second, in those cases where researchers use organic data generated in the case of daily life and available in the Web (and do not build a specific tool to collect data), the larger possibilities opened up by the use of organic data suggest a tendency towards an alliance between researchers and providers and the designers of online infrastructures. The sensitive nature of the organic data and the necessity to obtain permission and access to use them imply an intrinsic alliance between the providers and designers of online infrastructures and social scientists. Furthermore, social research can contribute to helping infrastructure designers develop tools in ways that generate more useful organic data for research needs. The mass of information produced as a consequence of actions designed for other ends has become a contended source of research and analysis, and it can be used to produce very sophisticated knowledge. Two examples of the commercial type are centre cards and Google Mail. Both attain the possibility to store and elaborate these information threads by paying "something" to the users (a gift after a certain number of purchases or free services). In this way, they use the "natural" behaviour of the users to elaborate marketing profiles. This is probably a new frontier in the research—the possibility of storing and elaborating information produced independently of direct research aims.

In terms of "interactivity" in the methodology and results, ICTs and the World Wide Web facilitate the establishment of a channel for a more continuous relationship with informants. It was a standard practice in the cases analysed to build a website dedicated to the research that contains information about the project's development. Moving forward, Web 2.0 opens up possibilities to develop more participative and collaborative research methodologies[17]. As part of its layout, a Web 2.0 site can allow, through the mechanisms of interactivity and easy intervention, informants to provide data for the empirical research directly or/and interpret and debate the data and results themselves.

DISCUSSION

Research collaboration has always depended on the dominant media matrix (Johns, Chen, & Hall, 2004), and it has changed over time, depending on the communicational capacities of each conjuncture. The adoption of ICTs represents the latest stage in this development. Although ICTs are rapidly evolving and still in an expanding phase, theoretical reflections and empirical analysis of their results in the form of e-research collaboration have been undertaken (Anandarajan & Anandarajan, 2010).

Initial empirical analysis focused on specific cases or on cases in disciplinary fields where the use of ICTs was intensive. This chapter aimed to expand the current stage of knowledge by providing a comparative empirical analysis of three case studies from the field of social and political science.

This field has no particular proclivity towards e-research collaboration in contrast to other ICT-intensive disciplines. Even if the ICTs have opened up great potential for development in the field and future trends can be drafted, at this stage, research in this field generally has neither a high technological profile nor expertise. Furthermore, most universities lack the institutional support to promote and support a technical infrastructure. Hence, analyses of cases linked to other fields that are more ICT-intensive may arrive at diverse findings.

The analysis was developed in cases of global or international scope, that is, collaboration that involved researchers based in different regions of the world that are not in spatially proximity. Prior

to the spread of ICT communication, research collaboration was more dependent on physical meetings and spatial-proximity encouraged collaboration (Hagstrom, 1965). With the spread of ICTs, the three cases analysed suggest that ICTs facilitate the overcoming of geographical barriers. The three cases show that the use of ICTs are intensive and play an important role in supporting e-research collaboration of global scope. Furthermore, the analyses also shed light on the fact that the emerging global e-research collaboration could assume very diverse forms in terms of group configuration. ICTs are suitable to support very diverse common goals. As it has been presented in detail, e-research collaboration can take the form of specific projects, loose networks and very large communities.

According to Siemens (2010), in order to strengthen collaboration, it is important not to be over-reliant on e-research tools and to find a balance between e-research tools and physical meetings. This chapter explored whether Siemens' findings, in terms of the relevance of physical meetings, are independent of the scale and complexity of the collaboration that has been established, and whether the establishment of such a balance between communication tools and physical meetings has a regular pattern in terms of scale and the complexity of collaboration. This includes an increase in physical encounters, depending on the scale and/or the complexity of collaboration established. In order to explore these questions, an empirical analysis of a case comparison of three cases, all of a diverse scale and specification of collaboration, was developed (see Table 2).

CONCLUSION

According to the findings, there is no common pattern or incremental parallel evolution of the need for physical encounters with the scale and/or complexity of the collaboration established. Instead, it seems that the need for physical encounters depends

Table 2. Cases comparison based

	Scale	Complexity and collaboration specificity	Communication tools	Physical encounters
Research project	Small	Specific and limited (empirical research project)	E-mail and chat	None
International network	Large	Intermediary (collective reflection)	Mailing lists, interactive website (low use), chat, e-mail and phone.	Network seminars, common participation in larger conferences and promoter groups meetings.
Commons	Very large	Lax and plural (sharing a space and pool around common interests)	Wiki pages and mailing lists	Does not target the whole community.

Source: author elaboration

on the combination between scale and complexity of collaboration, that is, depending on the overall type of grouping.

Both the small- and large-scale cases did not require physical encounters, while the case situated in the middle was very much physical encounter-dependent. The same could be said in terms of specificity and complexity of the collaboration: Neither the project that involved a more specific and complex interaction nor the one that had a vaguer target involved any physical meetings; however, the inter-medium case was dependent on physical meetings.

In other words, high complexity could be achieved using communication tools if the scale of the group is small, while very large groups can collaborate using communication tools if their target is a loose collaboration. However, if the collaboration involves both a large group and a considered complexity of collaboration, establishing a balance between communication tools with the requirement of physical meetings becomes a relevant issue.

In contrast to Siemens (2010), these research findings suggest that the relevance of a balance between e-research tools and physical meetings depends on the conditions of the collaboration in terms of the existing balance between scale and complexity of collaboration.

Finally, the systematisation of experience when comparing the three case studies suggests

the above presented findings. However, in order to validate this hypothesis, further research in terms of verifying statistical significance over a large N analysis may be required.

REFERENCES

Anandarajan, M., & Anandarajan, A. (2010). *E-research collaboration: Theory, techniques and challenges*. Berlin, Germany: Springer.

Benkler, Y. (2006). *The wealth of networks: How social production transforms markets and freedom*. New Haven, CT: Yale University Press.

Capó, S., William, A., Arteaga, C., Belén, A., & Manuela, Y. (2010). *La sistematización de experiencias: Un método para impulsar procesos emancipadores*. Caracas, Venezuela: Fundación Editorial El Perro y la Rana.

de Solla Price, D. J. (1963). *Little science, big science*. New York, NY: Columbia University Press.

Dutton, W. H., & Jeffreys, P. W. (Eds.). (2010). *World wide research: Reshaping the sciences and humanities*. Cambridge, MA: MIT Press.

Edge, D. (1979). Quantitative measures of communication in science: A critical review. *History of Science, 17*, 102–134.

Fuster Morell, M. (2010). *Governance of online creation communities: Provision of infrastructure for the building of digital commons.* Unpublished dissertation. Florence, Italy: European University Institute.

Hackett, E. J. (2005). Introduction to the special guest-edited issue on scientific collaboration. *Social Studies of Science, 35*(5), 667–671. doi:10.1177/0306312705057569

Hagstrom, W. O. (1965). *The scientific community.* New York, NY: Basic Books.

Halfpenny, P., & Procter, R. (2009). Special issue on e-social science. *Social Science Computer Review, 27*(4), 459–466. doi:10.1177/0894439309332662

Hine, C. (2000). *Virtual ethnography.* Thousand Oaks, CA: Sage.

Hine, C. (Ed.). (2005). *Virtual methods: Issues in social research on the Internet.* Oxford, UK: Berg.

Hine, C. (Ed.). (2006). *New infrastructures for knowledge production: Understanding escience.* Hershey, PA: IGI Global.

Jankowski, N. W. (Ed.). (2009). *E-research: Transformation in scholarly practice.* New York, NY: Routledge.

Jirotka, M., Procter, R., Rodden, T., & Bowker, G. (2006). Special issue: Collaboration in e-research. *Computer Supported Cooperative Work, 15*(4), 251–255. doi:10.1007/s10606-006-9028-x

Johns, M. D., Chen, S. S., & Hall, G. J. (Eds.). (2004). *Online social research: Methods, issues, and ethics.* New York, NY: Peter Lang.

Lampe, C. (2010). *Keynote intervention at the international symposium on wikis and open collaboration.* Retrieved from http://www.wikisym.org/ws2010/Invited+speakers.

O'Reilly, T. (2005). *What is Web2.0? Design patters and business models for the next generation of software.* Retrieved from http://www.oreillynet.com/pub/a/oreilly/tim/news/2005/09/30/what-is-web-20.html.

Ribes, D., & Lee, C. (2010). Sociotechnical studies of cyberinfrastructure and eresearch: Current themes and future trajectories. *Computer Supported Cooperative Work, 19*(3), 231–244. doi:10.1007/s10606-010-9120-0

Rogers, R. (2009). *The end of the virtual: Digital methods.* Amsterdam, The Netherlands: Amsterdam University Press.

Siemens, L. (2010). Time, place and cyberspace: Foundations for successful e-research collaboration. In *M. Anandarajan & A. Anandarajan (2010). E-Research Collaboration: Theory, Techniques and Challenges.* Berlin, Germany: Springer.

Stokes, T. D., & Harley, J. A. (1989). Co-authorship, social structure and influence within specialties. *Social Studies of Science, 19*, 101–125. doi:10.1177/030631289019001003

ADDITIONAL READING

Axelrod, R. (1985). *The evolution of cooperation.* New York, NY: Basic Books.

Becker, M. C. (2001). Managing dispersed knowledge: Organizational problems, managerial strategies, and their effectiveness. *Journal of Management Studies, 38*, 1037–1051. doi:10.1111/1467-6486.00271

Benkler, Y. (2011). *The penguin and the leviathan: How cooperation triumphs over self-interest.* New York, NY: Crown Publishing Group.

Bollier, D. (2008). Los bienes comunes: Un sector soslayado de la creación de riqueza (The communal properties: An avoided sector of the wealth creation). In S. Helfrich (Ed.), *Genes, Bytes y Emisiones - Bienes Comunes y Ciudadanía* (Genes, Bytes and Emissions - Communal properties and Citizenship). Mexico: Ediciones Böll. Retrieved from http://www.boell latinoamerica.org/download_es/Bienes_Comunes_total_EdiBoell.pdf.

Boltanski, L., & Chiapello, E. (2005). *The new spirit of capitalism*. London, UK: Verso.

Brown, J., & Duguid, P. (1991). Organizational learning and communities of practice: Toward a unified view of working, learning, and innovation. *Organization Science, 2*(1), 40–57. doi:10.1287/orsc.2.1.40

Carusi, A., & Reimer, T. (2010). Virtual research environment collaborative landscape study. *JISC Virtual Research Environment Programme Report*. Retrieved June 7, 2010 from http://www.jisc.ac.uk/publications/reports/2010/vrelandscapestudy.aspx.

Castells, M. (2009). *Communication power*. Oxford, UK: Oxford University Press.

Coase, R. (1937). The nature of the firm. *Economica, 4*, 386–405. doi:10.1111/j.1468-0335.1937.tb00002.x

Cox, L., & Barker, C. (2002). *What the Romans have ever done for us? Academic and activist forms of movement theorizing*. Paper presented at 8th annual conference of Alternative Futures and Popular Protest. Retrieved August 31, 2011 from http://eprints.nuim.ie/428/1/AFPPVIII.pdf.

Genoni, P., Merrick, H., & Willson, M. (2006). Scholarly communities, e-research literacy and the academic librarian. *The Electronic Library, 24*(6), 734–746. doi:10.1108/02640470610714189

Granovetter, M. (1983). The strength of weak ties: A network theory revisited. In Collins, R. (Ed.), *Sociological Theory (Vol. 1*, pp. 201–233). San Francisco, CA: Jossey-Bass. doi:10.2307/202051

Helfrich, S. (Ed.). (2008). *Genes, bytes y emisiones - Bienes comunes y ciudadanía* (Genes, bytes and emissions - Communal properties and citizenship). Retrieved from August 31, 2011 from http://www.boell.

Hess, C., & Ostrom, E. (Eds.). (2007). *Understanding knowledge as a commons: From theory to practice*. Cambridge, MA: The MIT Press.

Hine, C. (2007). Multi-sited ethnography as a middle range methodology for contemporary STS. *Science, Technology & Human Values, 32*(6), 652–671. doi:10.1177/0162243907303598

Knorr-Cetina, K. (1999). *Epistemic cultures: How the sciences make knowledge*. Cambridge, MA: Harvard University Press.

Kollock, P. (1999). The economies of online cooperation: Gifts and public goods in cyberspace. In Smith, M., & Kollock, P. (Eds.), *Communities in Cyberspace* (pp. 219–240). London, UK: Routledge.

Lee, D. (2003). Constructing the commons: Practical projects to build the information commons. *Knowledge Quest, 31*(4), 13–15.

Lessig, L. (1999). *Code and other laws of cyberspace*. New York, NY: Basic Books.

Liang, L. (2004). A guide to open content licences. *Piet Zwart Institute*. Retrieved August 31, 2011 from http://www.pzwart.wdka.hro.nl/mdr/research/lliang/open_content_guide.

Melucci, A. (1996). *Challenging codes*. Cambridge, UK: Cambridge University Press. doi:10.1017/CBO9780511520891

Moulier-Boutang, Y. (2007). *Le capitalisme cognitive: La nouvelle grande transformation*. Paris, France: Editions Amsterdam.

Orlikowski, W. J. (2007). Sociomaterial practices: Exploring technology at work. *Organization Studies, 28*(9), 1435–1448. doi:10.1177/0170840607081138

Orlikowski, W. J., & Scott, S. V. (2008). Sociomateriality: Challenging the separation of technology, work and organization. *The Academy of Management Annals, 2*, 433–474. doi:10.1080/19416520802211644

Powell, W. W. (1990). Neither market nor hierarchy: Network forms of organization. *Research in Organizational Behavior, 12*, 295-336. Retrieved August 31, 2011 from http://www.stanford.edu/~woodyp/papers/powell_neither.pdf.

Rheingold, H. (1993). *The virtual community: Homesteading on the electronic frontier*. Reading, MA: Addison-Wesley.

Ribes, D., & Finholt, T. A. (2009). The long now of infrastructure: Articulating tensions in development. *Journal of the Association for Information Systems, 10*(5), 375–398.

Santos, B. de S. (Ed.). (2007). *Another knowledge is possible*. London, UK: Verso.

Wellman, B. (2001). Physical place and cyberplace: The rise of personalized networking. *International Journal of Urban and Regional Research, 25*, 227–252. doi:10.1111/1468-2427.00309

KEY TERMS AND DEFINITIONS

Research Collaboration Links to Physical Encounters: Frequency and type of physical meetings as part of the research collaboration process.

Research collaboration scale: Number of researchers involved in the research collaboration.

Research collaboration: Researchers working together over a period of time to solve a research question or to achieve a research goal.

Research Commons: A community composed of a galaxy of individuals and research groups that collaboratively builds and shares a common resource.

Research Network: A set of loosely connections, activities and research relationships around common research interests.

Research Project: A group of researchers centred around a specific research goal.

Specification and Complexity of the Research Collaboration: Level of definition of the common goal (if the common goal is clearly defined around a specific common target *versus* if the collaboration is left open to what emerges from the interaction around common interests) and the level of interaction that is involved (from developing a final outcome together versus sharing a space).

ENDNOTES

[1] European University Institute. (2011). *Researcher's Guide 2011-2012*. Retrieved from http://www.eui.eu/Documents/DepartmentsCentres/SPS/RulesForms/ResearchersGuide2011-2012.pdf.

[2] IGOP. (2011). *Website*. Retrieved from http://igop.uab.es/.

[3] The data presented results from visiting stages and participative observation at the aforementioned centers, taking place in the period from 2008 to 2010.

[4] IOL. (2011). *Mailing list information page*. Retrieved from http://www.iol.ie/~mazzoldi/toolsforchange/sm.html.

[5] Harvard. (2011). *Mailing list information page*. Retrieved from http://lists.hmdc.harvard.edu/index.cgi?info=apsa_itp.

[6] Google. (2011). *Mailing list information page*. Retrieved from http://groups.google.com/group/getarticles/about?hl=en.

[7] Zephoria. (2011). *Blog page*. Retrieved from http://www.zephoria.org/thoughts/.

[8] Orgtheory. (2011). *Blog page*. Retrieved from http://orgtheory.wordpress.com/.

[9] Zotero. (2011). *Website Zotero*. Retrieved from http://www.zotero.org/. PLOS. (2011). *Website public library of science*. Retrieved from http://www.plos.org/.

[10] For the online interaction research project, virtual ethnography was developed through e-mail exchange, chats and voice conferences. For the Networked Politics international network, online ethnography was conducted for the mailing list (network@lists.euromovements.info) and the web and wiki www.networked-politics.info and www.openelibrary.info and participant observation at seminars on the Networked Politics Project: Barcelona October 2006; Berlin, June 2007; and Berkeley, 6-7 December 2008. For the Wikipedia Commons, virtual ethnography was developed on the Research Committee

and wiki-research mailing list and in the pages dedicated to research on meta. Participative observation was developed in Wikimania 2009 in Buenos Aires and at the Wikimania and Wikisym conferences 2010 in Poland.

[11] Medialab. (2011). *Project website*. Retrieved from http://www.medialab.sciences-po.fr/en/projects-en/online-interactions-and-behavior/.

[12] Networked Politics. (2011). *Website network*. Retrieved from http://www.networked-politics.info/.

[13] Wikipedia research commons is composed of: Academic Studies on Wikipedia (http://en.wikipedia.org/wiki/Wikipedia:Academic_studies_of_Wikipedia); Wiki Research Bibliography (http://meta.wikimedia.org/wiki/Wiki_Research_Bibliography); Zotero group on Wikipedia research (http://www.zotero.org/groups/wikipedia_research/items); Wikipedia research (http://meta.wikimedia.org/wiki/Research); Research Committee of the Wikimedia Foundation (http://meta.wikimedia.org/wiki/Research_Committee); Aca Wiki (http://acawiki.org/), Wikipedia research mailing lists (https://lists.wikimedia.org/mailman/listinfo/wiki-research-l), amongst others.

[14] Academic Studies. (2011). *Wikipedia*. Retrieved 26 March 2011 from http://en.wikipedia.org/wiki/Wikipedia:Academic_studies_of_Wikipedia.

[15] Academic Studies. (2011). *Wikipedia*. Retrieved 26 March 2011 from http://en.wikipedia.org/wiki/Wikipedia:Academic_studies_of_Wikipedia.

[16] Wikimedia. (2011). *Research network*. Retrieved from http://meta.wikimedia.org/wiki/Wikimedia_Research_Network.

[17] ICTs have several technological generations. The latest ICT tendency is found in the concept of Web 2.0. Web 2.0, initially proposed by O'Reilly (2005), refers to a second generation of ICT-based services, such as social networking sites, wikis, and communication tools that emphasize online collaboration and sharing amongst "users" to build up the site content. It also differs from early web development (retrospectively labeled Web 1.0) in that it moves away from static websites, the use of search engines, and surfing from one website to the next, and towards a more dynamic and interactive World Wide Web.

Compilation of References

Kacsuk, P., & Sipos, G. (2005). Multi-grid, multi-user workflows in the P-GRADE portal. *Journal of Grid Computing, 3*(3-4), 221–238. doi:10.1007/s10723-005-9012-6

Aasman, J. (1995). *Modeling driver behaviour in Soar*. Leidschendam, The Netherlands: KPN Research.

Acedo, F. J., Barroso, C., Casanueva, C., & Galan, J. L. (2006). Co-authorship in management and organizational studies: An empirical and network analysis. *Journal of Management Studies, 43*(5), 957–983. doi:10.1111/j.1467-6486.2006.00625.x

Ackerman, M. (2000). The intellectual challenge of CSCW: The gap between social requirements and technical feasibility. *Human-Computer Interaction, 15*, 179–203. doi:10.1207/S15327051HCI1523_5

ACLS. (2006). *Our cultural commonwealth: The final report of the American council of learned societies commission on cyberinfrastructure for the humanities and social sciences*. Washington, DC: American Council of Learned Societies Commission on Cyberinfrastructure for the Humanities and Social Sciences.

Agichtein, E., Castillo, C., Donato, D., Gionis, A., & Mishne, G. (2008). *Finding high-quality content in social media*. Paper presented at the ACM Web Search and Data Mining Conference. Palo Alto, CA.

Aitchison, C., & Lee, A. (2006). Research writing: Problems and pedagogies. *Teaching in Higher Education, 11*(3), 265–278. doi:10.1080/13562510600680574

Aleman-Meza, B., Nagarajan, M., Ramakrishnan, C., Ding, L., Kolari, P., Sheth, A. P., et al. (2006). Semantic analytics on social networks: Experiences in addressing the problem of conflict of interest detection. In *Proceedings of the 15th International Conference on World Wide Web,* (pp. 407-416). New York, NY: ACM Press.

Allan, R. J. (2011). Clouds and Web 2.0 services supporting research. *Daresbury Laboratory*. Retrieved 1 September 2011 from http:// 193.62.125.70/ NWGrid/ Clouds/.

Allan, R. J., & Yang, X. (2008). Using role based Access Control in the Sakai Collaborative Framework. *Daresbury Laboratory*. Retrieved 1 September 2011 from http:// epubs.cclrc.ac.uk/ work-details? w=50402.

Allan, R. J. (2009). *Virtual research environments: From portals to science gateways*. Oxford, UK: Chandos Publishing.

Allee, V., & Schwabe, O. (2009). *Measuring the impact of research networks in the EU: Value networks and intellectual capital formation*. Paper presented at the European Conference on Intellectual Capital. Haarlem, The Netherlands.

Allee, V. (2008). Value network analysis and value conversion of tangible and intangible assets. *Journal of Intellectual Capital, 9*(1), 5–24. doi:10.1108/14691930810845777

Allport, A., Styles, E., & Hsieh, S. (1994). Shifting intentional set: Exploring the dynamic control of tasks. In Umita, C., & Moscovitch, M. (Eds.), *Attention and performance XV: Conscious and Nonconscious Information Processing* (pp. 421–452). Cambridge, MA: MIT Press.

Anandarajan, M., & Anandarajan, A. (2010). *E-research collaboration: Theory, techniques and challenges*. Berlin, Germany: Springer-Verlag.

Ancona, D., & Caldwell, D. (1990). Information technology and work groups: The case of new product teams. In Galegher, J., Kraut, R., & Egido, C. (Eds.), *Intellectual Teamwork: Social and Technological Foundations of Cooperative Work* (pp. 173–190). Hillsdale, NJ: Erlbaum.

Anderson, C. (2006). *The long tail: How endless choice is creating unlimited demand*. London, UK: Random House Business Books.

Anderson, J. R., Reder, L. M., & Lebiere, C. (1996). Working memory: Activation limitations on retrieval. *Cognitive Psychology*, *30*(3), 221–256. doi:10.1006/cogp.1996.0007

Anderson, T., & Kanuka, H. (2003). *E-research: Methods, strategies and issues*. Boston, MA: Pearson Education.

Andriessen, J., Baker, M., & Suthers, D. (2003). *Arguing to learn: Confronting cognitions in computer-supported collaborative learning environments*. Dordrecht, The Netherlands: Kluwer.

Appelbaum, S. H., Marchionni, A., & Fernandez, A. (2008). The multitasking paradox: Perceptions, problems and strategies. *Management Decision*, *46*(9), 1313–1325. doi:10.1108/00251740810911966

Apple. (2011). *Microsoft's web page for business*. Retrieved 1 September 2011 from http:// www.apple.com/ uk/ business/ solutions/.

ARCS. (2011). NeAT projects. *Australian Research Collaboration Service*. Retrieved February 24, 2011, from http:// www.arcs.org.au/ index.php/ services/ research-community-projects/ 266-research-community-custom-projects-redone.

Asur, S., & Huberman, B. A. (2010). *Predicting the future with social media*. Retrieved from http:// www.hpl.hp.com/ research/ scl/ papers/ socialmedia/ socialmedia.pdf.

Atkins, D. E., Droegemeier, K. K., Feldman, S. I., Garcia-Molina, H., Klein, M. L., & Messerschmitt, D. G. (2003). *Revolutionizing science and engineering through cyberinfrastructure. Report of the National Science Foundation Blue-Ribbon Advisory Panel on Cyberinfrastructure*. Arlington, VA: National Science Foundation.

Atkinson, I. M., du Boulay, D., Chee, C., Chiu, K., Coddington, P., & Gerson, A. … Zhang, D. (2007). Developing CIMA-based cyberinfrastructure for remote access to scientific instruments and collaborative e-research. In *Proceedings of the Australasian Symposium on Grid Computing and Research (AusGrid)*, (vol 68), (pp. 3-10). Ballarat, Australia: IEEE Press.

Augustine, V., & Robinson, D. (2010). Using virtual machines for collaborative research. In *Proceedings of the ESEM, 2010*, 1–4. doi:10.1145/1852786.1852836

Back, M. D., Stopfer, J. M., Vazire, S., Gaddis, S., Schmukle, S. C., Egloff, B., & Gosling, S. D. (2010). Facebook profiles reflect actual personality, not self-idealization. *Psychological Science*, *21*, 372–374. doi:10.1177/0956797609360756

Bacon, J. (2009). *The art of community: Building the new age of participation*. Sebastopol, CA: O'Reilly Media.

Baddeley, M. C., Curtis, A., & Wood, R. (2004). An introduction to prior information derived from probabilistic judgments: Elicitation of knowledge, cognitive bias and herding. *Geological Society, 239*, 15-27.

Baddeley, A., Chincotta, D., & Adlam, A. (2001). Working memory and the control of action: Evidence from task switching. *Journal of Experimental Psychology*, *130*(4), 641–657. doi:10.1037/0096-3445.130.4.641

Baddeley, A., & Logie, R. H. (1999). Working memory: The multiple-component model. In Miyake, A., & Shah, P. (Eds.), *Models of Working Memory: 110 Annual Review of Information Science and TechnFology Mechanisms of Active Maintenance and Executive Control* (pp. 28–61). Cambridge, UK: Cambridge University Press.

Bairoch, A. (2009). *The future of annotation/biocuration*. Paper presented at the 3rd Biocuration Conference. Berlin, Germany.

Baker. (2010). *The influence and impact of Web 2.0 on e-research infrastructure, applications and users*. Retrieved 1 September 2011 from http://www.research3.org.

Baker, J. R., & Moore, S. M. (2008). Distress, coping, and blogging: Comparing new MySpace users by their intention to blog. *Cyberpsychology & Behavior*, *11*, 81–85. doi:10.1089/cpb.2007.9930

Balacheff, N., & Kaput, J. (1996). Computer-based learning environments in mathematics. In Bishop, A. J., Klements, K., Keitel, C., Kilpatric, J., & Laborde, C. (Eds.), *International Handbook on Mathematics Education* (pp. 469–501). Dortdrecht, The Netherlands: Kluwer.

Baltes, B. B., Dickson, M. W., Sherman, M. P., Bauer, C. C., & LaGanke, J. (2002). Computer-mediated communication and group decision making: A metaanalysis. *Organizational Behavior and Human Decision Processes*, *87*(1), 156–179. doi:10.1006/obhd.2001.2961

Bar-Anan, Y., De Houwer, J., & Nosek, B. A. (2010). Evaluative conditioning and conscious knowledge of contingencies: A correlational investigation with large samples. *Quarterly Journal of Experimental Psychology*, *63*, 2313–2335. doi:10.1080/17470211003802442

Barga, R., & Gannon, D. (2007). Scientific versus business workflows. In *Workflows for E-Science: Scientific Workflows for Grids* (pp. 9–16). Berlin, Germany: Springer.

Barjak, F., & für Wirtschaft, H. (2006). *Team diversity and research collaboration in life sciences teams: Does a combination of research cultures pay off?*. Fachhochschule, Nordwestschweiz: Hochschule für Wirtschaft.

Barjak, F., Wiegand, G., Lane, J., Kertcher, Z., Poschen, M., Procter, R., et al. (2007). *Accelerating transition to virtual research organization in social science (AVROSS): First results from a survey of e-infrastructure adopters*. Paper presented at the Third International Conference on e-Social Science. Ann Arbor, MI. Retrieved February 24, 2011, from http://ess.si.umich.edu/papers/paper141.pdf.

Barjak, F., Lane, J., Kertcher, Z., Poschen, M., Procter, R., & Robinson, S. (2009). Case studies of e-infrastructure adoption. *Social Science Computer Review*, *27*(4), 583–600. doi:10.1177/0894439309332310

Barnett, C. (2004). Pro-poor dissemination: Increasing the impact of research. *Development in Practice*, *14*(3), 432–439.

Barry, K. M., Cavers, D. A., & Kneale, C. W. (1975). Recommended standards for digital tape formats. *Geophysics*, *40*(2), 344–35. doi:10.1190/1.1440530

Beare, R. (2007). Investigation into the potential of investigative projects involving powerful robotic telescopes to inspire interest in science. *International Journal of Science Education*, *29*(3), 279–306. doi:10.1080/09500690600620938

Becher, T., & Trowler, P. R. (2001). *Academic tribes and territories*. Philadelphia, PA: Society for Research into Higher Education & Open University Press.

Beers, P. J., Kirschner, P. A., Boshuizen, H. P. A., & Gijselaers, W. H. (2007). ICT-support for grounding in the classroom. *Instructional Science*, *35*(4), 535–556. doi:10.1007/s11251-007-9018-5

Bélanger, F. (1999). Workers' propensity to telecommute: An empirical study. *Information & Management*, *35*(3), 139–153. doi:10.1016/S0378-7206(98)00091-3

Belanger, F., & Collins, R. (1998). Distributed work arrangements: A research framework. *The Information Society*, *14*, 137–152. doi:10.1080/019722498128935

Bell, G., Hey, T., & Szalay, A. (2009). Computer science: Beyond the data deluge. *Science*, *323*(5919), 1297–1298. doi:10.1126/science.1170411

Benbunan-Fich, R., & Truman, G. E. (2009). Multitasking with laptops during meetings. *Communications of the ACM*, *52*(2), 139–141. doi:10.1145/1461928.1461963

Benkler, Y. (2006). *The wealth of networks: How social production transforms markets and freedom*. New Haven, CT: Yale University Press.

Berlingerio, M., Coscia, M., Giannotti, F., Monreale, A., & Pedreschi, D. (2010). As time goes by: Discovering eras in evolving social networks. In *Proceedings of Advances in Knowledge Discovery and Data Mining* (pp. 81–90). ACM. doi:10.1007/978-3-642-13657-3_11

Berners-Lee, T., & Cailliau, R. (1990). *WorldWideWeb: Proposal for a hypertexts project*. Retrieved from http://www.w3.org/Proposal.html.

Berners-Lee, T., Hendler, J., & Lassila, O. (2001). The semantic web. *Scientific American Magazine*. Retrieved from http://www.scientificamerican.com.

Berners-Lee, T. (2006). Linked data. *International Journal on Semantic Web and Information Systems*, *4*(1), W3C.

Berners-Lee, T., & Fischetti, M. (1999). *Weaving the Web*. San Francisco, CA: Harper.

Berners-Lee, T., Hendler, J., & Lassila, O. (2001). The semantic Web. *Scientific American*, *284*, 35–43. doi:10.1038/scientificamerican0501-34

Beyer, H., & Holtzblatt, K. (1998). *Contextual design: Defining customer centered systems*. New York, NY: Academic Press.

Bierema, L. L., & Merriam, S. B. (2002). E-mentoring: Using computer mediated communication to enhance the mentoring process. *Innovative Higher Education*, *26*, 211–227. doi:10.1023/A:1017921023103

Biggs, J. B., & Collis, K. F. (1982). *Evaluating the quality of learning: The SOLO taxonomy*. New York, NY: Academic Press.

Bilder, G. W. (2009). Video presentation of CrossRef by its boss: Geoff W. Bilder. In *Proceedings of the 1st Conference on Open Access Scholarly Publishing*. Lund, Sweden. Retrieved from http:// river-valley.tv/ tag/ geoff-bilder/.

Birnbaum, M. H. (1999). Testing critical properties of decision making on the Internet. *Psychological Science, 10*, 399–407. doi:10.1111/1467-9280.00176

Birnbaum, M. H. (2000). SurveyWiz and FactorWiz: JavaScript web pages that make HTML forms for researchers on the Internet. *Behavior Research Methods, Instruments, & Computers, 32*, 339–346. doi:10.3758/BF03207804

Birnbaum, M. H. (2004). Human research and data collection via the Internet. *Annual Review of Psychology, 55*, 803–832. doi:10.1146/annurev.psych.55.090902.141601

Birnbaum, M. H., & Wakcher, S. V. (2002). Web-based experiments controlled by JavaScript: An example from probability learning. *Behavior Research Methods, Instruments, & Computers, 34*, 189–199. doi:10.3758/BF03195442

Birnholtz, J. P. (2006). What does it mean to be an author? The intersection of credit, contribution, and collaboration in science. *Journal of the American Society for Information Science and Technology, 57*(13), 1758–1770. doi:10.1002/asi.20380

Birnholtz, J. P. (2007). When do researchers collaborate? Toward a model of collaboration propensity. *Journal of the American Society for Information Science and Technology, 58*(14), 2226–2239. doi:10.1002/asi.20684

Bishop, L. (2005). Protecting respondents and enabling data sharing: Reply to Parry and Mauthner. *Sociology, 39*(2), 333–336. doi:10.1177/0038038505050542

Bizer, C., Heath, T., & Berners-Lee, T. (2009). Linked data - The story so far. *Journal on Semantic Web and Information Systems, 5*(3), 1–22. doi:10.4018/jswis.2009081901

Bîzoi, M., Suduc, A. M., & Gorghiu, G. (2010). Teachers' perception on developing and implementing virtual experiments. In *Proceedings of 1st International Multi-Conference on Innovative Developments in ICT (INNOV 2010)*, (pp. 133-136). Science and Technology Publications.

Bîzoi, M., Suduc, A. M., Gorghiu, G., & Gorghiu, L. M. (2009). Analysis of 1000 days of collaborative activities in two multinational educational projects. *WSEAS Transactions on Advances in Engineering Education, 6*(10), 337–346.

Black, J., & Hearne, S. (2008). *Effective leadership of international virtual project teams*. Denver, CO: PMI Global Congress.

Blackwell, J. E. (1989). Mentoring: An action strategy for increasing minority faculty. *Academe, 75*, 8–14. doi:10.2307/40249734

Blanke, T., Dunn, S., & Hedges, M. (2007). *Arts and humanities e-science - From ad hoc experimentation to systematic investigation*. Paper presented at the Third IEEE International Conference on e-Science and Grid Computing. New York, NY.

Blecken, A., Bruggemann, D., & Marx, W. (2010). *Usability evaluation of a learning management system*. Paper presented at the 43rd Hawaii International Conference on Systems Sciences. Hawaii, HI.

Blitzer, C. (1966). This wonderful machine: Some thoughts on the computer and the humanities. *ACLS Newsletter, 17*(4).

Bloom, B. S., Krathwohl, D. R., & Masia, B. B. (1956). *Taxonomy of educational objectives: The classification of educational goals*. New York, NY: Longmans.

Bloor, D. (1976). *Knowledge and social imagery*. London, UK: Routledge.

Boardman, P. C., & Corley, E. A. (2008). University research centers and the composition of research collaborations. *Research Policy, 37*(5), 900–913. doi:10.1016/j.respol.2008.01.012

Bollier, D. (2002). Reclaiming the commons. *Boston Review*. Retrieved March 10, 2011 from http:// bostonreview.net/ BR27.3/ bollier.html.

Bollier, D. (2003). Artists, technology and the ownership of creative content. *Cultural Commons Portal*. Retrieved March 10, 2011 from http:// www.culturalcommons.org/ comment-print.cfm?ID=10.

Bond, C. E., Shipton, Z. K., Gibbs, A. D., & Jones, S. (2008). Structural models: Optimizing risk analysis by understanding conceptual uncertainty. *First Break, 26*, 65–71.

Borgman, C. (2006). What can studies of e-learning teach us about collaboration in e-Research? Some findings from digital library studies. *Computer Supported Cooperative Work, 15*(4), 359–383. doi:10.1007/s10606-006-9024-1

Borgman, C. L. (2007). *Scholarship in the digital age: Information, infrastructure, and the internet*. Cambridge, MA: The MIT Press.

Bos, N., Zimmerman, A., Olson, J., Yew, J., Yerkie, J., & Dahl, E. (2007). From shared databases to communities of practice: A taxonomy of collaboratories. *Journal of Computer-Mediated Communication, 12*(2). doi:10.1111/j.1083-6101.2007.00343.x

Botella, C., Gallego, M. J., Garcia-Palacios, A., Baños, R. M., Quero, S., & Alcañiz, M. (2009). The acceptability of an Internet-based self-help treatment for fear of public speaking. *British Journal of Guidance & Counselling, 37*(3), 297–311. doi:10.1080/03069880902957023

Botella, C., Gallego, M. J., García-Palacios, A., Baños, R. M., Quero, S., & Guillen, V. (2008a). An Internet-based self-help program for the treatment of fear of public speaking: A case study. *Journal of Technology in Human Services, 26*(2-4), 182–202. doi:10.1080/15228830802094775

Botella, C., Quero, S., Baños, R. M., García-Palacios, A., Bretón-López, J., Alcañiz, M., & Fabregat, S. (2008b). Telepsychology and self-help: The treatment of phobias using the Internet. *Cyberpsychology & Behavior, 11*(6), 659–664. doi:10.1089/cpb.2008.0012

Boud, D., & Lee, A. (2005). Peer learning as pedagogic discourse for research education. *Studies in Higher Education, 30*(5), 501–516. doi:10.1080/03075070500249138

Boud, D., & Lee, A. (2008). *Changing practices of doctoral education*. London, UK: Routledge.

Boyack, K. W., Klavans, R., & Borner, K. (2005). Mapping the backbone of science. *Scientometrics, 64*(3), 351–374. doi:10.1007/s11192-005-0255-6

Bozeman, B., & Corley, E. (2004). Scientists' collaboration strategies: Implications for scientific and technical human capital. *Research Policy, 33*(4), 599–616. doi:10.1016/j.respol.2004.01.008

Bravo, B. R., & Alvite, M. L. (2007). E-science and open access repositories in Spain. *OCLC Systems & Services, 23*(4), 363–371. doi:10.1108/10650750710831501

Brereton, P., Kitchenham, B. A., Budgen, D., Turner, M., & Khalil, M. (2007). Lessons from applying the systematic literature review process within the software engineering domain. *Journal of Systems and Software, 80*(4), 571–583. doi:10.1016/j.jss.2006.07.009

Brody, T., Harnad, S., & Carr, L. (2006). Earlier web usage statistics as predictors of later citation impact. *Journal of the American Society for Information Science and Technology, 57*(8), 1060–1072. doi:10.1002/asi.20373

Brooks, C., Lee, E. A., Liu, X., Neuendorffer, S., Zhao, Y., & Zheng, H. (Eds.). (2005). *Heterogeneous concurrent modeling and design in java*. Berkeley, CA: University of California.

Brown, J. S., Collins, A., & Duguid, P. (1989). Situated cognition and the culture of learning. *Educational Researcher, 18*(1), 32.

Bruner, J. S. (1996). *Culture of education*. Cambridge, MA: Harvard University Press.

Buchanan, T., & Smith, J. L. (1999). Using the Internet for psychological research: Personality testing on the World Wide Web. *The British Journal of Psychology, 90*, 125–144. doi:10.1348/000712699161189

Buckland, M. K. (2008). Reference library service in the digital environment. *Library & Information Science Research, 30*, 81–85. doi:10.1016/j.lisr.2008.03.002

Buder, J., & Bodemer, D. (2008). Supporting controversial CSCL discussions with augmented group awareness tools. *International Journal of Computer-Supported Collaborative Learning, 3*(2), 123–139. doi:10.1007/s11412-008-9037-5

Buffardi, L. E., & Campbell, W. K. (2008). Narcissism and social networking web sites. *Personality and Social Psychology Bulletin, 34*, 1303–1314. doi:10.1177/0146167208320061

Burbidge, M., & Grout, I. (2006). *Evolution of a remote access facility for a PLL measurement course*. Paper presented at the 2nd IEEE International Conference on e-Science and Grid Computing. New York, NY.

Burgess, P. W. (2000). Real world multitasking from a cognitive neuroscience perspective. In Monsell, S., & Driver, J. (Eds.), *Control of Cognitive Processes: Attention and Performance XVIII* (pp. 465–472). Cambridge, MA: MIT Press.

Bush, V. (1945). As we may think. *Atlantic Monthly, 176*(1), 101–108.

Busstra, M. C., Geelen, A., Noroozi, O., Biemans, H. J. A., de Vries, J. H. M., & van 't Veer, P. (2010). Timing of information presentation in interactive digital learning material affects student's learning outcomes and appreciation of the material: a pilot study in the domain of nutritional research education. In *Proceedings of World Conference on Educational Multimedia, Hypermedia and Telecommunications 2010,* (pp. 3091-3100). Chesapeake, VA: AACE.

Byrne, J. R., & Tangney, B. (2010). *CAWriter: A CSCW/ CSCL tool to support research students' academic writing.* Paper presented at the British Computer Society HCI2010. Retrieved from http:// www.scss.tcd.ie/ crite/ publications/ sources/ CAWriter_ ByrneJR.pdf.

Cabon, P., Coblentz, A., & Mollard, R. (1990). Interruption of a monotonous activity with complex tasks: Effects of individual differences. In *Proceedings of the Human Factors Society 34th Annual Meeting,* (pp. 912-916). HFS Press.

Callon, M. (1986). Some elements of a sociology of translation: Domestication of the scallops and the fishermen of St. Brieuc Bay. In *Power, Action and Belief: A New Sociology of Knowledge* (pp. 196–233). London: Routledge & Kegan Paul.

Cambridge. (2011). *The University of Cambridge VLE home page.* Retrieved 1 September 2011 from http:// camtools.caret.cam.ac.uk.

Cantner, U., & Rake, B. (2011). *International research networks in pharmaceuticals: Structure and dynamics.* Paper presented at the Mannheim. New York, NY.

Capó, S., William, A., Arteaga, C., Belén, A., & Manuela, Y. (2010). *La sistematización de experiencias: Un método para impulsar procesos emancipadores.* Caracas, Venezuela: Fundación Editorial El Perro y la Rana.

Carletta, J. (2007). Unleashing the killer corpus: Experiences in creating the multi-everything AMI meeting corpus. *Language Resources and Evaluation Journal, 41*(2), 181–190. doi:10.1007/s10579-007-9040-x

Carlson, S., & Anderson, B. (2007). What are data? The many kinds of data and their implications for data re-use. *Journal of Computer-Mediated Communication, 12*(2). doi:10.1111/j.1083-6101.2007.00342.x

Carnap, R. (1947). *Meaning and necessity.* Chicago, IL: The University of Chicago Press.

Carpenter, J., Wetheridge, N., Smith, N., Goodman, M., & Struijvé, O. (2010). *Researchers of tomorrow.* London, UK: British Library/JISC.

Carusi, A., & Reimer, T. (2010). Virtual research environment: Collaborative landscape study. *JISC.* Retrieved from http:// www.jisc.ac.uk/ media/ documents/ publications/ vrelandscapereport.pdf.

Casanueva Roche, C., Escobar Pérez, B., & Larrinaga González, C. (2007). Red social de contabilidad en españa a partir de los tribunales de tesis. *Revista Española De Financiación y Contabilidad, 136,* 707–726.

Catteddu, D., & Hogben, G. (2009). *Cloud computing - Benefits, risks and recommendations for information security.* Retrieved 1 September 2011 from http:// www.enisa.europa.eu/ act/ rm/ files/ deliverables/ cloud-computing-risk-assessment.

Cha, M., Haddadi, H., Benevenuto, F., & Gummadi, K. P. (2010). *Measuring user influence in Twitter: The million follower fallacy.* Paper presented at the 4th International AAAI Conference on Weblogs and Social Media. Washington, DC.

Chandrasekaran, B., Josephson, J. R., & Benjamins, V. R. (1999). What are ontologies, and why do we need them? *IEEE Intelligent Systems, 14,* 20–26. doi:10.1109/5254.747902

Chan, T. W. (2010). How east Asian classrooms may change over the next 20 years. *Journal of Computer Assisted Learning, 26,* 28–52. doi:10.1111/j.1365-2729.2009.00342.x

Chan, T., Roschelle, J., Hsi, S., Kinshuk, , Sharples, M., Brown, T., & Hoppe, U. (2006). One-to-one technology-enhanced learning: An opportunity for global research collaboration. *Research and Practice in Technology Enhanced Learning, 1*(1), 3–29. doi:10.1142/S1793206806000032

Chibelushi, C. C., & Bourel, F. (2002). *Facial expression recognition: A brief tutorial overview.* Retrieved from http:// homepages.inf.ed.ac.uk/ rbf/ CVonline/ LOCAL_COPIES/ CHIBELUSHI1/ CCC_FB_ FacExprRecCVonline. pdf.

Chompalov, I., Genuth, J.,, & Shrum,. (2002). The organization of scientific collaborations. *Research Policy, 31*, 749–767. doi:10.1016/S0048-7333(01)00145-7

Chopra, P. (2009). *Neural network base code*. Retrieved on 3 January, 2010 from http://paraschopra.com/.

Chowdhury, G. G., & Chowdhury, S. (2003). *Introduction to digital libraries*. London, UK: Facet Publication.

Christensen, K. (1988). *The new era of home-based work*. Boulder, CO: Westview Press.

Clark, D. B., D'Angelo, C. M., & Menekse, M. (2009). Initial structuring of online discussions to improve learning and argumentation: Incorporating students' own explanations as seed comments versus an augmented-preset approach to seeding discussions. *Journal of Science Education and Technology, 18*(4), 321–333. doi:10.1007/s10956-009-9159-1

Clark, D. B., Sampson, V., Weinberger, A., & Erkens, G. (2007). Analytic frameworks for assessing dialogic argumentation in online learning environments. *Educational Psychology Review, 19*(3), 343–374. doi:10.1007/s10648-007-9050-7

Clarke, S., Harrison, A., & Searle, S. (2009). *Scholarly information repository services at Monash University*. Paper presented at the International Association of Technical University Libraries (IATUL) 30th Annual Conference. Leuven, Belgium.

Coffin, C., & O'Halloran, A. K. (2009). Argument reconceived. *Educational Review, 61*(3), 301–313. doi:10.1080/00131910903045948

Cohen, J. (1968). Weighed kappa: Nominal scale agreement with provision for scaled disagreement or partial credit. *Psychological Bulletin, 70*(4), 213–220. doi:10.1037/h0026256

Cole, B. (2007). *Opening address by chairman of the national endowment for the humanities*. Paper presented at the Using New Technologies to Explore Cultural Heritage Conference. Retrieved April 13, 2011 from http://www.neh.gov/ DigitalHumanities/ Conference_07Oct/ DH_Conference.html.

Cole, C., Spink, A., & Waller, M. (2008). Multitasking behaviour. In Cronin, B. (Ed.), *Annual Review of Information Science and Technology* (pp. 93–118). Medford, NJ: Information Today.

Cole, J., Henrick, G., & Cole, J. (2011). *Moodle 2.0 for business: Beginner's guide*. Birmingham, UK: Packt Publishing.

Comercher, M. (2006). *E-learning concepts and techniques*. Bloomsburg, PA: Bloomsburg University.

CoP. (2011). *The communities of practice web site*. Retrieved 1 September 2011 from http://www.communities.dl.ac.uk.

Corbel, A., Jaillon, P., Serpaggi, X., Baker, M., Quignard, M., Lund, K., & Séjourné, A. (2002). DREW: Un outil internet pour créer situations d'appretissage coopérant. (DREW: An internet tool for creating cooperative learning situations) In Desmoulins, C., Marquet, P., & Bouhineau, D. (Eds.), *EIAH2003 Environnements Informatique pour l'Apprentissage Humains* (pp. 109–113). Paris, France: INRP.

Council the European Union. (2001). *Report from the education council to the European council: The concrete future objectives of education and training systems*. Retrieved from http://ec.europa.eu/education/policies/2010/doc/rep_fut_obj_en.pdf.

Cowie, R., Douglas-Cowie, E., Tsapatsoulis, N., Votsis, G., Kollias, S., Fellenz, W., & Taylor, J. G. (2001). Emotion recognition in human-computer interaction. *IEEE Signal Processing Magazine, 18*(1), 32–80. doi:10.1109/79.911197

Cox, D., & Greenberg, S. (2000). *Supporting collaborative interpretation in distributed groupware*. Paper presented at the CSCW. Philadelphia, PA.

Cragin, M. H., Palmer, C. L., Carlson, J. R., & Witt, M. (2010). Data sharing, small science, and institutional repositories. *Philosophical Transactions of the Royal Society A: Mathematical, Physical and Engineering Sciences, 368*(1926), 4023-4038.

Creswell, J. W. (2005). *Educational research* (2nd ed.). Upper Saddle River, NJ: Pearson Education Inc.

Cumming, J. (2008). *Representing the complexity, diversity and particularity of the doctoral enterprise in Australia*. Sydney, Australia: The Australian National University.

Dandurand, F., Shultz, T. R., & Onishi, K. H. (2008). Comparing online and lab methods in a problem-solving experiment. *Behavior Research Methods, 40*, 428–434. doi:10.3758/BRM.40.2.428

David, P. A. (2004). Towards a cyberinfrastructure for enhanced scientific collaboration: Providing its 'soft' foundations may be the hardest part. *Oxford Internet Institute, Research Report No.4, August 2004.* Retrieved June 30th 2011, from http:// www.oii.ox.ac.uk/ resources/ publications/ RR4.pdf.

David, P. A., den Besten, M., & Schroeder, R. (2006). How open is e-science? In *Proceedings of the Second IEEE International Conference on e-Science and Grid Computing (e-Science 2006)*, (pp. 1-8). IEEE Press.

David, P. A. (2006). Towards a cyberinfrastructure for enhanced scientific collaboration: Providing its 'soft' foundations may be the hardest part. In Kahin, B., & Foray, D. (Eds.), *Advancing Knowledge and the Knowledge Economy* (pp. 431–454). Cambridge, MA: MIT Press.

David, P. A., & Bunn, J. A. (1988). The economics of gateway technologies and network evolution. *Information Economics and Policy, 3,* 165–202. doi:10.1016/0167-6245(88)90024-8

Davis, N., & Tearle, P. (1998). A core curriculum for telematics in teacher training. In *Proceedings of the 15th IFIP World Computer Congress – Teleteaching 1998 Distance Learning, Training and Education*, (vol 1), (pp. 239-248). ACM Press.

De Jong, F. P. C. M., Veldhuis-Diermanse, A. E., & Lutgens, G. (2002). Computer-supported learning in university and vocational education. In Koschman, T., Hall, R., & Miyake, N. (Eds.), *CSCL 2: Carrying Forward the Conversation* (pp. 111–128). Hillsdale, NJ: Erlbaum.

De Roure, D. (2010). *Semantic grid and sensor grid: Insights into the e-research ecosystem.* Paper presented at the 4th IEEE International Conference on Digital Ecosystems and Technologies (IEEE DEST 2010). New York, NY.

De Roure, D., & Frey, J. (2007). *Three perspectives on collaborative knowledge acquisition in e-science.* Paper presented at the Workshop on Semantic Web for Collaborative Knowledge Acquisition (SWeCKa). Hyderabad, India.

De Roure, D., Baker, M. A., Jennings, N. R., & Shadbolt, N. R. (2003). The evolution of the grid. In Berman, F., Fox, G., & Hey, A. J. G. (Eds.), *Grid Computing: Making the Global Infrastructure a Reality* (pp. 65–100). West Sussex, UK: Wiley.

de Solla Price, D. J. (1963). *Little science, big science.* New York, NY: Columbia University Press.

De Wever, B., Schellens, T., Valcke, M., & Van Keer, H. (2006). Content analysis schemes to analyse transcripts of online asynchronous discussion groups: A review. *Computers & Education, 46*(1), 6–28. doi:10.1016/j.compedu.2005.04.005

Deelman, E., Blythe, J., Gil, Y., Kesselman, C., Mehta, G., & Vahi, K. (2003). Mapping abstract complex workflows onto grid environments. *Journal of Grid Computing, 1*(1), 25–39. doi:10.1023/A:1024000426962

Delgado López-Cózar, E., Torres-Salinas, D., Jiménez-Contreras, E., & Ruiz-Pérez, R. (2006). Análisis bibliométrico y de redes sociales aplicado a las tesis bibliométricas defendidas en españa (1976-2002): Temas, escuelas científicas y redes académicas. *Revista Espanola la de Documentacion Cientifica, 29*(4).

DEST. (2006). *An Australian e-research strategy and implementation framework: Final report of the e-research coordinating committee.* Sydney, Australia: Australian Government.

Dillenbourg, P. (1999). Introduction: What do you mean by collaborative learning? In Dillenbourg, P. (Ed.), *Collaborative Learning: Cognitive and Computational Approaches* (pp. 1–19). Oxford, UK: Pergamon.

DiNucci, D. (1999). Fragmented future. *Print, 53*(4), 32.

Diviacco, P. (2007). *Perspective in distributed, web based seismic data handling for collaborative scientific research.* Paper presented at the 69th EAGE International Conference. London, UK.

Diviacco, P. (2005). An open source, web based, simple solution for seismic data dissemination, and collaborative research. *Computers & Geosciences, 31*(5), 599–605. doi:10.1016/j.cageo.2004.11.008

Diviacco, P. (2011). *Towards a collaborative research data space in Geophysics.* Mediterranean Marine Sciences.

Diviacco, P., Lowry, R., & Leadbetter, A. (2011b). Collaborative work and tools towards wide scientific community driven metadata model and vocabulary building. In *Geophysical Research Abstracts* (*Vol. 12*). Vienna, Austria: EGU.

Diviacco, P., & Pshenichny, C. A. (2010). Concept-referenced spaces in computer-supported collaborative work. In *Geophysical Research Abstracts (Vol. 12)*. Vienna, Austria: EGU.

Diviacco, P., & Pshenichny, C. A. (2011). A case study on the use of event bushes as a formal representation for computer supported collaborative work in the geosciences. In *Geophysical Research Abstracts (Vol. 12)*. Vienna, Austria: EGU.

Diviacco, P., Rebesco, M., & Camerlenghi, A. (2006). Late pliocene mega debris flow deposit and related fluid escapes identified on the antarctic peninsula continental margin by seismic reflection data analysis. *Marine Geophysical Researches, 27*(2), 109–128. doi:10.1007/s11001-005-3136-8

Dix, A., Finlay, J., & Abowd, G. D. (2004). *Human-computer interaction*. Upper Saddle River, NJ: Prentice Hall.

Doerry, E. (1996). *An empirical comparison of co-present and technologically-mediated interaction based on communicative breakdown*. PhD Dissertation. Eugene, OR: University of Oregon.

Dove, M. T., & de Leeuw, N. H. (2005). Grid computing and molecular simulations: The vision of the eMinerals project. *Molecular Simulation, 31*(5), 297–301. doi:10.1080/08927020500065801

Dubinsky, E., & Tall, D. (1991). Advanced mathematical thinking and the computer. In Tall, D. O. (Ed.), *Advanced Mathematical Thinking* (pp. 231–248). Berlin, Germany: Kluwer.

DuBrin, A., & Barnard, J. (1993). What telecommuters like and dislike about their jobs. *Business Forum, 18*(3), 13.

Dukette, D., & Cornish, D. (2009). *The essential 20: Twenty components of an excellent health care team*. Pittsburgh, PA: RoseDog Books.

Dummet, M. (1993). *Origins of analytical philosophy*. London, UK: Duckworth.

Dutton, W. H., & Jeffreys, P. W. (Eds.). (2010). *World wide research: Reshaping the sciences and humanities*. Cambridge, MA: MIT Press.

Dutton, W. H., & Meyer, E. T. (2009). Experience with new tools and infrastructures of research: An exploratory study of distance from, and attitudes toward, e-research. *Prometheus, 27*(3), 223–238. doi:10.1080/08109020903127802

Dux, P. E., Ivanoff, J., Asplund, C. L., & Marois, R. (2006). Isolation of a central bottleneck of information processing with time-resolved fMRI. *Neuron, 52*(6), 1109–1120. doi:10.1016/j.neuron.2006.11.009

Dyfour-Janvier, B., Bednarz, N., & Belanger, M. (1987). Pedagogical considerations concerning the problem of representation. In Janvier, C. (Ed.), *Problems of Representation in Teaching and Learning of Mathematics* (pp. 109–122). London, UK: Lawrence Erlbaum Associates.

Dyke, G., Lund, K., & Girardot, J.-J. (2009). Tatiana: An environment to support the CSCL analysis process. In *Proceedings of the International Conference on Computer Supported Collaborative Learning,* (pp. 58-67). Rhodes, Greece: ACM.

Dyke, G., Lund, K., Jeong, H., Medina, R., Suthers, D. D., van Aalst, J., et al. (2011). Technological affordances for productive multivocality in analysis. In *Proceedings of the International Computer Supported Collaborative Learning,* (pp. 454-461). Hong Kong, China: ACM.

Dyke, G., Lund, K., & Girardot, J.-J. (2010). Tatiana: Un environnement d'aide à l'analyse de traces d'interactions humaines. *Technique et Science Informatiques, 29*(10), 1179–1205. doi:10.3166/tsi.29.1179-1205

Eco, U. (1981). Guessing: From Aristotle to Sherlock Holmes. *Versus, 30*.

Edgar, B. D., & Willinsky, J. (2010). A survey of the scholarly journals using open journal systems. *Journal Scholarly and Research Communication*. Retrieved June 27, 2011, from http:// pkp.sfu.ca/ files/ OJS Journal Survey.pdf.

Edge, D. (1979). Quantitative measures of communication in science: A critical review. *History of Science, 17*, 102–134.

Edwards, P., Farrington, J. H., Mellish, C., Philip, L. J., Chorley, A. H., & Hielkema, F. (2009). E-social science and evidence-based policy assessment: Challenges and solutions. *Social Science Computer Review, 27*(4), 553–568. doi:10.1177/0894439309332305

Egan, G. F., Liu, W., Soh, W.-S., Hang, D., Wang, L., Chen, K., & Ong, Y. S. (2005). *Australian neuroinformatics research grid computing and e-research*. Paper presented at ICNC 2005, (pp. 1057-1064). ICNC Press.

e-IRG. (2009). *E-IRG white paper 2009*. Retrieved February 24, 2011, from http:// www.e-irg.eu/ images/ stories/ publ/ white-papers/ e-irg_white_paper_2009_final.pdf.

Ekman, P. (1980). *The face of man: Expressions of universal emotions in a New Guinea village*. New York, NY: Garland STPM Press.

Ellis, J., & Kvavilashvili, L. (2000). Prospective memory in 2000: Past, present and future directions. *Applied Cognitive Psychology, 14*(7), 1–9. doi:10.1002/acp.767

Ellison, N. B., Steinfield, C., & Lampe, C. (2007). The benefits of Facebook "friends": Social capital and college students' use of online social network sites. *Journal of Computer-Mediated Communication, 12*, 1143–1168. doi:10.1111/j.1083-6101.2007.00367.x

Engelbrecht, P. C., & Dror, E. I. (2009). How psychology and cognition can inform the creation of ontologies in semantic technologies. In Y. Kiyoki, T. Tokuda, H. Jaakkola, X. Chen, & N. Yoshida (Eds.), *Proceeding of the 2009 Conference on Information Modeling and Knowledge Bases XX*, (pp. 340-347). Amsterdam, The Netherlands: IOS Press.

Engelhardt, W., & Zimmerman, J. (1982). *Theory of earth science*. Cambridge, UK: Cambridge University Press.

Engelmann, T., Dehler, J., Bodemer, D., & Buder, J. (2009). Knowledge awareness in CSCL: A psychological perspective. *Computers in Human Behavior, 25*(4), 949–960. doi:10.1016/j.chb.2009.04.004

Engeström, J. (2009). *Building sites around social objects*. Paper presented at the Web 2.0 Expo. San Francisco, CA.

Engestrom, Y. (1987). *Learning by expanding. An activity-theoretical approach to developmental research*. Helsinki, Finland: Orienta-Konsultit Oy.

Ensher, E. A., Heun, C., & Blanchard, A. (2003). Online mentoring and computer-mediated communication: New directions in research. *Journal of Vocational Behavior, 63*, 264–288. doi:10.1016/S0001-8791(03)00044-7

Erhut, S., & Mokros, J. R. (1984). Professors as models and mentors for college students. *American Educational Research Journal, 21*, 399–417.

Erman, N., & Todorovski, L. (2010). Analyzing the structure of the EGOV conference community. *Electronic Government*, 73-84.

Ertl, B., Kopp, B., & Mandl, H. (2008). Supporting learning using external representations. *Computers & Education, 51*(4), 1599–1608. doi:10.1016/j.compedu.2008.03.001

ESFRI. (2006). *European roadmap for research infrastructures report*. Retrieved April 3, 2011 from http:// ec.europa.eu/ research/ infrastructures/ pdf/ esfri/ esfri_roadmap/ roadmap_2006/ esfri_roadmap_2006_en.pdf.

ESFRI. (2008a). *European roadmap for research infrastructures, update*. Retrieved April 3, 2011 from http:// ec.europa.eu/ research/ infrastructures/ pdf/ esfri/ esfri_roadmap/ roadmap_2008/ esfri_roadmap_update_2008.pdf.

ESFRI. (2008b). *European roadmap for research infrastructures, social sciences and humanities roadmap working group report*. Retrieved April 12, 2011 from http:// ec.europa.eu/ research/ infrastructures/ pdf/ esfri/ esfri_roadmap/ roadmap_2008/ ssh_report_2008_en.pdf.

European Commission. (1997). *Framework programme: Information society programme for technologies and skills acquisition: Proposal for a research agenda*. Brussels, Belgium: European Commission.

Faccioni, M., & Panzarasa, P. (2006). Knowledge transfer within affiliation networks. In *Proceedings of the IEEE International Engineering Management Conference*, (pp. 226-230). IEEE Press.

Faily, S., & Flechais, I. (2010). Designing and aligning e-science security culture with design. *Information Management & Computer Security, 18*(5), 339–349. doi:10.1108/09685221011095254

Farooq, U., Ganoe, C., Carroll, J., & Giles, L. (2007). Supporting distributed scientific collaboration: Implications for designing the CiteSeer collaboratory. In *Proceedings of the 40th Annual Hawaii International Conference on System Sciences (HICSS 2007)*. IEEE Computer Society.

Farooq, U., Merkel, C., Nash, H., Rosson, M., Carroll, J., & Xiao, L. (2005). Participatory design as apprenticeship: Sustainable watershed management as a community computing application. In *Proceedings of the 38th Annual Hawaii International Conference on System Sciences (HICSS 2005)*. Hawaii, HI: HICSS Press.

Feinberg, J. (2009). *Wordle*. Retrieved February 22, 2011, from http://www.wordle.net.

Feyerabend, P. (1975). *Against method.* London, UK: Verso.

Fink, J. L., Kushch, S., Williams, P. R., & Bourne, P. E. (2008). Biolit: Integrating biological literature with databases. *Nucleic acids research, 36*(2), W385-W389. Retrieved February 24, 2011, from http:// nar.oxfordjournals.org/ content/ 36/ suppl_2/ W385.full.

Fisch, K. (2006). *Did you know?* Retrieved from http:// thefischbowl.blogspot.com/ 2006/ 08/ did-you-know.html.

Fischer, G., Rohde, M., & Wulf, V. (2007). Community-based learning: The core competency of residential, research-based universities. *Computer-Supported Collaborative Learning.* Retrieved from http:// l3d.cs.colorado. edu/ ~gerhard/ papers/ final-iJCSCL07-rhode-wulf.pdf.

Fischer, F., & Mandl, H. (2005). Knowledge convergence in computer-supported collaborative learning: The role of external representation tools. *Journal of the Learning Sciences, 14*(3), 405–441. doi:10.1207/s15327809jls1403_3

Fischer, G. (2003). *Meta-design: Beyond user-centered and participatory design. Human-Computer Interaction: Theory and Practice* (p. 88). New York, NY: Horwood.

Fisher, C., & Sanderson, P. (1996). Exploratory sequential data analysis: Exploring continuous observational data. *Interaction, 3*(2), 25–34. doi:10.1145/227181.227185

Fitzgerald, S., Hanks, B., & McCauley, R. (2010). Collaborative research in computer science education: A case study. In *Proceedings of SIGCSE, 2010,* 305–309.

Foerde, K., Poldrack, R. A., & Knowlton, B. J. (2007). Secondary task effects on classification learning. *Memory & Cognition, 35,* 864–874. doi:10.3758/BF03193461

Fogel, J., & Nehmad, E. (2009). Internet social network communities: Risk taking, trust, and privacy concerns. *Computers in Human Behavior, 25,* 153–160. doi:10.1016/j.chb.2008.08.006

Foster, N. F., & Gibbons, S. (2005). Understanding faculty to improve content recruitment for institutional repositories. *D-Lib Magazine, 11*(1). Retrieved February 24, 2011, from http:// www.dlib.org/ dlib/ january05/ foster/ 01foster.html.

Foster, I., & Kesselman, C. (1998). *The grid: Blueprint for a new computing infrastructure.* New York, NY: Morgan-Kaufman.

Fox, G. C., Pierce, M. E., Mustacoglu, A. F., & Topcu, A. E. (2007). Web 2.0 for e-science environments. In *Proceedings of the Third International Conference on Semantics, Knowledge and Grid,* (pp. 1-6). IEEE Press.

Fragopanagos, N., & Taylor, J. G. (2005). Emotion recognition in human-computer interaction. *Neural Networks: Emotion and Brain, 18*(4), 389–405.

Francesco, D. (1994). *Aspetti logico-linguisitici dell' impresa scientifica.* Paper presented at Introduzione alla Filosofia della Scienza. Bompiani, Italy.

Freeman, L. C. (1979). Centrality in social networks conceptual clarification. *Social Networks, 1*(3), 215–239. doi:10.1016/0378-8733(78)90021-7

Frege, G. (1892). *Über sinn und bedeutung.* Milano, Italy: Bompiani.

Frey, F. (2002). *Condor dagman: Handling inter-job dependencies.* Retrieved from http:// cs.wisc.edu/ condor/ dagman/.

Frodeman, R. (1995). Geological reasoning: Geology as an interpretive and historical science. *Bulletin of the Geological Society of America, 107,* 960–968. doi:10.1130/0016-7606(1995)107<0960:GRGAAI>2.3.CO;2

Fry, J. (2006). Coordination and control across scientific fields: Implications for a differentiated e-science. In Hine, C. (Ed.), *New Infrastructures for Knowledge Production: Understanding e-Science* (pp. 167–188). Hershey, PA: IGI Global. doi:10.4018/978-1-59140-717-1.ch008

Fry, J., Schroeder, R., & den Besten, M. (2009). Open science in e-science: Contingency or policy? *The Journal of Documentation, 65*(1), 6–32. doi:10.1108/00220410910926103

Fuster Morell, M. (2010). *Governance of online creation communities: Provision of infrastructure for the building of digital commons.* Unpublished dissertation. Florence, Italy: European University Institute.

Gaffney, D., Pearce, I., Darham, M., & Nanis, M. (2010). *Presenting 140Kit: An open, extensible research platform for Twitter.* Retrieved from http:// www.webecologyproject.org/ 2010/ 07/ presenting-140kit/.

Galison, P. L., & Stump, J. D. (1996). *The disunity of science: Boundaries, context and power.* Palo Alto, CA: Stanford University Press.

Gao, J. (2010). Developing a web-based collaborative research environment for undergraduates. *Journal of Computing Sciences in Colleges, 26*(2), 39–46.

Gardner, H. (1985). *The mind's new science: A history of cognitive revolution.* New York, NY: Basic Books.

Gareis, C., & Nussbaum-Beach, S. (2007). Electronically mentoring to develop accomplished professional teachers. *Journal of Personnel Evaluation in Education, 20*, 227–246. doi:10.1007/s11092-008-9060-0

Genoni, P., Merrick, H., & Willson, M. (2006). Scholarly communities, e-research literacy and the academic librarian. *The Electronic Library, 24*(6), 734–746. doi:10.1108/02640470610714189

Gentil-Beccot, A., Mele, S., & Brooks, T. (2009). Citing and Reading behaviours in high-energy physics: How a community stopped worrying about journals and learned to love repositories. *Scientometrics, 84*(2), 345–355. doi:10.1007/s11192-009-0111-1

Georgieva, G., Todorov, G., & Smrikarov, A. (2003). *A model of a virtual university: Some problems during its development.* Paper presented at the 4th ACM International Conference on Computer Systems and Technologies: E-Learning. New York, NY.

Gershenfeld, N., Krikorian, R., & Cohen, D. (2004). The Internet of things. *Scientific American, 291*, 76–81. doi:10.1038/scientificamerican1004-76

Giaccardi, E. (2005). Metadesign as an emergent design culture. *Leonardo, 38*(4), 342–349. doi:10.1162/0024094054762098

Giaccardi, E., & Fischer, G. (2008). Creativity and evolution: A metadesign perspective. *Digital Creativity, 19*(1), 19. doi:10.1080/14626260701847456

Gilbert, A. (2004). Can't focus on the teleconference? Join the club. *C-Net.* Retrieved on January 3, 2010 from http:// news.cnet.com/ Cant-focus-on-the-teleconference-Join-the-club/ 2100-1022_3-5494304.html.

Gillie, T., & Broadbent, D. (1989). What makes interruptions disruptive? A study of length, similarity, and complexity. *Psychological Research, 50*, 243–250. doi:10.1007/BF00309260

Ginzburg, C. (1989). *Clues, myths and the historical method.* Baltimore, MD: Johns Hopkins University Press.

Gladstones, W. H., Regan, M. A., & Lee, R. B. (1989). Division of attention: The single-channel hypothesis revisited. *Quarterly Journal of Experimental Psychology: Human Experimental Psychology 41*(A), 1-17.

Gleditsch, N. P., Metelits, C., & Strand, H. (2003). Posting your data: Will you be scooped or will you be famous? *International Studies Perspectives, 4*(1), 89–97.

Goble, C., Stevens, R., & Bechhofer, S. (2005). The semantic web and knowledge grids. *Drug Discovery Today, 2*(3), 225–233. doi:10.1016/j.ddtec.2005.08.005

Godfrey, J., Holliman, E., & McDaniel, J. (1992). SWITCHBOARD: Telephone speech corpus for research and development. In *Proceedings of ICASSP, 1992*, 517–520.

Goldenberg-Hart, D. (2004). *Libraries and changing research practices.* Retrieved April 15, 2011 from http:// www.arl.org/ forum04/ #proceedings.

Golder, S., & Huberman, B. A. (2005). The structure of collaborative tagging systems. *HP Labs Technical Report.* Retrieved august 2011 from http://www.hpl.hp.com/ research/idl/papaers/tags.

Good, B. M., & Wilkinson, M. D. (2006). The life sciences semantic web is full of creeps! *Briefings in Bioinformatics, 7*, 275–286. doi:10.1093/bib/bbl025

Goodman, B. A., Drury, J., Gaimari, R. D., Kurland, L., & Zarrella, J. (2006). *Applying user models to improve team decision making.* Retrieved April 10, 2008 from http:// mitre.org/ work/ tech_papers/ tech_papers_07/ 06_1351/.

Gorghiu, G., Gorghiu, L. M., Suduc, A. M., Bîzoi, M., Dumitrescu, C., & Olteanu, R. L. (2009). Related aspects to the pedagogical use of virtual experiments. In *Proceedings of the Fifth International Conference on Multimedia & ICTs in Education*, (pp. 809-813). Lisbon, Portugal: ACM.

Gorghiu, G. (2009). VccSSe: Virtual community collaborating space for science education - An European project experience under socrates comenius 2.1 action. In Gorghiu, G., Gorghiu, L. M., Glava, A. E., & Glava, C. C. (Eds.), *Education 21* (pp. 7–16). Cluj Napoca, Romania: Casa Cărții de Știință Publishing House.

Gorghiu, G., Bîzoi, M., Gorghiu, L. M., & Suduc, A. M. (2011). Promoting the European cooperation with the view of improving the methodologies for science teaching and learning using virtual instrumentation. In Bolte, C., Gräber, W., & Holbrook, J. (Eds.), *Making Science Lessons Popular and Relevant - Examples of Good Practice*. Münster, Germany: Waxmann Verlag.

Gosling, S. D., Gaddis, S., & Vazire, S. (2007). *Personality impressions based on Facebook profiles*. Paper presented at the International Conference on Weblogs and Social Media. Boulder, CO.

Gray, P., & Tehtani, S. (2003). Technologies for disseminating knowledge. In Holsapple, C. (Ed.), *Handbook on Knowledge Management - Knowledge Matters* (pp. 109–127). Berlin, Germany: Springer-Verlang.

Green, T. (1989). Cognitive dimensions of notations: People and computers V. In *Proceedings of the Fifth Conference of the British Computer Society Human-Computer Interaction Specialist Group*, (p. 443). BCS Press.

Green, T., & Blackwell, A. (1998). *Cognitive dimensions of information artefacts: A tutorial*. Paper presented at the BCS HCI Conference. London, UK.

Greengard, S. (2002). Moving forward with reverse mentoring. *Workforce*, *81*, 15.

Greenhow, C., Robelia, B., & Hughes, J. E. (2009). Learning, teaching, and scholarship in a digital age: Web 2.0 and classroom research: What path should we take now? *Educational Researcher*, *38*(4), 246–259. doi:10.3102/0013189X09336671

Gruber, T. R. (1995). Toward principles for the design of ontologies used for knowledge sharing. *International Journal of Human-Computer Studies*, *43*(4-5), 907–928. doi:10.1006/ijhc.1995.1081

Hackett, E. J. (2005). Introduction to the special guest-edited issue on scientific collaboration. *Social Studies of Science*, *35*(5), 667–671. doi:10.1177/0306312705057569

Haggard, D., Dougherty, T., Turban, D., & Wilbanks, J. (2011). Who is a mentor? A review of evolving definitions and implications for research. *Journal of Management*, *37*(1), 280–304. doi:10.1177/0149206310386227

Hagstrom, W. O. (1965). *The scientific community*. New York, NY: Basic Books.

Häkkinen, P., & Jarvela, S. (2006). Sharing and constructing perspectives in web-based conferencing. *Computers & Education*, *47*, 433–447. doi:10.1016/j.compedu.2004.10.015

Halfpenny, P., & Procter, R. (2009). Special issue on e-social science. *Social Science Computer Review*, *27*(4), 459–466. doi:10.1177/0894439309332662

Halfpenny, P., Procter, R., Lin, Y.-W., & Voss, A. (2009). Developing the UK-based e-social science research program. In Jankowski, N. (Ed.), *E-research: Transformation in Scholarly Practice* (pp. 73–90). New York, NY: Routledge.

Hallowell, R. (2007). *Crazy busy: Overstretched, overbooked, and about to snap! Strategies for handling your fast-paced life*. New York, NY: Ballantine Books.

Hameed, A., Preece, A., & Sleeman, D. (2003). Ontology reconciliation. In Staab, S., & Studer, R. (Eds.), *Handbook on Ontologies in Information Systems* (pp. 231–250). Berlin, Germany: Springer Verlag.

Hamilton, B., & Scandura, T. (2003). E-mentoring: Implications for organizational learning and development in a wired world. *Organizational Dynamics*, *31*(4), 388–402. doi:10.1016/S0090-2616(02)00128-6

Hammond, M., Hawtin, R., Gillam, L., & Oppenheim, C. (2010). *Cloud computing for research: Report to JISC*. Retrieved 1 September 2011 from http://www.jisc.ac.uk/ whatwedo/ programmes/ researchinfrastructure/ usingcloudcomp.aspx.

Handy, S., & Mokhtarian, P. (1995). Planning for telecommuting: Measurement and policy issues. *Journal of the American Planning Association. American Planning Association*, *61*(1), 99–111. doi:10.1080/01944369508975623

Hanson, N. R. (1971). *Observation and explanation: A guide to philosophy of science*. New York, NY: Harper & Row.

Harasim, L., Hiltz, S. R., Teles, L., & Turoff, M. (1995). *Learning networks: A field guide to teaching and learning online*. Cambridge, MA: MIT Press.

Hargittai, E. (2007). Whose space? Differences among users and non-users of social network sites. *Journal of Computer-Mediated Communication*, *13*, 276–297. doi:10.1111/j.1083-6101.2007.00396.x

Harper, D. (1987). *The nature of work: Working knowledge.* Chicago, IL: University of Chicago.

Harrer, A., Zeini, S., & Ziebarth, S. (2009). *Integrated representation and visualisation of the dynamics in computer-mediated social networks.* Paper presented at 2009 International Conference on Advances in Social Network Analysis and Mining. Athens, Greece.

Haythornthwaite, C., Kazmer, M. M., Robins, J., & Shoemaker, S. (2000). Community development among distance learners: Temporal and technological dimensions. *Journal of Computer-Mediated Communication, 6*(1). Retrieved from http://www.ascusc.org/jcmc/vol6/issue1/haythornthwaite.html

Haythornthwaite, C., Lunsford, K. J., Bowker, G. C., & Bruce, B. C. (2006). Challenges for research and practice in distributed, interdisciplinary collaboration. In Hine, C. (Ed.), *New Infrastructures for Knowledge Production: Understanding e-Science* (pp. 143–166). Hershey, PA: IGI Global. doi:10.4018/978-1-59140-717-1.ch007

Headlamwells, J., Gosland, J., & Craig, J. (2006). Beyond the organization: The design and management of e-mentoring systems. *International Journal of Information Management, 26*, 372–385. doi:10.1016/j.ijinfomgt.2006.04.001

He, B., Ding, Y., & Ni, C. (2011). Mining enriched contextual information of scientific collaboration: A meso perspective. *Journal of the American Society for Information Science and Technology, 62*(5), 831–845. doi:10.1002/asi.21510

Henninger, D. (2010). Commentary – World. *Wall Street Journal.* Retrieved from http://www.wsj.com.

Henty, M., Weaver, B., Bradbury, S. J., & Porter, S. (2008). *Investigating data management practices in Australian universities.* Canberra, Australia: Australian Partnership for Sustainable Repositories (APSR).

Herrero, R. S. H. (2000). La terminología del análisis de redes problemas de definición y de traducción. *Politica y Sociedad, 33*, 199.

Herron, T. L., & Young, G. R. (2000). E-research moving behavioral accounting research into cyberspace. *Advances in Accounting Behavioral Research, 3*, 265–280. doi:10.1016/S1474-7979(00)03035-0

Hey, A. J. G., Tansley, S., & Tolle, K. M. (2009). *The fourth paradigm: Data-intensive scientific discovery.* Palo Alto, CA: Microsoft Research.

Hey, T., & Hey, J. (2006). e-Science and its implications for the library community. *Library Hi Tech, 24*(4), 515–528. doi:10.1108/07378830610715383

Hey, T., & Trefethen, A. (2003). The data deluge: An e-science perspective. In *Grid Computing: Making the Global Infrastructure a Reality* (pp. 809–824). New York, NY: Wiley.

Hey, T., & Trefethen, A. (2008). E-science, cyberinfrastructure, and scholarly communication. In Olson, G. M., Zimmerman, A., & Bos, N. (Eds.), *Scientific Collaboration on the Internet* (pp. 15–31). Cambridge, MA: MIT Press.

Hickson, I. (2011). *HTML5: A vocabulary and associated APIs for HTML and XHTML.* W3C Editor's Draft 16 February 2011. Retrieved from http:// dev.w3.org/html5/ spec/ Overview.html.

Hine, C. (2000). *Virtual ethnography.* Thousand Oaks, CA: Sage.

Hine, C. (Ed.). (2005). *Virtual methods: Issues in social research on the Internet.* Oxford, UK: Berg.

Hine, C. (Ed.). (2006). *New infrastructures for knowledge production: Understanding escience.* Hershey, PA: IGI Global.

Hinze-Hoare, V. (2007). CSCR: Computer supported collaborative research. *University of Southampton.* Retrieved on October 14, 2008 from http:// arxiv.org/ abs/ 0711.2760.

Hogan, M. J., Kelly, C., & Craik, F. (2006). The effects of attention switching on encoding and retrieval of words in younger and older adults. *Experimental Aging Research, 32*(2), 153–183. doi:10.1080/03610730600553935

Hollingsworth, D. (1994). The workflow reference model. *Workflow Management Coalition.* Retrieved from http://www.wfmc.org.

Holstein, W. J. (2006, June 7). The workplace. *International Herald Tribune,* p. 22.

Holz, H. J., Applin, A., Haberman, B., Joyce, D., Purchase, H., & Reed, C. (2006). *Research methods in computing: What are they, and how should we teach them?* Retrieved from http:// www.dcs.gla.ac.uk/ publications/ PAPERS/ 8445/ sigsce-final.pdf.

Hopwood, N., & McAlpine, L. (2007). *Exploring a theoretical framework for understanding doctoral education.* Retrieved from http:// ogpr.educ.ubc.ca/ Doctoral%20ed/ Documents/ Hopwood%20 &%20%20 MacAlpine%20 (2007).pdf.

Hoschka, P. (1998). CSCW research at GMD-FIT: From basic groupware to the Social Web. *ACM SIGGROUP Bulletin, 19,* 5–9.

Houghton, J., & Oppenheim, C. (2010). The economic implications of alternative publishing models. *Prometheus, 28*(1), 41–54. doi:10.1080/08109021003676359

Hsu, C. L., & Lin, J. C. (2008). Acceptance of blog usage: The roles of technology acceptance, social influence, and knowledge sharing motivation. *Information & Management, 45,* 65–74. doi:10.1016/j.im.2007.11.001

Huddle. (2011). *Huddle's web site.* Retrieved 1 September 2011 from http://www.huddle.com.

Hume, D. (1910). *An enquiry concerning human understanding.* New York, NY: P. F. Collier & Son.

Humphreys, L. M., Krishnamurthy, B., & Gill, P. (2010). *How much is too much? Privacy issues on Twitter.* Paper presented at the Conference of the International Communication Association. Singapore.

Huws, U., Korte, W., & Robinson, S. (1990). *Telework: Towards the elusive office.* Chichester, UK: John Wiley and Sons.

IMS-CP. (2011). Instructional management system content package, version 1.2. *Public Draft 2 Specification.* Retrieved from http:// www.imsglobal.org/ content/ packaging/.

IMS-LD. (2011). Instructional management system learning design, version 1. *Specification.* Retrieved from http:// www.imsglobal.org/ learningdesign/.

IMS-MD. (2011). *Instructional management system meta-data. version 1.3, final specification.* Retrieved from http:// www.imsglobal.org/ metadata/.

Iñiguez, L., Muñoz Justicia, J., Peñaranda, M. C., & Martínez, L. M. (2006). La psicología social en españa: Estructuras de comunidades. *Redes: Revista Hispana Para El Análisis De Redes Sociales, 10.*

Ishizaka, K., Marshall, S. P., & Conte, J. M. (2001). Individual differences in attentional strategies in multitasking situations. *Human Performance, 14*(4), 339–358. doi:10.1207/S15327043HUP1404_4

Jacobson, M. J., & Wilensky, U. (2006). Complex systems in education: Scientific and educational importance and implications for the learning sciences. *Journal of the Learning Sciences, 15*(1), 11–34. doi:10.1207/s15327809jls1501_4

Jain, A. K., & Li, S. Z. (2005). *Handbook of face recognition.* Secaucus, NJ: Springer-Verlag New York.

Jakubowicz, A. (2007). Bridging the mire between e-research and e-publishing for multimedia digital scholarship in the humanities and social sciences: An Australian case study. *Webology, 4*(1). Retrieved April 16, 2011 from http:// www.webology.org/ 2007/ v4n1/a38.html.

Jankowski, N. (2007). Exploring e-science: An introduction. *Journal of Computer-Mediated Communication, 12*(2). Retrieved June 15th 2011, from http:// jcmc.indiana. edu/ vol12/ issue2/ jankowski.html.

Jankowski, N. W. (Ed.). (2009). *E-research: Transformation in scholarly practice.* New York, NY: Routledge.

Janssen, J., Erkens, G., Kanselaar, G., & Jaspers, J. (2007). Visualization of participation: Does it contribute to successful computer-supported collaborative learning? *Computers & Education, 49*(4), 1037–1065. doi:10.1016/j. compedu.2006.01.004

Janvier, C. (1987). Representation and understanding: The notion of function as an example. In Janvier, C. (Ed.), *Problems of Representation in Teaching and Learning of Mathematics* (pp. 67–72). London: Lawrence Erlbaum Associates.

Jäschke, R., Hotho, A., Schmidtz, C., Ganter, B., & Stumme, G. (2008). Discovering shared conceptualizations in folksonomies. *Web Semantics Science Services and Agents on the World Wide Web, 6*(1), 38–53. doi:10.1016/j.websem.2007.11.004

Java, A., & Song, X. (2007). Why we Twitter: Understanding microblogging usage and communities. In *Proceedings of the Joint 9th WEBKDD and 1st SNA-KDD Workshop,* (pp. 56-65). Baltimore, MD: WEBKDD Press.

Jiménez Contreras, E. (2000). Los métodos bibliométricos aplicaciones y estado de la cuestión. *Cuadernos De Documentación Multimedia, 10,* 4.

Jiménez, F., Zabala-Iturriagagoitia, J. M., & Zofío, J. L. (2007). Efficiency in public research centers: Evaluating the spanish food technology program. *Working Papers in Economic Theory.* Retrieved from http:// ideas.repec. org/ p/ uam/ wpaper/ 200704.html.

Jirotka, M., Procter, R., Hartswood, M., Slack, R., Simpson, A., & Catelijne, C. (2005). Collaboration and trust in healthcare innovation: The eDiaMoND case study. *Computer Supported Cooperative Work, 14*(4), 369–398. doi:10.1007/s10606-005-9001-0

Jirotka, M., Procter, R., Rodden, T., & Bowker, G. (2006). Special issue: Collaboration in e-research. *Computer Supported Cooperative Work, 15*(4), 251–255.doi:10.1007/s10606-006-9028-x

Johns, M. D., Chen, S. S., & Hall, G. J. (Eds.). (2004). *Online social research: Methods, issues, and ethics*. New York, NY: Peter Lang.

Johnson, C. M. (2001). A survey of current research on online communities of practice. *The Internet and Higher Education, 4*(1), 45–60. doi:10.1016/S1096-7516(01)00047-1

Johnson, S. (1998). Teleworking service management – Issues for an integrated framework. In *Teleworking: International Perspectives* (pp. 185–206). New York, NY: Routledge.

Johnson, W. B. (2007). *On being a mentor: A guide for higher education faculty*. New York, NY: Lawrence Erlbaum Associates.

Joiner, R., & Jones, S. (2003). The effects of communication medium on argumentation and the development of critical thinking. *International Journal of Educational Research, 39*(8), 861–971. doi:10.1016/j.ijer.2004.11.008

Jonassen, D. H., Carr, C., & Yueh, H.-P. (1998). Computers as mindtools for engaging learners in critical thinking. *TechTrends, 43*(2), 24–32.doi:10.1007/BF02818172

Jones, R. M., Laird, J. E., Nielsen, P. E., Coulter, K., Kenny, P., & Koss, F. (1999). Automated intelligent pilots for combat flight simulation. *Artificial Intelligence Magazine, 20*, 27–42.

Kabassi, K., & Virvou, M. (2004). Personalised adult e-training on computer use based on multiple attribute decision making. *Interacting with Computers, 16*, 115–132. doi:10.1016/j.intcom.2003.11.006

Kalfoglou, Y., & Schorlemmer, M. (2003). Ontology mapping: The state of the art. *The Knowledge Engineering Review, 18*(1), 1–31. doi:10.1017/S0269888903000651

Kanade, T., Cohn, J., & Tian, Y. (2000). Comprehensive database for facial expression analysis. In *Proceedings of the Fourth IEEE International Conference on Automatic Face and Gesture Recognition (FG 2000)*, (pp. 484-490). Grenoble, France: IEEE Press.

Kanselaar, G., De Jong, T., Andriessen, J., & Goodyear, P. (2000). New technologies. In P. J. R. Simons., J. L. Van der Linden., & T. Duffy (Eds.), *New Learning,* (pp. 55-82). Dordrecht, The Netherlands: Kluwer Academic Publishers.

Kaput, J. J. (1994). The representational roles of technology in connecting μathematics with authentic experience. In R. Biehler, R. W. Scholz, R. Strasser, & B., Winkelman (Eds.), *Didactics of Mathematics as a Scientific Discipline: The State of the Art,* (pp. 379- 397). Dordrecht, The Netherlands: Kluwer Academic Publishers.

Karasti, H., Baker, K. S., & Halkola, E. (2006). Enriching the notion of data curation in e-science: Data managing and information infrastructuring in the long term ecological research (LTER) network. *Computer Supported Cooperative Work: The Journal of Collaborative Computing, 15*(4), 321–358. doi:10.1007/s10606-006-9023-2

Katz, J. S., & Martin, B. R. (1997). What is research collaboration? *Research Policy, 26*(1), 1–18. doi:10.1016/S0048-7333(96)00917-1

Kelly, K. (2008). World wide brain. *Age*. Retrieved March 10, 2011 from http:// businessnetwork.theage. com.au/ articles/ 2005/ 11/ 18/ 3491.html.

Kelso, J. (2003). eVOC: A controlled vocabulary for unifying gene expression data. *Genome Research, 13*, 1222–1230. doi:10.1101/gr.985203

Kemmis, S., & Wilkinson, M. (1998). Participatory action research and the study of practice. *Action Research in Practice: Partnerships for Social Justice in Education*, 21-36.

Kennan, M. A., & Kingsley, D. A. (2009). The state of the nation: A snapshot of Australian institutional repositories. *First Monday, 14*(2). Retrieved February 24, 2011, from http:// firstmonday.org/ htbin/ cgiwrap/ bin/ ojs/ index. php/ fm/ article/ view/ 2282/ 2092.

Kennan, M. A. (2007). Academic authors, scholarly publishing, and open access in Australia. *Learned Publishing, 20*(2), 138–146. doi:10.1087/174148507X185117

Khalil, M. (2008). Promoting success: Mentoring students with disabilities using new technologies in higher education. *Library Hi Tech News, 25*(1), 8–12. doi:10.1108/07419050810877490

Khare, R. (2006). Microformats: The next (small) thing on the semantic Web? *IEEE Internet Computing, 10*, 68–75. doi:10.1109/MIC.2006.13

Khatibi, V., & Montazer, G. A. (2009). *Study the role of web services in adoption of e-resarch process.* Paper presented at the International Conference on Engineering Education (lCEED 2009). Kuala Lumpur, Malaysia.

Khosrowabadi, R., Heijnen, M., Wahab, A., & Chai Quek, H. (2010). *The dynamic emotion recognition system based on functional connectivity of brain regions.* Paper presented at the 2010 IEEE Intelligent Vehicles Symposium. San Diego, CA.

Kiesler, S. (1986). The hidden messages in computer networks. *Harvard Business Review, 64*(1), 46–60.

Kim, B., Nam, D., Suh, Y., Lee, J., Cho, K., & Hwang, S. (2007). Application parameter description scheme for multiple job generation in problem solving environment. In *Proceedings of the International Conference on e-Sceince and Grid Computing,* (pp. 509-515). IEEE Press.

Kim, Y., Kim, E., Kim, J. Y., Cho, J., Kim, C., & Cho, K. W. (2006). e-AIRS: An e-science collaboration portal for aerospace applications. In *Proceedings of the High Performance Computing and Communications Conference,* (vol 4208), (pp. 813-822). IEEE Press.

Kim, A. J. (2000). *Community building on the Web.* Berkley, CA: Peachpit Press.

King, D. W., & Tenopir, C. (2011). Some economic aspects of the scholarly journal system. *Annual Review of Information Science & Technology, 45*, 295–366.

King, G. (2007). An introduction to the dataverse network as an infrastructure for data sharing. *Sociological Methods & Research, 36*(2), 173–199. doi:10.1177/0049124107306660

Kirakowski, J. (1994). *SUMI.* Retrieved Oct, 2010, from http:// sumi.ucc.ie/ index.html.

Kirakowski, J., & Claridge, N. (2008). *WAMMI.* Retrieved Oct, 2010, from http:// www.wammi.com/ about.html.

Kirschner, P. A., Beers, P. J., Boshuizen, H. P. A., & Gijselaers, W. H. (2008). Coercing shared knowledge in collaborative learning environments. *Computers in Human Behavior, 24*(2), 403–420. doi:10.1016/j.chb.2007.01.028

Kirschner, P. A., Buckingham-Shum, S. J., & Carr, C. S. (Eds.). (2003). *Visualizing argumentation: Software tools for collaborative and educational sense making.* Dordrecht, The Netherlands: Kluwer.

Klenk, N. L., Hickey, G. M., & MacLellan, J. I. (2010). Evaluating the social capital accrued in large research networks: The case of the sustainable forest management network (1995-2009). *Social Studies of Science, 40*(6), 931–960. doi:10.1177/0306312710374130

Kling, R., & Callahan, E. (2003). Electronic journals, the internet, and scholarly communication. *Annual Review of Information Science & Technology, 37*(1), 127–177. doi:10.1002/aris.1440370105

Kling, R., & McKim, G. (1999). Scholarly communication and the continuum of electronic publishing. *Journal of the American Society for Information Science American Society for Information Science, 50*(10), 890–906. doi:10.1002/ (SICI)1097-4571(1999)50:10<890::AID-ASI6>3.0.CO;2-8

Klobas, J. (2006). *Wikis: Tools for information, work and collaboration.* Oxford, UK: Chandos Publishing.

Koedinger, K. R., Cunningham, K., Skogsholm, A., & Leber, B. (2008). An open repository and analysis tools for fine-grained, longitudinal learner data. In *Proceedings of the First International Conference on Educational Data Mining,* (pp. 157-166). ACM.

Koper, R. (2001). Modelling units of study from a pedagogical perspective: The pedagogical metamodel behind EML. *Technical Report OUNL June.* Retrieved from http:// dspace.ou.nl/ bitstream/ 1820/ 36/ 1/ Pedagogical%20 metamodel%20 behind%20 EMLv2.pdf.

Korporaal, G. (2009). *AARNet 20 years of the internet in Australia: 1989-2009.* Sydney, Australia: AARNet.

Korta, Kepa, & Perry, J. (2011). Pragmatics. In E. N. Zalta (Ed.), *The Stanford Encyclopedia of Philosophy.* Palo Alto, CA: Stanford University.

Koschmann, T. (1996). Paradigm shifts and instructional technology: An introduction. In Koschmann, T. (Ed.), *CSCL: Theory and Practice of an Emerging Paradigm* (pp. 1–23). Mahwah, NJ: Lawrence Erlbaum Associates.

Kosonen, K., Ilomäki, L., & Lakkala, M. (2008). *Developing and applying design principles for knowledge creation practices.* Paper presented at the International Conference for the Learning Sciences. New York, NY.

Kötter, R. (2001). Neuroscience databases: Tools for exploring brain structure-function relationships. *Philosophical Transactions of the Royal Society B, 356,* 1111–1120. doi:10.1098/rstb.2001.0902

Kovács, G., & Spens, K. M. (2005). Abductive reasoning in logistics research. *International Journal of Physical Distribution and Logistics Management, 35*(2), 132–144. doi:10.1108/09600030510590318

Kram, K. E. (1985). *Mentoring at work: Developmental relationships in organizational life.* Glenview, IL: Scott Foresman.

Kranich, N. (2004). *The information commons: A public policy report.* Retrieved March 10, 2011 from http://www.fepproject.org/policyreports/infocommons.II.html.

Kraut, R. (1989). Telecommuting: The trade-offs of home work. *The Journal of Communication, 39*(3), 19–47. doi:10.1111/j.1460-2466.1989.tb01038.x

Kravcik, M., Kaibel, A., Specht, M., & Terrenghi, L. (2004). Mobile collector for field trips. *Journal of Educational Technology & Society, 7*(2), 25–33.

Kreifeldt, J. G., & McCarthy, M. E. (1981). Interruption as a test of the user computer interface. In *Proceedings of the 17th Annual Conference on Manual Control,* (pp. 655-667). ACM.

Kreijns, K., Kirschner, P. A., & Jochems, W. (2003). Identifying the pitfalls for social interaction in computer-supported collaborative learning environments: A review of the research. *Computers in Human Behavior, 19*(3), 335–353. doi:10.1016/S0747-5632(02)00057-2

Krige, J., & Pestre, D. (1997). *Science in the twentieth century.* Newark, NJ: Harwood Academic.

Kripke, S. A. (1972). Naming and necessity. In Davidson, D., & Harman, G. (Eds.), *Semantics of Natural Language.* Dordrecht, The Netherlands: Reidel. doi:10.1007/978-94-010-2557-7_9

Kuhn, T. S. (1962). *The structure of scientific revolutions.* Chicago, IL: University of Chicago Press.

Kwak, H., Lee, C., Park, H., & Moon, S. (2010). What is twitter, a social network or a news media? In *Proceedings of the 19th International conference on World Wide Web,* (pp. 591–600). ACM.

Kyvik, S., & Smeby, J.-C. (1994). Teaching and research: The relationship between the supervision of graduate students and faculty research performance. *Higher Education, 28*(2), 227–239. doi:10.1007/BF01383730

Lahl, O., Göritz, A. S., Pietrowsky, R., & Rosenberg, J. (2009). Using the world-wide-web to obtain large-scale word norms: 190,212 ratings on a set of 2,654 German nouns. *Behavior Research Methods, 41,* 13–19. doi:10.3758/BRM.41.1.13

Lakatos, I. (1970). Falsification and the methodology of scientific research programmes. In Lakatos & Musgrave (Eds.), *Criticism and the Growth of Knowledge.* Cambridge, UK: Cambridge University Press.

Lakkala, M., Rahikainen, M., & Hakkarainen, K. (2001). *Perspectives of CSCL in Europe: A review.* Retrieved from http://www.euro-cscl.org/site/itcole/D2_1_review_of_cscl.pdf.

Lampe, C. (2010). *Keynote intervention at the international symposium on wikis and open collaboration.* Retrieved from http://www.wikisym.org/ws2010/Invited+speakers.

Lange, P. G. (2007). Publicly private and privately public: Social networking on YouTube. *Journal of Computer-Mediated Communication, 13,* 361–380. doi:10.1111/j.1083-6101.2007.00400.x

Lanningham, S. (2006). *DeveloperWorks interviews: Tim Berners-Lee.* Retrieved from http://www.ibm.com/developerworks/podcast/dwi/cm-int082206txt.html.

Lassi, M., & Sonnenwald, D. H. (2010). *Identifying factors that may impact the adoption and use of a social science collaboratory: A synthesis of previous research.* Retrieved from http://informationr.net/ir/15-3/colis7/colis710.html.

Laterza, V., Carmichael, P., & Procter, R. (2007). The doubtful guest? A virtual research environment for education. *Technology, Pedagogy and Education, 16*(3), 249–267. doi:10.1080/14759390701614363

Latour, B., & Woolgar, S. (1979). *Laboratory life: The construction of scientific facts.* Princeton, NJ: Princeton University Press.

Laudel, G. (2002). What do we measure by co-authorships? *Research Evaluation*, *11*(1), 3–15. doi:10.3152/147154402781776961

Laurillard. (2010). Supporting teacher development of competencies in the use of learning technologies. In *Proceedings of the International Conference on ICT in Teacher Education: Policy, open Educational Resources and Partnership*, (pp. 63-74). St. Petersburg, Russia: ACM.

Lave, J., & Wenger, E. (1991). *Situated learning: Legitimate peripheral participation*. Cambridge, UK: Cambridge University Press.

Law, J., & Hassard, J. (1999). *The actor network theory*. Oxford, UK: Blackwell Publishing.

Lawlor, D. A., Davey Smith, G., & Ebrahim, S. (2004). Commentary: The hormone replacement-coronary heart disease conundrum: Is this the death of observational epidemiology? *International Journal of Epidemiology*, *33*(3), 464–467. doi:10.1093/ije/dyh124

Lawrence, K. (2006). Walking the tightrope: The balancing acts of a large e-research project. *Computer Supported Cooperative Work*, *15*(4), 385–411. doi:10.1007/s10606-006-9025-0

Lazar, J., Feng, J. H., & Hochheiser, H. (2009). *Research methods in human-computer interaction*. New York, NY: Wiley.

LEAD. (2008). *Lead evaluation report*. Retrieved 1 September 2011 from http:// www.lums.lancs.ac.uk/ files/ evaluation.pdf.

Lee, A., & Aitchison, C. (2009). Writing for the doctorate and beyond. In Boud, D., & Lee, A. (Eds.), *Changing Practices of Doctoral Education* (pp. 87–99). London, UK: Routledge.

Lee, B., Kwon, O., & Kim, H. (2011). Identification of dependency patterns in research collaboration environments through cluster analysis. *Journal of Information Science*, *37*(1), 67–85. doi:10.1177/0165551510392147

Lee, D. (2003). Constructing the commons: Practical projects to build the information commons. *Knowledge Quest*, *31*(4), 13–15.

Lee, F. J., & Anderson, J. (2001). Does learning of a complex task have to be complex? A study in learning decomposition. *Cognitive Psychology*, *42*, 267–316. doi:10.1006/cogp.2000.0747

Lee, S., & Bozeman, B. (2005). The impact of research collaboration on scientific productivity. *Social Studies of Science*, *35*(5), 673. doi:10.1177/0306312705052359

Leonard, D., & Becker, R. (2008). Enhancing the doctoral experience at the local level. In Boud, D., & Lee, A. (Eds.), *Changing Practices of Doctoral Education*. London, UK: Routledge.

Leonard, D., Brands, P., Edmondson, A., & Fenwick, J. (1998). Virtual teams: Using communications technology to manage geographically dispersed development groups. In Bradley, S., & Nolan, R. (Eds.), *Sense and Respond: Capturing Value in the Network Era* (pp. 285–298). Boston, MA: Harvard Business School Press. doi:10.1142/9789814295505_0014

Leppisaari, I., & Tenhunen, M. (2009). Searching for e-mentoring practices for SME staff development. *Service Business*, *3*, 189–207. doi:10.1007/s11628-008-0060-4

Lerman, K. (2006). *Social networks and social information filtering on Digg*. Retrieved from http:// arxiv.org/ PS_cache/ cs/ pdf/ 0612/ 0612046v1.pdf.

Lerman, K., & Galstyan, A. (2008). *Analysis of social voting patterns on Digg*. Paper presented at WOSN 2008. Seattle, WA.

Leshem, S. (2007). Thinking about conceptual frameworks in a research community of practice: A case of a doctoral programme. *Innovations in Education and Teaching International*, *44*(3), 287–299. doi:10.1080/14703290701486696

Lesh, R., Mehr, M., & Post, T. (1987). Rational number relations and proportions. In Janvier, C. (Ed.), *Problems of Representation in Teaching and Learning of Mathematics* (pp. 41–58). London: Lawrence Erlbaum Associates.

Leydesdorff, L. (2004). Clusters and maps of science journals based on bi-connected graphs in journal citation reports. *The Journal of Documentation*, *60*(4), 371–427. doi:10.1108/00220410410548144

Leydesdorff, L., & Rafols, I. (2009). A global map of science based on the ISI subject categories. *Journal of the American Society for Information Science and Technology*, *60*(2), 348–362. doi:10.1002/asi.20967

Leymann, F., & Roller, D. (2000). *Production workflow: Concepts and techniques*. Upper Saddle River, NJ: Prentice Hall.

Li, H., & Liu, L. (2007). A decentralized resource discovery based on keywords combinations and node clusters in knowledge grid. In *Proceedings of the Intelligent Computing 3rd International Conference on Advanced Intelligent Computing Theories and Applications,* (pp. 738-747). Qingdao, China: Springer.

Lin, C.-P., Liu, K.-P., & Niramitranon, J. (2008). Tablet PC to support collaborative learning: An empirical study of English vocabulary learning. In *Proceedings of IEEE International Conference on Wireless, Mobile, and Ubiquitous Technology in Education 2008,* (pp. 47–51). Beijing, China: IEEE Press.

Linden, A., & Fenn, J. (2003). *Understanding Gartner's hype cycles.* Strategic Analysis Report R-20-1971. New York, NY: Gartner Research.

Lipponen, L. (2002). Exploring foundations for computer-supported collaborative learning. In Stahl, G. (Ed.), *Computer Support for Collaborative Learning: Foundations for a CSCL Community* (pp. 72–81). Hillsdale, NJ: Erlbaum.

Littlejohn, A., & Pegler, C. (2006). *Preparing for blended e-learning: Understanding blended and online learning.* London: Routledge.

Little, R. J. A., & Rubin, D. B. (1987). *Statistical analysis with missing data.* New York, NY: Wiley.

Logan, G. D. (2004). Working memory, task switching, and executive control in the task span procedure. *Journal of Experimental Psychology. General, 133*(2), 218–236. doi:10.1037/0096-3445.133.2.218

Loizou, N. (2002). A post-well analysis of recent years exploration drilling in the Atlantic Margin. In *Sharp IOR E-Newsletter, no. 3.* London, UK: DTI Oil and Gas Directorate.

Lojeski, K. S., Reilly, R., & Dominick, P. (2007). Multitasking and innovation in virtual teams. In *Proceedings of the Hawaii International Conference on System Sciences,* (p. 44b). IEEE.

LOM. (2002). Learning technology standards committee of the IEEE. *Draft Standard for Learning Object Metadata.* Retrieved from http:// ltsc.ieee.org/ wg12/ files/ LOM_1484_ 12_1_v1_ Final_Draft.pdf.

Looi, C.-K., Ogata, H., & Wong, L.-H. (2010). Technology-transformed learning: Going beyond the one-to-one model? In *Proceedings of the 18th International Conference on Computers in Education,* (pp. 175–176). Putrajaya, Malaysia: ACM.

Looi, C.-K., So, H.-J., Toh, Y., & Chen, W. (2010). The Singapore experience: Synergy of national policy, classroom practice and design research. *Computer-Supported Collaborative Learning, 6*(1).

Looi, C.-K., Seow, P., Zhang, B., So, H.-J., Chen, W., & Wong, L.-H. (2010). Leveraging mobile technology for sustainable seamless learning: A research agenda. *British Journal of Educational Technology, 41,* 154–169. doi:10.1111/j.1467-8535.2008.00912.x

Lopez-Fernandez, O., & Rodriguez-Illera, J. L. (2009). Investigating university students' adaptation to a digital learner course portfolio. *Computers & Education, 52,* 608–616. doi:10.1016/j.compedu.2008.11.003

López-Ferrer, M. (2008). *Aplicación del análisis de redes a un estudio bibliométrico sobre psiquiatría, psicología general y psicología experimental.* València, Spain: Universitat de València.

López-Ferrer, M., & Osca Lluch, J. (2009). Una aproximación a la psicología en españa desde el análisis de redes sociales. *Revista de Historia de la Psicología, 30*(4), 55–73.

López-Ferrer, M., Velasco Arroyo, E., & Osca-Lluch, J. (2009). Spanish research groups in economy and management: A network analysis approach. *International Journal of Competitive Intelligence, Strategic. Scientific and Technology Watch, 2*(1), 45–59.

Lotka, A. J. (1926). The frequency distribution of scientific productivity. *Journal of the Washington Academy of Sciences, 16*(12), 317–323.

Lowry, R., Bermudez, L., & Graybeal, J. (2006). *Semantic interoperability: A goal for marine data management.* Paper presented at ICES CM 2006: Environmental and Fisheries Data Management, Access, and Integration. Maastricht, The Netherlands.

Ludäscher, B., Altintas, I., Berkley, C., Higgins, D., Jaeger, E., & Jones, M. (2006). Scientific workflow management and the Kepler system. *Concurrency and Computation, 18*(10), 1039–1065. doi:10.1002/cpe.994

Ludewig, T., Hauser, J., Gollnick, T., & Paap, H. (2004). *JUSTGrid – A pure Java HPCC grid architecture for multi-physics solvers using complex geometries.* Paper presented at the 42nd AIAA Aerospace Sciences Meeting and Exhibit. Washington, DC.

Lund, K., Prudhomme, G., & Cassier, J.-L. (2007). Using analysis of computer-mediated synchronous interactions to understand co-designers' activities and reasoning. In *Proceedings of the International Conference on Engineering Design*. Paris, France: IEEE Press.

Lynch, C. (2009). Jim Gray's fourth paradigm and the construction of the scientific record. In Hey, A. J. G., Tansley, S., & Tolle, K. M. (Eds.), *The Fourth Paradigm: Data-Intensive Scientific Discovery*. Palo Alto, CA: Microsoft Research.

Lynch, C. A., & Lippincott, J. K. (2005). Institutional repository deployment in the united states as of early 2005. *D-Lib Magazine, 11*(9), 1082–9873. doi:10.1045/september2005-lynch

Lyons, M., Akamatsu, S., Kamachi, M., & Gyoba, J. (1998). Coding facial expressions with gabor wavelets. In *Proceedings of the Third International Conference on Face & Gesture Recognition (FG 1998)*, (p. 200). ACM.

Malone, T. (1997). Is 'empowerment' just a fad? Control, decision-making, and information technology. *Sloan Management Review, 38*(2), 23–35.

Mangan, M. A., & Reips, U.-D. (2007). Sleep, sex, and the Web: Surveying the difficult-to-reach clinical population suffering from sexsomnia. *Behavior Research Methods, 39*, 233–236. doi:10.3758/BF03193152

Margolis, S. V., Claeys, P. F., & Kyte, F. T. (1991). Microtektites, mictokrystites and spinels from a late pliocene asteroid impact in the southern ocean. *Science, 251*, 1594–1597. doi:10.1126/science.251.5001.1594

Markauskaite, L., & Reimann, P. (2008). Enhancing and scaling-up design-based research: The potential of e-research. In *Proceedings of International Conference for the Learning Sciences*, (pp. 27-34). Utrecht, The Netherlands: ACM.

Markauskaite, L., Aditomo, A., & Hellmers, L. (2009). *Co-developing eresearch infrastructure: Technology-enhanced research practices, attitudes and requirements*. Retrieved February 24, 2011, from http://www.intersect.org.au/docs/eResearch%20survey%20full%20reportv1.0_noelene.pdf.

Markauskaite, L., Hellmers, L., Kennan, M. A., & Richardson, J. (2009). *eResearch practices, barriers and needs for support: Preliminary study findings from four NSW universities*. Paper presented at the 3rd eResearch Australasia Conference. Retrieved February 24, 2011, from http://www.eresearch.edu.au/docs/2009/era09_submission_55.pdf.

Markauskaite, L., Aditomo, A., & Hellmers, L. (2011). *Co-developing eresearch infrastructure: Technology-enhanced research practices, attitudes and requirements. Full technical report: Round 2*. Sydney, Australia: Intersect & the University of Sydney.

Martín, J. I. S., del Olmo Martínez, R., & Gutiérrez, J. P. (2006). Estudio de la red de participaciones en tribunales de tesis doctorales de organización y gestión de empresas en españa. In *Actas del X Congreso de Ingeniería de Organizción*, (pp. 183-184). Valencia, Spain: University of Valencia

Martinez, A., De la Fuente, P., & Dimitriadis, Y. (2003). Towards an XML-based representation of collaborative action. In *Proceedings of International Conference on Computer Supported Collaborative Learning Conference*, (pp. 14-18). Bergen, Norway: ACM.

Martinez, A., Harrer, A., & Barros, B. (2005). Library of interaction analysis tools. *Deliverable D.31.2 of the JEIRP IA*. New York, NY: KaleidoScope. Mce_sid. (2011). *Full schema for the structured information data (instantiation component) of a Mulce corpus*. Retrieved from http://lrl-diffusion.univ-bpclermont.fr/mulce/metadata/mce-schemas/mce_sid.xsd.

Martone, M. E., Gupta, A., & Ellisman, H. (2004). e-Neurosceince: Challenges and thiriumphs in integrating distributed data from molecules to brains. *Nature Neuroscience, 7*, 467–472. doi:10.1038/nn1229

Matute, H., Vegas, S., & Pineño, O. (2002). *Utilización de un videojuego para estudiar cómo interfiere lo nuevo que aprendemos sobre lo que ya sabíamos*. Paper presented at 1er Congreso Online del Observatorio para la Ciber-Sociedad. Retrieved from http://www.cibersociedad.net/congreso/comms/g10matute-el-al2.htm.

Matute, H., Vadillo, M. A., & Bárcena, R. (2007). Web-based experiment control software for research and teaching on human learning. *Behavior Research Methods, 39*, 689–693. doi:10.3758/BF03193041

Matute, H., Vadillo, M. A., Vegas, S., & Blanco, F. (2007). Illusion of control in internet users and college students. *Cyberpsychology & Behavior, 10*(2), 176–181. doi:10.1089/cpb.2006.9971

Maxwell, T. W., & Smyth, R. (2011). Higher degree research supervision: From practice toward theory. *Higher Education Research & Development, 30*(2), 219–231. doi:10.1080/07294360.2010.509762

McCotter, S. S. (2001). The journey of a beginning researcher. *Qualitative Report*, 6(2), 1–22.

McFarlane, D. C. (1997). *Interruption of people in human-computer interaction: A general unifying definition of human interruption and taxonomy*. Washington, DC: Naval Research Laboratory. Retrieved on January 5, 2009 from http:// www.interruptions.net/ literature/ McFarlane-NRL-97.pdf.

McFarlane, D. C. (2002). Comparison of four primary methods for coordinating the interruption of people in human-computer interaction. *Human-Computer Interaction*, 17(1), 63–139. doi:10.1207/S15327051HCI1701_2

McGraw, K. O., Tew, M. D., & Williams, J. E. (2000). The integrity of web-delivered experiments: Can you trust the data? *Psychological Science*, 11, 502–506. doi:10.1111/1467-9280.00296

Meadows, A. J. (1998). *Communicating research*. San Diego, CA: Academic Press.

Mele, S. (2009). *SCOAP3: Sponsoring consortium for open access publishing in particle physics*. Paper presented at the First Conference on Open Access Scholarly Publishing. Lund, Sweden. Retrieved from http:// river-valley.tv/ media/ conferences/ oaspa2009/ 0301-Salvatore_Mele/.

Memon, M. S., Memon, A. S., Streit, A., Riedel, M., Schuller, B., & Rambadt, M. ... Kranzlm, D. (2010). Exploring the potential of using multiple e-science infrastructures with emerging open standards-based e-health research tools. In *Proceedings of the 10th IEEE/ACM International Conference on Cluster, Cloud and Grid Computing*, (pp. 341-348). IEEE Press.

Meriluoto, J. (2003). *Knowledge management and information system*. Paper presented at ICE 2003 Conference. Helsinki, Finland.

Meyer, D. E., Kieras, D. E., Lauber, E., Schumacher, E. H., Glass, J., & Zurbriggen, E. (1995). Adaptive executive control: Flexible multiple-task performance without pervasive immutable response-selection bottlenecks. *Acta Psychologica. Discrete and Continuous Information Processing*, 90(1/3), 163–190.

Meyer, E. T. (2009). Moving from small science to big science: Social and organizational impediments to large scale data sharing. In Jankowski, N. (Ed.), *E-Research: Transformation in Scholarly Practice* (pp. 147–159). New York, NY: Routledge.

Meyer, E. T., & Schroeder, R. (2009). Untangling the web of e-research: Towards a sociology of online knowledge. *Journal of Informetrics*, 3(3), 246–260. doi:10.1016/j.joi.2009.03.006

Miao, Y., Fleschutz, J. M., & Zentel, P. (1999). Enriching learning contexts to support communities of practice. In *Proceedings of the 1999 Conference on Computer Support for Collaborative Learning, (CSCL 1999)*. Stanford, CA: International Society of the Learning Sciences.

Microsoft. (2011). *Microsoft's web page for business*. Retrieved 1 September 2011 from http:// www.microsoft.com/ business/ en-gb/ Pages/ default.aspx.

Mifsud, L., & Mørch, A. I. (2010). Reconsidering off-task: A comparative study of PDA-mediated activities in four classrooms. *Computer Assisted Learning*, 26, 190–201. doi:10.1111/j.1365-2729.2010.00346.x

Miles, S., Groth, P., Branco, M., & Moreau, L. (2007). The requirements of using provenance in e-science experiments. *Journal of Grid Computing*, 5(1), 1–25. doi:10.1007/s10723-006-9055-3

Mislove, A., Lehmann, S., Ahn, Y., Lazer, D., Lin, Y., Onnela, J., & Rosenquist, J. N. (2010). *Mapping the conversation: Political topics and geography on Twitter*. Retrieved from http://election.ccs.neu.edu/.

Mislove, A., Lehmann, S., Ahn, Y., Onnela, J., & Rosenquist, J. N. (2010). *Pulse of the nation: U.S. mood throughout the day inferred from Twitter*. Retrieved from http:// www.ccs.neu.edu/ home/ amislove/ twittermood/.

Mislove, A., Marcon, M., Gummadi, K. P., Druschel, P., & Bhattacharjee, B. (2007). *Measurement and analysis of online social networks*. Paper presented at IMC 2007. San Diego, CA.

Miyake, A., & Shah, P. (Eds.). (1999). *Models of working memory: Mechanisms of active maintenance and executive control*. Cambridge, UK: Cambridge University Press.

Molina, J. L. (2009). Panorama de la investigación en redes. *Redes: Revista Hispana Para El Análisis De Redes Sociales*, 17, 11.

Molina, J. L., Muñoz Justicia, J., & Domènech Argemí, M. (2002). Redes de publicaciones científicas un análisis de la estructura de coautorías. *Redes*, 1, 3.

Monahan, T., McArdle, G., & Bertolotto, M. (2008). Virtual reality for collaborative e-learning. *Computers & Education, 50*, 1339–1353. doi:10.1016/j.compedu.2006.12.008

Monsell, S. (2003). Task switching. *Trends in Cognitive Neuroscience, 7*(3), 134–140. doi:10.1016/S1364-6613(03)00028-7

Moreira, B. L., Goncalves, M. A., Laender, A. H. F., & Fox, E. A. (2009). Automatic evaluation of digital libraries with 5SQual. *Journal of Informetrics, 3*, 102–123. doi:10.1016/j.joi.2008.12.003

Morel, C. M., Serruya, S. J., Penna, G. O., & Guimaraes, R. (2009). Co-authorship network analysis: A powerful tool for strategic planning of research, development and capacity building programs on neglected diseases. *PLoS Neglected Tropical Diseases, 3*(8), e501. doi:10.1371/journal.pntd.0000501

Morris, C. (1971). *Foundations of the theory of signs.* Chicago, IL: University of Chicago Press.

Mouley, G. L. (1970). *The science of educational research.* London, UK: Van Nastrand Reinhold.

Moya-Anegón, F., Vargas-Quesada, B., Herrero-Solana, V., Chinchilla-Rodriguez, Z., Corera-Alvarez, E., & Munoz-Fernandez, F. J. (2004). A new technique for building maps of large scientific domains based on the cocitation of classes and categories. *Scientometrics, 61*(1), 129–145. doi:10.1023/B:SCIE.0000037368.31217.34

Mueller, S. (2004). Electronic mentoring as an example for the use of information and communication technology in engineering education. *European Journal of Engineering Education, 29*(1), 53–63. doi:10.1080/03043790320001229304

Mulce Platform. (2011). *Multimodal learning and teaching corpora exchange.* Retrieved from http:// mulce. univ-bpclermont.fr:8080/ PlateFormeMulce/.

Mulce. (2010). *French national research project 2006-2010.* Retrieved from http:// mulce.org.

Mulce-SR. (2011). *Static repository for the Mulce collection.* Retrieved from http://lrl-diffusion.univ-bpclermont. fr/ mulce/ metadata/ repository/ mulce-sr.xml.

Muller, M. J. (2003). Participatory design: The third space. In *Proceedings of HCI,* (pp. 1051-1068). HCI Press.

Muller, M. J., Matheson, L., Page, C., & Gallup, R. (1998). Methods & tools: Participatory heuristic evaluation. *Interaction, 5*(5), 18. doi:10.1145/285213.285219

Munneke, L., Andriessen, J., Kanselaar, G., & Kirschner, P. (2007). Supporting interactive argumentation: Influence of representational tools on discussing a wicked problem. *Computers in Human Behavior, 23*(3), 1072–1088. doi:10.1016/j.chb.2006.10.003

Myers, J., & McGrath, R. (2007). *Cyberenvironments: Adaptive middleware for scientific cyberinfrastructure.* Paper presented at the 6th International Workshop on Adaptive and Reflective Middleware. New York, NY.

Nadin, M. (1987). Pragmatics in the semiotic frame. In Stachowiak, H. (Ed.), *Pragmatik: Handbuch pragmatischen denkens* (pp. 148–170). Hamburg, Germany: Felix Meiner.

NaturalPoint. (2010). *Optical motion capture specialists.* Retrieved on January 4, 2010 from http://www.naturalpoint.com.

NCRIS Committee. (2008). *Review of the national collaborative research infrastructure strategy's roadmap.* Sydney, Australia: DEEWR.

NCRIS. (2011). *eResearch infrastructure.* Sydney, Australia: National Collaborative Research Infrastructure Strategy. Retrieved February 24, 2011, from https:// www. pfc.org.au/ bin/ view/ Main/ WebHome.

NeISS Public. (2011). *The NeISS public web site.* Retrieved 1 September 2011 from http:// weaver.dl.ac.uk:8080/ portal/ site/ neiss_public.

NeISS. (2011). *National e-infrastructure for social simulation web site.* Retrieved 1 September 2011 from http:// www.neiss.org.uk.

Nentwich, M. (2003). *Cyberscience: Research in the age of the internet.* Vienna, Austria: Austrian Academy of Science.

NeSC. (2007). *Definition of e-science.* Retrieved 10 January, 2010, from http://www.nesc.ac.uk/nesc/define.html.

Neto, M., Fernandes, C., Ferreira, A. S., & Fernandes, L. M. (2010). Enterprise information portals: potential for evaluating research for knowledge management and human capital assets using social network analysis. In *Proceedings of the 11th European Conference on Knowledge Management.* Portugal: ECKM Press.

Newell, A., & Simon, H. (1972). *Human problem solving.* Englewood Cliffs, NJ: Prentice Hall.

Newman, D., Bechhofer, S., & De Roure, D. (2009). *myExperiment: An ontology for eResearch.* Paper presented at the Workshop on Semantic Web Applications in Scientific Discourse in Conjunction with the International Semantic Web Conference. Washington, DC.

Nielsen, J. (1994). *Heuristic evaluation. Usability Inspection Methods* (pp. 25–62). New York, NY: Wiley.

Nilles, J. S. (2000). *Integrating telework, flextime, and officing for workforce 2020.* Indianapolis, IN: Hudson Institute.

Nolan, R., & Galal, H. (1998). Virtual offices: Redefining organizational boundaries. In Bradley, S., & Nolan, R. (Eds.), *Sense and Respond-Capturing Value in the Network Era* (pp. 299–320). Boston, MA: Harvard Business School Press.

Noroozi, O., Biemans, H. J. A., Mulder, M., & Chizari, M. (2010a). Analyzing learning processes and outcomes in computer-supported collaborative learning in the domain of nutritional research methodology education. In J. Baralt, N. Callaos, W. Lesso, A. Tremante, & F. Welsch (Eds.). *Proceedings of the International Conference on Society and Information Technologies,* (pp. 55-60). Orlando, FL: IEEE.

Noroozi, O., Biemans, H. J. A., Mulder, M., & Chizari, M. (2010b). Students' knowledge construction in computer-supported learning environments: A comparative study in the domain of nutritional research methodology education. In D. Gibson & B, Dodge (Eds.). *SITE Book of Abstracts: 21st International Conference on Society for Information Technology & Teacher Education,* (p. 83). San Diego, CA: ACM.

Noroozi, O., Biemans, H. J. A., Weinberger, A., Mulder, M., Popov, V., & Chizari, M. (2011). Supporting computer-supported argumentative knowledge construction in multidisciplinary groups of learners. In L. Gómez Chova, D. Martí Belenguer, & A. López Martínez (Eds.), *Proceedings of the 3rd International Conference on Education and New Learning Technologies,* (pp. 1937-1945). Barcelona, Spain: ACM.

Noroozi, O., Biemans, H. J. A., Busstra, M. C., Mulder, M., & Chizari, M. (2011). Differences in learning processes between successful and less successful students in computer-supported collaborative learning in the field of human nutrition and health. *Computers in Human Behavior, 27*(1), 309–318. doi:10.1016/j.chb.2010.08.009

Noroozi, O., Busstra, M. C., Mulder, M., Biemans, H. J. A., Geelen, M.M.E.E., van't Veer, P. & Chizari, M. (in press). Online discussion compensates for suboptimal timing of supportive information presentation in a digitally supported learning environment. *Educational Technology Research & Development.* doi: 10.1007/s11423-011-9217-2.

Noroozi, O., Mulder, M., Biemans, H. J. A., & Chizari, M. (2009). Factors influencing argumen¬tative computer supported collaborative learning (ACSCL). In F. Salajan (Ed.), *Proceedings of the 4th International Conference on E-Learning,* (pp. 394-403). Toronto, Canada: ACM.

Noroozi, O., Weinberger., Biemans, H. J. A., Mulder, M., & Chizari, M. (in press). Argumentation-based computer supported collaborative learning (ABCSCL). A systematic review and synthesis of fifteen years of research. *Educational Research Review.* doi: 10.1016/j.edurev.2011.11.006.

Nosek, B. A. (2005). Moderators of the relationship between implicit and explicit evaluation. *Journal of Experimental Psychology, 134,* 565–584.

Noss, R., & Hoyles, C. (1992). Looking back and looking forward. In Hoyles, C., & Noss, R. (Eds.), *Learning Mathematics and Logo* (pp. 431–470). Cambridge, MA: MIT Press.

Noss, R., & Hoyles, C. (1996). *Windows on mathematical meanings: Learning cultures and computers.* Dordrecht, The Netherlands: Kluwer Academic Publishers.

Novak, J. D. (1998). *Learning, creating and using knowledge.* New York, NY: Lawrence Erlbaum.

NYU. (2011). *The ATLAS network pilot at New York University.* Retrieved 1 September 2011 from http://www.nyu.edu/ its/ connect/ w11/ atlas.html.

O'Conaill, B., & Whittaker, S. (1997). Characterizing, predicting, and measuring video-mediated communication: A conversational approach. In Finn, K. E., Sellen, A. J., & Wilbur, S. B. (Eds.), *Video-Mediated Communication* (pp. 107–132). Mahwah, NJ: Lawrence Erlbaum Associates, Inc.

O'Connail, B., & Frohlich, D. (1995). Time space in the workplace: Dealing with interruptions. In *Proceedings of the Conference on Human Factors in Computing Systems,* (pp. 262-263). ACM.

O'Reilly, T. (2005). What is Web 2.0: Design patterns and business models for the next generation of software. *International Journal of Digital Economics, 65,* 17–37.

Oinn, T., Addis, M., Ferris, J., Marvin, D., Senger, M., & Greenwood, M. (2004). Taverna: A tool for the composition and enactment of bioinformatics workflows. *Bioinformatics (Oxford, England), 20*(17), 3045–3054. doi:10.1093/bioinformatics/bth361

OLAC. (2007). Open language archives community. *University of Pennsylvania.* Retrieved from http:// www. language-archives.org/.

Olmeda-Gómez, C., Perianes-Rodríguez, A., Ovalle-Perandones, M. A., & de Moya-Anegón, F. (2009b). Colegios visibles: Estructuras de coparticipación en tribunales de tesis doctorales de biblioteconomía y documentación en españa. *El Profesional De La Informacion, 18*(1), 41–49. doi:10.3145/epi.2009.ene.06

Olmeda-Gómez, C., Perianes-Rodriguez, A., Ovalle-Perandones, M. A., Guerrero-Bote, V. P., & de Moya Anegon, F. (2009a). Visualization of scientific co-authorship in spanish universities from regionalization to internationalization. *Aslib Proceedings, 61*(1), 83–100. doi:10.1108/00012530910932302

Olson, G. M., & Olson, J. S. (1997). Research on computer-supported cooperative work. In Helander, M., Landauer, T. K., & Prabhu, P. (Eds.), *Handbook of Human-Computer Interaction* (2nd ed.). Amsterdam, The Netherlands: Elsevier.

Olson, G. M., Zimmerman, A., & Bos, N. (2008). *Scientific collaboration on the internet.* Cambridge, MA: The MIT Press.

Olson, J. S., Ellisman, M., James, M., Grethe, J. S., & Puetz, M. (2008). Biomedical informatics research network (BIRN). In Olson, G. M., Zimmerman, A., & Bos, N. (Eds.), *Scientific Collaboration on the Internet.* Cambridge, MA: MIT Press.

O'Reilly, T. (2005). *What is Web2.0? Design patters and business models for the next generation of software.* Retrieved from http://www.oreillynet.com/pub/a/oreilly/ tim/news/2005/09/30/what-is-web-20.html.

Orlowski, W. (1992). Learning from notes: Organizational issues in groupware implementation. In *Proceedings of CSCW 1992.* CSCW Press.

Osca, J., Civera, C., Tortosa, F., Vidal, Q., Ortega, P., García, L., & José, J. (2005). *Difusión de las revistas españolas de psicología en bases de datos nacionales e internacionales.* Retrieved from http:// biblioteca. universia.net/ html_bura/ ficha/ params/ title/ difusion-revistas-españolas-psicologia-bases-datos-nacionales-internacionales/ id/ 1198502. html.

Osswald, A. (2008). E-science and information services: a missing link in the context of digital libraries. *Online Information Review, 32*(4), 516–523. doi:10.1108/14684520810897395

Osuna, C., Dimitriadis, Y., & Martínez, A. (2001). Using a theoretical framework for the evaluation of ksequentiability, reusability and complexity of development in CSCL applications. In *Proceedings of the European Computer Supported Collaborative Learning Conference.* Maastricht, The Netherlands: ACM.

Oxford. (2011). *WebLearn VLE home page.* Retrieved 1 September 2011 from http://weblearn.ox.ac.uk.

Paay, J., Sterling, L., Vetere, F., Howard, S. T., & Boettcher, A. (2009). Enginering the social: The role of shared artifacts. *International Journal of Human-Computer Studies, 67,* 437–454. doi:10.1016/j. ijhcs.2008.12.002

Packard, B. W. L. (2003). Student training promotes mentoring awareness and action. *The Career Development Quarterly, 51,* 335–345. doi:10.1002/j.2161-0045.2003. tb00614.x

Palloff, M. R., & Pratt, K. (2004). Learning together in community: Collaboration online. In *Proceedings of the 20th Annual Conference on Distance Teaching and Learning.* Retrieved on September 30, 2009, from http:// www.uwex.edu/disted/ conference/Resource_library/ proceedings/04_1127.pdf.

Pang, B., & Lee, L. (2008). Opinion mining and sentiment analysis. *Foundations and Trends in Information Retrieval, 2,* 1–135. doi:10.1561/1500000011

Papadimitriou, D. (2009, August 1st). Future Internet: The cross-ETP vision document. *European Technology Platform.*

Papert, S. (1980). *Mindstorms: Children, computers, and powerful ideas.* New York, NY: Basic Books.

Paré, A., Starke-Meyerring, D., & McAlpine, L. (2009). The dissertation as multi-genre: Many readers, many readings. In C. Bazerman, A. Bonini, & D. Figueiredo (Eds.), *Genre in a Changing World,* (pp. 179-193). Fort Collins, CO: Parlor.

Parikh, M., & Verma, S. (2002). Utilizing internet technologies to support learning: An empirical analysis. *International Journal of Information Management, 22,* 27–46. doi:10.1016/S0268-4012(01)00038-X

Parry, O., & Mauthner, N. (2005). Back to basics: Who re-uses qualitative data and why? *Sociology, 39*(2), 337–342. doi:10.1177/0038038505050543

Pashler, H. (1994). Dual-task interference in simple tasks: Data and theory. *Psychological Bulletin, 116*(2), 220–244. doi:10.1037/0033-2909.116.2.220

Pashler, H. (2000). Task switching and multitask performance (tutorial). In Monsell, S., & Driver, J. (Eds.), *Control of Cognitive Processes: Attention and Performance* (pp. 277–309). Cambridge, MA: MIT Press.

Pasini, E. (1997). Arcanum artis inveniendi: Leibniz and analysis. In *Analysis and Synthesis in Mathematics.* Dordrecht, The Netherlands: Kluwer. doi:10.1007/978-94-011-3977-9_2

Patel, V. L., Arocha, J. F., & Zhang, J. (2004). Thinking and reasoning in medicine. In Holyoak, K. (Ed.), *Cambridge Handbook of Thinking and Reasoning.* Cambridge, UK: Cambridge University Press.

Paterson, M., Lindsay, D., Monotti, A., & Chin, A. (2007). DART: A new missile in Australia's e-research strategy. *Online Information Review, 31*(2), 116–134. doi:10.1108/14684520710747185

Payette, S., Blanchi, C., Lagoze, C., & Overly, E. (1999). Interoperability for digital objects and repositories. *D-Lib Magazine, 5*(5), 1082–9873. doi:10.1045/may99-payette

Pea, R., Gomez, L., Edelson, D., Fishman, B., Gordin, D., & O'Neil, D. (1997). Science education as a driver of cyberspace technology development. In Cohen, K. C. (Ed.), *Internet Links for Science Education: Student–Scientist Partnerships* (pp. 189–220). New York, NY: Plenum. doi:10.1007/978-1-4615-5909-2_12

Pearce, N. (2010). A study of technology adoption by researchers. *Information Communication and Society, 13*(8), 1191–1206. doi:10.1080/13691181003663601

Peirce, C. S. (1931). *Collected papers*. Cambridge, MA: Harvard University Press.

Perianes-Rodríguez, A., Chinchilla-Rodriguez, Z., Vargas-Quesada, B., Olmeda-Gomez, C., & Moya-Anegon, F. (2009). Synthetic hybrid indicators based on scientific collaboration to quantify and evaluate individual research results. *Journal of Informetrics, 3*(2), 91–101. doi:10.1016/j.joi.2008.12.001

Perianes-Rodríguez, A., Olmeda-Gomez, C., & Moya-Anegon, F. (2010). Detecting, identifying and visualizing research groups in co-authorship networks. *Scientometrics, 82*(2), 307–319. doi:10.1007/s11192-009-0040-z

Perren, L. (2003). The role of e-mentoring in entrepreneurial education and support: A meta-review of academic literature. *Education + Training, 45*(8/9), 517-525.

Peters, S. (2009). *BBC Radio 4 interview*. Retrieved 1 September 2011 from http:// www.lums.lancs. ac.uk/ news/ 17271/ sue-peters-bbc/.

Pham, T. V., Dew, P. M., & Lau, L. M. (2006). Enabling e-research in combustion research community. In *Proceedings of the Second IEEE International Conference on e-Science and Grid Computing.* IEEE Press.

Phoenix. (2011). *The Phoenix integration web site.* Retrieved 1 September 2011 from http://www.phoenix-int.com.

Pierson, M., Shepard, M., & Leneway, R. (2009). Distributed collaborative research model: Meaningful and responsive inquiry in technology and teacher education. *Journal of Computing in Teacher Education, 25*(4), 127–133.

Pignotti, E., Edwards, P., Preece, A., Gotts, N., & Polhill, G. (2004). FEARLUS-G: A semantic grid service for land-use modelling. In *Proceedings of the ECAI-04 Workshop on Semantic Intelligent Middleware for the Web & the Grid,* (vol 111). IEEE Press.

PKP. (2010). *Public knowledge project*. Retrieved from http:// pkp.sfu.ca/ about.

Polanyi, M. (1966). *The tacit dimension*. New York, NY: Anchor Day Books.

Popper, K. (1963). *Conjectures and refutations*. London, UK: Routledge.

Popper, K. (1979). *Die beiden grundprobleme der erkenntnistheorie*. Milano, Italy: Il Saggiatore.

Powell, A., Nilsson, M., Naeve, A., Johnston, P., & Baker, T. (2008). DCMI abstract model. *Dublin Core Metadata Initiative*. Retrieved from http:// dublincore.org/ documents/ abstract-model/.

Pratt, W., Reddy, M. C., McDonald, D. W., Tarczy-Hornoch, P., & Gennari, J. H. (2004). Incorporating ideas from computer-supported cooperative work. *Journal of Biomedical Informatics, 37*(2), 128–137. doi:10.1016/j.jbi.2004.04.001

Prieto, J., Fernández-Ballesteros, R., & Carpintero, H. (1994). Contemporary psychology in Spain. *Annual Review of Psychology, 45*(1), 51–78. doi:10.1146/annurev. ps.45.020194.000411

Pritchard, A. (1969). Statistical bibliography or bibliometrics. *The Journal of Documentation, 25*, 348.

Prosser, D. C. (2005). Fulfilling the promise of scholarly communication – A comparison between old and new access models. In *Die Innovative Bibliothek: Elmar Mittler zum 65* (pp. 95–106). Berlin, Germany: Geburtstag.

Prudhomme, G., Pourroy, F., & Lund, K. (2007). An empirical study of engineering knowledge dynamics in a design situation. *Journal of Desert Research, 3*, 333–358. doi:10.1504/JDR.2007.016388

Pshenichny, C. A. (2002). Investigation of geological reasoning as a new objective of geosciences. *Earth Science Computer Applications, 17*(11), 1–3.

Pshenichny, C. A. (2004). Classical logic and the problem of uncertainty. *Geological Society, 239*, 111-126.

Pshenichny, C. A. (2009). The event bush as a semantic-based numerical approach to natural hazard assessment (exemplified by volcanology) 2009. *Computer and GeoSciences, 35*(5), 1017–1034. doi:10.1016/j.cageo.2008.01.009

Putnam, H. (1975). *Mind, language and reality: Philosophical papers* (*Vol. 2*). Cambridge, UK: Cambridge University Press. doi:10.1017/CBO9780511625251

Racherla, P., & Hu, C. (2010). A social network perspective of tourism research collaborations. *Annals of Tourism Research, 37*(4), 1012–1034. doi:10.1016/j.annals.2010.03.008

Ratliff, K. A., & Nosek, B. A. (2010). Creating distinct implicit and explicit attitudes with an illusory correlation paradigm. *Journal of Experimental Social Psychology, 46*, 721–728. doi:10.1016/j.jesp.2010.04.011

Ravenscroft, A., & McAlister, S. (2008). Investigating and promoting educational argumentation: Towards new digital practices. *International Journal of Research & Method in Education, 31*(3), 317–335. doi:10.1080/17437270802417192

Razum, M., Schwichtenberg, F., Wagner, S., Hoppe, M., Agosti, M., et al. (2009). eSciDoc infrastructure: A fedora-based e-research framework. In *Proceedings of ECDL 2009*, (pp. 227-238). ECDL Press.

Reffay, C., & Betbeder, M.-L. (2009). Sharing corpora and tools to improve interaction analysis. In *Proceedings of the 4th European Conference on Technology Enhanced Learning*, (pp. 196-210). Springer.

Reffay, C., Teplovs, C., & Blondel, F.-M. (2011). Productive re-use of CSCL data and analytic tools to provide a new perspective on group cohesion. In *Proceedings of International Conference* on *Computer Supported Collaborative Learning*. Hong Kong, China: ACM.

Reffay, C., Chanier, T., Noras, M., & Betbeder, M.-L. (2008). Contribution à la structuration de corpus d'apprentissage pour un meilleur partage en recherche. *Sciences et Technologies de l'Information et de la Communication pour l'Éducation et la Formation, 15*, 185–219.

Reijers, H. A., Song, M., Romero, H., Dayal, U., Eder, J., & Koehler, J. (2009). A collaboration and productiveness analysis of the BPM community. *Business Process Management. Proceedings, 5701*, 1–14.

Reips, U. D. (2002). Standards for Internet-based experimenting. *Experimental Psychology, 49*, 243–256. doi:10.1026//1618-3169.49.4.243

Reips, U. D., & Neuhaus, C. (2002). WEXTOR: A Web-based tool for generating and visualizing experimental designs and procedures. *Behavior Research Methods, Instruments, & Computers, 34*, 234–240. doi:10.3758/BF03195449

Reips, U.-D., & Garaizar, P. (2011). Mining Twitter: Microblogging as a source for psychological wisdom of the crowds. *Behavior Research Methods, 43*, 635–642. doi:10.3758/s13428-011-0116-6

Research Information Network. (2011). *Reinventing research? Information practices in the humanities report.* Retrieved April 15, 2011 from http:// www.rin.ac.uk/ our-work/ using-and-accessing-information-resources/ information-use-case-studies-humanities.

Ribes, D., & Bowker, G. (2009). Between meaning and machine: Learning to represent the knowledge of communities. *Information and Organization.* Retrieved from http://www.sis.pitt.edu/~gbowker/publications/Ribes%20Bowker%20-%20Between%20Meaning%20and%20Machine.pdf.

Ribes, D., & Finholt, T. A. (2009). The long now of infrastructure: Articulating tensions in development. *Journal of the Association for Information Systems, 10*(5), 375–398.

Ribes, D., & Lee, C. (2010). Sociotechnical studies of cyberinfrastructure and eresearch: Current themes and future trajectories. *Computer Supported Cooperative Work, 19*(3), 231–244. doi:10.1007/s10606-010-9120-0

Riedel, M., & Terstyanszky, G. (2009). Grid interoperability for e-research. *Journal of Grid Computing, 7,* 285–286. doi:10.1007/s10723-009-9138-z

Roberts, T. S. (2005). Computer-supported collaborative learning in higher education: An introduction. In Roberts, T. S. (Ed.), *Computer-Supported Collaborative Learning in Higher Education* (pp. 1–18). Hershey, PA: IGI Global.

Rogers, R. (2009). *The end of the virtual: Digital methods.* Amsterdam, The Netherlands: Amsterdam University Press.

Romera Iruela, M. J. (1996). Citas y referencias bibliográficas en el sistema de comunicación científica. *Revista Complutense De Educación, 7*(1), 243–270.

Rosas, S. R., Kagan, J. M., Schouten, J. T., Slack, P. A., & Trochim, W. M. K. (2011). Evaluating research and impact: A bibliometric analysis of research by the NIH/NIAID HIV/AIDS clinical trials networks. *PLoS ONE, 6*(3). doi:10.1371/journal.pone.0017428

Roschelle, J., Patton, C., & Tatar, D. (2007). Designing networked handheld devices to enhance school learning. *Advances in Computers, 70,* 1–60. doi:10.1016/S0065-2458(06)70001-8

Rosen, C. (2008). The myth of multitasking. *The New Atlantis, 20,* 105-110. Retrieved on February 4, 2010 from http:// www.thenewatlantis.com/ publications/ the-myth-of-multitasking.

Rosen, C. (2007). Virtual friendship and the new narcissism. *New Atlantis (Washington, D.C.), 17,* 15–31.

Rourke, L., Anderson, T., Garrisson, D. R., & Archer, W. (2001). Methodological issues in the content analysis of computer conference transcripts. *International Journal of Artificial Intelligence in Education, 12,* 8–22.

Rowlands, I., & Nicholas, D. (2006). The changing scholarly communication landscape: An international survey of senior researchers. *Learned Publishing, 19*(1), 31–55. doi:10.1087/095315106775122493

Rubinstein, J. S., Meyer, D. E., & Evans, J. E. (2001). Executive control of cognitive processes in task switching. *Journal of Experimental Psychology. Human Perception and Performance, 27*(4), 763–797. doi:10.1037/0096-1523.27.4.763

Rummel, N., & Spada, H. (2005). Learning to collaborate: An instructional approach to promoting collaborative problem solving in computer-mediated settings. *Journal of the Learning Sciences, 14*(2), 201–241. doi:10.1207/s15327809jls1402_2

Russell, B. (1905). *On denoting: Mind* (*Vol. 14*). Oxford, UK: Basil Blackwell.

Ryan, A., Cohn, J. F., Lucey, S., Saragih, J., Lucey, P., de la Torre, F., & Rossi, A. (2009). Automated facial expression recognition system. In *Proceedings of the IEEE International Carnahan Conference on Security Technology.* IEEE Press.

Sacks, H., Schegloff, E. A., & Jefferson, G. (1974). A simplest systematics for the organisation of turn-taking for conversation. *Language, 50,* 696–735. doi:10.2307/412243

Sakai. (2011). The Sakai project web site. Retrieved 1 September 2011 from http://sakaiproject.org/.

Sakaki, T., Okazaki, M., & Matsuo, Y. (2010). Earthquake shakes Twitter users: Real-time event detection by social sensors. In *Proceedings of the 18th International World Wide Web Conference.* New York, NY: ACM.

Salmon, G. (2004). *E-moderating: The key to teaching and learning online* (2nd ed.). London, UK: Routledge.

Salmon, W. C. (1990). *Four decades of scientific explanation.* Minneapolis, MN: The University of Minnesota Press.

Salvucci, D. D., Kushleyeva, Y., & Lee, F. J. (2004). Toward an ACT-R general executive for human multitasking. In *Proceedings of the Sixth International Conference on Cognitive Modeling*, (pp. 267-272). ACM.

Sargent, M. (2006). *An Australian e-research strategy and implementation framework*. Canberra, Australia: E-Research Coordinating Committee.

Scardamalia, M., & Bereiter, C. (1987). *The psychology of written composition*. Hillsdale, NJ: Lawrence Erlbaum Associates, Inc.

Scardamalia, M., & Bereiter, C. (1996). Computer support for knowledge-building communities. In Koschmann, T. (Ed.), *CSCL: Theory and Practice of an Emerging Paradigm* (pp. 249–268). Mahwah, NJ: Erlbaum.

Schellens, T., & Valcke, M. (2006). Fostering knowledge construction in university students through asynchronous discussion groups. *Computers & Education, 46*(4), 349–370. doi:10.1016/j.compedu.2004.07.010

Scherz, Z., & Oren, M. (2006). How to change students' images of science and technology. *Science Education, 90*, 965–985. doi:10.1002/sce.20159

Schlosser, L. Z., Knox, S., Moskovitz, A. R., & Hill, C. E. (2003). A qualitative examination of graduate advising relationships: The advisee perspective. *Journal of Counseling Psychology, 50*, 178–188. doi:10.1037/0022-0167.50.2.178

Schmidt, W. C. (1997a). World-wide web survey research: Benefits, potential problems, and solutions. *Behavior Research Methods, Instruments, & Computers, 29*, 274–279. doi:10.3758/BF03204826

Schmidt, W. C. (1997b). World-wide web survey research made easy with www survey assistant. *Behavior Research Methods, Instruments, & Computers, 29*, 303–304. doi:10.3758/BF03204832

Schroeder, R. (2008). E-sciences as research technologies: Reconfiguring disciplines, globalizing knowledge. *Social Sciences Information. Information Sur les Sciences Sociales, 47*(2), 131–157. doi:10.1177/0539018408089075

Schultz-Jones, B. (2009). Examining information behavior through social networks: An interdisciplinary review. *The Journal of Documentation, 65*(4), 592–631. doi:10.1108/00220410910970276

Schweickert, R., & Boggs, G. J. (1984). Models of central capacity and on currency. *Journal of Mathematical Psychology, 28*(3), 223–281. doi:10.1016/0022-2496(84)90001-4

Seidel, E., Allen, G., Merzky, A., & Nabrzyski, J. (2002). GridLab: A grid application toolkit and testbed. *Future Generation Computer Systems, 18*(8), 1143–1153. doi:10.1016/S0167-739X(02)00091-2

Seringhaus, M., & Gerstein, M. (2007). Publishing perishing? Towards tomorrow's information architecture. *BMC Bioinformatics, 8*(1). Retrieved February 24, 2011, from http://www.biomedcentral.com/content/pdf/1471-2105-8-17.pdf.

Severance, C., Hardin, J., Golden, G., Crouchley, R., Fish, A., & Finholt, T. (2007). Using the Sakai collaborative toolkit in e-research applications. *Concurrency and Computation, 19*(12), 1643–1652. doi:10.1002/cpe.1115

Shannon, C. E., & Weaver, W. (1949). *A mathematical model of communication*. Chicago, IL: University of Illinois Press.

Shapiro, M. A., So, M., & Park, H. (2010). Quantifying the national innovation system: Inter-regional collaboration networks in South Korea. *Technology Analysis and Strategic Management, 22*(7), 845–857. doi:10.1080/09537325.2010.511158

Sharma, M., & Urs, S. R. (2008). Network of scholarship: Uncovering the structure of digital library author community. *Digital Libraries: Universal and Ubiquitous Access to Information, 5362*, 363–366. doi:10.1007/978-3-540-89533-6_45

Sharples, M. (1999). *How we write*. London, UK: Routledge.

Sharples, M., Goodlet, J., & Pemberton, L. (1989). *Developing a writer's assistant. Computers and Writing: Models and Tools* (p. 22). New York, NY: Ablex.

Shelley, C. (1996). Visual abductive reasoning in archaeology. *Philosophy of Science, 63*(2), 278–301. doi:10.1086/289913

Shepherd, D. (2007). *The access grid in collaborative arts and humanities research, final report of the arts and humanities research council (AHRC) workshops: E-science*. Retrieved April 16, 2011 from http://www.ahessc.ac.uk/files/active/0/AG-report.pdf.

Sheriff, R. E. (1973). *Encyclopedic dictionary of exploration geophysics*. Tulsa, OK: The Society of Exploration Geophysics.

Shibata, H., & Hori, K. (2002). *A framework to support writing as design using multiple representations*. Retrieved from http:// www.ai.rcast.u-tokyo.ac.jp/ ~shibata/ pdf/ Shibata2002d-IW-APCHI.pdf.

Shibata, H., & Hori, K. (2008). Cognitive support for the organization of writing. *New Generation Computing, 26*(2), 97–124. doi:10.1007/s00354-008-0037-9

Shneiderman, B. (2008). Science 2.0. *Science, 319*, 1349–1350. doi:10.1126/science.1153539

Shneiderman, B., & Plaisant, C. (2009). *Designing the user interface: Strategies for effective human-computer interaction* (5th ed.). Boston, MA: Addison-Wesley Longman Publishing Co.

Siemens, L. (2010). Time, place and cyberspace: Foundations for successful e-research collaboration. In *M. Anandarajan & A. Anandarajan (2010). E-Research Collaboration: Theory, Techniques and Challenges*. Berlin, Germany: Springer.

Sierra, G. (2003). Deconstrucción de los tribunales del CSIC en el período 1985-2002: Profesores de investigación en el área de física. *Apuntes De Ciencia y Tecnología, 7*, 30–38.

Single, P. B., & Reis, R. M. (2009). *Demystifying dissertation writing: A streamlined process from choice of topic to final text*. New York, NY: Stylus Pub Llc.

Slof, B., Erkens, G., Kirschner, P. A., Jaspers, J. G. M., & Janssen, J. (2010). Guiding students' online complex learning-task behavior through representational scripting. *Computers in Human Behavior, 26*(5), 927–939. doi:10.1016/j.chb.2010.02.007

Smith, H., Luckin, R., Fitzpatrick, G., Avramides, K., & Underwood, J. (2005). *Technology at work to mediate collaborative scientific enquiry in the field*. Paper presented at the 12th International Conference on Artificial Intelligence in Education (AIED 2005). New York, NY.

Smith, M. K., Barton, M., Bass, M., Branschofsky, M., McClellan, G., Stuve, D., et al. (2003). Dspace: An open source dynamic digital repository. *D-Lib Magazine, 9*(1). Retrieved February 24, 2011, from http:// www.dlib.org/ dlib/ january03/ smith/ 01smith.html.

Smith-Jentsch, K., Scielzo, S., Yarborough, C., & Rosopa, P. (2008). A comparison of face-to-face and electronic peer-mentoring: Interactions with mentor gender. *Journal of Vocational Behavior, 72*, 193–206. doi:10.1016/j.jvb.2007.11.004

Smykla, E., & Zippel, K. (2010). Literature review: Gender and international research collaboration. *OISE, 936970*. Retrieved from http:// www.archive.org/ stream/ logarithmischtr0 0bremgoog/ logarithmischtr0 0bremgoog_ djvu.txt.

Snowdon, D., Churchill, E., Frécon, E., & Roberts, D. (2004). Communication infrastructures for inhabited information spaces. *Inhabited Information Spaces, Computer Supported Cooperative Work. Computer Science, 29*, 233–267.

Soloway, E. (1993). Reading and writing in the 21st century. *Communications of the ACM, 36*(5). doi:10.1145/155049.155052

Sorensen, A. A., Seary, A., & Riopelle, K. (2010). Alzheimer's disease research: A COIN study using co-authorship network analytics. In *Proceedings of the 1st Collaborative Innovation Networks Conference (Coins2009)*, (pp. 6582-6586). COINS Press.

Specia, L., & Motta, E. (2007). Integrating folksonomies with the semantic web. In *Proceedings of the European Semantic Web Conference (ESWC 2007)*. Innsbruck, Austria: Springer.

Spink, A., Alvarado-Albertorio, F., Naragan, B., Brumfield, J., & Park, M. (2007). Multitasking information behavior: An exploratory study. *Journal of Librarianship and Information Science, 39*(3), 177–186. doi:10.1177/0961000607080420

Spink, A., & Cole, C. (2006a). New directions in human information behaviour. In *Annual Review of Information Science and Technology* (p. 116). Berlin, Germany: Springer.

Spink, A., & Cole, C. (2006b). Human information behaviour: Integrating diverse approaches and information use. *Journal of the American Society for Information Science and Technology, 57*(1), 25–35. doi:10.1002/asi.20249

Spink, A., & Cole, C. (2007). Multitasking framework for interactive information retrieval. In *New Directions in Cognitive Information Retrieval* (pp. 99–112). Berlin, Germany: Springer.

Spink, A., Ozmutlu, H. C., & Ozmutlu, S. (2002). Multitasking information seeking and searching processes. *Journal of the American Society for Information Science and Technology, 53*(8), 639–652. doi:10.1002/asi.10124

Spink, A., & Park, M. (2005). Information and non-information task interplay. *The Journal of Documentation, 61*(4), 548–554. doi:10.1108/00220410510607516

Spitzmüller, C., Neumman, E., Spitzmüller, M., Rubino, C., Keeton, K., Sutton, M., & Manzey, D. (2008). Assessing the influence of psychosocial and career mentoring on organizational attractiveness. *International Journal of Selection and Assessment, 16*(4), 403–415. doi:10.1111/j.1468-2389.2008.00444.x

Stacey, E., & Gerbic, P. (2003). Investigating the impact of computer conferencing: Content analysis as a manageable research tool. In G. Crisp., D. Thiele., I. Scholten., S. Barker., & J. Baron (Eds.), *Interact, Integrate, Impact: Proceedings of the 20th Annual Conference of the Australasian Society for Computers in Learning in Tertiary Education*. ASCLTE Press.

Stanek, D., & Mokhtarian, P. (1998). Developing models of preference for home-based and center-based telecommuting: Findings and forecasts. *Technological Forecasting and Social Change, 57*, 53–74. doi:10.1016/S0040-1625(97)00070-X

Star, S. L., & Griesemer, J. R. (1989). Institutional ecology, translations and boundary objects: Amateurs and professionals in Berkeley s museum of vertebrate zoology. *Social Studies of Science, 19*(4), 387–420. doi:10.1177/030631289019003001

Steels, L. (2006). Collaborative tagging as distributed cognition. *Pragmatics & Cognition, 14*(2), 275–285. doi:10.1075/pc.14.2.09ste

Stegmann, K., Weinberger, A., & Fischer, F. (2007). Facilitating argumentative knowledge construction with computer-supported collaboration scripts. *International Journal of Computer-Supported Collaborative Learning, 2*(4), 421–447. doi:10.1007/s11412-007-9028-y

Stergiou, C., & Signanos, D. (1996). *Neural networks*. Retrieved on June 28, 2010 from http:// www.doc.ic.ac.uk/~nd/ surprise_96/ journal/ vol4/ cs11/ report.html#The Back-Propagation Algorithm.

Steyvers, M., Tenenbaum, J. B., Wagenmakers, E.-J., & Blum, B. (2003). Inferring causal networks from observations and interventions. *Cognitive Science, 27*, 453–489. doi:10.1207/s15516709cog2703_6

Stokes, T. D., & Harley, J. A. (1989). Co-authorship, social structure and influence within specialties. *Social Studies of Science, 19*, 101–125. doi:10.1177/030631289019001003

Strategic Roadmap. (2011). *2011 strategic roadmap for Australian research infrastructure discussion paper*. Canberra, Australia: Australian Government. Retrieved April 7, 2011 from http:// www.innovation.gov.au/ SCIENCE/ RESEARCHINFRASTRUCTURE/ Pages/ default.aspx.

Strayer, D. L., & Johnston, W. A. (2001). Driven to distraction: Dual-task studies of simulated driving and conversing on a cellular telephone. *Psychological Science, 12*(6), 462–466. doi:10.1111/1467-9280.00386

Strunk, W. Jr. (2006). *The elements of style*. New York, NY: Filiquarian Publishing.

Suchman, L. A. (1987). *Plans and situated actions: The problem of human-machine communication*. Cambridge, UK: Cambridge University Press.

Suduc, A. M., Bîzoi, M., & Filip, F. G. (2009). Exploring multimedia Web conferencing. *Informatica Economică, 13*(3), 5–17.

Suduc, A. M., Bîzoi, M., & Gorghiu, G. (2008). Virtual instrumentation environment used in the VccSSe project. In *Postępy Eedukacji* (pp. 364–370). Warsaw, Poland: Praca Zbiorowa Pod Redakcją Zespołu Ośrodka Kształcenia Na Odległość OKNO PW.

Suh, B., Hong, L., Pirolli, P., & Chi, E. H. (2010). *Want to be retweeted? Large scale analytics on factors impacting retweet in Twitter network*. Paper presented at the Second IEEE International Conference on Social Computing (SocialCom 2010). Minneapolis, MN.

Sun, W.-J., & Jiang, A.-X. (2009). *The collaboration network in china's management science*. Paper presented at the Management Science and Engineering Conference. Moscow, Russia.

Susskind, J. M., Littlewort, G., Bartlett, M. S., Movellan, J., & Anderson, A. K. (2007). Human and computer recognition of facial expressions of emotion. *Neuropsychologia, 45*, 152–162. doi:10.1016/j.neuropsychologia.2006.05.001

Suthers, D. (2001). Collaborative representations: Supporting face to face and online knowledge-building discourse. In *Proceedings of the 34th Annual Hawaii International Conference on System Sciences (HICSS-34)*, (vol 4). Maui, HI: HICSS Press.

Suthers, D. D., Lund, K., Rosé, C., Dyke, G., Law, N., & Teplovs, C. (2011). Towards productive multivocality in the analysis of collaborative learning. In *Proceedings of CSCL 2011*, (pp. 1015-1022). Hong Kong, China: ACM.

Suthers, D. D. (2006). Technology affordances for intersubjective meaning making: A research agenda for CSCL. *International Journal of Computer-Supported Collaborative Learning, 1*(3), 315–337. doi:10.1007/s11412-006-9660-y

Suthers, D. D., & Hundhausen, C. D. (2003). An experimental study of the effects of representational guidance on collaborative learning processes. *Journal of the Learning Sciences, 12*(2), 183–219. doi:10.1207/S15327809JLS1202_2

Swan, A. (2010). *The open access citation advantage: Studies and results to date*. Southampton, UK: University of Southampton.

Swan, A., & Brown, S. (2005). *Open access self-archiving: An author study*. Truro, UK: Key Perspectives Limited.

Tan, K. L. L., Lambert, P. S., Turner, K. J., Blum, J., Gayle, V., & Jones, S. B. (2009). Enabling quantitative data analysis through e-infrastructure. *Social Science Computer Review, 27*(4), 539–552. doi:10.1177/0894439309332647

Tapscott, D., Ticol, D., & Lowy, A. (2000). *Digital capital: Harnessing the power of business webs*. Cambridge, MA: Harvard Business School Press.

Tauberer, J. (2006). What is RDF? *O'Reilly XML from Inside Out*. Retrieved February 4th, 2011 from http://www.xml.com/ pub/ a/ 2001/ 01/ 24/rdf.html.

Taverna-2. (2011). *The Taverna-2 web site*. Retrieved 1 September 2011 from http:// www.taverna.org.uk/ documentation/ taverna-2-x/.

Taylor, C. (1992). *To follow a rule in critical perspectives*. Chicago, IL: University of Chicago Press.

Taylor, I., Shields, M., & Wang, I. (2003). Triana applications within grid computing and peer to peer environments. *Journal of Grid Computing, 1*(2), 199–217. doi:10.1023/B:GRID.0000024074.63139.ce

Tesone, D., & Gibson, J. (2001). E-mentoring for professional growth. In *Proceedings IEEE International Professional Communication Conference*. IEEE Press.

Thelwall, M. (2008). Social networks, gender and friending: An analysis of MySpace member profiles. *Journal of the American Society for Information Science and Technology, 59*, 1321–1330. doi:10.1002/asi.20835

Thelwall, M. (2009). MySpace comments. *Online Information Review, 33*, 58–76. doi:10.1108/14684520910944391

Thelwall, M., Wilkinson, D., & Uppal, S. (2010). Data mining emotion in social network communication: Gender differences in MySpace. *Journal of the American Society for Information Science and Technology, 61*, 190–199.

Thompson, L., Jeffries, M., & Topping, K. (2010). E-mentoring for e-learning development. *Innovations in Education and Teaching International, 47*(3), 305–315. doi:10.1080/14703297.2010.498182

Tomasello, M. (1999). *The cultural origins of human cognition*. Cambridge, MA: Harvard University Press.

Tonta, Y., & Darvish, H. R. (2010). Diffusion of latent semantic analysis as a research tool: A social network analysis approach. *Journal of Informetrics, 4*(2), 166–174. doi:10.1016/j.joi.2009.11.003

Torkjazi, M., Rejaie, R., & Willinger, W. (2009). *Hot today, gone tomorrow: On the migration of MySpace users*. Paper presented at the WOSN 2009. Barcelona, Spain.

Trefil, J. (2001). *The encyclopedia of science and technology*. London, UK: Routledge.

Trochim, W. M. K. (1989). An introduction to concept mapping for planning and evaluation. *Evaluation and Program Planning, 12*(1), 1–16. doi:10.1016/0149-7189(89)90016-5

TSB. (2011). *The TSB connect web site*. Retrieved 1 September 2011 from https:// ktn.innovateuk.org/ web/ guest.

Tsukada, K., Okada, K. I., & Matsushita, Y. (1994). The multi-project support system based on multiplicity of task. In Proceedings *of the 18th Annual International Computer Software and Applications Conference*, (pp. 358-363). ACM.

Turner, M. (1984). *Enclosures in Britain 1750-1830*. London, UK: Macmillan.

Uhlir, P. F., & Schroeder, P. (2007). Open data for global science. *Data Science Journal, 6*, 36–53. doi:10.2481/dsj.6.OD36

Underwood, J., Smith, H., Luckin, R., & Fitzpatrick, G. (2008). E-science in the classroom – Towards viability. *Computers & Education, 50*, 535–546. doi:10.1016/j.compedu.2007.07.003

Universities Australia. (2010). *Australian universities data snapshot 2010*. Retrieved February 24, 2011, from http:// www.universitiesaustralia.edu.au/ resources/ 389.

Vadillo, M. A., Bárcena, R., & Matute, H. (2006). The internet as a research tool in the study of associative learning: An example from overshadowing. *Behavioural Processes, 73*, 36–40. doi:10.1016/j.beproc.2006.01.014

Vadillo, M. A., & Matute, H. (2009). Learning in virtual environments: Some discrepancies between laboratory- and Internet-based research on associative learning. *Computers in Human Behavior, 25*, 402–406. doi:10.1016/j.chb.2008.08.009

Vadillo, M. A., & Matute, H. (2011). Further evidence on the validity of web-based research on associative learning: Augmentation in a predictive learning task. *Computers in Human Behavior, 27*, 750–754. doi:10.1016/j.chb.2010.10.020

Valenciano Valcarcel, J., Devis-Devis, J., Villamon, M., & Peiro-Velert, C. (2010). Scientific cooperation in the field of physical activity and sport science in Spain. *Revista Espanola la de Documentacion Cientifica, 33*(1), 90–105.

Van Amelsvoort, M. (2006). *A space for debate: How diagrams support collaborative argumentation-based learning*. Dissertation. Utrecht, The Netherlands: Utrecht University.

Van Damme, C., Hepp, M., & Siorpaes, K. (2007). *Folksontology: An integrated approach for turning folksonomies into ontologies*. Paper presented at the 4th European Semantic Web Conference. Innsbruck, Austria.

Van de Sompel, H., Payette, S., Erickson, J., Lagoze, C., & Warner, S. (2004). Rethinking scholarly communication. *D-Lib Magazine, 10*(9), 1082–9873. doi:10.1045/september2004-vandesompel

Van Eijl, P., & Pilot, A. (2003). Using a virtual learning environment in collaborative learning: Criteria for success. *Educational Technology, 43*(2), 54–56.

Vander Wal, T. (2004). *Folksonomy*. Retrieved from http:// vanderwal.net/ folksonomy.html.

Vavoula, G. N., & Sharples, M. (2007). Future technology workshop: A collaborative method for the design of new learning technologies and activities. *International Journal of Computer-Supported Collaborative Learning, 2*(4), 393–419. doi:10.1007/s11412-007-9026-0

VEC. (2011). *The VEC web site*. Retrieved 1 September 2011 from http:// www.stfc.ac.uk/ News+ and+ Events/ 13880.aspx.

Veerman, A. L. (2000). *Computer supported collaborative learning through argumentation*. PhD Dissertation. Utrecht, The Netherlands: Utrecht University.

Vega, V. (2009). Seminar on the impacts of media multitasking on children's learning & development. *Stanford University*. Retrieved on February 4, 2010 from http:// multitasking.stanford.edu/ Multitasking Background Paper.pdf.

Velden, T., Haque, A., & Lagoze, C. (2010). A new approach to analyzing patterns of collaboration in co-authorship networks: Mesoscopic analysis and interpretation. *Scientometrics, 85*(1), 219–242. doi:10.1007/s11192-010-0224-6

Veldhuis-Diermanse, A. E. (2002). *CSCLearning? Participation, learning activities and knowledge construction in computer-supported collaborative learning in higher education*. PhD dissertation. Wageningen, The Netherlands: Wageningen University.

Veldhuis-Diermanse, A. E., Biemans, H., Mulder, M., & Mahdizadeh, H. (2006). Analysing learning processes and quality of knowledge construction in networked learning. *Journal of Agricultural Education and Extension, 12*(1), 41–58. doi:10.1080/13892240600740894

Velterop, J. (2009). *Nano publications*. Paper presented at the first Conference on Open Access Scholarly Publishing. Lund, Sweden. Retrieved from http://river-valley.tv/ media/ conferences/ oaspa2009/ 0201-Jan_ Velterop/.

Verhulsdonck, G. (2007). Issues of designing gestures into online interactions: Implications for communicating in virtual environments. In *Proceedings of the 25th Annual ACM International Conference on Design of Communication (SIGDOC 2007)*, (pp. 26-33). ACM.

Vernberg, D., Snyder, C. R., & Schuh, M. (2005). Preliminary validation of a hope scale for a rare health condition using web-based methodology. *Cognition and Emotion*, *19*, 601–610. doi:10.1080/02699930441000256

Vinkler, P. (1987). A quasi-quantitative citation model. *Scientometrics*, *12*(1), 47–72. doi:10.1007/BF02016689

Vlaar, P. W. L., Van Fenema, P. C., & Tiwari, V. (2008). Co-creating understanding and value in distributed work: How members of onsite and offshore vendor teams give, make, demand, and break sense. *MIS Quaterly*, *32*(2), 227–255.

Vygotsky, L. S. (1962). *Thought and language*. Cambridge, MA: MIT Press.

Wald, C. (2010). *Scientists embrace openness*. Retrieved from http://sciencecareers.sciencemag.org/career_magazine/previous_issues/articles/2010_04_09/caredit.a1000036.

Walker, S., & Creanor, L. (2009). The STIN in the tale: A socio-technical interaction perspective on networked learning. *International Forum of Educational Technology & Society*, *12*(4), 305–316.

Waller, M. J. (1997). Keeping the pins in the air: How work groups juggle multiple tasks. In *Advances in Interdisciplinary Studies of Work Teams* (*Vol. 4*, pp. 217–247). Stamford, CT: JAI Press.

Walther, J. B. (1994). Anticipated ongoing interaction versus channel effects on relational communication in computer mediated interaction. *Human Communication Research*, *20*(4), 473–501. doi:10.1111/j.1468-2958.1994.tb00332.x

Walton, C., & Barker, A. (2004). An agent-based e-science experiment builder. In *Proceedings of the 1st International Workshop on Semantic Intelligent Middleware for the Web and the Grid*, (pp. 247-264). Valencia, Spain.

Wasserman, S. (1994). *Social network analysis: Methods and applications*. Cambridge, UK: Cambridge University Press.

Waugh, N. C., & Norman, D. A. (1965). Primary memory. *Psychological Review*, *72*, 89–104. doi:10.1037/h0021797

Weinberger, A. (2003). *Scripts for computer-supported collaborative learning effects of social and epistemic cooperation scripts on collaborative knowledge construction*. PhD Dissertation. München, Germany: München University.

Weinberger, A., Stegmann, K., Fischer, F., & Mandl, H. (2007). Scripting argumentative knowledge construction in computer-supported learning environments. In F. Fischer., H. Mandl., J. Haake., & I. Kollar (Eds.), *Scripting Computer-Supported Communication of Knowledge - Cognitive, Computational and Educational Perspectives*, (pp. 191-211). New York, NY: Springer.

Weinberger, A., Ertl, B., Fischer, F., & Mandl, H. (2005). Epistemic and social scripts in computer-supported collaborative learning. *Instructional Science*, *33*(1), 1–30. doi:10.1007/s11251-004-2322-4

Weinberger, A., & Fischer, F. (2006). A framework to analyze argumentative knowledge construction in computer-supported collaborative learning. *Computers & Education*, *46*(1), 71–95. doi:10.1016/j.compedu.2005.04.003

Weng, C., Gennari, J. H., & Fridsma, D. B. (2007). User-centered semantic harmonization: A case study. *Journal of Biomedical Informatics*, *40*(3), 353–364. doi:10.1016/j.jbi.2007.03.004

Wenger, E. (1998). Communities of practice: Learning as a social system. *Systems Thinker*, *9*(5), 1–5.

Wenger, E. C., & Snyder, W. M. (2000). Communities of practice: The organizational frontier. *Harvard Business Review*, *78*(1), 139–146.

Wenger, E., McDermott, R., & Snyder, W. (2002). *Cultivating communities of practice: A guide to managing knowledge*. Cambridge, MA: Harvard Business School Press.

Wenger, E., White, N., & Smith, J. D. (2009). *Digital habitats: Stewarding technology for communities*. Portland, OR: Cpsquare.

Westfall, R. (1998). The microeconomics of remote work. In Igbaria, M., & Tan, M. (Eds.), *The Virtual Workplace* (pp. 256–287). Hershey, PA: IGI Global.

Whitehill, J., Bartlett, M., & Movellan, J. (2008). *Automatic facial expression recognition for intelligent tutoring systems*. Paper presented at the CVPR Workshop on Human Communicative Behavior Analysis. New York, NY.

Whitley, R. (2000). *The intellectual and social organization of the sciences*. Oxford, UK: Clarendon Press.

Whyte, W. F. (1989). *Advancing scientific knowledge through participatory action research.* Retrieved from http:// intranet.catie.ac.cr/ intranet/ posgrado/ Met%20 Cual%20 Inv%20accion/ Semana%204/ Whyte,%20 W.%20 Advancing%20 Scientific%20 Knowledge%20 Through.pdf.

Wickens, C. D. (1992). *Engineering psychology and human performance.* New York, NY: HarperCollins.

Wilkins-Diehr, N. (2007). Special issue: Science gateways – Common community interfaces to Grid resources. *Concurrency and Computation, 19*(6), 743–749. doi:10.1002/cpe.1098

Williams, E. (2010). *Keynote.* Paper presented at Chirp, the official Twitter Developer Conference. San Francisco, CA.

Wills, G., Gilbert, L., Chen, X., & Bacigalupo, D. (2010). Technical review of using cloud for research (TeciRes). *Report to JISC.* Retrieved 1 September 2011 from http://www.jisc.ac.uk/ whatwedo/ programmes/ researchinfrastructure/ cloudcomptechreview.aspx.

Wilson, A., Rimpilainen, S., Skinner, D., Cassidy, C., Christie, D., & Coutts, N. (2007). Using a virtual research environment to support new models of collaborative and participative research in Scottish education. *Technology, Pedagogy and Education, 16*(3), 289–304. doi:10.1080/14759390701614413

Wilson, T. D. (2000). Human information behaviour. *Informing Science, 3*(2), 49–56.

Wolfram, S. (2002). *A new kind of science.* Champaign, IL: Wolfram Media.

Wong, L.-H., & Looi, C.-K. (2010). Vocabulary learning by mobile-assisted authentic content creation and social meaning making: two case studies. *Journal of Computer Assisted Learning, 26*, 421–433. doi:10.1111/j.1365-2729.2010.00357.x

Wood, C. C. (1993). A cognitive dimensional analysis of idea sketches. *Cognitive Science Research Paper, 275.* Retrieved from http:// www.cogs.susx.ac.uk/ cgi-bin/ htmlcogsreps? csrp275.

Woodgate, D., & Fraser, D. S. (2005). E-science and education 2005: A review. *Joint Information Systems Committee (JISC).* Retrieved 10 January, 2010, from http://www.jisc.ac.uk/uploaded_documents/ACF2B4.pdf.

Woo, G. (1999). *The mathematics of natural catastrophes.* London, UK: Imperial College Press. doi:10.1142/9781860943867

Woolgar, S. (2004). *Social shaping perspectives on e-science and e-social science: The case for research support.* Oxford, UK: University of Oxford.

Wouters, P., & Beaulieu, A. (2007). Critical accountability: Dilemmas for interventionist studies of e-science. *Journal of Computer-Mediated Communication, 12*(2). doi:10.1111/j.1083-6101.2007.00339.x

Wu, P. H. J., Heok, A. K. H., & Tamsir, I. P. (2007). Annotating web archives - Structure, provenance, and context through archival cataloguing. *New Review of Hypermedia and Multimedia, 13*(1), 55–75. doi:10.1080/13614560701423620

Xie, H. I. (2006). Evaluation of digital libraries: Criteria and problems from users' perspectives. *Library & Information Science Research, 28*, 433–452. doi:10.1016/j.lisr.2006.06.002

Xie, H. I. (2008). Users' evaluation of digital libraries (DLs): Their uses, their criteria, and their assessment. *Information Processing & Management, 44*, 1346–1373. doi:10.1016/j.ipm.2007.10.003

Xu, B., Lin, H., Chiu, L., Hu, Y., Zhu, J., Hu, M., & Cui, W. (2011). Collaborative virtual geographic environments: A case study of air pollution simulation. *Information Sciences, 181*, 2231–2246. doi:10.1016/j.ins.2011.01.017

Yan, E., & Ding, Y. (2009). Applying centrality measures to impact analysis: A coauthorship network analysis. *Journal of the American Society for Information Science and Technology, 60*(10), 2107–2118. doi:10.1002/asi.21128

Yan, E., Ding, Y., & Zhu, Q. (2010). Mapping library and information science in China: A coauthorship network analysis. *Scientometrics, 83*(1), 115–131. doi:10.1007/s11192-009-0027-9

Yang, X., & Allan, R. (2006). Web-based virtual research environments (VRE): Support collaboration in e-science. In *Proceedings of the 2006 IEEE/WIC/ACM International Conference on Web Intelligence and Intelligent Agent Technology,* (pp. 1-4). IEEE Press.

Yelling, J. A. (1977). *Common field and enclosure in England 1450-1850.* Hamden, CT: Archon Books.

Zettsu, K., Nakanishi, T., Iwazume, M., Kidawara, Y., & Kiyoki, Y. (2008). Knowledge cluster systems for knowledge sharing, analysis and delivery among remote sites. In *Proceeding of the 2008 Conference on Information Modelling and Knowledge Bases XIX*, (pp. 282-289). Amsterdam, The Netherlands: IOS Press.

Zhang, Z. (1999). Feature-based facial expression recognition: Sensitivity analysis and experiments with a multilayer perceptron. *International Journal of Pattern Recognition and Artificial Intelligence*, *13*(6), 893–911. doi:10.1142/S0218001499000495

Zucker, U., Radig, B., & Wimmer, M. (2008). *Facial expression recognition – A comparison between humans and algorithms*. Retrieved on January 7, 2010 from http:// www9-old.in.tum.de/ people/ wimmerm/ lehre/ sep_zucker/ sep_zucker.pdf.

About the Contributors

Angel A. Juan is an Associate Professor of Optimization, Simulation, and Data Analysis in the Computer Science Department at the Open University of Catalonia (UOC). He is also a Researcher at the Internet Interdisciplinary Institute (IN3), as well as a frequent Lecturer at the Technical University of Catalonia and at the Autonomous University of Barcelona. Dr. Juan holds a Ph.D. in Applied Computational Mathematics (UNED), an M.S. in Information Systems and Technology (UOC), and an M.S. in Applied Mathematics (University of Valencia). He completed predoctoral internships at Harvard University and at University of Alicante, as well as a postdoctoral internship at the MIT Center for Transportation and Logistics. His research interests include Applied Optimization, Randomized Heuristics, Computer Simulation, Educational Data Analysis, and Mathematical e-Learning. He has published over 100 peer-reviewed papers in international journals, books, and proceedings regarding these fields. Currently, he is the coordinator of the CYTED-IN3-HAROSA@IB Network and Editorial Board Member of both the *International Journal of Data Analysis Techniques and Strategies* and the *International Journal of Information Systems and Social Change*. He is also a member of the INFORMS society. His website is: http://ajuanp.wordpress.com.

Thanasis Daradoumis is Associate Professor at the Department of Cultural Technology and Communication, University of the Aegean, Greece. He is also Joint Professor at the Department of Computer Science, Multimedia, and Telecommunications at the Open University of Catalonia, Spain, and Collaborating Professor at the Hellenic Open University. He holds a PhD in Computer Science from the Polytechnic University of Catalonia, Spain, a Masters in Computer Science from the University of Illinois, and a Bachelors in Mathematics from the University of Thessaloniki, Greece. His research focuses on e-learning and network technologies, Web-based instruction and evaluation, distributed and adaptive learning, CSCL, CSCW, interaction analysis, and grid technologies. He serves in the editorial board of several international conferences and journals, and he has coordinated or participated in various European and International R & D projects. He is co-director of the DPCS (Distributed Parallel and Collaborative Systems) Research Laboratory (http://dpcs.uoc.es/). He has written over 100 papers.

Meritxell Roca is Associate Director of the Internet Interdisciplinary Institute – IN3, at the Open University of Catalonia (UOC). She is also an Associate Professor of Communication at the Blanquerna School of Communication and Blanquerna School of Health Studies at the Ramon Llull University (URL). She holds a Ph.D. in Communication and Humanities (URL), an M.S. in Communication – Journalism (URL), and postgraduate courses in International Relations and Knowledge Society. She has also been a Visiting Associate Professor at the Annenberg School for Communication (University of Southern California). Currently, her research interests are the future of television in a digital environment, open source and free software productive model, and teenagers' media consumption in a multiplatform and multiscreening scenario. She is a member of the Spanish WIP (World Internet Project) research team.

Scott E. Grasman is Professor and Department Head of Industrial and Systems Engineering at Rochester Institute of Technology. He previously spent 10 years in the Department of Engineering Management and Systems Engineering at Missouri University of Science and Technology. He has served as Adjunct Professor of Operations and Manufacturing Management in the Olin Business School at Washington University in St. Louis, and completed a sabbatical in Statistics and Operations Research at the Public University of Navarre in Spain, as well as a two month appointment as Visiting Research Scholar at IN3 – the Open University of Catalonia. He received his B.S.E., M.S.E., and Ph.D. degrees in Industrial and Operations Engineering from the University of Michigan. In addition to academia, he has relevant industrial experience in industrial collaborations on research and curriculum activities. His is the author or co-author of over 100 technical papers, receiving multiple best conference paper awards, and he serves in reviewer/editorial roles for various technical journals and books.

Javier Faulin is a Professor of Operations Research and Statistics at the Public University of Navarre (Pamplona, Spain). He also collaborates as an Assistant Professor at the UNED local center in Pamplona. He holds a Ph.D. in Economics and Business from the University of Navarre (Pamplona, Spain), a M.Sc. in Operations Management, Logistics, and Transportation from UNED (Madrid, Spain), and a M.Sc. and BSc in Mathematics from the University of Zaragoza (Zaragoza, Spain). He has extended experience in distance and Web-based teaching at the Public University of Navarre, at UNED (Madrid, Spain), at the Open University of Catalonia (Barcelona, Spain), and at the University of Surrey (Guilford, UK). His research interests include logistics, vehicle routing problems and simulation modelling, and analysis, especially techniques to improve simulation analysis in practical applications. He has published more than 40 papers in international journals, books, and proceedings about logistics, routing, and simulation. Similarly, he has taught many courses on-line about Operations Research (OR) and Decision Making, and he has been the academic advisor of three PhD students and more than 25 students finishing their master thesis. Furthermore, he has been the author of more than 100 works in OR conferences. He is an Editorial Board Member of the *International Journal of Applied Management Science (IJAMS)* and *International Journal of Operations Research and Information Systems (IJORIS)*, and an INFORMS member.

* * *

Anindito Aditomo is a Lecturer at the Faculty of Psychology, the University of Surabaya, Indonesia. Anindito received an Australian Development Scholarship in 2006 to complete his masters program at the Centre for Research on Computer Supported Learning and Cognition (CoCo), Sydney University. He is currently pursuing a PhD, also at CoCo, funded by the University of Sydney International Scholarship. His PhD project focuses on the assessment of knowledge about science and the nature of such knowledge. His broader academic interests are on understanding how people learn and develop in educational contexts, especially in technology-rich settings. Over the past year he has been involved in an ARC Discovery Project that aims at developing ways to automatically assess and visualize university students' online collaborative writing processes.

Rob Allan obtained a Ph.D. in Theoretical Atomic Physics from University of Newcastle upon Tyne in 1983. He is Leader of the HPC and Grid Technology Group in the Computational Science and Engineering Department at STFC's Daresbury Laboratory. Rob's background is as a researcher doing large scale computational modelling. He has an interest in distributed ICT service development and deployment and user interfaces for research, mainly in the natural sciences. He has also developed numerical algorithms and parallel computing and Grid tools for users of high performance computing resources. Rob has a practical knowledge of Grid and Web services middleware and helped to set up STFC's e-Science Centre and the UK's Grid Support Centre. He has co-authored a number of research papers, technical reports and books. He has more recently written a book entitled *Virtual Research Environments: From Portals to Science Gateways* published by Woodhead Publishing (2009).

Paul Arthur is inaugural Chair of the Australasian Association for Digital Humanities and Series Editor of *Anthem Scholarship in the Digital Age* (Anthem Press, London and New York). An advocate for digital research in the humanities, he studied at the University of Western Australia and held research fellowships in Europe, North America, and Australia before taking up the position of Deputy Director of the National Centre of Biography and Deputy General Editor of the *Australian Dictionary of Biography* at the Australian National University. He has published widely on digital research methods in the arts and social sciences and on the history of technology and media.

Barry Barrios is a Graduate Student at Northwestern University in the Department of Industrial Engineering and Management Sciences. He received his bachelor's degree in Physics from MIT. His current research interest focuses on vehicle routing problems and humanitarian logistics. Recently he has been working on scheduling flow-shop problems and the multi-depot vehicle routing problem. As an undergrad, he was awarded several academic scholarships, including the American Physical Society Minority Scholarship and the Hispanic College Fund (Lockheed Martin Scholar).

Marie-Laure Betbeder is Associate Professor of Computer Science at the LIFC Laboratory in Besançon, France. For the last ten years, she's been involved in the domains of Technology Enhanced Learning and Computer-Supported Collaborative Learning. Her early works were focused on the tailorability of computer artefacts as a support for learning environments. Since 2007 she has worked on the French national project Mulce, whose main objective is to provide structure and tools to share "Learning and Teaching Corpora." She is now involved in another French national project aiming at proposing an environment for controlled language writing support.

Harm J. A. Biemans is an Associate Professor at the Education and Competence Studies Chair Group, Wageningen University, The Netherlands. His research interests concern Competence Development, Competence-Based Education, Educational Psychology, Educational Development and Evaluation, and Computer-Supported Collaborative Learning. He studied Educational Psychology at Tilburg University and earned a PhD from Radboud University Nijmegen for his dissertation on Prior Knowledge Activation and Self-Regulation. He is the daily supervisor of several PhD students and has published many articles in international peer-reviewed scientific journals and books.

Mihai Bizoi is working at the Automatic Control, Informatics, and Electrical Engineering Department, Electrical Engineering Faculty, Valahia University of Targoviste, Romania. He was/is involved as a teacher training or technical expert in different ICT projects (research and educational) at the national and international level. His current research interests include communications-driven decision support systems, group decision support systems, Web development, Web collaborative technologies, e-learning technologies, and educational use of ICT. As author or co-author, he has published over 40 papers in journals or proceedings of international conferences and is member of prestigious professional associations such as ACM and IEEE.

Maria C. Busstra is an Assistant Professor in the Division of Human Nutrition, Wageningen University, The Netherlands. Her research interests concern Human Nutrition and Epidemiology, and Digital Learning Materials related to this topic. Her PhD dissertation at Wageningen University focused on the Design and Evaluation of Digital Learning Material for Academic Education in Human Nutrition. She has presented many papers at international conferences and published many articles in international peer-reviewed scientific journals.

Jake Rowan Byrne is a PhD candidate in the School of Computer Science and Statistics at Trinity College, Dublin. His current research is conducted at Trinity's Centre for Research in IT in Education (a joint initiative between the School of Education and the School of Computer Science and Statistics). His research looks at developing tools and cognitive supports for PhD candidates using a participatory design approach. This ranges from management tools on the functional level to cognitive scaffolds to support higher level thinking. He is also involved in a volunteer programme (Bridge-to-College) that provides under-privileged students with the opportunity to develop their collaboration skills through technology mediated projects.

Luis Casillas is Associate Professor at the Department of Computer Sciences, University of Guadalajara, Mexico. He holds a PhD in Information and Knowledge Society from the Open University of Catalonia (Spain), a Masters Degree in Information and Knowledge Society from the Open University of Catalonia (Spain), a Masters Degree in Information Systems from the University of Guadalajara (Mexico), and a Bachelor's Degree in Informatics from the University of Guadalajara (Mexico). His research focuses in bioinspired intelligent systems, collaboration analysis, and complex networks analysis. He serves in the Editorial Board of international conferences and journals. He is currently working in the content updating for the academic programs of computer science at the University of Guadalajara, using novel approaches based in complex networks analysis and coordinating experts' collaboration throughout automatic mechanisms.

Mohammad Chizari is a Professor at the Agricultural Extension and Education Chair Group, College of Agriculture, Tarbiat Modares University, Tehran, Iran. His research interests concern Sustainable Agriculture, Adult Education, E-Learning, and Distance Education. He earned his PhD at Mississippi State University. He is currently active in various boards, councils, organisations, and committees, and was recognised by TMU several times as a distinguished researcher and teacher. Furthermore, he is a member of the governors for the *Journal of Extension Systems*. He has presented many papers in international conferences and published many articles in international peer-reviewed scientific journals. He has supervised many MSc theses as well as several PhD dissertations.

Kum Won Cho received his Ph.D degree from KAIST in Aerospace Engineering in 2000. His research interests include: e-science, high performance computing / Grid computing, numerical methods for partial difference equations. Kum Won Cho is currently Head of the KISTI e-Science Division and Steering Committee of PRAGMA(Pacific Rim of Applications and Grid Middleware Assembly). Kum Won Cho has had experience with numerical analysis code development including 3-dimensional Navier-Stokes, structured, unstructured, and Chimera mesh generation, and unsteady moving body simulation. Kum Won Cho has had expertise in the performance issue of numerical analysis code including efficiency improvement by profiling, loop recording, memory issue, parallel efficiency, and numerical code development based on Grid computing environment.

Rob Crouchey obtained a PhD in Mathematics (Statistics) from Imperial College London, in 1991. He is the Director of Lancaster University Management School's (LUMS) Centre for e-Science where he currently directs research projects on the deployment of the Sakai collaboration environment for knowledge exchange between Lancaster University and small and medium sized enterprises. Rob also lectures on econometrics in the LUMS Economics Department. He has published many applied research papers as well as writing and editing several books. He currently represents the UK's Royal Statistical Society on the Government Statistical Service Methodology Advisory Committee (GSS MAC). His research interests include statistical modeling, development of collaboration tools, data base management, and using grid computing systems.

Paolo Diviacco holds a PhD in Geophysics of the Lithosphere and a University Degree in Geology. He coordinates the Geophysical Data Processing and Data Integration Group at the Istituto Nazionale di Oceanografia e di Geofisica Sperimentale (OGS), Trieste, Italy, and is the author of many publications in the field of collaborative systems and geophysical data processing and interpretation. He is involved in many large-scale international collaborative e-research projects where he has the chance to test the ideas and the tools he develops. He has a special interest in the philosophical aspects of e-reseach and of the development of tools that could support collaborative activities in environments that cross multiple scientific domains.

Gregory Dyke is a Post-Doc Researcher in the Language Technologies Institute at Carnegie Mellon University. His research interests focus on all aspects of social computing, particularly within collaborative learning situations. He completed his PhD in 2009 on the modelling of analytic representations in CSCL. During that time he authored Tatiana, a tool for helping researchers to create analytic representations. Since then he has expanded his work to focus on (semi-)automated analysis and visualisation of time-oriented data and on automated analysis of online discourse.

Alex Forcada is a student of the University of Zaragoza (Aragon, Spain). He started Industrial Engineering in 2006 and moved to Munich (Bavaria, Germany) to study the academic year 2010-11 as an Erasmus Student in the Technical University of Munich (TUM). He has worked as a teacher in different private academies. He has studied several Operations Research subjects at the TUM and in the G9 virtual campus with the on-line methodology. Currently, he is still in Munich writing his final thesis.

Mayo Fuster Morell is currently a postdoctoral researcher at the Institute of Govern and Public Policies (Autonomous University of Barcelona) and Visiting Scholar at the Internet Interdisciplinary Institute (Open University of Catalonia). Mayo has been selected as Postdoctoral Fellow at the Berkman Center for Internet and Society at Harvard University during the Academic Year 2011-2012. She is a Member of the Research Committee of the Wikimedia Foundation and collaborates in research projects with Science Po and Barcelona Media. She recently concluded her PhD thesis at the European University Institute (Title: "Governance of Online Creation Communities: Provision of Infrastructure for the Building of Digital Commons"). She co-wrote the books *Rethinking Political Organisation in an Age of Movements and Networks* (2007, Icaria: Barcelona), *Activist Research and Social Movements* (2005, El Viejo Topo: Barcelona), and *Guide for Social Transformation of Catalonia* (2003, Edicions Col·lectives: Barcelona).

Pablo Garaizar is an Assistant Professor in Computer Engineering at the University of Deusto (Bilbao, Spain) since 2003. He works as a Researcher at the DeustoTech Learning Research Unit of the Faculty of Engineering of the University of Deusto, and directs projects that explore new ways of using Information and Communication Technologies to enhance learning at Catedra Telefónica-Deusto since 2010. His research interests include Internet based research, Social Network Sites (SNS), Web development, and associative learning. His work has been published in journals that combine Computer Engineering and Psychology such as *Behavior Research Methods*.

Adina Elena Glava, PhD, works at Department of Sciences of Education, Faculty of Psychology and Sciences of Education, at Babeş-Bolyai University of Cluj-Napoca. She has great experience in working on various European transnational projects, as she was involved in different projects on Tempus, Socrates, Phare, and LLP frameworks, since 2002. Her area of interest is oriented on curriculum development, cognitive and metacognitive perspectives in education, early education, preschool education, e-learning, and inclusion education. Between 2006 and 2009, she was local coordinator of the European Socrates Comenius 2.1 Project: "VccSSe – Virtual Community Collaborating Space for Science Education," which provides the necessary support for the presented chapter.

Gabriel Gorghiu is an Associate Professor in the Automatic Control, Informatics, and Electrical Engineering Department, Electrical Engineering Faculty, and also at Teacher Training Department, at Valahia University Targoviste. He has great experience in working on various European transnational projects, as he was involved in different projects on Tempus, World Bank, Socrates, and LLP frameworks, since 1995. His area of interest is oriented on data processing, processes and phenomena modeling, educational technologies, e-learning, interaction, and virtual communication, Web-based learning platforms, and using ICT for educational purposes. Between 2006 and 2009, he coordinated the European Socrates Comenius 2.1 Project: "VccSSe – Virtual Community Collaborating Space for Science Education," which provides the necessary support for the presented chapter.

Leonie Hellmers is Communications and Grant Development Manager, Intersect Australia Ltd. She worked in the digital humanities as a project lead, manager, and advocate for 15 years, variously for the National Portrait Gallery, the National Gallery of Australia, Fairfax, Brainwa@ve, and for a consortium led by the University of NSW as founding Project Director of the Dictionary of Australian Artists Online. Previously, she delivered communication solutions for the Australia Council, Australian Heritage Commission, and the private sector, and worked extensively as a journalist and broadcaster. Hellmers has a BA in Fine Arts, Literature, and Politics from the University of Sydney.

Mary Anne Kennan is a Senior Lecturer in the School of Information Studies at Charles Sturt University in Australia. Her teaching and research are broadly in the fields of information and communication in the digital environment. Her recent PhD research investigated scholarly communications, open access, and institutional repositories. She continues to research in this area while developing new research connections in the eResearch domain. She is interested in further exploring how new opportunities for multidimensional information flows, developing connectedness, social inclusion, and participation arise from the interactions between people, information, and technology. Prior to becoming an academic, Kennan worked for 25 years in libraries and the information world in diverse positions, the most recent as director of the Frank Lowy Library at the Australian Graduate School of Management.

Vahid Khatibi is a PhD Student of Industrial Engineering in the Faculty of Engineering of University of Tehran, Iran. He received his B.Sc. degree in Computer Software Engineering from University of Applied Science and Technology, Tehran, Iran, in 2006, and his M.Sc. degree in Information Technology Engineering from Tarbiat Modares University, Tehran, Iran, in 2009. His areas of research include information systems engineering, Knowledge Discovery and Data mining (KDD), intelligent decision support systems, Business Intelligence (BI), Information Technology Management (ITM), and Knowledge Management (KM). Additional details about him can be found at http://www.vahid-khatibi.com/.

Maria Kordaki holds a PhD in Educational Technology, a Masters in Education, a diploma in Civil Engineering, and a Bachelor in Mathematics from the University of Patras, Greece. She is Assistant Professor of Educational Technology in the Department of Cultural Technology and Communication, University of the Aegean, Greece. During the last decade she also served as Collaborative Professor in the Hellenic Open University as well as Adjunct Professor in the Department of Computer Engineering and Informatics and in the Department of Mathematics, University of Patras, Greece. Her research focuses on the use of social and constructivist learning theories in the design of educational software and technology-supported learning design, towards critical and creative thinking within various educational settings including: paper and pencil, online, blended, collaborative, and technology-based learning. She also serves in the Editorial Board of various international and national conferences and journals. Finally, she has published over 150 scientific papers and 9 books.

Junehawk Lee received the BS degree in Computer Science and the MS degree in Biosystems from Korea Advanced Institute of Science and Technology (KAIST), Daejeon, Korea, in 2003 and 2005, respectively. He is currently a Senior Researcher at Supercomputing Center in Korea Institute of Science and Technology Information (KISTI). He is currently working on developing research environment regarding bioinformatics and computational biology. He also has interests in high performance computing and high throughput computing.

Fernando Lera-López is an Associate Professor of Applied Economics in the Department of Economics at the Public University of Navarre (Pamplona, Spain). He has also collaborated as an Assistant Professor at the UNED local center in Tudela. He has been General Coordinator of the School of Business and Economics (UNED, Spain) in this local center. Nowadays, he collaborates as an Assistant Professor at the UNED local center in Pamplona. He holds a PhD and a MS in Economics and Business from the University of Navarre (Pamplona, Spain). He has extended experience in distance and Web-based teaching at the Public University of Navarre and at UNED (Madrid, Spain). His research interests include economic analysis about environmental problems related to transportation and logistics and the information and communication technologies adoption and its effects at national and firm levels. He has published more than 25 papers in international journals and books about these topics.

Diego López-de-Ipiña is an Associate Professor in Computer Engineering at the University of Deusto (Bilbao, Spain) since February 2011. He is the Principal Researcher of the DeustoTech-Internet Research Unit and the Head of the "MORElab: Envisioning Future Internet" research group, both belonging to the Faculty of Engineering of the University of Deusto. He received his PhD from the University of Cambridge, UK, in 2002, in the area of Sentient Computing. His main research areas are ubiquitous computing, semantic service middleware, human-environment interaction, and future internet (internet of things and linked data). He has directed over 10 research projects involving the application of Web 2.0 and Semantic Web to novel application areas such as industrial electronics, ambient assisted living, and eLearning. He has published in journals such as *IEEE Transactions on Industrial Electronics, Personal and Ubiquitous Computing,* and *Journal of Universal Computer Science.*

Mayte Lopez Ferrer belongs on the Spanish Council for Scientific Research, CSIC. At the moment she works in INGENIO, Institute for Innovation and Knowledge Management, joint Institute of the Spanish Council for Scientific Research and the Polytechnic University of Valencia. She is Graduate in Documentation from the Carlos III University of Madrid and PhD in Documentation, from the University of Valencia. She has worked as a Researcher in other institutes of the Spanish Council for Scientific Research, CSIC, and she has been a Lecturer at the University of Valencia and of the Open University of Catalonia (UOC) in their respective Degrees of Documentation. Her areas of interest are bibliometrics and social network analysis applied to scientific activity.

Helena Matute is a Professor of Psychology at the University of Deusto (Bilbao, Spain). She has also been a Visiting Scholar at the universities of Málaga (Spain), Gent (Belgium), Sydney (Australia), and Queensland (Australia). She is the Founder and Director of Labpsico, the Experimental Psychology Laboratory at Deusto University, where she has directed over 10 research projects and doctoral theses on topics related to the psychology of learning, causal illusions, and Internet-based research. Her work has been published in the main journals of her area of expertise, including, among others, the *Journal of Experimental Psychology: General, Psychological Science, The Quarterly Journal of Experimental Psychology*, and *Psychological Science.*

Gholam Ali Montazer is an Associate Professor in the Department of Information Technology at School of Engineering, Tarbiat Modares University (TMU), Tehran, Iran. He received his B.Sc. degree in Electrical Engineering from Kh. N. Toosi University of Technology, Tehran, Iran, in 1993, and his M.Sc. and Ph.D. degrees in Electrical Engineering from Tarbiat Modares University, Tehran, Iran, in 1995 and 1999, respectively. His areas of research include soft computing approaches such as Artificial Neural Network (ANN), Fuzzy Set Theory (FST), Rough Set Theory (RST), evolutionary computation and their applications in pattern recognition, e-learning systems, and e-commerce environment. He is the Editor-in-Chief of Iranian *Journal of Information Technology (JIT)* as well as an Editorial Board Member for *International Journal of Information Science and Management (IJISM)* and *Journal of Science and Technology Policy (JSTP)*. He has received many national and international awards such as the Kharazmi International Award (KIA) in 2005, and Islamic Educational, Scientific, and Cultural Organization (ISESCO) recognized him as the distinguished researcher in Information Technology (IT) in 2004.

Martin Mulder is a Professor at the Education and Competence Studies Chair Group, Wageningen University, The Netherlands. His research interests include competence theory and research, human resource development, computer-supported collaborative learning, competence of entrepreneurs, competence of open innovation professionals, and interdisciplinary learning in the field of food quality management education. He leads an education and research program on competence development, has published over 400 articles, chapters, and books with his co-workers in the field of learning and work, is Editor of the *Journal of Agricultural Education and Extension*, and is a Member of editorial committees of various peer-reviewed journals in the field of education, training, and development (amongst which are the *Journal of International Training and Development*, the *Journal of European Industrial Training*, and *Vocations and Learning*).

Dukyun Nam received the BS degree in Computer Science and Engineering from Pohang University of Science and Technology (POSTECH), Korea, in 1999, and the MS and PhD degrees in Engineering from KAIST ICC (formerly, Information and Communications University), Daejeon, Korea, in 2001 and 2006, respectively. He is currently a Senior Researcher at the Korea Institute of Science and Technology Information (KISTI). His research interests include distributed systems, high performance computing, high throughput computing, cyber environment, and problem solving environment.

Omid Noroozi is a PhD student at the Education and Competence Studies Chair Group, Wageningen University, The Netherlands. His research interests include collaborative learning, e-learning and distance education, Computer-Supported Collaborative Learning (CSCL), argumentative knowledge construction in CSCL, argumentation-based CSCL, CSCL scripts, and transactivity within agri-food Sciences. He graduated in 2005 from Tarbiat Modares University in Iran with an MSc in Agricultural Extension and Education. He has been following a PhD program on Argumentation-Based CSCL within Agri-Food Sciences in Higher Education since 2008. He has presented many papers at international conferences and published various articles in international peer-reviewed scientific journals.

Vitaliy Popov is a PhD Student at the Education and Competence Studies Chair Group, Wageningen University, The Netherlands. His research interests include intercultural communication (ethno-psychological analysis of group and individual behavior) and educational practice (collaborative learning, computer-supported collaborative learning). He graduated in June 2006 from Moscow State University of Agro-Engineering with an MSc in Education. Since 2008, he has been following a PhD program on Computer-Supported Intercultural Collaboration in higher education. He has presented various papers in international conferences, seminars, and congresses.

Sam Redfern is a graduate of the National University of Ireland, Galway, and holds a B.A., M.Sc. and Ph.D. He has worked as a Lecturer in Galway since 1996, and has managed funded research projects in the areas of Collaborative Virtual Environments (CVEs), auditory display, and Computer Supported Co-Operative Work (CSCW). His academic publications in international journals, conferences, and books include work in digital image processing, various types of artificial intelligence, graphics, CSCW, CVEs, and "serious games."

Christophe Reffay is Associate Professor of Computer Science at the Educational Science laboratory STEF of the *École Nationale Supérieure* of Cachan, France. He is involved in the domains of Technology Enhanced Learning and Computer Supported Collaborative Learning. His work is dedicated to collaboration analysis and tool conception to capture, analyse, and represent social activity in collaborative learning environments. He conducted social network analysis on communication data issued from the "Simuligne" experiment. Since 2007, he has been involved in a French national project (mulce.org) whose main objective is to provide structure and tools to share "Learning and Teaching Corpora." His current interests are social network analysis, indicators for collaboration in technology enhanced learning environments, and research data sharing.

Jim Richardson studied and lectured in mathematics, then worked in information technology, including the development of eResearch. He is now retired.

Paul Smith has a B.Sc and Ph.D from the National University of Ireland, Galway, and has conducted more than 7 years of research and development into virtual communication and artificial intelligence, working closely with game engine and optical motion capture technology, and publishing in a number of international conferences. His current interests include Collaborative Virtual Environments (CVEs), virtual interaction technologies, computer graphics, and computer games development. He is currently employed as a Lead Graphics Developer for a Galway-based real-time 3D simulation and social game development company.

Alastair Robertson obtained a Ph.D. in Management from Lancaster University in 2005. He is Senior Research Fellow at Lancaster University Management School's (LUMS) Centre for e-Science where he currently manages various cloud-based software developments focusing around the enhancement of e-research tools for business researchers and other related stakeholders (e.g. regional development authorities). Specifically focusing around Small and Medium Sized Enterprises (SMEs), Alastair lectures on e-business management and market research methods. Alastair also holds an Honorary Research Fellowship at the Department of Management Science at LUMS, and is also a consultant for the Lancaster Centre for Forecasting within this department. Principle research interests are technology adoption among SME businesses and households with special focus in the psychological aspects of adoption.

Brendan Tangney is a Fellow of Trinity College, Dublin, where he is a Senior Lecturer in the School of Computer Science and Statistics. He is Co-Director of Trinity's Centre for Research in IT in Education (a joint initiative between the School of Education and the School of Computer Science and Statistics). He has held visiting positions in the Universities of Sydney and Kyoto and worked in industry in Dublin and Tokyo. He is a recipient of Trinity's Provost's Teaching Award for Excellence and Innovation in Teaching and Learning and is a Member of the Editorial Boards of *Computers and Education* and the *AACE Journal of Computers in Mathematics and Science Teaching*.

Miguel A. Vadillo is an Assistant Professor in Psychology at the University of Deusto (Bilbao, Spain) since 2005, where he also works as a Researcher at the Labpsico Research Unit of the School of Psychology and Education. He has been Visiting Scholar at the State University of New York at Binghamton and the Universiteit Gent (Belgium). His research interests include associative learning, causal reasoning, and Internet-based research. His work has been published in the main journals of his area of expertise, including, among others, the *Journal of Experimental Psychology: General*, the *Quarterly Journal of Experimental Psychology*, and the *Psychonomic Bulletin and Review*.

Index